THE ROUTLEDGE HANDBOOK OF PACIFISM AND NONVIOLENCE

Interest in pacifism—an idea with a long history in philosophical thought and in several religious traditions—is growing. *The Routledge Handbook of Pacifism and Nonviolence* is the first comprehensive reference designed to introduce newcomers and researchers to the many varieties of pacifism and nonviolence, to their history and philosophy, and to pacifism's most serious critiques. The volume offers 32 brand new chapters from the world's leading experts across a diverse range of fields, who together offer a broad discussion of pacifism and nonviolence in connection with virtue ethics, capital punishment, animal ethics, ecology, queer theory, and feminism, among other areas. This *Handbook* is divided into four sections: (1) Historical and Tradition-Specific Considerations, (2) Conceptual and Moral Considerations, (3) Social and Political Considerations, and (4) Applications. It concludes with an Afterword by James Lawson, one of the icons of the nonviolent American Civil Rights movement. The text will be invaluable to scholars and students, as well as to activists and general readers interested in peace, nonviolence, and critical perspectives on war and violence.

Andrew Fiala is Professor of Philosophy and Director of the Ethics Center at Fresno State University, USA. A former president of Concerned Philosophers for Peace, his publications include *The Just War Myth* (2008), *Public War, Private Conscience* (2010), *The Bloomsbury Companion to Political Philosophy* (editor, 2015), *Ethics: Theory and Contemporary Issues*, 9th edition (with Barbara MacKinnon, 2017), and *Transformative Pacifism* (forthcoming).

ROUTLEDGE HANDBOOKS IN PHILOSOPHY

For a full list of published Routledge Handbooks in Philosophy, please visit www.routledge.com/Routledge-Handbooks-in-Philosophy/book-series/RHP

Routledge Handbooks in Philosophy are state-of-the-art surveys of emerging, newly refreshed, and important fields in philosophy, providing accessible yet thorough assessments of key problems, themes, thinkers, and recent developments in research.

All chapters for each volume are specially commissioned, and written by leading scholars in the field. Carefully edited and organized, *Routledge Handbooks in Philosophy* provide indispensable reference tools for students and researchers seeking a comprehensive overview of new and exciting topics in philosophy. They are also valuable teaching resources as accompaniments to textbooks, anthologies, and research-orientated publications.

RECENTLY PUBLISHED:

THE ROUTLEDGE HANDBOOK OF PHILOSOPHY OF PAIN
Edited by Jennifer Corns

THE ROUTLEDGE HANDBOOK OF MECHANISMS AND MECHANICAL PHILOSOPHY
Edited by Stuart Glennan and Phyllis Illari

THE ROUTLEDGE HANDBOOK OF METAETHICS
Edited by Tristram McPherson and David Plunkett

THE ROUTLEDGE HANDBOOK OF EVOLUTION AND PHILOSOPHY
Edited by Richard Joyce

THE ROUTLEDGE HANDBOOK OF LIBERTARIANISM
Edited by Jason Brennan, Bas van der Vossen, and David Schmidtz

THE ROUTLEDGE HANDBOOK OF COLLECTIVE INTENTIONALITY
Edited by Marija Jankovic and Kirk Ludwig

THE ROUTLEDGE HANDBOOK OF PACIFISM AND NONVIOLENCE
Edited by Andrew Fiala

THE ROUTLEDGE HANDBOOK OF PACIFISM AND NONVIOLENCE

Edited by Andrew Fiala

NEW YORK AND LONDON

First published 2018
by Routledge
711 Third Avenue, New York, NY 10017

and by Routledge
2 Park Square, Milton Park, Abingdon, Oxon, OX14 4RN

Routledge is an imprint of the Taylor & Francis Group, an informa business

© 2018 Taylor & Francis

The right of Andrew Fiala to be identified as the author of the editorial material, and of the authors for their individual chapters, has been asserted in accordance with sections 77 and 78 of the Copyright, Designs and Patents Act 1988.

All rights reserved. No part of this book may be reprinted or reproduced or utilized in any form or by any electronic, mechanical, or other means, now known or hereafter invented, including photocopying and recording, or in any information storage or retrieval system, without permission in writing from the publishers.

Trademark notice: Product or corporate names may be trademarks or registered trademarks, and are used only for identification and explanation without intent to infringe.

Library of Congress Cataloging-in-Publication Data
Names: Fiala, Andrew, 1966– editor.
Title: The Routledge handbook of pacifism and nonviolence / edited by Andrew Fiala, Ph.D.
Other titles: Handbook of pacifism and nonviolence
Description: New York : Routledge, 2018. | Series: Routledge handbooks in philosophy | Includes bibliographical references.
Identifiers: LCCN 2017036718 | ISBN 9781138194663 (hardback)
Subjects: LCSH: Pacifism. | Nonviolence.
Classification: LCC JZ5548 .R68 2018 | DDC 303.6/6—dc23
LC record available at https://lccn.loc.gov/2017036718

ISBN: 978-1-138-19466-3 (hbk)
ISBN: 978-1-315-63875-1 (ebk)

Typeset in Bembo
by Apex CoVantage, LLC

CONTENTS

Notes on Contributors   *ix*
Acknowledgements   *xv*

    Introduction   1
    Andrew Fiala

PART I
Historical and Tradition-Specific Considerations   5

1 A History of the Idea of Pacifism and Nonviolence: Ancient to Modern   7
   Duane L. Cady

2 Nonviolence and Pacifism in the Long Nineteenth Century   15
   Michael Allen Fox

3 Pacifism in the Twentieth Century and Beyond   30
   Andrew Fiala

4 Christian Pacifism   43
   Daniel A. Dombrowski

5 Peace and Nonviolence in Islam   54
   Ramin Jahanbegloo

6 Philosophy of Nonviolence in Africa *Gail M. Presbey*	64
7 Nonviolence in the Dharma Traditions: Hinduism, Jainism, and Buddhism *Veena R. Howard*	80
8 The Gandhi-King Tradition and *Satyagraha* *Barry L. Gan*	93

PART II
Conceptual and Moral Considerations — **103**

9 Pacifism and the Concept of Morality *Robert L. Holmes*	105
10 Peace: Negative and Positive *David Boersema*	116
11 The Pacifist Critique of the Just War Tradition *Cheyney Ryan*	125
12 Contingent Pacifism *Paul Morrow*	142
13 Humanitarian Intervention and the Problem of Genocide and Atrocity *Jennifer Kling*	154
14 Virtue Ethics and Nonviolence *David K. Chan*	168
15 Personal Pacifism and Conscientious Objection *Eric Reitan*	179
16 Pacifism: Does It Make Moral Sense? *Jan Narveson*	191
17 Pacifism as Pathology *José-Antonio Orosco*	199

PART III
Social and Political Considerations — 211

18 The Triumph of the Liberal Democratic Peace
    and the Dangers of Its Success — 213
    Fuat Gursozlu

19 Human Rights and International Law — 225
    Robert Paul Churchill

20 Hospitality, Identity, and Cosmopolitanism: Antidotes
    to the Violence of Otherness — 238
    Eddy M. Souffrant

21 Warism and the Dominant Worldview — 249
    Duane L. Cady

22 The Military-Industrial Complex — 255
    William Gay

23 Feminism and Nonviolent Activism — 268
    Danielle Poe

24 Queer Oppression and Pacifism — 281
    Blake Hereth

PART IV
Applications — 293

25 Care Theory, Peacemaking, and Education — 295
    Nel Noddings

26 Becoming Nonviolent: Sociobiological, Neurophysiological,
    and Spiritual Perspectives — 307
    Andrew Fitz-Gibbon

27 The Death Penalty and Nonviolence: Justice Beyond Empathy — 318
    Lloyd Steffen

28 Ecology and Pacifism — 331
    Mark Woods

29 Animals, Vegetarianism, and Nonviolence   343
    Christopher Key Chapple

30 Children, Violence, and Nonviolence   355
    Jane Hall Fitz-Gibbon

31 Peace Pedagogy from the Borderlines   371
    Renee Bricker, Yi Deng, Donna A. Gessell, and Michael Proulx

    Afterword: Nonviolence and the Non-Existent Country   384
    James M. Lawson, Jr.

Index   *393*

CONTRIBUTORS

David Boersema is Emeritus Professor of Philosophy at Pacific University. Among his publications is *Philosophy of Human Rights: Theory and Practice* (Westview Press, 2011). He served as Executive Director of the Concerned Philosophers for Peace from 2004 to 2012 and as CPP President from 2016 to 2017.

Renee Bricker is Associate Professor of History at the University of North Georgia, Dahlonega campus, United States of America. Her chapter "Talking with the Dead: Using Social Media in the Early Modern Classroom" will appear in *Creating the Premodern in the Postmodern Classroom*.

Duane L. Cady, PhD, is Professor Emeritus of Philosophy at Hamline University in St. Paul, Minnesota. He is the author of *From Warism to Pacifism: A Moral Continuum* (Temple University Press, 1989; 2nd edition, 2010) and *Moral Vision: How Everyday Life Shapes Ethical Thinking* (2005), co-author of *Humanitarian Intervention: Just War vs. Pacifism* (1996), and co-editor of three anthologies.

David K. Chan is Professor of Philosophy at the University of Wisconsin–Stevens Point, with research interests in moral psychology, virtue ethics, the ethics of war, medical ethics, and Greek philosophy. He has published books on the ethics of war and on action theory, including *Action Reconceptualized: Human Agency and Its Sources* (Lexington Books, 2016) and *Beyond Just War: A Virtue Ethics Approach* (Palgrave Macmillan, 2012). Chan edited a special issue of *Philosophy in the Contemporary World* on "War, Peace and Ethics" (19:2, Fall 2012). Relevant articles include "Just War, Noncombatant Immunity, and the Concept of Supreme Emergency," *Journal of Military Ethics* 11 (2012) and "The Ethics of War and Law Enforcement in Defending Against Terrorism," *Social Philosophy Today* 28 (2012).

Christopher Key Chapple is Doshi Professor of Indic and Comparative Theology, and Director, Master of Arts in Yoga Studies at Loyola Marymount University. His research interests focus on the renouncer religious traditions of India: Yoga, Jainism, and Buddhism. He has published several books on these topics, including *Karma and Creativity* (SUNY, 1986) and *Nonviolence to Animals, Earth, and Self in Asian Traditions* (SUNY, 1993), as well as edited/co-authored volumes such as *Hinduism and Ecology* (with Mary Evelyn Tucker, Harvard, 2000), *Jainism and Ecology* (Harvard, 2000), *Yoga and Ecology* (Deepak Heritage, 2009), and *In Praise of Mother Earth: The Prthivi Sukta of the Atharva Veda* (with O. P. Dwivedi, winner, translation prize, Dharma Academy of North America, 2011). He also is editor of the journal *Worldviews: Global Religions, Culture, and Ecology* (Brill).

Robert Paul Churchill is Romeo Elton Professor of Moral Philosophy at George Washington University, where he has served as chair of the department and director of the Peace Studies Program. He earned his doctorate at Johns Hopkins University with a dissertation on civil disobedience. Publications include *Democracy, Social Values and Public Policy* (co-edited with Carrow and Cordes, Praeger, 1998), *The Ethics of Liberal Democracy* (edited, Berg, 1994), and *Human Rights and Global Diversity* (Prentice Hall, 2005). He is working on two books, *Women in the Crossfire: Understanding and Ending Honor Killing* and *Universal Human Rights: A Defense*.

Yi Deng is Assistant Professor of Philosophy at the University of North Georgia, Dahlonega campus, United States of America. She works primarily in social and political philosophy. Her recent article, "Kant's Publicity Principle as Dynamic Consent," will be included in the proceedings of the 12th International Kant Congress.

Daniel A. Dombrowski is Professor of Philosophy at Seattle University. He is the author of 18 books and over 150 articles in scholarly journals in philosophy, theology, classics, and literature. His latest books are *Rethinking the Ontological Argument: A Neoclassical Theistic Perspective* (Cambridge: Cambridge University Press, 2006); *Contemporary Athletics and Ancient Greek Ideals* (Chicago: University of Chicago Press, 2009); and *Whitehead's Religious Thought: From Mechanism to Organism, from Force to Persuasion* (Albany: SUNY Press, 2017). His main areas of intellectual interest are metaphysics and philosophy of religion from a neoclassical or process perspective. He is the editor of the journal *Process Studies*.

Andrew Fiala is Professor of Philosophy and Director of the Ethics Center at Fresno State University, USA. A former president of Concerned Philosophers for Peace, his publications include *The Just War Myth* (2008), *Public War, Private Conscience* (2010), *The Bloomsbury Companion to Political Philosophy* (editor, 2015), *Ethics: Theory and Contemporary Issues*, 9th edition (with Barbara MacKinnon, 2017), and *Transformative Pacifism* (forthcoming).

Andrew Fitz-Gibbon is Professor of Philosophy, Chair of the Philosophy Department, and Director for the Center for Ethics, Peace and Social Justice at the State University of New York College at Cortland. He is the author, co-author, or editor of 13 books in philosophy, ethics, spirituality, and nonviolence, including *Love as a Guide to Morals* (Rodopi, 2012) and *Talking to Terrorists, Non-Violence, and Counter-Terrorism: Lessons for Gaza from Northern Ireland* (Palgrave MacMillan, 2016).

Jane Hall Fitz-Gibbon has a PhD in interdisciplinary studies. She works in crisis intervention at a school for children with special needs and has cared for over 100 children in the foster care system. Her latest books are *Welcoming Strangers: Nonviolent Re-parenting of Children in Foster Care* (Transaction, 2016) and *Corporal Punishment, Religion and United States Public Schools* (Palgrave MacMillan, 2017).

Michael Allen Fox is Adjunct Professor, School of Humanities, University of New England, Australia, and Professor Emeritus of Philosophy, Queen's University, Canada. His books include

Nuclear War: Philosophical Perspectives (co-edited with Leo Groarke; Peter Lang, 2nd ed., 1987), *Understanding Peace: A Comprehensive Introduction* (Routledge, 2014), and most recently, *Home: A Very Short Introduction* (Oxford University Press, 2016).

Barry L. Gan is Professor of Philosophy and Director of the Center for Nonviolence at St. Bonaventure University. Gan has been editor of *The Acorn: Journal of the Gandhi-King Society* since 1990. He is the author of a number of articles and books, including *Violence and Nonviolence, An Introduction* (Rowman and Littlefield, 2013) and *Nonviolence in Theory and Practice*, 3rd edition (co-edited with Robert L. Holmes, Waveland Press, 2011).

William Gay is Professor Emeritus of Philosophy at the University of North Carolina at Charlotte. He has published seven books and over 100 journal articles and book chapters on issues of violence, war, peace, and justice from the perspectives of language and political philosophy. He also has edited book series on the philosophy of peace and on contemporary Russian philosophy. He has been an active member of Concerned Philosophers for Peace since 1981 and, among other roles, has served as its President and as its Executive Director.

Donna A. Gessell is a Professor of English at the University of North Georgia, Dahlonega campus, United States of America. Her article "Judith Ortiz Cofer and the Ecology of Creating Identity" will appear in an upcoming special edition of the *South Atlantic Review*.

Fuat Gursozlu is Assistant Professor of Philosophy at Loyola University Maryland, where he teaches social and political philosophy and ethics. He is the author of several articles on pluralism and violence, nonviolent political protest, and radical democracy, including "Pluralism, Identity, and Violence" in Gail Presbey and Greg Moses (eds.), *Peace Philosophy and Public Life* (Rodopi, 2014). He is editor of *Peace, Culture and Violence: Contesting Violence Building Peace* (Brill, forthcoming), and he is working on a book project entitled *Agonistic Peace and Democracy*.

Blake Hereth is a PhD student in philosophy at the University of Washington and a councilperson on the APA's Graduate Student Council. His primary areas of research are pacifism and the ethics of self-defense, animal ethics, and intersectional philosophy of religion. He recently defended the existence of animals in the afterlife in *Paradise Understood* (Oxford University Press, 2017) and has a forthcoming defense of radical pacifism in *Social Theory and Practice*.

Robert L. Holmes is Emeritus Professor of Philosophy at the University of Rochester. He is a past president of Concerned Philosophers for Peace and a former holder of the Rajiv Gandhi Chair in Peace and Disarmament at Jawaharlal Nehru University in New Delhi, India. He is author of *Basic Moral Philosophy*, 4th edition (Cengage, 2007), *Morality and War* (Princeton, 1989), and *Pacifism: A Philosophy of Nonviolence* (Bloomsbury, 2016), as well as co-editor (with Barry Gan) of *Nonviolence in Theory and Practice*, 3rd edition (Waveland, 2011).

Veena R. Howard is Assistant Professor of Philosophy and Religion and Director of the Peace and Conflict Program at Fresno State University. She is the author of *Gandhi's Ascetic Activism: Renunciation and Social Action* (SUNY, 2013) and a number of articles on religion and nonviolence.

Ramin Jahanbegloo is Executive Director of the Mahatma Gandhi Centre for Nonviolence and Peace Studies and the Vice-Dean of the School of Law at Jindal Global University, Delhi,

India. He has studied or worked at the Sorbonne, in Iran, at Harvard, and at the University of Toronto. He is the winner of the Peace Prize from the United Nations Association in Spain (2009) and more recently the winner of the Josep Palau i Fabre International Essay Prize. Among his 27 books in English, French, Spanish, Italian, and Persian are *Gandhi: Aux Sources de la Nonviolence* (Felin, 1999), *Penser la Nonviolence* (UNESCO, 2000), *The Spirit of India* (Penguin, 2008), *Beyond Violence* (Har-Anand, 2008), *Leggere Gandhi a Teheran* (Marsilio, 2008), *The Gandhian Moment* (Harvard University Press, 2013), *Introduction to Nonviolence* (Palgrave, 2013), *Talking Philosophy* (Oxford University Press, 2015), and *Gadflies in the Public Space* (Lexington Press, 2017).

Jennifer Kling is Assistant Professor of Philosophy at Siena Heights University. Her research focuses on moral and political philosophy, particularly issues in war, self- and other-defense, international relations, and feminism. Her most recent publication is in *Journal of Global Ethics*, and she is currently working on a book titled *War Refugees: Risk, Justice, and Moral Responsibility* (under contract with Lexington Books).

James M. Lawson, Jr. is one of the leading figures in the struggle of African Americans for equality and civil rights. He studied Gandhi's nonviolent philosophy during a visit to India. Upon his return, he worked with Martin Luther King, Jr., the Southern Christian Leadership Conference, and as a mentor for the Student Nonviolent Coordinating Committee. He has continued to train people in the practice of nonviolence in Los Angeles and elsewhere.

Paul Morrow is a postdoctoral scholar in the Program in Political Philosophy, Policy, and Law at the University of Virginia. His research focuses on the role of norms in explaining, and preventing, large-scale crimes. His articles have appeared in *Humanity*, *Social Theory and Practice*, and the *Royal Institute of Philosophy Supplement to Philosophy*.

Jan Narveson is Distinguished Professor Emeritus at the University of Waterloo. He is author of many articles and books, including a number of key articles offering a moral critique of pacifism. His books include *The Libertarian Idea* (orig. Temple University Press, 1989; republished Broadview, 2001), *Moral Matters* (Broadview, 1993; 2nd, expanded edition, 1999), *Respecting Persons in Theory and Practice* (Rowman and Littlefield, 2002), *You and the State* (Rowman and Littlefield, 2008), and (with co-author James P. Sterba) *Is Liberty Compatible with Equality?* (Cambridge University Press, 2010). In 2003, Narveson was inducted as an Officer of the Order of Canada.

Nel Noddings is Lee Jacks Professor of Child Education, Stanford University. She is the author of 21 books and about 300 articles and chapters, including *Caring: A Relational Approach to Ethics and Moral Education* (University of California Press, 1984/2013) and *Peace Education: How We Come to Love and Hate War* (Cambridge University Press, 2012). She is past president of the National Academy of Education, the Philosophy of Education Society, and the John Dewey Society. She is the holder of six honorary doctorates.

José-Antonio Orosco is Associate Professor of Philosophy at Oregon State University in Corvallis, Oregon. He is the author of *Cesar Chavez and the Common Sense of Nonviolence* (University of New Mexico, 2008) and *Toppling the Melting Pot: Immigration and Multiculturalism in American Pragmatism* (Indiana University Press, 2016).

Contributors

Danielle Poe is a Professor of Philosophy at the University of Dayton. She is the editor of *Philosophy of Peace* (Special Book Series in VIBS, published by Brill). Her research and teaching interests are in contemporary issues of peace and justice. Her recent work includes *Maternal Activism: The Ethical Ambiguity Faced by Mothers Confronting Injustice* (SUNY, 2015); "Justice and Joy" in *Peace Review: A Journal of Social Justice* (2015); "Asking to Be Welcomed: Luce Irigaray and the Practice of Receiving Hospitality" in *Journal for Peace and Justice Studies* (2014); and "Responding to Violence and Injustice Using Non-Violence: Martin Luther King, Jr., Leymah Gbowee, and Dorothy Stang" in *Global Change, Peace and Security* (2014).

Gail M. Presbey is Professor of Philosophy at the University of Detroit Mercy. She has edited or co-edited the following: *The Philosophical Quest: A Cross Cultural Reader* (McGraw Hill, 2000), *Thought and Practice in African Philosophy* (Konrad Adenauer, 2002), *Philosophical Perspectives on the "War on Terrorism"* (Rodopi, 2007), and *Peace Philosophy and Public Life* (Rodopi, 2014). She has held a two-year Fulbright Senior Scholar position at the University of Nairobi, Kenya, and a Fulbright research grant hosted by World Peace Center at MIT, Pune, India, where she studied Gandhian nonviolence.

Michael Proulx is Associate Professor of History at the University of North Georgia, Dahlonega campus, United States of America. His research investigates the development of institutional authorities in the classical world. He recently published a chapter titled "Color, Adornment, and Social Conflict: Fashioning Cultural Identity in Ancient Greece and Rome," in *The Use of Color in History, Politics, and Art* (2016).

Eric Reitan is Professor of Philosophy at Oklahoma State University. He is the author of numerous articles as well as three books: *The Triumph of Love: Same-Sex Marriage and the Christian Love Ethic* (Cascade, 2017), *God's Final Victory: A Comparative Philosophical Case for Universalism* (with John Kronen, Continuum, 2011), and *Is God a Delusion? A Reply to Religion's Cultured Despisers* (Wiley-Blackwell, 2009), which was named a Choice Outstanding Academic Title of 2009.

Cheyney Ryan is Senior Fellow in the Program on Ethics, Law, and Armed Conflict at Oxford University. Ryan is the author of a number of books and articles, including *The Chickenhawk Syndrome: War, Sacrifice, and Personal Responsibility* (Roman and Littlefield, 2009).

Eddy M. Souffrant is a faculty member of the Department of Philosophy at the University of North Carolina at Charlotte. He teaches Ethics, Social and Political Philosophy, and Ethics and International Affairs. He has research and teaching expertise in the areas of African American, Francophone, and Caribbean philosophy. His recent publications examine the issues of collective responsibility, conceptions of political identities, applied ethics, and international ethics. He is currently working on a manuscript that explores the intersection of international development, ethics, and disaster. His publications include *Identity, Political Freedom, and Collective Responsibility: The Pillars and Foundations of Global Ethics* (Palgrave MacMillan, 2013).

Lloyd Steffen is Professor of Religion Studies and University Chaplain at Lehigh University in Bethlehem, Pennsylvania. He is the author and editor of 11 books, including *Holy War, Just War: Exploring the Religious Meaning of Religious Violence* (Rowman and Littlefield, 2007), *Ethics and Experience: Moral Theory from Just War to Abortion* (Rowan and Littlefield, 2012), *Executing Justice: The Moral Meaning of the Death Penalty* (Wipf and Stock Publishers, 2006), and (with D. Cooley)

The Ethics of Death: Religious and Philosophical Perspectives in Dialogue (Fortress Press, 2014). Steffen has served as the NGO representative to the United Nations for the Religious Coalition for Reproductive Choice. He directs the Lehigh University Center for Dialogue, Ethics and Spirituality and the Lehigh Prison Project.

Mark Woods is a professor of philosophy at the University of San Diego. He is the author of the book *Rethinking Wilderness* (Broadview, 2017) as well as numerous articles in the field of environmental philosophy and the field of the ethics of war and peace. He is especially interested in how these fields intersect, and he is working on a new book on the environmental ethics of war and peace.

ACKNOWLEDGEMENTS

Special thanks to Dr. Veena Howard for her input and enthusiasm for this project. Also thanks to Jacqueline Alvarez for her assistance in editing, and thanks to the scholars and collaborators in Concerned Philosophers for Peace.

INTRODUCTION

Andrew Fiala

Pacifism is a complex topic comprising a variety of arguments, commitments, and applications. Nonviolence is a closely related and similarly complex idea. Pacifism is typically used in a narrow sense to mean opposition to war, while nonviolence typically describes a method and means, and in some cases a virtue or even a way of life. Many of the greatest proponents of pacifism and nonviolence have been religious: Leo Tolstoy, Mohandas K. Gandhi, and Martin Luther King, Jr., for example. But opposition to war can also be grounded in nonreligious moral argument. Significant secular pacifists and critics of war include William James, Jane Addams, Bertrand Russell, and Albert Einstein. This book provides a comprehensive overview of the ideas of pacifists and proponents of nonviolence in many traditions, while also providing examples of how these ideas can be applied in various cases.

Pacifism often begins with a basic presumption against war. Robert Holmes—an author whose work is included in the present volume—states, "There is a moral presumption against war, and unless that presumption is defeated, war is wrong" (Holmes 2017: XVIII). Such a claim runs counter to those who would defend war and who see defensive violence as justifiable. Jan Narveson—another author whose work is included here—has argued that when pacifism is understood as complete rejection of war and violence, it is self-refuting, self-defeating, and potentially self-contradictory (Narveson 2013). Other critics (see Orosco in the present volume) have worried that pacifism allows injustice to proceed. Defenders of nonviolence and pacifists have responded by qualifying, justifying, and explaining the critique of war and the war-system—and by demonstrating the power of nonviolent social protest. Diverse forms of pacifism have emerged in the literature: personal pacifism, contingent pacifism, just war pacifism, and so on. The debate about pacifism has become rich and complicated and has often developed in dialogue with the just war tradition, as Cheyney Ryan explains in his contribution to the present volume.

One important question in all of this is how deep a commitment to nonviolence ought to go. Some argue that it should extend all the way down to animals and ecosystems. We might also wonder how nonviolence connects to moral education, child-rearing, theories of punishment, and issues related to gender and sexuality. Pacifist insight and critiques of violence also connect to political issues such as theories of liberal democracy and historical progress, human rights concerns, worries about atrocities and genocide, and critiques of warism and the military-industrial complex. At the same time, nonviolence can be understood in connection with religious traditions, spiritual practices, and virtue ethics.

There is a rich and well-established tradition that builds upon the work of Gandhi and King in order to advocate for the use of nonviolence as a strategy of political activism. This approach is not passive or inactive (and pacifism is often unfortunately conflated with a kind of passivity). It is also possible to imagine a way of life that is based in nonviolence—and in the affirmation of values that are positive and life-affirming. Thus we can recognize nonviolence as a broader concept that is connected to ideas about human flourishing and the good life. Nonviolence has often been understood in relation to a larger account of the moral life. As Martin Luther King explained, "Nonviolence in its truest sense is not a strategy that one uses simply because it is expedient at the moment; nonviolence is ultimately a way of life that men live by because of the sheer morality of its claim" (King 1958/2010: 76).

Nonviolence is a negative term: it rejects or condemns violence. Pacifism appears to be more affirmative: it espouses peace or peacemaking. The term comes from the Latin *pacificus*—or as employed in the Bible's Sermon on the Mount (Matthew 5:9), *pacifici*—which means to make, build, or create peace (*pax-* means peace; *-facio* means to make). The Gospel text says "*beati pacifici*"—blessed are the peacemakers. Despite this heritage, we still need further explanation about what counts as peace, what counts as war, and what counts as violence or nonviolence. Once we understand the concepts in question, it remains to be seen whether there are good arguments to be offered in support of these ideas and commitments—from the standpoint of moral theory, religion, culture, and so on. It is easy to see that pacifism and nonviolence demand careful thought and critical reflection.

This *Handbook* offers a definitive collection of such reflective work. It offers original essays on pacifism, nonviolence, and the philosophy of peace, written by leading scholars in the field (including some new and emerging voices). This book focuses on historical, social, religious, and ethical issues arising in the philosophical study of pacifism and nonviolence. Unlike the field of peace studies, which focuses on empirical work in the social sciences aimed at understanding the power of nonviolent social movements and ways to build peace, the philosophical approach to pacifism and nonviolence, featured here, is concerned with conceptual analysis and abstract argument. Unlike work that is focused on the justification of violence and war—in what is called just war theory—pacifism and nonviolence offer a critique of war and violence, while also offering a vision of what a peaceful and just world ought to look like.

Some critics contend that pacifism and nonviolence are utopian, since the real world seems to be wracked with violence. Whether this is true is the subject matter of some of the essays in this volume. But even if the charge of utopianism is true, there is value in imagining a world to aspire toward: the world as it ought to be. James Lawson—a leading figure in the nonviolent American civil rights struggle—suggests in his contribution to this volume that advocates of peace and nonviolence live in a non-existent country. They work nonviolently, as Lawson has done, to make the dream a reality.

Pacifism and nonviolence have a long history in the world's religious and philosophical traditions. While pacifism is historically associated with religious traditions, the commitment to nonviolence is also found in sources in the philosophical tradition. Philosophers tend to prefer nonviolent methods of persuasion over more coercive measures. This basic commitment to nonviolence in argumentation extends all the way back to Socrates. Philosophers have developed ideas about justified violence that include a prima facie condemnation of violence as unreasonable and unproductive. While there is a rich debate among just war theorists about the justification of violence, pacifism has an equally rich set of philosophical concepts and arguments. Ethicists and political philosophers have carefully examined the logic and morality of pacifism and nonviolence, as well as the application of these ideas to problems in the real world. This volume provides a broad overview of the topic with contributions from scholars who have spent their careers thinking about these issues.

Ironically, some peace activists and scholars of peace and nonviolence have rejected the term "pacifism," despite their own interest in peace and commitment to nonviolence (see Cortright 2008). Such critics worry that pacifism has become a meaningless term that ought to be avoided. Thus we might prefer the neologism "nonviolentism" as a way of avoiding what they see as unfortunate connotations of "pacifism." Holmes coined the term "nonviolentism" in the 1970s (see Holmes 2013: 157) to describe a broad commitment to nonviolence. But even that term is subject to qualification. Barry Gan distinguishes between a broad and comprehensive commitment to nonviolence and a selective rejection of some forms of violence (see Gan 2013: 68). Others distinguish between pacifism and pacific-ism, using the former term to refer to an absolute rejection of war and violence and using the latter term to mean a less absolutist critique of war (see Alexandra 2006). Other scholars have imported Gandhian terminology such as *ahimsa* and *satyagraha* into their work on nonviolence and their critiques of war and violence. These terminological distinctions are important for conceptual clarity; however, there is no consensus in the usage of these terms among authors who generally write and argue about nonviolence and pacifism.

Nor indeed is there agreement about what we mean by "peace," "violence," or "war." Thus even though "peace is not a great mystery," as Michael Fox puts it (Fox 2014: XV), peace remains a complicated concept. Peace can be defined both positively (as what provides for a rich and harmonious communal life) and negatively (as the absence of war) (see Galtung 1969). The term "violence" has been employed to describe both overt, concrete acts of deliberate harm and more subtle and insidious structures of "institutional violence." In the era of cyberwarfare, the war on terrorism, asymmetric warfare, drone warfare, and so on, the concept of war itself has been stretched and modified in various ways.

This *Handbook* examines pacifism and nonviolence from a variety of perspectives—including discussions of terminological and semantic issues. Of course, terminological disputes are less important than the substantive commitment to peace and nonviolence and the implications that this has for both theory and practice. One goal of the *Handbook* is to make it clear that pacifism is a legitimate moral position, that it has a deep history, and that it ought to remain a central concern of scholars and activists who are concerned with violence, war, and social justice. Another goal of this volume is to demonstrate the fecundity of nonviolence by showing how it can be applied to a range of concrete issues.

Pacifism and nonviolence have long been important for activists. Peace activism and strategies of nonviolence have been developed in recent decades—following upon successful examples in the work of Gandhi and King, along with Cesar Chavez, Lech Walesa, Nelson Mandela, the Dalai Lama, and others. There has also been a long-standing and fundamental commitment to pacifism on the part of certain religious groups (Jains, Quakers, etc.), with some denominations coming closer to pacifism in recent decades (as for example in the case of Roman Catholicism). The global community has less tolerance for war (and especially for war crimes) under developing ideas in international law. And there is a growing chorus of people who condemn violence in social institutions, in the family, and in our treatment of nonhuman beings. Although war and violence continue to afflict us, we are increasingly aware of the futility of war and the vicious cycles of violence. We are more sensitive to the damage that war causes to noncombatants, to soldiers (in the form of post-traumatic stress disorder), and to the ecosystem. We are increasingly aware of problems such as structural or institutional violence. And yet violence remains a temptation for activists, and political structures continue to prepare for war. And so, the subject matter of this *Handbook* remains importantly relevant.

This book is organized into four main parts. Part One includes essays in the history of pacifism and nonviolence as well as essays focused on diverse religious and cultural traditions. Part Two contains essays on pacifism in moral theory and the morality of pacifism. Part Three offers essays that connect pacifism and nonviolence to issues in social and political philosophy. Part Four applies pacifism and nonviolence to concrete issues. The volume concludes with an essay by Reverend James Lawson, a student of Gandhian nonviolence who worked with Dr. Martin Luther King, Jr. during the American civil rights movement.

Readers of this book should be able to read individual chapters in any order: each chapter offers a self-contained focus on its topic. Authors were selected in order to obtain a diversity of viewpoints and methodological approaches—including those of philosophers and scholars of religion. This volume includes top names in the field, including authors who have dedicated their entire careers to this topic and who have written books and articles that have defined the philosophical study of pacifism and nonviolence. The book also includes new and emerging authors, whose work will continue to push scholarship in this arena. Many of the scholars included in this volume are active in Concerned Philosophers for Peace, an organization that continues to hold conferences and publish work on pacifism, nonviolence, and peace philosophy.

Works Cited

Alexandra, A. (2006). "On the Distinction between Pacifism and Pacificism," in B. Bleisch and J.-D. Strub (eds.), *Pazifismus: Ideengeschichte, Theorie und Praxis*. Bern, Stuttgart and Wien: Haupt, 107–124.
Cortright, D. (2008). *Peace: A History of Movements and Ideas*. Cambridge: Cambridge University Press.
Fox, M. A. (2014). *Understanding Peace*. New York: Routledge.
Galtung, J. (1969). "Violence, Peace, and Peace Research." *Journal of Peace Research* 6 (3): 167–191.
Gan, B. (2013). *Violence and Nonviolence: An Introduction*. Lanham, MD: Rowman and Littlefield.
Holmes, R. (2013). *The Ethics of Nonviolence: Essays by Robert Holmes*, edited by P. Cicovacki. London: Bloomsbury.
Holmes, R. (2017). *Pacifism: A Philosophy of Nonviolence*. London: Bloomsbury.
King, M. L., Jr. (1958/2010). *Stride Toward Freedom*. Boston: Beacon.
Narveson, J. (2013). "Pacifism: 50 Years Later." *Philosophia* 41 (4): 925–943.

PART I

Historical and Tradition-Specific Considerations

1
A HISTORY OF THE IDEA OF PACIFISM AND NONVIOLENCE
Ancient to Modern

Duane L. Cady

Although the words "pacifism" and "nonviolence" have found common usage gradually since the mid-nineteenth century, the idea they refer to can be found in documents dating back nearly three millennia. Pacifism arises initially as moral opposition to violence, especially mass violence. Although much of our contemporary world presumes the moral rightness of war as a central function of the nation-state (see Cady 1989/2010), moral resistance to mass violence, along with moral preference for society being orderly from within by cooperation rather than ordered by force from without, can be traced back to antiquity. The effort here is not to describe past events wherein pacifism succeeded or failed to resolve conflict, struggle against oppression, or establish thriving peaceful societies by nonviolent means. That history is important, but here the focus is on the *idea* of pacifism, a moral history of humans aspiring to harmonious living and the absence of war.

It seems the earliest documented philosophy of nonviolence appears in India among Jaina believers as early as the ninth century BCE. In the early sixth century BCE the Jaina reformer Vardhmana Mahavira systematized existing Jaina beliefs including ethical principles based on nonviolence accepted by followers of Jainism to this day. Jaina ascetics were to aim at complete mental and physical detachment from worldly affairs. This required a vow of nonviolence, the highest virtue of Jainism, and is the first of the five great vows: nonviolence, truth, non-stealing, celibacy, and non-possession. The basic vow of nonviolence includes not only avoiding physical injury but avoiding mental and verbal injury as well, and it serves as the moral basis for life itself.

Lao Tzu, the "old master" of Chinese philosophy usually credited with writing the *Tao Te Ching* and founding Taoism, dates to the sixth century BCE, though many scholars have questioned his historicity and speculate that work attributed to him may actually be a collection of pieces from many contributors. In any event the *Tao Te Ching* is a compilation of aphorisms and wisdom stories often enigmatic or paradoxical in expression. Readers are called to be wary of human willfulness because it has allowed us to distort our true nature. We are called to "return" to the divine way to discover our true selves, to go with the flow in simplicity and humility, and to be skeptical of willful and activist leaders. The Taoist social and political perspective advocates nonviolence and we are told that "weapons are instruments of evil, not the instruments of a good ruler," yet this is not absolute pacifism since "when he uses [weapons] unavoidably, he regards calm restraint as the best principle" and does not regard victory as praiseworthy, "for to praise victory is to delight in the slaughter of men" and "he who delights in the slaughter of men will not succeed in the empire" (Lao Tzu quoted in Holmes 1990: 14).

The great Hindu synthesis, *The Bhagavad-Gita*—Sanskrit for "Song of the Lord"—was written in the fourth or fifth century BCE. This 700-verse Hindu scripture is a dialogue between the warrior Prince Arjuna and his charioteer Krishna, the Hindu God Vishnu. Arjuna is reluctant to kill his own relatives in a civil war and Krishna counsels him to do his duty. The setting is a battlefield and the advice for the prince is bravery over cowardice. Literalists interpret the *Gita* as a divine reminder of caste obligation, but Thoreau, Gandhi, and many scholars read it as an allegory for the human struggle between good and evil within the self. Life is a battle of sorts, and when we let go of ego attachment—the sense of possession that makes us selfish, jealous, and violent—we travel the way of Truth, of detachment, of harmony, even with different religious traditions. We learn to live in truth without fear.

Moving from Eastern to Western antiquity, we find the familiar presumption of the legitimacy of war among ancient Greeks. Heraclitus, a pivotal pre-Socratic thinker at the turn of the sixth and fifth centuries BCE, tells us that "war is the father and king of all" (Heraclitus quoted in Nahm 1964: 71). Strife is a fundamental source of nature for Heraclitus. The scant and fleeting harmony found in nature is due to tensions among conflicting natural beings. For the most part ancient Greeks took war for granted as natural and inevitable, and a culture of war and the warrior was central to the Golden Age.

The Peloponnesian War between Athens and Sparta began in 431 BCE and continued for nearly thirty years between the young Athenian democracy and the old Spartan oligarchy. The best thinkers of the time disapproved of the war. Thucydides thought it was a needless war of rival ambitions. He blamed both sides (Thucydides 1900: 169), recounting one particularly telling episode in which Athenian military leaders explain themselves to the people of Melos, islanders in the Aegean Sea who had tried to remain neutral in the Athens/Sparta war:

> You and we both know that in the discussion of human affairs the question of justice only enters where there is equal power to enforce it, and that the more powerful exact what they can and the weak grant what they must. . . . Your subjection will give us an increase in security as well as an extension of empire. For of the gods we believe and of men we know, that by a law of their nature, wherever they can rule they will. This law was not made by us and we are not the first to have acted upon it. We did but inherit it and shall bequeath it to all time, and we know that you and all mankind, if you were as strong as we are, would do as we do.
>
> *Thucydides: 173*

With this as their justification, the Athenians destroyed Melos by killing all men of military age and enslaving the women and children. This is war realism, the position that morality is irrelevant in war. In matters of conflict, groups do what they can to prevail. Describing the civil war in Corcyra, Thucydides tells us that once war begins dire necessity takes over, bringing brutality. "War is a hard master, and most men grow to be like the lives they lead" (Thucydides: 175). While discussing the dominant view of war held by most ancient Greeks, Thucydides opens a critical examination of warism, the notion—often a presumption—that war is normal, natural, and morally acceptable.

The greatest ancient Greek playwrights took anti-war positions during the Peloponnesian War. In *The Trojan Women*, Euripides dramatizes the suffering of innocents with a veiled historical account from hundreds of years before the sacking of Melos. Contemporary Athenian audiences would have made the connection to the then recent Athenian massacre. Aristophanes, the great comic dramatist, wrote and produced *Lysistrata* (literally, "the peacemaker"), during the Peloponnesian War. In this sarcastic anti-war play, Lysistrata organizes Athenian women with a vow to withhold affection from men until the end of the senseless war. The play reflects gender roles associated with war and peace: the women want peace; the men do not. The consequences for the men prompt much laughter and provoke anti-war reflections. To this day readings of *Lysistrata* are held to protest nations as they launch themselves into war.

Ancient Greeks also begin developing the idea of moral restraint in war. The Roman scholar Cicero makes reference to the predominant ancient Greek tribes coming together as equals to recognize and observe rules of war designed to limit cruelty (see Stawell 1936: 14–15). Plato also outlines grounds for restraint in battle with perhaps the earliest systematic theoretical explanation of war in his *Republic*. He offers ideas on creating and maintaining peace as well as argues for the necessity of moral restrictions on the fighting of war.

Plato's *Republic* is his consideration of the good life. Early on it becomes clear that the best life for human beings happens in cooperative communities. Since none of us are self-sufficient, good lives are based on human interdependence. Plato's Socrates outlines a simple society where goods and services are shared to mutual advantage of all citizens, and where basic needs are met in part by forgoing luxuries. Calling this "the true city, like a healthy individual," Socrates is pressed to consider a luxurious city, one committed to the unlimited acquisition of wealth (Socrates calls it "fevered"). It is with the city dedicated to wealth that Socrates finds the origin of war (Plato, *Republic*: 72b–73e).

The society based on accumulating wealth requires a guardian class of watchdog warriors, censorship, government lies, eugenics, and the abolition of the family. And it requires war. Although scholars disagree on Plato's own ideal society, two points on war are very clear. One, war originates in the drive for wealth, and two, war is best avoided. Additionally, if it cannot be avoided, it must be restrained. Plato's main worry about war concerns Greeks. In *Republic* 470e–471b, the dialogue concerns relations among the "good and civilized" Greeks. Plato suggests that strife among Greeks will not be called war, since quarrels among Greeks will occur with the hope of reconciliation.

> Being Greeks they will not ravage Greece, they will not burn the houses, nor will they maintain that all the inhabitants of each city are their foes, men, women, and children, but only a few, those who caused the quarrel. For all these reasons, as the majority are their friends, they will not ravage the country or destroy the houses. They will carry their quarrel to the point of compelling those who caused it to be punished by those who were guiltless and the victims of it.
>
> *Plato,* Republic: *471*

Although Plato does not extend such moral restraint beyond Greek enemies, he does lay the groundwork for a wider application of the immunity of innocents and the principle of proportionality, the notion that the evil of war must not go beyond the good likely to come of it. Clearly morality is relevant to war for Plato. War realism is rejected and seeds of a just war tradition are planted.

Plato also highlights anti-warism in the *Crito*, an early dialogue that captures the historical Socrates' objections to war. Pacifism is not necessarily the same as anti-warism, but the critique of violence is obviously connected to the critique of war. After his trial and conviction for corrupting the youth of Athens and for teaching religion contrary to that of the city, Socrates awaited his execution. Some of his friends were convinced that they could help him escape to another city, but they had a problem: convincing Socrates that his escape would be just. Socrates argues that we should never do injustice nor should we retaliate against it. We must never do evil, and we must never return evil for evil, no matter what we may have suffered (Plato, *Crito*: 48b–c). Many scholars dismiss this as merely rhetorical, a point made only "for the sake of argument," but Gregory Vlastos, perhaps the leading Plato scholar of the twentieth century, tells us this is an original moral insight, namely, that suffering injustice does not give one a moral justification to retaliate with violence (Vlastos 1991: 190). This undercuts virtually all justifications for violence and war throughout history. It is an especially remarkable insight for its time because punishing enemies was not only tolerated but glorified in ancient Greek culture (Vlastos 1991: 180).

Unlike Socrates, Aristotle does not reject violent retaliation against violence, but he does follow Plato's call for moral restraint in war. In his *Politics*, Aristotle critiques those "aiming at domination, as in Sparta and Crete," two places where "both education and most of the laws are organized for war" (Aristotle, *Politics*, 1324b8–1325a6). With justice as his goal Aristotle finds that a good political system "does not aim at war or domination over enemy states" since a good system has "no enemies or wars" (Vlastos 1991). He further challenges the glorification of war in his *Nicomachean Ethics*, saying:

> No one chooses to fight a war, and no one continues it, for the sake of fighting a war; someone would have to be a complete murderer if he made his friends his enemies so there could be battles and killings.... [We] fight wars only so that we can be at peace, and not for empire.
>
> *Aristotle,* Nicomachean Ethics: *1177b6–11*

Alexander the Great consolidated the disparate Hellenic city-states into his empire only to have it swallowed by the Romans. From the end of the second century CE until the fall of imperial Rome at the end of the fifth century the empire was always at war, along the frontiers and even among rivals within. Romans such as Cicero considered ethical limitation in war. In *De Officiis* Cicero speaks of observing "the rights of war." He says, "The only excuse, therefore, for going to war is that we may live in peace unharmed; and when the victory is won, we should spare those who have not been blood-thirsty and barbarous in their warfare" (Cicero 1913: 37).

Despite fierce persecution of early Christians by the Romans, the most devoted followers of the crucified first-century rabbi Jesus of Nazareth practiced pacifism to the extreme of nonresistance to evil. Christianity was pacifistic for its first 300 years, with Christians understanding Jesus as having taught pacifism: "You have heard it was said, 'an eye for an eye and a tooth for a tooth,' but I say to you, do not resist an evil doer. If anyone strikes you on the right cheek, turn the other also" and "You have heard that it was said 'you shall love your neighbor and hate your enemy,' but I say to you, 'love your enemies and pray for those who persecute you'" (Matthew 5: 38–39; 43–34). At first Christians did not participate in war, but things changed with the conversion of Emperor Constantine in 313 along with his declaration of toleration of Christianity. One scholar suggests that the church conquered the empire only to be conquered by its captive (Stawell 1936: 35).

In the fourth century the church adopted the teachings of Augustine on the just war, a code built upon earlier ideas of Plato and Cicero with Christian additions. Jesus' words "resist not evil" were interpreted to require a spiritual attitude of love that did not preclude killing physically. This view of Christian morality insisted that attitudes, not actions, were right or wrong. As long as hate was avoided, salvation could be preserved despite killing. The life of the soul was paramount, the life of the body secondary, so much so that destroying physical life may even benefit a sinner. War requires the intention of restoring justice and building peace, and war must avoid massacre, looting, and atrocities; that is, war must be both just to enter and justly fought, and just war requires right authority—the emperor—to decide when to fight. With the union of the church and the empire, war can be morally accepted, even morally required.

Pacifism was rarely seen for the next twelve centuries, but returns with the Anabaptists, including Mennonites and others during the Reformation. Only isolated "heretical" objections to mass violence arise during this millennium-long medieval era, one dominated by ecclesiastical authority. Clergy members were exempt from military service, but others had no option but to participate in war. The wars between Christians during this time were among the worst the world had seen. The reemergence of pacifist thought came with Rationalist and Protestant revolt against the "senselessness and cruelty of trying to establish harmony by bloodshed," by rejecting the Crusades and later wars to expand territory among princes of Europe (Stawell 1936: 74).

> The crusade which originated in the [Middle Ages] differs from the just war in several respects. The cause is more than just, it is holy.... The authority of the Prince is not necessary. The war may be fought under the authority of God or His representatives on earth.
>
> *Bainton 1964: 249*

Between the time of the early church to the Middle Ages, Christian evaluation of war moved from the refusal to participate in war of extreme pacifism, to reluctant participation in just war, and finally to enthusiastic participation in holy war (Bainton 1964: 248).

The Crusades were driven by twin goals: the defeat of Islam and the unification of Christianity. They failed at both. Wars against the Muslim world precipitated East-West wars among Christians, opening Europe to Islamic advances while fragmenting Christendom. While Christianity and Islam came from the same Abrahamic roots in ancient Hebrew sacred texts, leaders and followers of both dug in for a long and bitter enmity that for the most part has endured. Early Christian pacifism was largely dormant as medieval ecclesiastical dominance broke apart into a mosaic of small Christian principalities, the national monarchies from which the pattern of modern Europe began to emerge (Windass 1964: 59). By the start of the sixteenth century kings and princes in the fragmented Christian Europe began to assert their own "divine" authority. A Crusading zealotry joined political nationalism, resulting in each "sovereign" autocrat determining when war is just.

Desiderius Erasmus was the most articulate critic of warism during the Renaissance. His critique of war exemplifies the humanistic, emotional, and intellectual spirit of the Renaissance itself. In writing his *Complaint of Peace* (1517), Erasmus shows his sense of humor as he cuts to the quick: "Who is there that does not think his own cause just?" With a simple question he challenges the basis of just-warism by rejecting the notion that political leaders can themselves decide whether war is just.

> We have borrowed much from the laws of the Caesars.... Wishing to perfect our work we twist the teachings of the gospel to suit it. Roman law allows us to counter force with force and press our own claims to the utmost.... It glorifies war, provided it be just, and by definition it is just provided the prince declares it to be so, although the prince may be a child or a fool.
>
> *quoted in Stawell 1936: 88*

Countering the argument that war is lawful because force is lawful in punishing wrongdoers, Erasmus reminds us that "in the courts a man is condemned and suffers according to law" but "in battle each party treats the other party as guilty" (quoted in Stawell 1936: 88). Erasmus uses pacifist arguments of various sorts as he objects to the warism of his time. He expresses concern for the suffering of innocents and he challenges the notion that war has pragmatic value: "If you cannot have the mind of a statesman, you might at least show the sense of a shopkeeper." Erasmus believes the practical costs of conquering a town by force are higher than the costs of building a new one, making war a waste of resources. At the same time Martin Luther, a contemporaneous rival to Erasmus, sarcastically mocked pacifists as naïve, and insisted that "war is in itself Godlike, and as natural and necessary to the world as eating and drinking" (quoted in Stawell 1936: 96).

During the period that the church broke apart into clusters of kingdoms and principalities, multiplying political rivalries, the technology of war developed apace. The invention of gunpowder along with novel ideas of putting it to use expanded the possibilities of war and often made dangerous leaders even more dangerous. Explosives under the command of princes and kings claiming "divine" authority to declare war made life in Europe "nasty, brutish, and short," as Thomas Hobbes would famously describe it in his *Leviathan* some years later. In this period guns were objects of beauty, most cities and towns were built as fortresses as a matter of course, and battle was brutish. Animalistic military virtues of strength, obedience, and courage anchored a revitalized and growing cult of war characteristic of dominant culture. The Renaissance Humanism of Erasmus was fueled by the warism predominant at the time.

For Erasmus, reason is human and battle is brutish, animalistic. We develop our higher selves by cultivating the virtues of intellect, by pursuing the life of the mind as opposed to stooping to our lower, barbarian selves, our animal nature expressed by physical fighting and killing. In his mind it is obvious that conflict is to be settled humanely by discussion and agreement or arbitration; only brutes would resort to war. Erasmus undercut the popular culture's fascination with war through satire, in hopes of cultivating disgust for war and violence (Windass 1964: 60–63). *Complaint of Peace*, *Praise of Folly*, and many of his colloquies show Erasmus' wit as he exposes the brutal underbelly of war.

The Age of Enlightenment brought protests against the persistence of European religious wars. People were tired of the carnage no matter the reasons and causes for the battles. Social and political theorists of the time reflected a spirit of reason and a disposition to promote thoughtful ways to peace. Plans for European and world peace were written. War was taken to be a problem. The solution? Internationalism. There had been suggestions of various means to resolve conflict without war before. Maximilien de Bethume, Duc de Sully, chief administrator to Henry IV of France, and William Penn, founder of Pennsylvania, come to mind as notable advocates for an international federation of sovereign princes of Europe for the purpose of resolving conflict short of war. Unfortunately the gap between theory and practice prevailed: European princes couldn't bring themselves to forgo nationalism for the sake of peace, or perhaps they couldn't bring themselves to give up their individual sovereignty and bow to the authority of an institutionally organized Europe. Since governments would not be subject to an international federation, the need to preserve a "balance of power" provided the excuse to build their individual military capabilities, every nation playing off against every other, even at the expense of neighbors.

Immanuel Kant wrote his "Idea for a Universal History from a Cosmopolitan Point of View" in 1784, following upon other plans for peace offered by authors such as Abbé St. Pierre and Rousseau. It is paradigmatic of Enlightenment internationalism. Kant's position is both rational and practical. According to Kant, the biggest problem for humanity is achieving a universal civil society. Human beings flourish only within free societies, that is, societies where limits to freedom are minimal and necessary to safeguard the freedoms of others. Everyone loves freedom without limits, but experience teaches that we cannot thrive in wild freedom. By trial and error we discover "that which reason could have told us at the beginning and with far less sad experience, to wit, to step from the lawless condition of savages into a league of nations" (Kant 1963: 16). Kant tells us this idea was laughed at by Jean-Jacques Rousseau; it seems fantastic to this day, yet, as Kant underscores his point, nations must come to this point just as individuals had to "give up their brutish freedom and to seek quiet and security under a lawful constitution" (Kant 1963: 19).

As Kant sees it, humanity—as individuals as well as the species—is evolving along a spectrum from brutish to rational behavior. The transition is uneven, but the general trend is from violent imposition of will toward arbitration, compromise, and cooperation among individuals and among states as well. His "Perpetual Peace" (1795/1963) is a more detailed account of human moral progress toward internationalism, within Europe in particular. Individuals and nations must learn how to self-impose restrictions on our freedom out of respect for the freedom of other individuals and nations. We create laws to do this, but because we legislate them for ourselves they free us. Experience then confirms what reason dictates: "Reason, from its throne of supreme legislative authority, absolutely condemns war as a legal recourse and makes a state of peace a direct duty, even though peace cannot be established or secured except by a compact among nations" (Kant 1963: 100). Without a legitimate international forum, war is inevitable. "But by war and its favorable issue in victory, right is not decided" (Kant 1963). Thus Kant condemns war on practical as well as rational grounds.

Near the end of "Perpetual Peace" Kant agrees with Hobbes in reminding us that before government, no individual or collective had more right than another in claiming any particular part of the Earth. Remarkably, Kant delineates many examples of inhospitable and unjust behavior committed by "the civilized" world.

> The injustices they show to lands and peoples they visit (which is equivalent to conquering them) is carried by them to terrifying lengths. America, the lands inhabited by the Negro, the Spice Islands, the Cape, etc. were at the time of their discovery considered by these intruders as lands without owners, for they counted the inhabitants as nothing.
>
> *Kant 1963: 103–104*

Kant does not discuss what recourse victims of colonization may rightly undertake, but he does emphasize the failure and futility of war, practically and morally, and makes clear that international law is "indispensable for the maintenance of the public human rights and hence also of perpetual peace" (Kant 1963: 105). Nations as well as individuals must subject themselves to principles and rules of order that respect the rights of their peers and give up claims to superiority, moral or political. If they do not, conflict will prevail and the arbitrary and brutal condition of war will persist.

Works Cited

Aristotle. (1995). "Politics and Nicomachean Ethics," in T. Irwin and G. Fine (eds.), *Aristotle: Selections*. Indianapolis: Hackett.
Bainton, R. H. (1964). *Studies on the Reformation*. London: Hodder and Stoughton.
Cady, D. (1989/2010). *From Warism to Pacifism: A Moral Continuum*. Philadelphia: Temple University Press.
Cicero. (1913). *De Officiis*. New York: MacMillan, Loeb Classic Library.
Heraclitus. (1964). *Selections from Early Greek Philosophy*, edited by M.C. Nahm. New York: Appleton Century Crofts.
Kant, I. (1795/1963). "'The Idea for a Universal History from a Cosmopolitan Point of View,' and 'Perpetual Peace'," in L.W. Beck (ed.), *On History*. Indianapolis: Bobbs-Merrill.

Lao Tzu. (1990). "The Way of Lao Tzu," in R.L. Holmes (ed.), *Nonviolence in Theory and Practice*. Belmont, CA: Wadsworth, 10–13.
Plato. (1997). "Republic," in J. Cooper (ed.), *Plato: Complete Works*. Indianapolis: Hackett.
Stawell, F. M. (1936). *The Growth of International Thought*. London: Thornton Butterworth.
Thucydides. (1900). "History of the Peloponnesian War," in B. Jowett (trans.), *Thucydides*, 2nd ed., vol. 2. Oxford: Clarendon Press.
Vlastos, G. (1991). *Socrates: Ironist and Moral Philosopher*. Ithaca, NY: Cornell University Press.
Windass, S. (1964). *Christianity and Violence*. London: Sheed and Ward.

2
NONVIOLENCE AND PACIFISM IN THE LONG NINETEENTH CENTURY

Michael Allen Fox

Overview of the Period

Dividing history into decimalized segments (decades, centuries) is convenient but at the same time often appears a bit artificial and arbitrary. As one scholar observes, "History is not a theater where the curtain suddenly falls" (Osterhammel 2014: 918). The nineteenth century proves the point, overlapping those that come before and after in interesting and significant ways, which enhance an understanding of its contributions to world peace. For this reason, the present discussion begins in the late eighteenth century and ends in the early twentieth. Space limitations permit highlighting only some major peace developments of the "long nineteenth century," but it is hoped that the flavor of the period will stand out clearly.

Major figures (for example, Immanuel Kant, Jane Addams, and Mohandas Gandhi) are considered in some detail. Others of note are briefly considered, while many who are only mentioned by name may be taken as representative of a larger group of theorists/activists working toward similar ends. The birth and evolution of European and Anglo-American peace societies and movements is a theme that runs through the century, but attention will also be paid to developments that occurred elsewhere in the world. Ideas and organizations devoted to nonviolence and peace unquestionably flourished during this period, and they both reflected the interdependence of nations and contributed to a fledgling sense of international community. This sense of community was also forged by economic realities of the time, revolutionary ideals, and attempts to think more broadly about human nature and to inspire the pursuit of something new: a set of shared global values.

As argued elsewhere (Fox 2014), the meaning of peace embraces much more than the absence of war and other forms of organized and chaotic violence, plus opposition to war. We miss capturing the creativity and productivity of peace if we overlook its everyday, ongoing presence in our lives—in the small contributions made by people everywhere. These include getting along, trusting one another, being kind, considerate, and supportive, and building community for the present and future. Because of this dynamic aspect, characterizing the peace accomplishments of a given era is like trying to capture motion with a still photograph—it can at best yield a glimpse of peace within that time frame, just as it provides only part of the story of peace overall. Antony Adolf asserts in *Peace: A World History* that a broad perspective on peace enables us to take a "panoramic view . . . across cultures and centuries," as well as to "zoom in on issues of permanent or periodic importance" (Adolf 2009: 2). He goes further to suggest that events in the history of peace, just like those in the history of war, were occasioned by concrete circumstances and cultural changes, and in doing so introduces a historicist dimension into the study of peace. Adolf makes us aware that "peace strategies did not come about in a vacuum, they were outgrowths of pacifist, civil disobedience and other traditions that predate and inform them" (Adolf 2009: 9). This entails that contributions to peace are historically contextual and continuous (or evolving), and should be viewed diachronically rather than synchronically.

Peace movements of the nineteenth century waxed and waned in response to wars and their impact upon public life. But the spirit of constructive optimism runs through these movements, in spite of the fact that wars unleash patriotic fervor that represses dissent and makes proponents of nonviolence and peace into unpopular scapegoats of the moment. This demonstrates that the yearning for peace is a deep-seated human impulse whose expression abides among conscientious individuals and groups and flourishes more widely as conditions permit.

Sandi Cooper, in her history of European pacifism, identifies three nineteenth-century periods of development (Cooper 1991). In the first, 1815–50, peace groups formed in the UK, the US, Switzerland, France, and Belgium. Initially the formation was religious, but more secular approaches soon emerged. During the second interval, 1850–70, momentum for peace recovered from the midcentury wars and advocacy organizations spread across Europe. Of this period, she writes that "a lively international debate among conservative, radical, and socialist voices crossed European borders" (Cooper 1991: 7), which drew many more nationalities into the fold. The third phase, 1871–1914, saw a dramatic expansion of the movement within various older states and its extension to newer states. Membership became strongly democratized, embracing workers, women, educators, students, and others, and now cut across socio-economic classes. Major international peace structures and congresses ushered in the twentieth century. This last wave of peace activity was in turn swept away by the colonialist, imperialistic, civil, revolutionary, independence, and genocidal events and world wars of the twentieth century.

The long nineteenth century reminds us, therefore, of the ambiguity found in the processes of history—of how the quest for peace can coexist with yet be eclipsed and overwhelmed by the impulse to make war. And it remains something of a miracle—as well as a testimonial to the strength and endurance of the peace movement—that the United Nations plus many NGOs dedicated to promoting peace, reconciliation, and conflict resolution exist today, and that a limited but fairly sophisticated and generally operative framework of international law and justice has carried over into the contemporary world.

Peace movement scholars and historians sometimes go to considerable lengths to distinguish between nonviolence and pacifism. David Cortright, for instance, argues that "pacifism and nonviolence . . . are conceptually and politically distinct" (Cortright 2008: 211). But we should not overlook their interdependence. *Nonviolence* is an orientation toward the world and other beings that inhabit it of harm avoidance or minimization of harm when it proves unavoidable. Nonviolence is also understood by some as a strategy and policy for bringing about social transformation by moral force, relying on behaviors that oppose violence and avoid causing harm themselves, or else cause the least harm in the situation. *Pacifism*—whether categorical and absolute or circumstantial and selective—is opposition to war and violence as means of settling disputes. Pacifism as an ongoing commitment entails dedication to nonviolent conduct in everyday life. Nonviolence, in turn, when most broadly applied, includes eschewing the resort to war. These conclusions follow because the causes of war can be traced to the smallest level of interactions from which animosities, misunderstandings, and hostilities grow, on the one hand, and on the other, because nonviolence cannot consistently be limited just to pragmatic calculations about effectively getting one's own way. It follows that *pacifism and nonviolence need to be seen as coordinated means to the betterment of life on the planet*. Furthermore, for some utopian, nonconformist, and/or religious communities, nonviolence is an expression of basic belief reinforced by a commitment to equality and practices of nonresistance to authority and aggression. And there are groups for which pacifism may stem from a principled, more general refusal to take part in the affairs of the larger society.

There is a general tendency to identify major historical events, such as the American and French Revolutions (1765–83 and 1789–99 respectively), with the violent conflicts they gave rise to. This interpretation fits readily into the dominant belief system that pictures humans as innately aggressive and violent, with the implication that history is the story of conflict and war. More careful examination of these revolutionary "mega-events," however, reveals that they are made up of many lesser events, and that prevalent among them are sub-events of a nonviolent sort that propelled historical change as much as, or more than, the violent ones. Everyone knows the saying "the pen is mightier than the sword," and the revolutions mentioned previously illustrate its truth as well as any other examples one can think of. Both uprisings may be thought of as combinations of nonviolent and violent happenings. The violent ones we know of as local skirmishes followed by full-scale mobilizations, armed hostilities, and war, featuring great brutality and larger-than-life military heroes, such as George Washington and Napoléon Bonaparte, emerging to claim victory and being venerated ever after. Mark Kurlansky, a careful historian of ideas, offers the skeptical opinion that "the great lesson from the history of revolutions is that a shooting war is not necessary to overthrow the established power but is often deemed necessary to consolidate the revolution itself" (Kurlansky 2006: 80). Whether war is ever "necessary" may be debated, alongside the question of who gets to decide what an individual revolution consists in. But as early US president John Adams observed in 1818:

> The [American] Revolution was effected before the war commenced. The Revolution was in the minds and hearts of the people.... This radical change in the principles, opinions, sentiments, and affections of the people, was the real American Revolution.
> *Adams 1856: 282*

Well, then, how *did* revolution enter "the minds and hearts of the people"? This is a process that could be (and has been) explained at great length, but it has to do, basically, with the dissemination of ideas about human nature, fundamental freedoms, rights, and values, a sense of public good and civic duty, contractual participation in society, and fair representation in political life. These ideas stemmed from many sources—from John Locke, the Baron de Montesquieu, and Jean-Jacques Rousseau, to Benjamin Franklin, Thomas Paine, and Thomas Jefferson.

The French Revolution also had its roots in Enlightenment ideas (and ideals) of popular sovereignty and the inalienable rights of human beings. Writers such as Denis Diderot, Rousseau, and Nicolas de Condorcet—known as the *Philosophes*—contributed to the advancement of subversive and transformative views concerning political and social reform, which were promulgated in their articles in the *Encyclopédie, ou dictionnaire raisonné des sciences, des arts et des métiers* (*Encyclopedia, or Systematic Dictionary of the Sciences, Arts, and Crafts*), published in thirty-five volumes between 1751 and 1780.

The force of this intellectual background led to Europe's being convulsed by a period of war that lasted well into the nineteenth century, for which the French Revolution and Napoleonic ambitions served as major catalysts. These conflicts were brought to a close by the Congress of Vienna (1814–15), which stabilized the balance of power through negotiation, compromise, and consensus and served as the basis for international relations in the region up until the outbreak of World War I. A larger framework of ongoing meetings and treaties, known as the Concert of Europe, resolved numerous hostilities up until the mid-nineteenth century, and eventually included, at one time or another, Great Britain, the countries of western Europe, Russia, and even the Ottoman Empire. Although this coalition of interests did not survive the revolutions of 1848 and the European wars of the second half of the nineteenth century, notions of European union, international law, and permanent institutions to promote cooperation and address grievances received important momentum from this experiment.

The Evolving Peace Movement

As a result of these major revolutions, certain ideas about political life gained credibility and growing support during the nineteenth century. Preeminent among them was the notion that an educated citizenry, composed of equals, has the right and responsibility to legitimize governments and hold their representatives to account. This belief in the power of the people was readily tapped into by the peace movement. As Cooper explains:

> Along with countless other issues ... peace became a citizen's mission—a subject of private conferences, of specialized periodicals, of national and international societies, of university and school curricula, and of challenges to parliamentary candidates. ... Peace was claimed as a citizen's right as well as a necessity of modern life ... that well-run governments must struggle to establish.
>
> *Cooper 1991: 5, 6*

The first half of the nineteenth century saw the rise of an organized peace movement in the public sphere in several countries, as already noted—each with its own meetings and agendas, political action programs, and publications. Peace societies were established in 1815 in New York and Massachusetts, and in London a year later, in Ohio in 1820 (the Cincinnati-based Female Peace Society), in France in 1821, and in Switzerland in 1830. Female Auxiliary Peace Societies were set up in Leeds, Tavistock, and Huddersfield during the 1820s. By midcentury, a series of international Peace Congresses had been held, in London (1843, 1851), Brussels (1848), Paris (1849), and Frankfurt (1850). The 1848 Congress was convened by American Elihu Burritt, who had also founded a League of Universal Brotherhood two years earlier. Various luminaries began to throw their support behind these conferences, such as Alexis de Tocqueville and Victor Hugo in the case of the Paris international, where Hugo essentially proposed the formation of a United States of Europe.

An additional stimulant to the movement during this period was the publication of Percy Bysshe Shelley's *The Masque of Anarchy* (Shelley 1990). Although it did not appear in print until 1832, the work was penned in 1819 in response to the Peterloo Massacre in Manchester, when a militia attacked an unarmed crowd protesting against living conditions and the denial of voting rights. *The Masque of Anarchy* is considered by many to be the most important political poem in the English language as well as "perhaps the first modern statement of the principle of nonviolent resistance" (Wikipedia 2017). Whether or not it was the first, Shelley's poem had a formative impact on the thought of both Henry David Thoreau and Mohandas Gandhi.

Thoreau was an activist and strong voice in the US anti-slavery movement, but he was also an opponent of the Mexican-American War (1846–48) and spoke out against colonialist mistreatment of First Nations. Politically, he is best known and most influential worldwide because of his essay on civil disobedience (first published as "Resistance to Civil Government," 1849), in which he called on conscientious citizens to revolt and engage in nonviolent struggle against unjust or corrupt governments. (Gandhi will be discussed in the next section.)

Early in the second half of the century, a split had begun to appear, in France and elsewhere, between those who believed that political freedom, democracy, social justice, and national liberation are the prerequisites of peace, and those who thought peace and prosperity themselves are the means to these ends. This difference of approaches defined a fundamental opposition that continues to resonate into the present—between revolutionists and radicals, on the one hand, and moderates and gradualists, on the other; between those who want to "change (or overthrow) the system" and those who choose to "work within the system." Another division in the movement also began to assert an ongoing influence, namely, that between opponents of war on moral grounds and those who sought the remedy for armed conflict in better, more rational institutions. The second half of the nineteenth century saw the rise of organized labor (unions) in the UK and the US as well. While much of the early history of this movement is marred by violence, the strategy of unions over time focused on the use of nonviolent means of effecting change, such as strikes, non-cooperation in the workplace, working to rule, picketing, boycotts, and collective bargaining.

The year 1867 proved to be a pivotal moment, as it saw the founding of two major rival groups in France: the progressivist International and Permanent League of Peace, led by Frédéric Passy (co-winner of the first Nobel Peace Prize in 1901), and the more activist International League of Peace and Liberty, whose guiding lights were Edmond Potonié-Pierre and Charles Lemonnier. It was on Lemonnier's initiative that a new Peace Congress was convened in Geneva. Presided over by none less than Giuseppe Garibaldi, it attracted "more than six thousand attendees of nearly all political, religious, and economic creeds" (Adolf 2009: 136).

An Institute of International Law was established in Ghent in 1873 (following on the Franco-Prussian War of 1870–71) by a group of distinguished jurists from eleven countries, representing Europe, North America, and South America. This organization, which won the 1904 Nobel Peace Prize, has endured and is now located in Geneva and meets every two years to review the current state of affairs, make recommendations to governments, and take other actions to promote and develop international law.

In 1879, Priscilla Peckover, who came from a Quaker banking family, established a peace society in Wiesbech, Cambridgeshire, which grew to 6,000 members. She edited and financed a peace journal for fifty years, was very active internationally, and linked her English group to others in Spain, France, Germany, Denmark, Italy, and Switzerland.

Elsewhere, the first Japanese peace society (Nihon Heiwa-kai) was founded in 1889, followed by those in Australia (1900), Canada (1904), and New Zealand (1910), taking peace organizations well beyond Europe. This groundswell continued until just prior to World War I, when there were "190 peace societies, some with thousands of members, in dozens of countries," which shows that during the long nineteenth century, "pacifism broadly defined emerged as a significant international presence" (Cortright 2008: 43). As many as 300,000 French citizens alone, male and female, were members of peace societies.

During the century-plus under discussion, more than seventy-five international conferences were held in seven nations (Belgium, France, Germany, Italy, the Netherlands, the UK, and the US). Sponsorship by governments and their official representation at these meetings increased. Did all these conferences amount to anything? They did. As one source comments:

> Peace conferences tried to end war—and to stop impending wars. . . . [They] created a general appreciation of international cooperation, the principle of international arbitration was established, and some specific organizations were created, e.g. the Red Cross in 1864 and the International Olympic Committee in 1894. . . . Today's peace

movement has no international structure under which anything like the "universal" peace conferences of the 19th and early 20th centuries could be organized.

Friends of Peace Monuments n.d.

Universal peace conferences, so-called, began life in 1889, coinciding with the centenary of the French Revolution and the Paris Exposition (at which the Interparliamentary Union was established), and continued on a regular basis for the next fifty years. In 1891–92, a group of 100 or so peace societies came together to form an International Peace Bureau in Berne (and this group won the 1910 Nobel Peace Prize). It is generally agreed that around 1903, the word "pacifism" was first coined by French lawyer and writer Émile Arnaud, and it quickly entered common usage. By 1905, there were "over 90 treaties either containing arbitration clauses or directly promising to use arbitration" (Cooper 1989: 233). Such was the momentum the peace movement had gained by the turn of the century.

No discussion of nonviolence and peace in the long nineteenth century would be complete without reference to the crucial role played by religious belief. Religion has depressingly often been a cause of divisiveness, violence, and warfare. But it also contains fertile tendencies toward nonviolence and pacifism (Armstrong 2014). Many religions, including Judaism, Christianity, Islam, Hinduism, Sikhism, Jainism, Buddhism, and Bahá'í, have teachings about nonviolence and adherents who practiced it in the past and continue to do so. Most of the earliest peace organizations had a religious foundation, as noted earlier. Important religious antiwar groups that deserve special mention are the so-called historic peace churches—Quakers (Society of Friends), Church of the Brethren, and Anabaptists (Amish, Hutterites, Mennonites). In addition, many others also shaped the peace culture of the nineteenth century and beyond, such as Unitarians, Methodists, Baptists, Congregationalists, Presbyterians, Doukhobors, Moravians, Christadelphians, and Shakers (United Society for Believers in Christ's Second Appearing).

Both Protestantism and Catholicism, as they evolved during the nineteenth and early twentieth centuries, shaped the nonviolence and pacifist movements in fundamental respects. One tendency of special note was the advent of "social Christianity," a renewed dedication to improving people's living conditions and preventing war—widely recognized as interconnected obligations. Several Protestant organizations, such as the Christian Social Union in Great Britain and the National Council of Churches in the US, had their origins in this period of ferment. The Catholic Church, through the tenure of a series of more activist popes, took a strong stand in support of social justice and peace. Pope Leo XIII (1878–1903) espoused an antiwar position, and Pope Benedict XV (1914–22) even rejected the theory of just war that had been an integral aspect of theological doctrine since the Middle Ages. As recorded in the present essay, themes and principles derived from various religious sources helped form the outlooks of important individual figures, just as they do today.

Conscientious objection to military service, or at least armed military service, predates the nineteenth century, as does its legal recognition by some governments. It was also a feature of the nonviolence/pacifism movement in the period under discussion, for example in the US Civil War and in World War I—by which time there were substantial numbers of both religious and nonreligious opponents of war.

Some Prominent Peace Pioneers

Immanuel Kant (1724–1804), considered by many to be the most influential philosopher of the Enlightenment, lived only four years into the nineteenth century, yet his impact on thought and culture in that century was immense, just as it continues to be today. Kant held that the chief guideline for conduct is always to act in accordance with principles that can be willed as universal and exceptionless. In this spirit, Kant asserts, in his late essay "To Perpetual Peace: A Philosophical Sketch," that "the right to go to war is meaningless," not just because it would lead to mutual annihilation, but more importantly because it cannot be derived from "independent, universally valid laws" (Kant 1983: 117). Accordingly, it is no surprise to discover the key to universal peace in just such a principle:

> [F]rom the throne of its moral legislative power, reason absolutely condemns war as a means of determining the right and makes seeking the state of peace a matter of unmitigated duty. But without a contract among nations peace can neither be inaugurated nor guaranteed. A league of a special sort must therefore be established, one that we can call a *league of peace* (*foedus pacificum*), which will be distinguished from a *treaty of peace* (*pactum pacis*) because the latter seeks merely to stop *one* war, while the former seeks to end *all* wars forever.
>
> Kant 1983: 116–117

This league, he adds, will be a "free federation," rather than some form of super-governmental authority, for it will be voluntarily entered into and participated in by those whose behavior is rationally self-directed. We might now say such participants realize their self-interest coincides with that of others, so as to form a universal interest with which all can identify; but Kant, on the contrary, believes that reason ascertains the universal interest *directly*, not via some circuitous route. Peace, then, as well as being inherently desirable, is what reason freely chooses to will, inasmuch as it instantiates the highest moral obligation: to treat others as one would be treated, namely, as ends-in-themselves, and not merely as means to one's own ends.

In keeping with his general approach, Kant's theory of peace assumes that an appeal to the dictates of reason will triumph in the end, assuring the betterment of the human condition and the creation of an international community of equals. It must be said, however, that the peace movement went in a different direction, to the extent that the necessity of a super-state with the authority to enforce measures controlling violence and war became a central feature of its discourse; and the lack of this authority is of course often cited today as a shortcoming of the United Nations. Aside from this issue, some organizations, such as the French League of Public Good (founded in 1850), also espoused principles of social justice, identifying economic and other forms of inequality as potential causes of war, and promoting the idea that they must be addressed through nonviolent reforms in order to bring about world peace.

Kant's philosophy as well as his specific proposals about peace have nevertheless helped shape the cosmopolitanism (sense of world citizenship) that has energized many peace movements and initiatives from his time onward. His preference for categorical over conditional or consequentialist rules of conduct seems compatible with an absolute pacifist stance. Kant's way of thinking also promotes the view that in the dialectical interplay between our native endowments, reason can triumph over aggression. Finally, he observes that nations characterized by participatory democracy are less likely to engage in warfare with one another—a hypothesis that is widely held and appears to have empirical support (Hegre 2014).

What we see from Kant onward is the genesis of the idea that peace, rather than war, might actually be in the best interest of nations on political, economic, social, and individual grounds. John Stuart Mill, the great utilitarian and defender of liberty and democracy, crystallizes this outlook as well as any thinker of his time:

> It is commerce which is rapidly rendering war obsolete, by strengthening and multiplying the personal interests which are in natural opposition to it. And it may be said

without exaggeration that the great extent and rapid increase of international trade, in being the principal guarantee of the peace of the world, is the great permanent security for the uninterrupted progress of the ideas, the institutions, and the character of the human race.

Mill 2004: 175

Views such as this were frequently uttered during the nineteenth century, but were far from being universally accepted. Prominent socialists absented themselves from the capitalism and free trade cheering section, advocating instead for nonviolent reforms in the interest of avoiding class conflict and promoting greater equality among citizens. Richard Owens in England and Charles Fourier in France, among others, planned to establish experimental cooperative communities wherein resources and opportunities (for work, education, housing, participatory democracy, purchasing power, and the like) would be fairly distributed and evenly beneficial to all. These approaches, which favored progress through incremental change, were tried out in England and the US with some degree of success. They were later condemned by Karl Marx and Friedrich Engels as "utopian," when they issued the call for revolutionary overthrow and radical transformation of all existing social, economic, and political institutions. The same current of opposition would be maintained by later figures in the radical socialist movement, such as Mikhail Bakunin, V.I. Lenin, and Rosa Luxemburg.

Count Leo Tolstoy (1828–1910) believed that the state is a vehicle of oppression and ideological and economic enslavement. Wars, therefore, amount to nothing more than attempts to exploit the lives and energies of ordinary people in order to advance the interests of one state against those of other states. Tolstoy proposed numerous arguments in support of his view that wars are illogically rationalized, chaotic, and largely unplanned, but this controversial perspective, while novel and interesting, takes second place to his anarchistic and absolutist pacifism. As we have seen, many peace movements and conferences took place during the long nineteenth century. Yet in a 1901 letter to Bertha von Suttner, Tolstoy declared that "the sole solution to the question [of war] is for the citizens to refuse to be soldiers.... The disappearance of war ... [has] no need of conferences of peace societies" (Tolstoy 1910: 372–373). While treating the well-intentioned movements of his day with disdain, and perhaps displaying naïveté in regard to the need to organize efforts against war, Tolstoy's outlook does connect with principles both ancient and modern: political disobedience and withdrawal of consent. It is now more or less orthodoxy within the framework of strategic nonviolent protest and opposition that disobeying unjust laws and imposed conditions is morally obligatory, as well as that in the absence of the consent of those who are ruled or governed, any central authority loses its legitimacy and ability to control its subjects. Activists from Thoreau (who influenced Tolstoy) to Gandhi to Gene Sharp have developed this fruitful line of argument.

Born a countess in the Austro-Hungarian Empire, Bertha von Suttner (1843–1914) followed an unusual and unpredictable route through life, from aristocratic daughter of an Austrian field marshal, to employment as a governess, to new status as a baroness, to novelist and intellectual, to leader of the international peace movement. She was never in thrall to her family's military background, and held the view, shared by many peace advocates of the late nineteenth and early twentieth centuries, that war is not an inevitable aspect of human nature but an irrational institution that is antithetical both to the growing trend toward the interdependence of nations and to the currents of evolutionary and historical progress. In accordance with these beliefs, she wrote: "Universal peace is not a question of possibility, but of necessity. It is not only the aim, but the normal condition of civilization" (von Suttner, cited in Cohen 2010). Her pacifist novel *Die Waffen Nieder!* (*Lay Down Your Arms!*), published in 1889 (von Suttner 1972), became a bestseller, was translated into sixteen languages, and attracted more than one million readers. She then co-published for several years a popular monthly magazine of the same name containing peace movement news. Von Suttner was instrumental in persuading the industrialist Alfred Nobel to financially support the peace movement and to establish a special prize for peace work. She later received the Nobel Peace Prize for 1905, the first woman to be so honored.

Von Suttner not only carried major responsibilities in important peace organizations of her time, but also helped resolve political and religious conflicts within them. At the same time she conducted voluminous correspondence (in three languages) with prominent decision-makers and other literary and public figures. She was one of the architects of the First Hague Peace Conference of 1899, which led to the establishment of the Permanent Court of Arbitration at The Hague. Much of her activity revolved around campaigns against militarism, racism, sexism, violence, and other war-nurturing tendencies, while promoting cooperative and peace-enhancing ideals such as democracy, tolerance, equal rights, and world citizenship. According to one source, "Her many activities helped to remove the labels of 'utopians' and unrealistic 'idealists' from those involved in peace activism by gaining the support of respected world leaders and intellectuals for the movement" (Encyclopedia of World Biography 2016). This was far from an easy task, however, and it is important to note that many pacifists, peace activists, and proponents of nonviolence were subjected to public ridicule, often harsh criticism, ostracism, and worse for practicing what they believed in, and exhibited courage and resilience in the face of condemnation.

A Nobel Peace Prize co-recipient in 1931, Jane Addams (1860–1935) was a towering figure in the movement for social equality in the US, best known for her role in the establishment (with Ellen Gates Starr) of Hull House in Chicago, a community center complex dedicated to improving the lives of immigrants and working-class individuals more generally and to promoting a range of social, legal, and public policy reforms. Activities at this settlement house included free classes in cultural and academic subjects and in various practical skills, as well as enrichment programs for children, free concerts, and art exhibitions. This institution also pioneered in providing vital neighborhood resources such as cooperative housing for young working women, playground space, public baths, a gymnasium, a kindergarten and daycare center, infant care, shops, a café, clubs, and a performance theater.

Addams presents a good example of someone who understood and appreciated the interrelated nature of social issues. She would rank high on the list of people who "walk the walk" as well as "talk the talk," or who "think globally, act locally," in that she chose to live in the same setting where she implemented her ideas. She pursued a multi-tiered agenda that embraced legislation to address child labor, women's suffrage, racial equality, strike mediation, urban sanitation, adequate medical care for women and children, juvenile courts, and educational reform (including compulsory education). In all of this, her unified objective was to bring about "a moral change which would create peace and contentment where there had previously been only divisive exploitation" (Reynolds 1989: 257). It is no surprise, therefore, that Addams opposed war and became a prominent leader in the international peace movement (in particular, as chair of the Women's Peace Party, and subsequently president of the Women's International League for Peace and Freedom). She recognized that war is hugely wasteful of resources of all kinds and undermines the essential human bonds that people form in peaceful interaction with one another, when they rise above cultural and other challenges to form personal connections. This outlook is reflected in one of her many publications, *Newer Ideals of Peace* (Addams 1907), in which she argues that from the standpoint of social evolution, peace is progressive and brings about social harmony, while war is regressive, fragmenting, and socially stunting.

Because of her strong opposition to US entry into World War I, Addams suffered considerable vitriolic abuse and loss of reputation. In spite of this, she worked hard on behalf of a mediation process to end the war, and after it ended, to raise consciousness of the need for food aid to Germany and eastern Europe. Although the kind of progressivism she endorsed seems to have been killed off, like many other ideals, by the "war to end all wars," Addams' writings have gained in stature from the reassessment of recent scholars, who see them as important original contributions to American pragmatism and the ethics of care.

A shy, unassuming man and an indifferent student, Mohandas K. Gandhi (1869–1948) studied law in England. After a shaky start to his legal career, he took up a contract position in South Africa in 1893 and, as an Indian, immediately came face-to-face with racial discrimination, which he vowed to oppose. He did so in ways both small and big, refusing to remove his turban in court and to vacate a first-class train compartment, then taking on the court case against legislation to prevent Indians from voting. He stayed in South Africa until 1914, and there he underwent an awakening of both his courage and creativity as a strategist for social change, becoming a leader in the movement to block legislation in the Transvaal that would severely restrict the rights of Indians. His actions included organizing civil disobedience and ultimately negotiating a compromise that allowed Indians certain rights.

During this formative period, Gandhi developed some of his signature concepts and practices. Among them was a devotion to truth in all things (his autobiography was later to be subtitled *The Story of My Experiments with Truth* [Gandhi 1993]). Gandhi's personal evolution seemed to flow from a belief in the unity of human nature (whereby those who cause suffering to others also cause it to themselves); adherence to a program of publicly transparent projects, patiently pursued; faith in the indestructibility and invincibility of the truth (truth-force or *satyagraha*); and the need to reconcile means and ends through the use of nonviolent resistance to injustice (*ahimsa*).

Gandhi's work for change in South Africa included publishing a newspaper, providing medical services to British troops during the Boer War, a protest march of Indian coal miners, public burning of "pass" documents, being jailed and abused, and founding a self-sufficient settlement community. Alongside all of this activity, he also wrote a book on Indian independence (Gandhi 1910).

A Global View of Nineteenth-Century Nonviolence and Pacifist Activity

It is easy to overlook or be unaware of some "peaceful facts" near at hand, such as that neither Sweden nor Switzerland has engaged in any war since the time of Napoléon, nor Iceland since 1256. Less clear, perhaps, is that we seldom do justice to the groups, ideals, and practices supporting peace that lie beyond the usual frame of reference provided by Western culture. Some acknowledgment of these must be recorded here.

To begin with, a great variety of warless societies and sub-societies exist around the globe, according to an impressive list of scholars (Mead 1940; Melko 1973; Montagu 1978; Howell and Willis 1989; Bonta 1993; van der Dennen 1995; Boulding 2000; Fry 2007; University of Alabama at Birmingham 2016). The features setting such groups apart are belief systems supportive of nonviolence, nonviolent practices in everyday interactions, conflict avoidance, and well-tested methods of conflict resolution. In this respect, they carry on traditions that pre-date but also span the nineteenth century, and in many cases continue today. Peaceful societies on record are "geographically diverse and range in size from small communities (e.g., the La Paz Zapotec [Mexico]) to populations in the thousands or tens of thousands (e.g., the Semai [Malaysia] or the Fipa [Tanzania])" (Baszarkiewicz and Fry 2008: Box 1). The confederation of Six Nations—Mohawks, Oneidas, Onondagas, Cayugas, Seneca, and Tuscarora—has observed its "Great Law of Peace" for several centuries (see Fox 2014: 55). Most examples of peaceful cultures are found in the anthropological literature. Within the commonplace categories of assessment, these would be designated as pacifist communities—and they have been when left undisturbed. But this does not adequately capture their inner spirit, because what we call pacifism is a response to the prospect of war, whereas within the societies themselves, nonviolence, cooperative co-dependence, and membership of a spiritual community are the fundamental norms that define their way of life and focus their daily behavior.

It has already been mentioned that there were early peace societies in Japan. Individuals within the Japanese peace movement worthy of recognition include Uchimura Kanzō, a Christian evangelist and teacher who strongly opposed the Russo-Japanese War (1904–5), and Abe Isoo, a socialist, feminist, Unitarian preacher, and antiwar activist during the same conflict. Kanzō established a "nonchurch" form of Christianity guided by his belief that established churches are allies of the militaristic state. In addition, the founding of the Japanese Society of International Law (1897) fostered the expansion and codification of the law of nations.

In Africa, many traditional institutions and procedures exist for resolving disputes nonviolently, meting out justice according to group-held principles and beliefs, and restoring post-conflict harmony to the community. These were practiced during the long nineteenth century, just as before and after, and some have been described as "among the most effective anywhere in the world" (Somjee 2010).

A group of New Zealand Maori conducted a campaign of nonviolent resistance to British land seizure during the period 1879–81, in defense of a North Island settlement known as Parihaka. Actions included removing surveyors' marks, plowing seized lands, rebuilding fences torn down by soldiers, meeting armed forces with singing and dancing children, sitting resolutely in unarmed groups, and offering food to the invaders. Hundreds were jailed and expelled from their homes (which were then looted and destroyed). Nonviolent resistance continued episodically after this period and the village was eventually rebuilt. Kurlansky (2006) maintains that the Maori commitment to nonviolence in this episode prevented genocide, as the cost of invasion became prohibitive to the British. In any case, the events unfolding at Parihaka are considered landmarks on the rough road to reconciliation in New Zealand.

What the Long Nineteenth Century Contributed to World Peace

Prior to World War I, there had been no major wars in Europe for forty-three years, and so one finds reference in the literature to "the 19th century long peace" (Stevenson n.d.). One book on the Great War even designates it as "the war that ended peace" (MacMillan 2014). But as this historical era unfolded, industrialization, new weapons technology, and the rise of nationalism, militarism, alliances, and colonialist ambitions spurred arms races and lent a sense of urgency to the quest for peace and disarmament. In Europe and elsewhere, the growing peace movement stressed that peace should be considered the norm of international relations, and that war is not only wasteful but also antithetical to progress (Cooper 1991).

From the late nineteenth century until the beginning of World War I, peace advocates increasingly engaged in a critique of militarism, which had accompanied the rise of nationalism in Europe and the reactionary response to it by "already well-armed repressive states" such as Italy, Spain, and Hungary (Cortright 2008: 96). Disarmament, or at least arms reduction, became an essential feature of the antiwar agenda, especially after studies began to appear that documented the economic, social, and human costs of weapons production and use and the futility of war. A powerful early work of this kind was Jan de Bloch's *The Future of War in Its Technical, Economic, and Political Relations* (de Bloch 1899). Norman Angell popularized the internationalist case against war and received the 1933 Nobel Peace Prize for his work. He argued in *The Great Illusion* (Angell 1910) that in an integrated world economy, interstate armed conflict ceases to be of potential benefit to any nation. Philosopher-psychologist William James took a different tack. James, who opposed all war, nonetheless endorsed the common assumptions that humans are innately bellicose and that war builds character. He therefore seeks, in the celebrated essay "The Moral Equivalent of War" (James 1910), a substitute form of activity that will satisfy the drive toward aggressive violence in our species, and that will also improve (male) citizens. Although he finds the solution in a distastefully conceptualized program of "human warfare against nature" (James 1910: 467), subduing it for the benefit of society, James's idea of alternate national service nonetheless has lasting value for the evolution of a nonviolent world.

Some philanthropists of the time began to help fund essential empirical investigations into the conditions of conflict avoidance and resolution. Prominent among these was wealthy American industrialist Andrew Carnegie. The Carnegie Endowment for International Peace was established in 1910 in Washington, DC. (The Endowment's first president, Elihu Root, received the Nobel Peace Prize for 1912.) Its centers and considerable influence have since spread to Russia, China, Europe, the Middle East, and India. Carnegie was a believer in international law and strong organizations, and he held that rationality expressed through study and research would provide the answer to the riddle of war.

In retrospect, it can be said that this vision, expressed by Carnegie and endorsed by many others, survived the numerous wars of the late nineteenth century and the massive armed conflicts of the twentieth to reassert itself and become the basis for today's European Union and United Nations. It is an interesting fact, a paradox worth celebrating, that during the darkest moments of modern history—the two world wars—although peace was obliterated, the quest for peace was not, and even gained new urgency and commitment. Kent Shifferd accurately observes that "in spite of and in the midst of the slaughter of the last two hundred years, the last two centuries have been the most creative years for the development of peace in the 6000-year history of the war system" (Shifferd 2011: 126). He regards this as a phenomenon in need of analysis, but urges that the rise of democracy is a crucial factor.

In many ways, the nineteenth century was a period of ferment and re-evaluation of accepted norms. Peace advocates of the nineteenth century (and beyond) were (and today still are) devoted to other causes as well, such as the abolition of slavery, religious tolerance, equal rights for women, universal education, labor law reform, public sanitation, the temperance movement, and the campaign against capital punishment. Some of these causes achieved their goals or at any rate markedly advanced them during this period.

Cortright offers the following list of breakthroughs attributable to the nineteenth- to early twentieth-century peace movement:

> The laws of war were crafted and refined, governments sponsored the Hague peace conferences, dozens of bilateral treaties and arbitration agreements were signed, and a Permanent Court of Arbitration was created. . . . The understanding of what causes war and the requirements for peace advanced, as peace advocates gained a greater appreciation for the role of international law, arbitration, and institutionalized cooperation among nations. Democratic freedom, self-determination, and social justice were recognized as vital components of peace.
>
> Cortright 2008: 43

One shouldn't assume, however, that social justice or the decent treatment of colonized peoples were of concern to *all* advocates of nonviolence and pacifism, because not everyone perceived the connections between these campaigns and the pursuit of peace. Nor did those who sought peace always embrace nonviolence and pacifism. US President Theodore Roosevelt, who won the 1906 Nobel Peace Prize for brokering a treaty that stopped Japan and Russia from making war on each other, had very little use for pacifists and wasn't above fomenting revolution in Panama in order to get the great canal built. Be this as it may, the contributions listed by Cortright have reverberated into the present and help form the groundwork for modern agreements, negotiations, and conflict resolution procedures.

At the end of his magisterial 900-plus-page global study of the long nineteenth century, historian Jürgen Osterhammel reflects on this period, confessing, "All in all, the picture is ambiguous and contradictory even for Europe." He insists that "nevertheless, it was a century of emancipation or, more plainly put, a century of revolt against coercion and humiliation" (Osterhammel 2014: 917). But in spite of all the well-documented achievements, peace advocacy and peace work were overwhelmed in 1914 by the deep dynamics of conflict waiting to play out on the world stage with crushing effects. This in no way shows or suggests that nonviolence and peace are either weak or superficial historical energies, but rather reveals the colossal size of the transformation from warism to pacifism that confronts our species. Cooper observes that the peace movement of the long nineteenth century:

> cannot be faulted for the coming of war in 1914; it never claimed it would be able to prevent war.... What the peace movement articulated was a vision of a system of international security grounded in human institutions ... [and] the rule of law.
>
> *Cooper 1989: 234*

Yet it remains an enduring puzzle how an enormous and snowballing dedication to the pursuit of peace and forces leading relentlessly to world war could materialize on parallel pathways; and we must ask ourselves whether any important historical lessons can be gained from studying this phenomenon. The answer is unclear. The great nineteenth-century German philosopher G.W.F. Hegel (Hegel 1980) stated that the rational side of humanity simply takes a very long time to work itself out and assert itself, following circuitous and unpredictable paths. Whether we share his faith in the inherently progressive nature of this process is of course another story altogether.

Works Cited

Adams, J. (1856). "Letter to Hezekiah Niles (13 February 1818)," in C.F. Adams (ed.), *The Works of John Adams*, vol. 10. Boston: Little Brown, 282.
Addams, J. (1907). *Newer Ideals of Peace*. New York: Macmillan.
Adolf, A. (2009). *Peace: A World History*. Cambridge, UK: Polity Press.
Angell, N. (1910). *The Great Illusion: A Study of the Relation of Military Power in Nations to Their Economic and Social Advantage*. London: William Heinemann.
Armstrong, K. (2014). *Fields of Blood: Religion and the History of Violence*. London: Bodley Head.
Baszarkiewicz, K., and D. P. Fry (2008). "Peaceful Societies," in L. Kurtz (ed.), *Encyclopedia of Violence, Peace, and Conflict*, 2nd ed., vol. 2. Amsterdam: ScienceDirect and Elsevier, 1557–1570.
Bonta, B. D. (1993). *Peaceful Peoples: An Annotated Bibliography*. Metuchen, NJ: Scarecrow Press.
Boulding, E. (2000). *Cultures of Peace: The Hidden Side of History*. Syracuse: Syracuse University Press.
Cohen, L. R. (2010). "Suttner, Bertha von," in N.J. Young (ed.), *Oxford International Encyclopedia of Peace*, Online Edition. Oxford: Oxford University Press, 70, item 2. http://www.oxfordreference.com/view/10.1093/acref/9780195334685.001.0001/acref-9780195334685.
Cooper, S. E. (1989). "Peace Movements of the Nineteenth Century," in L. Pauling, E. Laszlo, and J.Y. Yoo (eds.), *World Encyclopedia of Peace*, vol. 2. Oxford: Pergamon Press, 230–234.
Cooper, S. E. (1991). *Patriotic Pacifism: Waging War on War in Europe, 1815–1914*. New York: Oxford University Press.

Cortright, D. (2008). *Peace: A History of Movements and Ideas*. Cambridge, UK: Cambridge University Press.
De Bloch, J. (1899). *The Future of War in Its Technical, Economic, and Political Relations*, translated by R.C. Long. Boston: Ginn and Company (published for the International Union).
Encyclopedia of World Biography. (2016). "Bertha von Suttner Facts." Available at: www.biography.yourdictionary.com/bertha-von-suttner
Fox, M. A. (2014). *Understanding Peace: A Comprehensive Introduction*. New York: Routledge.
Friends of Peace Monuments. (n.d.). "More Than 150 International Peace Conferences over the Years." Available at: http://peace.maripo.com/p_conferences.htm
Fry, D. P. (2007). *Beyond War: The Human Potential for Peace*. Oxford: Oxford University Press.
Gandhi, M. K. (1910). *Indian Home Rule*. Phoenix, South Africa: International Printing Press.
Gandhi, M. K. (1993). *An Autobiography, or the Story of My Experiments with Truth (1927–9)*, translated by M.H. Desai. Boston: Beacon Press.
Hegel, G. W. F. (1980). *Lectures on the Philosophy of World History: Introduction (1837)*, translated by H.B. Nisbet. Cambridge: Cambridge University Press.
Hegre, H. (2014). "Democracy and Armed Conflict." *Journal of Peace Research* 51, March: 159–172.
Howell, S., and R. Willis (eds.) (1989). *Societies at Peace: Anthropological Perspectives*. New York: Routledge.
James, W. (1910). "The Moral Equivalent of War." *McClure's Magazine* 463 (8), August. Available at: www.unz.org/Pub/McClures-1910aug-00463
Kant, I. (1983). "To Perpetual Peace: A Philosophical Sketch (1795)," in T. Humphrey (trans.), *Perpetual Peace and Other Essays on Politics, History, and Morals*. Indianapolis: Hackett, 107–144.
Kurlansky, M. (2006). *Non-Violence: The History of a Dangerous Idea*. London: Jonathan Cape.
MacMillan, M. (2014). *The War That Ended Peace: The Road to 1914*. New York: Random House.
Mead, M. (1940). "Warfare Is Only an Invention—Not a Necessity." *Asia* 40: 415–421. Available at: http://users.metu.edu.tr/utuba/Mead.pdf
Melko, M. (1973). *52 Peaceful Societies*. Oakville, ON: Canadian Peace Research Institute Press.
Mill, J. S. (2004). *Principles of Political Economy, with Some of Their Applications to Social Philosophy* (1848), abridged ed., S. Nathanson (ed.). Indianapolis: Hackett.
Montagu, A. (ed.) (1978). *Learning Non-Aggression: The Experience of Non-Literate Societies*. New York: Oxford University Press.
Osterhammel, J. (2014). *The Transformation of the World: A Global History of the Nineteenth Century*, translated by P. Camiller. Princeton: Princeton University Press.
Reynolds, R. C. (1989). "Nobel Peace Prize Laureates: Jane Addams (1931)," in L. Pauling, E. Laszlo, and J.Y. Yoo (eds.), *World Encyclopedia of Peace*, vol. 3. Oxford: Pergamon Press, 256–259.
Shelley, P. B. (1990). *The Mask of Anarchy 1832*. Oxford: Woodstock Books.
Shifferd, K. D. (2011). *From War to Peace: A Guide to the Next Hundred Years*. Jefferson, NC: McFarland.
Somjee, S. (2010). "African Peace Traditions," in N.J. Young (ed.), *Oxford International Encyclopedia of Peace*, Online Edition. Oxford: Oxford University Press, 1, item 8. www.oxfordreference.com/view/10.1093/acref/9780195334685.001.0001/acref-9780195334685
Stevenson, D. (n.d.). *Europe Before 1914*. London: British Library. Available at: www.bl.uk/world-war-one/articles/europe-before-1914
Tolstoy, L. (1910). "Leo Tolstoy to Bertha von Suttner, 28 August 1901," in B. von Suttner (ed.), *Memoirs of Bertha von Suttner: The Records of an Eventful Life*, vol. 1. Boston: Ginn and Company, 372–373.
University of Alabama at Birmingham, Department of Anthropology. (2016). "Peaceful Societies: Alternatives to Violence and War." Available at: https://cas.uab.edu/peacefulsocieties
Van der Dennen, J. M. G. (1995). *The Origin of War: The Evolution of a Male- Coalitional Reproductive Strategy*, 2 vols. Groningen: Origin Press.
Von Suttner, B. (1972). *Lay Down Your Arms! The Autobiography of Martha von Tilling*, translated by T. Holmes (orig. pub. 1894), rev. 2nd ed. New York: Garland.
Wikipedia. (2017). "The Masque of Anarchy." http://en.wikipedia.org/wiki/The_Masque_of_Anarchy

Further Reading

Alonso, H. H. (1993). *Peace as a Women's Issue: A History of the U.S. Movement for World Peace and Women's Rights*. Syracuse: Syracuse University Press. (Focuses on ideologies and personalities within the US feminist peace movement.)

Ceadel, M. (1996). *The Origins of War Prevention: The British Peace Movement and International Relations, 1730–1854*. Oxford: Oxford University Press. (Discusses from a British perspective how the fatalistic view of war as beyond human control was overthrown and peaceful alternatives proposed in its place.)

Hippler, T., and M. Vec (eds.) (2015). *Paradoxes of Peace in Nineteenth Century Europe*. Oxford: Oxford University Press. (Explores how peace has been used as a polemical concept to promote different political agendas, with special reference to the nineteenth century.)

Howlett, C. F., and R. Lieberman (2008). *A History of the American Peace Movement from Colonial Times to the Present*. Lewiston, NY: Edwin Mellen Press. (A historical survey of the antiwar movement aimed at remaking US society, based on primary and secondary sources.)

Stearns, P. N. (2014). *Peace in World History*. New York: Routledge. (An examination of human experiments in pursuing peace from earliest times to the present, revealing history through the lens of peace rather than of war.)

3
PACIFISM IN THE TWENTIETH CENTURY AND BEYOND

Andrew Fiala

Pacifism comes into its own as a philosophical idea and political movement in the twentieth century. Philosophers took up pacifism as an object for philosophical analysis. Pacifist parties and peace movements worked in earnest to abolish war. Nonviolent activism was successful. Peace and nonviolence became the object of sustained reflection. Scholars and activists clarified the power of nonviolence and the ongoing challenge of violence in all of its forms, including cultural violence, institutional violence, and structural violence. In the early part of the century important philosophers and scholars reflected on pacifism and often engaged in peace activism: William James, Jane Addams, John Dewey, Bertrand Russell, Albert Einstein, and others. After the Second World War, pacifism and peace activism focused on the problem of the Cold War and the absurdity of nuclear weapons. Throughout this period, peace activists honed their skills, learning from Gandhi and others. The field of peace studies developed in an effort to systematically understand how peace is made and violence can be diminished.

By the end of the twentieth century, an extensive scholarly literature had developed that focused on philosophical puzzles regarding pacifism in ethics and with regard to those aspects of political and social life that contribute to peace. In the twenty-first century, pacifism is still a fruitful subject of critical reflection. The non-pacifist alternative of the just war tradition has been honed and shaped by pacifist critique. Committed pacifists have developed a set of concepts and an intellectual apparatus that helps them understand their own commitments and ideals. In the twentieth century we get detailed accounts of "the military-industrial complex," "militarism," "warism," and "war crimes," as well as theories of contingent pacifism, just war pacifism, political pacifism, personal pacifism, and other concepts described throughout the present anthology.

This chapter considers two phases of the development of pacifism. The first phase developed under the shadow of Tolstoy and in relation to the First and Second World Wars. The second phase developed during the Cold War and includes pacifism as a response to nuclear weapons as well as the successful application of strategies of nonviolence in liberation movements. A third phase is currently under development, as we respond to the end of the Cold War and the ongoing "war on terrorism." Also in recent years, there has developed an all-inclusive critique of violence that considers the ubiquity of structural violence and cultural violence, building on the work of Johan Galtung, one of the giants of peace studies (see Galtung 1969 and 1990). In general, in the twentieth century we see a productive dialectic between pacifism and its critics;

and in general, the world has become sympathetic to the insights of advocates of pacifism and nonviolence.

Early Twentieth Century: From Tolstoy to the Second World War

There have long been a variety of people who are committed to nonviolence and opposed to war in a variety of cultures. There have also been sustained efforts to build peace and end war. Important philosophers have contributed to peace movements and the critique of war and violence: Erasmus, Kant, and Bentham. Religious thinkers such as the Quakers, Mennonites, and other Protestants also had a profound influence on the development of peace philosophy and pacifism. A longer genealogy of pacifism would examine the pacifism of American abolitionists, religious visionaries, and advocates of nonresistance and civil disobedience, such as Adin Balou, Bronson Alcott, and Henry David Thoreau.

One of the seminal thinkers for the development of twentieth-century pacifism is Leo Tolstoy. Tolstoy's nonresistant pacifism was based upon a close reading of the Christian Gospels. He explained, "Jesus said, simply and clearly, that the law of resistance to evil by violence, which has been made the basis of society, is false, and contrary to man's nature; and he gave another basis, that of non-resistance to evil, a law which, according to his doctrine, would deliver man from wrong" (Tolstoy 1885: 40). This idea of nonresistant pacifism would set the stage for reflection upon pacifism in the twentieth century. Tolstoy influenced Gandhi (who named one of his early communes "Tolstoy Farm"). Gandhi and Tolstoy corresponded. Gandhi modified nonresistance and transformed it into active but nonviolent resistance. This idea influenced Martin Luther King, Jr., James Lawson, and other nonviolent activists in the twentieth century. Jane Addams was influenced by Tolstoy, as was James and Dewey. Addams traveled to Russia to meet Tolstoy; James wrote of Tolstoy in his *Varieties of Religious Experience*. And although Dewey studied Tolstoy, he rejected Tolstoy's approach to life as requiring too much of an "all or nothing" choice (Dewey 1990). Dewey's critique of pacifism—especially the "professional pacifists" of the WWI era—held that "the efforts of pacifists" were "idle gestures in the air." Dewey wanted to see war made pragmatically effective—not abolish it. He said in 1917 that the future of pacifism lies:

> in seeing to it that the war itself is turned to account as a means for bringing these agencies into being. To go on protesting against war in general and this war in particular, to direct effort to stopping the war rather than to determining the terms upon which it shall be stopped, is to repeat the earlier tactics after their ineffectualness has been revealed.
>
> *Dewey 1917: 359*

Dewey, like others of his generation, thought that war could be used to end war. He supported American efforts in World War I (also called "the war to end all wars"). Committed pacifists rejected this idea.

Addams, James, and Dewey were members of the Anti-Imperialist League (along with Mark Twain, who mocked the cynicism of war, and Andrew Carnegie, who put his fortune behind philanthropic efforts to abolish war). Members were not necessarily pacifists even though they opposed American imperialism, including wars in the Philippines and elsewhere. In their work in different ways, Addams and James each advocated the development of a moral alternative to war. In a speech from 1910, published in 1911, entitled "A Moral Equivalent of War," James discusses "Tolstoi's pacificism" (James 1911: 283). Reprints of this essay update the spelling, writing "pacifism" instead of "pacificism." But this shows us that there was no agreement about the proper name for what we are describing here—whether it was pacific-ism or pacifism. The concept and terminology of pacifism was under development during this time. Scholars tend to agree that the term "pacifism" was coined by Émile Arnaud in 1901 at an international peace conference. Arnaud published a pamphlet in 1906, *Le Pacifisme et ses Détracteurs*, in which pacifism is described as the banner under which war is suppressed and a humane life is defended (Arnaud 1906). James's usage of the term "pacificism" in 1910 shows that the idea was already spreading quickly. By the time of the First World War, Russell, Dewey, and others were arguing about the idea and employing the term "pacifism."

Some authors have attempted to contrast pacifism and pacific-ism in a technical fashion. Dower explains—building upon the work of Taylor and Ceadel—that pacific-ism is focused on creating conditions for peace (which can also be open to limited and just wars), while pacifism is a moral rejection of violence (Dower 2009). In this sense, James would be a pacific-ist if he were not completely opposed to war, while being interested in imagining alternatives and preventing war. Indeed, James's idea about a moral equivalent of war was primarily interested in finding ways to channel the human interest in warlike activity—in more peaceful and productive ways.

James died before the outbreak of World War I, but Addams and Dewey lived through it. The First World War caused philosophers to pick sides. Addams was opposed to the war. She supported Woodrow Wilson when he promised to keep the U.S. out of the war. She felt betrayed by Wilson when the U.S. entered the war. Addams connected her pragmatic hope for peace to democracy and the empowerment of women and the oppressed masses, who usually suffered silently from the horrors of war. Addams and her Women's Peace Party worked to end the war and eventually ended up creating the Women's International League for Peace and Freedom.

As mentioned, Dewey supported the Great War. But Dewey's student Randolph Bourne criticized Dewey for his support of the war. Bourne famously argued that "war was the health of the state"—and combined his critique of war with a general critique of militarized states (Bourne 1918). He was especially disappointed with the way the American intelligentsia threw its support behind the war effort. Bourne argued that once war breaks out, critical thinking stops, pacifism is viewed as absurd, and everyone is forced to join in as a cog in the "great wheel" of the militaristic state (Bourne 1917: 12).

Bourne's critique of militaristic states had parallels with Marxist critiques of the relation between war and the state, as found for example in the work of Karl Liebknecht—who published his *Militarism and Anti-Militarism* in 1907 (resulting in a yearlong imprisonment). Marxists like Liebknecht saw militarism as an adjunct of capitalism. Liebknecht claimed that standing armies and escalating militarism was a threat to peace. He was involved in "anti-militarism," which involved advocating for universal disarmament and establishing international relations based upon proletarian interests. One of Liebknecht's colleagues, Rosa Luxemburg, explained in an article entitled "The Meaning of Pacifism" in 1911:

> Militarism in both its forms—as war and as armed peace—is a legitimate child, a logical result of capitalism, which can only be overcome with the destruction of capitalism, and hence whoever honestly desires world peace and liberation from the tremendous burden of armaments must also desire socialism.
>
> *Luxemburg 1911: n.p.*

The socialist pacifism of Liebknecht and Luxemburg developed alongside the anarchism of the early part of the century. Like the socialists, the anarchists were critical of the state's power to make war. While anarchists and socialists often advocated the use of violence to overthrow the state, there were anarcho-pacifists whose rejection of violence was connected to a critique of political power in all its forms. One important example is Emma Goldmann, the American anarchist. Goldmann stated in an essay first published in 1908, "The fact is that Anarchists are the only true advocates of peace, the only people who call a halt to the growing tendency of militarism" (Goldmann 1998: 52). She explained further:

> I believe that militarism—a standing army and navy in any country—is indicative of the decay of liberty and of the destruction of all that is best and finest in our nation. The steadily growing clamor for more battleships and an increased army on the ground that these guarantee us peace is as absurd as the argument that the peaceful man is he who goes well armed.
>
> *Goldmann 1998: 54*

Goldmann further explained her complaint against the bourgeois pacifists as follows: "Nor is it enough to join the bourgeois pacifists, who proclaim peace among the nations, while helping to perpetuate the war among the classes, a war which in reality is at the bottom of all other wars" (Goldmann 1998: 355).

Before concluding this discussion of pacifism through the First World War, we should mention Bertrand Russell and Albert Einstein, two of the most prominent intellectuals of the twentieth century, each of whom was committed to pacifism. Each was opposed to the First World War, although they modified their position with regard to the Second World War. Einstein was one of the few intellectuals in the German sphere of influence to sign a document opposing the First World War. He continued his peace activism throughout his life. At one point he said, "I am not only a pacifist but a militant pacifist. I am willing to fight for peace. Nothing will end war unless the peoples themselves refuse to go to war" (Einstein 1981: 125). In 1928, he said:

> It seems to be an utterly futile task to prescribe rules and limitations for the conduct of war. War is not a game; hence one cannot wage war by rules as one would in playing games. Our fight must be against war itself. The masses of people can most effectively fight the institution of war by establishing an organization for the absolute refusal of military service.
>
> *Einstein 1981: 90*

Einstein was one of the most famous proponents of war resistance and refusal of military service. Later, in the 1930s, Einstein corresponded with Sigmund Freud regarding humanity's warlike propensity. Freud's response focused on the psychological tendency toward aggression. But Freud said that civilized men like he and Einstein "are therefore bound to resent war, to find it utterly intolerable. With pacifists like us it is not merely an intellectual and affective repulsion, but a constitutional intolerance, an idiosyncrasy in its most drastic form" (quoted in Einstein 1981: 202). Freud suggested that as the revulsion toward war grew and developed, the rest of humanity might "turn pacifist" (Einstein 1981).

Like Freud and Einstein, Russell was opposed to the mechanical brutality and insipid patriotic fervor of modern war. Russell was one of the most important philosophers of the early part of the twentieth century. His work on logic and philosophy of language was groundbreaking. In 1901 he reports a mystical conversion experience—prompted by an encounter with a young child—that opened his mind to pacifism:

> Having been an Imperialist, I became during those five minutes a pro-Boer and a Pacifist. Having for years cared only for exactness and analysis, I found myself filled with

semi-mystical feelings about beauty, with an intense interest in children, and with a desire almost as profound as that of the Buddha to find some philosophy which should make human life endurable.

Russell 2010: 137

Russell subsequently wrote numerous polemics against war, including pacifist tracts. He worked with the No Conscription Fellowship and the Union of Democratic Control—both of which were opposed to the First World War. During the war he was fired from Cambridge, arrested, and sentenced to six months in prison. In one of his anti-war essays he argued that the juridical attempt to justify war was lazy and formulaic. While not affirming absolute pacifism, Russell offered a critique of war that could be described as utilitarian: he focused on "the balance of good which it [war] is to bring to mankind" (Russell 1915: 130). In general Russell claimed that the just war idea no longer applied in modern times. In the midst of the First World War he argued that the idea of self-defense is manipulated as an excuse for war. And he argued against the idea of going to war in defense of democracy: "To advocate democracy by war is only to repeat, on a vaster scale and with far more tragic results, the error of those who have sought it hitherto by the assassin's knife and the bomb of the anarchist" (Russell 1915: 138). Russell further admits his admiration for Tolstoy and the principle of nonresistance: "The principle of non-resistance contains an immense measure of wisdom if only men would have the courage to carry it out" (139).

But Russell was no absolutist. He does not oppose all war—he defended the Second World War as the only available response to Nazism. Nonetheless, even during that war, Russell continued to call himself a pacifist, albeit a "relative political pacifist" (for example, in the article "The Future of Pacifism" 1943–4). This position meant for him that wars were usually not the best means for fighting for justice (with the exception of the war against the Nazis), and moreover, that there was a political solution to the problem of war. For Russell, the solution was to be a sort of world government that held a monopoly on force and that was committed to liberal principles of justice, as well as a complete transformation of social and political life. As he explained in *Why Men Fight*, the book he composed while in prison:

The fundamental problem for the pacifist is to prevent the impulse towards war which seizes whole communities from time to time. And this can only be done by far-reaching changes in education, in the economic structure of society, and in the moral code by which public opinion controls the lives of men and women.

Russell 2004: 97

After the First World War, by the 1920s, pacifism (*Pazifismus*) was the object of serious philosophical analysis for Max Scheler, the German phenomenologist who offered a detailed account in 1926/7 (published posthumously in 1931—translated as Scheler 1976; 1977). One of Scheler's interests was the question of history and progress toward peace. A variety of important thinkers—Hobbes, Hegel, Nietzsche, and Spengler—claimed that war and violence are necessary features of human nature, that history proceeds through war, that war strengthens the state, and that peace is effeminate and war is heroic. Scheler pointed out that none of that is necessarily true; indeed, he supposed that as the human race continued its spiritual development, peace was more likely. Scheler connects the philosophy of peace to an account of the philosophy of history. Scheler is also important as a source of attempts to analyze the concept of pacifism, which is typical of twentieth-century philosophical approaches. He enumerated eight forms of pacifism: (1) heroic-individual pacifism (based on nonresistance), (2) Christian pacifism (based on natural law and the unifying efforts of the Catholic church), (3) economic-liberal pacifism (based upon the peace of free trade), (4) juridical pacifism (based upon legal systems grounded in Kant, socialism, and the growth of international treaties and institutions), (5) Communist pacifism (based in hope for the end of class struggle), (6) imperial world pacifism (based in the pacifying tendencies of imperial power—as in the *pax Romana*), (7) international capitalistic bourgeois pacifism (based in the unifying common interests of the international capitalists), and (8) cultural pacifism (based in cosmopolitanism and an educational effort at humanization).

Other analytic frameworks have been offered, outlining varieties of pacifism. But Scheler's work, like that of Russell and the others mentioned here, reminds us that pacifism is a fruitful area of philosophical exploration.

The Second World War and Beyond

The Second World War posed a problem for pacifists. Quakers and other members of historic peace churches remained opposed to the war. But philosophical pacifists such as Russell and Einstein eventually acknowledged that a war against Nazism could be justified. Philosophers continued to reflect, even during the war, on the concept of pacifism. Paul Weiss presented an analysis in 1943 that explained a variety of types of pacifism: religious pacifism, cynical pacifism, sentimental pacifism, political pacifism, and ethical pacifism. Weiss concluded that there was room for ethical pacifism within the division of labor in society. He wrote:

> If it is our choice to be contemplative men—scientists, philosophers, artists, or godly—we cannot in full conscience take part in that worldwide and permanent war, of which the present is but an episode, which proceeds by subjugating some men and nations in order to attain an eventual good for all. We must be and remain pacifists, in this war and those that follow, holding steadfast to our obligation to pursue ultimate ideals with fidelity, impartiality, and for all mankind.
>
> *Weiss 1943: 491*

But Weiss also laid out objections against pacifism that hold *in extremis*—when civilization itself is at stake. He concludes:

> No man can remain an ethical pacifist or a militarist when civilization is in the process of being finally extinguished; no man can be really contemplative or practical when it has already been extinguished.
>
> *Weiss 1943: 496*

This sort of argument explains the stakes for pacifists during the Second World War.

After the war concluded and the true devastation was measured—including the potential devastation of atomic weapons—pacifism re-emerged in earnest. Russell's pacifism continued to develop through the Second World War and on through the 1960s. One problem for Russell was the presence of nuclear weapons. After the atomic bombs were dropped on Japan, in an article printed in the *Glasgow Forward* on August 18, 1945, Russell soberly reflected on the power of the bomb. He concluded:

> Mankind are faced with a clear-cut alternative: either we shall all perish, or shall have to acquire some slight degree of common sense. A great deal of new political thinking will be necessary if utter disaster is to be averted.
>
> *Russell 1945: 310*

Russell's proposed solution was stronger international institutions. Such a solution was also imagined by Einstein. Einstein's pacifism was tied to his criticisms of nationalism and militarism. He advocated disarmament and was a supporter of the League of Nations as well as the United Nations. Einstein did advocate for the Manhattan Project because he was convinced that the Germans would get the bomb first. But Einstein remained committed to the abolition of war. In an article published in 1952, explaining his support for the American atomic bomb project, Einstein maintained, "I have always been a convinced pacifist. To kill in war is not a whit better than to commit ordinary murder" (Einstein 1982: 165). Claiming Gandhi as an inspiration, Einstein concluded, "Only the radical abolition of wars and of the threat of war can help" (Einstein 1982: 166). To create this outcome, Einstein maintained that peacetime had to cease being a mere preparation for war. Disarmament and de-escalation were necessary.

Russell and Einstein worked together to establish a conference of concerned scientists opposed to nuclear war—the Pugwash Conference on Science and World Affairs (held in 1957). The so-called "Russell-Einstein Manifesto" (1955) considered the destructive power of hydrogen bombs and the potential of nuclear war to end the human race. The manifesto stated:

> Here, then, is the problem which we present to you, stark and dreadful and inescapable: shall we put an end to the human race; or shall mankind renounce war? People will not face this alternative because it is so difficult to abolish war.

The threat of nuclear war contributed to the development of a doctrine known as "just war pacifism," which held that nuclear war and the general threat of total wars meant that there could no longer be a just war. As Robert Holmes argues, modern warfare is wrong, since modern war inevitably kills innocent persons and killing innocent persons is wrong. Thus for Holmes, "modern war is presumptively wrong" (Holmes 1989: 189).

As mentioned previously, Einstein indicated his admiration for Gandhi. And as we also mentioned previously, during the early part of the twentieth century, Gandhi's efforts at nonviolent social activism were shown to bear fruit. Other chapters in this book discuss this in more detail. But it is worth pausing for a moment to point out that Gandhi seemed to think that his approach could have even been useful in response to Hitler and Nazism. Gandhi exchanged letters with Martin Buber, the great Jewish thinker, that focused on this question (Buber 1957). Gandhi stated, "If there ever could be a justifiable war in the name of and for humanity, a war against Germany, to prevent the wanton persecution of a whole race, would be completely justified" (Gandhi 1938: n.p.). Buber explained his own position as follows: "I am no radical pacifist: I do not believe that one must always answer violence with nonviolence. I know what tragedy implies; when there is war, it must be fought" (Buber 2005: 293). But Buber was an advocate of peace and dialogue. He even imagined that this could work in the Arab-Israeli conflict. He explained his vision of a real peace as follows: "A peace that comes about through the cessation of war, hot or cold, is no real peace. Real peace, a peace that would be a real solution is organic peace. A great peace means cooperation and nothing less" (Buber 2005: 276).

Despite his sympathy for Gandhi and pacifism, Buber did not agree with nonviolence in response to evil threats such as Nazism. Nor perhaps did the Christian pacifist Dietrich Bonhoeffer. Bonhoeffer was persecuted by the Nazis for his pacifism and war resistance. According to the standard account of Bonhoeffer's life and death, he renounced his pacifism and conspired in a plot to kill Hitler—for which he was executed. Recent scholarship has challenged this account, claiming that Bonhoeffer was not actively engaged in violence: his arrest and execution were for his war resistant activity and his work to save the Jews, and not because of the plot he was associated with (see Nation, Siegrest, and Umbel 2013). This theory of Bonhoeffer's pacifism remains contentious. Defenders of realism look at Bonhoeffer's participation in the plot to kill Hitler as an example of the failure of pacifism; but pacifists will prefer the alternative interpretation, which views Bonhoeffer as a hero of nonviolence to the end.

A detailed consideration of whether Gandhian *satyagraha* would work against Nazis—or whether Bohnoeffer and other Christian pacifists remained committed to nonviolence in the midst of atrocity—is a question we cannot pursue further here. But we should note that Gandhi's ideas about nonviolent social protest spread and were woven together with Christian pacifism. By the 1960s, nonviolent social protest had become part of the mainstream of social activism, embodied in the work of Martin Luther King and the U.S. Civil Rights Movement—and put into practice in other anti-colonial and civil rights protests around the globe, including in revolutions against the Soviet Union and in Eastern Europe, Africa, and Latin America.

While Christian pacifism is discussed in more detail in another chapter, we should note that the twentieth century produced a significant amount of scholarship focused on Christian pacifism. Christian pacifists in the twentieth century include Dorothy Day, A.J. Muste, Thomas Merton, Daniel and Philip Berrigan, John Howard Yoder, Myron Augsburger, Cesar Chavez, and Stanley Hauerwas.

We cannot discuss each of these figures here. But we can highlight a few, noting that Christian pacifists were among the most radical—and most effective—forces for social change in the twentieth century. Day and her Catholic Worker Movement provide one inspirational example. Day linked pacifism with Christian charity and a general opposition to injustice and greed that was based upon Jesus's Sermon on the Mount. Her model of Catholic nonviolence and social justice activism has a close connection with the work of Cesar Chavez, who drew upon his understanding of Latino Catholicism as an inspiration for his own nonviolent activism (see Orosco 2008). Another significant twentieth-century pacifist was A.J. Muste, who argued that pacifism was intimately tied to the idea that God is love. Muste worked with the Fellowship of Reconciliation, through which he influenced Martin Luther King, Jr., another one of its members. It was Muste, for example, who helped to send James Lawson to India, where he studied Gandhian nonviolence. Lawson was a Methodist minister who was also a conscientious objector during the Korean War. When Lawson returned from India, he worked with King and the Nonviolent Student Coordinating Committee. Day, Muste, King, and Lawson recognized the need for organized nonviolent action and for the creation of institutions of peace as a replacement for the war system.

Christian pacifists developed the strategy of nonviolent direct action and civil disobedience based upon the idea that when the civil law conflicted with the higher moral or religious law, the law should be broken—as King explained in his "Letter from Birmingham Jail" (King 1986: 93). Civil disobedience grounded in Christian teaching points toward a higher law of the Kingdom of God. Related to this is the Christian pacifist call for a nonviolent revolution against existing social, political, economic, and racial systems. Muste, for example, once said, "In a world built on violence, one must be a revolutionary before one can be a pacifist; in such a world a non-revolutionary pacifist is a contradiction in terms, a monstrosity" (Muste quoted in Danielson 2014: 103). At the heart of twentieth-century Christian pacifism is a commitment to a theology that makes no compromises with the secular world. Hauerwas has argued, for example, that pacifism is an explicitly theological doctrine that calls all other values—including the values of patriotism and nationalism—into question. Hauerwas follows ideas found in Bonhoeffer, as well as in the writings of Yoder and others, to reach the conclusion that a commitment to Jesus requires pacifism. In an essay reflecting on September 11 he wrote, "Christian nonviolence is not a strategy to rid the world of violence, but rather the way Christians must live in a world of violence" (Hauerwas 2004: 203).

There are of course Christians who are not pacifists. The twentieth century featured a lively debate among Christians about war and nonviolence. While pacifists argue that the original Christian message is a pacific one, there are a wide variety of defenders of the just war tradition who ground their approaches in the Augustinian tradition that claims that war can be used as a tool that is intended to create the peace of *tranquilitas ordinis*. These Christian realists and just war theorists include Reinhold Niebuhr, Elizabeth Anscombe, Paul Ramsey, James Turner Johnson, Jean Bethke Elshtain, and George Weigel. One influential work is Anscombe's essay "War and Murder." Anscombe argues that a false interpretation of Christianity leads to pacifism (Anscombe 1981: 55). Christian pacifism is based upon a "false picture" of Jesus and a fallacious reading of the New Testament. According to Anscombe, Christian ethics requires defense of the innocent, which can justify war; and the doctrine of double effect allows some innocent people to be killed in pursuit of a justified war.

Perhaps the most famous Christian who argues against pacifism is C.S. Lewis. In his essay "Why I Am Not a Pacifist" (an address he gave in 1940 to a society of pacifists) he considers the nature of obedience to authority, while also discussing the question of whether war produces more harm than benefit. With regard to the question of harms and benefits, he argues that there is no way of knowing whether this is true. He concludes, "History is full of useful wars as well as of useless wars" (Lewis 2001: 74). He also argues that pacifists are merely tolerated by liberal regimes—and that a liberal regime in which pacifism is preeminent would be defeated by a totalitarian regime waiting to pounce. He concludes, "Pacifism of this kind is taking the straight road to a world in which there will be no Pacifists" (Lewis 2001: 78). These are standard objections to pacifism. George Orwell made a similar and stronger point when he called pacifism a "bourgeois illusion" that is "dishonest and intellectually disgusting" (Orwell 1942: n.p.).

Lewis's more specifically Christian argument appeals to a view of life that points beyond the material world. He says, "The doctrine that war is always a greater evil seems to imply a materialist ethic, a belief that death and pain are the greatest evils. But I do not think they are" (Lewis 2001: 77). Lewis further notes that the prevailing opinion of mainstream Christianity has been in support of war, including in the writings of Augustine and Aquinas. And he interprets the supposed pacifism of Jesus in a very concrete and limited way: the doctrine of turning the other cheek is for individual relations and has nothing to do with war.

As the Cold War dawned and nuclear weapons appeared on the scene, Christian debate moved further in the direction of just war pacifism. The nature of warfare in an age of advanced technology makes it unlikely that any war can be just. Nuclear deterrent strategy, for example, deliberately targets noncombatants, thus violating one of the basic principles of *jus in bello*. This critique is grounded in a larger ethical ideal that is closely associated with the ideals of what might be called Christian personalism. This is the idea that persons have intrinsic value. The personalist critique holds that modern warfare assaults the sacred dignity of the person in many ways: by using mass conscript armies, by vilifying and demonizing the enemy, and by using weaponry that makes killing abstract and impersonal. Along these lines, Pope John Paul II advocated a sort of pacifism in his idea of the "gospel of life." John Paul links the critique of war to a broad critique of all sorts of killing, condemning abortion, euthanasia, suicide, and the death penalty. And he marks as a sign of hope our growing awareness of the importance of nonviolent approaches to social conflict:

> Among the signs of hope we should also count the spread, at many levels of public opinion, of a new sensitivity ever more opposed to war as an instrument for the resolution of conflicts between peoples, and increasingly oriented to finding effective but "non-violent" means to counter the armed aggressor.
>
> *John Paul 1995: para. 27*

The current pope, Francis, has reiterated his call for a Christian commitment to nonviolence. In his "World Peace Day" address (January 2017) he states:

> I ask God to help all of us to cultivate nonviolence in our most personal thoughts and values. May charity and nonviolence govern how we treat each other as individuals, within society and in international life.... Violence is not the cure for our broken world.
> *Francis 2017: n.p.*

Unlike Lewis and Anscombe, who reject a pacifist interpretation of the Gospels, Francis explicitly embraces Jesus's teachings of nonviolence. He cites the nonviolent accomplishments of Gandhi, Abdul Ghaffar Khan, Martin Luther King, Mother Teresa, and John Paul II. And he calls for Christians to engage in "peacebuilding through active nonviolence." Of course, there remains a vigorous debate among Christians and in Catholicism about Christian pacifism. But it is hard to deny that the recent popes have shifted toward a commitment to some version of pacifism.

Related to Christian pacifism is the pacifism and nonviolence of thinkers and activists in other religious traditions. In addition to Gandhi, we might also note Abdul Ghaffar Khan, a Muslim who worked with Gandhi and taught *satyagraha* to the Pashtun peoples. Other inspirational figures include the Vietnamese Buddhist monk Thich Nhat Hahn and the Tibetan Buddhist Tenzin Gyatso, better known as the Dalai Lama. But many nonviolent activists and parties have no famous single champion. Nonviolent activism can be found in movements by indigenous peoples across the world, including in the work of women seeking equality, oppressed people seeking liberty, and others concerned with social justice. As an example of this, we might note the movement known as "the Arab Spring," which began as a series of nonviolent protests by Muslim youth that erupted across North Africa and the Middle East in 2011.

During the twentieth century, pacifism became conceptually distinguished from a different sort of commitment to nonviolence. Indeed, scholars such as Robert Holmes identified a concept called "nonviolentism," which Holmes seems to have coined in 1971 (Holmes 2013: 157). This is a broader concept than pacifism since nonviolentism opposes violence in general and not just war. Yet nonviolent social protestors need not be morally opposed to war: they may simply be strategic in their use of violence. However, in the Gandhi-King tradition, the prevailing idea is that there ought to be a unity of means and end: if one is aiming toward justice and peace, one ought to utilize peaceful tactics. And indeed, during the 1960s, there was a developing conjunction between civil rights activism and anti-war activism. Since the end of the Cold War, pacifists and social activists have focused on defending human rights, strengthening international institutions, and criticizing the excesses of militarism. Today there are a wide range of pacifisms and nonviolentisms that are grounded in a variety of religious, ethical, and political doctrines. Pacifism and nonviolence are also connected to critique of a variety of practices and ideas, with connections to feminism, environmentalism, and so on. Pacifism and nonviolentism has also been conceived in connection with a larger life-affirming ethic. Albert Schweitzer, for example, describes a larger ethical idea based upon the principle of "reverence for life," an idea that led him to vegetarianism. As Schweitzer puts it, "Ethics is responsibility without limit toward all that lives" and "a man is truly ethical only when he obeys the compulsion to help all life that he is able to assist and shrinks from injuring anything that lives ... Life as such is sacred to him" (Schweitzer 2002: 73–74).

Conclusion: Beyond the Twentieth Century

When the Cold War ended, there was great hope that the logic of nonviolence would prevail. Francis Fukuyama predicted "the end of history." Successful nonviolent campaigns brought about the end of the Soviet Empire. In Czechoslovakia this was called the velvet revolution or the gentle revolution. There was hope for global disarmament and the growth of peaceful globalization connected to the spread of liberal-capitalism and democracy. Unfortunately, violence and war did not go away. Terrorism and mass violence continues to plague the world, and war was declared against terrorism. Ongoing conflicts remain unsolved. The geopolitical situation has remained fractious. Nuclear weapons and other weapons of mass destruction continue to exist. And technological developments have changed the nature of warfare, which now includes cyberwar, drone attacks, precision guided missiles, missile defense systems, and so on. Throughout this period, international organizations have continued to grow, including international tribunals that try war crimes and international peacekeeping forces that intervene under the developing idea of humanitarian intervention and the responsibility to protect innocent people who are being persecuted and slaughtered by their own governments. If the era of total and global wars appears to be over, there still remains significant violence and the ongoing challenge of justifying military responses to violence.

Philosophers and activists continue to reflect on the nature of violence and the question of peace. A significant amount of scholarship has developed that is focused on the question of justice in war and the just war tradition. Scholarship on peace has also grown to include a field known as "peace studies," which often focuses on empirical inquiries. Guided by the work of seminal thinkers such as Gene Sharp and Johan Galtung, we now have a deep and comprehensive understanding of the power of nonviolence. Philosophers have continued to probe and question the ethics of pacifism: many of the key authors in the ongoing debate about the ethics of pacifism and peace philosophy are included in this anthology. One conclusion to be derived from the past 25 years of conversations about peace, war, and violence is that these things are philosophically complex. There are varieties of pacifism. Peace and violence are complicated topics with multiple meanings, iterations, and applications.

The theory and practice of pacifism and nonviolence has benefited from a long century of debate. The world has benefited, as well, from the work of nonviolent activists and theorists of nonviolence. In 2011, the psychologist Steven Pinker published a book explaining "why violence has declined" (Pinker 2011). The good news is that the empirical data show us that violence is declining. Pinker's complex thesis about the decline in violence includes reflections on psychology, politics, and philosophy. Although he does not directly attribute the decline of violence to the development of pacifism and nonviolence outlined here, the implication is clear. The work of many of the authors and activists cited in this chapter and discussed in the rest of this anthology have been instrumental in changing our attitudes about violence, in clarifying the power and value of nonviolence, and in helping us to understand how we can build a global culture of peace. There is still much work to be done on behalf of peace. But thanks to the heroic efforts of those discussed in this chapter, we are already on our way toward a better world.

Works Cited

Anscombe, G. E. M. (ed.) (1981). "War and Murder," in *Ethics, Religion, and Politics*. Minneapolis: University of Minnesota Press, 51–61.
Arnaud, E. (1906). *Le Pacifisme et ses Détracteurs*. Paris: Aux Bureaux de la Grande Revue.
Bonhoeffer, D. (1956). *No Rusty Swords*. New York: Harper and Row.
Bourne, R. (1917). "War and the Intellectuals" (pamphlet published by American Union against Militarism). Available at Google Books: https://books.google.com/books?id=Sn4_AQAAMAAJ&dq=bourne+war+and+the+intellectuals&source=gbs_navlinks_s (Accessed October 23, 2017).
Bourne, R. (1918). "The State." Available at: http://fair-use.org/randolph-bourne/the-state/ (Accessed October 23, 2017).

Buber, M. (1957). *Buber, Pointing the Way*. New York: Harper Brothers.
Buber, M. (2005). *A Land of Two Peoples: Martin Buber on Jews and Arabs*. Chicago: University of Chicago Press.
Danielson, L. (2014). *American Gandhi: A.J. Muste and the History of Radicalism in the 20th Century*. Philadelphia: University of Pennsylvania Press.
Dewey, J. (1917). "The Future of Pacifism." *The New Republic* (July 28): 358–360.
Dewey, J. (1990). "Tolstoy's Art," in J. Boydston (ed.), *Dewey Later Works: 1925–1953*, vol. 17. Carbondale, IL: SIU Press, 381–392.
Dower, N. (2009). *The Ethics of War and Peace*. Cambridge: Polity Press.
Einstein, A. (1981). *Einstein on Peace*. New York: Crown Publishers.
Einstein, A. (1982/1954). *Ideas and Opinions*. New York: Three Rivers Press.
Francis, Pope. (2017). "World Peace Day Address." Available at Vatican website: https://w2.vatican.va/content/francesco/en/messages/peace/documents/papa-francesco_20161208_messaggio-l-giornata-mondiale-pace-2017.html (Accessed October 23, 2017).
Galtung, J. (1969). "Violence, Peace, and Peace Research." *Journal of Peace Research* 6 (3): 167–191.
Galtung, J. (1990). "Cultural Violence." *Journal of Peace Research* 27 (3): 291–305.
Gandhi, M. K. (1938/1994). "Statement of November 26, 1938," in *Gandhi Reader*. New York: Grove Press. Reprinted and available at: http://gandhiserve.org/information/writings_online/articles/gandhi_jews_palestine.html (Accessed October 23, 2017).
Goldmann, E. (1998). *Red Emma Speaks: An Emma Goldmann Reader*, 3rd ed. New York: Humanity Books.
Hauerwas, S. (2004). *Performing the Faith: Bonhoeffer and the Practice of Nonviolence*. Grand Rapids, MI: Brazos.
Holmes, R. (1989). *On War and Morality*. Princeton: Princeton University Press.
Holmes, R. (2013). *The Ethics of Nonviolence: Essays by Robert Holmes*, edited by P. Cicovacki. London: Bloomsbury.
James, W. (1911). "A Moral Equivalent of War," in W. James (ed.), *Memories and Studies*. New York: Longmans, Green and Co, 267–296.
John Paul II, Pope. (1995). "Evangelium Vitae." Available at Vatican website: http://w2.vatican.va/content/john-paul-ii/en/encyclicals/documents/hf_jp-ii_enc_25031995_evangelium-vitae.html (Accessed October 23, 2017).
King, M. L., Jr. (1986). "Letter from Birmingham Jail," in M.L. King (ed.), *Why We Can't Wait*. Boston: Beacon, 85–109.
Lewis, C. S. (2001). "Why I Am Not a Pacifist," in C.S. Lewis (ed.), *The Weight of Glory*. New York: HarperOne, 64–90.
Luxemburg, R. (1911). "The Meaning of Pacifism." Available at: www.marxists.org/history/etol/newspape/themilitant/socialist-appeal-1938/v02n14/luxemburg.htm (Accessed October 23, 2017).
Nation, M. T., A. G. Siegrist, and D. P. Umbel. (2013). *Bonhoeffer the Assassin? Challenging the Myth, Recovering His Call to Peacemaking*. Grand Rapids, MI: Baker Academic.
Orosco, J. A. (2008). *Cesar Chavez and the Common Sense of Nonviolence*. Albuquerque, NM: University of New Mexico Press.
Orwell, G. (1942). "Pacifism and the War." *Partisan Review* August-September. Available at: www.orwell.ru/library/articles/pacifism/english/e_patw (Accessed October 23, 2017).
Pinker, S. (2011). *The Better Angels of Our Nature: Why Violence Has Declined*. New York: Viking Books.
Russell, B. (1915). "The Ethics of War." *International Journal of Ethics* 25 (2), January: 127–142.
Russell, B. (1934–44). "The Future of Pacifism." *The American Scholar* 13 (1), Winter: 7–13.
Russell, B. (1945). "The Bomb and Civilization." Available at: www.humanities.mcmaster.ca/~russell/civbomb8.pdf (Accessed October 23, 2017).
Russell, B. (2004/1916). *Why Men Fight*. New York: Cosimo.
Russell, B. (2010/1975). *Autobiography*. New York: Routledge.
Russell, B., and A. Einstein. (1955). "Russell-Einstein Manifesto." Available at: https://pugwash.org/1955/07/09/statement-manifesto/ (Accessed October 23, 2017).
Scheler, M. (1976). "The Idea of Peace and Pacifism: Part 1." *Journal of the British Society for Phenomenology* 7: 154–166.
Scheler, M. (1977). "The Idea of Peace and Pacifism: Part 2." *Journal of the British Society for Phenomenology* 8: 35–50.
Schweitzer, A. (2002). "The Philosophy of Civilization," in M. Meyer and K. Bergel (eds.), *Reverence for Life: The Ethics of Albert Schweitzer for the Twenty-first Century*. Syracuse: Syracuse University Press, 70–90.
Tolstoy, L. (1885). *My Religion*, translated by H. Smith. New York: Thomas Y. Crowell and Co.
Weiss, P. (1943). "The Ethics of Pacifism." *The Philosophical Review* 51 (5): 476–496.

Further Reading

Brock, P., and N. Young. (1999). *Pacifism in the 20th Century*. Syracuse, NY: Syracuse University Press. (A definitive historical overview of pacifism in the twentieth century.)

Cortright, D. (2008). *Peace: A History of Movements and Ideas*. Cambridge, UK: Cambridge University Press. (A useful overview of peace movements, which points beyond pacifism and toward peace activism and nonviolence broadly construed.)

Kurlansky, M. (2006). *Nonviolence: 25 Lessons from the History of a Dangerous Idea*. New York: Modern Library. (A popular survey of the history of pacifism and nonviolence.)

4
CHRISTIAN PACIFISM

Daniel A. Dombrowski

The topic of the present article might seem to be a very particular one, but the case for Christian pacifism can escape the charge of parochialism for at least four reasons. First, the idea that war ought to be renounced comes to us from Christianity. Peter Brock ably shows that there is no known instance of non-vocational conscientious objection to participation in war, and no recorded advocacy of such objection, prior to the Christian era (Brock 1972). (The personal commitment to non-violence in ancient Hinduism and Buddhism was vocational in character in that it was applied in a way analogous to the medieval exemption of priests from warfare. One can be a vocational pacifist and still support just war theory, so long as others fight.) Second, although after the patristic period only a minority of Christians have been pacifists, between the patristic period and the nineteenth century in the West pacifism was nonetheless confined to those who were influenced by Christianity. Third, pacifism is a characteristic form of renewal in Christianity (as in some of the Franciscans, the Waldensians, the Quakers, etc.), hence current interest in pacifism has implications for Christianity, just as current renewal in Christianity has implications for non-Christian pacifism. And fourth, to the extent that Christian pacifism is defended on a rational basis that is distinguishable from a defense of it in terms of divine command theory, Christian pacifists and non-Christian pacifists travel along the same (or at least parallel) paths.

In the present chapter I will first make the case for Christian pacifism on a biblical basis (in dialogue with some just war theorists who tend to interpret Jesus as bellicose), and then I will make the case on a rational basis that is intended to appeal to all rational agents, even those who are not Christians or even theists. The rational case for Christian pacifism has both a negative formulation and a positive one.

It should be noted that some Christians, especially in the Protestant tradition, adopt a *sola scriptura* position wherein ethics is determined solely on the basis of divine commands from scripture. Other Christians, especially in Catholicism and Eastern Orthodoxy, rely on both scripture and rational argumentation in ethics. But this contrast should not be overemphasized in that there are many Protestant thinkers who see the need for rational argumentation in Christian ethics, on the one hand, and scripture remains very important in Catholic and Orthodox circles, on the other. As mentioned, in the present chapter I will present both scriptural and rational cases for Christian pacifism. The latter will rely on both natural law and deontological reasons, which I will argue are still very much based in the Christian intellectual tradition.

Some thinkers try to bridge the scriptural and rational approaches. For example, perhaps the most influential Christian pacifist religion has been the Society of Friends or Quakers, who arose in the seventeenth century in England under George Fox. Quakers believe, primarily on the basis of the image of God hypothesis in Genesis and the Gospel of John, that human beings are possessive of an inner light that makes them eminently worthy of respect. The fact that this inner light is identified with Johannine *logos* should not in this context escape our notice. That is, what it means to say that human beings are made in the image of God is to say that they can reason and hence be held accountable for their actions. A similar way of viewing things can be found in the Mennonites, another famous Christian pacifist version of Protestantism.

Biblical Background

In an old Charlton Heston movie, *Khartoum*, a Muslim man who has just been introduced to the beliefs of Christianity expresses astonishment when he first reads the Gospels. What surprises him is the apparent tension between the pacifism of Jesus and the belligerence of the Christians he has met, all of whom were fierce soldiers. We might be struck with the same sort of tension when we (re)read the Gospels. The sort of tension mentioned here is real, not apparent. Further, according to Christian pacifists, attempts of Christian theorists to assuage this tension by interpreting Jesus as bellicose seem doomed to failure.

The most striking feature of the life of Jesus, according to Christian pacifists, is his emphasis on love (*agape*). In fact, the greatest commandment a human being has is to love (e.g., Matthew 22: 34–40; Mark 12: 28–34; Luke 10: 25–29). And the sort of love he had in mind was extreme, as it was a love that did not demand love in return. When struck on one cheek by an evildoer, we are not to resist, but to offer the other cheek as well (e.g., Matthew 5: 38–42; Luke 6: 29). In fact, not only are we to suffer the injustices of evildoers, we should love them while they perpetrate that injustice (e.g., Matthew 5: 43–48; Luke 6: 35). Put quite simply, for Jesus the meek and the peacemakers are blessed (e.g., Matthew 5: 1–12; Luke 6: 17–49), not the violent, the vengeful, or the warmakers.

This was not an idle theory for Jesus. His praxis consistently illustrates his teachings. All of the passion narratives consistently exemplify his turning the other cheek. Peter had completely missed the point of Jesus's teaching when he used the sword against Malchus on the night Jesus was betrayed. He failed to realize that *all* (*pantes*) who draw the sword will die by it (see Matthew 26: 51–54; John 18: 10).

Granted, Jesus was not a political, or even a moral, theorist. But the thrust of his teachings and actions make it clear that when the question of a just Christian war is raised, the burden of proof is on the one who attempts to justify a war and yet claim to be a Christian. The onus is not on the pacifist, if what is meant by pacifism is an opposition to war or violence as a means of settling disputes or an attitude of non-violent resistance to evil. This claim regarding where the burden of proof lies is supported not only by Christian pacifists themselves, but also by one of the greatest defenders of just war theory, St. Thomas Aquinas. He frames his defense of just war theory in response to the following question: "Is it always a sin to wage war?" (Aquinas 1972: 2a2ae, 40, 1). The presence of the word "always" (*semper*) in this question suggests that normally war *is* sinful; or better, the burden of proof is on the person who would like to argue that waging war need not be sinful.

The very early Christians were universally pacifists (as Brock and Ramsey attest). This is one of the better-kept secrets in the Christian intellectual tradition. The first Christians who are known to have been soldiers are not found until 177 C.E. It can be argued that this early Christian pacifism was, in the main, a consistent deduction from the foundation laid by Jesus.

That is, it seems that Jesus, in disarming Peter, "had unbelted every soldier," to use Paul Ramsey's language (Ramsey 1961: XV–XVII). He also notes that by 403 C.E. *only* Christians could be soldiers in the Roman Empire, thereby bringing about the "social triumph" of Christianity, from Ramsey's just war perspective, in contrast to the "fall of Christianity," from a pacifist perspective.

It is legitimate to infer that Christian pacifism is in tension with just war theory, which is also largely the result of certain Christian thinkers who eventually bequeathed their view to international jurists. This tension very often surfaces in biblical interpretation. For example, regarding Jesus's words to Peter mentioned previously, Aquinas offers the following interpretation (relying on St. Augustine): what is meant by drawing the sword is to arm oneself and spill blood without command or lawful authority. According to Aquinas, in contrast to the Christian pacifist, Jesus was prohibiting *private* persons from using the sword when he chastised Peter, or at least those who do not have the authority of God behind them. Yet, as has been noted, Jesus quite simply says that *all* who draw the sword will die by it, not all who draw the sword without legitimate authority. At another point (Aquinas 1972: 2a2ae, 40, 2) Aquinas interprets this passage as an exhortation to all bishops and clerics. That is, when Jesus says "Put your sword back in its scabbard" to Peter, Peter becomes a symbol for all bishops and clerics, thus indicating an embrace of vocational pacifism, at the very least, if not pacifism per se.

It might also be objected that at one point Jesus *does* say that he did not come to bring peace on earth, but the sword. In context, however, he is doing anything but justifying war. The point of the passage in question seems to be to show the radical character of Jesus's calling. As he puts it, "He who loves father or mother more than me is not worthy of me" (Matthew 10: 35–39). In other words, Jesus brings the "sword" to cut the umbilical cord, not another person's head.

It has to be admitted that the Christian pacifist cringes when certain passages describing God as violent from the Hebrew scriptures and from the last book of the Christian scriptures are considered; and it must also be admitted that these passages seem to be at odds with the Jesus of the Gospels. But the pacifist need not violate the integrity of the Bible as a whole if the *agape* of the New Law *fulfills* the Old Law (e.g., Matthew 5: 17–20), which still leaves room for a certain continuity between the Old and New Testaments (e.g., both point to a monotheistic God who is omnibenevolent), as opposed to a total cleavage between the two.

Elizabeth Anscombe is an influential just war theorist who views with approbation scriptural passages that depict God as bloodthirsty (Anscombe 1978). In this regard she mentions Jesus's commendation of the centurion (Matthew 8: 5–13; Luke 7: 1–10). In all fairness it should be noted that Jesus does not chastise the soldier for his profession. But, as Anscombe herself notes, he does not commend his profession, either. Jesus only commends the soldier's *faith*.

Anscombe also refers to a passage where God is claimed to have power to destroy both body and soul in hell (Matthew 10: 28; Luke 12: 5). But to say that God *can* do these things is not necessarily to say that God *will* do them. That is, Jesus's pacifism seems to have implications for how we should view God. This conclusion is supported by the fact that this passage is immediately followed by the assurance that not even a sparrow falls without the concern of God.

Just war theorists differ in their attitude toward Christian pacifism. Some, like Ramsey, permit pacifism as an (inadequate) expression of responsible Christian service to the common good, whereas others, like Anscombe, see Christian pacifism as irresponsible. What is common to all Christian just war theorists, however, as I see things, is a halfhearted attempt to trace their justifications of the use of violence back to Jesus.

It might also be objected that the inability of Christian just war theorists to trace their case back to Jesus is not the serious problem that Christian pacifists allege it to be. Christianity, it will be correctly claimed, has never been slavishly attached to the conditions peculiar to a first-century Roman colony. Opponents of Christian pacifism might note that all of Jesus's disciples were Jews, but this does not mean that henceforth all of Jesus's followers would have to be Jews. So also, Jesus may have been a pacifist, but that fact *simpliciter* does not mean that all Christians must be pacifists. In response I would say that I am certainly not insisting on anything even closely resembling biblical fundamentalism. My claim is merely that the centrality of *agape* and non-violence in the Gospels sets a standard against which Christians who are not pacifists must contend.

Just war theory was born (within Christianity, at least, ignoring classical Greek and Roman predecessors) in the patristic era, and not before. The earliest Christians were pacifists, as has been noted, and not only because the Romans did not want them as soldiers. Their pacifism made sense in that Jesus himself was a pacifist. But with the decline of the Roman Empire, Christian leaders found themselves in a schizophrenic position, with one eye on Jesus's unbelting of Peter and Jesus's own non-violence and the other eye on all the real estate scattered throughout the empire. In order to rule such land and defend the people on it, Christian leaders after Constantine came to the conclusion that they would have to forcefully defend themselves against barbarians.

A final objection might be that the view of Jesus as a pacifist is at odds with the story of Jesus cleansing the temple. I assume that the image most people have of this story includes a whip in the hand of Jesus as he violently expels the moneychangers who had defiled the temple. This image is reinforced by depictions of this event by various famous artists (Giotto, El Greco, Rembrandt, Picasso, etc.). But it is not clear if this image, which is incompatible with the thesis that Jesus was a pacifist, can withstand scholarly analysis.

The synoptic Gospels (Matthew 21: 12–13; Mark 11: 15–17; Luke 19: 45–46) seem to point to one cleansing and John 2: 13–17 to another, perhaps earlier, cleansing. But whereas tradition and artistic representation have it that Jesus violently drove the moneylenders out of the temple with a whip, the texts seem to suggest something different. The whip is not mentioned at all in Matthew, Mark, or Luke. This in itself is worthy of note, given the prevalence in art history, and then in popular imagination, of the violent cord. All that is asserted is that Jesus drove out all who were buying or selling things in the temple. We have no indication how he drove them out. Did he say "Get out" or did he yell vehemently "Get Out!" Might not a "miracle man" scare off a crowd with mere words, especially when the traders probably already realized that they were in violation of the spirit, if not the letter, of the law? Or was it because of Jesus's upsetting of their tables and seats?

Such speculation, although interesting, is idle. We are not told how he drove them out. What is important to note is that, first, he did drive them out and, second, there is no indication in the synoptic Gospels that he did so violently or even physically. Jesus may have done "violence" to several tables and chairs, but there is no evidence to suggest that he struck another human being. Perhaps this upsetting of objects would force one to define very precisely what is meant by the term "pacifism." If it is taken as an opposition to war or violence as a means of settling disputes or resisting evil, then perhaps one should add that this non-violence is with regard to human beings, not inanimate things.

What of John's description of the cleansing of the temple? Finally, we come upon the infamous "whip." It was probably not a whip at all, but a lash made out of rushes (*phragellion ek schoinion*), of the sort still used to herd animals in parts of the Mideast today. But if Jesus hoped to drive the moneychangers out violently, why did he choose such an inadequate instrument? The answer to this question is again found in the text. There is no clear indication in John that Jesus drove out the moneychangers violently; in fact, there is no clear evidence in John that he drove them out at all. The use of the word "all" (*pantas*) may well refer to the sheep and cattle (*kai poiesas phragellion ek schoinion pantas exebalen ek tou hierou ta te probate kai tous boas*).

If he drove out the moneychangers at all, which is not clearly stated in John 2: 13–17, there is certainly no clear indication that he did so violently or even physically. Perhaps, and again this is only speculation, it was the boldness with which Jesus drove out the animals in the first cleansing of the temple (described in John) that made the moneychangers fear him so—remembering his reputation as a miracle man and their own cognizance of their violation of at least the spirit of the law—when he cleansed the temple a second time (described in the synoptic Gospels). In this second incident, one can imagine, all that Jesus needed to do was say "Get out" to drive out the moneychangers. At any rate, Jesus's pacifism remains intact. What is really noteworthy in this incident is that Jesus's feisty pacifism did not preclude his actively resisting evil, nor does it preclude his use of irony or an acid tongue.

Rational Defense: Negative Formulation

Some Christian pacifists do not so much offer a direct defense of their view as they "back into" Christian pacifism as a result of the failure of just war theory. If there are three major options regarding the relationship between morality and war (just war theory, pacifism, and *realpolitik*), and if the realist option has always been understandably anathema in Christian intellectual circles, then the failure of just war theory would have felicitous consequences for any effort to defend Christian pacifism.

If just war theory is seen as having two main components, *jus ad bellum* and *jus in bello*, then one wonders about the cogency of this theory when it is realized that most (perhaps all) wars fail to meet one or both of these criteria. It should be noted that according to the logic of just war theory, there is *at most* one just side in a war, which leaves open the possibility that there are wars in which both sides are unjust in that they both fail to meet the crucial *jus ad bellum* criterion of a just cause to fight for (quintessentially, self-defense). On this basis, I assume that most of the cases that are made in favor of *jus ad bellum* fail to convince even just war theorists.

But even if a convincing case for *jus ad bellum* could be made regarding some state that had been illegitimately attacked, it is crucial to notice that it is not assured (or even likely) that the aggrieved state would meet the strict criteria associated with *jus in bello*, especially the all-important criterion of non-combatant immunity. Any defensible concept of justice starts with the idea that each person should receive his or her due, hence it is hard to see how non-combatants are getting what they deserve when they are killed in time of war. Aquinas is a prominent Christian just war theorist who puts my point in the strongest terms: *Et ideo nullo modo licit occidere innocentum* (There is simply no justification for taking the life of an innocent person)—(Aquinas 1972: 2a2ae, 64, 6).

The logic of my position here is quite simple:

1. Christian just war theory has considered killing, or threatening to kill, innocent persons as illegitimate.
2. Modern warfare *depends* on weapons that either kill, or threaten to kill, innocent persons.
3. Therefore, one cannot use the Christian just war theory to justify the construction and/or use of weapons that kill, or threaten to kill, innocent persons.

In terms of killing innocent persons (as in premise 2), nuclear weapons immediately come to mind, as do devices in chemical/biological warfare. But my claim cuts deeper than these obvious cases. The logic of my argument here holds as well for most "conventional" modern weapons, affecting our judgments concerning the saturation bombings of English, French, Japanese, Chinese, and German cities in the Second World War, the devices used in the blockade of Germany at the end of the First World War and in the siege of Leningrad in the Second World War, the defoliants used in Vietnam to starve civilian populations (see Deuteronomy 9: 1–5 regarding fruit trees), the bombs dropped on hospitals in various wars, and so on. The list is enormous and quite cosmopolitan. The Russians murdered Poles in Katyn Forest, just as the Turks murdered defenseless Armenians locked in cages.

Has there been a just war in the twentieth and twenty-first centuries? I cannot think of a single one that clearly exhibits both *jus ad bellum* and *jus in bello*. The latter is honored more in the breach than in the observance. The former is sometimes found, but unfortunately not often enough in those cases where *jus in bello* obtains, as in the British fight in the Falklands. If a just war is to be found, it is only in these minor fights, but in the Falklands-Malvinas case *jus ad bellum* can only be established on the Hobbesian right to defend an empire, which is hardly a paradigmatic example.

It is ironic that the pacifist is often criticized for being impractical. One reply is that if one cannot easily produce an example of just war in a historical period full of wars, then what are we to *do* with this theory? Some might say that just war theory can function as an ideal, but here an egregious category mistake appears. The just war theory is not and never has been an ideal, even on the reasoning of just war theorists themselves, but an instrument to reach an ideal. Peace is that ideal, according to both Christian pacifists and Christian just war theorists. Whatever value war has, it is instrumental to the ideal of reaching peace.

Just war theorists are prone to forget that, on the grounds of their own theory, the injustice of the enemy's war aim is a necessary but not sufficient condition of the justice of one's own war aim. It is perhaps because these sufficient conditions for just war have seldom, if ever, been met that in the tenth and eleventh centuries soldiers in general had to perform penances for killing in battle. The extreme cynicism implied in the willingness to kill innocents should not hide the less extreme cynicism implied in the commonly heard justification for killing combatants, i.e., that combatants can be killed because they have "forfeited" their right to life. But if this is true, then why should the just warrior worry about right intention? (Right intention is a crucial feature for just war theorists like Aquinas.) Why does one even need right intention when killing, if the being to be killed no longer has a right to life or a right to be treated with respect?

The overall point to this negative formulation is that, once the moral defects in just war theory are emphasized, the stage is set for a (re)consideration of the pacifist roots of Christian intellectual life and Christian spirituality.

Rational Defense: Positive Formulation

The positive case for Christian pacifism can be stated in the terms of the following simple argument:

1. It is morally wrong to intentionally kill dignified subjects worthy of respect.
2. War by its very nature involves the intentional killing of dignified subjects who are worthy of moral respect (and it does so in large numbers).
3. Therefore, war is immoral.

Of course we are in contentious territory here, so mentioning a few of the criticisms that are likely is one of the demands of intellectual honesty. For example, one criticism that will be delivered against the first premise is that it implies not only opposition to killing in war, but also opposition to other sorts of killing, some of which might be acceptable to many reflective moral agents, as in voluntary euthanasia. This insightful objection causes a defender of the first premise to fine-tune it so as to make it clear that what is being morally prohibited is intentionally killing dignified subjects *without their consent* (see Dombrowski 1996).

A more serious challenge to the first premise will no doubt be delivered by those contemporary scholars who agree with Aquinas that in a just war, opposing soldiers are never killed intentionally. This objection relies, whether explicitly or implicitly, on Aquinas's famous (or infamous) principle of double effect (see Aquinas 1972: 2a2ae, 64, 7). According to this principle, an action in war can have two effects: one is intended and the other is foreseen but not intended. In a just war, it will be argued, the primary effect of one's actions must be good, as in defending the rights of non-combatants in one's own country, and it is this effect that is intended. The secondary effect of one's actions in war, the one that is foreseen but not intended, is that enemy soldiers will be killed in the effort to protect the rights of non-combatants in one's own country. Thus, on this line of reasoning, one can kill massive numbers of combatants in war without doing so intentionally such that the first premise is undermined.

The enormous amount of attention that the principle of double effect has received has centered on its use in attempting to justify the killing of non-combatants in war (e.g., see Walzer 2006: 153, 155, 192–193), but here the principle is being used to attempt to justify war itself. To be frank, the amount of exegetical effort and linguistic analysis that would be required to adequately explicate the meaning of "intention" here is probably not worth the effort. Clearly the overwhelming majority of killing that occurs in war is "intended" in the sense that it is not accidental (which is presumably what defenders of this principle mean when they misleadingly say that killing in war is "foreseen"). But defenders of the principle of double effect seem to have some other definition of "intention" in mind, a definition that serves to conveniently get them off the hook morally so that they can claim that war does not violate the fifth commandment from the Hebrew scriptures (see Exodus 20: 13). That is, along with other critics, I find the principle of double effect to be a piece of merely linguistic trickery. It would be more honest of just war theorists if they tried to justify the intentional killing of people in war, rather than denying that such killing is intentional.

Rapprochement with just war theorists can perhaps be found when some Christian pacifists argue for gradual disarmament in order to extricate ourselves from the immoral predicament we find ourselves in. For example, if I am choking a man I could immediately release him if it is brought to my attention that I am acting immorally. But if I am holding him hostage in a room whose only door is rigged with a bomb, upon realizing that I had acted immorally I would have to continue to hold him hostage for a while, until I could make it safe for him to leave. To paraphrase Iris Murdoch (in her novel *The Sacred and Profane Love Machine*), better Christians never would have gotten into the predicament we are in at present where millions of people around the world are in effect held hostage to the presence of nuclear and other weapons; but given this predicament, Christians could do no better than to gradually disarm. Although I am skittish regarding this sort of reasoning, it does point toward some sort of "just-war pacifism" that should not go unnoticed.

Table 4.1 helps to illustrate the different sorts of Christian pacifism that could be imagined. The *modes of approach* to pacifism consist in seeing it as permissible, or seeing it as a duty, or seeing it as supererogatory (i.e., above and beyond the call of duty). Whereas the *types* of pacifism include, first, nuclear pacifism, where just war theory would be considered a live option *except* when nuclear weapons and other weapons that killed, or threatened to kill, innocents came into play. The National Conference of Catholic Bishops seems to have adopted this view. Second, pacifism can be seen as an opposition to all war, even if innocents are not killed or threatened with death. And third, pacifism can be seen as an opposition to all violence as a means of settling disputes, or as a means of responding to evil, in all instances involving human beings, whether in

Table 4.1 Modes of Approach to Pacifism

Types of Pacifism	Modes of Approach to Pacifism		
	Permissible	*Duty*	*Supererogatory*
Nuclear Pacifism	A	B	C
Pacifism as Opposition to All War	D	E	F
Pacifism as Opposition to All Violence	G	H	I

war or not. This third type is often called complete or total pacifism. When mode of approach and type of pacifism are considered together, nine options ensue. B, E, and H, which claim that pacifism is a duty, are stronger claims than the other six, with E being a stronger claim than B, in that E opposes all war rather than only war that involves nuclear weapons (and other weapons that kill innocents), and H being a stronger claim than either B or E, in that H consists in an opposition to all violence, whether in war or not.

My position on A, B, and C should be already apparent. My defense of B (which claims that opposition to the construction or use of weapons that of necessity threaten non-combatants is a duty) is obvious. Option A trivializes the issue, as if to say that it is a matter of indifference whether one kills with one's bare hands, a gun, or a nuclear weapon. To say that one is *allowed* to be a pacifist with respect to nuclear weapons and such, which is what A says, but one is not morally required to be a pacifist, is, in effect, to offer a defense (albeit a weak one) of nuclear weapons. Option C also trivializes the issue, although not as much as A. To say that one is to be *commended* for being a pacifist with respect to nuclear weapons and such, as opposed to merely being permitted to be a nuclear pacifist, is some consolation to defenders of B. But it is only small consolation. C in effect ignores the intellectual rigor of B because C does not make nuclear pacifism a duty for individuals throughout a society, but rather only makes it a commendable option. And to say that nuclear pacifism is above and beyond the call of duty leads one to wonder what one's duty *is*. Does it not consist in avoiding killing or threatening to kill innocents?

B is more closely related to E than is usually noticed. Weapons of mass destruction are integrally related to the military strength of great powers and serve as a backdrop or threat behind the use of conventional weapons. This is why several countries around the world have sought or now seek to possess nuclear weapons. That is, the strength of B carries over into a defense of E. The United States' defense strategy, for example, *centers* on nuclear weapons. Any use of weapons by states possessing either nuclear weapons or other weapons that kill or threaten to kill innocents carries with it the implication that nuclear or other such weapons could be used if less powerful weapons fail.

D (which sees opposition to war as merely permissible) is a weak view that leaves one of the key questions unanswered: Can a nation with advanced technological means of destruction avoid either killing or threatening to kill innocents in war, or, what is even more unlikely, use weapons that do not kill or threaten innocents in an efficacious way without indirectly relying on weapons that do kill or threaten innocents? In any event, E is supported by the previous rational argument in defense of pacifism in its positive formulation. Perhaps it will be objected that this formulation sounds more Kantian than Christian. However, as many left-wing critics of Kant have noted (e.g., Goldmann 2011), behind the Kantian "respect for persons" version of the categorical imperative lies nothing other than the traditional Christian view of the human person as *imago Dei*, as made in the image of God. And F is problematic for reasons that are similar to the problems with C. That is, F trivializes Christian pacifism by ignoring the intellectual strengths in E and by failing to give adequate reasons against our duty not to intentionally kill human beings.

There is a worrisome contrast between a very popular reductionist view of human beings as merely accidental byproducts of evolutionary history with no real intrinsic value and no *telos*, on the one hand, and the view of human beings as intrinsically valuable, which undergirds the declaration of human rights by the United Nations, say, on the other. We might wonder about how to justify, over the long haul, paying our Amnesty International dues on the basis of the aforementioned reductionistic view. *Why* do human beings have inalienable rights to life if they are no more intrinsically valuable than any other sort of protoplasmic stuff? To put the point in commercial terms, given the gradual Weberian disenchantment of the world, in recent years we have been living off of the (human rights) capital of the Judeo-Christian ages without paying much of a premium.

I would like to make it clear that I am not claiming that all deontological views or all ethical views that rely on the concept of respect for persons are concealed theologies. But I am suggesting that many or most contemporary deontological views or "respect for persons" views are underdetermined. Consider the prominent example of John Rawls, whose view presupposes that human beings deserve moral respect: Rawls says very little about *why* this is so. His influential critique of utilitarianism is based on the idea that utilitarians do not respect the distinctness of persons, *each* of whom should be seen as worthy of moral respect. That is, one cannot submit human persons to the utilitarian calculus without leaving something out. Nicholas Wolterstorff notices that what seems to make human persons worthy of moral respect in Rawls is Rawls's belief in natural human rights. But Rawls discusses the natural rights basis of his view only twice, with the more informative passage found in a footnote (see Wolterstorff 2008: 15–16; Rawls 1999: 442–443, 447). This is why it is defensible to claim that if Rawls's view is not exactly a concealed theology, it *is* a concealed version of natural rights. The insurance premium metaphor in the previous paragraph seems quite appropriate.

H is, admittedly, a difficult position to consistently apply. Claiming to hold that all violence directed against human beings is immoral immediately opens one up to the charge of hypocrisy if mugged on the street, or if witness to a rape, where one might either fight or be tempted to fight. Yet the insistence of Jesus at the very least is enough for Christian pacifists to reject G, which suggests that opposition to all violence is merely permissible. The *issue* of complete pacifism cannot be a matter of indifference to Christians. The question is this: Must we adopt H, or is I (which sees opposition to all violence as supererogatory) acceptable? Running the risk of hypocrisy, not knowing how I would react when personally attacked, but hoping that I would have the courage to resist evil non-violently, let me try to defend H. As was noted earlier, *agape* is not an option or an elective for Jesus—which would play into the hands of I—but a command (*entole*—Matthew 22: 34–40). So also, Jesus orders us to "be perfect, as your father in heaven is perfect" (Matthew 5: 48). What these passages point out is that in many approaches to morality outside of Christianity, the sphere of supererogatory acts is quite large at the expense of duty's sphere. Christians are commanded (i.e., duty bound) to do things (e.g., feed the hungry, etc.) that from other perspectives would clearly be going above and beyond the call of duty. H makes more demands on us than B or E. This is a Christian's cross to bear and it is by no means easy to bear it with equanimity, although figures like Thomas Merton, Albert Schweitzer, Martin Luther King, Gandhi (as an anonymous Christian, i.e., someone who exhibits Christlike qualities without explicitly or formally identifying with any Christian denomination), the Berrigan brothers, Dorothy Day, and the like do a fine job of pointing the way.

Obviously some versions of Christian pacifism make the burden of this position easier to bear due to the promise of personal immortality. For example, being killed for one's pacifist beliefs might be easier to bear if one thought that one would thereby be rewarded eternally in heaven. Two comments are in order here. First, not all versions of Christianity require belief in personal immortality in that some versions encourage alternative views, as in a view that Charles Hartshorne calls "contributionism" (Hartshorne 1984: 32–37). This latter view does not hold out the (illusory) consolation found in belief in personal immortality in that the contributionist thinks that human beings as biological animals are obviously mortal and that any "immortality" they might have consists in the loving contributions they might make to the everlasting life of God. In fact, to think that *we* should live forever might be seen as hubristic in that what it means to be a theist in this view is to think that, despite the fact that all of us will die, God will live forever. Second, even among those Christian pacifists who do believe in personal immortality, it is not always (or even usually) the case that this belief provides the primary motivation for their pacifism. If all human beings deserve moral respect, then killing them is wrong regardless of whether one will be rewarded for not doing so or punished if one does.

Conclusion

In this chapter I have supplied reasons, persuasive reasons I hope, in defense of B and E, and in rejection of A, D, and G. I have also intimated how C, F, and I can be reluctantly tolerated, for the sake of argument, with a special tolerance for I, as long as these options are held temporarily (e.g., for the reason cited in the aforementioned room rigged with a bomb example) until pacifism is adopted at some point in the foreseeable future. But this reluctant tolerance of C, F, and I is not to be confused with the attempt to forthrightly offer a theory that is morally defensible. I also defend H, but with the humility (it is to be hoped not false pride) of one who has faltered in the past. To hold H one must say along with Augustine when he was thinking aright: "Late have I loved." The task is to talk in terms of various degrees of difficulty in fulfilling one's moral duties without destroying the irrefragable demands of duty itself. In our culture it takes more heroism to consistently hold H than E, and still less to hold B, which, with the resurgence of pacifism within Christianity, is hardly a heroic position to hold anymore. But even E and H are duties, at least if we take as normative the law of *agape* as Jesus is reported to have presented it. And if we do not take the law of *agape* as normative, there are nonetheless rational arguments (which rely implicitly on the Judeo-Christian tradition of human beings as *imago Dei*) to support B and E, at the very least. To hold even these two positions deserves the designation "pacifist."

The defender of H can have a tolerance of police forces if there is an assurance that when criminals are subdued they are not killed and that when incarcerated they are treated humanely with the possibility left open that they could be reconciled with the rest of society. The practicality of non-violent arrest and incarceration of criminals, or of resistance to an attacker without maiming or killing the attacker, need not be an overwhelming problem. Even in the worst possible case of a crazed gunman, the criminal can just as easily be hit with a sedative dart as a deadly bullet. And working seriously against the underlying causes of violent crime (especially the easy access to guns) is the best possible way to prevent the existence of crazed gunmen in the first place.

Neither the death nor the non-existence of a human being is necessarily evil. We do not mourn the time before our birth, nor do we need to mourn the painless death of a 90-year-old who lived a full life, especially when it is considered that a person who has lived a natural life span has had ample opportunity to contribute much that is significant to fellow human beings and to the everlasting divine life that is both omnibenevolent and has perfect memory. Once we realize that we are animals we should expect to die. But from this we do not have enough evidence to conclude that we do not have an obligation to avoid intentionally killing a human being. That is, although death simply as such is not an evil, premature or ugly or painful death surely *is* an evil, especially if such deaths are intended by moral agents.

As before, however, a consistent defense of Christian pacifism would have to challenge the concept of God (which has some biblical support) as an omnipotent tyrant who rules the world through *coercive power*. Instead, the concept of God that would be compatible with Christian pacifism is the one intimated in the Gospels who would exhibit agapic, *persuasive power* as a patient lure toward a better, less violent future (see Dombrowski 2017).

Bibliography

Anscombe, E. (1978). "War and Murder," in J. Rachels (ed.), *Moral Problems*, 3rd ed. New York: Harper and Row.
Aquinas, St. T. (1972). *Summa Theologiae*, Blackfriars ed. New York: McGraw-Hill.
Bainton, R. (1960). *Christian Attitudes Toward War and Peace*. Nashville, TN: Abington.
Brock, P. (1972). *Pacifism in Europe to 1914*. Princeton, NJ: Princeton University Press.
Cadoux, J. (1982). *The Early Christian Attitude to War*. New York: Seabury.
Day, D. (1942). "Our Country Passes from Undeclared War to Declared War." *The Catholic Worker* (January, 1942): 1, 4.
Dombrowski, D. (1991). *Christian Pacifism*. Philadelphia: Temple University Press.
Dombrowski, D. (1996). "Must a Pacifist Also Be Opposed to Euthanasia?" *Journal of Value Inquiry* 30: 261–263.
Dombrowski, D. (2002). "Rawls and War." *International Journal of Applied Philosophy* 16: 185–200.
Dombrowski, D. (2017). *Whitehead's Religious Thought: From Mechanism to Organism, from Force to Persuasion*. Albany: State University of New York Press.
Douglass, J. (1968). *The Non-Violent Cross*. New York: Macmillan.
Friesen, D. (2002). "Christian Pacifism and September 11." *Mennonite Life* 57 (3): 1–13.
Goldmann, L. (2011). *Immanuel Kant*, translated by R. Black. London: Verso.
Hartshorne, C. (1984). *Omnipotence and Other Theological Mistakes*. Albany: State University of New York Press.
Hauerwas, S. (1985). *Against the Nations*. Minneapolis: Winston.
Kinast, R. (1981). "Non-Violence in a Process Worldview." *Philosophy Today* 25: 279–285.
McSorley, R. (1985). *New Testament Basis of Peacemaking*. Scottdale, PA: Herald.
Merton, T. (1971). *Thomas Merton on Peace*. New York: McCall.
Murdoch, I. (1974). *The Sacred and Profane Love Machine*. New York: Viking.
Murphy, T. (2013). "The Pacifism of Duane Friesen." *Process Studies* 42: 110–131.
Musto, R. (1986). *The Catholic Peace Tradition*. New York: Orbis.
National Conference of Catholic Bishops. (1983). *The Challenge of Peace*. Washington, DC: United States Conference of Catholic Bishops.
Ramsey, P. (1961). *War and the Christian Conscience*. Durham, NC: Duke University Press.
Rawls, J. (1999). *A Theory of Justice*, revised ed. Cambridge: Harvard University Press.
Regan, T. (1972). "A Defense of Pacifism." *Canadian Journal of Philosophy* 2: 73–86.
Tolstoy, L. (1899). *The Kingdom of God Is Within You*, translated by Aline Delano. New York: Crowell.
Walzer, M. (2006). *Just and Unjust Wars*, 4th ed. New York: Basic Books.
Whitehead, A. N. (ed.) (1967). "From Force to Persuasion," in *Adventures of Ideas*. New York: Free Press 69–86.
Wink, W. (1992). *Engaging the Powers*. Minneapolis: Fortress.
Wolterstorff, N. (2008). *Justice: Rights and Wrongs*. Princeton: Princeton University Press.
Yoder, J. (1972). *The Politics of Jesus*. Grand Rapids, MI: Eerdmans.
Yoder, J. (1983). *What Would You Do?* Scottdale, PA: Herald.
Yoder, J. (1994). "How Many Ways Are There to Think Morally About War?" *Journal of Law and Religion* 11: 83–107.
Zahn, G. (1967). *War, Conscience, and Dissent*. New York: Hawthorn.

5
PEACE AND NONVIOLENCE IN ISLAM

Ramin Jahanbegloo

Although Islam is sometimes disparaged as a culture and religion of violence, there are deep resources within Islam for understanding and developing peace and nonviolence. In Islam, non-coercion is more important than violence, which requires strong moral justification and which must end at the first opportunity. This chapter considers concepts such as *salam* and *jihad*. One of the first things that a devout Muslim is likely to teach a non-Muslim is that Islam is a religion of peace, and not a doctrine of violence and cruelty. *Islam* and the Arabic term *salam* ("peace") derive from the same trilateral root, *sa-li-ma*, "to be safe, secure, free from any evil or affliction." As a noun derived from this root, *salam* denotes a condition of peace or safety while also connoting "freedom from faults and defects." For Muslims the related term *Islam*, conventionally translated as "surrender or submission to the will of God," suggests a state of peace and security that comes through renunciation of willfulness and resignation to a higher power (see Funk and Said 2009: 61).

This chapter explains how Islamic sources tend to view violence as a violation of the order of the universe. It considers how the Qur'an sees violence as a harmful interaction among human beings that violates the state of balance, peace and order created by God. It considers Islamic traditions of peaceful civil society and toleration in places such as Andalusia/Córdoba and under Akbar in India. The internal diversity of Islam includes Sufism, which tends to emphasize peace. The chapter explains how contemporary Islamic justifications of violence are often influenced by Western (non-Muslim) sources, including reaction to colonialism. Finally, the chapter reminds us that there is a connection in the twentieth century in India between Gandhi and nonviolent/tolerant interpretations of Islam. The example of India reminds us that Muslim advocates of nonviolence, such as Maulana Abul Kalam Azad and Khan Abdul Ghaffar Khan, were allied with Gandhi and the theory and practice of nonviolence.

Introduction

Since the tragic events of September 11, 2001, followed by the invasion of Iraq and the rise of the Islamic State, many people in the West have linked Islam with violence. Many have come to the erroneous conclusion that Islam is a religion of war and that it resists any form of peace and nonviolence. Islam is not the only civilization and religion that people distort and misunderstand. But it has become a focus of deep prejudice and unacceptable stereotyping. There are differences between Islam and other religions. But we should neither defend Islam and proselytize on its behalf nor engage in cheap Islamophobia. In either case, we end up with an oversimplified view which is imposed on a complex phenomenon. As with any other tradition, Islam has engaged in a somewhat rational, logical and social-historical response to the perennial challenges of violence, war and peace. And as with other traditions, Islamic societies and cultures throughout the ages have presented remarkable and profound internal diversities and variations. Each has interpreted concepts such as violence, nonviolence and peace, according to its proper engagement with Islam. One can question the authenticity of an interpretation of a tradition. One can also question the credentials of the various authorities. This occurs both between and within traditions. We should be fully conscious of the basic conceptual and structural difference between Islam, as a set of received precepts and practices, and the interpretative framework of Muslims in the social-historical context. All of this complexity of interpretation is on the table as we study concepts of nonviolence and peace in the Islamic context.

Understanding peace and nonviolence in the Islamic context can help create a better understanding of the role played by these values within the framework of reconciliation, peacebuilding, nonviolent transformation and conflict resolution in Islamic history. To do justice to the open-ended tradition of peacemaking and nonviolence in different Islamic contexts we need to differentiate between overgeneralizations activated by ideological insights and non-shared patterns of interpretation, on the one hand, and basic precepts and common horizons of peacemaking and nonviolent action within Islamic traditions, on the other. In many respects, the Islamic concepts of nonviolence and peace offer a view of harmonious development and social organization which are distinctively different from the Islamic fundamentalist takes on the zero-sum game of human relations in the pursuit of an ideal of religious purity. Moving beyond these attitudes and interpretations require awareness of visions, practices and experiences of nonviolent action and peacemaking in Islamic civilization as complementarities rather than polarities among Muslims themselves and with others.

Roots of Peace and Nonviolence in Islam

The Qur'an and the Sunna (the traditions) of the Prophet are the primary sources of inspiration and action for Muslims. They are the guides which set the tone for the moral vision of the individual and the community in Islam. Belief is continuously accompanied with ethical action. In other words, the integrity of the believer in face of adversity is derived from the sense of the divine and the guidance of God. The capacity of judgment with which human beings are endowed is a reminder that believers are beings "whom God has guided, and they are the possessors of minds" (Qur'an 39:17–18). As Toshihiko Izutsu, an outstanding Japanese authority on Islam, argues:

> In a certain sense the Koran as a whole is dominated by the very spirit of *hilm*. The constant exhortation to kindness (*ihsan*) in human relations, the emphasis laid on justice (*adl*), the forbidding of wrongful violence (*zulm*), the bidding of abstinence and control of passions, the criticism of groundless pride and ignorance—all are concrete manifestations of this spirit of *hilm*.
>
> *Izutsu 1964: 216*

The essence of Muslim ethics is, thus, closely related to the social and political actions of the Islamic community in light of the teachings of the Qur'an. Moreover, the Qur'an recognizes the fact that human beings need guidance in order to have an adequate ethical action and this is why God has sent them a Messenger. The Qur'an underlines: "We never punish until we have sent a Messenger" (Qur'an 17:15). So broadly speaking, the Qur'an invites the believer to moral betterment coupled with the awareness of the divine presence. It is, therefore, in such an ontotheological and ethical setting that ideas such as "peace," "nonviolence," "tolerance" and "respect" find their real meaning in the Islamic ethical framework. As such, the sense of wrong and right plays out in relation to the believer's conduct toward the Muslim *umma* or other communities of faith. "Let there be among you," observes the Qur'an, "a community that calls to the good (*al-khayr*), bidding virtue (*maruf*) and forbidding vice (*munkar*)" (Qur'an 3:104). What makes the Qur'an a compelling scripture across space and time is the conviction that it is both a spiritual and an ethical scriptural text, which invites Muslims to strive in the path of God and along with divine grace. This could lead to excellence and happiness, binding individual virtue to the duty of care toward the community and others. Moral virtue, therefore, is not an individual goal, but is affirmed as a communitarian and universal ethic. It is in this context of global moral responsibility that tensions between violence and nonviolence, peace and war, play an intense and crucial role. This is another way of saying that Islam is no more a "religion of the sword" than is Christianity or Judaism.

As mentioned previously, *Islam* is related to *salam*, whose root meaning is peace. The essential message of the Qur'an with regard to nonviolence and peace is formulated in terms of the presentation of Allah as a principle of All-Peace and a Creator of life which calls on humanity in general and Muslims in particular to practice peace and not destroy life. Moreover, next to patience, self-restraint and peace, the Qur'an stresses concepts such as inclusion and respect of the other. Abstaining from violence and practising peace are activities that reflect patience, peace, and an inner effort toward self-restraint in the believer. The Qur'an warns against corruption (*fasad*) from this state of peace and patience. It repeatedly invites Muslims to strive in the path of God on behalf of the weak (*al-mustad a fun*) and against the oppressors (*zalimun*). Hence, the authentic struggle or the "greater jihad" (*al-jihad al-akbar*) is a constant internal striving against one's baser self. The word "peace" is repeated sixty-seven times in the Qur'an, while the concept of "war" is only cited thirty-six times. In Sura 59:22–24 the Qur'an presents God as the Giver of Peace:

> Allah is He, than Whom there is no other god—Who knows (all things) both secret and open; He, Most Gracious, Most Merciful. Allah is He, than Whom there is no other god—the Sovereign, the Holy One, the Source of Peace, the Guardian of Faith, the Preserver of Safety, the Exalted in Might, the Irresistible, the justly Proud, Glory to Allah! (High is He) above the partners they attribute to Him. He is Allah, the Creator, the Originator, the Fashioner to Him belong the Most Beautiful Names: whatever is in the heavens and on earth, does declare His Praises and Glory: and He is the Exalted in Might, the Wise.

The word "peace" is mentioned a number of different times in other verses of the Qur'an. We can refer to the following examples: "And God calls [the human beings] into the abode of peace, and guides one who wills onto a straight way. Those who persevere in doing good, they will get the ultimate good" (10:25–26), or "O you who have attained to faith! Enter all wholly into peace, and follow not Satan's footsteps, for, verily, he is your open foe" (2:208). According to the Qur'an, the true faith in Allah as All-Peace is to attain peacefulness from within and from without; therefore, a faithful Muslim has to respect the sanctity of life and incline to peaceful manners as much as possible. Two verses of the Qur'an reflect this view: "If they incline to peace, you should incline to it and trust in God" (8:61) and "Do not kill the soul that God has made sacred, except by right" (6:151).

The Qur'an addresses the question of violence as a non-constructive way of establishing communication among human beings. Committing violence against any other human being is a violation of the state of balance and peace ordered and created by God. The Qur'an teaches the following:

> In consequence, We did ordain unto the children of Israel [and all believers who follow] that if anyone kills a human being—unless it be [in punishment] for murder or for spreading damage on earth—it shall be as though he had killed all humankind: whereas, if anyone saves a human life, it shall be as though he had saved the lives of all humankind.
>
> *5:32*

In addition, the Qur'an provides a solid foundation for abstaining from violence. This simply means that non-coercion has primacy over violence and war, which both require strong moral justifications to be practised and must end at the first opportunity. This view is underlined in numerous Qur'anic verses through the entire Holy Book:

> And among the humankind there is the one whose views on this world life would please you, and would cite God as witness to what is in his [/her] heart, and he [/she] is the most contentious of adversaries in dispute. As this one gets away, he [/she] goes about the earth spreading damage and destroying tilth and progeny; and God does not love causing damage. And whenever he [/she] is told, "Be conscious of God," he [/she] adds arrogance to guilt; and for him [/her] hell will be well-deserved, and how vile a resting place!
>
> *2:204–206*

or

> Even if you draw forth your hand towards me to kill me, I shall never draw forth my hand towards you to kill you; I fear God, the Lord of the whole universe. Let you bear my wrong-doings as well as yours, and then you would be destined for fire and that is the requital of evildoers.
>
> *5:28–29*

Violence and Nonviolence in Islamic History

War and violence are considered by Islam's ethical framework only as forms of self-defense against aggression and not as preferred means. From the historical point of view, the Prophet Muhammad is considered a reluctant practitioner of violence and he is very often portrayed as someone who seeks to end wars, even against the urging of his Companions (see Hashmi 1996: 141–174; Kelsay 1993: 46–47; Aslan 2006: 84–87). However, after the Prophet's death in 632 AD, his successors did not follow his path as peacemakers, but mostly as conquerors and builders of an Islamic empire. This violent adventure started with a civil war, often called by the name of *Fitna*, which marked the downfall of a unified Islamic community and ended with the two tragic murders of the Prophet's cousin, the Fourth Rightly Caliph, Ali ibn Abi Talib (599–661 AD), and his grandson, Husayn ibn Ali (626–680 AD), which has been ever since the main cause of schism between Sunni and Shia Muslims. With the rise to power of the Umayyad dynasty, conquests in Asia, as well as in North Africa, and Transoxiana, northern India and southern

Spain continued. Their successors, the Abbasids, followed the same politics of violence and war. Admittedly, as in the case of many other Abrahamic religions, from the Prophet Muhammad's death to the Mongol invasion of Baghdad in 1258 and beyond, caliphs and dynasties presided over the Muslim world in Asia, Africa and Europe with a spirit of violence aimed at promoting the expansion of Islam.

With the spread of Islam and the rise of Islamic sovereignties around the world, a disagreement developed among Islamic jurists on the necessity of war and violence in light of different interpretations of the Qur'an. Here is one account of some of this history, presented by a contemporary Egyptian interpreter of Islam, Mohamad Fathi Osman:

> The distinguished jurist Sufyan al-Thawri (d. 161H./778) in Iraq, was among others who persistently emphasized that *"jihad"* is only a religious duty in case of defense. However, others like al-Awza'i (d. 157H./774) in Syria, Abu Hanifa (d. 150H./767) in Iraq, and a pillar of the Hanafi school Muhammad ibn al-Hasan al-Shaybani (d. 189H./804) represented the expansionist trend, and held that war is legitimate to spread the message of Islam in a land that its authorities do not accept voluntarily the faith or the payment of a tribute *"jizya."* The obligation for such a war is collective and considered according to the ability to fulfill its *"fard kifaya."* The whole Muslim community, *"umma,"* is held responsible for this obligation and whenever any part of it is able to fulfill it, this would be a fulfillment for the entire community, differently from the case of responding to an attack on the Muslims, when every Muslim individual in this case is held responsible for defending the attacked people and land *(fard 'ayn)*. Since the Byzantines turned to attack the Muslim lands instead of receiving the Muslim attacks, the trend for aggressive war increased and prevailed, especially when it was supported by the distinguished jurist al-Shafi'i (d. 204H./820). The distinguished jurist Malik ibn Anas (d. 179H./795) in Medina seemed through his answers to questions about jihad under the Umayyads not wholeheartedly supportive, but merely not objecting in consideration of the late detrimental development against the Muslims at the Byzantine borders.
>
> *Osman quoted in Heft 2004: 64–65*

Thus we see that the Muslim understanding of peace and nonviolence developed and changed within the process of Islamic history. With the defeat of the armies of two great empires, those of Christian Byzantium and Sassanian Persia, the prophecy of Muhammad and the Islamic values which burst out of the Arabian Peninsula turned into a new and strong civilization with new political, juridical and cultural imperatives and values. For several long centuries, the relative value of peace, war and nonviolence was discussed in notable Islamic urban and cultural centres like Damascus, Córdoba, Cairo, Baghdad, Istanbul, Isfahan and Delhi. However, the greatest spiritual insights on peace and the most valuable experiences in tolerance and nonviolence were achieved in the Spanish region of Andalusia and during the reign of Akbar in India. What is considered the "Andalusian Convivencia" is also known to historians of Islam as the Iberian Umayyad golden age, which lasted from 929 to 1031 AD. This period was characterized by the coexistence among different faiths and the development of a culture of tolerance and peace which found its apogee in the peaceful and philosophical dialogue of two great philosophers of the medieval period: Ibn Rushd, the Muslim, and Moses Maimonides, the Jew. These two great Cordobán philosophers symbolized the universal coexistence of cultural and religious traditions of al-Andalus, a tradition which was almost unique in its time. As such, until the beginning of the twelfth century, Córdoba, capital of al-Andalus, was one of the most cultured and tolerant cities in Europe. Herein lies the importance of what can be called the "Córdoba Paradigm" as a universally accepted social pattern and intercultural experience and as a public sphere where European Jews, Christians and Muslims did manage to live, work and learn together and promote an enduring culture of tolerance. Dominant historiographic trends in Islamic studies centre their analyses either on the distant past (early Islam) or on contemporary Islam and forget the Andalusian legacy by perceiving it as something exclusively Spanish, isolated from the rest of the Muslim world. Despite this historical forgetfulness the Andalusian experience still serves as a strong legacy and a social and political attitude in peacemaking which tried to bring the Western and the Muslim worlds closer to each other.

The reign of Akbar the Great in the Indian Peninsula during the sixteenth and early seventeenth centuries was also represented by an attempt to practice peace and tolerance among different religions and by uniting them through their shared belief in the almighty. With Akbar the Great, once again, the Islamic experience of peace and nonviolence became reality. According to Amitabh Pal:

> The tolerant and pluralistic spirit of the Sufis most profoundly had an impact on the great Mughal emperor Akbar, two of whose closest friends were the children of a Sufi saint . . . Akbar adopted the Sufi notion of peace and tolerance toward all his reigning creed and went beyond by conceptualizing Din-I-Ilahi, a syncretic moral code that sought to incorporate the best from the region's religions.
>
> *Pal 2011: 69*

Akbar was convinced of the need for two things: first, to liberate Islam from the domination of the Muslim clerics, and second, to find a way to break away from the notion of superiority of Islam over other religions. As Craig Considine argues:

> Akbar the Great's departure from orthodoxy [appeared] in a letter from 1582 to King Philip II of Spain. Rather than learning only from Muslim scholars in his court, Akbar stated that he mingled with "learned men of all religions, thus depriving profit from their exquisite discourses and exalted aspirations." Akbar added that too many people do not investigate their religious arguments and instead blindly "follow the religion in which [they] were born and educated, thus excluding [themselves] from the possibility of ascertaining the truth, which is the noblest aim of the human intellect." In challenging people to open their minds to knowledge outside of their own religious traditions, Akbar insinuated that no single religion has a monopoly on the truth.
>
> *Considine 2013: n.p.*

Though Akbar's pluralist vision for Indian society was short-lived and his great-grandson Aurangzeb would end the religious tolerance and peaceful manners of his ancestor, the peaceful and nonviolent legacy of Akbar, as that of the experience of Andalusian Islam, found their ways in the thoughts and actions of Islamic practitioners of nonviolence in twentieth century.

Modern Figures of Nonviolence in Islam

Among the significant historical and philosophical developments that accompanied the transformation of Islam in the nineteenth and twentieth centuries was the rise of pan-Islamic consciousness in the Islamic world. This was accompanied by a worldwide movement which, from the eighteenth century until today, has generally been expressed in two contradictory ways: a return to the principles of peace and tolerance, on the one hand, and the use of violence against Western civilization and "infidels," on the other. Robinson explains:

> Islamists saw the real danger as Western civilisation itself. Their real enemies were the secular or modernist élites in Muslim societies who collaborated with Western political, economic and cultural forces, and enabled Western influence to flourish in their societies. Their prime aim was to take power themselves so that their societies could be sealed off from these corrupting influences. They would then be able to introduce their Islamic system in which the Quran and the *shari'a* were sufficient for all human purposes. This was a system to match capitalism or socialism; it envisaged the Islamisation of economics, knowledge and so on—it was an ideology.
>
> *Robinson 2005: 85*

This Islamic movement of revival, which reaches into the present time, was presented by ideologues and religious leaders such as Hassan-al Banna, Seyyed Qutb, Maulana Mawdudi and Ruhollah Khomeini, and more recently by Usama Bin Laden, the leader of Al-Qaeda, and by the leader of the so-called Islamic State (in Syria and Iraq), Abu Bakr al-Baghdadi. These expressions of Islamic violence, however, stem less from the Islamic tradition of tolerance and peace and a "soft-reading" of the Qur'an, than from the impact of Western colonialism and imperial adventure on Muslim societies. Moreover, the Islamic experience of intolerance has become, via the Western ideological and intolerant reading of Islam, political and ontological barriers for the understanding of Islamic trends of nonviolence in the past hundred years.

Despite that more violent interpretation of Islam, a rival nonviolent Islamic interpretation developed, for example, in India. Amitabh Pal explains:

> A little-known fact in the West is the number of prominent Muslims who joined with Gandhi in the Indian freedom struggle against the British, adopting his values of nonviolence and religious harmony.... Gandhi himself followed a strand of Hinduism that with its emphasis on service and on poetry and songs bore similarities to Sufi Islam.
>
> *Pal 2011: 125*

Among these, we can consider the two Indian Muslim figures of Maulana Abul Kalam Azad and Khan Abdul Ghaffar Khan.

Maulana Azad will not only be remembered in the history of India in particular and Islam in general for the role he played in the Indian national liberation movement, but he will also be considered a Muslim leader who stood for dialogue among Muslims and Hindus. The evolution of Azad's outlook from Islamic revivalism to nonviolence was undoubtedly determined by his friendship and collaboration with Mahatma Gandhi and by the rise of the communal problems in the Indian liberation movement. Through Gandhi, Azad learned that communal harmony played an important role in the future of India. He believed that despite religious, ethnic and linguistic differences, India was one nation. Azad believed that the "two-nation theory" offered "no solution of the problem of one another's minorities, but [could] only lead to retribution and reprisals by introducing a system of mutual hostage" (Azad 2010: 34). Like Gandhi, Azad considered Hindu-Muslim unity a necessary principle for the national reconstruction of India. In his famous address to the Agra session of the Khilafat Conference on August 25, 1921, he referred to Hindu-Muslim unity as a moral imperative for the future of India. He proclaimed:

> If the Muslims of India would like to perform their best religious and Islamic duties ... then they must recognize that it is obligatory for the Muslims to be together with their Hindu brethren ... and it is my belief that the Muslims in India cannot perform their best duties, until in conformity within the injunctions of Islam, in all honesty, they establish unity and cooperation with the Hindus. This belief is based on the imperative spirit of Islam.
>
> *quoted in Grover 1992: 208–209*

Azad foresaw the idea of Islam in relation with the two concepts of peace and nonviolence and with the necessity of interfaith dialogue and coexistence among different religions. The concepts of nonviolence and peace were logically connected in Azad's mind to his conception of religious pluralism. Azad's main distinction between the spirit of religion (*Din*) and its outward expressions (*Shari'a*) provided him a theoretical justification for his idea of oneness of God, the concept of unity of humanity and universal peace in the world. The foundation of Azad's religious pluralism was that the divine has many aspects, but the human and the divine are united in an expression of love. In his commentary on *Surat-ul-Fatiha*, also called *Um-ul-Quran* (core of the Qur'an), Azad outlined the essence of his ideas on what he considered to be "the God of Universal Compassion." "[It] is clear," writes Azad:

> that the mind which the *Surat-ul-Fatiha* depicts is a type of mind which reflects the beauty and the mercy of the God of Universal Compassion. It is in no sense fettered by prejudices of race or nation or other exclusive groupings. It is a mind imbued with Universal Humanism. This is the true spirit of the Quranic invitation.
>
> *Grover 1992*

The entire argument of Azad was to present Muslims with the fact that the fundamental teaching of the Qur'an is mercy and forgiveness (*Rahmat*). Therefore, it followed for him that these attributes of God should also be uncalculated in humans. It is interesting to see up to what point Azad's "*tafsir*" (interpretation) of the Qur'an keeps its closeness to the text, while at the same time it is inspired by the Sufi perception of God through "*Kashf*" (personal revelation). Azad's faith in the essential unity of humanity and in the oneness of all religions stemmed essentially from the Sufi concept of "the unity of existence" (*wahdat-al-wujud*). Truth, for Azad, was one and the same everywhere. The mistake was to equate particular forms of Truth with Truth itself. Actually, Azad's conception of "Truth" is very close to that of Mahatma Gandhi, where Truth and nonviolence are the two sides of the same medal. Seen from this angle, Azad's most important book, *Tarjuman-ul-Qur'an*, illustrates Azad's firm beliefs in tolerance and dialogue. It is in this book that Azad's idea of religious pluralism is expressed powerfully by the concept of oneness of faiths (*Wahdat-I-Din*). For Azad, God as the "cherisher" and "nourisher" (*Rabb*) transcends all fragmentations and divisions of humanity in race, color and religion. As a result, the path of universal God (*Rabb-ul-Alameen*) is "the right path" (*Sirat-al-Mustaqeem*), which belongs to no particular religion. Therefore, for Azad, there is no room for violence and intolerance in Islam.

Khan Abddul Ghaffar Khan, another Muslim collaborator of Mahatma Gandhi, has the same view of Islam and its nonviolent message for humanity. Peace and nonviolence were at the centre of Ghaffar Khan's theory and practice of Islam. At first, Ghaffar Khan's aim was to uplift his people by building schools in villages and bringing the Pashtuns together. Later when he began working with Gandhi, he took up the effort for India's independence from Britain as well as supporting a united India that was not partitioned by separating Muslims off into Pakistan. This idea was closely linked with his desire for an independent Pashtun homeland—a desire that still remains in many Pashtuns' hearts until this day, especially those living in areas officially under Pakistan's rule. Ghaffar Khan described himself in the following terms:

> As a young boy, I had had violent tendencies; the hot blood of the Pathans was in my veins. But in jail I had nothing to do except read the *Qur'an*. I read about the Prophet Muhammad in Mecca, about his patience, his suffering, his dedication. I had read it all before, as a child, but now I read it in the light of what I was hearing all around me about Gandhiji's struggle against the British Raj.
>
> *Easwaran 1984: 170*

As Gandhi's Muslim counterpart, Ghaffar Khan not only brought support of his own people for the end of domination by the British, but he also contributed with bringing an appeal to the Indian independence movement from the Indians who were Muslim. For Ghaffar Khan it was clear from the very beginning that devotion to one's own religion did not mean denouncing other faiths, but it was a source of strength and inspiration to recognize the own and to expand the view of the self, and to include the broader humanity in all its diversity. As in the case of Maulana Azad, harmony among Hindus and Muslims was a key aspect of Ghaffar Khan's vision, for the simple reason that he interpreted Islam as a religion of peace, nonviolence, love and service. That is why he founded in the 1920s a nonviolent army by the name of Khudai Khidmatgar or "Servants of God," which was committed to peaceful resistance to colonial rule. Khan Abdul Ghaffar Khan's army, which was composed of men and women, required its members to take an oath to refrain from violence. It was a difficult oath for those facing active provocation and violence; however, the Khudai Khidmatgar kept their word because of their courage and sense of honor. The British regarded the Servants of God as a threat and therefore undertook active measures of suppressing their activism: killings and torture were common practice, and the Pashtuns paid with their lives but did not take up violent means to defend themselves (Johansen 1997: 53–71). Like Gandhi, Ghaffar Khan combined principled nonviolence with strategic nonviolence. This allowed him and his supporters to declare themselves nonviolent in thought and practice. There was a moral superiority in putting down arms even though they had them and knew how to use them—for the greater good, namely, peace and self-determination in the region. Khan Abdul Ghaffar Khan applied religious means to achieve his goals and the entire discourse was framed not as "a contest between secular activism and religious faithfulness . . . but as a debate . . . between two forms of religious faithfulness" (Johansen 1997: 66). Khan Abdul Ghaffar Khan was a prime example of a peaceful and nonviolent Muslim who created a nonviolent army, which was a first in human history. As he himself repeated, his thoughts and actions were rooted in the verses of the Qur'an and they had a great impact on Mahatma Gandhi.

Conclusion

Many consider Khan Abdul Ghaffar Khan and Maulana Azad to be figures of exception in the modern history of Islam. As such, many around the world continue to believe that Islam and nonviolence cannot coexist. Also, for many Muslims around the world, nonviolence symbolizes the withdrawal from political struggle against the West, which could lead to the collapse of Islam. To such people, nonviolent Islam represents an embarrassment which needs to be suppressed. The truth is that in Islam, like in all other great religions, extremism and fanaticism cannot prepare the way of peace and harmony. We need to understand, however, that if there has been a misunderstanding and stereotyping of Islam and Muslims in the past century, it is mainly due to the permanence of war and violence in the Middle East in particular and in the Islamic world in general. But we should not forget that the major victims of these violent conflicts and killings have been the Muslims themselves. One of the major reasons for these atrocities is the absence of information on nonviolent Islam and on Muslims who have been and continue to be practitioners of nonviolence in the world. Nonviolent Islam could give fresh life to democratic aspirations of Muslims around the world. It may also help steer Muslim public spaces away from violent forms of political Islam, opening the way to peaceful democracies in the Middle East and North Africa.

Works Cited

Aslan, R. (2006). *No God but God: The Origins, Evolution and Future of Islam*. New York: Random House.
Azad, M. A. K. (2010). *Words of Freedom*. Delhi: Penguin Books India.
Considine, C. (2013). "Finding Tolerance in Akbar, the Philosopher-King." *The Huffington Post* October 4.
Easwaran, E. (1984). *A Man to Match His Mountains: Badshah Khan, Non-violent Soldier of Islam*. Petaluma, CA: Nilgiri Press.
Funk, N. C., and A. A. Said (2009). *Islam and Peacemaking in the Middle East*. Boulder: Lynne Rienner Publishers.
Grover, V. (1992). *Political Thinkers of India*, vol. 17. New Delhi: Deep and Deep.
Hashmi, S. H. (1996). "Interpreting the Islamic Ethics of War and Peace," in T. Nardin (ed.), *The Ethics of War and Peace*. Princeton: Princeton University Press.
Izutsu, T. (1964). *God and Man in the Koran: Semantics of the Koranic Weltanschauung*. Tokyo: Keio Institute of Cultural and Linguistic Studies.
Johansen, R. C. (1997). "Radical Islam and Nonviolence: A Case Study of Religious Empowerment and Constraint among Pashtuns," *Journal of Peace Research* 34 (1), February 53–71.
Kelsay, J. (1993). *Islam and War: A Study in Comparative Ethics*. Louisville, KY: Westminster John Knox Press.
Osman, M. F. (2004). "God Is the All-Peace, the All- Merciful," in J.L. Heft (ed.), *Beyond Violence: Religious Sources of Social Transformation in Judaism, Christianity and Islam*. New York: Fordham University Press.
Pal, A. (2011). *Islam Means Peace: Understanding the Muslim Principle of Nonviolence Today*. Santa Barbara: Praeger.
Robinson, F. (2005). "Islam and the West: Clash of Civilisations?" in R. Boase (ed.), *Islam and Global Dialogue: Religious Pluralism and the Pursuit of Peace*. Burlington, VT: Ashgate.

Further Reading

Hashmi, S. (ed.) (2002). *Islamic Political Ethics: Civil Society, Pluralism, and Conflict*. Princeton: Princeton University Press. (A collection of essays focused on topics in ethics and political philosophy in Islamic context, including civil society, boundaries, pluralism, and war and peace.)
Kelsay, J., and J. T. Johnson (eds.) (1991). *Just War and Jihad: Historical and Theoretical Perspectives on War and Peace in Western and Islamic Tradition*. Westport, CT: Greenwood Press. (A collection of essays by scholars versed in just war ethics focused on connections between Islamic and Western sources.)
Paige, G. D., S. A. Chaiwat, and S. Gilliatt (eds.) (2001). *Islam and Nonviolence*. Honolulu: Center for Global Nonviolence. Available at: http://nonkilling.org/pdf/b3.pdf. (A collection of essays from a global seminar on Islam and nonviolence.)

6
PHILOSOPHY OF NONVIOLENCE IN AFRICA

Gail M. Presbey

This chapter surveys contributions to the philosophy of nonviolence and nonviolent strategies for social change in Africa. The focus includes conflict resolution, cessation of personal violence and war, notions of positive peace, and prevention of escalation of conflict. The African continent is large and its history is long, so this chapter cannot claim to be comprehensive, but it can serve as an introductory overview. This chapter uses the continental definition of Africa. It begins with ancient Egypt and North Africa, where the oldest written texts can be found, and includes sub-Saharan Africa (see Mazrui 1986 for the definition of Africa). Africa as a continent has influenced and has been influenced by regional and international developments. This chapter covers Africa in this larger and interactive context.

Histories of philosophy written up until the time of Kant usually incorporated ancient Egypt, Africa, and Asia in general into their historical narratives. Around the time of Kant and Hegel that changed, and Africa and Asia were then written out of that history (in part because the definition of philosophy became narrower, and in part due to the racism spread by practices of the transatlantic slave trade).[1] Scholars in Europe and Africa in the twentieth century have finally reinstated African thought as part of the history of philosophy.

Emphasis on studying and championing Africa could be found in the nineteenth century in the writings and actions of early proponents of "Pan-Negroism" like Edward Wilmot Blyden (originally from St. Thomas in the Caribbean but having lived in Liberia since 1851). Blyden's thought developed over time. Eventually he emphasized the promotion of the African personality, which he contrasted to the European personality. The African was naturally conciliatory, a gentle and good-natured peacemaker, who serves humankind and endures suffering (carrying the cross of Jesus). This was in contrast to the European personality that was harsh, individualistic and self-assertive, competitive, combative, and intolerant. The Europeans were non-religious and materialistic and thought that they served humanity by ruling humanity. Blyden converted from Christianity to Islam because he decided that Islam was better suited to African culture and he regretted how Euro-American missionary Christianity was forced upon Africans. Blyden developed into a cultural nationalist who thought Africa had everything it needed. His book, *African Life and Customs* (1908/1994), said the African way of life was wise and balanced.[2]

In the twentieth century North Atlantic academics pushed to incorporate African topics. As African countries gained independence in the 1950s and '60s, African scholars rushed to explore African philosophical ideas, values, history, and culture so as to fill a void in Eurocentric academic studies inherited from the colonizers. Many African traditions survived to contemporary times, albeit sometimes in modified form. Some of these studies are relevant to peace studies and the philosophy of nonviolence.

In the African context, the concept of nonviolence has been expressed as (or intertwined with) mutual respect and care. It shows itself in practices of hospitality to strangers, de-escalating conflict, and/or bringing together opponents. In African contexts one can see an emphasis on nonviolence in:

- the Egyptian idea of *ma'at*
- practices of noncooperation
- early North African Christian philosophers' writings and personal witness
- West African cultural and ethical values as expressed in the Ifa
- Gandhian nonviolent theory and activism (which began in South Africa)
- the concept of *ubuntu* in the work of Mandela, Tutu, and others
- and especially in the work of women and activists who challenge colonialism, slavery, and patriarchy.

Ancient Egypt

Some of the earliest written texts come from ancient Egypt. It is fitting that we look for the beginnings of philosophical thought in general, and a philosophy of nonviolence, in ancient Egypt.[3] An important term in Egyptian philosophy is *ma'at*. The etymology of *ma'at* shows it was first related to physical straightness, levelness, evenness, or correctness, but later developed as a more abstract principle of truth as well as a life-generating principle and force, and was considered to be the opposite of "unrealness, disorder, incorrectness, violence, injustice, in a word, evil" (Karenga and Assmann 2004: 7). Some of the most interesting ancient Egyptian texts are those in which their authors criticize Egyptians for not living up to the moral ideals of *ma'at*. For example, the anonymous author of *Dialogue of a Man and his Soul* (2200–2050 BCE) chronicles a "non-Ma'atian situation in the land" by noting: "Compassion has perished, Violence assaults everyone" (in Karenga: 74). Tomb inscriptions are places where persons often list their virtues and vices, thus giving voice to the moral code they intended to live up to. The Autobiography of Hotepheryakhet (a fifth-dynasty priest of Abusir) explains that he had "not done violence to anyone" (Karenga: 165). Karenga finds many admonitions against violent actions in ancient Egyptian texts, including comments such as "He who is silent toward violence undermines the offerings" (Karenga: 300) and "One should not rely on violence but live in peace" (Karenga: 365).

Jan Assmann translates *ma'at* as "connective justice" (Assmann 2003: 126). This phrase "connective justice" is Assmann's way of explaining the Early and Middle Kingdom Egyptian concept that there is a reciprocal relation between doing and faring well. Reward for good action was not dispensed by gods; although Ma'at was described as a winged goddess, she did not reward and punish human actions. Instead, human social action ensured the connection between doing and faring well (Assmann 2003: 238–240). Assmann sums up the connection between *ma'at* and justice, saying, "Ma'at is the law liberating the weak from oppression at the hands of the strong" (Assmann 2003: 153). As Maybee argues in her article analyzing the ancient Egyptian text *Instruction of Any*, the scribe Any proposes an ethics based on the importance of relationships of care, not unlike contemporary feminist approaches to ethics. Through respect toward others and concern for their needs, conflict is avoided or de-escalated (Maybee 1999: 166–167).

The Tale of the Eloquent Peasant (ca. 1985–1773 BCE) centers on a peasant who argues against systemic injustice. He attempts to get justice through the courts for the offense he suffered (a low-level administrator entraps him and takes his goods as a fine, basically a form of "legal robbery," deception, and duplicity). This is an early version of the nonviolent technique of sitting indefinitely at the door of one who wronged you. This is similar to the Gandhian technique of *dharna* (see Bondurant 1965: 118): the peasant refuses to take "no" (or silent indifference) as an answer and gives nine speeches until he receives recognition of the injustice. Chike Jeffers says that the peasant, Konanup, uses an "argument from dysfunction" that, through pinpointing the injustices he is suffering, sheds light on what good governance should be like (Jeffers 2013: 422, 432–434). Karenga notes that this "tale" was taught in schools in Egypt, and he considers it evidence that there was "an active tradition of critique and redress of grievance" in Egypt, as well as an ethic of care and responsibility and a conviction that justice should have no class bias (Karenga: 71).

Early acts of civil disobedience were engaged in by Egyptians in Egypt, even if they were written about in the Hebrew language by Israelites. Daube finds "the earliest example in world literature of conscientious disobedience" in the book of Exodus (1: 15–21) when the midwives refused to kill the male newborn Jewish babies, under the decree of the Egyptian Pharaoh (Daube 2008: 208, 2005: 122). He notes that the midwives did not admit their disobedience, which is considered by some to be a central part of the definition of civil disobedience, but Daube does not agree with drawing the definition of "civil disobedience" so narrowly (Daube 2005: 121). Dykstra argues that contrary to popular belief, the midwives (Shiprah and Puah) were Egyptian women who were allies of Israel, not Hebrew women. The Egyptian midwives did not cooperate with Pharaoh's decree and instead let the Hebrew children live. Their act is one of refusal to carry out genocide. The story follows a common theme in the Bible of "women who lie for their people" (Dykstra 2002: 168). Dykstra says that the women took advantage of a stereotype that the Pharaoh held about Hebrews, by telling him that the Hebrew women gave birth quickly, before they could arrive on the scene to carry out the Pharaoh's orders. Dykstra notes that some later church fathers like Augustine and Gregory thought that lying was never justified and so did not appreciate the midwives' heroism. But Dykstra notes that these men have not taken into consideration the power dynamics. The women lied because they lacked power. They are heroes nonetheless, she argues, because they feared God and felt compelled to act according to basic moral principles, which meant that they engaged in "radical action for life" (Dykstra 2002: 172).

Dykstra notes that as a direct result of the Egyptian midwives' action, Moses' mother puts Moses in a basket in the river, and then due to the influence of Moses' sister, Pharaoh's daughter contradicts her father the Pharaoh's decree when she rescues Moses from the river and raises him as her own son (Dykstra 2002: 173, 178). Dykstra also argues that many Egyptian women helped Hebrew women prepare to leave in the Exodus by providing them with supplies and needed resources (Dykstra 2002: 185–187). Of course, she realizes the difficulties in treating the stories in these ancient texts as history in a contemporary sense, but she does see them as clear role models.

Ancient, Medieval, and Early Modern North Africa

Ancient North Africa was closely mixed with the greater Mediterranean world (and what we now call the Middle East) as Christian, Jewish, and later Muslim philosophers influenced each other. Augustine is an important example. He was born in Thasgate (now called Souk Ahras, Algeria), and became bishop of Hippo, forty miles from his home town. Masolo argues that Augustine should be recognized as a North African philosopher. As he says, there is no doubt about Augustine's Berber heritage (an ethnic group indigenous to Africa), and he writes *City of God* from the perspective of an outsider to the Roman Empire. Masolo even suggests there is an "African nationalist attitude in the *Confessions*" (Masolo 2004: 59). Augustine is often considered the founder of the just war theory.[4] Egan argues that a fuller study of Augustine would more accurately represent Augustine as critical of war rather than as an apologist for it. For example, when Pope John Paul II wrote an Apostolic letter on Augustine he quoted Augustine as saying, "There is more glory in killing the wars themselves with a word than in killing men with the sword; and there is more glory in achieving or maintaining peace by means of peace than by means of war" (see Egan 1999: 53).

Grey has analyzed the concepts of violence and nonviolence in ancient North Africa by scrutinizing Augustine's evaluation of the actions of his contemporaries. In one case, an angry mob lynches a corrupt tax official. Augustine argues that the lynching was violent because only the state can punish. This position insists on a monopoly of state violence, rather than a nonviolent stance (according to our contemporary definitions), and it insists that people should not give vent to their frustrations and outrage in this way. Grey's point is that in ancient North Africa, "violence" was considered irrational and illegitimate, while "force" could be rational and justified. But just what counted as violence was up for debate, because, "for ancient authors, identifying and labeling acts as violent was neither value-neutral nor completely objective. Nor is the boundary between violent and nonviolent, between violence and force, fixed. Rather, that boundary could shift according to circumstances and perspective" (Grey 2013: 230). The definitions of violent and nonviolent were fluid, and mostly depended on ideas of "who is entitled to act in what ways toward whom" (Grey 2013: 227).

Another famous North African philosopher is Origen, born in Alexandria, Egypt, in 185 CE. Masolo says, "Several things define Origen as an African. First, eminent historians and commentators of his time refer to him as 'the African'" (Masolo 2004: 53). Masolo considers this evidence that Origen was a Punic or a Berber like Augustine.[5] Masolo reviews several ways in which Origen's Christian philosophy (of the Trinity, and his theory of personhood) show the influence of classical Egyptian philosophy (Masolo 2004: 55–56). Egan focuses on Origen's emphasis on nonviolence. In his work *Against Celsus*, she explains, he considers the Christian call to convert swords into plowshares and spears into pruning hooks, and insists that Jesus' call to turn the other cheek now takes the place of the earlier admonition to take an eye for an eye (Egan 1999: 27). Origen argued against Celsus, insisting that Christians help rulers not by slaying in battle but by being pious. Even pagans exempt their priests who serve at shrines from service in the army. Origen says, "Those who attend on certain gods, as you account them, keep their hands free from blood, that they may ... offer the appointed sacrifices to your gods" (in Egan 1999: 28), and he uses this point to argue that Christians should likewise be seen as exempt from military service. Origen was persecuted, imprisoned, and tortured by Decius. He died after his release from prison. Cadoux notes that Origen's arguments against army service did not depend on the idea of refusing idolatry but were instead based on prohibition against shedding blood, showing that early Christians took Jesus' admonitions against violence literally (in Egan 1999: 28).

In addition to Christian sources, North and West Africa included Muslim philosophy. During the medieval period Africa had several important centers of learning, including Timbuktu (in present-day Mali). One important example of African thought can be found in the manuscript *Munyat al-murīd*, which counsels avoidance of violence.[6] Another focus is Ethiopia. Sumner provides translation and analysis of medieval and early modern Ethiopian texts written in Ge'ez (a precursor to Amharic). Many of these texts are Christian adaptations of earlier Greek or Arabic texts. One of them, *Life and Maxims of Skendes* (written in the early sixteenth century), includes the sayings of the wise Skendes (a mythical character), put in the form of answers to 100 questions. Several of the topics comment on resisting evil and avoiding strife and violence. For example, when the questioners complain to Skendes that "there are people who like strife more than peace!" he answers by saying, "Dogs far prefer the bad smell of dirt to the sweet scents of the royal palace, for their food is the garbage. It is the same for the evil-hearted" (Sumner 1985: 209). To win over a person with evil desires, Skendes counsels tolerance and patience (208). He also counsels his followers to avoid violent acts:

> God does not send epidemics, death, famine, hardships and great distresses into the world as so many blessings, but when you act against your brother, and your brother against you, then God sends these disasters to the world as a punishment. However, the source of these disasters is yourself.
>
> 210

While Skendes attributes desire for violence to the work of the devil, he does not devise a way to resist oppression nonviolently, counseling forbearance in the context of oppression.

Twentieth-Century West Africa

To see more of a focus on the practice of active nonviolence, we turn to the twentieth century and the struggles of Africans to win liberation from European colonization. Many African traditions of governance and socialization incorporated wisdom and practices to promote harmonious living. Many scholars have studied African traditions of peace, nonviolence, and reconciliation.[7] For example, Oguejiofor of Nigeria studied African proverbs and myths (Oguejiofor 2007). While he draws on sources across the continent, he also includes a study of West African sources, and notes that the Igbo considered human life to be sacred. The Nri myth says that God commanded the land (Ala) to grow food, and in exchange for this food humans must work to cultivate the food, and to agree to refrain from murder. Even if it is not deliberate, the spilling of blood is an offense that demands compensation.

African traditions nurtured and repaired social relationships: these traditions continue to be important contemporary tools for creating peace (see Coe, Palmer, and el Shabazz 2013). Oluwole notes that communal wisdom passed down through the centuries has been debated over the years, and if it is accepted now, that is not a sign that Africans placidly accept authority. Oral expression can improve over time and respond to public criticism (Oluwole 1997: 6–9). She is concerned that when people call some aspect of African culture "traditional" they may be thinking it is "archaic" in contrast to the "modern" (Oluwole 1997: 41). She is also concerned that some African philosophers have asserted that traditional Africa was not adversarial and that oral expression, because it had accommodation as its goal, was not "strict" philosophy. She debunks these ideas, showing that the Ifa writings of the Yoruba contain arguments in which two opposing hypotheses are put forward and one is justified as the better argument. Oluwole thinks that accommodationism—being forebearing, coping, and open to other points of view—can be appreciated while developing and transmitting strict philosophy. Intellectual modesty and not forcing views down the throats of others is a sign of a true intellectual. In contrast, Western approaches to philosophy, with its preoccupation with absolute certainty coupled with force, results in hard-heartedness (Oluwole 1997: 43–48, 105). Insofar as not all African philosophical texts come to the exact same conclusions, that is from Oluwole's point of view a sign of intellectual freedom in Africa. Yoruba texts do not quest for absolute certainty because they think that humans are not wise enough to know everything (Oluwole 1997: 93, 102). Oluwole's description of Yoruban epistemologies presents a kind of nonviolent epistemology.[8]

Kwame Gyekye of Ghana has described the Akan system of governance as one that prioritizes consensus and the resolution of conflict. There are proverbs that advocate collaboration and discourage the abuse of power by any ruler. A chief must consult lineage heads (who in turn consult the people), and an unpopular leader who does not respond to people's needs can be de-stooled (removed from his position/impeached) (Gyekye 2010a: 242–258). There are elaborate patterns of indirect communication that soften harsh language and have formal intermediaries (called *okeyame* or linguists) between the chief and the people who reword requests and responses to requests, with mutual respect and agreement as the goal of communication. Many of the skills used in contemporary mediation can be found in these traditional practices (Yankah 1995: 51–57). Also, communitarianism is a goal. While individuals are respected, the goal of all people is the flourishing of the community and there is special care for those who are needy or vulnerable. There are practices to reduce conflict, or to shorten conflict if it breaks out (Gyekye 2010b: 198). Proverbs and their respective symbols (such as the crocodile with two heads and one stomach, conveying that despite competition, all concerns and interests are common) reassert the main point that the flourishing of individuals is tied up with the community.

There is a long history of nonviolent struggle in Gold Coast/Ghana, and an articulated philosophy of nonviolence. Nonviolent action in Ghana precedes the arrival of Kwame Nkrumah, who explicitly referred to international Gandhian developments in nonviolent strategies for political change. For example, people of the Gold Coast (as it was then called) would not comply with the 1852 poll tax. A century of nonviolent resistance including tactics of tax resistance, parallel government, and boycott finally resulted in independence from colonial rule (see Presbey 2013).

This idea of a peaceful African personality described earlier in Blyden's work continues in the philosophical work of Nkrumah's book *Consciencism*. As Ramose explains, Nkrumah describes the "African personality" as based upon a cluster of African humanist principles embodied in African traditional societies. These principles are supported by two ethical principles, "promote life and avoid killing" and "life is mutual aid" (Ramose 2017: 201). Ramose considers these two ethical principles the core message of philosophical consciencism as advocated by Nkrumah. In pursuit of this abundant life Nkrumah searched for alternatives to capitalism, which Nkrumah explained was harmful to both egalitarianism and African traditional social practices (Nkrumah 1970: 78). As Gyekye explains, Nkrumah received a master's degree in philosophy from the University of Pennsylvania, and was enrolled as a doctoral student in philosophy in Britain, but did not finish his studies due to his involvement in African politics. Nkrumah coins the word "consciencism" to describe a philosophy that comes to be due to a crisis of the African "conscience"—possibly understood, Gyekye suggests, as African personality, character, or collective conscience (Gyekye 2017: XIII–XIV).

While in the U.S., Nkrumah started a publication called *The African Interpreter*. The first issue called for Gandhi to be released from jail. In 1943 Nkrumah took part in a debate at Bryn Mawr, hosted by the Department of Philosophy, where he argued that Africans should not aid Britain in the war effort (Sherwood 1996: 78, 80), a position close to Gandhi's stance as part of the "Quit India" movement of the same time period. When Nkrumah participated in the Fifth Pan-African conference, held in Manchester, England in 1945, he noted that all assembled there agreed to win Africa's independence "based on the Gandhist technique of non-violent non-cooperation, in other words, the withholding of labor, civil disobedience, and economic boycott" (Nkrumah 1963: 134–135; see Adi and Sherwood 1995).

Nkrumah had published a pamphlet, *What I Mean by Positive Action* (1962), in which he took many of the ideas that he found in C.V.H. Rao's book, *Civil Disobedience Movements in India*, and presented them with some new terminology to the people of Ghana. When the Positive Action campaign took place in 1950–51, it used nonviolent methods including a large general strike. In a series of articles in the *Nation* magazine (later put into one book), C.L.R. James explained how he and other leaders understood the developments in Ghana as experiments in nonviolent action—even if he was not a pacifist, he at least agreed that strategically, the nonviolent methods were the best and most effective option at the time (James 1992: 294, 1959: 8).

As the leader of independent Ghana, Nkrumah took seriously his role of proponent of Pan-Africanism. He thought that a united African continent could better resist colonialism and prosper. He held important conferences where nonviolence was advocated as a philosophy and a strategy. Nkrumah hosted a Pan-African conference in 1960 that drew prominent nonviolent activists like Ralph Abernathy and A.J. Muste (Sutherland and Meyer 2000).[9]

The story of how Nkrumah used nonviolent strategies, which he called "Positive Action," is well known (Nkrumah 1957: 115–121). Also well known is the fact that he later abandoned nonviolence, both practicing violence against his internal enemies, and after his ouster as president, advocating the need for violent revolution (Ramose 2017: 204–205; Presbey 2006). Why did Nkrumah change? There are probably many reasons. Ahlman provides an overview of the influence of Algerians who came to Ghana and influenced Nkrumah to give up his devotion to the idea of nonviolent action. Frantz Fanon, supporter of the liberation movement in Algeria, had defended the use of violence in the Algerian context. He and other Algerians, in a series of conference presentations, as well as in articles published in Nkrumah's own newspaper, the *Evening News*, argued that violence was needed to end European rule in Africa. Fanon received an ambassadorship to Ghana, and so continued his influence not only on Nkrumah but on other new heads of newly independent African states. Ahlman thinks that Nkrumah was not only influenced by Fanon but also by the continually breaking news of colonial atrocities such as Patrice Lumumba's assassination, French nuclear testing in the Sahara, and the Sharpeville massacre in South Africa. Nkrumah renounced nonviolence. In his book, *Handbook for Revolutionary Warfare*, he said that war was logical and inevitable anywhere, including in Africa (see Presbey 2006). Alhman insists that the debates about violence and nonviolence in Ghana in the late '50s and early '60s were not just debates about tactics: "Rather, these debates should be read as part of a broader moral and methodological dialogue over what an independent Africa should look like and how best to construct it" (Ahlman 2010: 82).

Fanon, the Martinican of African descent who became a philosopher and psychiatrist as well as a practicing revolutionary, is well known for his justification of revolutionary violence. He was personally involved in the fight in Algeria. However, there have always been many commentators who have noted that Fanon, as a humanist who wanted individuals and societies to thrive in a healthy environment, always advocated only short periods of violence that would hopefully lead to a more humane government. In the appendix to *Wretched of the Earth*, he explained how acts of violence harmed perpetrators and victims alike (Fanon 1963: 249–310). In his conclusion he cautioned readers not to mimic Europe:

> Leave this Europe where they are never done talking of Man, yet murder men everywhere they find them, on the corner of every one of their own streets, in all the corners of the globe.... Europe undertook the leadership of the world with ardor, cynicism and violence.... So, my brothers, how is it that we do not understand that we have better things to do than to follow that same Europe?
>
> *Fanon 1963: 311–312*

Fanon calls for a new humanism instead of European hypocrisy and lip service to a humanism Europeans deny with their violent actions.[10]

Additionally, the success of the Cuban revolution, based on a quick violent overthrow, and Cuba's willingness to intervene in several African countries with covert armed groups (as in Congo) and military assistance (as in Angola), contributed to the turn away from nonviolence. Philosophers have recently shown new interest in the philosophical ideas of Amilcar Cabral, a theorist and armed revolutionary who fought the Portuguese in Cape Verde and Guinea-Bissau (Rabaka 2014).

A more recent emphasis on nonviolent action in West Africa comes from a Nobel Peace Prize winner from Liberia, Leymah Gbowee. In the documentary *Pray the Devil Back to Hell*, Gbowee and the other women in her movement "Women of Liberia Mass Action for Peace" explain how they used nonviolent methods such as public vigils and sit-ins to encourage seemingly intransigent men on two sides of a political and military dispute to come together at the bargaining table and agree to end their fighting. They helped to end a fourteen-year-old civil war, and brought Christians and Muslims together in unity to end the fighting (film by Reticker 2008). Frykholm includes Gbowee in her study of nonviolent protest, drawing parallels between Gbowee and M.L. King, focusing on both as prophets guided by their dreams and religious experience (Frykholm 2016). In her book on the Liberian war, Abramowitz considers Gbowee a healer. She notes that Gbowee, as well as Etmuniah Tarpeh (recently minister of education in Liberia) had been NGO employees (psychosocial workers) teaching people trauma-surviving skills before they took on larger leadership roles. Abramowitz thinks this larger network of psychosocial work should be recognized for its contribution to Liberia's peaceful emergence from years of war (Abramowitz 2014: 220–223). Press' study of Liberia shows how fragmented and hidden attempts to oppose Charles Taylor's tyranny changed as alliances were built and people became more public, finally able to engage in mass demonstrations. He also highlights the role of the Catholic Church in Monrovia and the leadership role of Archbishop Michael Kpakala Francis, and the role of new human rights organizations and an attorney named Toe (who had cited both Gandhi and Martin Luther King, Jr., as his inspiration) (Press 2015). He explains how women used their status as mothers to ensure that rebels would listen to them.

As Gbowee reflected on the biblical saying "blessed are the peacemakers," she shared:

> Jesus in his wisdom really knew that peacemaking meant speaking the truth to power, and sometimes keeping your emotions in check in order to speak the truth. When everyone else is picking up arms, you are choosing to use the right word and you are choosing non-violence.
>
> *Gbowee and Makgoba 2014: 156*

She also emphasized the need for forgiveness and reconciliation:

> We are 3.4 million people, we are not a lot of people—the piece of space that we inhabit is a space we will continue to inhabit, whether we hate or love each other. God is testing us to be in that space.... We need to get to the place where we are not waiting for someone to apologize. In some instances, we need to step up and offer forgiveness if we are to move forward. It begins with forgiving ourselves and then forgiving our political leaders. Because until we do that, all we will have to give our children is a country full of conflict, mixed-up history, and a lot of hate.
>
> *Gbowee and Makgoba 2014: 155*

Nkiru Nzegwu, a U.S.-based philosopher from Nigeria, argues that the Igbo traditionally respected women, but that British colonization brought male dominance, with changes in laws and the courts disadvantaging women, even stripping them of their rights within marriage (Nzegwu 2006). She considers the "colonially imposed patriarchal structure" to be the source of current problems in Igboland, such as "a culture of violence, brutality, political excesses, and gargantuan social problems" (Nzegwu 2006: 20). And yet contemporary men have constructed a fictive tradition, presuming that their current dominance is an African tradition. She insists that reintegrating women back into positions of social leadership can help to undo the current harms and rebuild Igbo society.

Contemporary movements for peace abound; one is led by a philosophy professor from Nigeria, Fr. Emmanuel Edeh, who, after writing about Igbo metaphysics in 1985, has more recently devoted himself to founding and running a Centre for Peace, Justice, and Reconciliation at Elele in Rivers State, Nigeria. In his earlier book he grappled with the Igbo version of the problem of evil. *Omenani* is the Igbo term that describes being "in harmony with the totality of all that is" (Edeh 1985: 103). A communitarian outlook would see that evil hurts the community, and social offenses are considered a kind of pollution that harms the central community ideals of love, humanity, and brotherhood. To combat evil, mutual recognition and acceptance of each other is very important. For the Igbos, the wind has symbolic power and is considered a Wind God who has the power to blow away evil.

Twentieth-Century South Africa

Mohandas K. Gandhi formed his theory and practice of nonviolent action in South Africa, where he lived from 1894 to 1914. He explained that black South Africans had already been practicing nonviolent non-cooperation with unjust colonial systems. Some of Gandhi's nonviolent tactics were adaptations of Hindu traditions, such as *hartal* (day of mourning, which has similarities to a general strike but is done with a different mindset and mood) and *dharna* (vigiling at the door of one who has done wrong) (Bondurant 1965: 105–120). He was also encouraged by the British suffragettes, writing about their tactics in his newspaper, *Indian Opinion*. A few months prior to Gandhi's large *satyagraha* action of 1913, the women of Bloemfontein—a group consisting of Colored (mixed race) as well as black Africans—organized themselves nonviolently to resist the pass laws there (Walker 1982; Gasa 2007). Gandhi's earlier reticence to involve women in his nonviolent protests changed during this year. When we take into account the size of the Bloemfontein women's resistance, and the extent to which local black African and Colored intellectuals were involved in discussing the developments along with Gandhi, we can see that the development of *satyagraha* as a tactic was a larger social development, and not an Indian idea that just happened to be tried out in Africa.

The African National Congress (called the SANNC when it first formed in 1912) committed itself to using nonviolent action to bring justice and an end to segregation. When the apartheid government took power in 1948, the ANC continued its use of nonviolence. After the Nationalist Party was voted in, and apartheid segregation laws were passed, the ANC organized the Defiance Campaign. Participants went through lengthy training in nonviolence. Gandhi's son Manilal was involved in the movement. Nelson Mandela was in a group of fifty-two men who defied the pass laws and were arrested. Altogether over 8,000 people were arrested as part of the campaign. Albert Luthuli was the head of the ANC at the time. He was also chief of Grouville, but due to his involvement with the Defiance Campaign, the government removed him from his post as chief. In 1956 he was arrested for treason, although he was released in 1957. He received the Nobel Peace Prize in 1960. He remained president of the ANC until 1967.

In his memoir, *Let My People Go*, Luthuli tells how as a teacher of teachers at Adams College in the 1920s he publicly criticized the emphasis on educating Africans only for manual labor. He tried to educate himself in religion, philosophy, and sociology through personal reading (Luthuli 1962: 35–37). In this book he explains his philosophy of nonviolence and his personal commitment to nonviolent means as part of his self-expression as a Christian. He explains that his goal and that of the ANC was to "bring the white man to his senses, not to slaughter him," if they could only encourage a "change of heart" (Luthuli 1962: 113). While this was a tall order, he noted that in 1949 the African and Indian communities were fighting each other violently, and yet in 1952 they came together in the Defiance Campaign in unison to denounce injustice. He also shares keen insights (based on his personal experience as an activist and leader) regarding nonviolence's success as a tactic. From his perspective, nonviolence was working because it interrupted white South Africans' narrative of blacks as unruly and dangerous, thereby justifying police and military repression. In recounting what happened during the Defiance Campaign, Luthuli explains that the South African government used agent provocateurs in Kimberley and Port Elizabeth, because if the protest movement could be castigated as having broken into a riot, police could move in and quell it. From Luthuli's perspective, these developments proved that the government couldn't defeat nonviolence: "The challenge of non-violence was more than they could meet. It robbed them of the initiative" (Luthuli 1962: 127).

Mandela, who was in charge of the ANC Youth League during the early 1960s, famously said after the Sharpeville Massacre that he was departing from adherence to nonviolence. He said, "If the government reaction is to crush by naked force our non-violent demonstration, we will have to seriously reconsider our tactics" (in Sampson 1999: 148–149). After that point, the ANC created an armed wing called Umkhonto we Sizwe. To avoid creating deep animosity he wanted his attacks on apartheid infrastructure to avoid casualties. Mandela was soon arrested and imprisoned for planning acts of sabotage. There remains a debate in the literature regarding whether Luthuli himself agreed with (or merely acquiesced with) the abandonment of strict nonviolence. Couper has written that Luthuli maintained his commitment to nonviolence, noting that when Luthuli accepted Mandela's challenge, he did so, saying on March 25, 1962: "I would urge our people not to despair over our methods of struggle, the militant, nonviolent techniques. So far we have failed the methods—not the method us" (in Couper 2009: 339).

Mandela was finally released from prison in 1990. Mandela would not agree to "renounce violence" (unless the government did so as well) and that was part of the reason the apartheid government kept holding him. But Mandela expressed great appreciation of nonviolent tactics and wrote an article in 1990 reflecting on the importance of Gandhi's legacy. In this article Mandela tried to narrow the chasm seen between their two positions, by suggesting that his own position had been to limit violence to sabotage "because it did not involve the loss of life" and highlighting the fact that Gandhi had said in his writings that violence was better than cowardice (Mandela 1999: n.p.). Mandela asserted that "violence and nonviolence are not mutually exclusive; it is the predominance of the one or the other that labels a struggle" (Mandela 1999). Despite Mandela's not being a pacifist, he is well known for his emphasis on reconciliation of all races and ethnicities in South Africa, and it is on this basis that he has a reputation as a peacemaker. Kök Arslan and Turhan focus on his unitive leadership style and his "peace traits" of "*forgiveness, dissolving vindictiveness*, and *empathetic capacities*" (Kök Arslan and Turhan 2016: 30).

After apartheid ended, Desmond Tutu and others began a process of truth and reconciliation for the country. Tutu emphasized the philosophy of *ubuntu*, an African humanistic and communitarian philosophy, as the basis for mutual respect and reconciliation. Being an Anglican minister, Tutu also developed his ideas in the context of Christian theology. He has continued to preach the message of peace and reconciliation into contemporary times. In his 2004 book *God Has a Dream*, he says he wants his readers to realize that God loves our enemies and does not share our hatreds and prejudices. God wants humans to overcome the divisions they have created between each other. We need to realize that every human being is precious. Then we need to take concrete steps toward reconciliation, which involves confession and forgiveness, and making a new start. This is needed on the interpersonal level as well as the international level (Tutu 2004).[11]

Mogobe Ramose wrote about the importance of the concept of *ubuntu* for African philosophy. In order to be fully human, we must share with those in need. He refers to the Sotho proverb "*Motho ke motho ka batho*," which means that "to be human is to affirm one's humanity by recognizing the humanity of others, and on that basis, establish human relations with them" (Ramose 1999: 154). And so, this concept of *ubuntu* (or "*botho*" in the Sotho language) entails both peaceful relations and the end of exploitation. Ramose considers this African insight to be humanness (rather than "humanism," which has a different set of connotations in the European context) (Ramose 1999: 155). Ntate Koka, a participant in the 1970s Black Consciousness Movement in South Africa, makes the connection between *ubuntu* and peace explicit: "There can be no peace in Africa until our humaneness is realized. Unless I realize that my beingness hangs on the beingness of the other" (Koka, in Vervliet 2009: 22).

Writing about contemporary African philosophy of education, Yusef Waghid of Stellenbosch University in South Africa sees an important role for the concept and practice of *ubuntu*.

> *Ubuntu* can play a dualistic role, of, on the one hand, contributing toward healing ethnic–political conflict, and on the other, undermining corruption and chauvinistic governance on the African continent. As a humanistic concept, *ubuntu* can engender cooperative and harmonious human relations; as a philosophical concept, *ubuntu* can contribute toward cultivating the respect and care that are required to produce a morally worthwhile African society; and as a politico–ideological concept, *ubuntu* can engender human interdependence for transformed socio-political action.
>
> Waghid 2013: 2

Reflecting on contemporary problems of terrorism, Waghid thinks that education can play an important role in reducing terrorism. First of all, some radical terror groups have misappropriated the concept of "jihad," so education could correct misconceptions. But additionally, Waghid thinks that terrorism rises due to people's misrecognition of each other, and also due to the consequences of exclusion that causes deprivation and grievance. Education can help people to compassionately imagine and recognize each other and then to be respectful of each other. When we know ourselves and others better, we can then recognize our common humanity. Waghid therefore hopes that the promotion of *ubuntu* can help to prevent atrocities in Africa.

While the concept of *ubuntu* is an old one, contemporary discussions of *ubuntu* are shaped by current political events and even globalization. South African philosopher Leonard Praeg notes that *ubuntu* is now in the South African Constitution, thereby changing its character (Praeg 2014a: 114; see Graness 2015). There are many supporters but also many critics of either the concept *ubuntu* or its usage in contemporary contexts. While the story of South Africa's "peaceful transition" is to a certain extent a myth and an oversimplification (see Nixon 1994; Praeg 2014b), and while protest and dissatisfaction with ongoing injustices in South Africa show that *ubuntu* has not fully been realized (see Odendaal), this is often the case with moral ideals. Despite their not being realized, they can serve as a goal.

Conclusion

Throughout the many centuries that Africans have philosophized, their metaphysics and ethics have emphasized the need for humane respect and care for all persons, manifested concretely in peaceful coexistence. In Africa, as on other continents, there is often a chasm between ideals and lived reality. It is nevertheless helpful to learn about and learn from the centuries of wisdom shared on the topics of peace, justice, and nonviolence that can be found in the works of African scholars and peace activists.

A common theme in African thought is the dignity of the human person, respect for life, and the need for relationships based on mutual respect and care. African philosophers have provided insights into causes of conflict and ways to de-escalate tensions and address underlying causes. They have emphasized communitarian values and fulfilling people's basic needs. They eschew exploitation as a way of avoiding conflict in the first place. And they show how relationships that have been harmed can be mended through forgiveness and reconciliation. The insights, life experience, and reflections of Africans are surely valuable lessons for all people.

Notes

1 African philosophers had been critical of the practice of slavery in prior centuries. For example, in *Miraj al-Sud* (written in 1615 CE) we have Timbuktu-based philosopher Ahmad Baba advancing arguments against race-based slavery (Baba 2000: 23–53). Wilhelm Anton Amo, the philosophy professor (and physician) from Gold Coast (contemporary Ghana) was brought to Europe by a missionary and raised by Duke Anton Ulrich. He wrote two dissertations (the first, in 1729 at University of Halle, being a treatise against slavery, and the second, at University of Wittenberg, a critique of Descartes) (Abraham 2004). Park explains (Park 2013), among other points, that Kant based many of his ideas about the abilities of Africans from a book written by Edward Long, who used as his sources on Africans' character and abilities colonial landholders in Jamaica like Samuel Estwick who had slaves (Park 2017). Toussaint Louverture and the Haitian independence struggle nurtured Hegel's philosophical reflections on the importance of freedom (and the necessity of violence to free oneself from bondage) as Hegel expressed them in the "Lordship and Bondage" section of *The Phenomenology of Mind*; nevertheless, Hegel subsequently wrote Africa out of the history of philosophy (Buck-Morss 2000: 842–846). Slavery as an institutional practice was rejected slowly by European colonial governments throughout the nineteenth century, urged along as it was by writings and public talks by former slaves like Olaudah Equiano in England and Frederick Douglass in the United States.
2 While Blyden took over certain concepts of race from scientific racists, he insisted races were different, not hierarchical (van Hensbroek 2004: 83). While one should be suspicious of any theory that assigns negative attributes to another group and saves the good attributes for one's own group (for example, white racists assign negative traits to black Africans and imagine themselves to be the opposite of blacks, denying human attributes found in all persons, even themselves; and negritude is sometimes criticized as doing something similar), at least Blyden's account of African personality tells us that being peaceful and conciliatory was considered a virtue and a trait of a superior person. For Africans to have more influence in the world would lead to a more peaceful world.
3 Theophile Obenga notes that the verb "rekh" means "to know" and "to learn." The noun "rekh" means philosopher, wise man. Rekhet means philosophy, accurate knowledge, and good judgment. "Sat" means wisdom and prudence, sagacious behavior, awareness of principles of moral conduct and sociable behavior (Obenga 2004: 34). The Inscription of Antef (twelfth dynasty; 1991–1782 BCE) gave the definition of a philosopher:

> [He is the one] whose heart is informed about these things which would be otherwise ignored, the one who is clear-sighted when he is deep into a problem, the one who is moderate in his actions, who penetrates ancient writings, whose advice is [sought] to unravel complications, who is really wise, who instructed his own heart, who stays awake at night as he looks for the right paths, who surpasses what he accomplished yesterday, who is wiser than a sage, who brought himself to wisdom, who asks for advice and sees to it that he is asked advice.
>
> *Obenga 2004: 35; translated by the German Egyptologist Hellmut Brunner*

4 Augustine's contribution depends on four letters of Augustine's, and was made famous by a later theorist, Gratian of Bologna, who wrote the *Decretum* in 1148, which became part of the canon law of the Catholic Church.
5 Origen was not a Greek, since references point out his mastery of Greek language and philosophy (and they would not have done so if he were Greek). He also wrote in Latin, which was the preferred language of African intellectuals. Also, Origen was expelled from Antioch when all Egyptians were expelled (Masolo 2004: 53).
6 As explained in the Introduction to the online version of this text: "In *Munyat al-muñd* (The desire of the aspirant), Baba ibn Ahmad al-Alawi al-Maliki al-Maghribi al-Shingiti presents an explanation of the lives and activities of the Sufi Tijānī order. The Tijāniyyah originated in North Africa in the 1780s and was soon established in West Africa. Here the author stresses the importance of individuals and groups within society paying attention to avoiding violence" (al-Shingiti, World Digital Library Link: www.wdl.org/en/item/9677/ (accessed 14 July 2017)).
7 When we use the word "traditions," we have to be careful. "Traditions" are not necessarily old or irrational. They are values and practices that are repeated because people continue to find them meaningful. They can be dynamic and change over time, even if the change is slow and is not noticed by contemporary practitioners. Traditions can also be "invented" (that is, a new or recent practice or interpretation is imaginatively given a long history). While current practitioners may presume that their iteration of an idea or practice is long-standing, scholars can often more carefully account the nuances of its history. Taking all of this into account, we should be reticent to represent Africa using tradition and modernity as a dichotomy, and realize the fluid and interpenetrating aspect of these various influences on human action, societies, and their institutions.
8 This epistemological open-mindedness is similar to what Chakravarthi Ram-Prasad called "multiplism," which Ram-Prasad connects to Jain teachings of "non-one-sidedness" as well as Gandhi's writings (Ram-Prasad 2003).
9 A good source regarding Nkrumah's stands on nonviolence is Bill Sutherland, an African American who had been a conscientious objector during the Second World War, and who co-founded the Congress of Racial Equality (CORE). During the 1950s he desired to flee the McCarthyism that was growing in the U.S. and to become part of promising developments in Africa. Both he and Bayard Rustin joined other anti-nuclear activists trying to stop French nuclear testing in the desert of Upper Volta.
10 Fanon was influenced by Jean-Paul Sartre (and one could say that Sartre was influenced by him). Scholars have shown that nevertheless Sartre reluctantly embraced violence in a limited way and only as a last resort, always insisting that one's humanistic values should not be lost. Both Fanon and Sartre emphasized that an act of violence against oppressors can be an affirmation of the human being and their freedom to act to end oppression and birth a new humanity. While definitely not a nonviolent "purist," Sartre emphasized, as did Camus, that one risks eroding one's own humanity if one too glibly uses violent means to the end of liberation (Santoni 2003).
11 Philosophers, among others, became involved in the TRC process, with Wilhelm Voerword, a philosopher at Stellenbosch, joining with Canadian philosopher Trudy Govier to describe the theory behind the TRC process and to point out the challenges of achieving reconciliation (Govier and Verwoerd 2002). Lötter wrote a book-length philosophical study of the high cost of violence in South Africa and a roadmap to peace by focusing on justice and healing, emphasizing the need to face apartheid's pain and undo its harm (Lötter 1997).

Bibliography

Abraham, W. (2004). "Anton Wilhelm Amo," in K. Wiredu (ed.), *A Companion to African Philosophy*. Malden, MA: Blackwell, 191–199.
Abramowitz, S. A. (2014). *Searching for Normal in the Wake of the Liberian War*. Philadelphia: University of Pennsylvania Press.
Adi, H., and M. Sherwood. (1995). *The 1945 Manchester Pan-African Congress Revisited*. London: New Beacon Books.
Ahlman, J. S. (2010). "The Algerian Question in Nkrumah's Ghana, 1958–1960: Debating 'Violence' and 'Nonviolence' in African Decolonization." *Africa Today* 57 (2), Winter: 67–84.
Assmann, J. (2003). *The Mind of Egypt: History and Meaning in the Time of the Pharaohs*. Cambridge, MA: Harvard University Press.

Baba, A. (2000). *Mi'raj al-Su'ud: Ahmad Baba's Replies on Slavery*, annotated and translated by J. Kunsick and F. Kanck. Rabat: Institute of African Studies.
Blyden, E. W. (1908/1994). *African Life and Customs*. Baltimore, MD: Black Classic Press.
Bondurant, J. (1965). *Conquest of Violence*, revised ed. Los Angeles, CA: University of California Press.
Buck-Morss, S. (2000). "Hegel and Haiti." *Critical Inquiry* 26 (4), Summer: 821–865.
Coe, K., C. T. Palmer, and K. el Shabazz. (2013). "The Resolution of Conflict: Traditional African Ancestors, Kinship, and Rituals of Reconciliation." *African Conflict and Peacebuilding Review* 3 (2), Special Issue on Peace Education, Memory, and Reconciliation in Africa, Fall: 110–128.
Couper, S. (2009). "'An Embarrassment to the Congresses?' The Silencing of Chief Albert Luthuli and the Production of ANC History." *Journal of Southern African Studies* 35 (2), Liberation Struggles, Exile and International Solidarity, June: 331–348.
Daube, D. (2005). "The Women of the Bible and Greece," in R. Holmes and B. Gan (eds.), *Nonviolence in Theory and Practice*, 2nd ed. Long Grove, IL: Waveland Press, 119–128.
Daube, D. (2008). *The Deed and the Doer in the Bible: David Daube's Gifford Lectures*, vol. 1. West Conshohocken, PA: Templeton Foundation Press.
Dykstra, L. A. (2002). *Set Them Free: The Other Side of Exodus*. Maryknoll, NY: Orbis Books.
Edeh, E. M. P. (1985). *Towards an Igbo Metaphysics*. Chicago: Loyola University Press.
Egan, E. (1999). *Peace Be with You: Justified Warfare or the Way of Nonviolence*. Maryknoll, NY: Orbis Books.
Fanon, F. (1963). *The Wretched of the Earth*. New York: Grove Press.
Frykholm, A. (2016). *Christian Understandings of the Future: The Historical Trajectory*. Minneapolis, MN: Augsburg Fortress Publishers.
Gasa, N. (2007). "Let Them Build More Gaols," in N. Gasa (ed.), *Women in South African History*. Cape Town: Human Sciences Research Council Press, 129–151.
Gbowee, L., and T. Makgoba (2014). "Nonviolence and Peacemaking." *The Ecumenical Review* 66 (2): 154–156.
Govier, T., and W. Verwoerd. (2002). "Trust and the Problem of National Reconciliation." *Philosophy of the Social Sciences* 32 (2): 178–205.
Graness, A. (2015). "Review article of Leonhard Praeg and Siphokazi Magadla (eds.), 'Ubuntu: Curating the Archive'." *South African Journal of Philosophy* 34 (1): 143–147.
Grey, C. (2013). "Shock, Horror, or Same Old Same Old? Everyday Violence in Augustine's Africa." *Journal of Late Antiquity* 6 (2), Fall: 216–232.
Gyekye, K. (2010a). "Traditional Political Ideas, Their Relevance to Development in Contemporary Africa," in K. Wiredu and K. Gyekye (eds.), *Person and Community: Ghanaian Philosophical Studies I*, 2nd printing. Washington, DC: Council for Research and Values in Philosophy, 241–256.
Gyekye, K. (2010b). "Moral Foundations of an African Culture," in K. Wiredu and K. Gyekye (eds.), *Person and Community: Ghanaian Philosophical Studies I*, 2nd printing. Washington, DC: Council for Research and Values in Philosophy, 193–206.
Gyekye, K. (2017). "Foreword," in M. O. Ajei and K. Gyekye (eds.), *Disentangling Conscienticism: Essays on Kwame Nkrumah's Philosophy*. Lanham, MD: Lexington Books, XI–XV.
James, C. L. R. (1959–60). "Notes on the Life of George Padmore." *The Nation* October 2, 9; November 13, 27; December 4, 1959.
James, C. L. R. (1992). *The C.L.R. James Reader*, edited by A. Grimshaw. Cambridge, MA: Blackwell.
Jeffers, C. (2013). "Embodying Justice in Ancient Egypt: The Tale of the Eloquent Peasant as a Classic of Political Philosophy." *British Journal for the History of Philosophy* 21 (3): 421–442.
Karenga, M., and J. Assmann (2004). *Maat: The Moral Ideal in Ancient Egypt*. New York: Routledge.
Kök Arslan, H., and Y. Turhan (2016). "Reconciliation-oriented Leadership: Nelson Mandela and South Africa." *All Azimuth* 5 (2), July: 29–46.
Lötter, H. (1997). *Injustice, Violence and Peace: The Case of South Africa*. Amsterdam: Rodopi.
Luthuli, A. (1962). *Let My People Go: The Autobiography of Albert Luthuli*. New York: McGraw-Hill.
Mandela, N. (1999). "The Sacred Warrior." *Time Magazine* December 31.
Masolo, D. A. (2004). "African Philosophers in the Greco-Roman Era," in K. Wiredu (ed.), *A Companion to African Philosophy*. Malden, MA: Blackwell, 50–65.
Maybee, J. E. (1999). "'The Instruction of Any': An Ancient Egyptian Philosophical Theory of Ethics." *African Philosophy* 12 (2): 149–174.
Mazrui, A. (1986). *The Africans: A Triple Heritage*. Boston: Little, Brown, and Company, 23–38.
Nixon, R. (1994). *Homelands, Harlem and Hollywood: South African Culture and the World Beyond*. London: Routledge.

Nkrumah, K. (1957). *The Autobiography of Kwame Nkrumah*. London: New World Paperback.
Nkrumah, K. (1962). "What I Mean by Positive Action" (pamphlet, 5 pages). Accra, Ghana: Ministry of Information and Broadcasting.
Nkrumah, K. (1963). *Africa Must Unite*. London: Heinemann.
Nkrumah, K. (1970). *Consciencism: Philosophy and Ideology for Decolonization*, revised ed. New York: Monthly Review Press.
Nzegwu, N. (2006). *Family Matters: Feminist Concepts in African Philosophy of Culture*. Albany, NY: State University of New York Press.
Obenga, T. (2004). "Egypt: Ancient History of African Philosophy," in K. Wiredu (ed.), *A Companion to African Philosophy*. Malden, MA: Blackwell, 31–49.
Odendaal, A. (2016). "South Africa's Incomplete Peace," in O. Richmond, S. Pogodda, and J. Ramovi (eds.), *The Palgrave Handbook of Disciplinary and Regional Approaches to Peace*. London: Palgrave Macmillan UK, 287–298.
Oguejiofor, J. O. (2007). "Resources for Peace in African Proverbs and Myths." Available at: www.abibi-tumikasa.com/forums/showthread.php/34275-Resources-for-Peace-in-African-Proverbs-and-Myths (Accessed 14 July 2017).
Oluwole, S. B. (1997). *Philosophy and Oral Tradition*. Ikea, Lagos, Nigeria: African Research Konsultancy (ARK) Publications.
Park, P. K. J. (2013). *Africa, Asia, and the History of Philosophy: Racism in the Formation of the Philosophical Canon, 1780–1830*. Albany, NY: State University of New York Press.
Park, P. K. J. (2017). "Kant's Colonial Knowledge and His Greek Turn." Presentation at the American Philosophical Association conference, Baltimore, MD, January.
Praeg, L. (2014a). *Ubuntu: Curating the Archive*, edited by S. Magadla, Thinking Africa Series. Pietermaritzburg: University of KwaZulu-Natal Press.
Praeg, L. (2014b). "Rethinking Girardian Reconciliation: South Africa and the Myth of the Exception," in V. N. Redekop and T. Ryba (eds.), *René Girard and Creative Reconciliation*. Lanham, MD: Lexington Books, 215–228.
Pray the Devil Back to Hell. Directed by Gini Reticker, produced by Abigail Disney, distributed by Balcony Releasing (US) ro★co films (International).
Presbey, G. (2006). "Strategic Nonviolence in Africa: Reasons for Its Embrace and Later Abandonment by Nkru-mah, Nyerere, and Kaunda," in D. Boersema and K. Gray Brown (eds.), *Spiritual and Political Dimensions of Nonviolence and Peace*. Amsterdam: Rodopi, 75–101.
Presbey, G. (2013). "The Role of Nonviolent Resistance in Ghana's Independence Movement (1890s–1950s)," in M. Bartkowski (ed.), *Rediscovering Nonviolent History: Civil Resistance in Liberation Struggles and Nation-Making*. Boulder: Lynne Rienner, 51–70.
Press, R. M. (2015). *Ripples of Hope: How Ordinary People Resist Repression Without Violence*. Amsterdam: Amsterdam University Press.
Rabaka, R. (2014). *Concepts of Cabralism: Amilcar Cabral and Africana Critical Theory*. Lanham, MD: Lexington Books.
Ram-Prasad, C. (2003). "Nonviolence and the Other: A Composite Theory of Multiplism, Heterology and Heteronomy Drawn from Jainism and Gandhi." *Angelekai: Journal of the Theoretical Humanities* 8 (3): 3–22, December.
Ramose, M. B. (1999). *African Philosophy Through Ubuntu*. Harare, Zimbabwe: Mond Books.
Ramose, M. B. (2017). "The Ethics of Liberation in Nkrumah's Consciencism," in M. Odei Ajei and K. Gyekye (eds.), *Disentangling Consciencism: Essays on Kwame Nkrumah's Philosophy*. Lanham, MD: Lexington Books, 201–212.
Sampson, A. (1999). *Mandela: The Authorized Biography*. London: Harper Collins.
Santoni, R. (2003). *Sartre on Violence: Curiously Ambivalent*. University Park, PA: Pennsylvania State University Press.
Sherwood, M. (1996). *Kwame Nkrumah: The Years Abroad 1935–1947*. Legon, Ghana: Freedom Publications.
"South African Blacks Boycott Apartheid in Port Elizabeth, 1985–86." *Global Nonviolent Action Database*. Available at: http://nvdatabase.swarthmore.edu/content/south-african-blacks-boycott-apartheid-port-elizabeth-1985-86 (Accessed 2 November 2017)
Sumner, C. (1985). *Classical Ethiopian Philosophy*. Addis Ababa: Commercial Printing Press.
Sutherland, B., and Meyer, M. (2000). *Guns and Gandhi in Africa: Pan-African Insights on Nonviolence, Armed Struggle and Liberation in Africa*, foreword by Archbishop Desmond Tutu. Trenton, NJ: Africa World Press.

Tutu, D. (2004). *God Has a Dream: A Vision of Hope for Our Time*. New York: Image Books and Doubleday.
van Hensbroek, P. B. (2004). "Some Nineteenth Century African Political Thinkers," in K. Wiredu (ed.), *A Companion to African Philosophy*. Malden, MA: Blackwell, 78–89.
Vervliet, C. (2009). *The Human Person, African Ubuntu and the Dialogue of Civilisations*. London: Adonis and Abbey Publishers Ltd.
Waghid, Y. (2013). *African Philosophy of Education Reconsidered: On Being Human*. New York: Routledge.
Walker, C. (1982). *Women and Resistance in South Africa*. London: Onyx.
Yankah, K. (1995). *Speaking for the Chief: Okyeame and the Politics of Akan Royal Oratory*. Bloomington and Indianapolis: Indiana University Press.

7
NONVIOLENCE IN THE DHARMA TRADITIONS
Hinduism, Jainism, and Buddhism

Veena R. Howard

If one were asked to identify a single concept that is broadly shared among India's various philosophical and religious texts and popular practice, it would be *dharma*. Dharma is derived from its Sanskrit root, *dhr*, meaning, "to hold," "to support," or "to sustain," and it defies a single definition and a definite interpretation. The term is used most prevalently in Hindu, Jain, and Buddhist traditions (also known as Dharma traditions) to encompass ethics, law, duty, personal calling, and religion. Within the codes of *dharma*—morality and disciplines of Indic traditions—nonviolence (*ahimsa*) holds the essential and the primary place. The Hindu epic *Mahabharata*'s popular Sanskrit phrase *ahimsa parmo dharma* translates as "nonviolence is the greatest duty or virtue," meaning it is the greatest duty of human beings to not harm any living being. The list of five essential disciplines, shared by Hinduism, Jainism, and Buddhism, includes nonviolence, truth, non-stealing, sexual control, and non-possession, with nonviolence preceding the other four disciplines in order and importance. The Hindu Yoga System's five disciplines (*yamas*), namely nonviolence (*ahimsa*), truth (*satya*), non-stealing (*achaurtya*), control of the senses (*brahmacharya*), and non-possession (*aparigraha*), are identical with Jain Dharma's five *anuvratas* or vows. Buddha Dharma's *Panc Sila*, or five ethical precepts, contain a slight variation. In Buddhism four precepts are identical with the Jain and Hindu traditions, but Buddhism includes abstaining from intoxication instead of non-possession.

Broadly speaking, these virtues and codes of ethics are meant to create order and harmony in one's self and society. The concept of *dharma* signifies the harmonious order of the cosmos where harmony in the self and society requires the ethical conduct of humans. The codes of *dharma* provide individuals with moral and ethical rules (but these rules are not static in the Kantian sense of ethical imperatives) that guide them to interact with one another in various situations for the purpose of keeping order in the society. Even though Hindu, Jain, and Buddhist religious and philosophical traditions provide nuanced interpretations of the concept, they simultaneously share its core meaning as "ethics," the harmonizing force of the society.

The notion of *dharma* is dynamic. *Dharma* as "ethics" encompasses moral principles that guide human conduct, laws that maintain order, and duties that lead to individual fulfillment and social harmony. For example, Mahatma Gandhi used the concept of *dharma* in terms of ethics and sought to live according to its ethical disciplines. He held that "*dharma* means morality. I do not know any *dharma* which is opposed to, or goes beyond morality. *Dharma* is morality practiced to its ultimate limits" (Pushparaj 2005: 109–110). Yet he also transformed the components of *dharma*'s ethical disciplines into tools for his nonviolent activism. For example, the method of *satyagraha* (meaning truth-force, but generally known as passive resistance) was based on truth and nonviolence. Gandhi sought to practice all five disciplines in his personal life and made *ahimsa* and *satya* (nonviolence and truth) central to his strategy to obtain freedom for India.

Many texts of the Dharma traditions analyze and elaborate on the value of nonviolence in personal life and in interpersonal relations. The Jain tradition takes the *dharma* of *ahimsa* to an extreme level, prohibiting any form of violence (which will be discussed later in the chapter). Such a strict adherence to the *dharma* of nonviolence becomes problematic when it is in conflict with the duty of self-defense or the protection of one's clan or country. Two crucial questions arise: How do these traditions reconcile the personal ethical *dharma* (virtue) of nonviolence with the *dharma* (duty) to protect one's family or nation? Can this virtue be translated into a policy or practice for confronting social and political challenges? In order to address these questions, this chapter will (1) provide a brief overview of Hindu, Jain, and Buddhist religions' approaches to nonviolence in personal life as well as in social and political situations; (2) explore the dilemma of practicing the *dharma* of nonviolence in the face of dire situations such as injustices and war through analyzing the war context and philosophy of the *Bhagavad-Gita*, which ostensibly instructs the warrior of his duty (*dharma*) to fight the righteous battle; and (3) analyze Gandhi's unconventional allegorical interpretation of war in the *Bhagavad-Gita* to elaborate on how Gandhi's interpretation not only situates active nonviolence within a religious framework, but also reconciles the two meanings of the *dharma* of nonviolence—*virtue* to avoid causing harm to fellow beings and *duty* to confront social and political injustices.

Jainism: Nonviolence Is the Highest Vow

Jainism has existed on the Indian subcontinent for over three millennia as a parallel system of philosophy and religion alongside Hinduism. Unlike any other religion, nonviolence (*ahimsa*, which literally means non-harming) defines Jainism, a religion that coexisted with other Dharma traditions and has been influential in shaping the ethos of Indian culture. Jainism extends the duty of nonviolence toward not only humans but all living beings, from miniscule insects to mighty mammals. In his book *The Virtue of Nonviolence: From Gautama to Gandhi*, Nicholas F. Gier notes, "Jainism offers us the first and unarguably most extreme conception of nonviolence" (Gier 2006: 29). The practice of nonviolence is linked to the Jain belief that all beings have a soul; therefore, it is the absolute imperative of spiritual life to avoid speech, thought, and deeds that have the potential to cause harm.

According to the Jain Sutras, texts compiled based on the teachings of Lord Mahavira:

> All living beings desire happiness, and have revulsion from pain and suffering. They are fond of life, they love to live, long to live, and they feel repulsed at the idea of hurt and injury to or destruction of their life. Hence no living being should be hurt, injured, or killed.
>
> All things breathing, all things existing, all things living, all things whatsoever, should not be slain, or treated with violence, or insulted, or tortured, or driven away.
>
> He who hurts living beings himself, or gets them hurt by others, or approves of hurt caused by others, augments the world's hostility towards himself.
>
> *Jain Sutras 1983: 187–188*

Nonviolence is so crucial to the Jain philosophy of liberation from karmic bondage that Jain thinkers have scrupulously categorized the value of various life forms. Life and souls dwell in rocks, drops of water, flowing streams, radiant sunbeams, flickering flames, viruses, fungi, insects, plants, reptiles, birds, and mammals, including humans. The *Tattvartha Sutra* places these souls into a hierarchy according to the number of senses possessed by various species: humans and animals are on the top (possessing five senses) and worms and vegetables on the bottom (having only one sense, of touch).

Jain monks and nuns take extreme measures to avoid all forms of violence, including the practices of sweeping paths before walking on them, plucking their hair because cutting hair may kill lice, avoiding fermented food and drinks and root vegetables out of the fear that the fermentation process causes violence to microorganisms, and eating only picked fruits rather than cutting vegetables. An even more extreme form of this vow of nonviolence involves not consuming any food or drink because eating and digesting also cause violence. Jain teachings are scrupulous about identifying how the process of digesting and eating causes violence not only to the food that is digested but also to the microorganisms used in the digestive process. This practice is known by Jains as *Sallekhana* (thinning out the passions) and to critics as "suicide" because this observance culminates in the slow death of the practitioner. Jain monks or nuns take this vow to purify their soul from karmic bondage by avoiding any physical and mental activities. Their focus is not on hurting themselves, because the vow is taken voluntarily with full deliberation and a joyful mind.

However, the vow of nonviolence for Jain householders, or laymen and laywomen, is not as strict. Jain householders seek to avoid violence by consuming vegetarian meals and avoiding any form of unnecessary violence to plants, animals, or humans. Even though the Jain laity is advised to avoid occupations and conflicts that may involve violence, historically they may kill in self-defense (i.e., in the instances of political warfare by Jain kings in the medieval period) (Gier 2006: 29). Jain laypeople prepare vegetarian food for the monks and nuns so that the monastics can avoid causing violence even to plants. Jains are generally pacifists, as most are advised to avoid enlisting in war or working in military industries.

Jainism is also uniquely cognizant of intellectual violence, which is a type of violence caused by pressing individual views on others. The ancient doctrine of *anekantavada* (literally meaning "many sidedness" or "non-absolutism") is based on the view that truth is complex and can be expressed through many viewpoints. The famous parable of the "Six Blind Men," a story that is also found in Hindu and Buddhist texts, illustrates this point. According to this parable, six blind men approach an elephant. One blind man feels the sturdy leg and declares the elephant to be a tree. Another feels its tail and takes it to be a snake. Another grabs the elephant's ear and uses it as a fan, and so on. Each is convinced of his experience, and yet none of the blind men is completely correct. Similarly, humans may think they have understood a situation, but the complexity of truth always defies simple explanations.

In the modern era, Jain scholars and thinkers are reimagining the value of Jain nonviolence, especially to address the ecological crisis. Jain thinkers believe that extending the vow of nonviolence to all living beings can serve as a model to avoid modern lifestyles and choices that cause human and environmental violence. Jainism's long tradition of creating animal hospitals exemplifies the philosophy of caring for all sentient beings, and it may serve as a model to confront violence toward humans, animals, and the environment. While Jainism's monastic traditions are committed to avoiding all forms of nonviolence for individual spiritual liberation, Jain laypeople are looking to a broader application of the Jain vow of nonviolence. The entire purpose of Jain religion throughout history has been to avoid actions that may cause violence and to offer solutions for disrupting the insidious forces of violence.

Buddhism: *Ahimsa* as the Ethical Precept

While the Jain concept of *ahimsa* is *sui generis* and is fundamental to Jain ethics and religiosity, Buddhism holds more nuanced views on nonviolence. Siddhartha Gautama, the Buddha, lived during the sixth century BCE, at the same time as Lord Mahavira, the most recent Jain Tirthankara (enlightened being). Jainist and Buddhist views of nonviolence influenced Hinduism, the dominant tradition of India, and shaped the subcontinent's culture. The Buddha's teachings included the four Noble Truths and the Eightfold path to attain freedom from *samsara* (the cycle of death and rebirth). This path required that followers live a life of morality and simplicity. Many serious followers observe the vows of celibacy and renunciation and choose to become monks and nuns. Thus, it is not surprising that in the popular opinion Buddhists are perceived as calm, meditative, and peaceful.

The five ethical precepts (*Panch Shila*)—abstaining from violence, lying, stealing, sexual misconduct, and the consumption of intoxicating substances—structure the core of ethics of the Buddha *Dhamma* (the Pali rendering of *Dharma*, which translates to the "teachings of the Buddha"). Prohibition of violence toward all sentient beings is the first ethical precept. The *Dhammapada*, which is believed to be composed of the Buddha's own words, instructs followers to avoid acts that cause injury to other beings:

> All men [beings] tremble at punishment, all men fear death. Likening others to oneself, one should neither slay nor cause to slay. All men tremble at punishment; all men love life. Likening others to oneself one should neither slay nor cause to slay.
> *The Dhammapada 1950: X: 1–2*

The Buddha warns against harsh speech and certain occupations that cause violence to humans and animals, including the trade of weapons and animal slaughter. Consistent with the other Dharma traditions, Buddhism also emphasizes the painful repercussions of violent acts, not only in this life but in the next life as well. Such accumulation of bad *karmas* perpetuates the wheel of *samsara*, but acts of compassion lead to peace: "He who seeking his own happiness does not inflict pain (strikes with a stick) on beings who (like himself) are desirous of happiness obtains happiness after death" (*The Dhammapada* 1950: X: 4).

In Jain teachings, *ahimsa* (abstaining from harming any living beings) is always motivated by the will to avoid the accumulation of sinful *karmas* (because the goal is freedom from constrains of all *karmas*), but in Buddhism the emphasis is often on the positive virtues of *metta* (loving-kindness) and *karuna* (compassion), even when punishing heinous actions. (In Jainism consequences of actions are inescapable.) S. Tachibana, a Buddhist scholar, emphasizes that compassion is connected to nonviolence: "We ought not hurt mentally and physically our fellow creatures as well as our fellow men, but to love and protect them" (Gier 2006: 53). The Buddha is said to have transformed a notorious, violent bandit by emphasizing this type of compassion rather than punishment of the bandit's crimes. The story of the serial killer Angulimala (literally, "the one with the garland of fingers"), who was known for brutally killing any passerby and then severing and stringing the fingers of the dead into a garland that he wore around his neck, features the Buddha appeasing the criminal's hatred with compassion. The transformed bandit chooses the life of a monk and takes the vow of compassion and loving kindness (Cho 2009). Unlike Jainism's belief that one must suffer the consequences of bad actions, the bandit was not judged for his past heinous actions by the Buddha and was celebrated as a noble being who changed his course of life. The Jain version of extreme nonviolence, requiring extreme renunciation, has also been questioned by Buddhists. Historically, Buddhists often criticize the practice of self-mortification (including that of fasting to death) in order to avoid any form of violence because it overlooks compassion for the self. (The instances of self-immolation of monks in protest of the Vietnam War are said to be exceptions to the Buddhist view of nonviolence.) *Ahimsa*, adjoined with compassion, asks of its followers not merely to withdraw from violence but to actively engage with acts of compassion, as the Buddha did in the case of the bandit.

Even though popular portrayals of Buddhism are peaceful and the tradition's overall ideal is pacifist, conventionally, Buddhism is not dogmatic about nonviolence. According to Mahinda Deegalle, Pali canonical texts do not offer justification for any form of violence, but their approach to nonviolence is considered pragmatic, as the Buddha always taught the Middle Way in all aspects of life (Deegalle 2002). Jain monks and nuns take the absolute vow of non-harming, Buddhist monks also commit to all five precepts and help all sentient beings. However, in various countries like Korea, Japan, Tibet, Bhutan, and Burma (also known as Myanmar), monks have served in armies and fought wars. In the modern era, Venerable Wiranthu has been leading an anti-Muslim campaign in Myanmar. In his book *The Origins of Religious Violence*, Gier critiques Venerable Wiranthu, who accuses Muslims of being "crude and savage." Gier explains, "In a perverse application of Buddhist ethics to Muslims, he [Wiranthu] stated: 'You can be full of kindness and love, but you cannot sleep next to a mad dog'" (Gier 2014: 68). Wiranthu justifies violence as necessary to tame the supposed madness of Muslims in Burma. Simultaneously, the current Burmese leader Aung San Suu Kyi, who was influenced by Gandhi and has deeply studied Buddhist texts, believes in the Buddhist virtue of loving-kindness:

> Some have questioned the appropriateness of talking about such matters as *metta* (loving-kindness) and *thissa* (truth) in the political context. But politics is about people and what we had seen ... proved that love and truth can move people more strongly than any form of coercion.
>
> Gier 2014: 89

Nevertheless, in recent years, she has been criticized by human rights groups for not speaking out against violent Buddhist groups more vehemently.

However, the Burmese militaristic monks are not a new phenomenon; martial tendencies are found in various East Asian Buddhist traditions. For example, Gier brings attention to various Buddhist traditions that integrated martial practices into their religious regimen. For example, there has been a historical overlap between Buddhism and military practices in Japan: "Zen Buddhism had always maintained close connection with the Japanese military, and it had a special vigor and masculinity that appealed to the samurai warriors" (Gier 2014: 192). D.T. Suzuki, who was the catalyst for bringing Zen to the United States, revived the connection between "Zen and the samurai sword" and has been said to have "urged Buddhists to support imperial warfare" (Gier 2014: 192). However, not all scholars agree with the views, as they cite Suzuki's postwar writings that highlight how he saw war as an act of exploitation. Indeed, Zen teachings and its strict regimen help cultivate the strong will, deep focus, and devout commitment of the samurai, and that power has been summoned to support imperial warfare. However, in general the Zen power of the sword is not to harm others but to contribute to peace.

Such apparently contradictory viewpoints about violence are found in various Buddhist texts that condone some violent actions by attributing them to compassionate motivations. In some legends of Mahayana Buddhism ("the Great Vehicle," a popular form of Buddhism), a Bodhisattva (Being of Wisdom) defends future beings by preemptively killing the would-be murderer. Thus, the Bodhisattva not only protects the would-be victims but also defends the would-be murderer from the torments of hell. This act of killing is considered compassionate, not violent.

In its overarching philosophy, Buddhism advocates the *dharma* of nonviolence, compassion, and loving-kindness, and even necessary acts of violence are motivated by compassion for sentient beings.

Hinduism: *Ahimsa* as Yogic Discipline (*Yama*)

Hindu Dharma, which is historically the oldest tradition on the India subcontinent, upholds the virtue and discipline of *ahimsa* as the highest duty/virtue. In the Hindu law books, nonviolence is one of the ten components of universal ethics. Other ethical codes include truth, patience, self-control, control of anger, forgiveness, etc. In the Yoga System of Hindu philosophy, *ahimsa* is the first of the five disciplines (*yamas*): nonviolence, truth, non-stealing, restraint of the senses, and non-avarice. These restraints are identical to the five Jain vows and similar to the five Buddhist ethical precepts. They are prerequisites for embarking on the spiritual path and, at the same time, they are foundational to a harmonious personal and social life.

More broadly, in Hinduism, the Law of Karma dictates that social harmony and sustainable justice cannot be obtained by violent means. The concept of *karma* (literally "action") is central to Hindu ethics, as in the other Dharma traditions, and it is understood as the principle of cause and effect. It is inextricably linked to the theory of reincarnation and the wheel of *samsara* (the cycle of life, death, and rebirth) in Buddhism. Each thought and action produces moral reverberations whose effects resound not only in this life but in next lives as well. S. Radhakrishnan, a prominent scholar of Indian philosophy, summarizes the Law of Karma: "All acts produce their effects which are recorded in both organism and environment. . . . Good produces good, evil, evil. Love increases our power of love, hatred, our power of hatred" (in Howard 2008: 139). The Law of Karma and belief in the system of reincarnation makes it impossible to think that violence and revenge can lead to sustainable justice. It is almost impossible to discern whether or not a certain experience (good or bad) caused by another is a result of a previous life's actions. Any use of violence for either taking revenge or seeking justice has the potential to create more negative actions. Violence perpetuates the cycle of retribution and it must be interrupted through compassion and forgiveness. Texts of Hinduism often prohibit violence against other sentient beings, including nonhuman animals.

Furthermore, the roots of Hindu ethics of respecting all life lie in the philosophy of Advaita (non-dualism), the notion of ontological identity and the unity of the Self and the Other. In a general understanding of Hinduism, universal *atman* (literally Self or Spirit) connects all sentient beings, and dictates that within each resides a divine essence. An understanding of this non-dualistic philosophy reveals that the Other is none other than our very own Self.

Given the difficulty of practicing nonviolence (in deed, speech, and thought) as a policy, it is not surprising that nonviolence is celebrated as the highest virtue or duty (*dharma*) in various Hindu texts. Ahimsa has also been translated as "abstention from cruelty." The Hindu epic of the *Mahabharata* (Dutt XIII: 116.38–39) lauds its high status:

> Ahimsa [nonviolence] is the highest dharma, Ahimsa is the best tapas [religious austerity]. Ahimsa is the greatest gift. Ahimsa is the highest self-control. Ahimsa is the highest sacrifice. Ahimsa is the highest power. Ahimsa is the highest friend. Ahimsa is the highest truth. Ahimsa is the highest teaching.
>
> Howard 2008: 135

Ironically, the main narrative of the *Mahabharata* centers on the world's deadliest war. The epic contains the account and an apparent endorsement of the bloodiest battle recorded in any religious literature, by the divine incarnation of Lord Krishna. In the *Bhagavad-Gita*, Lord Krishna himself persuades the warrior Arjuna to fight against his cousins who wronged his wife and family and usurped his right to the kingdom. Even though nonviolence is celebrated as highest duty, Hinduism is not pacifist, so necessary violence—such as violence for sustaining harmony and peace (another meaning of *dharma*)—has a place in the tradition. Nonviolence guides personal moral conduct, but political actions at times have to involve violence, as they do in the *Mahabharata*, when all other means have been exhausted.

In recent history, militaristic actions by some Hindu groups against the British and Muslims have been justified by invoking the *Bhagavad-Gita* and selected Hindu religious myths of warring gods and goddesses against evil demons. Some of the religious and political leaders of the nineteenth century blamed Hindu, Jain, and Buddhist philosophies of nonviolence and pacifism for India's plight of slavery and oppression under foreign regimes. Paying no heed to the Hindu axiom of "nonviolence as the highest *dharma*," and ignoring Lord Krishna's various attempts to avert the looming war in the epic of the *Mahabharata*, some of the activists justified the *Bhagavad-Gita*'s call to fight as a template for condoning violence.

As we discussed earlier, Jain, Buddhist, and Hindu Dharma traditions emphasize the *dharma* of nonviolence, but at the same time grapple with the question of necessary violence when confronted with oppression and injustice. In the following section, I use the example of Gandhi's interpretation of the *Bhagavad-Gita* to underscore the dilemma of observing the virtue of nonviolence in the face of violence and the problem of choosing between nonviolence and violence. Furthermore, I will explore how Gandhi's unique reinterpretation of the *Bhagavad-Gita* for his nonviolent fight against the British regime sought to resolve the dilemma of choosing between violent and nonviolent action. Gandhi's writings show that he was deeply influenced by the Jain, Buddhist, and Yogic emphasis on the *dharma* of nonviolence. His unique rendering of nonviolence as weapon seeks to reconcile the *dharma* (virtue) of nonviolence and the *dharma* (duty) of defending against violence. His synthesis of Jain and Buddhist teachings with Hindu ideology of the unity of all beings renders his interpretation consistent with the ethos of *dharma* of nonviolence (as duty and virtue) for sustaining harmony. This synthesis has the potential to provide a model for reading ancient texts that advocate "just" war by paying attention to the moral mandates of nonviolent traditions.

Gandhi's Reading of the *Bhagavad-Gita*: An Attempt to Resolve the Dilemma in the *Dharma* of Nonviolence and Justice

The *Bhagavad-Gita* (*The Song of the Lord*) is an ancient and globally influential text; it occupies a high status within the sacred canon of Hinduism because it contains a direct message from the incarnation of the god Lord Krishna. Some scholars and pacifists find it alarming how easily and unequivocally Lord Krishna summons the warrior Arjuna to fight the civil war between two sets of cousins for which he has stationed himself in the battlefield. In the beginning of the text, Arjuna feels reluctant and morally conflicted in the face of the horror of civil war. He explains his psychological state, fearing the ensuing horror: "As I look upon these kinsmen, O Krishna, assembled here eager to fight, my limbs fail, my mouth is parched, a tremor shakes my frame and my hair stands on end" (Gandhi 2000: 30). The terrible sin of killing his relatives and gurus troubles Arjuna: "Alas! What a heinous sin we are about to commit . . . we are prepared to slay our kith and kin" (Gandhi 2000: 33). He announces to his charioteer Krishna: "I shall not fight." In response, Lord Krishna (who has chosen the role of Arjuna's charioteer) mocks Arjuna's conflict and his hesitancy to battle with his "evil" cousins, and chides the warrior for his "unmanliness."

The divine Krishna's categorical command, "Get up, Arjuna, with the resolve to fight," has led some contemporary Western scholars and pacifists to condemn the text as an overt endorsement of war (Rao 2002: 118). It has been argued that the god is mocking the compassion and piety of a warrior and provoking him to kill members of his own family. Furthermore, some Hindu nationalists who fought in India's independence movement interpreted the *Gita*'s call to fight literally, and, unlike Gandhi, they did not rule out the use of arms, when necessary (Howard 2013: 47–48). Many readers who encounter the *Gita* for the first time also draw the conclusion that the text justifies war.

Although the teaching is set against a backdrop of the battlefield, it is revered by Hindus for its awe-inspiring theophany, deep psychological insights, multi-faceted yoga philosophy, and complex *dharma* ethics. Gandhi's symbolic interpretations of the war context of Krishna's admonition to Arjuna is not meant to advocate violent action. Instead, the war symbolizes the deep lessons of the *karma* yoga philosophy, or performing action with selflessness and equanimity. Devout Hindus often extrapolate symbolic meanings from the battlefield context and Krishna's call to perform duty—even in dire situations like war. The epic war is symbolic of the constant battle between the forces of good and evil, as Gandhi termed it.

Many religious leaders of the twentieth century like Gandhi invoked the wisdom of *the Song of the Lord* when battling against inner demons of desire, greed, and instincts of animosity in personal lives. Krishna's call also inspired some Indian activists to actively rise against the evils of British imperialism. But it is a well-known fact that Gandhi rejected violence as a method, which seemed at odds with the *Gita*'s call to fight the war with conventional weapons. Some of Gandhi's contemporary activists and leaders, such as B.G. Tilak and Sri Aurobindo, interpret Krishna's call as non-passive "action," but do not rule out physical and violent means if all else fails. Political, secular, and academic readings of the *Gita* as a war-justifying treatise have resulted from the questions concerning justified war and the present-day popular rhetoric of "holy war." Traditional philosophical interpreters (such as Shankaracharya and Madhavacharya) and many contemporary thinkers (including H.P. Blavatsky, a Russian author and a co-founder of the Theosophical Society) perceive the text as a treatise that conveys psychological and philosophical truths, instead of a dialogue that sanctions religious warfare (Howard 2013: 41–44; Minor 1986: 18–24). For the purpose of examining the question of whether the *Gita* justifies war, it is important for readers to attain a more nuanced understanding of the text and to consider how Hindus traditionally interpret this teaching when seeking inspiration and solace in difficult times. Such nuanced readings have the potential to give us valuable insights as we engage with the question of justified violence.

Many modern intellectuals, such as Henry David Thoreau, Albert Schweitzer, and Gandhi, expressed appreciation for the *Gita* in accordance with a more philosophical and positive interpretation of the text (Friedrich 2008; Meyer 2002). Gandhi called the sacred text his "guiding light" and used it to inspire *nonviolent* activism. Such dichotomous responses invite us to consider the following questions: Does Lord Krishna's call to battle represent the command of an angry god? Does the *Bhagavad-Gita* provide justification for all wars? What consequential actions (including war) have been historically inspired by this text? In the contemporary milieu of interreligious interactions, the ideas of "just war" and "holy war" carry great relevance and gravity. Therefore, it is all the more critical to engage with such questions by considering Indian hermeneutic traditions that concentrate on the questions of metaphysics and ethics while also critically analyzing the content and context of the text. Lord Krishna's call to fight is considered within the larger context of the *Mahabharata*. It is not a categorical sanctioning of war.

A brief overview of the context is essential in understanding the dilemma of choosing nonviolence in the time of war. The context reveals that the battle was fought only as the last option, when all other means had been exhausted. In advocating the battle, the text also takes into account the ensuing horrors caused by violence.

An examination of the context reveals that the *Gita*'s context of battle is more nuanced and complex than a simple endorsement of warfare. The text consists of 700 verses contained within the epic *Mahabharata*—the longest epic in the world, at about 100,000 verses—and was composed around 300 BCE to 200 CE. Reading it outside this historical and textual context is like pulling Christ's Sermon on the Mount from the greater context of the Bible. The *Gita* appears at the beginning of the epic's great civil war, but it is independently revered as a sacred text.

The *Mahabharata* provides a detailed account of events preceding the war, recounting the atrocities (*adharma*) caused by the Kauravas (100 sons of Dhritrashtra) on the Pandavas (five sons of Pandu) for assuming their lawful right to the kingdom. The cruelties include an attempt by the Kauravas to kill the Pandavas by burning their house, usurping the Pandavas' rightful kingdom, molesting the Pandavas' queen in the public court, and exiling them for thirteen years from their land. The Pandavas had been patient and pardoning and made many efforts for peace before the war. Disasters associated with warfare were seriously considered by Lord Krishna and the Pandava leaders. However, despite negotiations and reconciliatory attempts by Lord Krishna himself, the Pandavas are forced into the sinful conflict of war, only as a last resort.

When the trumpets of war resonate across the battlefield, Arjuna, the leader of the Pandava army, decides not only to turn his back on his duty as a warrior but also on his immediate family, whose very existence depends upon his actions. Dejected and desperate, he asks Lord Krishna's guidance, which marks the beginning of the teaching.

What is noteworthy about Krishna's response is that in the entire 700-verse text, only five times does he explicitly tell Arjuna to fight. Furthermore, Krishna never prompts the warrior to incite the fight, nor does he provoke him into doing his duty to seek justice and revenge against the evildoers. Instead, Krishna imparts lessons that teach that one should treat friend and foe as equals, practice self-control and detachment without ego, and understand the immortality of the Self and the unity of all beings—messages that seem out of place in a speech exhorting violence and inspiring a dejected and demoralized warrior to fight the war. However, the *Mahabharata*'s detailed accounts of the atrocities and horrors caused by his opponents remind both Arjuna and the reader that passivity will not bring peace or justice.

Beyond the literal story line, the text is a treatise on philosophical themes, including the nature of the self and the divine (*atman* and *brahman*), sacred duty (*dharma*), many paths of union with the divine (*yoga*), and the right course of action (*karma*) to achieve peace and harmony with Self and the environment.

> Desire, anger, and greediness
> comprise the three gates of hell
> Truly destructive of the Self,
> So one should renounce this triad
> BG 2015: 16: 21

This command is similar to how Buddhism teaches followers to avoid three vices (delusion, hatred, and greed), which perpetuate the suffering in the cycle of *samsara* (worldly existence). The entire *Bhagavad-Gita* meanders through various philosophical and ethical vistas, as if the guide, Lord Krishna, intends to steer Arjuna to the field of righteous/ethical action (*dharmakshetre*) and away from the field of battle (*kurukshetre*):

> Know that the enemy is this:
> desire, anger, whose origins

> are in the quality of passion,
> all consuming, greatly harmful
> > BG 2015: 3: 37

To some readers, Lord Krishna's imparting such philosophical and ethical lessons to a soldier on the battlefield might seem odd; however, they are consistent with the implied message of the *Mahabharata*. Kings and warriors of the high ranks were, along with their military education, educated in ethics by sages because they were the guardians of their land and required moral as well as martial strength. It is not inconsistent with the viewpoints of Plato, who proposed the ideal of a philosopher-king in *Republic*: "Our guardian is soldier and philosopher in one" (Plato 1969: 525 b). The dharma-king, by definition, is both a soldier and philosopher. Moreover, despite the overt theme of war, the *Mahabharata* enunciates *ahimsa* (nonviolence) as the highest *dharma*, and the *Gita* upholds it among the highest virtues. Violence can be inevitable at times to confront evil forces, but it is never holy. Even though Jain and Buddhist traditions are better known for upholding pacifist views, the lay ethic of polity in these traditions includes violence when it is necessary to destroy the evil, as we saw earlier.

Wrestling with the *Gita*'s content and context is not a modern secular and academic phenomenon—a literal or simplistic interpretation has seldom been entertained by the devout. Traditional and indigenous analyses of the *Bhagavad-Gita* take into consideration metaphorical and symbolic meanings of the text as well as lexical meanings, contextual denotations, and the time and space in which the message is delivered. Prominent commentaries on the *Bhagavad-Gita* by philosophers and activists—from the medieval philosophers Adi Shankaracarya and Ramanuja to contemporary activists Sri Aurobindo and Gandhi—serve as models that point to the multi-dimensional nature of its subtle and hidden meanings. Textual commentaries spanning from the eighth to the nineteenth and twentieth centuries were primarily oriented toward justifying theological and philosophical viewpoints. Some emphasized devotion to a personal god and non-duality of the Self and Divine, while others highlighted the *Gita*'s teaching of developing a state of equanimity.

> He who is one with foe and friend,
> And one in honor and disgrace,
> In cold and heat, joy and anguish,
> freed from attachments to results
> > BG 2015: 12: 18

In essence, Lord Krishna's philosophical and ethical teachings are more central to the discourse than his call to "fight."

However, some nineteenth- and twentieth-century Hindu reformers and activists did leverage Krishna's call to "fight" as a summons for the devout to actively resist unjust British rule. For example, the renowned leaders in India's independence movement, including Sri Aurobindo and B.G. Tilak, did not rule out violent actions to expedite the end of the British rule (Danino 2002: 48). Unlike his contemporary militant activists who looked to the *Bhagavad-Gita* for inspiration to fight against the imperial regime, Gandhi found a different sort of inspiration from the same text. Gandhi provided a more nuanced and symbolic interpretation of Krishna's call to "fight" as a battle within one's self against the baser impulses and sensual desires that assault the mind. He provides an allegorical interpretation, saying, "It is a battle between the innumerable forces of good and evil, which become personified in us as virtues and vices. The Kauravas represent the forces of Evil, the Pandavas the forces of Good" (Gandhi 2000: 27). Furthermore, Gandhi, who read the *Gita* every day and translated the text with his own commentary, understood "fight" as "action" rather than passivity: "We should spend every minute of our waking life in doing work which has fallen to our lot" (Gandhi 2000: 89). Since the *Gita* teaches the interconnectedness of all beings, he argued that justice is to be sought only through nonviolence and forgiveness. Thus, the political manipulations of the text asserted a nonviolent active resistance rather than a passive defeat.

In contemporary India, the *Gita*'s ritual reading is common in Hindu religious circles, and chanting of the Song at funerals is meant to provide solace to minds overcome by suffering. Modern saints utilize its message to impart ethical lessons, providing tools for coping with conflict and turmoil in our existence. Simultaneously, some extreme political groups invoke the text for their ominous agenda against certain religious groups or secular liberal ideologies. Like any religious text, the *Gita* can be manipulated to fit an agenda. It is important to consider this as we encounter notions of "holy war" in various traditions.

How the *Gita*'s call "to fight the war" has most commonly been interpreted by Hindus is essential to understanding the dilemma of *dharma* of choosing violence only when it is used to prevent more violence. The context of *Mahabharata* demonstrates that war was the last resort when all other means of reasonable and nonviolent reconciliation had been exhausted. War cannot be characterized as "just" or "holy" (though it can be a necessary duty) because it conflicts with Hinduism's notion of *karma* and the greater philosophy of the unity of all beings (*sarvabhuta-ātma-bhutātma*). The message of the *Gita* is to act selflessly for performing one's duty so that all actions become *sadhana* (spiritual practice). Gandhi argues through an allegorical interpretation of the *Gita*'s war context that it is necessary to observe the use of battle rhetoric in broader traditional and contemporary contexts, in which references to fighting are more about symbolic triumph than literal violence. Traditionally, Hindu thinkers use the symbolism of fighting one's inner selfish desires, which are the true enemies for the one who practices *dharma* ethics. In contemporary contexts, fighting also conveys determination, as in fighting cancer, fighting one's addictions, fighting to score in a sport in the face of imminent defeat.

Conclusion

The preceding analysis points to the danger of reading religious texts too literally and offers a more nuanced study that points to spiritual messages embedded in the *Gita*. It cautions against any haphazard inferences or reductionist interpretations that support the ideology of holy war, specifically within the present interreligious context. Religious discourse is seldom literal; it invites readers to consider deeper meanings of sacred texts. The metaphor of life as a battle or struggle requires participation rather than passivity.

Gandhi read the *Gita*'s call to fight as the moral mandate to fight for sustaining justice; however, he was aware of the moral dilemmas of prohibiting violence in all situations. The *Bhagavad-Gita* underscores the moral predicament that arises when considering violence and nonviolence in a time of war. Gandhi, who had trust in the power of nonviolence, deliberates on a situation where violence to stop violence becomes the duty of the votary of *ahimsa*:

> Suppose a man runs amuck and goes furiously about sword in hand, and killing anyone that comes his way, and no one dares to capture him alive. Anyone who dispatches this lunatic will earn the gratitude of the community and be regarded as a benevolent man. From the point of view of ahimsa it is the plain duty of everyone to kill such a man.
> *CWMG 2001: vol. 36: 449*

Gandhi's views and the *Gita*'s teachings are not inconsistent with Jain and Buddhist exceptions to nonviolence (such as in situations where violence becomes essential to disrupt the forces of carnage). Gandhi had many Jain friends and studied the texts of various Dharma traditions. He was aware that living requires causing harm, and that often the customary understanding of *ahimsa* equates it with the avoidance of any conflicts. Absolute nonviolence toward all living creatures is impossible and its practice requires the highest level of self-control (Howard 2013: 57–59). Understood merely as self-control or self-limitation for spiritual goals, it may lead one to conquer the seductions of ego, but it can also translate into complete passivity and therefore indifference to, or even the deliberate avoidance of, sociopolitical issues. Gandhi is known for his pacifist ideologies; however, he hardly used the term pacifism. For Gandhi, practicing nonviolence was to fight against structures of violence—racial, social, and economic—which required active participation, not a passive attitude. Drawing inspiration from the *Gita*, Gandhi interpreted the *dharma* of nonviolence as both virtue and duty to sustain justice. Gandhi makes this proclamation: "The purest way of seeking justice against the murderers is not to seek it.... Their punishment cannot recall the dead to life" (Howard 2008: 139). Gandhi's views were not only in conflict with the war narrative of the *Mahabharata*, but they came in conflict with a judicial system that includes the execution of murderers. Against Gandhi's own wishes and pleas for commutation by his sons, for instance, his own murderer was executed. This is a prime modern-day example of the conflict between the ideology of nonviolence and the reality of a legal system that at times necessitates violence in the name of justice.

Gandhi's interpretation is consistent with Hindu Dharma's ethics and the moral vows and precepts of Jainism and Buddhism, which are religions that hold their own forms of exceptions to passive nonviolence when faced with the forces of oppression. Gandhi's allegorical interpretation of the *Bhagavad-Gita* seeks to resolve the dilemma inherent in the absolute practice of nonviolence by interpreting it as a "powerful weapon." His rendering underscores the need for a more contextual, nuanced understanding of representations of violence in religious texts. It calls on readers to rethink the popular usages of terms like "just war" and "holy war." Ultimately, in Dharma traditions, a war is only just when it resists and confronts violence through nonviolent means, and using violence is only acceptable when it sustains harmony and procures justice.

It becomes clear that there is much diversity in the Dharma traditions: nonviolence is almost non-negotiable in Jainism, it is the first ethical precept in Buddhism, and it is the central virtue and duty in Hinduism. In his practice of nonviolence, Gandhi was deeply influenced by Jainism's adamant emphasis on nonviolence, but his interpretation is more like the Buddha's version of nonviolence. For Gandhi, nonviolence was not simply a negative practice but required positive acts of compassion. According to Gandhi:

> There is as much difference between *ahimsa* and compassion as there is between gold and the shape given to it, between a root and the tree which sprouts from it. Where there is no compassion, there is no *ahimsa*. The test of *ahimsa* is compassion. The concrete form of *ahimsa* is compassion.
>
> *CWMG 2001: vol. 45: 285*

Inspired by the *Gita*'s call to fight in the face of adversity, Gandhi reimagines the war context as a symbol of striving for justice and the virtue of *ahimsa* as a tool to fight injustice. In doing so, he upholds the Hindu definition of *dharma* as the principle of cosmic harmony. He was aware of both the shared and unique religious and moral ideologies of the Dharma traditions, and he provides one contemporary attempt to synthesize this diversity in his rendering of nonviolence as a moral (*dharmic*) method to confront violence.

Work Cited

Cho, F. (2009). "Buddhism," in J. Lyden (ed.), *The Routledge Companion to Religion and Film*. New York: Routledge, 162–177.

Danino, M. (2002). "Sri Aurobindo and the Gita," in S.J. Rosen (ed.), *Holy War: Violence in the Bhagavad-Gita*. Virginia: Deepak Heritage, 43–58.

Deegalle, M. (2002). "Is Violence Justified in the Theravada Buddhism?" Available at: www.academia.edu/960858/Is_Violence_Justified_in_Theravada_Buddhism (Accessed 7 February 2017).

The Dhammapada (first pub. 1950). Translated and edited by S. Radhakrishnan. New Delhi: Oxford University Press.

Flood, G. D., and C. Martin. (2015). *The Bhagavad Gita: A New Translation, Contexts, Criticism*. New York: W.W. Norton.

Friedrich, P. (2008). *The Gita Within the Walden*. New York: State University of New York Press.

Gandhi, M. K. (2000). *The Bhagavad-Gita According to Mahatma Gandhi*, edited by J. Strohmeier. Berkeley: Berkeley Hills Books.

Gandhi, M. K. (2001). *The Collected Works of Mahatma Gandhi* (*CWMG*), 98 vols. [electronic book]. Delhi: Publication Division Ministry of Information and Broadcasting, Government of India.

Gier, N. F. (2006). *The Virtue of Nonviolence: From Gautama to Gandhi*. New York: State University of New York Press.

Gier, N. F. (2014). *The Origins of Religious Violence: An Asian Perspective*. Lanaham, MD: Lexington Books.

Howard, V. (2008). "Nonviolence and Justice as Inseparable Principles: Gandhian Perspective," in M.K. Duffy and D. Nash (eds.), *Justice and Mercy Will Kiss: The Vocation of Peace Making in a World of Many Faiths*. Marquette, WI: Marquette University Press, 135–143.

Howard, V. R. (2013). *Gandhi's Ascetic Activism: Renunciation and Social Action*. Albany, NY: State University of New York Press.

Jain, Pushparaj. (2005). "Mahatma Gandhi's Notion of Dharma: An Explication," in A. Vohra, A. Sharma, and M. Miri (eds.), *Dharma: The Categorical Imperative*. New Delhi: D.K. Printworld Ltd, 103–111.

Jain Sutras, translated by Jyoti Prasad Jain. (1983). *Religion and Culture of the Jains*, 3rd ed. New Delhi: Bharatiya Janapith.

The Mahabharata (9 vols.) (1994). Translated by M.N. Dutt. Delhi: Parimal Publications.

Meyer, M., and K. Bergel (eds.) (2002). *Reverence for Life: The Ethics of Albert Schweitzer for the Twentieth Century*. New York: Syracuse University Press.

Minor, R. (ed.) (1986). *Modern Interpreters of the Bhagavad-Gita*. Albany, NY: State University of New York Press.

Plato. (1969). *Republic* in *Plato in Twelve Volumes*, Vols. 5 and 6, translated by P. Shorey. Cambridge, MA: Harvard University Press.

Rao, R. N. (2002). "Pursuing the Gita from Gandhi to Doniger," in S.J. Rosen (ed.), *Holy War: Violence in the Bhagavad-Gita*. Virginia: Deepak Heritage, 117–126.

8
THE GANDHI-KING TRADITION AND *SATYAGRAHA*

Barry L. Gan

In 1936 Mahatma Gandhi met on two separate occasions with African American leaders—at that time called Negro leaders—in the United States. The first of these meetings was with Howard Thurman, professor and dean at Howard University. It took place on February 21, 1936, and it ended with a prescient remark by Gandhi: "It may be through the Negroes that the unadulterated message of non-violence will be delivered to the world" (Gandhi 1999: vol. 68: 237). At the time, Martin Luther King, Jr. was 7 years old.

A few months later Benjamin Mays met with Mahatma Gandhi. Though neither of them knew it then, it was a historic meeting. Gandhi was living at the Sevagram Ashram, and Mays, who had recently received his doctorate in theology from the University of Chicago, was visiting from the United States. As with the earlier interview, the meeting was recorded by Gandhi's secretary, Mahadev Desai, and it consisted of Gandhi responding to questions about nonviolence that Mays posed to Gandhi (Gandhi 1999: vol. 70: 261–264).

The meeting was historic because a few years after this meeting, in 1940, Benjamin Mays became president of Morehouse College, an all-Negro college for men in Atlanta, Georgia. And a few years after that, in 1944, 15-year-old Martin Luther King, Jr. began his college career at Morehouse. While King attended Morehouse College, he came to regard Mays as one of the great influences in his life, as King wrote later in his book *Stride Toward Freedom* (King, Jr. 1958: 145).

So, King knew of Gandhi during his undergraduate years at Morehouse College, but his reading of Nietzsche left him with grave concerns about the ability of Christian love—*agape*—to address social problems. It wasn't until shortly after Gandhi's assassination in January of 1948 that King became genuinely interested in learning more about Gandhi. A talk that King attended in 1950, given by the longtime president of Howard University, Mordecai Johnson, sparked his interest. Of Johnson's speech, King said:

> His message was so profound and electrifying that I left the meeting and bought a half-dozen books on Gandhi's life and works. Like most people, I had heard of Gandhi, but I had never studied him seriously.
>
> *King, Jr. 1958: 96*

King claimed that Gandhi's philosophy convinced him that his skepticism about Christian love's ability to address social problems was unwarranted. He concludes:

> I came to feel that [Gandhi's philosophy of nonviolent resistance] was the only moral and practically sound method open to oppressed people in their struggle for freedom.
>
> King, Jr. 1958: 97

Gandhi's *Satyagraha* as a Way of Life

What is Gandhi's philosophy of nonviolent resistance? And how does it compare with the strategies and tactics that King developed?

Gandhi's philosophy of nonviolent resistance is called *satyagraha*. However, *satyagraha* is not merely a philosophy of nonviolent resistance. The *Oxford-American Dictionary* defines *satyagraha* as "a policy of passive political resistance, especially that advocated by Mahatma Gandhi against British rule in India" (Oxford 2010: 1581), but this, too, is a definition that Gandhi himself would reject. *Satyagraha* is first and foremost a way of conducting oneself in the world, and secondly, Gandhi insisted that there was nothing passive about it.

Gandhi said, "God is Truth, Truth is God." And he meant that quite literally. He believed that God comprised all of reality, that reality comprised Truth, and that to understand all of reality was to realize God. He believed that we should pursue God, pursue Truth. His term for the pursuit of Truth is *satyagraha*. Literally, *satyagraha* means holding on to truth. *Satya* means Truth, and *graha* means grasping. Gandhi, in one of his writings (Gandhi 1999: vol. 20: 39–45), offered three examples of *satyagrahis*, people who practice *satyagraha*: (1) Socrates, (2) Daniel in the lions' den, and (3) Prahlad. Prahlad is a mythical figure, the son of a king who commanded that he be worshipped by everyone. But Prahlad insisted upon worshipping the Hindu god Vishnu rather than worshipping his father. For this rejection Prahlad's father attempted many times in many ways to have his son killed, but his son's devotion to Vishnu saved Prahlad from death each time. Gandhi's examples reveal that first, a *satyagrahi* is committed to Truth; second, a *satyagrahi* will not abandon the Truth as she sees it, even if it involves suffering unto death; and third, a *satyagrahi* refuses to harm or injure others in the name of Truth. Thus, *satyagraha* is not merely a form of nonviolent resistance—though it can be—because neither Socrates nor Daniel nor Prahlad was intentionally resisting anything; each was simply engaged in the pursuit of what he perceived to be the Truth. Nor was there anything passive about their commitment to Truth. Daniel actively pursued his perception of the Truth by worshipping his God despite an injunction calculated to entrap him for doing so. Socrates actively pursued his interrogation of city elders in a pursuit of wisdom by helping them to recognize the limits of their own knowledge. Prahlad persisted in his worship of Vishnu. None sought to harm others by his practice.

An instance from Gandhi's own life illustrates well these central features of *satyagraha*. Early in the 1982 film *Gandhi* is a scene that shows Gandhi being unceremoniously thrown from a train in Maritzburg, South Africa. Gandhi had refused to move from his first-class seat, for which he had purchased a ticket, and as an Indian in 1890s South Africa, he was not allowed to sit there. Gandhi later described this event as the turning point in his life, when he ceased being a shy and ineffectual attorney and turned his attention to bringing himself and others closer to Truth.

But what the 1982 film doesn't show is what happened the following day. Gandhi had to take a stagecoach to continue his journey. The person in charge of the stagecoach, called the leader, refused to seat Gandhi inside the coach with the other passengers, who were white. As Gandhi puts it, he pocketed the insult and sat up top with the driver. But when the coach stopped for the afternoon, the leader wanted to smoke. So he left the coach to sit next to the driver and asked Gandhi to sit at his feet, on the rail. Gandhi at this point refused to change his seat, and the leader began to beat him. But Gandhi clung to the rail and refused to be budged even as the leader attempted to pull him from his seat. Eventually the passengers themselves intervened and insisted that Gandhi be allowed to ride in the coach.

This image of Gandhi is perfect *satyagraha*: Gandhi clinging to the rail of the stagecoach, being pulled and beaten as he refuses to loosen his grip. Here is the person who believes he is grasping Truth and refusing to let go of it. But he does not harm others for the sake of his Truth. In fact, in refusing to cooperate, he endures harm himself. His commitment to Truth requires that if need be, he, not others, suffers for it. That is his duty.

So, *satyagraha*: grasping Truth, and suffering, if necessary, for one's beliefs. But there is more. *Sat* means being or reality. Gandhi believed that insofar as each life is a part of reality, each life holds a piece of the truth, and the destruction or diminution of other lives precludes one from grasping more of the Truth. Truth, Gandhi thought, cannot be grasped fully by any finite being, and it is therefore incumbent upon all people not to destroy or harm other life, for to destroy life is also to destroy what is, and each act of destruction precludes one from ever gaining the entire Truth. This is the root of Gandhi's commitment to nonviolence. Nonviolence is the only means by which Truth can be pursued, for to act other than nonviolently is to destroy Truth. Thus we must be united in our pursuit of Truth; we cannot obtain Truth by the destruction of one another.

In making such claims Gandhi is following closely the Jain tradition. No doubt he strongly inclined toward the Jain tradition because of his great admiration and respect for his mother, who, though she was Hindu, had a Jain monk as a close friend and spiritual adviser. His devotion to major Jain precepts is quite evident in his *History of the Satyagraha Ashram*, which he began to write in 1932 but never finished (Gandhi 1999: vol. 56: 142–192). In his draft he identifies vows and practices that were expected of all those living in the Satyagraha Ashram. In the order he lists them, they are (1) Truth, (2) prayer, (3) *ahimsa* or love (*ahimsa* is the principle of non-harm to any living thing), (4) *brahmacharya* or chastity (which for Gandhi means control of all the senses), (5) non-stealing and non-possession or poverty, (6) bread labor, (7) *swadeshi* (production and consumption of locally produced goods only), (8) removal of untouchability, (9) a commitment to agriculture, (10) a hesitant commitment to a dairy to provide milk for the ashram, (11) a commitment to education and a number of precepts regarding education, and finally, (12) *satyagraha*. The five major Jain vows are contained within the practices listed previously: *ahimsa*, *satya*, *brahmacharya*, *asteya* (non-stealing), and *aparagraha* (non-possession) (Sharma 2012: 4–9).

Gandhi left off writing his *History of the* Satyagraha *Ashram* just as he turned to discuss *satyagraha*. In what little he wrote explicitly about *satyagraha* in the *History* he says that "[t]he Ashram came into existence to seek the Truth by adhering to truthful conduct," and three times he uses the word *weapon* to describe one aspect of *satyagraha*. But he is quick to assert, too, that "man's adherence to truth is also *satyagraha*" (Gandhi 1999: vol. 56: 192). But why does he speak of *satyagraha* as a weapon?

Gandhi's *Satyagraha* as a Weapon

Gandhi, as we have seen, understood nonviolence was a way of life. It is an end in itself insofar a nonviolent life preserves Truth. But it is also a means to that end. Gandhi's refusal to move from his seat on the stagecoach is a simple example of this means: one perceives what one believes to be the Truth, one clings to it, even when others disagree, and one suffers for it, if necessary. But this means of clinging to truth, when well designed, is itself a strategy for helping others to see the Truth as one sees it. Gandhi's famous Salt March is a case in point.

Although the Salt March itself was in one sense a single action—a march to the sea to make salt—it was but one tactic of a larger strategy designed to enable Indians to recognize their own abilities to cling to Truth, to suffer if necessary for it, and to become empowered by their practice of clinging to Truth, of *satyagraha*. Gandhi's decision to march to the sea with approximately eighty other members of his ashram was an assertion of Gandhi's view of the Truth, that Britain had no right to tax Indians on salt. Rather than argue with the British about this, he gave them a choice, in essence, saying: Change the law, or I will make salt myself, and I will encourage others to do so. If you don't like it, you can punish me, but I hope that my suffering for what I believe will cause you to reconsider your position. I am willing to suffer for what I believe, but I am not willing to make you suffer for it.

The series of actions began with a letter that Gandhi wrote to Lord Irwin, the British viceroy of India. Near the beginning of the letter, Gandhi wrote:

> My personal faith is absolutely clear. I cannot intentionally hurt anything that lives, much less fellow human beings, even though they may do the greatest wrong to me and mine. Whilst, therefore, I hold the British rule to be a curse, I do not intend harm to a single Englishman or to any legitimate interest he may have in India.
> *Gandhi 1999: vol. 48: 362*

Later in the letter he continued:

> I know that in embarking on non-violence I shall be running what might fairly be termed a mad risk. But the victories of truth have never been won without risks, often of the gravest character. Conversion of a nation that has consciously or unconsciously preyed upon another, far more numerous, far more ancient and no less cultured than itself, is worth any amount of risk.
> *Gandhi 1999: vol. 48: 365–366*

Gandhi concludes the letter by indicating that unless Lord Irwin could see his way to taking steps to eliminate the salt tax, he intended to begin a march nine days later in defiance of the tax, which Gandhi argued posed an unfair and immoral burden on the poor of India especially. Irwin replied to Gandhi that he was sorry to see Gandhi contemplating an illegal action. And so, on at 6:30 a.m., March 12, 1930, Gandhi began the Salt March.

The march began at Gandhi's Sabarmati ashram, near Ahmedabad, with a group of about eighty people. Each of the twenty-four days that Gandhi marched, approximately ten miles each day, he stopped in one village in the morning and another in the evening and spoke to the inhabitants of the village. He arranged in advance to receive information about each village just prior to his arrival. The information included details about the numbers of men and women in the village, the numbers in each different religious and ethnic group, the amount of salt consumed in the village, the numbers of untouchables, the numbers of cattle, spinning wheels, and more. When he spoke, he spoke not just about salt but also of the importance of *swadeshi*, of religious tolerance, and of eliminating untouchability. The march ended near the sea at Dandi, north of Mumbai.

Gandhi had expected to be arrested prior to or during the march (see Gandhi 1999: vol. 48: 394). It didn't happen until a month after the conclusion of the march. Following his arrest, many of his followers, trained in nonviolence, launched a raid upon the Dharasana Salt Works, near where Gandhi's march had ended. Gandhi had intended to lead the raid, but his arrest interfered. The violence to which the nonviolent protesters were subjected at Dharasana roused the indignation of many, including Britons, against British rule in India. However, by this time

Gandhi had encouraged tens of thousands of Indians to begin making their own salt, and he had spoken to tens of thousands of Indians on the issues that he thought confronted Indians: independence from Britain, religious tolerance, *swadeshi*, and the elimination of untouchability. Salt-making and other forms of resistance by Indians continued across the country and led ultimately to a series of negotiations with Nehru and Gandhi over many months while they were both in different prisons. Eventually Gandhi was released from prison to attend a conference in London (Brown 1989: 236–254).

Gandhi's strategy—his weapon of *satyagraha*—was to pursue what he believed was correct, to encourage the British to accept his actions, and, if the British chose not to, to suffer the penalty for violating their law. He had acted similarly years earlier when he first established his ashram on the Sabarmati River. He had invited an untouchable family to live in the ashram. Some neighbors of the ashram objected, and donors ceased their donations (Jack 1956: 125–127). For Gandhi, in both these instances and in many more, it was simply a matter of pursuing Truth. But there was political strategy behind it all: a person willing to undergo suffering for one's beliefs is winsome to others, not so much to those who oppose those beliefs but more so to those who sit on the sidelines and have no strong commitments one way or another. They—and sometimes those who had previously opposed one's actions—are won over. And in being won over, the opposition loses support and the people nonviolently pursuing Truth gain in power, in influence, in credibility. The Salt March roused the conscience of the world and the spirit of countless Indians. It was daring; it was provocative, and it was nonviolent. The strength of Gandhi's Salt March strategy derived from the purity of his motives. He was out to convert people by example, not to defeat them by conquest. Gandhi thoroughly appreciated the potential of this dynamic, and he understood the strategy so well that he was sometimes viewed as being a politician in a religious posture rather than a religious man engaged in a politics. Regardless, the strategy worked well enough that it was adopted by civil rights activists in the United States in the 1940s, 1950s, 1960s, and beyond.

King

One of the leading civil rights activists in the United States since 1950 has been the Reverend James Lawson, a man who became friends with Martin Luther King, Jr. shortly after the Montgomery Bus Boycott ended in 1956. Lawson had spent time in India in the 1950s in an effort to understand Gandhi better, and he succeeded a few years later in convincing King to visit India. Says Lawson:

> Violence has a very simple dynamic. I make you suffer more than I suffer. I make you suffer until you cry, "Uncle!" Then you surrender. That's what a war is. It's violence. The difference with nonviolence is that we don't want to beat the opponent up. We don't think it does any good.
>
> *Ackerman and DuVall 2000*

In contrast, the dynamic of nonviolence, well understood by Lawson and Martin Luther King, Jr., who became friends in the late 1950s, is that of doing what one believes is right, what one wants to see happen, and suffering for it if necessary. This captures the strategy employed by Gandhi in the decades immediately before the civil rights movement accelerated in the U.S.

King employed this strategy quite successfully in the Montgomery Bus Boycott even though he wasn't the person who organized the boycott. As is well known, Negroes in Montgomery, Alabama took to walking or carpooling to work rather than accepting the indignity of being forced to sit in the backs of public buses. Their actions offered a choice to the city of Montgomery and the bus company: change your law or face our refusal to participate in the bus system. And in the end, although the city and state did not change their minds about the law, the self-suffering of the Negroes over the course of about a year helped to convince the Supreme Court of the United States to declare the city law a violation of the U.S. Constitution. King grasped the strategy well. On one January evening in 1956, just after his house had been bombed, a large crowd of angry Negroes gathered outside his home with sticks, guns, tools, anything that could be used as a weapon. They were ready to march on the white citizens of Montgomery. King assembled them in front of his house and spoke to them, saying:

> My wife and my baby are all right. I want you to go home and put down your weapons. We cannot solve this problem through retaliatory violence. We must meet violence with nonviolence. Remember the words of Jesus: "He who lives by the sword will perish by the sword." We must love our white brothers no matter what they do to us. We must make them know that we love them. Jesus still cries out across the centuries, "Love your enemies." That is what we must live by. We must meet hate with love. Remember, if I am stopped, this Movement will not stop, because God is with this Movement. Go home with this glowing faith and this radiant assurance.
>
> *King 1993: 119–120*

These remarks were extemporaneous, yet they capture perfectly the spirit of Gandhi's notion of *satyagraha*: do what we are doing because we believe it is right; suffer if necessary, but cling to Truth.

King pursued similar strategies in all his campaigns. For example, during the Birmingham campaign, which aimed to integrate the downtown businesses of Birmingham, Alabama, King's efforts deliberately provoked an excitable and racist police chief to arrest numerous protesters. But before the direct action began, King and others made good faith efforts to negotiate a solution to the segregation. Ultimately, though, with an uncompromising city government, and with his campaign out of money, King elected to get himself arrested and jailed as well. While in jail, he wrote on scraps of newspaper his famous "Letter from Birmingham Jail." In this letter King outlined four steps that must be a part of any nonviolent campaign (King, Jr. 2013: 105). They are, first, collection of the facts. This involves an aggrieved party gathering together the facts that led to the grievance. This is a step that Gandhi also regularly pursued, early on. Second, the aggrieved party should enter negotiations with those in position to alleviate the conditions that led to the grievance. Gandhi and King both pursued this avenue with vigor, always prior to and even during any subsequent protests or direct action. Third, the aggrieved party should undertake self-purification. For King, this involved impressing upon everyone the importance of nonviolence, of not striking back when struck. It involved training sessions where people who would be subjected to violence could practice not responding violently or provocatively to insults and beatings. It also involved heavy reliance upon religious and moral beliefs that it is more important to do what is right than to pursue what is materially beneficial. This understanding reflects the understandings of the *satyagraha* exemplars whom Gandhi held up: Socrates, Daniel, and Prahlad. Finally, and fourth, failing successful negotiations, direct action would be undertaken.

In subsequent years, the King Center expanded upon King's four steps and suggested these six steps (King Center 2014):

1. Information gathering. This is the same step that King originally named.
2. Education. This is an expansion on the first step, urging not just education of the aggrieved party but also education of a wider public as to the nature of the grievance.

3. Personal commitment. This is roughly the same step as King's self-purification, but it has a less spiritual overtone. It is also a way for leaders to assess the relative degrees of commitment among those in the aggrieved party.
4. Negotiation. Again, this is the same step King originally named.
5. Direct action. And again, this is the same step King originally named.
6. Reconciliation. Just as this was always part of Gandhi's approach, this was also always a part of King's approach, though he didn't mention it in his "Letter from Birmingham Jail."

Here, for example, is how King urged reconciliation following the Montgomery Bus Boycott:

> I would be terribly disappointed if anybody goes back to the buses bragging about we, the Negroes, have won a victory over the white people.... If that is a victory, it will be a victory for justice and a victory for goodwill and a victory for the forces of light.
> *King 1956a: n.p.*

And:

> Our duty in going back on the buses is to destroy this superior-inferior relationship.... It is our duty to act in the manner best designed to establish man's oneness.
> *King 1956b: n.p.*

King's strategic nonviolence was rooted in Christianity. He admired Gandhi and applied Gandhi's ideas to the racial situation in America because he saw that they were rooted in an ethic of love, *agape*, that was itself an intrinsic part of Christianity. He said:

> [Gandhi] was probably the first person in history to lift the love ethic of Jesus above mere interaction between individuals to a powerful effective social force on a large scale. Love, for Gandhi, was a potent instrument for social and collective transformation. It was in this Gandhian emphasis on love and nonviolence that I discovered the method for social reform that I had been seeking for so many months.
> *King, Jr. 1958: 96–97*

One of King's biographers described it this way: "Christ had furnished him with the spirit; now Gandhi had showed him how it could work" (Oates 1994: 32).

Gandhi, King, and *Satyagraha*

Gandhi and King are probably more similar than most realize, but there is one striking difference. Gandhi was already 36 or 37 years old when he undertook his first major nonviolence campaign. King was assassinated at age 39, by which time he had already helped lead the Montgomery Bus Boycott, the Albany campaign, the Birmingham and Selma campaigns, the Jacksonville campaign, and the Chicago campaign. He was in the midst of organizing the Poor People's March to Washington while assisting with the sanitation workers' strike in Memphis. All the while he was pastor at a church, first in Montgomery and then in Atlanta, where he gave weekly sermons. In short, he had accomplished much by the age at which Gandhi's major efforts were just getting underway. The differences between them that one is inclined to notice—Gandhi's relatively ascetic life and his communal life at an ashram, and his many varied concerns, from economics to the untouchables to disease eradication and *swadeshi*—were all activities of the second half of Gandhi's life, begun for the most part after the age of 36 or so. King, up until age 36 or so, had focused almost entirely on matters of segregation and racial injustice. However, in those final years of his short life King did widen that focus to much broader considerations—poverty, militarism, consumerism, all similar to Gandhi's later concerns.

So just as Gandhi had begun his life with concerns about the relative inequality of the Indians with respect to the British, King began his life with concerns about the relative inequality of Negroes with respect to white America. However, as Gandhi came to see, the inequality was symptomatic of a growing dependence on and desire for material goods produced outside of one's home community, symptomatic of viewing violence as a way of addressing social and economic problems. King, too, began to see this interconnectedness around the time he was awarded the Nobel Peace Prize in 1964. His receipt of that prize caused him to view his responsibilities in the world as wider than a responsibility only to the plight of African-Americans. So he also turned his attention to the Vietnam War, and in August of 1965 he spoke out against the war publicly for the first time. Many of his friends and allies urged him not to do so, and by the time he made his most famous speech against the war, on April 4, 1967, many civil rights movement leaders and others turned against him, worried that he jeopardized his own stature as a civil rights leader by taking a stand against the U.S. government, which had often been his ally in enforcing civil rights. Whitney Young, the leader of the Urban League, told King that his "speeches would cost the movement dearly when it came to White House support. [King responded that] 'what you're saying may get you a foundation grant, but it won't get you into the kingdom of heaven'" (Oates 1994: 432). Like Gandhi, King was committed to Truth, come what may. Had Gandhi been alive at the time, he likely would have added King to his list of exemplars of *satyagraha*.

The final campaign that King helped to organize in his life, the Poor People's Campaign, was his first national campaign, and it deliberately incorporated concerns of both whites and blacks. Like Gandhi, King was coming to see the interrelatedness of so many forms of violence. In his April 4, 1967, speech against the war in Vietnam, King said:

> We must rapidly begin the shift from a thing-oriented society to a person-oriented society. When machines and computers, profit motives and property rights, are considered more important than people, the giant triplets of racism, extreme materialism, and militarism are incapable of being conquered.
>
> King, Jr. 1967

It might just as easily have been Gandhi speaking. Both had recognized from their starts the evils of prejudice against certain classes of people. But both had moved from seeking acceptance from the powers-that-be in their cultures and from seeking material well-being to recognizing the dangers of people hungry to consume for the sake of consumption. Both had moved from hesitantly supporting wars that they thought were being fought for good causes to opposing war altogether. And what bound them together in their movement against these perceived evils was their commitment to Truth, which also bound them together in recognizing nonviolence as the only means by which Truth could be obtained.

Works Cited

Brown, J. M. (1989). *Gandhi: Prisoner of Hope*. New Haven: Yale University Press.
Gandhi, M. (1999). *The Collected Works of Mahatma Gandhi* (Electronic Book), 98 vols. New Delhi: Publications Division Government of India. Available at: www.gandhiashramsevagram.org/gandhi-literature/collected-works-of-mahatma-gandhi-volume-1-to-98.php (Accessed 17 July 2017).

Holmes, R. L., and B. L. Gan. (2013). *Nonviolence in Theory and Practice*. Long Grove, IL: Waveland.
Jack, Homer A. (1956). *The Gandhi Reader*. New York: Grove Press.
King, C. S. (1993). *My Life with Martin Luther King, Jr.* New York: Henry Holt.
King, Jr., M. L. (1956a). "Address to Holt Street Baptist Church." Available at: https://kinginstitute.stanford.edu/king-papers/documents/address-mia-mass-meeting-holt-street-baptist-church (Accessed 17 July 2017).
King, Jr., M. L. (1956b). "We Are Still Walking." Available at: https://kinginstitute.stanford.edu/king-papers/documents/we-are-still-walking (Accessed 17 July 2017).
King, Jr., M. L. (1958). *Stride Toward Freedom: The Montgomery Story*. New York: Harper & Row.
King, Jr., M. L. (1967). "Beyond Vietnam: A Time to Break the Silence," delivered April 4, at the New York: Riverside Church. Available at: http://kingencyclopedia.stanford.edu/encyclopedia/documentsentry/doc_beyond_vietnam.1.html (Accessed 14 January 2017).
King, Martin Luther, Jr., "Letter from Birmingham Jail," in *Nonviolence in Theory and Practice*, (2013) 3rd edition, edited by Robert L. Holmes and Barry L. Gan. Long Grove, Illinois: Waveland Press.
The King Center. (2014). "Six Steps of Nonviolent Social Change." Available at: www.thekingcenter.org/king-philosophy#sub3 (Accessed 10 October 2016).
Lawson, J. (2000). "Nashville," segment from Peter Ackerman, and Jack DuVall, *A Force More Powerful*, produced by Steve York, PBS.
Oates, S. B. (1994). *Let the Trumpet Sound: A Life of Martin Luther King, Jr.* New York: Harper.
Oxford Dictionary of English. (2010). Oxford: Oxford University Press.
Sharma, I. C. (2012). "The Ethics of Jainism," in R.L. Holmes and B.L. Gan (eds.), *Nonviolence in Theory and Practice*, 3rd ed. Long Grove, IL: Waveland Press.

Further Reading

Cicovacki, P. (2015). *Gandhi's Footprints*. New Brunswick, NJ: Transaction Publishers. (Considers Gandhi's legacy and spiritual teachings.)
Gan, B. L. (2013). *Violence and Nonviolence: An Introduction*. Lanham, MD: Rowman and Littlefield. (Provides a detailed account of the difference between strategic (selective) nonviolence and nonviolence as a comprehensive way of life.)
Gandhi, M. (1993). *An Autobiography: The Story of My Experiments with Truth*. Boston: Beacon Press. (Gandhi's account of his path to nonviolence.)
King, Jr., M. L. (1986). *A Testament of Hope: The Essential Writings and Speeches of Martin Luther King, Jr.*, edited by J. Washington. New York: Harper Collins. (A compilation of texts by King.)

PART II

Conceptual and Moral Considerations

9
PACIFISM AND THE CONCEPT OF MORALITY

Robert L. Holmes

This chapter seeks to clarify the relationship of pacifism to the concept of morality, and thereby to clarify the issues dividing pacifists and warists. It does so, first, by clarifying what pacifism is; second, by showing the importance of the distinction between individuals and collectivities to the problem of war; and third, by clarifying the concept of morality. There has evolved the idea that different moralities apply to the conduct of individuals and collectivities, and that when they conflict, as they seem clearly to do in the case of war, collective morality supersedes individual morality. I shall argue that there is no reason to postulate a collective morality. The conduct of nation states (the collectivity mainly relevant to the problem of war) is simply the conduct of appropriately authorized individuals within the state. The killing and destruction of war must therefore be justified by the actions of the individuals who authorize, support and engage in war, and they have a moral responsibility to produce that justification. To try to justify the collective violence of war by reference to a collective morality, as the just war theory implicitly does, violates the very concept of morality. Morality, I propose, is a perspective from which to guide the conduct of individual persons and to foster the good, not of any particular nation state, or even of a collection of nation states, but of humankind the world over.

The earliest declaration of an essentially pacifist position was probably by the ancient Chinese philosopher Mo Tzu, who wrote that to obey the will of Heaven "is to use righteousness [as opposed to force] as the method of control." If that is done, he said, "a ruler of a big state will not attack a small state. A ruler of a large family will not usurp a small family. The strong will not plunder the weak" (Chan 1963: 220). Contemporary pacifism need not be grounded in religion, as Mo Tzu's was, and may be defended as an essentially ethical or philosophical position. I shall take it to be a nonreligious opposition to war that does not necessarily involve a broader commitment to nonviolence, but much of what follows could readily be adapted to religious pacifism and principled nonviolence.

All wars cause death and destruction, and most leave ruin, dislocation and injustice in their wake as well. Because these are incompatible with peace in any meaningful sense, contemporary pacifism seeks a peace that goes beyond the mere absence of war. It seeks a positive peace, which can be understood as a world that embodies justice, prosperity and the highest good for all. Pacifism is not passivism. Because it contextualizes war rather than abstracting it from its overall effect on the quality of human life, pacifism cannot fully be understood apart from the concept of morality.

If pacifism is taken as an active commitment to promoting positive peace, the gap between pacifism and warism narrows. "Warism" is Duane Cady's term for the view that some wars are morally justified in principle and in fact (Cady 2010: 17). Since most warists support the promotion of the good of their own society (usually characterized as national interest), the difference between warists and pacifists to that extent concerns the means to that end, warists contending and pacifists denying that the good in question sometimes requires going to war. Promotion of the broader end of global peace, as opposed to simply the national interest of one's own country, still separates pacifists from most warists.

Although sometimes used interchangeably with pacifism, *pacificism* holds only that war can and should be abolished (see Holmes 2017: 241–243). It does not entail pacifism. One might think that war should be abolished but that until such time as that can be achieved, wars may justifiably be fought, which is consistent with warism. The other component of pacificism—the view that war *can* be abolished—is a factual claim. On the assumption that should (or ought) implies can, that factual claim is presupposed by the first component.[1] That is, it makes sense to hold that war should be abolished only if it can be abolished. Pacifists and pacificists agree that war can be abolished. But pacifists say in addition that war in the modern world is impermissible, which is not necessarily held by pacificists.

Pacifism as a global perspective also contrasts with purely personal pacifism, which is a refusal to participate in war that does not necessarily extend to opposing the participation of others. There might be many reasons for such a position. Just as one might think that gambling, recreational drug use and skydiving are justifiable but avoid them because of the risks, so one might think that war is justifiable but for prudential reasons not want to be part of it. Such prudential pacifism, as it might be called, is grounded in the fact that it is arguably in one's self-interest not to be killed in war, and the risk of that happening is obviously greater if one goes to war than if one does not. Even if you refuse to participate in war because you believe it is wrong, you might refrain from judging that others should do likewise because you think that responsible persons should make up their own minds on issues as momentous as whether to kill other human beings. However, if you are a member of the clergy and clergy are exempt from war, you might hold that one need not (and perhaps ought not) participate in war even though others may do so. Other biblical grounds for exemption from war include everything from the fact that one has built a house, planted a new vineyard or become engaged, to the fact that one is just plain faint-hearted (Deuteronomy 20). Faint-hearted people are not necessarily pacifists, but they do not make good soldiers.

An individual can participate in war or not, but an individual cannot—*as* an individual—wage a war, any more than an individual alone can sing a duet or perform a symphony. That can only be done by a group. Other than in attenuated or metaphorical senses, war is the organized, systematic use of force by groups to try to resolve their differences by killing. They tacitly consent to this. War is a cooperative undertaking of collectivities. The paradigm case of war is the mutual infliction of death and destruction by the armies of states whose governments seek thereby to attain their ends. Trying to attain one's ends, as Clausewitz saw, means trying to compel an adversary to comply with one's will, which usually means forcing him or her to yield, surrender or sue for peace. But it may not. Some wars are genocidal in intent, as were some of the Old Testament wars where the aim was the annihilation and extermination of an enemy (see Deuteronomy 20–22). Few wars in the modern world have that express intent, though enemies often impute it to one another, and even fewer, if any, have been successful in actually killing every last member of a target group. As one moves away from the paradigm of interstate war, the boundaries of the concept of war begin to blur, giving rise to different conceptions of war (such as limited war, conventional and nuclear war, and guerilla war) to the point where it becomes unclear whether the violence in question constitutes war any longer. Because the relevant moral issues are clearest in war between states, that will be our focus.

Social Ontology and the Value of Collectivities

The foregoing considerations make clear that in thinking about war there is an important distinction between the individual and the collectivity. The distinction involves many complexities, but we can sketch its relevance to the problem of war. The rudimentary collectivity is the family. It probably antedates larger groups that emerged as humankind evolved. These include (not necessarily in this order) tribes, clans, villages, towns, cities, societies and states. The relationship of the individual to collectivities became complex as subgroups formed within the larger groups, particularly in the case of societies and states. An individual today can be a member of many groups, often with varying degrees of attachment to them and with different responsibilities and privileges determined by the roles played in them. In addition to being a citizen, one can, among other things, be single or married; Christian, Jew or Muslim; and Republican or Democrat, as well as make a living in callings as divergent as law enforcement, teaching or trash collecting.

At some point collectivities were deemed to have value. That value typically consisted in their role in helping to promote the security of the individuals making them up. But with the enlargement of collectivities, the individuals whose interests the collectivity served were often only a subset of all those who made up the collectivity. In ancient Greek city-states the well-being of citizens (not slaves) was paramount; in the Middle Ages it was that of the nobility (not serfs). With the rise of nation-states, monarchs and their families were initially privileged. For that reason, the preservation of autocracy became paramount, particularly following the American and French Revolutions, when the "people" were perceived as a threat to the established social order. But even in America, the foremost democracy, white males were privileged, not women or slaves. For Nazis it was Aryans, for white supremacists the white race, and for communists the world proletariat whose interests dominated. Within religion, the Israelites are a biblically chosen people, and both religious and secular Zionism promote the interests of the Jewish people. Genders are also deemed to have rights, as implied in Mary Wollstonecraft's eighteenth-century work *Vindication of the Rights of Woman*. The conviction that the collectivity one most strongly identifies with should be protected and preserved, if not given privileged treatment, provides a major source of conflict among those identifying with divergent collectivities.

In the modern world, ever-larger collectivities came to be seen as invested not only with value but also with *interests, rights* and *duties*. As modern nation states formed, they were deemed to have rights superseding those of individual persons. This had long been true of villages, communities and even families (as evident in so-called honor killings). But with the advent of nation states, the number of individuals over whom the collectivity is deemed to have rights rose to hundreds of thousands and in some cases hundreds of millions. Matters become even more complex when states themselves became members of even larger collectivities. By the turn of the nineteenth century, the idea had taken hold that all states—not just those that voluntarily assumed obligations in the manner of the Holy Alliance—are subject to obligations and duties to other states. These obligations and duties are not necessarily rooted in individual or Christian morality. They are grounded in alleged group rights possessed by larger collectivities whose members are states. A prescient analysis in 1900 effectively makes this point in anticipating much of the current preoccupation with humanitarian intervention:

> The practice [of intervention] shows clearly that states have proceeded from the basis of a group right; the higher interests of the community of nations as opposed to those

> of the individual political unit.... They have assumed that the society of states has certain rights which each state is bound to respect. Their action is based on the principle that there are certain obligations which states owe to each other, and which no state is at liberty to violate ... and that the practice of intervention is a means admissible for enforcing these higher claims against the individual state.
>
> Lingelbach 1900: 29

It remained only for intervention to be limited to the prevention or termination of gross human rights violations to provide the foundation for humanitarian military intervention in the late twentieth and early twenty-first centuries.

Today, the organizations to which states are thought to have obligations include such organizations as the UN, NATO or the European Union. Such organizations represent groups of collectivities. This socio/political/metaphysical ramification is presumed to confer the rights of mega-collectivities over the particular collectivities that make them up. Not only is the state thought to have rights over individual persons residing within its territory, it is presumed to have rights with regard to other states and they with regard to it.

Individual and Collective Moralities

As states were conceptualized to have rights, duties and interests, the idea emerged of two moralities, one governing the conduct of individuals, the other governing the conduct of states—an *individual morality* and a *collective morality*. Today, states as well as individuals are presumed to act rightly or wrongly and to have rights and obligations. The standards of right and wrong, and the rights and obligations, are often at variance with those of individuals. The right to kill millions of people with weapons of mass destruction if deemed necessary is claimed by many states (and the capacity to do so is coveted by states that do not have that capacity) but not by individuals.[2] On the other hand, virtues like patience, love and forgiveness are valued by individuals but not by states. And as states come to be thought of as having national interests, those interests also readily conflict with the interests of individuals. When that happens, the interests of the state are often thought to override those of the individual. This is particularly true in fascist philosophies but is characteristic even of some just war philosophies. In supreme emergencies, it has been said, the rights of innocent persons may be overridden in order to preserve the state.

Every state arrogates to itself rights over its subjects.[3] Rights are entitlements. Every state considers itself entitled to make demands (e.g., to pay taxes), set prohibitions (e.g., against treason) and impose penalties (e.g., imprisonment or death). But if a state also has rights with regard to other states (such as a right to self-defense as stipulated in Article 51 of the UN Charter), then it may sometimes kill the subjects of other states in the course of exercising that right. This is not usually expressed as a right over the individual subjects of other states, but it is tantamount to having such a right. In the case of war, it may consider itself entitled to kill them (or such of them as are under arms), just as it may, if it has a death penalty, kill individual members of its own state or others within its jurisdiction. There are virtually no acts that a state can undertake vis-à-vis other states that do not affect individual subjects of those states. The command of collective violence is part of the very conception of the modern nation state. It is called law enforcement when directed against its own subjects, and war when directed against other states. In the case of law enforcement, it is intended to prevent, curtail or punish the performance of specific wrongs. In the case of war, it is intended to punish the violation of rights, provide for self-defense, or—increasingly in the twenty-first century—to avert humanitarian disasters to others. In both cases, the state's presumed right of collective self-defense is a major justification for the use of violence.

However, it is one thing to note how historically the state has come to be viewed as governed by a different morality from individuals. It is another to show that such a view is justified. Let us assume for the moment that a different morality does apply to states than to individuals. We may then distinguish three theses.

The first thesis is:

1. *The state should conduct itself by the same morality as individuals.*

This claim does not specifically affirm that there are two moralities. It only entails that collective morality, if there is such a thing, should be set aside in favor of individual morality when it comes to the conduct of states. This was set forth explicitly, perhaps for the first time, by Czar Alexander I in the Holy Alliance among Russia, Austria and Prussia in 1815 at the end of the Napoleonic War. He proclaimed the determination of Russia and its allies "to adopt no other rule of conduct, either in the government of their respective countries, or in their political relations with other governments than the precepts of the holy religion [Christianity] of justice, charity, and peace." He stated further that these principles, "far from being applicable exclusively to private life, ought on the contrary to control the resolutions of princes, and to guide their steps as the sole means of establishing human institutions" (Hazen 1928: 11). Although the Czar did not specifically identify two moralities as such, his proclamation reflects an awareness of the essentials of the distinction between them.

The second thesis says:

2. *Individual morality overrides the collective morality of the state if the two conflict.*

This claim presumes that there are two moralities and implies that the state may properly be governed by collective morality unless or until such time as that morality conflicts with individual morality. If the two conflict, individual morality takes precedence. It would be difficult to justify war if one accepts thesis (1) or (2). Caring, compassion, honesty, truthfulness, trust, respect for persons, regard for the right to life and respect for property are among the values of individual morality. Killing, destruction, treachery, lying, secrecy, spying and a willingness to countenance the killing of innocents are all features of war. These directly conflict with individual morality. If one contends that there are two moralities and wants to justify war, then one must, at the least, hold that collective morality predominates in the case of war.

We may represent that as a third thesis:

3. *The collective morality of the state overrides individual morality if the two conflict.*

German historian Heinrich Treitschke repudiated both (1) and (2) in the later nineteenth century, whereas US president Woodrow Wilson reaffirmed at least (2) and possibly (1) in the early decades of the twentieth century. Realists, for their part, in the nineteenth and twentieth centuries, scoffed at both (1) and (2), which they considered naïvely idealistic, and some of them would reject (3) as well, insofar as it implies that morality applies to states. Realism holds that morality is either inapplicable to states or applicable but of limited or no relevance.

With respect to war, the justification of collective violence has been endowed with the sanctity of a moral theory. It is the just war theory (JWT). In that theory, it is the *state* (i.e., the collectivity) that must have a just cause, legitimate authority and right intention, and which must proceed with proportionality as a last resort; and it is the state that must conduct war with discrimination and proportionality. Individual soldiers do the killing. But the circumstances in which they do their killing determine whether the war (as waged by their state) is a just war. And it is whether the state is fighting a just war that is the main concern. Just war theorists evaluate war in this light. Pacifists, if they were to accept the view that there are two moralities, would accept (1) or (2) and reject (3).

We have been assuming for the sake of argument that there are two moralities. It is time to examine that claim more closely. Specifically, we want to ask whether there is such a thing as collective morality. To answer this requires clarifying the very concept of morality.

The Concept of Morality

The term "moral," as others have noted, is ambiguous. It can be used to contrast with immoral, as in "that was the moral thing to do," in which case it is roughly synonymous with morally right. But it can also be used to contrast with nonmoral, as in "moral considerations outweigh prudential considerations." In that case it sets moral considerations off from other sets of consideration used to judge acts, such as those of law, religion, etiquette or prudence. A related but distinguishable ambiguity attends the use of the noun "morality." When preceded by the definite article, as in "the morality of abortion" or "the morality of capital punishment," it sometimes implies an endorsement of those practices, as though their rightness were presumed. At other times, it simply refers to the moral considerations relevant to assessing whether those practices are right or wrong. Thus, the phrase "the morality of war" might be taken to mean the presumed rightness or justifiability of war or to mean the considerations relevant to deciding *whether* war is right or wrong.

By contrast, when preceded by the indefinite article, as in "a morality of self-sacrifice," the term often refers to whatever values or principles characterize a particular group. In this sense, there may be many moralities of a collective sort: the morality of the Homeric age, of Periclean Athens, or Sparta, and of Taoist and Confucian moralities in ancient China. When Lenin said that young people should be taught communist morality, he implied that there was more than one kind of morality and that communist morality was superior to the others. The phrase "honor among thieves" implies that there is a morality of sorts among thieves, just as there clearly is a set of values and duties among the Mafia, at least as portrayed by the entertainment industry.

A morality, in this sense, is empirically verifiable. It is the accepted values and practices of a group. They can be studied and the moralities of different groups compared and contrasted. To do so is the business of anthropology and descriptive ethics. In this descriptive sense it is perfectly intelligible to speak of collective morality.

In social groups of any appreciable size, morality in this sense may be called a tribal morality. Tribal morality has two dimensions. One governs the interpersonal relations of members of the group (the in-group) to one another. The other governs the relations of the group as a whole to other groups (the out-groups). Anthropologist Frantz Boaz sums this up as follows:

> The one outstanding fact is that every human society has two distinct ethical standards, the one for the in-group, the other for the out-group. Everybody has close association with some group, however, constituted, and as such has certain duties to other members of the group. The ethical standards in the group, as long as a person is a member of that group, are the same everywhere. Murder, theft, lying find expression in every language. The concepts of "must" and "ought" . . . are probably universal. Co-operation of some sort always exists; so does subjection to a code of behavior that makes living together bearable. . . . Outside of the group the standards are entirely different. Murder,

theft, and lying, which are condemned in the in-group, are commendable insofar as they help to protect the interests of one's own group.

Boaz 1938: 22

What Boaz calls ethical standards are two dimensions of tribal morality, one governing the in-group and the other governing relations to the out-group. We may refer to them respectively as TM_1 and TM_2. If anthropologists are correct, every social group has these two moralities. TM_1 harmonizes the relations among individuals within the group, enabling them to live peacefully together. TM_2 effectively defines the group's relationship to other collectivities, its end being first and foremost the survival and self-interest of the group as a whole. TM_2 may involve cooperation with other groups, but historically it often has meant competition, struggle and warfare against them. And the values of the two differ markedly. Friendship, promise-keeping and honesty are valued by the in-group. Hostility, mendacity and violence are practiced when necessary toward out-groups.

The preceding are metaethical observations. Normative ethics enters the picture when one asks what *ought* to be the morality of a group that has a tribal morality. That TM_1 governs the relations among the in-group does not entail that it ought to. Nor does the fact that TM_2 governs the relations of the group to outside groups entail that it ought to. The fact that one can intelligibly ask such questions suggests that there is another morality in the background here, one that is more comprehensive than tribal morality in either of its dimensions. In this sense, we can speak of morality per se: the idea or concept of morality (M_3). Here we might cite, for example, W.K. Frankena's analysis in "The Concept of Morality" (Frankena 1976: 125–133). Tribal morality is culturally relative. M_3 is universal. It purports to govern the conduct of everyone, wherever they are and whatever society or cultural group they belong to. In this sense there is but one morality, not many. Subjectively M_3 represents a point of view that one may or may not adopt, but that if one does adopt gives weight—and perhaps final and authoritative weight—to certain kinds of considerations in one's conduct.

How these considerations are understood from an objective standpoint provides grist for moral philosophy. We see taking shape here the deontological and axiological perspectives and their permutations in utilitarianism, Kantianism, rights-based theories and virtue ethics.

If we accept the notion of a universal morality (M_3) in addition to the two versions of tribal morality, we can ask how it relates to the question of whether there is a collective as well as an individual morality. Who or what is governed by that one universal morality (M_3)? May it not prescribe one set of values and principles for states and another for individuals and hence support the idea of two moralities (individual and collective)? There is a measure of truth behind this suggestion. But only a measure. Perhaps the strongest argument for this position lies in the obligations associated with certain roles within society. It is often argued, for example, that corporations have duties to stockholders to maximize profits, and that to discharge these duties they may have to do things—like exacerbate inequalities in wealth—that seem unjust from the perspective of individual morality. And it might be argued that the state has a duty to defend its citizens, and that doing so sometimes requires going to war even though war conflicts with the tenets of individual morality.

Let us consider how those judgments should be understood. They cannot intelligibly be taken to mean that corporations and states act on their own, independently of individuals, or have duties independently of the duties of individuals. When we say that corporations have duties to stockholders, what this means is that certain persons holding management positions in corporations have duties defined by their roles (perhaps even included in their job descriptions), and these require trying to maximize profits. And when the state is said to have duties toward its citizens, what is meant is that certain individuals in government or the military have duties associated with their roles, and that sometimes fulfilling those duties requires going to war. When those decisions are made and acted upon, the state is said to go to war. But the decisions are those of individual persons, and the acts executing those decisions are those of individual persons. All of those decisions and acts are governed by morality per se. Only moral agents—conscious, living, rational beings—are governed by morality. Remove those qualities, which entail the capacity to act morally, and morality no longer applies. States do not have those properties. No state is a conscious living being. Lacking the necessary capacities to be moral agents, states *as collectivities* can no more be guided by morality than can rocks or oysters. We do speak of states acting. But that is merely shorthand for the actions of individual persons appropriately credentialed within the state to represent others. There is no action by any state at any time that is not the action of some individual or individuals having the appropriate social, political or legal relationship to others. Their acts count as acts of the state. There is nothing but their actions (and the actions of those who follow their orders or enact their policies).

So, we can explain everything we need to explain about the moral obligations of corporate managers and government and military leaders without postulating a separate morality either for them or for the collectivities they represent. This does not tell us one way or the other on the issue of precisely what they may justifiably do. Capitalists can argue that corporate managers are justified in maximizing profits at the expense of the poor, and socialists can argue that they are not. Warists can argue that government leaders and soldiers are justified in the killing and destruction they inflict, and pacifists can argue that they are not. All of this can be accommodated within M_3. There is no need to postulate a collective morality to try to justify the acts in question.

That every action is governed by morality does not mean that every action is *guided* by morality, any more than the fact that every use of a gun is governed by law means that every use of a gun is guided by law. The freedom and autonomy of moral agents allows them to ignore morality if they choose. Those who do so are amoral, but that does not exempt their conduct from being subject to moral judgment. One can be amoral and still immoral. It is even arguable that to disregard morality willfully is in itself immoral. One can choose to ignore morality, but one cannot choose not to be subject to it.

More specifically, primary acts are those of individual, conscious rational beings. Secondary acts are those of entities like groups or collectivities that devolve into primary acts. When we say that Iraq invaded Kuwait in 1990, or that the US attacked Iraq in 2003, we are talking about the acts of nation states. They are secondary acts. There is nothing to them beyond the actions of the individual heads of state who ordered the actions and those who supported and carried them out. Those are all primary acts, undertaken by conscious rational beings. Just as the acts of states are only secondary and explainable in terms of the primary acts of individual persons, so the acts of states are morally assessable only derivatively, in terms of the assessments of the acts of individuals. The acts of individual moral agents are basically assessable from a moral standpoint. They are, every one of them, right or wrong. The acts of states are morally assessable *only* derivatively, in terms of the acts of the individuals whose acts they consist of.

To sharpen the differences between morality per se and the two dimensions of tribal morality, I propose the following account of morality per se (M_3). In terms of our earlier distinctions, these represent criteria that are necessary for a frame of reference to be moral as opposed to nonmoral.

1. Morality extends to all conduct of rational agents, rendering that conduct in principle subject to moral assessment.
2. Morality precludes the possibility of incompatible moral judgments being correct at the same time.

3. Morality allows that ethical disagreements are always in principle capable of rational resolution, so that with sufficient factual knowledge and conceptual clarity it can be shown of disputants that

   a. one is mistaken,
   b. both are mistaken, or
   c. both are correct but actually judging of different things.

4. Morality is distinguishable from etiquette, law, religion and egoism.
5. Morality entails that moral considerations override all others.

As with most of philosophy, all of these are contestable. Statements (2) and (5) are particularly controversial, and I shall not argue for them here. The point is that these represent the essentials of a conception of morality—what I am calling morality per se—that is distinguishable from tribal morality. Tribal morality is culturally relative. Ethical relativism holds that what is morally right or wrong (as opposed to what is merely thought to be right or wrong) may vary fundamentally from person to person or culture to culture. Tribal morality is a form of ethical relativism. According to it, incompatible cross-cultural judgments may both be correct at the same time and ethical disagreements in principle incapable of rational resolution. Even if Boaz is correct that TM_1 is held by all societies, its values, as part of tribal morality, hold only for the in-group of that society. On all of these counts morality per se differs from tribal morality.

There is therefore a fundamental problem in the notion of collective morality as it has evolved with regard to war. Insofar as morality is a coherent, rational perspective by which to try to foster the good of humankind and its environment, the collective violence of warfare—the intentional causing of harm, death and destruction to human beings on a large scale—does violence to the very concept of morality. That does not in itself suffice to show that war is wrong. But it does show that the very frame of reference by which the permissibility of war is commonly assessed is misconceived. There is but one morality. If war is to be justified, it must be justified by the actions of the particular individuals who initiate, fight and support wars—living, breathing, conscious and rational human beings. Only they, barring the existence of divinities or intelligent aliens, can be moral agents. States cannot.

This means that the JWT is deeply flawed. Insofar as the JWT is intended to judge the actions of states, it is wedded to the collectivist perspective. According to the JWT, it is the state that does or does not have legitimacy, the state that does or does not have a just cause and that meets or fails to meet the various conditions of JWT. Some awareness of this can be seen among more recent theorists who shift from talking only about states to talking about just and unjust warriors. This is on the right track. For every individual is responsible for the rightness or wrongness of what he or she does. Whether they are soldiers or heads of state, individuals are responsible for the rightness or wrongness of every human being they kill or are responsible for having killed. And they are responsible for the harm and destruction they cause or assist others in causing and for every piece of destruction they cause. It matters not whether they do these things singly or in concert with others. It is the full implications of individual responsibility in this sense that pacifism would have us accept.

The Individual Perspective

There is a broader issue here. Metaphorically put, we always view the world through lenses of some sort. These include scientific, aesthetic, economic and moral lenses. Such lenses organize the world in terms of concepts of one sort or another. The concepts of space, time and causality, as Kant saw, are among the most fundamental of concepts, and we are so constituted as to be incapable of doing without them in our everyday lives. But nothing compels us to wear one set of lenses always to the exclusion of others. A few put on scientific lenses and view the world as governed by laws of nature only, or more specifically by the categories of relativity or quantum theory. Some view the social world in economic terms, as a set of interactions governed by the interplay of groups and socio-economic-financial structures. Others view the world through aesthetic lenses, in which beauty predominates, whether in the form of poetry, music or art, to whose expression they devote their lives. Some, like Pythagoras, conceptualize the world in mathematical terms; others, like Democritus, in material terms. Heraclitus sees it as a place of continual struggle.

Moral considerations do not apply to the interactions of atoms and subatomic particles or to the actions of chemicals or the movements of galaxies. Somewhere in between these—somewhere between the micro level of subatomic particles and the macro level of galaxies—are persons and their social and natural environments. These include the societies and nation states they have formed over millennia. Morality applies here if it applies anywhere. The categories of states and collectivities have evolved as a way of organizing our experience of the increasingly complex social and international world. They represent what may be called a social Kantianism. The concepts of states, races, and religious and ethnic or political groups operate in the social world in much the way in which space, time and causality do for Kant at the subjective level. Just war theory is one way of adapting one dimension of that world to morality. It is one way of making sense of warfare. But it is not the only way. Instead of focusing on such concepts as states, national interests, balance of power and deterrence, we can focus upon *individuals, children, families, the innocent, victims* and *human beings*. These also represent ways of conceptualizing, organizing and thinking about our experience of the world. And they lead directly to a different set of moral considerations than the just war theory. Philosophical pacifism argues for a reconceptualization not only of war, but of the broader, global social order. It makes individual persons, not states, the primary concern—not governments, corporations and other collectivities. It places the emphasis first and foremost on caring, compassion, sympathy, empathy and cooperation among individual persons. These qualities are foremost, not those of power and national interest. From the pacifist perspective, when collective actions are undertaken—as they unavoidably are, given the complexities of our social world—it is not national interest that is foremost, but the well-being of individual human beings. The relevant groups are children, mothers, fathers, families, the poor, the innocent, whoever they are, wherever they are and within whatever national boundaries they happen to fall. For many the relevant concerns extend to animals and the environment as well. A concern for the individuals comprising these groups—whatever other collectivities, such as states or races or religions they belong to—can be at the center of our thinking. It can be our starting point in making moral assessments. We do not have to start here. But we are free to do so. It is a matter of choice.

In conclusion, pacifism seeks a global peace beyond the mere absence of war. It sees this as morally required. It places full moral responsibility upon individuals for the decision they make as members of states. One cannot justify wars as the actions of collectivities governed by a different morality from individuals. States are not conscious moral agents. They do not literally act. They act only in a secondary sense, explicable in terms of the actions of individual persons with appropriate authorization with the state. Since only the actions of conscious rational beings are morally assessable, the actions of states are morally assessable only in a derivative sense. The rightness or wrongness of what they are said to do is always reducible to the rightness or wrongness of the acts of the particular individuals who authorize, carry out and support the policies of the state. This does not in itself settle the issue between pacifism and warism. But it does mean, if correct, that whether war can be morally justified depends upon whether the harm and death inflicted by individual human beings on one another in war can be morally justified.

Notes

1 The thesis that ought implies can is shorthand for the claim (put simply) that a person can be morally obligated to do something only if it is something that he or she can do.
2 I say this mindful that terrorist groups, and even some individuals, seek to kill large numbers of people, and might well do so with weapons of mass destruction if they were available. But this does not alter the fact that such acts are dramatically at variance with the standard values and principles of individual morality. They are not at variance with collective morality; indeed the capacity in question is highly prized as a means of deterrence. It must be said, however, that although many states strive mightily to acquire weapons of mass destruction, some do not.
3 I shall speak of subjects for the sake of simplicity, intending the term to cover citizens, residents, visitors and others subject to the supposed jurisdiction of the state.

Works Cited

Boaz, F. (1938). *What I Believe: The Personal Philosophies of Certain Eminent Men and Women of Our Time*, edited by C. Fadiman. New York: Simon and Schuster.
Cady, D. (2004). "The Challenge of Peace," in S. Hasmi and S. Lee (eds.), *Ethics and Weapons of Mass Destruction*. Cambridge: Cambridge University Press, 470–482.
Cady, D. (2010). *From Warism to Pacifism*, 2nd ed. Philadelphia: Temple University Press.
Chan, W. (ed.) (1963). "Mo Tzu's Doctrines of Universal Love, Heaven, and Social Welfare," in *A Sourcebook in Chinese Philosophy*. Princeton: Princeton University Press, 211–232.
Frankena, W. K. (1976). *Perspectives on Morality: Essays by William K. Frankena*, edited by K.E. Goodpaster. Notre Dame: University of Notre Dame Press.
Hazen, C. D. (1928). *Europe Since 1815* (Special Revised Edition 1815–1914). New York: Henry Holt and Company, 11.
Holmes, R. L. (2017). *Pacifism: A Philosophy of Nonviolence*. London: Bloomsbury.
Lingelbach, W. E. (1900). "The Doctrine and Practice of Intervention in Europe." *Annals of the American Academy of Political and Social Science* July, 1–32.

Further Reading

Brimlow, R. W. (2006). *What About Hitler? Wrestling with Jesus's Call to Nonviolence in an Evil World*. Grand Rapids, MI: Brazos Press. (A consideration of nonviolence as grounded in Christian teaching.)
Cady, D. (2010). *From Warism to Pacifism: A Moral Continuum*, 2nd ed. Philadelphia: Temple University Press. (An overview of the moral continuum that includes pacifism and positive peace.)
Fiala, A. (2008). *The Just War Myth: The Moral Illusion of War*. Lanham, MD: Rowman and Littlefield. (A critical account of the application of just war theory.)
Werner, R. (2007). "Pragmatism for Pacifists." *Contemporary Pragmatism* 4 (2), December: 93–115. (A critical, pragmatic argument against war and in favor of pacifism.)

10
PEACE
Negative and Positive

David Boersema

If asked to define "peace" most people end up saying something along the lines of it being the absence of war or violence. But this conception places violence as the central, basic concept, with peace being a secondary, derivative one. While concerns about being free *from* hostilities are, of course, important for peace, they reflect only what philosophers of peace call "negative peace," that is, peace in the sense of the absence of hostilities. But at least as important is "positive peace," the conditions for being free *to* fulfill one's potentials. Living in a state of poverty or prejudice or fear or degradation are forms of experiencing a life that is not peaceful. Murder is violent, but so, too, is starvation, at least for the person who is starving. Psychological, emotional, and economic abuses are experienced as violence just as much as physical blows are. To this extent, and for this reason, peace—especially peace as freedom *to* and not merely as freedom *from*—is intimately related to justice. Any genuine attempt to understand and promote peace requires addressing issues and questions of injustice, as both a form of violence and a cause of violence. This can include the pain that results from failure to fulfill one's potentials and aspirations, sometimes caused by direct harm or even injustice perpetrated by others that prevents that fulfillment.

One component that is relevant to understanding and addressing the complexity of peace is seeing the interrelations between *interpersonal* peace—peace with others—and *intrapersonal* peace—peace within oneself. It is difficult to have inner peace (within oneself) if one lives in a context of threats, intolerance, or discrimination. At the same time, it is difficult to get along with others and respond to conflict nonviolently if one lives in an inner state of confusion, humiliation, or rage. As Mohandas Gandhi noted, "It has always been a mystery to me how men can feel themselves honored by the humiliation of their fellow beings" and "I claim that human mind or human society is not divided into watertight compartments called social, political and religious. All act and react upon one another" (Gandhi 2017). To have a fuller understanding of peace in both the negative and positive senses, it is necessary to flesh out various conceptions and forms of both peace and violence, as well as to see how they relate to issues of justice, rights, and needs.

Basic Conceptions of Peace

In exploring the nature of peace, it is useful to distinguish three terms: conflict, violence, and force. Conflict involves incompatible desired outcomes. When two chess masters sit down to face each other, each one wants to win, but only one will; they have conflicting desired outcomes. This is conflict, but not violence nor force. Violence is one response to conflict, one form of behavior among many. There are others, such as negotiation, cooperation, compromise, changing perceptions, and even (nonviolent) persuasion. Nonviolent action can be forceful and, indeed, has been, as is witnessed by the work of Mohandas Gandhi in India and Nelson Mandela in South Africa. Violence is a form of force, but only one form; force is an energy or power used to bring about some change. While there is no single definition of violence with necessary and sufficient conditions, there are generally accepted and acknowledged aspects to violence: violence is force (whether physical or non-physical) used in a harmful or destructive way against some being that has an interest in not being harmed or destroyed. If one included the notion that, say, violence can be done to the environment, then having an interest in not being harmed or destroyed would need to be understood not in the sense of having an explicit, cognitive interest, but in the sense of being capable of suffering because of harmful or destructive actions.

Commonly, peace is typically taken to be a "secondary" concept, a derivative of the more primary concept of violence. That is to say, "peace" is typically defined as the absence of violence, rather than the other way around. Peace theorists have long spoken of peace as the absence of violence in a variety of ways. For example, they have distinguished between organized violence and unorganized violence, with peace subsequently defined along those terms. Organized violence, of course, includes war, whether between states or within them. Unorganized violence includes such direct, physical, personal violence as interpersonal killings, assaults, rapes, abuse, etc. In addition, there is structural violence, conditions or actions that are aspects of social structures or social institutions that—intentional or not—might harm people by preventing them from meeting their basic needs or interests. Such structures can be prevailing attitudes or practices, such as sexism, racism, ageism, etc., or they might be in the form of specific institutional policies or practices, such as discriminatory laws (e.g., ones that prohibit interracial marriage or require documentation of individuals based on religious affiliation).

The term "negative peace" is used, then, to speak of a state of affairs in which there is an absence of such violence, whether it is organized or unorganized. For instance, some would claim that, say, Canada is at peace today because it is not at war (that is, it is not engaged in organized violence). Others, however, claim that Canada is not really at peace because, although, yes, it is not explicitly at war with any other state, there still exists plenty of unorganized violence there. Not being openly at war, then, might be one form (or perhaps, let's say, a necessary condition) for Canada to experience negative peace, but it is not sufficient, because there is still a level of unorganized violence in Canada so that full negative peace does not exist there.

As we all know, however, there are other forms of violence besides and beyond direct, physical, personal violence. There are also indirect forms of violence that either shorten the life span of persons (or moral agents and patients) or that indirectly reduce the quality of life for them. There might be, for instance, social or economic structures in place that harm—directly or indirectly—the quality of life of persons (again, the notion of structural violence). This could be organized, in the sense of, say, restrictions of civil liberties or civil freedoms, or it could be unorganized in the sense of, say, a culture of racism or social practices that curtail opportunities for some persons. The term "positive peace" is used when speaking of the absence of these forms and types of indirect violence.

Underlying these two types or notions of peace—that is, negative peace and positive peace—are the works of the noted Norwegian peace theorist Johann Galtung. As a point of departure in speaking of peace, Galtung defines *violence* as a state in which "human beings are being influenced so that their actual somatic and mental realizations are below their potential realizations" (Galtung 1969: 167–191). Peace, then, would be a state in which those potentials are actualized.

This definition, or at least characterization, is the underpinning of the earlier notions of negative peace and positive peace. For Galtung, one's potentials are not realized, perhaps not even capable of being realized, in the context of war or other direct, physical violence. In addition, they are not realized, or perhaps even capable of being realized, in the context of social injustice and other forms of structural violence. People are no more at peace if they are threatened, intimidated, inappropriately discriminated against, barred from economic or educational opportunities, etc. than they are if they are physically attacked, for Galtung.

In addition to identifying violence as the differential between one's potentials and one's realizations, Galtung spells out six dimensions of violence that he claims can comprise this differential. One dimension is that of physical and non-physical (what he specifically identifies as psychological) violence. We all know that threats can be just as effective at times as actual attacks in influencing someone's behavior and actions. If a schoolyard bully can acquire another child's lunch money with a threat rather than with actually hitting and taking the money, the result is the same and the victim is just as much a victim (and, for Galtung, is just as much lacking in being at peace).

The second dimension of violence, for Galtung, is what he calls a negative vs. positive approach to influence. This is his way of speaking about negative vs. positive reinforcement, with negative reinforcement being punishment and positive reinforcement being reward. As with threats vs. attacks, rewards for "good" behavior (or policies) can bring about the same result as punishment for "bad" behavior. If the "good" behavior is in fact behavior that promotes (or fails to reduce) the differential between one's potentials and one's realizations, then that person, for Galtung, is not fully at peace.

A third dimension of violence focuses on whether or not there is an object that can be hurt. No one need actually be hurt for there to be a state of violence. Again, in cases of threats, no actual harm need occur for relevant agents to be subject to violence. Galtung remarks that the balance of power doctrine is based on efforts to obtain precisely this effect.

His fourth dimension is the flip side of the third; it focuses on whether or not there is a subject that acts to cause the violence. There might well be no specific actor or agent that causes the harm, even though harm is caused. For instance, economic structures and practices might well result in specific persons or groups being disadvantaged (and, hence, harmed in a way) without anyone (again, whether specific person or group) orchestrating the disadvantage. As Galtung puts it: if people are starving, violence is experienced, whether or not someone is trying to starve them.

Directly related to this concern is Galtung's fifth dimension of violence, namely, intended vs. unintended violence. As is often said, the road to hell is paved with good intentions. Some violence is and can be intended; other violence is and can happen even when not intended.

Finally, for Galtung, there is manifest and latent violence. Manifest, of course, is open, recognizable violence. Latent violence, on the other hand, is not open or directly recognized. As we all know, the prevalence, say, of biases or stereotypes can be latent yet harmful.

Action and Agents

Just as one speaks of negative peace as the absence of something (violence) and positive peace as the presence of something (conditions for the fulfillment of potentials), so too can one speak of positive and negative actions. A positive action is a case of something that is actually done or committed, whereas a negative action is a case of something not being done or committed. For instance, if one chooses to cast a vote during an election, that is a positive action, but if one chooses not to cast a vote during an election, that is a negative action. There are forms of not acting that are not the same thing as a negative action. If one does not cast a vote because one is a two-year-old child, that is a form of not acting, but it is not a negative action because casting votes is not within the arena of actions for a child. For an adult to choose not to vote, however, is a negative action. In the case of the adult, it is a choice to refrain from committing a positive action.

Positive actions are often referred to as acts of commission and negative actions are often referred to as acts of omission. The connection to peace and violence is that violence can occur—peace can be thwarted—by acts of omission just as much as by acts of commission. For example, if one strikes a child, that is an act of physical violence, or if one verbally berates a child that is an act of psychological or emotional violence. But if one simply ignores the physical or psychological or emotional needs of a child, that is also an act of violence, but an act of omission rather than an act of commission. Both moral theory and legal theory wrestle with acts of omission with respect to whether one can be found responsible (and to what extent) for such negative actions. If one commits a crime, for example, we assume that one is morally and legally responsible. But what if one "merely" witnesses a crime and does nothing about it? Again, how this relates to peace and violence is whether and to what extent violence can be a matter of not doing something (that is, omitting) as opposed to doing something (that is, committing).

Just as questions about the nature of actions (positive or negative) are relevant to peace and violence, so too is the question of who are the agents involved in those actions. Clearly, we identify particular individuals as relevant agents. Again, if I strike another person that is an act of violence that I have committed, or if I fail to help another person in a moment of need, that could be an act of violence that I am responsible for, since I omitted making a helpful positive action. However, we also identify other agents besides particular individuals, such as institutions or groups of people or whole nations or social structures. For instance, some have claimed that the legal system is structured in a way that is biased toward certain people. If this were true, it would be the system that is the agent of violence, not merely specific individual judges or other legal authorities. Or when we say that nations go to war, we do not mean specific individuals, but the social collective that we call "the nation."

With respect to peace and violence, just who the relevant agents are can obviously be important. The same action committed between two people might be one of violence depending upon who is involved. An insulting remark made by an adult to another adult could have a very different effect than that same insulting remark made by an adult to a child, and hence be an act of violence in one case but not necessarily in the other. This speaks to the importance of perspective as an element of peace and violence. The meaning of an action can be quite different depending upon context and upon the agents involved. We all recognize the difference between how an action is intended and how it is received. For example, one person might intend to say something as a joke, but the person hearing it might be offended. This can also be the case for acts of omission; one person might not greet another person upon meeting because that person is preoccupied, but the other person might take that failure of greeting as a snub. In both cases, the intended meaning is not the same as the received meaning. Where this can be relevant to peace and violence is in recognizing that an action—whether one of commission or omission—can be received as being violent even if it is not intended as such. And this relates back to agents of violence (or of peace). For instance, an institution—say an organization—in its hiring practices might not intend to be racist or sexist, but could be perceived as such because of who it actually hires over time.

Rights

A common and important approach to understanding peace and violence today is to relate these issues to the notions of rights and justice. With respect to rights, they fundamentally are the means we use to identify and secure either protections for us from the (possible) offenses of others, or empowerments for us to engage in the world. In the former case, rights function to say what others do not get to do; they protect us (for example, the right to be free of unreasonable search and seizure), while in the latter case, they function to say what we get to do; they empower us (for example, the right to freedom of expression). As will be noted later, these two functions relate directly to what are called negative rights and positive rights as well as to negative peace and positive peace.

We never merely "have a right," but we always have a right to something or other. That is to say, there is always some content to a right. That content involves some opportunities or goods or services. For example, if you have a right to the pursuit of happiness, it is understood not that you have the right to be happy but that you have the right to the opportunity to be happy. Or, to say that you have the right to be president of the United States someday really means that you have the right to try to become president. However, when we say that you have the right to an attorney, we do not simply mean that you have the right to try to get an attorney; rather, we mean that you have the right to the services (at least some) of an attorney. Likewise, if you have a right to an education, we do not simply mean that you have the right to try to get an education, but rather that you have the right to have some goods and services provided for you (such as books and teachers). Or if you have the right to health care, this is usually understood to mean not just that you can try to get health care, but that some goods and services need to be provided to you.

Rights entail duties on other agents; they regulate other agents' behavior. When your rights place a duty on other agents (or regulate the behavior of other agents) in the sense of requiring those other agents not to interfere with you, this is usually referred to as a negative right. All that this means is that other agents have the duty not to interfere with you; they just need to leave you alone. So, if you have the right to worship as you please, then the duty placed on others is to not do anything to interfere with you with respect to that. This is called a negative right because, in effect, the duty on others is negative; negative in the sense that nothing must be done (except to leave you alone).

By contrast, sometimes people claim that one agent's rights place duties on others that require some positive action by those others in order for that right to be realized. For example, earlier we noted that having a right to an attorney requires that others (in this case, the state) provide the right holder with the services of an attorney. In this case, it is not enough to simply leave the right holder alone and do nothing. Doing nothing is not the same thing as providing an attorney. This sort of right, in which something must be provided to the right holder, is usually said to be a positive right. It is said to be a positive right because some positive action, not mere noninterference, is required in order for the right to be realized.

There are various kinds or levels of right, with some referred to as basic rights. That is, there are some rights that are fundamental and necessary in order for other rights to be meaningful and even possible. For example, I have the right to vote, but that right presupposes and relies upon some other rights such as the right to self-determination and freedom of movement. But even those rights presuppose the more basic right of physical security. I cannot really exercise my right to vote if my personal security is at risk. I can talk about having a right, but enjoying that right is something else and requires physical security. While most everyone has argued for physical security as a basic right—and has seen physical security as a negative right, since the duty on you is simply to leave me alone—many have gone on to say that subsistence, or some minimum level of food, shelter, etc., is also a basic right. Subsistence rights are basic for exactly the same reasons that physical security rights are basic: no other rights are possible without them. The philosopher Henry Shue has remarked:

> No one can fully, if at all, enjoy any right that is supposedly protected by society if he or she lacks the essentials for a reasonably healthy and active life. Deficiencies in

the means of subsistence can be just as fatal, incapacitating, or painful as violations of physical security.

Shue 1996: 32

Subsistence rights, of course, are positive rights. Something (beyond noninterference) must be provided to an agent in order for those rights to be realized. This issue of subsistence rights relates back to matters of actions and agents. While, of course, everyone needs physical security and subsistence, some agents—for example, children or severely handicapped persons—especially need them, because they are not capable of securing them on their own. Such matters are, of course, related to issues of peace, both negative and positive. Security rights are directly related to negative peace in the sense of agents not being harmed by acts of commission (such as being killed) and subsistence rights are directly related to positive peace in the sense of agents not being harmed by acts of omission (such as being prevented access to basic needs for survival). If peace in a full sense is to be attained, or even pursued, then these various kinds of rights need to be realized.

Equality and Justice

As with the issue of rights, it is clear that equality and justice relate to peace and violence, especially with the understanding and realization of positive peace. But also, as with the issue of rights, the notions of equality and justice are complex. There are various concepts of equality. For example, there is the concept of numeric equality, meaning simply the same number. Where numeric equality matters to people might be in cases when something is to be distributed among a group and we believe that everyone should get the same as everyone else; that is, an equal distribution is a fair distribution. However, numeric equality is not always what we believe is fair, or a sense of equality that is important to us, because we might claim that one person deserves more than another. For instance, if one worker does a better job than another, we might well say that the first worker deserves higher pay than the other. Recognizing that numeric equality does not fully capture what we think is important, philosophers speak of the difference between *treating equally* and *equal treatment (or, equal consideration)*. For instance, suppose that there are three children in a family. The parents want to be sure not to show favoritism for any of the three, so for every child they give the exact same birthday present, say, a basketball. One of the children loves to play basketball, one is neutral about it, and one hates playing basketball. There is a sense in which all three children are treated equally by the parents; they all receive the same thing, a basketball. However, from the perspective of the children, there is not equal treatment; the gift of a basketball has very different meaning for each of them. In such a case, treating equally—that is, numeric equality—is not the same thing as equal treatment. There is not equal consideration of the different interests among the children, and so it is not received as being equal, whether or not it is intended as being equal.

Related to the distinction between treating equally and equal treatment (and simple numeric equality) is the issue of equal *in what respect*. Two people might be equal in various ways and unequal in various ways. It is not simple equality or inequality that matters, but equality that is relevant to certain concerns. For example, in both moral and legal contexts, we believe that people should have equal rights or equal opportunities. However, even this notion is not uncontroversial. For instance, some rights apply to only some people, not to all people. As an example, there are special legal benefits set aside for veterans, such as special low-interest loans from the government. Or there are parking spaces that are reserved only for handicapped people; in effect, they have the right to park in them, but no one else has that right. This case points to the fact that equality is one moral and social value, but it is one that we balance along with other moral and social values.

Equality is closely connected with justice, though not identical with it. As the previous examples show, there are cases in which we believe that inequality, or at least unequal treatment, is just and fair—as with providing special parking spaces for some individuals or special low-interest loans for some individuals. In particular, we relate equality both to *procedural* justice (that is, having fair procedures) and *substantive* justice (that is, fair outcomes of those procedures). For instance, if two teams receive equal treatment by the referees or umpires in a game, then whatever the outcome is (that is, whoever wins the game) is seen as just—because there was equal treatment in terms of process, although there was an unequal outcome (one team won and one team lost).

Procedural justice has to do with a just process. We think that a process is unjust if it is biased or skewed in some way or on some basis that we think is inappropriate or irrelevant. A just process is one that is not unjust. As was just mentioned, if we are playing some game and the referees or umpires seem to be favoring one team over another (say, by calling fouls on only one team even when both teams perform the same actions), then we think that this is unjust; that is, we think the rules of the game are not being applied to both teams justly. Or, in an election, if we think that some ballots or voters are being excluded for inappropriate or irrelevant reasons, we think that there is an injustice happening. (Not all exclusions would necessarily be unjust; if a particular person has failed to register to vote, then that person's ballot might be excluded, but this would not necessarily be an injustice.) As another example, if some law were applied differently to different persons for what seem to be inappropriate or irrelevant reasons, then, again, we would say that there is an injustice with the legal process (the law is not being applied in a just way). While procedural justice often involves upholding some sense of equality—for instance, treating like cases alike or weeding out irrelevant biases—equality of outcomes is not necessary for justice.

Besides procedural justice, the other broad sense of justice is substantive justice. This has to do with the substance, or outcomes, of interactions. Within substantive justice, there are several forms of justice. One form is called *distributive* justice. Distributive justice involves the just distribution of goods or services or other things of social value. Goods and services (say, money or objects or opportunities for education) can be distributed among people in many different ways. For instance, one person could own or possess all of them, or everyone could have exactly the same amount of each good or service, or there could be some other distribution. What would make the actual distribution just or unjust? What standards or criteria would determine whether a particular distribution of goods and services is just or unjust? Philosophers and others have given many different answers to these questions. One criterion that has been suggested is merit. As long as you deserve what is distributed to you, then the distribution is just. This, of course, depends on what counts as merit. Another criterion that has been suggested is luck. For instance, if two people play the lottery and one of them wins, it is not because that person deserves to win, but is lucky; however, since the process was fair and equal (it was a random drawing of numbers), then the outcome is just, at least not unjust. Another criterion that has been suggested is utility. This view is that whatever distribution of goods and services leads to the greatest happiness of the greatest number of people is the just distribution. Yet another criterion that has been suggested is need. This is the view that goods and services should be distributed in order to meet the needs of people. Of course, what those needs are would have to be made clear, as well as why some things are legitimate needs (as opposed to wishes or luxuries). In addition, there is the issue of how to justly distribute goods and services if there are not enough to meet everyone's needs (so that, by itself, need would not suffice).

The other major form of substantive justice is called *corrective* justice (sometimes called *retributive* justice). This form of justice has to do with what happens once an injustice has occurred. While distributive justice is focused on what we consider to be a fair distribution of goods and services, corrective justice is focused on what to do when an injustice has taken place. If we think that someone has acted in ways that violate accepted rules, then we might think of that as an injustice, either in terms of procedural justice or in terms of distributive justice. For instance, if someone commits a crime, we might think of that as a violation of social rules (hence, a violation of procedural justice) and as a result of that crime an unjust distribution of goods or services would be brought about (such as stealing someone else's money, resulting in a redistribution of goods). Other people claim that the criminal must be "brought to justice" and be given some form of punishment so that "justice can be served." This sense of justice, again, is corrective justice (or correcting an injustice that has happened).

The two broad forms of substantive justice, distributive and corrective, often overlap and speak to the notion of restorative justice. For instance, issues of reparation or affirmative action involve both forms. In the case, say, of past discrimination against minorities, there was an unjust distribution of goods and services (minorities were unfairly discriminated against). Acts of reparation (that is, repairing the damage, so to speak) or practices of affirmative action are steps toward corrective justice, toward correcting the injustice that occurred in the past.

These various forms of justice are, of course, related to the varied and multiple aspects of peace. Galtung argued that structural violence itself was injustice. To suffer injustice, whether procedural or substantive, is to suffer a form of violence. Again, one can be harmed by acts of commission that are procedurally unjust, such as being subject to laws that are inappropriately discriminatory (for example, having voter registration laws that take race into account) as well as by acts of omission (by not having fair voter registration laws upheld). Likewise, one can be harmed by acts of commission that are substantively unjust (for example, permits for public assembly that discriminate on the basis of religious affiliation) as well as by acts of omission (by not having such unfair permits overturned). Acts and forms of injustice are fundamental harms to agents and significant forms of violence.

Promoting Peace

It is important, of course, to recognize the varied facets and dimensions of peace—for example, the differences and interconnections between negative and positive peace, and interpersonal and intrapersonal peace—as well as the multiplicity of related issues and concerns: actions and agents, rights, equality and justice. But recognizing and understanding these are only one step. Also important is addressing the reduction or elimination of violence and the promotion and realization of peace. With respect to negative peace, one long-standing approach, at least in terms of international conflicts and nation-states as the relevant agents, has been to cope with the threat of violence. One means of coping has been in the guise of deterrence. An example of this was the policy of Mutual Assured Destruction during the Cold War of the late twentieth century between the United States and the Soviet Union. Here the means of coping with violence, and hence maintaining peace, was to threaten the opponent with severe retaliation of violence. While supporters referred to it as "peace through strength," critics often referred to this policy as the MAD doctrine and argued that this resulted at best in a state of negative peace, but that it did not promote positive peace. Détente, not deterrence, was said to be a better means toward reducing or eliminating international violence and threats of violence. Preventing conflict and violence, rather than merely coping with them, led, for example, to arms control talks and agreements. Where arms control or disarmament might reduce the means of conflict and violence, preventive diplomacy is claimed to reduce the incentives or causes of conflict and violence.

Peace theorists have noted that these same concerns and approaches also apply to interpersonal peace, that is, where the agents are not nation-states, but individuals or groups of individuals. Gene Sharp, in *The Politics of Nonviolent Action*, enunciated numerous ways in which individuals could respond to conflict nonviolently: peaceful protests, efforts at persuasion, symbolic acts of demonstration, petitions, lobbying, picketing, marches, withholding relevant funds, strikes, economic boycotts, etc. Some of these ways apply also to international agents; for example, instituting economic sanctions against an aggressive regime rather than (threats of) military strikes (Sharp 1973).

With respect to promoting and realizing positive peace, more needs to be said and done. First, recognizing that positive peace has to do with quality of life, not merely the absence of overt violence, points to a variety of steps. For example, because economic hardships detract from positive peace, working on eliminating those hardships is paramount. Likewise, because social stigmatization, isolation, and stereotyping can detract from positive peace, working on eliminating racist, sexist, and other forms of disrespect are crucial. Because lack of adequate health care detracts from positive peace, working on providing such health care is important. While these points can seem obvious, almost to the level of seeming to be trite, they are basic and true. Preventing harm is important, but so, too, is helping. They reinforce the notion that peace is a verb, not a noun. That is, peace is a state to be achieved, both intrapersonally and interpersonally. As Duane Cady has remarked: pacifism is not passivism. Genuine peace, both negative and positive, comes about through active engagement with one's social and natural environments (Cady 2010). This includes acknowledging that acts of omission—failing to do something—can sometimes be a form of violence, just as much as direct acts of committing violence. It also includes acknowledging that peace is ineliminably intertwined with matters of rights and needs, as well as the need to address social justice and equality.

Works Cited

Cady, D. L. (2010). *From Warism to Pacifism: A Moral Continuum*, 2nd ed. Philadelphia: Temple University Press, p. 24.
Galtung, J. (1969). "Violence, Peace, and Peace Research." *Journal of Peace Research* 6 (3): 167–191.
Gandhi, M. (2017). Quotations. Available at: www.mkgandhi.org (Accessed 7 July 2017).
Sharp, G., M. S. Finkelstein, and T. C. Schelling. (1973). *The Politics of Nonviolent Action*, Vol. 1–3. Manchester, NH: Porter Sargent Publisher.
Shue, H. (1996). *Basic Rights: Subsistence, Affluence, and U.S. Foreign Policy*, 2nd ed. Princeton: Princeton University Press.

Further Reading

Barash, D. P. (1991). *Introduction to Peace Studies*. Belmont, CA: Wadsworth. (A comprehensive treatment of kinds of violence, with a focus on building negative peace and positive peace.)
Fox, M. A. (2014). *Understanding Peace: A Comprehensive Introduction*. New York: Routledge. (A thorough and readable overview of multiple dimensions of peace and violence.)
Richmond, O. P. (2013). *Peace: A Very Short Introduction*. Oxford: Oxford University Press. (A very readable introduction to various aspects of peace, including negative and positive peace.)
Sawatsky, J., and H. Zehr. (2009). *Justpeace Ethics: A Guide to Restorative Justice and Peacebuilding*. Eugene, OR: Cascade Books. (A collection of essays on the interrelationships between peace and justice, with a focus on steps toward achieving positive peace.)
Stassen, G. H. (ed.) (2008). *Just Peacemaking: The New Paradigms for the Ethics of Peace and War*. Cleveland, OH: Pilgrim Press. (A collection of essays focused on practical steps toward achieving just positive peace.)

11
THE PACIFIST CRITIQUE OF THE JUST WAR TRADITION

Cheyney Ryan

The just war tradition, commencing with Augustine, began as a critique of the "turn the other cheek" pacifism of the first Christians. Since then, the identities of both just war thinking and pacifism have involved their mutual critique. Grotius was responding to the pacifist Mennonites in writing the first treatise on the laws of war, *De Indis*. He aimed to chart a course between "two extremes," that forbidding "all use of arms to the Christians" and that imposing no limits at all (Grotius 2012: 8). The codification of the laws of war in the late nineteenth century was a response to pacifist sentiments generated by Crimean and Franco-Prussian Wars. (One example is the Papal Postulatum of 1870, which attacked the "venal motives" of states with their large standing armies engaged in "hideous massacres.") World War I caused substantial doubts about war itself, which were met in turn by institutional attempts to maintain war while limiting it. Post-1945 Cold War debates asked whether nuclear weapons had rendered traditional just war thinking obsolete. Contemporary debates date from the Vietnam War. Opposition to that war in the United States came principally from the pacifist community. The pacifist Martin Luther King, Jr. was the major opposition figure until his assassination in 1968. Michael Walzer's *Just and Unjust Wars* (1977) appeared after the war but took inspiration from disagreement based on just war principles. Revisionist criticisms of Walzer have led in turn to skepticism about the just war framework itself, as it is been subjected to the demands of precision and coherence. The war on terrorism has prompted further discussion between pacifists and just war theorists.

So a specter haunts just war thinking—the specter of pacifism. But to speak of a "mutual critique" may be misleading. The just war tradition has long been ensconced in established institutions like the church and universities, aimed at providing guidance and reflection—if not apologies—for the warlike practices of the state. (Grotius's writings were subsidized by a Dutch mercantile corporation to justify its acts of piracy.) So there is a substantial literature articulating the just war position. By contrast, pacifism has been an outcast tradition, an affair of the marginalized. There are exceptions, like Erasmus. But championing pacifism has been an enterprise of the obscure, or a ticket to obscurity. Jane Addams was America's most admired woman until her strong antiwar views made her a subject of public opprobrium. Another great pacifist of World War I, Randolph Bourne, was a celebrated journalist until his views led to professional exile. For much of the twentieth century pacifists were legally prohibited from teaching in many American public universities. Hence the major pacifist voices, like John Howard Yoder, taught in religious schools. Only recently can one speak of a "pacifist critique" of just war thinking possessing the same kind of theoretical richness (see Yoder 2009).

Talk of "traditions"—as in the "just war tradition"—can also be misleading in suggesting more unity than has existed. Every tradition contains conflicting strands. Every tradition is a tradition of argument, including argument over what's part of the tradition. Pacifism too is a tradition of argument, and a complex one. All pacifists may be distinguished from just war theorists by the question they ask. Just war theory's main concern is "How can we distinguish just from unjust wars?" But the pacifist's concern is what Clausewitz termed "the question of war itself": "Is there any distinction between 'just' and 'unjust' wars?" As I construe it, pacifists are *unconditionally* opposed to all war. But that opposition takes two main forms. *Personal* pacifism privileges individual actions: war is never justified because the act of killing is never justified—even in self-defense. Personal pacifism begins with the first Christians and is generally religiously inflected; its politics is one of personal resistance. This is how most people construe "pacifism" today, hence the fixation in discussions of pacifism on personal self-defense. But this view was originally termed "non-resistance." "Pacifism" is a more recent term, first coined to mark a second form that I call *political* pacifism (see Brock 1972).

Political pacifism's focus is social institutions. It is opposed to war as a social practice—opposed to the *kind* of killing that war involves ("political" killing), much as death penalty opponents are opposed to the kind of killing it involves ("legal" killing). But just as death penalty opponents can oppose the practice of capital punishment while still condoning personal self-defense, political pacifists can oppose war as a social practice while still condoning personal self-defense. Personal pacifism's approach is from the bottom up; political pacifism's is from the top down. Political pacifism is more secular in origin, first found in figures like Erasmus and then developed by Enlightenment-influenced thinkers. Its politics is one of social movements.

Finally, we may distinguish two different objections political pacifists have to war. One focus is on war's *injustice*. It holds that both the prosecution of war (war making) and the preparation for war (war building) violate the rights of individuals and groups. Of special concern has always been conscription, which political pacifists see as a form of enslavement at the heart of war. Another focus is on war's *inhumanity*: this problem with war is that it takes on a life of its own, detached from all human agency in ways that render it both aimless and limitless.

This complexity means that there is no "just war" position *simpliciter* and no "pacifist" critique of "it." So discussion of that critique must be selective. Today's just war discussions begin with Walzer's *Just and Unjust Wars*, which is a logical reference point of contemporary pacifist discussion. But the greatest problem with that book is its ahistorical, monolithic picture of the just war tradition, one that has been uncritically accepted by later theorists. You cannot understand what pacifists have thought is wrong or self-contradictory about that tradition if you don't understand how it has developed over time, including the historical/political context of that development, and how pacifism has emerged at crucial points. So the first part of my critique will be a *genealogy* of the just war tradition from a pacifist perspective (also see Neff 2005; Anghie 2007).

I then turn to Walzer and his revisionist critics, though I deal with the latter only briefly. I could add praise for Walzer's achievement. But as my task here is critical I shall dwell entirely on his shortcomings—which I see as substantial. Walzer is praised for reviving "just war" discussion, but he can also be read as derailing the ethical discussion of war prompted by the Vietnam War. One expression of this is his indifference to the pacifist alternative, in contrast to past just war thinkers. He is also indifferent to the history of just war views and major tensions within them. So his work does not address them so much as *enact* them, rendering it deeply ambivalent in ways that have made it a fruitful target for others. Revisionist critics of Walzer have deepened the discussion in ways that enliven the argument between just war thinking and pacifism, leaving the latter open as a real possibility.

A Genealogy of Just War Thinking

Western pacifism begins with the "turn the other cheek" ethic of Jesus and the first Christians (leaving aside, for this chapter, a broader global discussion). This was a personal ethic but also a political one involving a larger rejection of the Roman Empire and its idolatry—its deification of worldly force. Ever since, pacifism has been both a critique of illicit violence and a critique of arrogant, predatory power, a call for both less brutal forms of relating to one another and more collaborative forms of authority. The "just war tradition" begun by Augustine mixed Christian and Roman ideas as part of the Constantinian reconciliation of church and empire. A defining feature of that tradition—and a focus of pacifist critique—has been just war theory's ambiguous relation to empire (see Parker and Brock 2009).

A fateful legacy of Hellenic thought was a twofold division between wars against other "civilized" peoples and wars against "savages." Something like this contrast continues to inform just war thinking (e.g. America's "War on Terror"—except now, the "savages" are dubbed the "bad guys," the "civilized" the "good guys"). This distinction defines two different conceptions of conflict. War between "civilized" peoples is "war" proper, construed as a discrete act, bound by rules, with a finite beginning and end, and akin to a civil strife insofar as the aim is ultimately reconciliation. By contrast, wars with "savage" peoples are "hostilities," an ongoing condition, bound by no rules, that only ends with the destruction of one of the parties. (Its impulse, then, is genocidal.) These may be identified with different notions of "self-defense." In war proper, self-defense is a discrete act—*repelling attack*. In hostilities self-defense is an ongoing project—*securing survival*. Debates about the "justification of self-defense" constantly muddle these together: endless, paranoid projects of national "survival" are constantly likened to fending off blows on a street corner. "Securing survival" has always been a rationalization of empire. "The motive of strategic security is usually seen by imperialists as defensive expansion against threats from other states or empires. The bigger the empire, the less secure it feels!" (Mann 2012: 21—referring to James 2006).

Moved by Christian humility, Augustine inaugurated what might be termed just war's reserved strand. War was a sad necessity in a sinful world, needed to restore a peace that would shelter the innocent. (For Augustine, war was about the defense of others, not oneself.) But war was never good or righteous in itself. It had to be waged without pride or malice. Since all taking of human life was sinful, it had to be atoned for afterwards, however much justified. From this came the notion of war as law enforcement, overseen by a common church. Furthermore, moral principles primarily assessed actions *after* the fact, for considerations of penance; they were not conceived as directing decisions to wage war or not (see Yoder 2009: 84–85).

In time, the picture of war moved from the mournful and tentative to the celebratory and certain. This is the ideal of "holy war" most dramatically evident in the Crusades (see Bainton 1960). Ever since, the reserved and aggressive strands have vied for the soul of just war thinking: does it enlist morality to counsel restraint, or weaponize morality to endorse aggression?

The Crusades were an attempt by the church in Rome to consolidate its dominance by mobilizing Christians to fight against a common enemy: Islam. The fight was soon extended to Jews, heresies, and the Eastern Church when it got in the way. With this, war achieved a new *political* function: binding people together by identifying a common enemy to kill. It was no longer something permitted but not obligatory, whose sacrifices were regrettable, aimed at welcoming the adversary back to the community. Now it was something mandatory, whose sacrifices were honorable, and whose aim was the very survival of the faith by destroying its enemies. Moral principles played an exhortatory function, rousing believers to action.

Christian pacifism reappeared in response to this. Sects like the Cathars and Albigenses introduced it into the medieval world, only to become the victims of a Crusade themselves. It fully emerged with the Anabaptists of the sixteenth century, the source of most subsequent Christian pacifism. They fundamentally rejected the reconciliation of Christianity and empire, arguing that the critique of Caesar should now be extended to the pope and religious establishments. The last Crusade, and the only successful one, was the reconquest of Spain in 1492. Three months later Christopher Columbus set sail for India, only to find the Americas. This "discovery" inaugurated international law in its modern sense—and the next major phase in just war thinking.

The tale is illustrative of how just war thinking's reserved side so easily becomes its aggressive one (see Tuck 2001 and Wood 2012). Violence against indigenous peoples led scholars like Vitoria to challenge holy war justifications of the conquest, with ideas about the "natural rights" of indigenous peoples that impacted later doctrines of individual rights. But then they proceeded to *justify* the conquest by appealing to the more defensive strand, arguing that the "right to self-preservation" gave Europeans the right to commercial endeavors, hence the right to war against those who frustrated them—and hence the right to dominion over lands and peoples defeated in war. Such thinking has remained remarkably resilient in the just war tradition. Grotius employed it in *De Indis* to justify the Dutch East India Company's act of piracy. It was a staple of nineteenth-century "free trade" imperialism: the Opium Wars, fought to introduce narcotics into China, were justified on these grounds.

European modernity has been defined by the dialectic between imperialism abroad and imperialism at home. The wealth flooding into Spain from its American conquests led its rulers to conclude they had the means to conquer the rest of Europe. This began the era of conflict that culminated in the Thirty Years' War. That war had two dimensions (see Cavanaugh 2009). It was principally an attempt by Catholic Spain to impose an empire on all Europe, but it also had a religious dimension from the passions of the Protestant Reformation in Germany. The religious dimension can be overstressed. In its quest for dominance, Catholic Spain attacked other Catholic countries and allied with Protestant ones. It was ultimately frustrated by a coalition led by the Dutch, the emergent center of nascent capitalism. The upshot was the creation of the European state system, and the next major formulation of just war principles.

War, States, and the State System

The Thirty Years' War (1618–1648) was Europe's first true hyper-war, or "total war," marked by its all-inclusiveness, its indiscriminateness, and ultimately its aimlessness—war took on a life of its own, absent any intelligible purpose. This made it a revolutionary event, generating popular revolt against rulers who had created a world so evidently absurd. Modernity has been defined by three such wars, each lasting about three decades. Each involved the attempt to impose an empire in Europe, similar to what Europeans imposed on non-Europeans. Each has resulted in Europeans treating each other as they had previously treated others. The second was the Napoleonic Wars (1792–1815): France sought to dominate Europe and nationalist fanaticism replaced religious fanaticism. The third was World Wars I and II (1914–1945): Germany sought Europe domination and each side treated each other like "savages," in the name of "civilization." Henceforth, the principal aim of just war theorizing became preventing war from becoming hyper-war, lest the entire system be destroyed. Each hyper-war would lead to new formulations of the just war framework.

The "state" emerged from an act of personification whereby the attributes of "sovereigns," i.e. princes, became the attributes of "sovereignty," possessed by the state. Bobbitt (Bobbitt 2002: 82–83) claims that this abstraction facilitated the war-making power of the state, but also rendered inherently problematic the state's legitimacy qua abstract. The promise of the state is security, but that promise has always been problematic—given that what states give us is 350 years of constant war! Tilly argues that the state is best understood as "the disease for which it purports to be the cure": it creates the threats from which it then saves us, like a "protection racket" (Tilly 1985). For Tilly, the rights we treasure are not secured by the state, they actually arose from *resistance* to the state and its war-making claims (Tilly 1999).

Hyper-war conflicted with the state's promise of security. The rulers' question became: "How can states war against each other without threatening the society of states as a whole?" The answer was to divide the world up (just as the pope had reconciled Spain and Portugal by dividing the Americas). Imperialism—and its ethic of holy war—were relegated to the non-European world, while Europeans conducted their own affairs via the restrained ethic of defensive war. Put crudely, imperialism at home was prohibited so as to facilitate imperialism abroad. As McNeill suggests, imperialism was a "safety valve" (McNeill 1963: 312). "Sovereignty" always had a twofold meaning, due to its double origins: as a kind of ownership, whose rights are akin to persons over their property, or as a kind of membership, whose rights are akin to citizens' rights to participate. Relations between European states were more like sovereignty as membership, restrained by common concerns; relations between Europeans and non-Europeans was more like sovereignty as ownership—unbridled and acquisitive.

This division proved unstable, introducing a rhythm into modern history. The Thirty Years' War was followed by the colonization of the Americas and India, the Napoleonic Wars were followed by imperialism in East Asia and Africa. The twentieth century's world wars are more ambiguous insofar as the 1945 settlement meant a rejection of formal imperialism. But the site of armed conflict moved again from Europe to the non-European world, East Asia and Africa and the Middle East.

The Treaty of Westphalia ending the Thirty Years' War founded the modern state system. Its key elements were, first, that Europe would never be a single empire but multiple states, and second, that Europe would not be ruled by a single faith, hence no state could crusade against another to impose its religion. But none of this applied to the non-European world, which was still subjected to empires ruled by a single faith. Later, "civilization" replaced "faith" as the holy cause: Europeans could not impose their model of civilization on each other, but they were permitted—indeed, they felt obliged!—to impose it on others.

The Thirty Years' War also gave us our two main political philosophies, both of which can be seen as responses to war's excesses. For liberalism, those excesses demonstrated the dangers of religious passion. The solution lay in separating religion from politics to prevent domestic factions from crusading against each other internally (civil conflict) and states from crusading against each other externally (international conflict). This foreshadowed later liberalism's separating the private from the public and the good from the right so as to cleanse politics of metaphysical claims—as incentives to holy war. For republicanism, war's excesses were not the product of unconstrained passions/ideals but of predatory power. The solution in both the domestic and international realms lay in keeping power dispersed. This has meant that republicans have been more concerned with the organization of the state, specifically with preventing the state from becoming an engine of illicit empire through coagulated power. Hence they have been more worried about war as enabling concentrated power as well as expressing it. Generally, discussions of republicanism in political philosophy have ignored its preoccupation with military matters. Hence they overlook the significance of the fact that republican ideas have flourished on the margins of empire, as in the American colonies (or the Italian city-states). "Self-defense," for this tradition, is not an abstract right but a specific response to the expansionist logic of imperialism (see Nabulsi 2005 and Deudney 2008).

All this bears on the status of self-defense. We're so used to the idea that states and their armies are necessary to defend us that it's noteworthy that a principal concern about the rise of the state was its *tension* with the right to self-defense. The consolidation of the state meant the disarming of the general populace and the concentration of violence in the hands of the state. Some, like Hobbes, saw this as the individual's alienating the right to self-defense to the state, in the name of civil peace; others saw it as maintaining the right as the *permission* to defend oneself, while restricting the right as the *power* to defend oneself. But this is problematic in two ways: what is to prevent the state from being a constant threat to its own citizens (tyranny) and to other states (anarchy)? As Rousseau later put it, "We have taken all kinds of precautions against private wars only to kindle national wars one thousand times more terrible, and in joining a particular group of men, we have really declared ourselves the enemies of the whole race" (Rousseau 2012: 294). The republican solution can be summarized as saying that "states" do *not* have the right to self-defense; rather, governments are delegated the power to maintain security on the condition it be exercised responsibly. But that delegation is not total—the people maintain their right to defend themselves against governments domestic and foreign by maintaining the right to bear arms.

The upshot was two quite different approaches to war. Liberalism has tended to focus on the act of war *making*, or the *conduct* of war, stressing war as an act of violence—"Is it just?" It is not so interested in the entity making war, the state. Its concern is what the state does, not what it is. By contrast, republicans have tended to focus on the act of war *building*, or the *constitution* of war—stressing war as an exercise of power. Hence the question: "Is it legitimate?" I stress these two orientations because a defining feature of today's just war theory is that it proceeds entirely in the liberal framework. It does not interrogate the state, or power generally, it does not consider how endless war-making is the inevitable result of endless war-building, or the arrangements by which all of this might be constrained.

The founder of the liberal approach to just war thinking is Grotius (1583–1645), who developed it in the course of defending Dutch imperialist practices. Grotius began by equating individuals and states as legal persons and maintaining there was no significant difference between the justifications for their respective violence. This is the origin of the so-called domestic analogy, so crucial today, which underlies liberalism's sanguine attitude to the state generally. Its importance rests as much in affirming an *instrumentalist* view of war, anticipated by Machiavelli and unquestioned today: war was an instrument of state purpose, much as personal violence is an instrument of individual purpose; henceforth, just war principles were conceived as guiding the proper employment of that instrument. Grotius further distinguished the "laws of nature," i.e. the rights that individuals possessed by the nature of things, from the "laws of nations," i.e. the rights that nations possessed via the mutual consent of states. Neff calls this the "greatest conceptual leap" in the history of international law because with it the morality of states is detached from that of interpersonal morality, as it was not in Augustine (Neff 2005: 85, 111–112). But there's a tension here insofar as the first says that individuals and states stand within the same moral framework, the second that they abide by different ones.

Soldiers are caught in the middle. Writes Neff, "This universalist view of natural law had the effect of placing just-war theorists in a dilemma which they never satisfactorily resolved" (Neff 2005: 56). Notions of individual responsibility implied that soldiers should carefully judge the lawfulness of any war in which their ruler ordered them to serve, but this could make waging any war a practical impossibility. We might call this the *soldier's dilemma*. It helps explain why in modern times soldiers have been a major source of pacifist sentiment, from the Levellers in the Puritan Revolution to former soldiers like Tolstoy and post–World War I dissenters like René Cassin (whose war experiences led him to found a pacifist organization of disabled veterans and ultimately to draft the Universal Declaration on Human Rights, leading to his Nobel Peace Prize).

The eighteenth century saw a dramatic rise in peace thinking, especially among Enlightenment thinkers who reacted against the imperialist machinations of France and Britain and the military's aristocratic pretensions. Rousseau and Kant were exemplary. Political pacifism proper, though, only emerged in the next century in response to the Napoleonic Wars. It is heir to both liberalism and republicanism. With liberalism, it worries about war and individual rights but holds that the two cannot be reconciled. War is intrinsically and irredeemably an insult to liberal values. With republicanism, it worries about war and centralized power, and claims that the one invariably leads to the other. War is intrinsically and irredeemably an insult to democratic values. The dominance of the liberal framework has meant that this second pacifist critique has been overlooked, but if anything it has been more important to pacifism given that tradition's anxieties about power generally.

The Ambivalent Nineteenth Century

The next hyper-war was the Napoleonic conflict, twenty-five years of almost uninterrupted fighting on a scale not seen since the barbarian invasions. This too was holy war, but now a crusade for abstract ideals like liberty, equality, and fraternity. It was also a crusade for *peace*: it was the first "war to end all wars" aimed at destroying the corrupt monarchical system seen as the source of war. Henceforth, war—especially cataclysmic, all-consuming war—would be justified as the solution to war (see Bell 2007). The social trauma of this raised questions about the viability of war itself, giving rise to modern political pacifism, which held that war was a product of the "war system." War was as much a matter of war building as of war making. But pacifism rejected as absurd the notion that this system could itself be destroyed by war—it would only be empowered by it.

In time, these wars produced modernity's two other political ideologies, nationalism and socialism. Both were partly reactions to imperialism. Napoléon's conquests inflamed the nationalism of the defeated and conquered, who saw an intrinsic clash between the claims of empire and those of national communities. Socialists rejected imperialism, opposing it to the global community of workers. The relation of both to pacifism was complex. Both shared pacifism's skepticism of the state, the one because it privileged the nation over statehood, the other because it privileged class over statehood. Nationalists sided with pacifists in holding that if war were truly defensive the problem of war would basically be solved. Socialists sided with pacifists in holding that when war occurred, workers were the cannon fodder. Jean Jaurès provides an interesting example: he was a pacifist, a nationalist, and socialist. Both nationalism and socialism would become bellicose, in part because they came to see the state as the rightful instrument of nations/classes, hence its machinations as serving these larger purposes.

Initially, the response of the rulers was twofold: creating the Concert of Europe, the first attempt at collective security arrangements, and returning to limited wars fought by aristocratic officers and professional troops. This meant an explicit return to the eighteenth-century ideals of Emer de Vattel. Peace prevailed in Europe, as militaries spent more time repressing riots and revolutions at home. But, as before, peace at home brought war abroad, where none of the rules applied. The War of Indian Independence (1857) was as brutal as anything the French inflicted on the Vendee. The Taipang Rebellion in China (1850–1864), provoked by Western incursions, was the largest conflict of the nineteenth century, with up to one hundred million killed.

European peace began to unravel with the Crimean War (1853–1856), the first of several conflicts prompted by the decline of the Ottoman Empire and British anxieties about the threat to India. It anticipated the methods of modern total war in many ways: railroads, trenches, blind artillery fire, and more effective weapons due to rifled barrels. All of these proved their murderous potential the next decade in the American Civil War. This led to the two main strands in the "laws of war." The Geneva Conventions (1864) addressed the victims of war, beginning with wounded soldiers (who had proliferated due to mass conscription). Their impulse was quasi-pacifist in seeing war as basically tragic, and all its soldiers victims, hence meriting concern whichever their side. Accompanying it was a new wave of pacifism proper, led by Crimean War veteran Leo Tolstoy. Later, in response to such peace sentiments, the Hague Conventions (1899–1907) dealt with the conduct of war, like restrictions on weapons. It all would prove futile against the increasing militarization of the late nineteenth century.

Historians debate the sources of militarism. Some identify them with bellicose imperialist policies meant to diffuse class tensions at home, themselves provoked by capitalist industrialization. Champions of war invoked the crackpot biology of social Darwinism, which held that war was a "natural" phenomenon and not a product of social systems (as Enlightenment critics held), a "survival of the fittest" between something called "races" (or "nations," racially construed). Critics of war invoked images from industry: war was the ultimate "machine," summarizing all the evil to which modernity was leading. What these shared was the sense that war was increasingly something that escaped human agency, an "autonomous force." It all seemed to confirm Clausewitz's contention that Napoleonic War had transformed—and exacerbated—the problem of war in ways that new international arrangements or laws would never contain.

Clausewitz held that in modern war, success at war making rested on war building, i.e. victory would go to who could mobilize the most resources, starting with soldiers. The main innovators were Germany and the United States. They instituted what might be called the "welfare-warfare bargain," or "war contract" for short. Citizens were promised social benefit and civil rights in peacetime in return for their bodies and treasure in wartime. Germany emphasized social benefits, in part to mollify its strong socialist movement. The United States emphasized civil rights—wartime participation was typically rewarded with the right to vote. Both championed the idea of the "nation": a quasi-racial, quasi-political entity whose uniqueness could be marked and celebrated in the narratives of historians. It wasn't particularly stable, though, especially in the United States. The disciplinary ethic of war grated against the democratic ethic of civic participation; conscription—a central feature of the nation-state—was hard to square with an ethic of personal liberty.

Thinking about war remained fundamentally divided. Eighteenth-century limited-war ideals persisted, especially among aristocratic elements wanting war to be left to them. They persisted in holding that the rules for how war was fought should be independent of why it was fought. But this fundamentally conflicted with Napoleonic notions of war as being fought for ultimate ideals, or Social Darwinist notions of war as about ultimate survival—why constrain a war fought for such stakes (see Witt 2013)? These ideas gave rise to notions that war should be constrained only by what was "necessary" or not—with the military, presumably, making that judgment. It is no surprise, then, that when war finally came all the limitations were forgotten.

The Warlike Twentieth Century

The third major hyper-war was World Wars I and II (1914–1945). These were straightforward imperialist conflicts (see Mann 2012). World War I especially seemed to vindicate Clausewitz's dark vision of modern war. War as the extension of politics became war as the negation of politics: a "Doomsday Machine" beyond all human agency, indifferent to human ends or limits.

The viciousness of the conflicts reflected the ultimacy of their crusades as "wars to end all wars" and to "defend civilization." Again, the holy war impulse brought profound social disruption: the Russian Revolution, from World War I, and the Chinese Revolution, from World War II. In both world wars, Europeans treated each other with the same lawlessness they'd treated non-Europeans before, hence any division between "civilized" and "savage" disappeared. The upshot of it all was the rise of the United States, significantly the first global power with a strong anti-imperialist tradition. Together, these wars resulted in a challenge to the imperialist project, in its traditional form at least, that had defined European politics since the discovery of the Americas.

The framework subsequently adopted by the League of Nations and United Nations to constrain hyper-war was modeled on the federal arrangements of the now dominant power, the United States. Both had elements of anti-imperialism. The post–World War I insistence on "self-determination" was taken as opposing imperialism's indifference to national claims. In practice it was highly disruptive of the existing state order, ultimately lending credence to Hitler's predations in the name of German "self-determination." The World War II settlement reversed things. State borders were deemed sacrosanct in rejection of imperialist expansiveness. The upshot would be the canonization of "national self-defense" in post-war thinking.

The road to "national self-defense" began with the minorities problem, after World War I. The question was how to protect minorities within the larger ("self-determining") nation-states. Russian concerns for persecuted fellow Slavs had been one of the war's causes. The solution was minority treaties whereby the international community via the League of Nations pledged to defend the rights of groups. It was a substantial intrusion on sovereign rights, hence one that the victorious powers did not apply to themselves. And it failed: expulsions of minorities by Nazis and others created a chronic refugee crisis in the late 1930s, followed by German genocides against its national minorities in the name of securing survival. Ironically, the post–World War II solution basically accepted the German model of ethnic homogeneity by adopting a "territorialist" solution giving each minority its own state with the right to defend itself—the principle of "self-help." But boundaries were not redrawn to fit nations, but rather boundaries were frozen and populations were "transferred" to them. Ethnically homogenous states were created in Central and Eastern Europe by the "transfer" of 31 million people, the largest in history. After World War I, shapers of the international order has resisted creating new states; after World War II the idea that every nation deserved a state to defend it proliferated new states—that in the non-European world repeated the history of expulsions, population flights, and refugees. Henceforth, the security of peoples became a matter of "national self-defense."

World Wars I and II inspired anti-imperialism in part because the colonies were enlisted to win the wars, hence empowered thereby. But the post–World War II settlement was ambivalent. As Winter notes, the peacemakers never decided if they were inaugurating a new international order or shoring up the dominant powers (Winter 2006). The United Nations Charter marked a return to the reserved vision of Augustine: peace was the norm, war the exception, justified only in exceptional circumstances—as community law enforcement, supervised by the United Nations, or the defense by states against immediate aggression. Of these, the community law enforcement principle was the more important, which did not assume that such enforcement needed to be "defensive." The UN police action in Korea began repulsing aggression, then expanded "to restore peace and security to the area." But the UN Security Council meant that all of this would be controlled by the dominant powers, lending a certain amount of cynicism to its global purpose and leaving it largely ineffective with the rise of Cold War tensions. As UN enforcement faded, "self-defense," now termed "national security," emerged as the all-purpose justification for war—thus what I've termed the canonization of national self-defense.

The implications for just war thinking were also ambivalent. Neither of the United Nations' models—war as community law enforcement or war as self-defense—conceived war as an exception to ordinary moral standards; neither fit easily with past notions that states and their soldiers were somehow "morally equal" once conflict began (anymore than cops and criminals are equal, or homeowners and intruders). Some argued for scuttling such notions altogether, others for keeping them on purely pragmatic grounds. What ultimately salvaged the principle of even-handedness was what Neff calls the "humanitarian revolution," whose origins trace to the compassionate ethic of Geneva and its tragic conception of war. Neff terms this another "major conceptual leap" and rightly so (Neff 2005: 315). Its focus was not states but soldiers, whose equality rested not in their rights as doers but in their victimhood as sufferers; indeed, its vision was skeptical of any talk of "rights" in war, not on realist grounds that war is basically amoral but on the grounds that war is so profoundly immoral. Conjoined with the privileging of "self-defense," this meant a tension—if not incoherence—in the structure of just war principles. Those of *jus ad bellum* reflected the rights-oriented claims of self-defense while those of *jus in bello* reflected the compassion-oriented claims of mutual sufferers. Again, soldiers were caught in the middle.

After the Napoleonic Wars, Britain and France quickly made peace so they could carve up the rest of the world. Some see the Cold War as a phony conflict enabling the aspirations of both sides, but this minimizes the risks it posed. In both the United States and Soviet Union the upshot was a profound disillusionment with war itself. A nuclear war could not be won in any meaningful sense of "won." Plus Vietnam and other conflicts seemed to confirm that military might no longer meant political success. The best expression of this climate was the increasing resistance of ordinary citizens to fight in wars: one study asks *Where Have All the Soldiers Gone?* (Sheehan 2009). It used to be that a "pacifist" was someone who resisted "serving their country." Now everyone did. The end of conscription across the Western world starting in the 1960s to 1970s marked the end of the "war contract" between the state and citizen at the heart of modern war politics. People questioned if the rights and benefits of citizenship warranted the sacrifices of military service, and if liberalism and democracy in peacetime required their suspension in wartime. This skeptical attitude frames contemporary discussions.

Contemporary Just War Thinking

The Vietnam War revived both pacifism and just war thinking. Martin Luther King, Jr.'s 1967 speech "A Time to Break the Silence" was the turning point in antiwar sentiment. King was a "true pacifist" in his words, as were antiwar leaders like Muste, Dellinger, Deming, and Day. They did not distinguish just from unjust wars; they claimed the illegitimacy of *all* war. When people of the 1960s generation first heard of "just war" ideals, it was in response to pacifist thinking and in *defense* of American aggression in Vietnam. Paul Ramsey's writings in the 1960s on "discrimination" and "proportionality," which began the recovery of just war principles, were marshaled in defense of American counterinsurgency practices, which he endorsed "without hesitation." In 1967, Ramsey wrote:

> No Christian and no moralist should assert that it violates the moral immunity of noncombatants ... to direct the violence of war upon vast Vietcong strongholds whose destruction unavoidably involves the collateral deaths of a great many civilians.
>
> *Ramsey 1967 reprinted in Ramsey 2002: 503*

Pacifists continued to press the question of what just war principles were for. The worry was not that they necessarily *endorsed* crimes like Vietnam, but that they were flaccid enough to be employed for any purpose. Wink charged that just war thinking was "morally slack" (Wink 2010). Yoder claimed that the attraction of the theory lay in its vagueness, making it a useful tool of the powerful. This led to a strange 1973–1974 debate between Gordon Zahn, a prominent pacifist, and James Turner Johnson, the leading historian of just war thinking. Zahn challenged Johnson to say what—*precisely*—just war principles would say about the Vietnam War (over a decade old by then). Turner began with the striking claim that "there never were very many theologians seriously working within the just war tradition, and now there are even fewer." He continued by saying that "classic just war doctrine as developed within Western Christian thought has comparatively little to say about what may be done in waging war," and concluded that pacifists were unreasonable in expecting this (2,000-year-old) tradition to yield practical judgments about an actually existing war (Johnson 1974; in response to Zahn 1973). Problems were compounded by the novelty of the Vietnam conflict. It was "not a 'test case' for applying just war standards," as Zahn assumed; it was "a 'test case' for finding out what they *are*, in the sense of what they require in this form of war that took almost everyone in the West by surprise" (Johnson 1974).

Walzer's Revival

The Vietnam War reawakened Americans to both liberal concerns about war and individual rights, and republican concerns about war and centralized power, both of which had been marginalized by Cold War hysteria. Republican concerns need stressing, as later political philosophy marginalized them to the point that central figures are all but forgotten. During World War I Randolph Bourne had seen war and its complicity with centralized state power as undermining democratic principles, indeed as threatening politics itself construed as the supervision of society by human agency. Once begun, war had an "inexorability" that escaped all practical will, threatening to make it limitless and endless. Late nineteenth-century thinkers had identified autonomous social forces the "machine." Lewis Mumford, one of America's leading public intellectuals, placed war at the heart of the social "mega-machine" that he also termed the "pentagon of power," in reference to the seat of what President Eisenhower called the "military-industrial complex." Bourne is little discussed, Mumford not all since the 1960s despite his standing as one of twentieth-century America's major public intellectuals (see Blake 1990). The draft came to exemplify both the problem of war and individual rights and war and centralized power, the latter harkening back to foundational republican concerns about the dangers of standing armies.

After Vietnam, Walzer's *Just and Unjust Wars* framed debate. But it took a while. It had little to say about such immediate concerns as the Reagan nuclear arms buildup or interventions in Central America. It only achieved importance fifteen years later with the first Gulf War, which officials explicitly packaged as a "just war" in attempting to lay the "Vietnam Syndrome" to rest. Ever since, it has been central to debates about which American invasions are just and which not.

Walzer privileged individual rights. "I want to suggest that the arguments we make about war are most fully understood . . . as efforts to recognize and respect the rights of individual and associated men and women" (Walzer 1977: XXXI). But Walzer approached the "just war tradition" as if it were a single, stable, and basically coherent thing. This reflected how he generally abstracted the discussion of war from larger debates in political philosophy. One upshot was ignoring the non-rights-oriented humanitarian tradition and its ethic of compassion of the Geneva tradition. This ignored the republican orientation and its concerns with centralized power as both expressing and expressed in war. Basically, "just war theory" was construed as addressing the conduct of war while ignoring the constitution of war. Hence Walzer's framework has little concern with the problem of the draft or war building generally. It had nothing to say about constitutional crises like Watergate due to executive overreach. Its conception of "just war" focused entirely on the justification of war as an act of violence and ignored the legitimacy of war as an exercise of power.

This helps explain Walzer's silence on pacifism, with which humanitarianism and republicanism are so closely linked. He does discuss non-violence as a tactic, but not pacifism's objections to just war principles. His indifference to power is further evidenced in his silence on the problem of imperialism, so central to both the pacifist and just war tradition. This may explain his slighting of the principal initiative at constraining war to emerge from World War II, the United Nations. Since the Concert of Europe, if not before, it had been recognized that laws of war enforced by self-policing states were not enough—especially to constrain imperialist predations within Europe. Some institutional mechanism was required. The twentieth century's two world wars increasingly confirmed this. Walzer says little about the United Nations and what he says is dismissive. To dwell on the meaning of the United Nations Charter "is today a kind of utopian quibbling" (Walzer 1977: XVIII). This partly reflects the reality of the United Nations' marginalization during the Cold War, but also his inattention to the problem of empire, as one of centralized power, which the federal arrangements of the United States Constitution partly meant to address, and which both the League of Nations and the United Nations meant to address in modeling themselves on those arrangements.

More generally, the problem of total war—and of war acquiring a life of its own—is absent from Walzer's discussion. You'd never know from reading it that he was writing near the end of the most warlike century in human history. This is crucial to pacifist doubts about the whole just war enterprise, doubts that were prominent in the 1960s: if the just war tradition is so great, how could it lead to the wars of the twentieth century? The fact that a tradition fails is not itself reason for scuttling it, but surely—after such failure—it is obliged to provide an explanation, and assurance of why it might not continue. My discussion has suggested this is not just a problem *about* the tradition, but *for* the tradition insofar as a main concern has been preventing the slide from war to hyper-war.

Still, there is a deep ambivalence in Walzer's vision that recommends it over some of his more sanguine critics. Sometimes his vision is positive: war can be a promoter of rights, fought respectfully of rights, so the problem is to demarcate just and unjust wars and fighting justly vs. unjustly. Much revisionist theory carries on this project, and in the same manner as Walzer. Its approach is not historical but anecdotal. It speaks of "war" and "soldiers" in the abstract, as if they were invariant across place and time, illustrated by cases chosen randomly from throughout the millennia. But sometimes Walzer's vision is darker, what I've elsewhere termed a "grim realism." This is especially true in speaking of soldiers, whose condition he describes as "military servitude" subject to "the thralldom of the trenches," while he speaks of war generally as a kind of "tyranny." This larger issue raised here is whether war is the "collective expression" of individual rights, or their denial. Writes Walzer:

> States exist to defend the rights of their members, but it is a difficulty in the theory of war that the collective defense of rights renders them individually problematic. The immediate problem is that the soldiers who do the fighting, though they can rarely be said to have chosen to fight, lose the rights they are supposedly defending.... "Soldiers are made to be killed," as Napoleon once said; that is why war is hell.
>
> *Walzer 1977: 136*

It's hard to see how war can be a "collective defense of rights" if those defending them lose those rights—through no fault of their own. It's hard to see how an enterprise (war) can be respectful of rights while also being a tyranny. On the one hand is war as Walzer *wishes* war would be; on the other is what war really *is*. The crucial point is to keep these distinct—for otherwise one is guilty of what Rousseau regarded as the primal sin of just war thinking, confusing "fact" with "right," rendering one a "miserable comforter" of the war makers.

Walzer lapses into this error most when he resorts to analogical thinking. The "domestic analogy," he says, is "indispensable" to just war thinking, despite the fact that, as he acknowledges, "international society as it exists today is a radically imperfect structure." Indeed: it is *so* "imperfect" that the analogy hardly holds at all. War is "like" domestic punishment, except that "neither the procedures nor the forms of punishment have ever been firmly established in customary or positive international law. Nor are its purposes entirely clear: to exact retribution, to deter other states, to restrain or reform this one?" So, it's like domestic punishment except it lacks all the features that make such punishment *legitimate*. War is "like" law enforcement, except "there are no policemen," just sovereign states acting on the principle of "self-help," their wars the equivalent of "citizen's arrests"—another name for which might be "taking the law into their own hands." And the "law" is a primitive one: civilized society treats different crimes differently, but international society treats every crime the same. "It is as if we were to brand as murder all attacks on a man's person, all attempts to coerce him, all invasions of his home." We do this, Walzer says, because otherwise the whole structure would collapse. International society "might be likened to a defective building, founded on rights; the whole thing shaky and unstable because it lacks the rivets of authority."

A case in point is the principle of "proportionality," which many pacifists have seen as the Achilles' heel of the entire framework. Just war principles prohibit the targeting of non-combatants; in this, war is like law enforcement. But then they allow that the foreseeable but unintended killing of innocents is permissible as "collateral damage" if it is "proportionate" to the good achieved. Massive questions confront all this, like what it means for something like a *state* to "foresee but not intend" killings (or anything, for that matter). But the main point is that this is completely *contrary* to the principles of law enforcement, which prohibit foreseeable innocent deaths as side effects even if the damage is "proportionate"—or "the lesser evil." The standard argument for this principle is that if you *don't* adopt it, you have to be a pacifist! So, the domestic analogy holds when it supports war, and it is suspended when it doesn't.

The basic problem here is that if states are "like" persons in some sense, they are equally unlike persons in being organized collectives—the very dimension that makes their acts war. Walzer acknowledges as much, suggesting that because of this their violence is more a "feudal raid," like the Vikings descending on Paris or the Magyars on Northern Italy, and their "self-defense" more like the counter-raids of Otto the First. This is why war even as an act of punishment "will more probably extend than cut off the violence." In summary, then: states are like *vigilantes*, armies like *posses*, and the "punishment" they inflict are like *lynchings* for even petty offenses, or shoot-outs, where rights are affirmed by the law of the gun. The better analogy, as Walzer at one point admits, is "the 'wild west'" of American fiction, which is why during the Vietnam War people found the best analogies to "international society" in films like *Hang 'Em High* or *The Wild Bunch*.

Again, we might want international society to be like a domestic legal system, but the upshot of the domestic analogy blurs the dream with the reality so as to blur the crucial questions: how do we realize that dream in reality, and why has the just war tradition thus far failed to do so?

The distance between theory and practice, or dream and reality, is most dramatic in its critique of aggression, at the heart of his just war theory. I've noted it was the first Gulf War that brought Walzer prominence. His condemnation of aggression seemed to speak to Iraq's invasion of Kuwait. But his account of *why* aggression was wrong had little relevance. According to it, communities must be defended and borders must be secured because they preserved a "common life." But Kuwait's borders had nothing to do with a "common life"; they were entirely an artifact of Western imperialism (Kuwait was almost one-fourth Palestinians, almost all exploited—see Schofield 1991). More generally, the post-1945 sanctification of borders was mainly to remove borders as a source of conflict by freezing them in place, partly by *denying* they rested on anything deeper (like a "common life")—much as the Westphalian settlements sought to remove religion as a source of conflict by denying it rested on anything higher.

More generally, Walzer regarded the state's defense of a "common life" as key to both its historical origins and moral standing. "Over a long period of time, shared experiences and cooperative activity of many different kinds shape a common life," which the state then protects against "external encroachment." The moral standing of any particular state depends upon "the reality of the common life it protects and the extent to which the sacrifices required by that protection are willingly accepted and thought worthwhile," so if states have standing now it is because "most states do stand guard over the community of their citizens, at least to some degree: that is why we assume the justice of their defensive wars" (Walzer 1977: 53–54). This is conjectural history to the extreme. States did not defend against encroachment, they are the products of encroachment, often against a common life that already existed (as noted, whatever "common life" post–World War II states protected was often due to forced population transfers); their legitimacy does not rest on the willingness of people to sacrifice for them, their survival rests on bribing or coercing people to do so; "most" states do not "stand guard" over their communities—in the twentieth century you were more likely to be killed by your own state than a foreign one. Walzer, like others, takes Poland's resistance to the Nazis as a paradigm of just war. If there was a "common life" in 1930s Poland, it did not include its Jewish population.

Revisionist Critiques

Today's revisionist just war theory is best placed by what it accepts and what it rejects from Walzer. Like Walzer, its methodology is ahistorical and anti-institutional. It has no interest in how war has changed over time, hence why the twentieth century was so extraordinarily warlike such as to render just war principles all but meaningless. It is not interested in the logic of the state or those international institutions aimed at addressing that logic. Hence it ignores the entire cluster of issues raised by the republican tradition involving war building as distinct from war making and its conduciveness to centralized power. And in so doing it leaves behind major questions raised by the Vietnam War about the *abuse* of the war-making power—and how democratic institutions can address them.

It departs from Walzer in its penchant for imaginary, hypothetical cases. This is especially risky in matters of war given the massive ideological mystifications surrounding an institution; untutored "intuitions" about it are almost sure to be false. More generally, bad arguments for some X only work *because* we can imagine some instances in which X might be justified. The question with war is not whether it could be justified in an imagined world but whether it is justified in the actual world. Ultimately, this returns us to the question of what—precisely—just war theorizing aims to do, and the persisting ambiguities of the just war tradition about this.

Where revisionist theory transcends and deepens the concerns in Walzer is in posing the question of whether a just war is possible. Walzer claims that ultimately our judgments about war rest on our commitment to the individual rights to life and liberty, while revisionism asks if our judgments are in fact compatible with that commitment. Where they are not, it urges revising the particular judgments we make in war—but raising thereby the question of our judgment of war generally: is it fundamentally an insult to individual rights? Thus revisionist theory remains open to the viability of pacifism in ways that previous discussions have not.

Basically, many of the challenges that revisionist theory has raised trade on the tensions, if not contradictions, in the just war tradition. It accepts Walzer's monolithic portrayal of that tradition and so takes itself to be opposing something simple and straightforward. By contrast, I take that tradition as a motley jumble of elements, arising from different sources. In its demand for greater precision and coherence, revisionist theory is best conceived not as refuting the past so much as providing a critical perspective on the past, on how its elements don't quite fit together.

For example, some of the problems raised by revisionists serve to highlight the enduring tension from Grotius onwards between the laws of nature and the laws of nations as a normative reference point. Hence its discussion of the obligations of soldiers returns us to the dilemma that Neff claimed has been present from start—the conflict between the individual conscience of the soldier (given that the laws of nature prohibit unjust killing) and the institutional imperatives of soldiering (given that the laws of nations oblige soldiers to obey their rulers). Other problems highlight the tensions in Grotius and after from how the violence of the state is both equated and contrasted with the violence of the person. The questions about national self-defense and its relation to personal self-defense first raised by Rodin can be construed in this light (Rodin 2005). The state's right to self-defense is sort of like the individual's right to self-defense in warranting lethal force, but it's unlike the individual's right insofar as what individuals defend is their lives whereas what states defend is their "sovereignty"—the meaning and importance of which continue to be debated. And even the issue of lethal force is complex. In domestic society, the individual right to self-defense implies the permissibility of lethal force but not necessarily the empowerment for lethal force, i.e. the right to bear arms. But in international society, the state's right to self-defense is equated with the right to the means of self-defense, creating an inherent tension between the right to self-defense and the right to security (of the type identified by the first liberal thinkers).

But revisionists' acceptance of Walzer's monolithic picture leads them to ignore other central tensions in just war thinking, especially more recent ones.

A great deal of revisionist discussion has focused on the apparent oddity that in matters of *jus ad bellum* everything rests on whether the war is just or unjust, while in matters of *jus in bello* the perspective on soldiers abstracts from that fact. Following Walzer, this is taken to be a timeless feature of the just war tradition which, also following Walzer, revisionism tries to make sense of in terms of individual rights. This results in one of their major partings of ways, Walzer holding that rights can make sense of treating combatants equally, revisionism claiming it cannot. But neither recognizes the fact noted previously, that in its modern form the equal treatment of combatants primarily derives from the humanitarian tradition's ethic of compassion. The suffering of soldiers is treated equally by the Geneva Conventions regardless of whether they fight justly or unjustly for the same reason that the suffering of patients is treated equally by physicians regardless of whether they were the cops or the criminals. Just as a physician in a hospital might regard the shootings he or she treated as a needless tragedy, the humanitarian ethic regards killing in war as a needless tragedy. The tensions within just war thinking, then, bespeak of our fundamentally different moral perspectives on war generally.

Future Questions

The dialogue between pacifism and just war thinking is just beginning because serious ethical reflection on war is just beginning. In itself, this is an astonishing fact. War has been one of the principal scourges—if not *the* principle scourge—of humanity for millennia. But only recently has it been subjected to serious ethical interrogation. A historical parallel is slavery, which received serious ethical interrogation only in its waning phase, contributing to its demise. I see the same thing happening to war.

How should the dialogue proceed? Both pacifism and just war thinking are products of their time, specifically the world of separate, increasingly territorially defined states that has constituted modernity. The first question confronting both is whether or to what extent we are entering a new political world constituted by a new type of state, or a movement beyond states, with the emergence of a new type of war. The principal theorist here for those attracted to pacifism is Kaldor, who explores what a commitment to nonviolence means in a world of "new wars" (Kaldor 2012). An important work related to this and the topics here is Jonathan Schell's *Unconquerable World* (2004). In keeping with these thinkers, my approach would place an emphasis on war building as well as war making. If states are no longer the organizers of war, who is? The rise of so-called non-state actors has been largely parasitic on the existence of states; ISIS would not exist, for example, without the support of Saudi Arabia and others. The question is whether such non-state actors augur something truly new or are just today's equivalent of pirates and privateers.

The bigger challenge is articulating a framework from which the relative claims of pacifism and just war thinking can be assessed. Oftentimes, just war argument has proceeded by simply assuming that if a claim leads to pacifism it must be rejected out of hand. There are practical reasons for proceeding thus, if, for example, one's role is to advise those already committed to war. But theoretically it is sheer dogmatism. Pacifists can also be dogmatic. What is needed is a framework that is open enough so as not to prejudge the question of pacifism vs. just war theory one way or the other, that is expansive enough to assess the many types of issues I've identified as dividing the two perspectives. These are not just ethical but historical and sociological as well, hence ones that transcend the traditionally more limited concerns of both frameworks. My name for this framework is *critical war theory*. It describes a direction that pacifists concerned with the ultimate validity of their viewpoint might pursue.

Works Cited

Anghie, A. (2007). *Imperialism, Sovereignty, and the Making of International Law*. Cambridge: Cambridge University Press.
Bainton, R. (1960). *Christian Attitudes Toward War and Peace: A Historical Survey and Critical Re-Evaluation*. Nashville, TN: Abingdon Press.
Bell, D. A. (2007). *The First Total War: Napoleon's Europe and the Birth of Warfare as We Know It*. New York: Houghton Mifflin.
Blake, C. N. (1990). *Beloved Community: The Cultural Criticism of Randolph Bourne, Van Wyck Brooks, Waldo Frank, and Lewis Mumford*. Raleigh: University of North Carolina Press.
Bobbitt, P. (2002). *The Shield of Achilles*. New York: Random House.
Brock, P. (1972). *Pacifism in Europe to 1914*. Princeton: Princeton University Press.
Cavanaugh, W. T. (2009). *The Myth of Religious Violence: Secular Ideology and the Roots of Modern Conflict*. Oxford: Oxford University Press.
Deudney, D. H. (2008). *Bounding Power: Republican Security Theory from the Polis to the Global Village*. Princeton: Princeton University Press.
Grotius, H. (2012). *On the Law of War and Peace*, edited by S. Neff. Cambridge: Cambridge University Press.
James, H. (2006). *The Roman Predicament: How the Rules of International Order Create the Politics of Empire*. Princeton: Princeton University Press.
Johnson, J. T. (1974). "Rationalizing the Hell of War." *Worldview* 17 (1), January: 43–47.
Kaldor, M. (2012). *New and Old Wars: Organized Violence in a Global Era*. Stanford: Stanford University Press.

McNeill, W. H. (1963). *The Rise of the West: A History of the Human Community*. Chicago: University of Chicago Press.
Mann, M. (2012). *The Sources of Social Power: Volume 3, Global Empires and Revolution, 1890–1945*. Cambridge: Cambridge University Press.
Nabulsi, K. (2005). *Traditions of War: Occupation, Resistance and the Law*. Oxford: Oxford University Press.
Neff, S. C. (2005). *War and the Law of Nations: A General History*. Cambridge: Cambridge University Press.
Parker, R. A., and R. N. Brock. (2009). *Saving Paradise: How Christianity Traded Love of This World for Crucifixion and Empire*. Boston: Beacon Press.
Ramsey, P. (1967/2002). "Is Vietnam a Just War?" (first appeared in *Dialog*, Winter 1967), reprinted in Ramsey's *Just War: Force and Political Responsibility*. Lanham, MD: Rowman and Littlefield.
Rodin, D. (2005). *War and Self-Defense*. Oxford: Clarendon Press.
Rousseau, J. J. (2012). *Rousseau: The Basic Political Writings*. Indianapolis: Hackett Publishing.
Schell, J. (2004). *The Unconquerable World: Power, Nonviolence, and the Will of the People*. New York: Holt Paperbacks.
Schofield, R. (1991). *Kuwait and Iraq: Historical Claims and Historical Disputes*. London: Royal Institute of International Affairs.
Sheehan, J. J. (2009). *Where Have All the Soldiers Gone? The Transformation of Modern Europe*. New York: Mariner Books.
Tilly, C. (1985). "War Making and State Making as Organized Crime," in P. Evans, D. Rueschemeyer, and T. Skocpol (eds.), *Bringing the State Back In*. Cambridge: Cambridge University Press, 169–191.
Tilly, C. (1999). "Where Do Rights Come from?" in T. Skocpol (ed.), *Democracy, Revolution, and History*. Ithaca: Cornell University Press, 55–72.
Tuck, R. (2001). *The Rights of War and Peace: Political Thought and the International Order from Grotius to Kant*. Oxford: Oxford University Press.
Walzer, M. (1977). *Just and Unjust Wars*. New York: Basic Books.
Wink, W. (2010). *The Powers That Be*. New York: Harmony.
Winter, J. (2006). *Dreams of Peace and Freedom: Utopian Moments in the Twentieth Century*. New Haven: Yale University Press.
Witt, J. F. (2013). *Lincoln's Code: The Laws of War in American History*. New York: Free Press.
Wood, E. M. (2012). *Liberty and Property: A Social History of Western Political Thought from the Renaissance to Enlightenment*. London: Verso.
Yoder, J. H. (2009). *Christian Attitudes to War, Peace, and Revolution*, edited by T.J. Koontz and A. Alexis-Baker. Grand Rapids, MI: Brazos Press.
Zahn, G. (1973). "War and Its Conventions." *Worldview* 16 (7), July: 25–33.

12
CONTINGENT PACIFISM

Paul Morrow

Contingent pacifism is an emerging moral position towards war and participation in war. First outlined by John Rawls, and subsequently elaborated by Larry May, Andrew Fiala, Saba Bazargan, and others, this position occupies a middle ground between just war theory and more absolute forms of pacifism. Contingent pacifists believe, centrally, that citizens of modern states have decisive moral reasons not to participate in any wars currently in prospect or already underway. These reasons are grounded in contingent, but stable, empirical facts that render all existing and prospective wars presumptively unjust.

In this chapter, I begin by reviewing the development of contingent pacifism as a distinct moral position towards war and participation in war. Next, I analyze some of the leading arguments that have been offered in favor of this position. Finally, I present a novel argument for contingent pacifism—one designed to show that this position is particularly well suited for individual men and women facing the possibility of enlistment or conscription into their nations' armed forces. Building on the work of philosopher L.A. Paul, I call this the argument from transformative experience. The argument holds that service in the armed forces is a transformative experience, one in which serious moral risks coincide with significant changes in individuals' knowledge and preferences. The decision of whether to undergo such a transformative experience, I contend, should be guided by a moral position that properly weighs these factors. Contingent pacifism, I conclude, is the moral position that best reconciles the various considerations relevant to the decision of whether to enter military service.

One preliminary clarification is in order. I understand contingent pacifism as a moral position towards war, rather than towards interpersonal violence generally. War is a contested concept; I take it to involve the coordinated use or credible threat of armed force by states or state-like actors, directed towards political aims, and subject to the laws governing armed conflict. My discussion will not address borderline cases, such as targeted killings, terrorist bombings, and cyberattacks. Though these cases deserve philosophical scrutiny, I do not think they pose significant challenges to the arguments for contingent pacifism considered here.

Defining Contingent Pacifism

The term "pacifism," as Cheyney Ryan has observed, is a comparative neologism (Ryan 2016). Like "trench foot," "air raid," and "concentration camp," it was coined during the series of conflicts that shook the English-speaking world in the late nineteenth and early twentieth centuries. Unlike those other terms, there existed a long tradition of reflection on the morality of war upon which early pacifists could draw when developing their views. This same history informs efforts by contingent pacifists to define their particular moral position today.

Some contingent pacifists suggest that historical texts offer complete arguments in favor of this position (May 2015). Others invoke traditional responses to war and the moral challenges of war in order to differentiate contingent pacifism from related views (Rawls 1999: 335). Here I will consider three conceptual distinctions commonly deployed in discussions of contingent pacifism. These are the distinction between personal and political pacifism, the distinction between opposition to individual wars and opposition to militarism more broadly, and the distinction between official accommodations for non-selective and selective conscientious objectors.

The distinction between personal and political pacifism is central to Cheyney Ryan's account of contingent pacifism. Personal pacifism, Ryan argues, has religious sources, particularly in the Christian teachings of the Gospels and the early church fathers. It involves opposition to killing as an act, as well as the ideal of maintaining peaceful relations with all. Political pacifism has secular sources, notably in the Enlightenment thought of Voltaire, Kant, and others. It involves a commitment to ending "war as a social practice," chiefly by reforming political institutions (Ryan 2016). Contingent pacifism, Ryan concludes, should be understood as a form of political, rather than personal, pacifism—both because the negative arguments it offers center on war and war-fighting, and because the positive prescriptions it sets out focus on institutions, rather than individuals (Ryan 2016).

Closely related to the distinction between personal and political pacifism is the distinction between opposition to individual wars and opposition to "militarism" or the "war-system." Andrew Fiala defines militarism as "a social, economic, and political system that is devoted to standing armies, the armaments industry, and constant preparation for war" (Fiala 2014: 467). Contingent pacifism, on Fiala's view, involves opposition to this system as a whole, and not simply opposition to one or more particular wars. Fiala reserves the term "contingently pacifist conclusions" for cases where individuals or groups oppose particular wars due to their perceived injustice but do not extend their criticism to the political conditions that make it possible for states to wage unjust wars (Fiala 2014: 467).

The third distinction is more fine-grained than the other two. It concerns the different kinds of conscience-based accommodations supported by particular versions of pacifism. In the United States, as in other countries, obtaining official conscientious objector status has traditionally required declaring opposition to all wars, past, present, and future. It has required, in other words, a commitment to absolute forms of pacifism. Contingent pacifists believe that individual men and women have decisive moral reasons to oppose all current and prospective wars, but need not oppose all past wars, or all possible future wars. Accordingly, Larry May has called for institutional recognition of *selective* conscientious objection—a form of official accommodation under which conscripts, and perhaps also serving members of a nation's armed forces, can request exemption from service on the basis of their sincerely held beliefs about the moral status of existing wars (May 2015: 240).

Contingent pacifists, as I have said, claim that these distinctions help differentiate their position both from absolute forms of pacifism and from leading versions of just war theory. One aim of this chapter is to offer additional support for the claim that contingent pacifism constitutes a distinct moral position. For now, however, I want briefly to explain how I understand claims of distinctness.

Contingent pacifism would be logically equivalent to one of its rival positions just in case the descriptive and normative claims central to these positions had the same extension in our world and in nearby possible worlds. So far as I know, no one has argued that contingent pacifism is equivalent in this sense to either absolute pacifism or to leading versions of just war theory. The assertions of equivalence worth taking seriously are those that hold that contingent pacifism is practically equivalent to absolute pacifism or just war theory—where practical equivalence means roughly that, across a broad range of cases, both positions give the same guidance to deliberating agents.

We can refine the question of practical equivalence by separating the different categories of deliberators addressed by absolute pacifists, contingent pacifists, and just war theorists. These different categories include potential military recruits, already serving soldiers and junior officers, military or civilian leaders, and civilian workers or voters. Contingent pacifism, in my view, is particularly well suited for individuals in the first of these categories, i.e. men and women facing the possibility of enlistment or conscription into military service. My discussion in the remainder of this article will focus mostly on cases of this kind.

Defending Contingent Pacifism: Arguments from the Impermissibility of Defensive War and the Rights of Soldiers

Some philosophers hold that contingent pacifism is only a stopover on the way to a more comprehensive form of opposition to war (Ryan 2016). On this view, contingent pacifism is valuable chiefly for the challenges it poses to certain widely accepted beliefs about the morality of war. I do not favor this account of the theoretical significance of contingent pacifism, but I agree that some of the most influential arguments for this position proceed by challenging existing orthodoxies. Here I will consider two such arguments: David Rodin's argument against the right of states to defend themselves against political aggression, and Larry May's argument from the right of soldiers not to be killed unnecessarily.

In his article "The Myth of National Self-Defense," David Rodin criticizes the "self-evident proposition" that "politically ordered societies—notably states—have the right to defend their sovereign independence and territorial integrity through war" (Rodin 2014: 88). Rodin's argument, if successful, has implications that extend to the highest levels of international law and governance. Here, I will focus on the guidance that Rodin's view provides for individual men and women contemplating enlistment or conscription into their nations' armed forces. Rodin's argument, I will suggest, not only identifies reasons for such individuals to embrace contingent pacifism, but also helps to clarify one way in which that position is contingent.

Rodin begins "The Myth of National Self-Defense" by noting that both just war theory and current international law grant broad permissions to states to defend their sovereignty through war. Normative constraints on the scale and destructiveness of such defensive actions exist, in the form of requirements of proportionality, necessity, and so on. These constraints, however, are significantly reduced in cases where the threat to the survival of a state as a sovereign entity is sufficiently serious (Rodin 2014: 71).

In order to justify this position, just war theorists and legal scholars typically employ one of two strategies, which Rodin terms the "analogical" and the "reductive" strategies (Rodin 2014: 74). Those who follow the analogical strategy hold that "the state itself possesses a right of defense analogous to the individual right of self-defense." Those who follow the reductive strategy hold that "national self-defense is the coordinated exercise of individual rights of defense" (Rodin 2014: 74).

In rejecting the orthodox view of the right of states to engage in self-defense, Rodin seeks to defeat both the analogical and the reductivist justifications of that right. The analogical justification is countered by a *reductio ad absurdum* argument. States, Rodin contends, are not substantially different from other kinds of valuable and valued communities, such as charities or employee-owned corporations. But it is preposterous to hold that these kinds of communities have a right of violent self-defense against takeover or dissolution. Accordingly, Rodin concludes, whatever value states create for or beyond their individual members, that value cannot ground an independent right of self-defense on behalf of states comparable to the right that individual persons have to defend themselves (Rodin 2014: 74–79).

Rodin's response to the reductivist justification of defensive war is more complex, and, in my view, more plausible. It also bears more directly on contingent pacifism. The response involves an analysis of conditional threats—i.e. threats in which the sacrifice of a lesser interest is the condition for preventing harm to a greater interest (Rodin 2014: 81). On Rodin's view, most defensive wars waged by modern states start from the refusal to sacrifice a lesser interest, namely, political sovereignty, and result in harm to a greater interest, namely, the lives and well-being of citizens. For this reason, Rodin argues, wars waged simply for the preservation of political sovereignty cannot be reduced to the coordinated exercise of individual rights of personal defense (Rodin 2014: 87).

There is a class of conflicts where the reductivist characterization of defensive force would be accurate. These are conflicts involving not just political, but genocidal, aggression. Here Rodin believes "coordinated, forceful defense" can be justified on reductivist grounds (Rodin 2014: 88). But he also believes that most defensive wars are not like this, and that "there are good reasons for denying that such acts of collective defense constitute acts of war" (Rodin 2014: 88).

If Rodin is right that most real or prospective defensive wars are morally impermissible because they are likely to cause more harm to the lives and well-being of citizens than peaceful concession would, this provides individual men and women with a reason to refuse to fight in such wars. This reason for refusal is qualified in two ways that clearly connect it with contingent pacifism. First, Rodin suggests that there is a need for more robust non-state, international institutions that could "interdict" against acts of political aggression (Rodin 2014: 89). The development of such institutions might cancel out the reasons that individual men and women currently have to avoid serving in their national militaries—for example, by making the likelihood of unjustified aggressive or defensive wars far smaller than it is currently.

Second, Rodin's argument supports contingent pacifism insofar as he accepts that genocidal, as opposed to merely political, aggression can permissibly be resisted by all members of the political community towards which it is directed. Although Rodin resists applying the term "war" to such acts of collective resistance, it seems to me that this is just the sort of conflict that a contingent pacifist could agree might render military service morally justified. That other forms of collective resistance, such as popular uprisings, would also be permissible in the face of such aggression does not undermine the fact that serving in an organized military might afford individuals the best opportunity to defend themselves and to effectively protect others. Accordingly, it seems that contingent pacifism could furnish the "new normative position intermediate between just war theory and pacifism" for which Rodin calls in his article's conclusion (Rodin 2014: 89).

David Rodin departs from both just war theorists and absolute pacifists in his critique of self-defense as a moral justification for war. Larry May similarly departs from existing theories in his analysis of the moral rights of combatants—most notably, their right against being killed unnecessarily. As with Rodin's argument, May's analysis provides support for contingent pacifism, as I shall explain.

Among the issues that divide theorists working within the just war framework, one of the most significant concerns the rights retained—or forfeited—by combatants in war. In his *Just and Unjust Wars*, Michael Walzer defends the traditional view that soldiers on all sides of a given war lose their right against being killed, simply by reason of being combatants (Walzer 2015). This view is usually referred to in terms of the "moral equality of combatants." Within the past two decades, an alternative line of thinking about the rights of combatants has gained traction, aided chiefly by the work of Jeff McMahan. McMahan, along with other so-called revised just war theorists, rejects the moral equality of combatants, and argues that only soldiers serving on the unjust side of a war, or who perform impermissible actions in war, lose their right against being killed (McMahan 2008; Frowe 2015).

In his *Contingent Pacifism*, May rejects both of these positions, arguing that there is a way in which combatants on all sides of a conflict are morally equal, but that this equality does not consist in an equal lack of a right against being killed. Instead, May suggests, "soldiers all have roughly the same *minimal* moral status" insofar as "all have the right not to be killed unnecessarily" (May 2015: 97).

Necessity is one of the standard criteria proposed by just war theory for assessing the permissibility of war, and of actions in war. May's use of this concept, however, is distinctive. His concern with the unnecessary killing of soldiers is not bound up with debates about what degree of defensive harm can permissibly be inflicted on soldiers who have forfeited their right against being killed—a major topic for revisionist just war theorists. Rather, May suggests that soldiers, even soldiers on the unjust side of a war, or soldiers performing unjust actions in war, do not forfeit their right against being killed unnecessarily. He describes this right against being killed "unnecessarily" as a "special right" that soldiers acquire as a compensation for the special vulnerabilities they incur in their role as soldiers (May 2015: 95). Most controversially, May suggests that soldiers hold this right not only against opposing forces, but also against their own commanders: "[S]oldiers should only take on this increased risk if it is clear that taking on a risk of death is strictly necessary for achieving a legitimate military objective" (May 2015: 95).

May's argument supports contingent pacifism in two ways. First, as May argues, even in an era of advanced weapons systems and sophisticated targeting procedures, there is no "guarantee that in a just war" the only soldiers killed will be "those who are posing an objective threat and of whom it can be said that it is necessary to kill them" (May 2015: 102). Soldiers and those contemplating becoming soldiers are "best advised to act cautiously and rarely if ever accede to the demands or requests of their State to fight in wars that will likely involve the killing of the innocent, for which no excuse may be available" (May 2015: 103).

A second kind of argument, but one which May does not press at length in his book, is that soldiers and recruits may be acting permissibly but unadvisedly in agreeing to serve in conflicts or military roles where their own rights against unnecessary killing may be violated. This concern is less likely to emerge in the case of small-scale, all-volunteer conflicts, but it becomes significant in cases of general mobilization for large-scale conflicts, of the kind familiar from the early twentieth century. It is connected with a concern for the moral exploitation of soldiers. In order to say more about these concerns, and about their connection to contingent pacifism, I will turn now to consider the transformative nature of military service.

Military Service as Transformative Experience

The arguments for contingent pacifism canvassed earlier in this chapter challenge widely held views on the morality of war. Readers who find those challenges compelling may be ready to embrace contingent pacifism. Those who think the arguments offered by May and Rodin fail may wonder whether any other, less radical, arguments favor this position. In this section and the next, I will develop an argument for contingent pacifism rooted in premises that are widely shared, and that builds on insights offered by both absolute pacifists and just war theorists. My argument starts from the idea that enlisting or accepting conscription into military service constitutes a *transformative experience*.

The concept of transformative experience was first articulated by philosopher L.A. Paul. In her work, Paul identifies a distinct category of experiences that are "epistemically" and "personally transformative." Such experiences both "giv[e] you new information" and "chang[e] how you experience being who you are" (Paul 2014: 17). Ordinary rules for rational decision-making cannot guide individuals' choices about whether to undergo such transformative experiences, Paul contends. This is because the changes in knowledge and values occasioned by such experiences cannot be confidently predicted before they take place, and cannot be reliably evaluated after they occur.

Paul explicitly considers the case of individuals facing enlistment or conscription into military service in her analysis of transformative experience. She describes such a case as follows:

> Consider a recruit's choice about whether to enlist. If the recruit has no experience of war, what it is like to be on the front lines of a battle can be a transformative experience, as the evidence of post-traumatic shock amongst veterans can testify to. If such an experience is transformative, as it likely is, and on the assumption that there is reasonable variation amongst the experiences of new recruits (some experience a newfound sense of glory and heroism, some experience fear, and so on), a new recruit who is likely to go to the front lines if he enlists cannot make a rational choice about whether to enlist based on his subjective projections for the future.
>
> *Paul 2014: 52–53*

So far, it seems that the decision faced by this potential enlistee is well fitted to the framework of transformative choice and transformative experience. But Paul continues:

> there is subjective value in life experience, and subjective value in heroism, and subjective value in sacrificing your comfort and happiness for the sake of your country. But if you can assume (and I admit this is not without justification!) that the negative value of the experience of being on the front lines is very likely to outweigh the positive value of all these other experiences, although you cannot actually know what it is like to be on the front lines at wartime, you can rationally choose to avoid it on this basis.
>
> *Paul 2014: 53–54*

As an analysis of the actual decision confronted by potential military enlistees, Paul's account has limitations. Some of these are explicit—as when Paul adds that she is assuming there is no compulsion involved in the recruit's choice (Paul 2014: 53). Other limitations are implicit—as when Paul shifts, within the first passage quoted, from considering the decision facing military recruits generally to considering the decision facing recruits who can expect to be deployed to the front lines of a conflict. My own view is that the decision of whether to enlist or accept conscription into the armed forces frequently does confront individuals as a genuinely transformative decision, rather than the no-brainer Paul depicts. In the remainder of this section, I will offer evidence for this view, focusing as Paul does on cases of voluntary enlistment. In particular, I will suggest that military enlistment is likely to be morally transformative, even as it produces broader changes in individuals' knowledge and preferences.

To begin, we may note that marketing materials for national militaries frequently present the choice to become a soldier as both personally and epistemically transformative. In the United States, the Army, Navy, Marines, and Air Force promise to help recruits discover their potential, become adults, see the world, and acquire lasting abilities. These promises are not substantially different from the promises that colleges and universities make to young men and women at the same age level—and for current recruits, as for those conscripts and volunteers who participated in the Second World War, service is directly tied to a promise of financial support for higher education.

Of course, the military's marketing materials and incentive packages provide only partial evidence of the transformative nature of military service. Further evidence comes from the testimony of individual soldiers describing or anticipating their combat experiences. Jeff McMahan begins his 2008 book *Killing in War* by presenting the reflections of one famous WWI recruit on this subject—Ludwig Wittgenstein. By facing combat, McMahan reports, Wittgenstein hoped to "finally become a decent human being" (McMahan 2008: 2). The fact that Wittgenstein would go on to become one of the most influential philosophers of the twentieth century might lead some to object that his reflections on the experience of combat cannot be representative. Historians tell us otherwise. Yuval Noah Harari has shown that the view of participation in war as both epistemically and personally transformative was pervasive across European societies for centuries before WWI (Harari 2008). Harari cites the recollections of a young British officer in the Napoleonic Wars who was told, prior to his first battle, that "in less than twenty-four hours hence, I might be wiser than all the sages and philosophers that ever wrote" (Harari 2008: 1). Subsequent examples of testimony from both officers and ordinary soldiers in a large range of conflicts support Harari's claim that war has very often been viewed by its participants as "the ultimate experience."

If these transformative features of military service—specialized training, world travel, and self-revelation—are beneficial, other transformative features of military service are costly. Traveling the world, for example, while in many ways an attraction, also entails separation from family for extended periods. For young recruits whose family consists chiefly of parents and siblings, this may be no different than going away to college. For soldiers with spouses and young children, however, the separation may be more difficult, particularly as family visits to sensitive areas are generally impossible, and as the timing of leaves and discharge may be unpredictable.

A second, and more significant, potential cost of military service consists in psychological effects. L.A. Paul rightly mentions post-traumatic stress disorder, or PTSD, as a risk confronting potential military recruits. Whereas Paul associates this risk with front-line combat experience, however, PTSD and other negative psychological effects also seem to be heightened for soldiers who do not face direct exposure to combat (Junger 2016: 87). This is important, since it suggests that even men and women considering enrolling for specialized service in non-combat branches of the military face the possibility of significant psychological damage.

A third feature of military service that is likely to be costly, and which Paul also mentions, is the possibility of killing and being killed or injured. Not all, and indeed not most, service members directly experience combat, as we have just seen. Nevertheless, the possibility for killing and being killed or injured extends outside of combat zones in a variety of ways: in the handling and storage of volatile munitions; in conducting training exercises or non-combat missions in hostile environments; and in guiding or making targeting decisions for remote weapons systems. Engaging in such activities is not as dramatic as the Somme-like picture of combat Paul provides, but it is more realistic as a representation of the types of risks to health, both physical and psychological, that today's recruits face.

Military service is not just epistemically and personally transformative. It also induces moral transformations. Enlisting for or accepting conscription into the armed services transforms an individual's moral relationships; it establishes new moral responsibilities, and exposes individuals to new moral risks. Paul's model of transformative experience is supposed to apply to choices not determined by prevailing legal or moral norms (Paul 2014: 19). This may be taken to suggest that the morally transformative features of military service count as reasons against using this model to analyze such choices. However, this need not be so. We can hold that enlisting for military service is frequently morally permissible, while still accepting that there are significant moral (as well as personal) costs for doing so. One way of understanding those changes in risks, responsibilities, and relationships is through the lens of exploitation. Michael Robillard and Bradley Strawser have argued that the position of military recruits within all-volunteer forces provides an exemplary case of moral exploitation, defined as "unfairly burdening someone with added moral responsibility or moral decision making" (Robillard and Strawser 2016: 172). Recruits, they say, are vulnerable to moral exploitation insofar as they bear outsize responsibility for *in bello* decision-making and outsize blameworthiness for infractions of *in bello* rules. The youthfulness and comparatively low socio-economic status of most new recruits render them still more vulnerable to moral exploitation, insofar as they "lac[k] important and relevant knowledge necessary for making an informed decision" (Robillard and Strawser 2016: 178).

The framework of transformative experience complicates this account of the moral costs of military service. It does so by suggesting that what Robillard and Strawser call "the heavy moral responsibilities that one takes on once one becomes a soldier" cannot be fully understood or assessed until one has had the relevant experiences (Robillard and Strawser 2016: 178). The moral costs of military service, like the non-moral costs, deserve to be included among the factors weighed in any decision to enter military service. In the next section, I will argue that the moral position of contingent pacifism is better equipped to reconcile these various factors than rival moral positions.

Extending Contingent Pacifism: The Argument from Transformative Experience

In order to understand what it means for a moral position to provide guidance to individuals facing a transformative decision, it is helpful to use the notion of deliberative norms. Deliberative norms are "norms concerning how we are supposed to *think* about—deliberate about, judge, value—certain kinds of things" (Brennan et al. 2013: 248). Such norms generally constitute a component of broader moral positions; they are grounded in the reasons that support those positions, but directed at specific types of practical problems that individuals embracing such positions are likely to confront.

One aim of L.A. Paul's analysis of transformative experiences is to argue that, in the case of decisions to undergo such experiences, there is a limit to what acceptable deliberative norms can demand of us. Deliberative norms that demand that we really understand how the choice to have a child, for example, will affect us before pursuing such a course are unacceptable, because such understanding only comes from actually undergoing the experience in question (Paul 2014: 71). Even mental simulations of the experience—what Paul terms "cognitive modeling"—cannot really fulfill this requirement, since such modeling cannot produce meaningful comparisons between present and future knowledge and preferences (Paul 2014: 71).

None of the major moral positions towards war and participation in war that I have discussed in this chapter require individuals contemplating military service to adopt unacceptable deliberative norms. In this respect, each of these positions is compatible with my characterization of enlistment into military service as a transformative choice. Nevertheless, there are considerable differences in the particular deliberative norms that absolute pacifism, traditional and revised just war theories, and contingent pacifism recommend for men and women considering enlistment for military service. Those differences do not exhaust these moral positions, which have implications for many other kinds of decisions besides that of whether to enlist or accept conscription into military service. Still, providing guidance to choices of this kind is a major aspiration of contemporary contingent pacifists. It is worth considering the implications of different pacifist and non-pacifist positions for such decisions here.

Absolute pacifism presents what philosophers might describe as a norm against deliberation, i.e. a norm that says it is wrong even to consider entering the military and undergoing the training in violence that this entails (Brennan et al. 2013: 251–252). Some versions of absolute pacifism may ground themselves in other kinds of reasons, such as the impermissibility of submitting to military authority, while issuing equivalent deliberative norms. While considering this case is instructive, I should note that many absolute pacifists would resist framing their position as giving guidance for a transformative choice, at least in Paul's sense. This is because many absolute pacifists deny that the decision to enlist or accept conscription into military service lies within the set of choices morally permitted to individuals (Ryan 2016).

Focusing on deliberative norms also helps clarify the distinction between traditional and revised forms of just war theory. Both forms of this theory recommend that potential combatants, either at the stage of enlistment or the stage of actually engaging in fighting, deliberate about the morality of their nation's cause. However, traditional just war theorists typically hold that both recruits and serving soldiers act permissibly in following their military or civilian leaders' assertions about the justness of particular conflicts—even when the evidential value of such assertions is unclear. So, Michael Walzer argues that ordinary soldiers serving on both sides of a conflict "are most likely to believe that their wars are just," and suggests on this basis that they should be regarded as "moral equals" (Walzer 2015: 127). Similarly, David Luban argues, in an article focusing specifically on the deliberative position of serving soldiers, that "soldiers [should] take heed whether the war they are asked to fight is manifestly unjust, but [should] obey the order to deploy when the fog of politics and war means that nothing is manifest" (Luban 2016).

Revised just war theorists resist Walzer and Luban's claims about the permissibility of deliberating in this fashion about the justness of one's nation's cause. Jeff McMahan argues that soldiers may sometimes be excused for failing to consider carefully the justness of their cause, but do not act permissibly in doing so (McMahan 2008: 112–115). McMahan does not directly challenge the legal permission soldiers enjoy to act in this way. He does suggest his moral arguments put pressure on this legal status quo. It's important to be clear about the distinction here. While traditional just war theorists suggest that recruits and enlisted soldiers are morally permitted to defer to the judgments of their leaders concerning the justness of their cause (except in cases of "manifest injustice"), revised just war theorists argue that such deference is not usually morally permitted, but is often excused.

Revised just war theorists present fairly demanding deliberative norms for individuals contemplating participation in war. Referring specifically to men and women who are already serving in their nation's armed forces, Jeff McMahan writes, "Given that what is at stake in their decision is of the utmost importance morally, it seems clear that it is morally incumbent upon them to deliberate carefully and to be confident of their ability to rebut the apparent presumption against fighting before they commit themselves to fight" (McMahan 2008: 150). The fact that most soldiers do not, as a matter of empirical fact, appear to engage in such deliberations before going to war, or to exhibit a baseline attitude of skepticism towards the justice of their nation's cause, does not make their actions permissible, but at most offers a partial excuse. It is considerations of this kind that lead McMahan closest to the contingent pacifist position, though he has not embraced it outright (McMahan 2008: 153; McMahan 2010).

It is not clear if revised just war theorists believe that the moral risk of participating in an unjust war is sufficient to make enlisting for military service, or accepting conscription, morally impermissible. Most of the aforementioned arguments concern soldiers already serving in their nations' armed forces, rather than individuals merely considering enlistment or facing conscription. If those theorists do take this view, then they will likely view the case from transformative experience as ill-founded, since that case excludes choices clearly ruled out by existing moral norms. If they do not take this view, they are likely to view the moral, epistemic, and personal costs of service that I have identified as too weak to ground such a prohibition. Either way, it seems that revised just war theory does not provide individual men and women contemplating enlistment or conscription with deliberative norms specifically attuned to the transformative features of their choice.

This difference between contingent pacifism and revised just war theory shows up still more clearly when we consider cases of conscription. Some revised just war theorists, notably Helen Frowe, argue that individual men and women should be held to a strict standard when it comes to allowing themselves to be conscripted for service in an unjust war. This view can be described alternatively as holding that a very high level of cost is reasonable for individuals to bear in order to avoid contributing to an unjust threat (Frowe 2015: 162–163n43).

The kind of choice Frowe considers here is a good example of what L.A. Paul calls a "choic[e] between transformative experiences." In such cases, "keeping the status quo is not an option"; rather, individuals must "pic[k] between equally revelatory options" (Paul 2014: 123). The experience of conscientious objection, even under a relatively benign regime of alternative civilian service, may be transformative if significant social stigma is attached to declaring CO status. In many historical cases, where hard labor or imprisonment has been imposed even on successful seekers of conscientious exemptions, the moral, epistemic, and personal costs have been even higher. Contingent pacifism, especially when informed by the model of transformative experience, can prepare potential conscripts to bear those costs, while providing a realistic depiction of the benefits, and harms, of accepting conscription.

Contingent pacifism, in my view, is the moral position that best reconciles the various considerations relevant to the decision of whether to enter military service. It incorporates full regard for moral considerations of the sort central to just war theory—without necessarily having to go beyond those to the more radical moral and legal claims made by Rodin, May, and others. At the same time, this position is attentive to the moral, epistemic, and personal transformations involved in this decision. It need not misrepresent that decision, in Paul's manner, as trivial or obvious. Though it holds that the transformative features of military service will usually incline in favor of abstention or conscientious objection, contingent pacifism acknowledges the possibility that some wars might be morally justified, and it allows that in such cases the reasons for participation in war may override the moral, epistemic, and personal costs of military service. Saba Bazargan reaches a similar conclusion after discussing what he calls the "epistemic argument" for contingent pacifism. According to this argument, "the prevalence of false-positive judgments regarding the justness of wars, combined with the devastating harmfulness of unjust wars, requires that we err on the side of caution by adopting strong presumptions against the permissibility of waging wars" (Bazargan 2014: 2).

Objections

The arguments for contingent pacifism that I have discussed in this chapter will likely prompt objections of several kinds. By considering some of those objections, we can get a better sense of the limits of this position, and of the reasons supporting it.

A first objection is that if every man and woman considering military service within a particular state embraced contingent pacifism, there would be no more effective armed forces, leaving that state defenseless against actual attacks or credible threats. In this form, the objection fails. After all, contingent pacifists allow that military service is permissible and may even be obligatory in some cases, notably cases of "existential threats" or "genocidal aggression" as discussed by Rodin. But the objection can be modified to evade such a response. In modified form, the worry is that without regular armies, trained and kept up even in peacetime, states will lack the ability to mobilize effectively against those threats that contingent pacifists believe do justify war and participation in war.

In response to this objection, we should first note that nations already face some "existential threats" that cannot be avoided with certainty even by means of routine military buildup. The chief example of such a threat is nuclear destruction. The existential risk posed by nuclear weapons has caused many to favor contingently pacifist conclusions during particular standoffs. It has prompted some to support contingent or absolute pacifism as responses to war generally.

More comprehensively, we can say that even if contingent pacifism were embraced by a large majority of military-aged men and women, the actual decisions on military service made by those individuals would not be identical. Due to many factors, including differences in assessments of the value of military service, as well as what Rawls called the burdens of judgment, it is likely that at any given time some individuals who embrace contingent pacifism will judge that the reasons supporting this position are overridden by other considerations favoring enlistment. Thus, it is unlikely that national militaries would cease to exist, or that their institutional knowledge would cease to be passed on, if contingent pacifism is widely embraced.

A second objection cuts in the opposite direction. Though I have suggested that contingent pacifism is particularly well suited for men and women facing enlistment or conscription into military service, this framing might be judged too narrow. In particular, it fails to capture the "anti-militarism" that Andrew Fiala and others consider central to this position. Promoting particular deliberative norms for potential conscripts or enlistees, the objection concludes, simply will not affect the majority of the social and political institutions that make it possible for nations to wage unjust wars.

It is true that the framework of transformative experience is less helpful for addressing the decision by a legislator to vote for a military funding bill than it is for guiding the decisions of potential conscripts or enlistees. Nevertheless, this framework has important implications for broader social and political institutions. By using the lens of transformative experience, we can see that some of the most beneficial features of military service, such as education and skills training, or exchange with foreign countries and cultures, are in no way unique to those who serve in the armed forces, but are regularly experienced by men and women who do not take on the moral and personal risks of military service. The argument from transformative experience thus amplifies demands from the earliest self-declared pacifists for the "moral equivalent to war," i.e. for institutions that can provide beneficial transformative experiences without imposing the heavy moral and personal costs of military service (James 2007). Redirecting resources to such programs may well help undermine existing social and political institutions favoring "warism."

A third objection holds that in my discussion of the various features of military service that prompt moral, epistemic, and personal transformations, I neglected the most important such feature. Military service, put briefly, entails commitment to a cause outside of and larger than oneself. This transformative feature of military service is emphasized in military recruiting materials, in the inscriptions on public monuments, and in the testimony offered by veteran soldiers. It is, according to proponents of military service, a uniquely valuable transformation—one that benefits both the individuals who undergo it and their political community at large.

In response to this objection, I want first to suggest that no all-things-considered benefits can arise, either for an individual service member or for his or her countrymen, from participation in an unjust war. This implies a certain priority in the considerations contingent pacifists recognize as relevant to decisions about service. The possibility that enlistment or conscription for military service might lead to participation, either on the front lines or in supporting roles, in unjust wars should take precedence in the deliberations of potential recruits over any merely personal or epistemic consequences of service.

A more substantive response is to reiterate the fact that military service is not the only way to benefit one's political community, or to advance any cause one cherishes. Military service is distinctive chiefly in that it involves heightened risks of psychological trauma, moral exploitation, and wrongful killing. The burden rests with the critics of contingent pacifism to show that there is something especially valuable about the experience of serving a greater cause even in the face of these risks that can shift the deliberative presumption in favor of military service. Simply to assert this begs the question against what I believe to be the most suitable moral position for individual men and women confronting this transformative choice.

Works Cited

Bazargan, S. (2014). "Varieties of Pacifism in War," in H. Frowe and G. Lang (eds.), *How We Fight*. Oxford: Oxford University Press, 1–17.

Brennan, G., L. Eriksson, R. Goodin, and N. Southwood. (2013). *Explaining Norms*. Oxford: Oxford University Press.

Fiala, A. (2014). "Contingent Pacifism and Contingently Pacifist Conclusions." *Journal of Social Philosophy* 45 (4), Winter: 463–477.

Frowe, H. (2015). *Defensive Killing*. Oxford: Oxford University Press.

Harari, Y. N. (2008). *The Ultimate Experience: Battlefield Revelations and the Making of Modern War Culture, 1450–2000*. New York: Palgrave MacMillan.

James, W. (2007). "The Moral Equivalent of War," in R. Kambler and D. Kolak (eds.), *William James: Essays and Lectures*. New York: Pearson Longman, 270–283.

Junger, S. (2016). *Tribe: On Homecoming and Belonging*. New York: Twelve.

Luban, D. (2016). "Knowing When Not to Fight," in S. Lazar and H. Frowe (eds.), *The Oxford Handbook of Ethics of War*. Oxford: Oxford University Press.

McMahan, J. (2008). *Killing in War*. New York: Oxford University Press.

McMahan, J. (2010). "Pacifism and Moral Theory." *Diametros* 23, March: 44–68.

May, L. (2015). *Contingent Pacifism*. New York: Cambridge University Press.

Paul, L. A. (2014). *Transformative Experience*. New York: Oxford University Press.

Rawls, J. (1999). *A Theory of Justice*, revised ed. Cambridge, MA: Harvard University Press.

Robillard, M., and B. Strawser. (2016). "The Moral Exploitation of Soldiers." *Public Affairs Quarterly* 30 (2), April: 171–195.

Rodin, D. (2014). "The Myth of National Self-Defense," in C. Fabre and S. Lazar (eds.), *The Morality of Defensive War*. Oxford: Oxford University Press, 69–89.

Ryan, C. (2016). "Pacifism," in S. Lazar and H. Frowe (eds.), *The Oxford Handbook of the Ethics of War*. Oxford: Oxford University Press.

Walzer, M. (2015). *Just and Unjust Wars*, 5th ed. New York: Basic Books.

13

HUMANITARIAN INTERVENTION AND THE PROBLEM OF GENOCIDE AND ATROCITY

Jennifer Kling

When Hitler rose to power, and it became evident that he was going to mobilize the power of the German state against German (and non-German) Jews, a number of concerned rabbis and political activists wrote to Gandhi asking for advice. Should the Jewish citizens of Germany fight back? Gandhi wrote that the Jews should engage in nonviolent action, and that surely such civil resistance would "convert the latter [the German gentiles (to use Gandhi's phrase)] to an appreciation of human dignity" (Gandhi 1938: n.p.). Needless to say, the nonviolent civil resistance of the Jews—of which there was a good amount—was unsuccessful (Bauer 1989). Over six million Jewish people died before the concentration camps were liberated at the end of World War II (Snyder 2010: 389).

In essence, Gandhi's letter urges two main conclusions: the Jews have to save themselves, and they should save themselves nonviolently. While such a commitment to political self-determination and pacifism is in most cases laudable, the common reaction to Gandhi in this case is often disbelief. Surely, in this case of attempted genocide, it is not required that the Jews save themselves, and surely it is not required that the Jews—or others, for that matter—save themselves using nonviolent methods. More generally, we tend to think that mass atrocities and attempted genocides call for humanitarian intervention by other states. (Nonviolent intervention if possible, military intervention if need be.) In this chapter, I discuss these two related claims in turn. What, if anything, justifies humanitarian intervention in certain states by other states? Ought such interventions, if justified, be pacifist in nature, or is it legitimate in some cases to intervene violently? To discuss these questions, I draw primarily on principles and arguments found in just war theory, pacifism, international relations, and analytic political philosophy more generally.

Against Intervention

John Stuart Mill (1859), somewhat like Gandhi, argues that the principle of political self-determination precludes any sort of intervention, military or otherwise, by a state in the domestic affairs of another state. In other words, a people get the government that they deserve and are willing to fight for; domestic politics should be left to a state's citizens, not interfered with, influenced, or controlled by outside political forces. Mill's argument for this principle of political self-determination, as stated, is dependent on his utilitarianism. However, we need not commit ourselves to utilitarianism to take the point. Mill argues that people are in the best position to tell what makes themselves happy; thus, we should, in general, defer to their judgment, even when we think they are mistaken. Allowing a people to choose their own form of government is a way of avoiding political paternalism. Furthermore, people will be made happier by having the choice. So even if, Mill claims, the people choose wrongly (i.e., they do not in fact choose the government best positioned to make them happiest), they will still be happier than if some other political entity had chosen their government for them. Thus, Mill advocates for the political principle of non-intervention.

Mill puts the argument for political self-determination (and thus the subsequent argument for the principle of non-intervention) in terms of utilitarianism, but we could equally well understand the argument in terms of rights. Humans have the right to autonomy, and so we have the right to choose our form of government. For anyone else—another state, a non-governmental institution, or an individual—to choose it for us would be for that entity to violate our autonomy rights. So, the principle of political self-determination is justified not only on utilitarian grounds, but also on rights-theoretic grounds. As Kant puts it, "No nation shall forcibly interfere with the constitution and government of another . . . a foreign power's interference would violate the rights of an independent people struggling with its internal ills. Doing this [intervening] would be an obvious offense and would render the autonomy of every nation insecure" (Kant 1983: 109). The rights of the people to political self-determination thus straightforwardly generate, for Kant, the political principle of non-intervention.

In the broad scheme of things, such a principle seems easily defensible; if a people want a constitutional monarchy, or a theocracy, or an oligarchy, who are we to tell them otherwise? To tell them otherwise seems not only to run counter to utilitarian and rights-theoretic reasoning, but also to be the height of condescending paternalism, an attitude as infuriating as it is outdated. To tell people what sort of government they ought to want, and worse, to interfere with their domestic politics in order to make sure they get the "right sort" of government, smacks of imperialism and colonialism, not to mention systemic racism and oppression. As Walzer points out, "As with individuals, so with sovereign states: there are things that we cannot do to them, even for their own ostensible good" (Walzer 1977: 89). The principle of political self-determination demands that states stay out of each other's domestic political affairs, that is, that states observe the principle of non-intervention.

On its face, we might think of the principle of non-intervention as the international political equivalent of the old interpersonal adage "mind your own business." Thus, it is not surprising that non-intervention, historically, has been linked to the political ideology of isolationism, i.e., the idea that it is best for one's state to be entirely self-reliant, to avoid any economic, social, political, or militaristic entanglements with other states (Chalberg 1995). Isolationists generally argue that their policies will help maintain a state of peace (Turku 2009: 6–7). On one commonsense view of peace, this appears to be correct; if a state refuses any responsibilities towards and engagements with other states, then that state is likely to be able to avoid conflicts with other states. Similarly, we tend to think that a good way to "keep the peace" in our personal lives is to avoid confrontation—this is why we (mostly) avoid discussing politics at the dinner table. But this understanding of peace, as simply a lack of conflict or confrontation, is not obviously correct. As King famously argues, "True peace is not merely the absence of tension: it is the presence of justice" (King, Jr. 1958/2010: 27). So, the question then becomes whether isolationism generally and non-interventionism more specifically are always conducive to justice, as they claim, or whether, in certain circumstances, they seek to avoid conflict at the expense of justice.

To put the question another way, is the principle of political self-determination absolute, or are there circumstances wherein intervention is permitted, or indeed, obligatory? We might think that the situation with the German Jews is one such case. Surely the German Jews tried to fight politically for the government they wanted; however, they lost, and the result was domestic, and soon afterwards international, genocide. Such an extreme injustice seems to call straightforwardly for humanitarian intervention: the principle of political self-determination and its affiliated principle of non-intervention, we might think, stops where mass atrocities and attempted genocides begin. Otherwise, we leave the German Jews, and more recently, the Tutsi in Rwanda, the Rohingya in Myanmar, and the Darfuri in Sudan, etc., to their fate.

In Favor of Intervention

While there is a strong intuitive pull towards the conclusion that extreme cases (such as mass atrocities and genocides) call for extreme measures (such as military interventions by other states), intuition is not the same as argumentation. Turning to the argument for humanitarian intervention, then, let us consider Walzer's well-known theory of intervention, found in his seminal *Just and Unjust Wars*. Walzer argues that the principle of political self-determination, following Mill's argument, should be reformulated as follows: "Always act so as to recognize and uphold communal autonomy" (Walzer 1977: 90). Normally, he claims, recognizing and upholding communal autonomy will require recognizing and upholding the political self-determination of states (i.e., it will require adhering to the principle of non-intervention); but because states and communities are not always identical, recognizing and upholding communal autonomy will sometimes require intervention. It is possible for a state to violate the autonomy of various communities of people within its borders, through either severe oppression, mass violence, or widespread enslavement and imprisonment, and when this happens, Walzer argues, other states can best prove their commitment to communal autonomy by intervening against the state in question on behalf of those threatened communities and their individual members (Walzer 1977: 90).

Given the often severe asymmetries between the sheer amount of military force a government can bring to bear on its people, versus the amount of military force a people can bring to bear on its government, Walzer's argument here is reasonable. As he writes, "Humanitarian intervention is justified when it is a response (with reasonable expectations of success) to acts 'that shock the moral conscience of mankind'" (Walzer 1977: 107). Such acts include mass atrocities, large-scale massacres, and genocides. In these sorts of extreme cases, it seems, as Walzer puts it, deeply cynical and troubling for other states to write off mass atrocities and attempted genocides as the result of people just not fighting hard enough for their communal autonomy (Walzer 1977: 101–108). Often, they fight valiantly and for long periods of time, only to be outgunned and subsequently interred (in political prisons, gulags, or internment camps), left to die, or killed outright. In such cases, defense of communal autonomy supports the right of other states to come to the assistance of the people who are fighting against—or simply being massacred by—their murderous state, rather than leaving the state in question to its atrocious and genocidal domestic devices.

There is some debate about whether a state's right to intervene is dependent on the people in the murderous state fighting back against their state, either violently or nonviolently. However, to say that the people have to be fighting back in order for an intervention to be justified, as though that is what makes them worthy of help, is mistaken. People who are being slaughtered by their government deserve help because they are people, not because they have proven themselves worthy by fighting back. However, this is not to say that people ought not fight back against severe oppression; perhaps Boxill (1976) is correct that people have an obligation to resist their own oppression. It is simply to say that the right to intervene is not dependent on people fulfilling their obligations (if they have them!) to resist. It is instead based on the right to defend communal autonomy when it is under threat.

The Rwandan Genocide

As a case in point, consider the Rwandan genocide. In the spring of 1994, the Hutu majority government began a genocidal campaign against the minority Tutsi (BBC News 2011). The genocide was planned by the core political elite of the Rwandan government and carried out by the Rwandan military and police forces, government-backed militias, and a large number of civilians (Independent Inquiry Commission 1999). An estimated 800,000 Rwandans, up to 70% of the Tutsi population of Rwanda, were slaughtered between April 1994 and June 1994, when the Rwandan Patriotic Front (RPF) took control of the country and ended the genocide (Harsch 1998: 4). After the RPF took control, an estimated two million Rwandans, many of them Hutus, were displaced and became refugees, many in neighboring Zaire (UN Refugee Agency 2000: 245–246). Despite violent and nonviolent resistance by Tutsi and Tutsi sympathizers, roughly 8,000 people a day were murdered during the genocidal 100-day period.

In response to the Rwandan genocide, many states called on the United Nations (UN) to intervene; however, no formal UN military intervention occurred. And furthermore, the UN peacekeepers in Rwanda at the time were withdrawn after ten soldiers were killed by genocidal Rwandan troops (Melvern 2004: 197). In a subsequent report assessing United Nations involvement in Rwanda before and during the genocide, it was found that the UN Security Council, the body responsible for determining whether to intervene, "lacked the resources" and "political will" to authorize a "robust peacekeeping force" that could have prevented the genocide (Independent Inquiry Commission 1999). Implicit in the report, but not stated outright, is that the UN ought to have authorized, not only an intervention of some sort or other, but a straightforwardly military intervention.

Was the international community morally correct to stay out of Rwanda? In the face of such a catastrophe, it seems that the better answer would have been to intervene in order to, if not stop the genocide, then at least lessen its severity. As Bill Clinton, the U.S. president at the time, put it, "I don't think we could have ended the violence, but I think we could have cut it down [if the U.S. had intervened]. And I regret it [not intervening]" (Chozick 2012). Of course, Clinton did not cause the Rwandan genocide. However, there is a real sense in which he, as the overall director of American foreign policy at the time, allowed it to occur. In line with Walzer's argument, Clinton could have used U.S. military power (just as other heads of state could have used their military power) to defend the communal autonomy of the Rwandan Tutsis. But he (and they) didn't. The same goes for the UN; while the UN's actions did not cause the genocide, its lack of responsiveness straightforwardly allowed the Rwandan genocide to occur and continue unchecked.[1] As Kofi Annan, who headed UN peacekeeping at the time of the Rwandan genocide, said, "There can be no more binding obligation for the international community than the prevention of genocide ... the international community clearly had the capacity to prevent those events [the Rwandan genocide], but failed to summon the will." He went on to say, "All of us must bitterly regret that we did not do more to prevent it. ... On behalf of the United Nations, I acknowledge this failure and express my deep remorse" (Harsch 2004: 3).

Both Clinton and Annan, as well as many other world leaders, seem to be expressing here the same intuition that we confronted previously, albeit in slightly different terms. When it is imminently possible to save hundreds of thousands of people, we should do so, regardless of national boundaries, and a lack of swift, decisive, preventative action is morally unacceptable. In broad theoretical terms, the prevention of genocide overrides the principle of non-intervention.

To say otherwise, interventionists argue, is to sacrifice people's lives and concrete communities either for the sake of abstract political rights, or because of—as in the Rwandan case—a lack of political will.

The Responsibility to Protect

In response to the Rwandan genocide and other mass atrocities, Annan, among others, called for a new global doctrine regarding intervention to be added to international law (Annan 1999). This doctrine, called the Responsibility to Protect (R2P), was endorsed by all member states of the UN at the 2005 World Summit (GCRP 2015: 1). While not yet an international law, strictly speaking, the R2P does have the status of an international "norm," in the sense that it has gained widespread acceptance in the international community. In its broad form, the R2P focuses on the responsibility of all states to protect people at risk, rather than on the moral or legal right of outside states to intervene in another state's domestic affairs (GCRP 2015). It thus attempts to avoid the difficult situation discussed previously, wherein people's rights to political self-determination must be weighed against other states' rights to commit acts of war unilaterally in the name of humanitarian intervention. By shifting the debate from state rights to state responsibilities, the R2P tries to elide some of the difficult legal and political questions posed by the explicit adoption of a state right to go to war in service of humanitarian intervention.

The Responsibility to Protect protects against four types of mass atrocity: genocide, ethnic cleansing, war crimes, and crimes against humanity (UN 2005: 30), each of which is spelled out in detail by the founding statute of the International Criminal Court (UN 1998). The R2P, considered as a global political commitment, is based on three broad "pillars" of action:

> **Pillar 1:** Every state has the responsibility to protect its populations from the four mass atrocity crimes.
> **Pillar 2:** The wider international community has the responsibility to encourage and assist individual states in meeting that responsibility.
> **Pillar 3:** If a state is manifestly failing to protect its populations, the international community must be prepared to take appropriate collective action in a timely and decisive manner and in accordance with the UN Charter.
>
> *UN 2005: para. 138–139*

Taken together, these three pillars set out a prevention method for mass atrocity. Insofar as Pillar 1 sets out the responsibilities of individual states in regard to their domestic populations, it goes against the traditional notion of sovereignty, according to which states have supreme authority within a territory (Wolff 1990: 20). Like the Universal Declaration of Human Rights (UDHR), which was adopted by the UN member states in 1948, the R2P circumscribes traditional state sovereignty in that it limits what states may do domestically. Although neither the UDHR nor the R2P have the status of positive international law, both are the subject of widespread international agreement, and as such, operate to tether individual states to a set of universal obligations regarding their internal affairs. The R2P thus revises the traditional notion of sovereignty: it maintains that sovereignty involves a "responsibility to protect" on the part of a state towards its own populations, a responsibility that the international community may assume when a state either perpetrates mass atrocities or cannot protect its populations from such crimes (International Commission on Intervention and State Sovereignty 2001: 12–13).

Some have tried to argue that the R2P strengthens rather than weakens sovereignty—as the 2009 Report of the UN Secretary-General puts it, "by helping States to meet their core protection responsibilities, the responsibility to protect seeks to strengthen sovereignty, not weaken it. It seeks to help States to succeed, not just to react when they fail" (UN 2009: 7–8). However, this seems to misunderstand the notion of strength at issue in traditional discussions of sovereignty. Traditionally, discussing the "strength" of sovereignty means discussing how able the sovereign (be it the king, the senate, the people, or the government or state as a whole) is to control its territory, and how rightful its authority is seen to be, both by its people and by other sovereigns. By contrast, the 2009 Report, in its use of "strength," seems to be referring to the ability of the sovereign to run a good state, i.e., one that protects its domestic populations. This usage thus assumes the revised understanding of sovereignty that the R2P explicitly argues for as a needed revision. So, whether we think the R2P actually strengthens or weakens sovereignty depends in large part on which conception of sovereignty we accept.

It is worth pointing out that the traditional notion of sovereignty comes out of the 1648 Peace of Westphalia, a series of peace treaties signed by the major and minor European powers. Designed to end the European wars of religion, the Peace of Westphalia established (among other things) the state right of political sovereignty, i.e., the right of states to govern themselves without outside interference, as well as the right of national political self-determination, discussed in Section I (Croxton 2013). The Peace of Westphalia was thus an attempt to end war by requiring states to respect each other's internal sovereignty. Given the peaceful purpose of sovereignty as it was originally conceived, the right of humanitarian intervention can be seen as a blow against peace insofar as it is a blow against traditional sovereignty. The R2P seeks to distance itself from this worry about the traditional doctrine of humanitarian intervention by arguing that it strengthens, rather than weakens, sovereignty. As noted, though, this argument depends on a false equivalency.

But the R2P not only attempts to revise the notion of sovereignty; it also sets out the responsibilities of the international community vis-à-vis individual states. Pillar 2 declares that the international community is responsible for helping individual states implement the kinds of programs necessary to prevent mass atrocity, such as diplomatic engagement, economic assistance, rule-of-law reform, and the building of inclusive political institutions, among other things (UN 2009: 9, 15). In other words, Pillar 2 changes the moral status of other states providing encouragement and assistance to a state under stress. Before the R2P, such aid was seen as supererogatory; a good thing to do, certainly, but not obligatory. With the R2P, such aid is morally required; to fail to help states "to build their capacity to protect" is to fail to fulfill one's obligations as a state in good standing in the international community (UN 2009: 15). Again, these obligations are not a matter of international law; but they are a matter of international agreement, and as such can be regarded as having normative, if not legal, force. These obligations help to situate the R2P in a primarily preventative role: the goal of Pillar 2 is to block the need for military intervention by blocking many of the social and political conditions that enable mass atrocities to occur. Again, this differentiates the R2P from the traditional doctrine of humanitarian intervention, which, as we have seen, tends to operate in a reactive capacity—once the mass atrocity or genocide is either occurring or about to occur, the right of other states to intervene overrides the state in question's right to sovereignty.

However, while the R2P is primarily preventative, it is not entirely so: Pillar 3 requires "timely and decisive" action by the international community in cases of threatened or occurring mass atrocity. If all else fails, the use of military force by the international community in order to stop the atrocity is explicitly permitted, if not required, by the R2P. Perhaps not unexpectedly, given the development of the R2P after not only the Rwandan genocide, but also the NATO bombing of Kosovo[2] such decisions to intervene with military force are to be made by the UN Security Council—individual member states are barred from taking unilateral military action

(UN 2009: 22). Essentially, through the adoption of the R2P, war is (appropriately) relegated to be used only a last resort in cases of mass atrocity and genocide, and can only be undertaken legitimately by the international community working together under the aegis of the UN Security Council.

But while these restrictions, considered as a whole, do severely restrict the scope and use of military force, they do not prohibit it. As stated in the 2009 Report, "Paragraph 139 [on which Pillars 2 and 3 are based] of the [2005] Summit Outcome reflects the hard truth that no strategy for fulfilling the responsibility to protect would be complete without the possibility of collective enforcement measures, including through sanctions or coercive military action in extreme cases" (UN 2009: 25). The R2P, although distinct from the traditional doctrine of humanitarian intervention, is thus still an argument for military intervention in cases of mass atrocity and genocide. The reasoning may be different, but the conclusion is roughly the same. The R2P prioritizes people's safety and security over state rights to political self-determination and self-governance, and so concludes that we ought to protect people everywhere from mass atrocity and genocide, with peaceful means if we can, with war if we must.

The Pacifist Response

In the face of mass atrocity and genocide, it now seems both intuitively clear and supported by a whole host of arguments that other states, as well as the international community as a whole, ought to intervene. However, the case for *military* intervention, specifically, has not yet been made (as we saw previously, it is stated, rather than argued for, in the R2P). Often, the move from "intervention" to "military intervention" happens so quickly as to be instantaneous; the assumption seems to be that nothing else can be done against the horrors of mass atrocity. Thus, the supposed pacifist response to mass atrocity and genocide, that we should never stage a military intervention (because it is always wrong to go to war), falls somewhat short of compelling. But to say only this is to dismiss the pacifist too quickly; there is more to say on behalf of pacifism here, in no small part because it seems straightforwardly false that nothing else can be done against the horrors of mass atrocity. True, but often forgotten, is the fact that "pacifist" does not mean "passive." As May writes:

> Being generally opposed to the recourse to war does not mean that one favors inaction in the face of tyrants or humanitarian crises. . . . The pacifist can be just as much an activist . . . as those who support war in such cases.
>
> May 2015: 62

The pacifist, although she can be, need not be committed to isolationism or strict non-interventionism; pacifism is perfectly compatible with, and in fact may be positively linked with, a nonviolent, or, more cautiously, a non-lethal, interventionist worldview.[3]

To see how pacifism might be positively linked with nonviolent or non-lethal interventionism, it is helpful to consider pacifism's root arguments. The pacifist argues, roughly, that it is always wrong to go to war because wars inevitably involve killing people, and killing people is morally prohibited (Norman 1988: 197–198). We need not go into the particular reasons for why killing people is wrong; different theorists differ here, and this is not the place to get into such deep waters (May 2015: ch. 1). For our purposes, it is enough to note that pacifists argue that the moral prohibition against killing is strong enough that it overrides the many moral and political reasons that governments and individuals often give for going to war (Nagel 1972: 126). Given the strength of this prohibition, it seems that pacifists might be committed not only to the claim that it is always wrong to go to war, but also to the further claim that people ought to stop others from going to war as well, if at all possible. Of course, the second claim is neither necessitated nor implied by the first. However, it does seem to be an objectionable sort of moral quietism to both argue that war is wrong and to refuse to try to convince other people that they ought not engage in it. More plausible, and certainly more historically accurate, is the pacifist who tries to convince others of her view; she not only decries war as immoral, she also tries to prevent other people—through nonviolent means—from engaging in war and other warlike activities, such as mass atrocity and genocide.[4]

The Danish Resistance

Thus, it is at least possible to consider adopting a strongly interventionist pacifism in response to the problem of mass atrocity and genocide. There are many interventionist actions that fall under the rubric of pacifism. Most dramatic, of course, is the use of one's own body as a human shield. Less dramatic, but possibly more effective in certain cases, are the strategies taken up by Denmark after their capitulation to Nazi Germany in World War II. While it is difficult to say whether the Danish case is, strictly speaking, an intervention—on the one hand, it was the Danish government interfering with the actions of the German government, but on the other hand, most (although not all) of the Danish actions took place on Danish soil and in regard to Danish citizens—it is nevertheless true that the nonviolent, non-lethal strategies employed by the Danes can provide a general rubric for pacifist resistance and intervention. After the German invasion of Denmark on April 9, 1940, the Danish government chose to collaborate with the German authorities in order to remain in power. The Danes then engaged in various kinds of wide-scale nonviolent resistance against the Nazi program (Hæestrup 1976–77). Although such resistance was never officially sanctioned by the Danish government, Danish intelligence officials contacted British intelligence officers soon after the invasion, and stayed in communication almost weekly throughout the occupation, passing along a large amount of significant military data (Lunding 1970: 68–72). This suggests that while the Danish government did not publicly endorse nonviolent resistance, they likely privately endorsed it; the Danish government certainly never publicly condemned, nor sought to stop, the flow of intelligence data from Denmark to Great Britain. And furthermore, this form of nonviolent resistance was arguably very successful; as Jespersen writes, Danish intelligence had a "significant strategic effect" on the war in Europe (Jespersen 2002: 2).

In addition to passing along significant military intelligence to the Allies, the Danes also disrupted attempts by the Nazis to deport Danish Jews, as well as non-Danish Jews who passed through Denmark, to concentration camps (United States Holocaust Memorial Museum n.d.). Throughout the course of the occupation, roughly 7,500 Danish Jews were smuggled to neutral Sweden, where they were granted asylum. Of the 500 Danish Jews who were deported to Czechoslovakia, 449 survived, due to Danish officials pressuring the Germans publicly throughout the war with concerns about their deported citizens (United States Holocaust Memorial Museum n.d.). Most notably, the Danish king, Christian X, threatened to wear a yellow Star of David on his coat when the German ambassador to Denmark floated the idea in conversation of requiring Danish Jews to don the yellow Star of David (Christian X, cited in Vilhjálmsson 2003). The suggestion was subsequently dropped, and Danish Jews were never required to publicly identify themselves during the occupation. (Nor did Christian X ever wear the yellow Star of David, contrary to popular myth.) Ultimately, the Danes proved with their actions that military force was not the only way to resist the genocide of the Jewish people; their nonviolent resistance and interventionist policies saved many lives.

Pacifist Intervention

Now, the Danes did not entirely prevent the Holocaust; but, it must be said, military intervention did not succeed in entirely preventing the Holocaust either. What the Danes did, rather, was resist and intervene using pacifist strategies to significantly lessen the horror of the Holocaust.[5] This suggests that it is not hand waving, or wishful thinking, which leads the pacifist to say that interventions need not be military interventions. Rather, pacifists are responding to historical evidence that pacifist interventions can be successful, if carried out publicly and by a large enough number of people. Imagine if the general strategy, by whole states, in response to Nazi aggression had been not only the smuggling of targeted groups and persons and the passing off of military intelligence, but also the use of more dramatic strategies such as creating walls of human shields, engaging in persistent economic slowdowns (through general strikes and the like), and generally making themselves ungovernable. As Walzer points out:

> No nonviolent struggle has ever been undertaken by a people trained in advance in its methods and prepared (as soldiers are in the case of war) to accept its costs. So it might be true . . . that resistance is as likely to [work] as military action is . . . and at a much lower cost in human lives.
>
> *Walzer 1977: 330*

And given the success of the Danes with no prior preparation, it seems that we can say not only that pacifist interventions might possibly work, but that they in fact have a somewhat reasonable chance of success.

So, pacifist interventionism—or interventionist pacifism—could be a fruitful path to pursue. It is important to note, though, that the possibility of a successful pacifist intervention depends on two things: first, convincing people that it is possible, and second, training people on how to engage in effective pacifist interventions. The first, if it occurs at all, will be the result of much argumentation and public debate. (This chapter could be seen as one entry in such a debate.) The second, however, is already being done through grassroots trainings worldwide. Bystander prevention training is becoming common on university campuses and in high schools around the world (Pfetsch et al. 2011; Gidycz, Orchowski and Berkowitz 2011), as are nonviolence trainings by grassroots Peace Teams in various states and countries (Meta Peace Team 2016). The legendary Gene Sharp has been training nonviolent civil resistance groups worldwide for decades, many of whom have subsequently passed on his teachings to others (Sharp 1970; Popovic 2015). Optimistically, these happenings can be seen as evidence for a slow shift towards pacifism, towards the idea that interventions do not have to be military in nature to be successful.

In addition to nonviolent intervention trainings, which primarily target adults, pacifists committed to intervening to prevent mass atrocity and genocide could also begin a campaign of teaching empathy worldwide, in particular to children. McFarland (2016) argues that prejudice is one of the root causes of mass atrocity, and Allport (1979) argues that prejudice partially comes about because of a lack of empathy. Both theorists suggest, although they admit the evidence is not conclusive, that empathy is learned primarily during childhood. Assuming these conclusions are roughly correct, early interventions across the world in order to teach empathy to children could be extraordinarily effective in preventing future mass atrocities and genocides. Or, at the very least, such interventions could help lessen the violence, by making people much less likely either to participate once atrocities start occurring, or to turn a blind eye and fail to protest in the presence of such atrocities. As McFarland points out, those who are highly empathetic are much more likely to resist atrocities, either in their own or in other states (McFarland, Webb, and Brown 2012). Admittedly, this is a much different sort of intervention than those who commonly discuss the doctrine of humanitarian intervention have in mind; like the R2P, it is proactive, but somewhat uniquely, it targets children rather than adults. However, if pacifists are serious about preventing mass atrocity and genocide, it seems that such interventions could be very effective. And again, it is an evidence-based practice that pacifists can point to when asked how they, with their strong commitment to nonviolence and non-killing, can possibly prevent, or at the very least ameliorate, mass atrocity.

Finally, pacifists could create an open-source database online for groups targeted by murderous states—such as is imagined by Stephenson in *Cryptonomicon* (1999). While not strictly speaking an intervention, insofar as it does not involve a violation of physical territory or political sovereignty, such a database could definitely serve the purpose that interventions are meant to serve—it could prevent or help stop mass atrocities and genocides. Such a database, and associated online systems, could detail how to resist nonviolently, how to forge papers, how to flee without being caught, how to create effective disguises, how to bribe officials, etc. It could also list safe places where targeted groups and persons could seek asylum, and could detail various methodologies for bringing sympathetic global attention to their plight. Often, it is not only fear that holds people who have been targeted in place, it is a lack of information about what to do and where to go. Simply by providing relevant and useful information free of charge to all, pacifists could, if not prevent such horrific violence from occurring, certainly cut it down. (It is important to emphasize again at this point that this, in essence, is what a military intervention would do, too; it would cut the violence down, not prevent it from occurring altogether.)

While such a technological intervention may sound futuristic and farfetched, there is some evidence that online databases and systems are already being used in ways close to this. Egyptian nonviolent civil resisters avoided being arrested, and coordinated their movement to overthrow Mubarak, primarily through online systems such as Google Docs, Facebook, Twitter, WhatsApp, and YouTube (Shapiro 2009; Lefkow 2011). In addition, global attention was brought to the tragedy of Aleppo by citizens of that city tweeting as their city burned around them, which helped lead to renewed peace talks between Bashar al-Assad (the Syrian president at the time of writing) and representative Syrian rebel leaders (Moore 2017). The global pressure that can be created through strategic publicity should not be underestimated, and pacifists are well situated to help targeted groups and peoples take advantage of this fact by enabling and encouraging them to make good use of the internet (Ali 2011).

Enabling Escape

In addition to the direct pacifist interventions I have so far discussed, there is another strategy that could be used by pacifists to prevent, or at least ameliorate, mass atrocities and genocides. Pacifists could urge their home states to open their borders to refugees. Such an open-door policy would not stop mass atrocity altogether, of course, but it would certainly help lessen the atrocities. In World War II, the United States refused to grant asylum to thousands of fleeing Jews, fearing that Nazi spies might be hiding among the Jewish refugees. Instead, the Jewish refugees were sent back to Europe, where many of them were interred in concentration camps and subsequently murdered (Gross 2015). If the United States had instead worked to resettle the Jewish refugees, either in the United States or in safe neighboring states, those needless deaths could have been avoided. And further, if the United States had not only opened its borders, but also worked nonviolently to help persecuted peoples escape the Nazi regime, it is possible that many of those targeted by the Nazis could have survived.

A state's willingness to engage in refugee resettlement is not an intervention *per se* because it is not one state physically (or even politically) intervening in the affairs of another state. Rather, it is one state changing its own domestic immigration policies in response to the actions of another state. Still, if other states were to open their doors to refugees in the event of a murderous state or regime arising, it could serve the purpose that interventions are meant to serve—it could prevent or help stop mass atrocities and genocides. Now, the United States, in particular, has long been against such open-door policies because of national security concerns. The current debate regarding accepting Syrian refugees into the United States, much like the old World War II debate, turns on worries that spies and terrorists will gain entry to the U.S. by disguising themselves as refugees (Kaplan and Andrews 2015; Seipel 2015). I suggest, though, that such concerns are unfounded, in part because they are factually inaccurate and in part because such a laser-like focus on national security concerns ignores the amount of good that the United States could do for refugees. The vetting process for refugees to enter the U.S. is one of the most comprehensive in the world, and as a result, the chances of an American being killed in a terrorist attack committed by a refugee is 1 in 3.64 *billion* a year (Cone 2015; Nowrasteh 2016: 1). And aside from these factual points, it is also the case that enabling refugees to escape by providing them with a safe haven would save them from persecution and death. Sometimes, we ought to help people just because we can, even when doing so requires us to put forth a certain amount of effort and take a certain amount of risk, because they are people who need the help (Singer 1972; Walzer 1977: 155–156).

By highlighting such facts and moral arguments, pacifists could put pressure on their home states to establish open-door policies towards refugees, in order to provide those targeted by murderous states and regimes with a safe haven to which to escape. The presence of such safe havens—for those able to run—would straightforwardly help to ameliorate, if not prevent, mass atrocities and genocides. Creating and implementing such generous refugee resettlement policies, while politically difficult, is thus one part of a plausible pacifist response to mass atrocity and genocide. (The other part being, as I discussed previously, the implementation of interventionist nonviolent strategies that help enable people to run.) In addition, such open-door policies would serve the purpose of allowing states to take a sort of middle road in response to mass atrocity, neither fully abandoning victims to their fate nor obviously intervening against another state's sovereignty.

Conclusion

None of what I have described is a perfect solution; at some point, so the argument goes, surely even the pacifist must concede that if nonviolent, or non-lethal, intervention fails, then we must be willing to step in with military force. Otherwise, we either abandon the victims of mass atrocities and genocides to their fate, or allow ourselves to die shielding them. It is precisely because neither of these options appears acceptable that the problem of mass atrocity and genocide is one of the most difficult sticking points for pacifism.

In this chapter, I have set out the shape of the current debate on humanitarian intervention as a whole, and have argued that pacifism has more to say about, and in response to, mass atrocity and genocide than is generally recognized. Ultimately, an interventionist pacifism might not be wholly satisfying, especially when we are viscerally confronted by the horrors of mass atrocities and genocides. However, it does not have to be silent in response to such horrors; as I have shown, pacifism can call for various kinds of effective nonviolent and non-lethal interventions and intervention-like policies and activities, and in general can say much more about the problem of mass atrocity and genocide than has often been assumed.

Notes

1 There is a moral difference between doing and allowing; sometimes, it is permissible to allow things to happen that it is impermissible to do (Bradley and Stocker 2005). But this distinction does not make a decisive moral difference here. It is undoubtedly worse to commit mass atrocities and genocides; however, it is also very bad to allow them to happen.
2 In 1999, the UN Security Council failed to authorize military action to stop ethnic cleansing being carried out in Kosovo by Serbian forces against ethnic Albanians. In response to this lack of action, NATO carried out a series of air strikes against Serbian military and government positions. The legitimacy of NATO's unilateral action has been debated ever since (Coleman 2007: 194–239)
3 Some claim that pacifism entails nonviolence, while others argue it entails merely non-lethality (Norman 1988; Reader 2000).
4 There have been a number of grassroots movements dedicated to anti-war pacifism throughout history. Recent examples include Code Pink: Women for Peace and the Non-Aligned Movement. Historical examples can be found in Beckwith (1845).
5 It is odd, in cases of genocide, to discuss the amount of horror produced, as though it can be quantified in any meaningful way. But of course, part of what makes mass atrocities so awful is that they force us to quantify horror, to talk in terms of numbers of the dead and dying, rather than about the mere fact that someone is dead or dying. Insofar as we must count the dead, though, it is—at least a bit—less horrific when there are fewer of them.

References

Ali, A. H. (2011). "The Power of Social Media in Developing Nations: New Tools for Closing the Global Digital Guide and Beyond." *Harvard Human Rights Journal* 24 (1): 185–219.
Allport, G. W. (1979). *The Nature of Prejudice*. New York: Basic Books.
Annan, K. (1999). "Two Concepts of Sovereignty." *The Economist* September 16. Available at: www.economist.com/node/324795 (Accessed 15 January 2017).
Bauer, Y. (1989). "Forms of Jewish Resistance During the Holocaust," in M.R. Marrus (ed.), *The Nazi Holocaust: Historical Articles on the Destruction of European Jews*, vol. 7. Westport, CT: Meckler, 34–48.
BBC News. (2011). "Rwanda: How the Genocide Happened." *BBC News* May 17. Available at: www.bbc.com/news/world-africa-13431486 (Accessed 20 February 2017).
Beckwith, G. C. (1845). *The Book of Peace: A Collection of Essays on War and Peace*. Philadelphia: American Peace Society.
Boxill, B. (1976). "Self-Respect and Protest." *Philosophy and Public Affairs* 6 (1): 58–69.
Bradley, B., and M. Stocker. (2005). "'Doing and Allowing' and Doing and Allowing." *Ethics* 115: 799–808.
Chalberg, J. C. (1995). *Isolationism: Opposing Viewpoints*. San Diego: Greenhaven Press.
Chozick, A. (2012). "In Africa, Bill Clinton Toils for a Charitable Legacy." *New York Times* September 4. Available at: www.nytimes.com/2012/09/05/us/politics/in-africa-bill-clinton-works-to-leave-a-charitable-legacy.html (Accessed 21 February 2017).
Coleman, K. P. (2007). *International Organisations and Peace Enforcement: The Politics of International Legitimacy*. Cambridge: Cambridge University Press.
Cone, D. (2015). "The Process for Interviewing, Vetting, and Resettling Syrian Refugees in America Is Incredibly Long and Thorough." *Foreign Policy* November 30. Available at: http://foreignpolicy.com/2015/11/30/the-process-for-interviewing-vetting-and-resettling-syrian-refugees-in-america-is-incredibly-long-and-thorough/ (Accessed 5 March 2016).
Croxton, D. (2013). *Westphalia: The Last Christian Peace*. Basingstoke, UK: Palgrave Macmillan.
Gandhi, M. (1938). "The Jews." Letter written from Segaon, November 20. Available at: www.jewishvirtuallibrary.org/lsquo-the-jews-rsquo-by-gandhi (Accessed 10 January 2017).
Gidycz, C. A., L. M. Orchowski, and A. D. Berkowitz. (2011). "Preventing Sexual Aggression Among College Men: An Evaluation of a Social Norms and Bystander Intervention Program." *Violence Against Women* 17: 720–742.
Global Centre for the Responsibility to Protect (GCRP). (2015). *The Responsibility to Protect: A Background Briefing*. New York: Global Centre for the Responsibility to Protect. Available at: www.globalr2p.org/publications/22 (Accessed 22 February 2017).
Gross, D. A. (2015). "The U.S. Government Turned Away Thousands of Jewish Refugees, Fearing That They Were Nazi Spies." *Smithsonian.com* November 18. Available at: www.smithsonianmag.com/history/

us-government-turned-away-thousands-jewish-refugees-fearing-they-were-nazi-spies-180957324/ (Accessed 11 June 2017).
Hæstrup, J. (1976–77). *Secret Alliance—A Study of the Danish Resistance Movement 1940–45*, vols. I, II and III. Denmark: Odense University Press.
Harsch, E. (1998). "OAU Sets Inquiry into Rwanda Genocide." *Africa Recovery* 12 (1): 4.
Harsch, E. (2004). "The World Reflects on Rwanda Genocide." *Africa Recovery* 18 (1): 3.
Independent Inquiry Commission. (1999). *Report of the Independent Inquiry into the Actions of the United Nations During the 1994 Genocide in Rwanda*. Geneva: UN Security Council. Available at: www.securitycouncilreport.org/atf/cf/%7B65BFCF9B-6D27-4E9C-8CD3-CF6E4FF96FF9%7D/POC%20S19991257.pdf (Accessed 20 February 2017).
International Commission on Intervention and State Sovereignty. (2001). *The Responsibility to Protect: Report of the International Commission on Intervention and State Sovereignty*. Ottawa, ON, Canada: International Development Research Centre. Available at: http://responsibilitytoprotect.org/ICISS%20Report.pdf (Accessed 11 February 2017).
Jespersen, K. J. V. (2002). *No Small Achievement: Special Operations Executive and the Danish Resistance, 1940–1945*, translated by C. Wade. Denmark: Odense University Press of Southern Denmark.
Kant, I. (1983). *Perpetual Peace, and Other Essays on Politics, History, and Morals*, translated with introduction by T. Humphrey. Indianapolis: Hackett Publishing Company.
Kaplan, T., and W. Andrews. (2015). "Presidential Candidates on Allowing Syrian Refugees in the United States." *New York Times* November 17. Available at: www.nytimes.com/interactive/2015/11/17/us/politics/presidential-candidates-on-syrian-refugees.html (Accessed 25 March 2016).
King, Jr., M. L. (1958/2010). *Stride Toward Freedom: The Montgomery Story*. New York: Harper.
Lefkow, C. (2011). "Social Media, Cellphone Video Fuel Arab Protests." *Sydney Morning Herald* February 22. Available at: www.smh.com.au/technology/social-media-cellphone-video-fuel-arab-protests-20110222-1b3fw.html (Accessed 27 February 2016).
Lunding, H. M. (1970). *Stemplet Fortroligt*, 3rd ed. Denmark: Gyldendal (Danish). Discussed in Jespersen, K.J.V. (2002). *No Small Achievement: Special Operations Executive and the Danish Resistance, 1940–1945*, translated by C. Wade. Denmark: Odense University Press of Southern Denmark.
McFarland, S. G. (2016). "Identification with All Humanity: The Antithesis of Prejudice, and More," in S.G. Sibley and F.K. Barlow (eds.), *Cambridge Handbook on the Psychology of Prejudice*. New York: Cambridge University Press, 632–654.
McFarland, S. G., M. Webb, and D. Brown. (2012). "All Humanity Is My Ingroup: A Measure and Studies of Identification with All Humanity." *Journal of Personality and Social Psychology* 103: 830–853.
May, L. (2015). *Contingent Pacifism: Revisiting Just War Theory*. Cambridge: Cambridge University Press.
Melvern, L. (2004). *Conspiracy to Murder: The Rwandan Genocide*. London and New York: Verso.
Meta Peace Team. (2016). *About Us*. Michigan: Meta Peace Team. Available at: www.metapeaceteam.org/about_us (Accessed 26 February 2017).
Mill, J. S. (1859). "A Few Words on Non-Intervention." *Fraser's Magazine*.
Moore, J. (2017). "Syria Peace Talks Between Rebels and Assad Regime Begin in Kazakhstan." *Newsweek* January 23. Available at: www.newsweek.com/syria-peace-talks-between-assad-regime-and-rebels-begin-kazakhstans-astana-546798 (Accessed 26 February 2017).
Nagel, T. (1972). "War and Massacre." *Philosophy and Public Affairs* 1 (2): 123–144.
Norman, R. (1988). "The Case for Pacifism." *Journal of Applied Philosophy* 5 (2): 197–210.
Nowrasteh, A. (2016). "Terrorism and Immigration: A Risk Analysis." *Cato Institute Policy Analysis no.* 798, September 13. Available at: www.cato.org/publications/policy-analysis/terrorism-immigration-risk-analysis (Accessed 11 June 2017).
Pfetsch, J., G. Steffgen, M. Gollwitzer, and A. Ittel. (2011). "Prevention of Aggression in Schools Through a Bystander Intervention Training." *International Journal of Developmental Science* 5 (1–2): 139–149.
Popovic, S. (2015). *Blueprint for Revolution*. New York: Spiegel and Grau.
Reader, S. (2000). "Making Pacifism Plausible." *Journal of Applied Philosophy* 17 (2): 169–180.
Seipel, A. (2015). "30 Governors Call for Halt to U.S. Resettlement of Syrian Refugees." *NPR* (National Public Radio) November 17. Available at: www.npr.org/2015/11/17/456336432/more-governors-oppose-u-s-resettlement-of-syrian-refugees (Accessed 25 March 2016).
Shapiro, S. M. (2009). "Revolution, Facebook-Style." *The New York Times Magazine* January 22.
Sharp, G. (1970). *Exploring Nonviolent Alternatives*. Boston: Porter Sargent.
Singer, P. (1972). "Famine, Affluence, and Morality." *Philosophy and Public Affairs* 1 (3): 229–243.

Snyder, T. (2010). *Bloodlands: Europe Between Hitler and Stalin*. New York: Basic Books.
Stephenson, N. (1999). *Cryptonomicon*. New York: Avon Books.
Turku, H. (2009). *Isolationist States in an Interdependent World*. London and New York: Routledge.
United Nations. (1948). *The Universal Declaration of Human Rights* [General Assembly resolution 217 A]. Geneva: United Nations. Available at: www.un.org/en/universal-declaration-human-rights/ (Accessed 19 February 2017).
United Nations. (1998). *Rome Statute of the International Criminal Court* [A/CONF.183/9]. Geneva: United Nations. Available at: www.icc-cpi.int/nr/rdonlyres/ea9aeff7-5752-4f84-be94-0a655eb30e16/0/rome_statute_english.pdf (Accessed 19 February 2017).
United Nations. (2005). *2005 World Summit Outcome* [A/RES/60/1]. Geneva: United Nations. Available at: www.un.org/womenwatch/ods/A-RES-60-1-E.pdf (Accessed 19 February 2017).
United Nations. (2009). *Implementing the Responsibility to Protect: Report of the Secretary-General* [A/63/677]. Geneva: United Nations. Available at: http://responsibilitytoprotect.org/implementing%20the%20rtop.pdf (Accessed 19 February 2017).
United States Holocaust Memorial Museum. (n.d.). *Rescue in Denmark*. Ushmm.org. Available at: www.ushmm.org/outreach/en/article.php?ModuleId=10007740 (Accessed 23 February 2017).
The UN Refugee Agency. (2000). *The State of The World's Refugees 2000: Fifty Years of Humanitarian Action—Chapter 10: The Rwandan Genocide and Its Aftermath*. Geneva: UNHCR. Available at: www.unhcr.org/3ebf9bb60.html (Accessed 20 February 2017).
Vilhjálmsson, V. Ö. (2003). "The King and the Star," in M.B. Jensen and S.B. Jensen (eds.), *Denmark and the Holocaust*. Denmark: Danish Center for Holocaust and Genocide Studies, 102–118.
Walzer, M. (1977). *Just and Unjust Wars*, 4th ed. New York: Basic Books.
Wolff, R. P. (1990). *The Conflict Between Authority and Autonomy*. Oxford: Basil Blackwell.

Further Reading

Holmes, R. L. (2016). *Pacifism: A Philosophy of Nonviolence*. New York: Bloomsbury. (A holistic philosophical defense of pacifism that incorporates historical and contemporary examples.)
Mill, J. S. (1859). "A Few Words on Non-Intervention." *Fraser's Magazine*. (One of the early philosophical discussions of the political principles of intervention and non-intervention.)
Pattison, J. (2010). *Humanitarian Intervention and the Responsibility to Protect: Who Should Intervene?* Oxford: Oxford University Press. (A contemporary discussion of the R2P doctrine that includes both normative analysis and empirical assessment.)
Stacy, H. (2007). "Humanitarian Intervention and Relational Sovereignty," in S.P. Lee (ed.), *Intervention, Terrorism, and Torture: Contemporary Challenges to Just War Theory*. New York: Springer Publishing, 89–104. (A historically informed discussion of the close links between the concepts of sovereignty and humanitarian intervention.)
Walzer, M. (1977). *Just and Unjust Wars*, 4th ed. New York: Basic Books. (The classic treatment of the Western just war tradition.)

14
VIRTUE ETHICS AND NONVIOLENCE

David K. Chan

Virtue ethics is not a rule-based ethics, and the choice of action by a virtuous agent requires the exercise of practical wisdom to judge what is right in the circumstances. Pacifism is the view that as a rule, violence should never be used against another human being, regardless of what that person is doing to oneself or others. Is there any reason to think that a virtue ethicist would advocate absolute pacifism? There are indeed actions that, according to Aristotle, are so evil in themselves that a person of good character would never choose to do them (Aristotle 1998: II.6).[1] However, it does not seem obvious that killing in self-defense would clear the bar to count as the kind of action that is ruled out absolutely, and which should not be chosen regardless of the circumstances. Thus, in this paper, I will discuss virtue ethics in relation to the rejection of the use of lethal violence. I will argue that, given how I apply virtue ethics, a person of good character will have a very strong intrinsic desire to avoid the killing of another human being, so that only in rare circumstances where the alternative to violence is immensely evil would the use of violence to prevent the evil be the morally appropriate choice for the person to make.

I shall first give a brief summary of a neo-Aristotelian version of virtue ethics. Then I will explain why I think that a virtuous agent would be strongly averse to killing human beings. I will go on to show that this does not mean that such an agent would never use violence on others, only that she would be very reluctant to do so. The circumstances in which she would do so are rare, but cannot be ruled out. For instance, virtuous agents may in very limited cases kill in self-defense despite a strong aversion to killing. The circumstances in which killings take place are found most of all in war, so I will close by discussing where the virtue ethics approach to war is positioned in relation to just war theory and pacifism.

Neo-Aristotelian Virtue Ethics

Virtue ethics has been contrasted with consequentialism and deontological ethics as being agent-focused rather than act-focused. What this means is that the criterion for right action in virtue ethics refers to the concept of a virtuous agent, not the consequences of the action (as in utilitarianism) or the maxim of the action (as in Kantian deontological ethics). Many accounts of virtue ethics draw from the writings of the ancient Greek philosopher Aristotle. There are, however, metaphysical assumptions in Aristotle's idea of a good human being that modern virtue ethicists seek to avoid. In particular, Aristotle sees each natural kind as having an essential nature that can be used to explain what the thing is and does, as well as to provide a standard for what its good is (Aristotle 1998: I.7). So humans are thought to have an essential nature that differentiates them from all other creatures, and a good human is one who does the activities that fulfill human nature in an exemplary manner. Given this view of human goodness, a list of human excellences or virtues can be provided that is independent of culture. These virtues are states of character that are stable and they motivate the agent to choose certain actions for their own sake. Virtuous actions are those that are performed as a constitutive part of a good human life. A human being is not born with virtues of character but acquires them by practicing virtuous actions in a process of habituation (Aristotle 1998: II.1). It is only after she has fully acquired the virtues that she does virtuous actions for their own sake and with full understanding.

The virtues of human beings dispose them to perform the activities that differentiate humans from other living things, and to do them well. Aristotle finds that humans are essentially rational animals, so the best human life involves doing activities that make use of the capacity to reason. Some of these activities are theoretical, such as doing mathematics, science, and philosophy. But another part of human reason is practical, wherein reason is used to decide about what the agent is to do. In order to decide well, the agent exercises the intellectual virtue of practical wisdom. The choice of an agent with practical wisdom is not determined by calculating consequences or following a rule. Instead, the agent has an intuitive ability gained through experience to judge correctly regarding the virtuous thing to do (Aristotle 1998: VI.11).

Two problems for virtue ethics are obvious, and contemporary virtue ethicists have given a variety of responses to the problems. The first problem is whether all humans have a nature in common, from which we can derive a universal list of virtues. Aristotle seems to reflect an intellectualist bias in holding reason to be the defining human characteristic, and insisting that one has to use reason well in order to live a good human life. Moreover, the list of virtues he came up with seems to reflect his cultural assumptions. We know that what was viewed as a virtue in the past or in one society is not necessarily viewed as a virtue in different times and places. Moreover, how he analyzes the virtues may not be how we think of them today. This becomes relevant later when I diverge from Aristotle's idea that the willingness to go to war to defend the state is a virtue of the citizen (Aristotle 1998: III.6).[2]

A second problem concerns the vagueness of the criterion for right action in virtue ethics. If moral decision-making is not rule-based, and there is no yardstick for measuring and comparing options to decide what is best, how is it done? The idea that it is a matter of intuition seems to make it subjective, leaving no public way of settling disagreement. Moreover, it is of little help to someone who needs guidance to be told to do what a virtuous person would do in the situation. If she is already virtuous, she does not need guidance. But if she is not, how can she tell what it is that a virtuous person would do, and who the virtuous person to consult is if she does not know what to do?

Virtue ethicists today have proposed different answers to these and other problems in Aristotle's virtue ethics. Some have moved away from Aristotle's account to consider virtues using a different framework. Others have tried to improve on Aristotle's account. The latter, who include all those who use Aristotle's account as the starting point for formulating virtue ethics, are known as neo-Aristotelians. They can however diverge from Aristotle in different ways, so there are many versions of neo-Aristotelian virtue ethics. In this paper, we cannot explore all the different accounts of virtue ethics. I will give some of my own views in order to address the question of whether a virtuous agent would use or avoid using lethal violence, taking an approach that is largely neo-Aristotelian.

Virtue and Killing

Prohibitions on murder are found in almost every society, so it is a test of any moral theory whether it can explain the basis for the intuition that murder is wrong. I say "murder" because most legal codes have exceptions in which killing is justified and not wrongful, such as killing in self-defense or when acting under the authority of the state (for instance, executioners and soldiers). For virtue ethics, the basis for the wrongness of unjustified killing has to rest on the character of the agent, and not so much on the nature of the act of killing or its consequences. A virtue ethicist has to explain why someone in possession of all the virtues would be disposed to refrain from actions that cause the deaths of other humans.

Having said previously that in virtue ethics, an agent exercises practical wisdom in choosing the appropriate thing to do in the circumstances rather than applying rules, the question of why killing is wrong is about why it would be inappropriate in most circumstances for a virtuous agent to choose to kill instead of choosing another available option that does not involve killing. How an agent makes such a choice is a matter of practical rationality in which a failure of reason rather than of character is possible. If an agent responds to a situation impulsively, or fails to consider or make salient an option, her choice would be irrational rather than vicious. The *moral* evaluation of her choice is one that examines the motivation behind her choice and her action, particularly the desires that she has for ends that are valued for themselves and not for the sake of something else. Such intrinsic desires are the ultimate sources of an agent's motivation to engage in practical reasoning and action thereafter. What she chooses and what she does, were she rational, depends on what her intrinsic desires are for and how strong they each are. If there is no practical irrationality in how she chooses and how she acts, then when she acts, her actions reflect her moral character, and reveal the kind of person that she is.

I am here suggesting that when Aristotle describes virtues of character as dispositions to think, feel, and act in certain ways (Aristotle 1998: II.3), these virtues consist of intrinsic desires of the agent. In moral psychology, desires need to be distinguished from intentions that concern what one is motivated to do after practical reasoning. (See Chan 2016 for accounts of desire and intention that differentiate between them as action-theoretic concepts on the basis of their roles in motivation and practical reasoning.) One can be motivated to do what one does not desire to do for itself because one intends to do it as the rational thing to do given one's ends. Intentions are formed by means-end reasoning and they may be revised when one receives relevant new information, but the intrinsic desires that are the ultimate sources of agency are much more stable. Such stability is what Aristotle attributes to character when he says that virtues and vices are formed through a habituation process and they are not easily changed once acquired. In my view, a person's character consists of her intrinsic desires and such desires, unlike intentions, take practice to acquire and change.

When I claim that a virtuous agent would strongly desire to refrain from killing human beings, this may be a conceptual claim or a descriptive claim or both. For Aristotle, any claim about what counts as a virtue is based on the concept of human good, as human virtues are defined as the characteristics of human beings that play a necessary part in making good lives possible. As I mentioned in the last section, we no longer accept Aristotle's metaphysical claims about what makes us human, and this leaves it an open question as to what should be included in a list of virtues. One could provide a naturalistic account based on biology that would sidestep his controversial metaphysical theses. Alternatively, one could engage in a historical description of human practices that grounds virtues in a moral tradition rather than in nature. An example of the naturalistic approach is found in Foot (2001), while MacIntyre (1981) is someone who has appealed to moral traditions.

I think however that we do not need to provide an account of human nature or human good in order to say what some of the *central* virtues and vices are. It is not as if we are unsure whether someone who cold-bloodedly murders an innocent person is a good or bad human being until philosophers pronounce on what makes us human. I grant that many character traits that motivate what humans do lie in a gray area, and to resolve whether these are virtues or vices requires philosophical assistance. But if virtues and vices consist of intrinsic desires that motivate choice and action, then I can safely say that a strong desire to refrain from killing human beings is found in any human being whom we would call virtuous. The evidence for this is both empirical and conceptual. Given that humans from the beginning of history are social, someone who is not motivated to avoid killing would be ill suited to live in human society.[3] Hence, rules that forbid murder exist in nearly every society. Moreover, there is ample evidence, from war for instance, that otherwise normal human beings who kill other humans are traumatized to an extent that gets in the way of human flourishing. Of course, to say this may seem question begging because there are those whom I would consider not "normal," who kill without remorse, and may even take pleasure in doing so. So is it a human vice that someone possesses in being indifferent to homicide?[4] In response, I can make a conceptual case. If we imagine, as a thought experiment, a comparison between two people who have exactly the same virtues (that is, the same intrinsic desires for a number of good ends) but differ in the single aspect that the first of them has the strong desire to refrain from killing and the second lacks this desire, I think it is intuitive and fairly uncontroversial to say that the first person is a better human being.

I do not have the space to expound further on the thought experiment I use here to support my view about the virtuous person's strong desire not to kill. But if I am right, a virtuous agent, who has to choose whether to kill another human being or not to do it, will be making that choice on the basis of a motivational set that includes a strong desire to avoid doing the killing. If she is not irrational in making the choice, what she chooses reflects on her character since the outcome of her deliberation takes into account all her ends and how strongly she desires to achieve those ends. How hard or easy it is for her to choose not to kill depends on how strongly she desires not to kill. This account of the practical choices of a virtuous agent does not show that such a person would never choose to kill. It does however show that it would take something exceptional to make killing the appropriate choice for a virtuous person. In the next section, I will explain what sort of circumstances could lead a virtuous person to make the choice to kill, and how carrying out that choice would affect her character.

Moral Dilemmas

Moral dilemmas are situations in which a person does wrong no matter which course of action (or inaction) she chooses, and even if she does not choose. Utilitarians deny there are such situations because they hold that agents ought morally to always choose the action that has the best outcome in terms of utility (in whichever way it is defined). An agent does the right thing if what she does has as good an outcome as any alternative open to her, even if she kills people in doing it. Deontologists, who see certain kinds of action to be morally wrong regardless of their consequences, likewise need not accept the possibility of moral dilemmas, as long as there is a ranking of moral duties so that when they conflict, it is clear which duty has priority and ought to be fulfilled. It would not be surprising if the duty not to kill ranks so high that it overrides just about every other duty with few exceptions. So in most instances, it is wrong both to kill and to choose to kill even if other duties can be fulfilled only by killing.

Aristotle holds that there are some actions that are so depraved and shameful that no virtuous person could act rightly in doing them. But to act rightly is to be motivated by an intrinsic desire concerning certain ends: a desire that is found in a person of virtuous character. If as I previously claimed, virtuous humans necessarily possess a strong desire not to kill other humans, then someone of good character could not be motivated by a desire to kill. She could however be motivated by an *intention* to kill—an intention that is formed as a result of practical reasoning that takes account of all desires she has that are relevant to the situation (see Chan 2016 for a discussion of intention formation). In acting on that intention, she does not do something that is the virtuous thing to do. She does not do the kind of action that is associated with a virtue of character, in the way that a courageous action, for instance, is associated with the virtue of courage. Thus, she does not act virtuously. Yet she is not a vicious person who desires to do that kind of action in doing it.

In saying this, I am suggesting that a virtue ethics that takes moral dilemmas seriously is one that cannot rule out the possibility that a virtuous person may kill from an intention to kill that is formed in correctly reasoning about her available options. To make such a choice is not a failure of virtue, but the result of bad moral luck that places the agent in a situation in which she does not have the option of doing what she would characteristically do to express her virtues.

The decision-making process of a virtuous agent is not done by weighing the consequences in the way that a utilitarian would. For one thing, I have explained that in becoming virtuous, the agent acquires from experience an intuitive ability to make good judgments about what the virtuous thing to do is, and this is a matter of practical wisdom, not of measurement and calculation. And furthermore, the virtuous thing to do may be that in which the overall consequences are worse, not better. A fanciful but illustrative example of how a virtuous person chooses in a dilemma is to suppose that she has to choose between saving her mother and a very important world leader, say a Nelson Mandela type of leader whose death will throw a part of the world into turmoil. Let's say both are drowning and she has only one float to throw out, and she cannot swim. To allow one or the other to die is to fail to perform a virtuous act of saving a life. Clearly, assuming she is aware of the facts, a consequentialist would throw the float out to save the world leader. Yet a virtuous agent acting in character may choose appropriately to save her mother and do so intuitively without as much as a second thought.

Now I do not think that the virtue of compassion that consists of a desire to save others as an end in itself, when they are in trouble or danger, is as central to virtuous character and human flourishing as the virtue that consists of a desire not to kill others.[5] So in the remaining sections of the paper, I will focus on the tragic dilemmas that could make it appropriate for a virtuous agent not just to fail to save lives but to choose to kill in self-defense and in war, despite having a strong desire not to kill.

One further point I need to make before I move on is the following: when a virtuous agent, because of the moral dilemma, does an action that is not the kind of action that is "in character" for her, she may not emerge with her character unscathed. Character is formed and changed by what the agent does. It is true that virtuous agents may not always be perfect in what they do but remain virtuous nevertheless. But Aristotle describes a virtuous person who has the misfortune of King Priam as not living a happy life (Aristotle 1998: I.9–10). Now he says that Priam, given his character, will make the best of the situation and will not do what is vicious. However, I have argued that a virtuous person in a moral dilemma may do what is vicious, though not in the way that a vicious person does it. She does not do it because she desires to do it (or because she is not sufficiently averse to doing it). But one's character is affected by what one does, and it may be changed due to repeatedly doing what is contrary to it, or even by doing something just once that is extremely contrary to it. If the desire not to kill is central to virtuous character and human flourishing, then killing in a moral dilemma, even though one in fact strongly desires not to kill, is likely to damage one's good character. Ethicists who subscribe to modern views of moral responsibility may find this unpalatable, but I think that a neo-Aristotelian virtue ethics has to allow that good character and good living are affected by luck or fortune that is not within the agent's control (see Nussbaum 1986). This is already obvious in how the process of habituation in forming one's character depends on the circumstances of one's birth and upbringing. To allow that character can be changed by what happens to someone later in her life is simply an extension of this view of character formation.

Killing in Self-Defense

What one is permitted to do to defend one's life is a matter of controversy both in law and in moral philosophy. A number of state legislatures in the United States have passed "Stand Your Ground" laws that treat killing as self-defense (and therefore exculpating) if the killer felt that his life was threatened by the person he killed, even if he could have avoided the alleged threat without killing the alleged assailant. The view of self-defense that such laws reflect is one that is at odds with traditional views that hold killing in self-defense to be justified only as a last resort. What makes these laws even more disturbing is that they are often combined with laws that permit the open display of firearms in public places. Given that others may feel unsafe when someone carries a gun in public, would they then be justified in acting in self-defense in attacking the person who is armed with a gun? And would their attempt to disarm that person be seen as a threat that justifies him to in turn use the gun in self-defense?

In thinking about the matter in this way, one gets into an examination of whether more lives are saved or lost as a result of the combination of "Stand Your Ground" and open carry laws. Such thinking may be appropriate for rule-utilitarians, but a virtue ethicist would approach the issue differently. What an agent-focused moral theory such as virtue ethics is mainly concerned with is not the balance of consequences of an action or law, but how the choice of killing is made by an agent and how acting on the choice affects her character. If I am right that virtuous agents have a strong desire not to kill, what would they do when they are faced with possible threats to their lives? Would they be disposed to be cautious about killing unnecessarily even in situations where their lives may be at risk?

The favored approach to the morality of killing in self-defense is one that grounds self-defensive killing as a right (Thomson 1991). To kill someone is to breach a duty to respect the right to life of another. Killing in self-defense would not however constitute such a breach if the person killed was liable to be killed because he had lost his right not to be killed. Two ways of accounting for the loss of the right not to be killed are the culpability view and the unjustified-threat view. The former view holds that the culpability of the aggressor in posing a lethal threat renders him liable to be killed. The latter view makes room for a broader range of cases in which killing in self-defense is justified, as the mere fact that the threat to one's life is unjustified (as one still has the right to life) is sufficient to make the aggressor liable to be killed, even in cases when he poses the threat innocently.[6]

What is not fully appreciated about these two accounts of the right to kill in self-defense is that for an agent to apply the criterion for the right, she needs to have knowledge that is often unavailable at the time that she exercises the right to kill in self-defense. There is likely to be uncertainty concerning both the culpability of an alleged aggressor, and whether one is being subject to a threat to one's right to life at all. If people who are not only innocent but who do not pose any actual threat may be killed in "self-defense" because they are viewed as possibly a threat, the right to kill in self-defense seems overly broad. It is unfair to place the burden of risk of being killed entirely on those merely perceived to be threats. To kill in self-defense without absolute certainty that the criterion for exercising the right is satisfied is to risk harming others in an unjustified way.

For anyone concerned to avoid doing the wrong thing, the moral risk involved in killing unjustifiably counts against using violence when one is uncertain about the existence of a threat or the culpability of the alleged aggressor. Although perfect knowledge is unrealistic, someone engaged in activities that risk harm to others is expected to take extra care to avoid mistakes. To kill someone as an act of self-defense is surely the type of action that requires an agent to guard against causing unnecessary harm. But the uncertainty regarding the nature of what one is facing means that a degree of moral risk is unavoidable when killing in self-defense. As Lazar (2009: 720) writes: "Self-defense is always a risky activity" for an agent to carry out because of "the possibility that he might harm [someone] unjustifiably."

Given all of this, we should turn away from accounts of self-defense that require the defender to know facts about the person who is seen as a threat, and towards an account that focuses on the agent who acts in self-defense. It is better to use a virtue ethics approach in which the motivations of an agent of virtuous character is the basis for deciding what she may rightly do in self-defense. Since acts of homicide are seriously damaging to a person's ability to flourish as a human being, and it is a vice for someone not to be sufficiently averse to killing, the virtuous person would be more careful about using violence when she is uncertain about whether there is a genuine threat and about whether there is culpability on the part of the alleged aggressor. The virtuous agent is someone who can judge well regarding the mean between a failure to defend oneself and an overreaction (see Aristotle's "doctrine of the mean," Aristotle 1998: II.6). Knowing that she is faced with an actual and culpable threat, killing may be the appropriate choice for a virtuous agent. But given her strong desire to avoid killing innocent people who pose no threat, the virtuous choice may often be to delay the use of violence and to attempt to ascertain the facts, even if doing so increases the risk that she may be unable to save herself from the threat. In other words, it is more important for a virtuous person to avoid the damage to her character that results from killing too readily in the face of possible threats, than to avoid the harm of losing her life. As Hursthouse (1995: 64) puts it, "There are some things a virtuous agent must die rather than do; this is recognized in common morality, which condemns at least some cases of saving one's own life by betraying or killing others." There is too great a moral risk in resorting quickly to violence in response to possible threats that may not be actual or culpable.

Virtue Ethics, Just War, and Pacifism

War is a great evil. Besides the fact that terrible suffering and huge losses of life are inevitable occurrences when war is unleashed, the soldiers who inflict death and destruction too suffer moral and psychological harm even if they survive the war physically. When a political leader declares war and sends out a military force to fight, he commits the soldiers in the force to carry out acts of killing that go against the desire not to kill—a desire that many acquire in peacetime as part of the process by which humans learn to flourish and lead good lives.[7] I have shown that a person of good character is one who has a strong aversion to killing other human beings. War would therefore undermine the character of the virtuous ones who are sent to fight in wars. Does this not mean that a virtue ethics approach to the morality of war would be indistinguishable from pacifism? Should it not always be viewed as wrong for soldiers to fight in a war?[8] Would it then not follow that it is an even greater wrong for political leaders to choose to fight a war since that would involve ordering large numbers of citizens to risk grave harm to their moral character?

But just as there are moral dilemmas in which a virtuous agent correctly chooses to kill despite a strong desire not to kill,[9] there are situations in which political leaders who are of good character may appropriately choose to engage in war despite its great evil. A virtue ethics approach to the morality of war takes the evil of war much more seriously than the tradition of just war theorizing, according to which nations have a right to go to war, even very destructive wars, when the requirements of *jus ad bellum* (justice in going to war) are satisfied. Many devastating wars in human history are considered by just war theorists to be wars that satisfy all the principles of *jus ad bellum*, including the principle of proportionality in which the good of achieving the just cause has to outweigh the evils in war. Although it might impress utilitarian thinkers, I do not think that satisfying proportionality is doing enough to take account of the nature of war as an extremely evil means to a good end (Chan 2012a).

On the other hand, the virtue ethics approach would not be so restrictive as to altogether rule out war in any circumstance. Obviously, the virtue ethics approach comes much closer to pacifism than just war theory. But the difference is that the virtue ethicist sees war as a tragic choice in which real-world circumstances prevent political leaders and soldiers from living their lives in a way that exemplifies complete virtue. Even though war is a great evil, there are evils worse than war that may have to be stopped by going to war. Whether war is the lesser evil is a matter of moral judgment that a political leader using practical (and political) wisdom is able to correctly decide. In choosing the evil of war, the leader is making a tragic choice in the kind of situation in which whatever she chooses, she goes against what she as a person of good character desires.

What kind of evil is worse than war? In my book, I cite the war against the evil of Nazism as a case in which a virtuous leader would rightly choose to resist evil by military means.[10] But I also believe that evils comparable to that of Hitler's regime are extremely rare, and most evils that have been dealt with by war are not greater evils than the evil of war itself. Thus, I think that most of the wars that apparently satisfy the requirements of just war theory would not be wars that a virtuous leader would choose to fight. In fact, the only cases in which war is the lesser evil are wars that are fought in the face of a "supreme emergency." The concept of a supreme emergency was used by Walzer to justify the violation of *jus in bello* (justice in the conduct of war) under the rare condition in which defeat by an evil enemy would be catastrophic and irreversible (Walzer 1977: 251–255). The phrase was coined by British Prime Minister Winston Churchill to justify terror bombing of civilian population centers in Germany at the time when Britain alone stood against the might of Nazi Germany with military defeat seemingly imminent. Following just war theory, Walzer accepts that in order for a war to be morally just, it should satisfy the *jus ad bellum* part, as well as the *jus in bello* part that has to do with the conduct of war. Not only must countries have justice in going to war, but they should also fight in a just manner. Thus, the supreme emergency exemption that he proposed is controversial. However, I think the line between what is and is not a supreme emergency is indeed morally significant— not for violating noncombatant immunity as Walzer suggests, but for going to war at all. In other words, supreme emergencies are the rare cases where a virtuous leader can appropriately choose the evil of war as the lesser evil, whereas when not in a supreme emergency, war is too evil to choose even if conditions of *jus ad bellum* are satisfied (Chan 2012b).[11]

It is clear then that my virtue ethics approach to the morality of war is much more restrictive about going to war than theories in the just war tradition. The reason the approach is not, however, a pacifist one is that there have been evils in the past, namely Nazism, that satisfy the threshold of a supreme emergency, and it seems unrealistic to think that there will never again be that kind of evil that makes war the lesser evil, however rare its occurrence may be. In line with virtue ethics, I do not think there is a way to measure and compare evils to decide whether war is the lesser evil. Instead, it is a matter decided by the virtuous agent using practical wisdom that is acquired through experience. Thus, there will not be a clear line between evils comparable to

Nazism and evils that are not. But I think that once the evil of war is fully taken into account, it is likely that worse evils than war are not a common occurrence in history.[12]

It bears repeating what I said earlier about the harm to a person's character when she chooses to do something that is evil, not because she desires to do it but because it is the lesser evil when faced with a moral dilemma. In getting her nation to fight a war with all the evil that war entails, she acts against her strong aversion both to killing by herself and to ordering others to kill. She does not get away with her character unscathed just because she is confronted with a tragic choice in which there is no option for her to act virtuously. In a more perfect world where she is never presented with a tragic choice between evils, she would satisfy her desire not to kill (or order others to kill) and her life and actions would be indistinguishable from those of a pacifist. Unlike a just war theorist or a believer in the right to kill in self-defense, she does not think that killing can be morally justified by satisfying a set of requirements that grounds a right to use life-threatening force. But when there is a Hitler-like evil that puts her nation in a rare supreme emergency, the virtuous leader will not shrink from doing what is needed to avert the evil even at the expense of her good character. Here, she will choose the lesser evil of war instead of the nonviolence of the pacifist.

Given that the pacifist would not choose to go to war when confronted with the need to stop the kind of evil that constitutes a supreme emergency for the state, is the pacifist exhibiting a vice?[13] The answer to this question depends on what the basis for pacifism in the face of such evil is. Someone who refuses to kill or to order killing on the basis of an absolute rule that forbids all violence is one who makes decisions on a basis that is alien to virtue ethics.[14] Her mistake, if it is one, lies in her moral theory—but in acting solely from a sense of duty, she may be exhibiting a vice in either not having desires that are part of virtuous character, or suppressing such desires so as to act from duty.[15] Alternatively, someone may be against going to war because in her judgment, a Hitler-like foe is the lesser evil compared to the evils entailed in fighting a war to stop that evil. It is possible that she is mistaken in her judgment, in which case she does not possess the virtue of practical wisdom. But it is also possible that fully virtuous people can disagree about what the appropriate choice in a moral dilemma is without exhibiting a vice. As moral decision-making in virtue ethics depends on the judgment of a virtuous agent, there is a lack of precision in the theory's criterion for right action as compared with utilitarianism and deontological ethics. This feature of virtue ethics is not a flaw but an advantage since it reflects the complexity of moral choices in the real world. Thus, if a person of virtuous character judges the evil of war to be worse than the evil of an enemy and refuses to declare war or to fight in one, the fact that another virtuous person judges differently does not mean that either is making an inappropriate choice.[16] But while disagreeing in a particular case, such people of virtue would not rule out in advance every possibility of fighting and killing on the basis of an absolute rule. Thus, they will not be absolute pacifists.

Notes

1 My approach to virtue ethics in this paper is neo-Aristotelian. Aristotle is the source of the main ideas found in virtue ethics. In his *Nicomachean Ethics*, he defines ethical virtue and examines a number of such virtues. [I shall follow convention in citing his text using Book (in Roman numeral), period, followed by Chapter (in Arabic numeral).]
2 Aristotle's view of courage as a civic virtue has its counterpart in contemporary ideas of military virtues that are associated with character-building in the armed forces.
3 Trivigno (2013) shares my belief that "resistance to killing is … psychologically important in the development and maintenance of virtue." He rests his case on clinical and social psychological studies that reveal the role of empathy in inducing altruism and in preventing sociopathic behavior.

4 If it is a vice, it is not one in Aristotle's ethics, which is unsurprising given how he relates the virtue of courage to actions undertaken in war. Perhaps some soldiers in ancient Greece were traumatized after killing in war but it was not considered a vice to not react in that way.
5 For my reasons for saying this, see Chan (2010). In brief, if we run a thought experiment of comparing two people with the same virtues, except that one has a strong desire not to kill but lacks the desire to save lives while the other has a strong desire to save lives but lacks the desire not to kill, I believe it is more intuitive to consider the former to be a better human being.
6 Nozick (1974: 34–35) provides an example of an innocent threat in the form of a fat man who is pushed (or blown) off a cliff and is about to crush you to death, unless you vaporize him with your ray gun.
7 Trivigno (2013) argues that the training that soldiers undergo is aimed as disabling their resistance to killing, and thereby causes them moral harm even before they are sent out to war.
8 Trivigno's view is that even preparing soldiers to be ready to fight is harmful to them, so he believes that virtue ethics lends support to pacifism. I will argue later that the moral harm to soldiers and to the leaders who order them to fight does not preclude the ethical choice of war as a response to evil in supreme emergencies.
9 Besides the possibility of killing in self-defense, a virtuous agent could be faced with a situation where the only options are to kill one person or allow a very large number of innocent people to die. Even though she is not a consequentialist, her desire to save lives may make it rational to choose to kill, despite her desire not to kill.
10 I also suggest in Chan (2012a) that once the Nazis have been rendered unable to perpetuate evil to the extent that their evil is worse than that of war, the continuance of the war would not be the appropriate choice for a virtuous leader.
11 The just war theory attempts to sanitize wars using restrictions on the conduct of war in non-supreme emergencies, but I think that a virtuous leader would not go to war in such cases. However, in a supreme emergency, the virtuous leader who goes to war will not disrespect noncombatant immunity in the way that Walzer thinks is permissible.
12 I make this claim with some trepidation, given the human capacity to do evil. I have been challenged on more than one occasion to say whether I consider the Islamic State (ISIS) to be the kind of evil that meets the threshold for war.
13 Thanks to Andy Fiala for suggesting that I address this question.
14 This claim may seem strange given that there are Christian pacifists whose moral views derive from a virtue tradition. However, it seems to me that religious pacifism is rooted in views regarding the inner moral worth or intrinsic value of human beings that are not an essential part of neo-Aristotelian virtue ethics.
15 In the latter case, she will suffer what Stocker (1976) calls "moral schizophrenia," in which her motivations fail to align with reasons for acting that derive from her moral theory.
16 Aristotle (1998: II.9) tells us that an agent may, without incurring blame, deviate from the mean, lying between two vices, that defines a virtue. Yet we cannot even be precise about how much deviation is acceptable, as the answer varies with the particular case.

Works Cited

Aristotle. (1998). *Nicomachean Ethics*. New York: Oxford University Press.
Chan, D. K. (2010). "A Reappraisal of the Doctrine of Doing and Allowing," in J. Campbell, M. O'Rourke, and H. Silverstein (eds.), *Action, Ethics, and Responsibility*. Cambridge, MA: MIT Press, 25–45.
Chan, D. K. (2012a). *Beyond Just War: A Virtue Ethics Approach*. Basingstoke: Palgrave Macmillan.
Chan, D. K. (2012b). "Just War, Noncombatant Immunity, and the Concept of Supreme Emergency." *Journal of Military Ethics* 11: 273–286.
Chan, D. K. (2016). *Action Reconceptualized: Human Agency and Its Sources*. Lanham: Lexington Books.
Foot, P. (2001). *Natural Goodness*. Oxford: Clarendon Press.
Hursthouse, R. (1995). "Applying Virtue Ethics," in R. Hursthouse, G. Lawrence, and W. Quinn (eds.), *Virtues and Reasons*. Oxford: Clarendon Press, 57–75.
Lazar, S. (2009). "Responsibility, Risk, and Killing in Self-Defense." *Ethics* 119: 699–728.
MacIntyre, A. (1981). *After Virtue*. Notre Dame: University of Notre Dame Press.
Nozick, R. (1974). *Anarchy, State, and Utopia*. New York: Basic Books.
Nussbaum, M. C. (1986). *The Fragility of Goodness*. Cambridge: Cambridge University Press.

Stocker, M. (1976). "The Schizophrenia of Modern Ethical Theories." *Journal of Philosophy* 73: 453–466.
Thomson, J. J. (1991). "Self-Defense." *Philosophy and Public Affairs* 20: 283–310.
Trivigno, F. V. (2013). "A Virtue Ethical Case for Pacifism," in M. Austin (ed.), *Virtues in Action*. Basingstoke: Palgrave Macmillan, 86–101.
Walzer, M. (1977). *Just and Unjust Wars*. New York: Basic Books.

15
PERSONAL PACIFISM AND CONSCIENTIOUS OBJECTION

Eric Reitan

For centuries there have been those who have personally renounced participation in war or violence as part of adopting a nonviolent way of life, but who have not endorsed a general moral requirement for others to do likewise. Atack (2001: 179) calls this stance "vocational pacifism," and characterizes it as a stance that conceives pacifism "as a way of life or vocation, binding only on those who choose it." Kemp (1995: 21) names it "personal pacifism," and defines it as the view that "given who one is, or what one has decided to become, it would be wrong to fight" even though no general prohibition on violence or war is endorsed. He goes on to note that the choice to be the kind of person for whom fighting would be wrong "may be a response to a vocation in the etymological sense, i.e. a calling, presumably from God, or it might be an individually made life choice." Ihara (1978: 369) does not use the "personal pacifism" label, but what he sets out to defend is the pacifism of someone who "does not believe that violence is always wrong," who asserts a right to use violence defensively, but who "also believes that a life of nonviolence is a morally preferable way of life" and who has made a commitment to such a life.

Individuals who fit these descriptions are *pacifists* in that they are committed to abstaining absolutely either from fighting in war or from violence more broadly. But their pacifism is *personal* in that their commitment is not based on endorsing a general principle that precludes war or violence. They are not what we might call "universal pacifists." They renounce war or violence in their own case as part of a life choice they do not see as obligatory for all.

In what follows, I will consider several questions about such "personal pacifism," questions whose importance becomes clearest once we consider the objection that charges personal pacifism with not being a morally significant stance. While I will consider this objection more fully in a later section, the basic charge is this: given that personal pacifism involves a decision to renounce violence or war-participation without endorsing a general moral obligation for others to do likewise, it cannot be a *principled* position but must be just a lifestyle preference, akin to avoiding action movies because one doesn't like them.

Were this charge correct, one would have good grounds for doubting that personal pacifism could be legitimately invoked as a basis for conscientious objector status. The goods of collective social life often call us to contribute in ways we don't like. (Few *enjoy* filing their tax returns.) Suppose the state is fighting a war and decides that a draft of healthy adults offers the best way to distribute the burdens of waging the war. The state might, out of respect for personal conscience, plausibly grant exemptions from military service to those who condemn all war or believe the current conflict does not satisfy just war principles. But if someone thinks the current war is just, would it be reasonable to recuse them from military service because they have a personal *distaste* for violence? That hardly seems sufficient to justify an exemption from a burden others are required to bear.

It is clearly *possible* for someone to refrain from all violence or war-participation simply out of some lifestyle preference. Hence, it is possible for there to exist versions of "personal pacifism" that are no more significant morally than a decision to avoid action movies out of distaste. But the important question is whether a personal commitment to nonviolence *has* to be nothing but such a psychological disinclination. Could a personal pacifist stance be justified by something more morally significant (and hence more deserving of moral respect), even if what justifies it is not a principle imposing a *general obligation* for others to do likewise? If so, could it be taken seriously as a basis for conferring conscientious objector status?

Distinctions

Before turning to these questions, it will help to make some preliminary distinctions. When distinguishing species of pacifism, one might focus on the scope of what is prohibited. So, for example, one might be an anti-war pacifist who does not object to violence in self-defense or in domestic policing; or one might be an "absolute" pacifist who thinks all violence is immoral (or one might adopt a position somewhere between these).

Personal pacifism, while necessarily narrow in scope in terms of *who* is to refrain from violence, admits of varying degrees of scope with respect to *what* is prohibited. Thus, a personal pacifist might be an anti-war personal pacifist (who has renounced fighting in war but not similarly renounced self-defense) or an absolute personal pacifist (who is committed to excluding all violence from her life).

It should be noted, also, that someone might combine universal pacifism at one level of scope with personal pacifism at another. For example, someone might think all war is wrong (and so be a universal pacifist with respect to war) while making a purely personal commitment to a nonviolent life without affirming a general obligation for others to do likewise (and so be a personal pacifist with respect to violence more broadly).

In this essay, I will focus mainly on versions of personal pacifism that (a) extend beyond mere refusal to fight in war to encompass a more general refusal to engage in unambiguously violent acts, and (b) are not paired with a commitment to universal pacifism at any level of scope. I say "unambiguously" violent in order to set aside gray area questions such as whether acts of physical coercion that can cause minor injury—such as a teacher pulling an aggressive schoolchild off a classmate—qualify as violence. One can certainly imagine those with a rather sweeping commitment to eschew violence who are prepared to engage in such uses of force.

Within this species of personal pacifism, there is a further distinction that Kemp makes (in the quote given previously) between (a) pacifism adopted as part of an explicit vocational role, presumably connected with broader social institutions or practices—such as, for example, the role of a Catholic priest, and (b) pacifism adopted as part of a more individual life choice, for reasons that are more strictly private. I will here reserve the term "vocational pacifism" for the former and refer to the latter as "individual pacifism," treating each as a species of personal pacifism.

Finally, as historian Brock (2001: 56) has noted, we must distinguish personal pacifism from expressions of universal pacifism that are tolerant of non-pacifist positions and do not proselytize on pacifism's behalf. Some who think war and violence are universally wrong might, Brock notes, be convinced that adherence to the universal pacifist principle "cannot be imposed on anyone, but must arise from a conviction of what is right." While believing their position correct, these pacifists adopt an attitude of tolerance towards those who disagree, leading to outward behavior similar to what one would expect to see from a personal pacifist. But such "tolerant pacifism" is not personal pacifism in either the vocational or individual form.

The Case against Personal Pacifism

There has been a tendency among philosophers to set aside personal pacifism as philosophically uninteresting. In *The Ethics of War and Peace*, for example, Lackey (1989: 6) says that this sort of pacifism "does not constitute a moral point of view" since "there is no way to have moral values without believing that these values apply to other people."

Narveson (1965) goes deeper in his classic essay, "Pacifism: A Philosophical Analysis." He argues that any non-universal pacifism at best lacks moral significance and at worst is incoherent. According to Narveson, if a moral principle applies to me, it applies to me for a reason—and so will apply to others for whom that reason obtains. If it is wrong for me to "meet force with force," it is wrong for any similarly situated individual. Any genuine pacifist must therefore say that "for whatever class of people he thinks [the pacifist principle] applies to, there is something positively wrong about meeting violence with force," such that when those "to whom the principle applies resort to force, they are committing a breach of moral duty" (Narveson 1965: 260).

This feature of moral principles, Narveson thinks, causes problems for what I am calling personal pacifism. Any principled commitment to eschew violence would have to invoke a rationale that would extend to all those who are similarly situated. Of course, there are some specific moral principles that personal pacifists would need to adopt in order to endorse their stance. They would need to adopt the principle that "we may, if we wish, prefer not to resist violence with force," but Narveson claims that this is a view non-pacifists could adopt—and then decide to resist violence with force since they lack the requisite preference. Likewise, he thinks many non-pacifists would agree that "there is something admirable or saintly" about the refusal to respond violently to a violent attack—so this kind of supererogatory endorsement of nonviolence couldn't serve as the principled commitment that distinguishes personal pacifists from non-pacifists. It has to be the conviction that violence is strictly prohibited, at least for the class of individuals to which the pacifist belongs (Narveson 1965: 260).

And this class cannot be simply the class of personal pacifists. Any principled commitment according to which the pacifist obligation only applies to pacifists generates, for Narveson, an untenable circularity (Narveson 1965: 261). Whether this charge of circularity is sound, his overall point has force: if only those who choose to take on an obligation have it, and there is no reason independent of their taking on the obligation why they should do so, one wonders on what basis they can truly be said to have an *obligation* at all. If nothing but personal whim generates the obligation, could not a change in whims eliminate it? And can something have the force of an obligation if its authority depends on individual whims?[1]

Narveson thus concludes that anyone who refrains from violence but "holds that no one *else* has this duty of pacifism" is not "holding pacifism as a moral principle or, indeed, as a principle at all." Rather, what we are left with is a "disinclination for violence" that is "essentially just a matter of taste" and "could hardly license a man to refuse military service if it were required of him" (Narveson 1965: 262). But is this conclusion warranted?

Vocational Pacifism

One clear weakness in Narveson's case is his failure to engage with vocational pacifism. The closest he comes to considering it is when he argues that it is "impossible to claim that your support of pacifism is a moral one if your position is that a certain selection of people, but no one else, ought not to meet force with force, even though you are unprepared to offer any reason whatever for this selection" (Narveson 1965: 262). His argument here rests entirely on dismissing the coherence of cases where the pacifist duty is applied to "only the Arapahoes, or only the Chinese, or only people more than six feet high" with "no reasons offered." Based on the rational incoherence of such cases, he affirms his desired conclusion that pacifism "must be the principle that the use of force to meet force is wrong as such, that is, that nobody may do so unless he has a special justification" (Narveson 1965: 263). But he reaches this conclusion without considering the following possibility: perhaps there is a vocationally designated class of persons for whom a reason *can* be given why they should never resort to violence, a reason related to their vocational responsibilities.

This oversight is not trivial, given the historic significance that just this sort of vocational pacifism has had in the Roman Catholic tradition.[2] Aquinas, for example, asserts that "[c]lerics and bishops are forbidden to take up arms, not as though it were a sin, but because such an action is incompatible with their state." According to Aquinas, military pursuits are at odds with the work of the priesthood, such that those who commit themselves to the priesthood are thereby barred from shedding others' blood. It is therefore "unbecoming for them to slay or shed blood, and it is more fitting that they should be ready to shed their own blood for Christ, so as to imitate in deed what they portray in their ministry." Acts of violence thus make clerics "unfit" to perform their duty, rendering it "unlawful for clerics to fight" (Aquinas 1947: ST II-II, Q. 40, Art. 2).

This argument is made in a context in which Aquinas treats war and violence as justifiable under appropriate conditions. As such, Aquinas is no universal pacifist. But because of their decision to commit to the priesthood, he thinks priests are obligated to refrain from violence. Of course, one might find Aquinas's argument uncompelling. But it would be a mistake to accuse Aquinas of singling out the clergy for *no reason*. As such, Narveson's conclusion that the only principled pacifism is universal is at best unsupported.

In fact, I think a stronger rebuttal is warranted, to the effect that certain vocations call for a commitment to eschewing violence beyond what is more generally required. But rather than stake the case for this in the domain of the priesthood, I want to consider Martin Luther King's argument for what amounts to vocational pacifism for the leaders of nonviolent social justice movements.

King did not always hold the view that those engaged in leadership of a nonviolent campaign are obligated to eschew violence. Early in his civil rights career, after his home was bombed, King sought (and was denied) a concealed carry permit (King 1998: 78–83). The intent was to have it for *personal* defense. He did not intend to use it to help fight bus segregation laws. King was already convinced by then that nonviolent methods offered the only real way forward for the civil rights movement. A violent movement would alienate the "uncommitted middle group" whose support was essential to win. But he believed that when "the Negro uses force in self-defense he does not forfeit support—he may even win it, by the courage and self-respect it reflects" (King 1986b: 33).

This view, however, did not last. While King never repudiated a right to self-defense, he became increasingly convinced, the more he came to understand nonviolent direct action, that its success required its agents to make a sweeping commitment to nonviolence that put aside even the right to use it in self-defense. The emerging sense of this first hit home for him in the wake of the bombing of his home (King 1998: 82). The idea finds vivid expression in an essay written towards the end of his career, in which he argued that those engaged in nonviolent direct action needed to be willing to suffer the unjust blows of others for the sake of long-term social change rather than defend themselves through violence. Even when violence is used only in defense, it threatens the integrity of the nonviolent campaign (King 1986a: 57).

Furthermore, King insists that the success of a nonviolent campaign calls for not merely an outward transformation in behavior but an inner transformation of the spirit, one that refuses to see the opponent as anything less than a potential friend, a prospective fellow member of the "beloved community" (King 1986a: 58). It is difficult, if not impossible, to reconcile the cultivation of such unconditional goodwill—even to enemies who wish you harm—with a willingness to do violence to them when they seek to do you harm.

Arguably, someone could forego a life commitment to nonviolence while participating effectively in one or two nonviolent campaigns. But King concluded that this was not something he, as a *leader* of a nonviolent movement, could do. Arguably, he became convinced that to be a leader of such a movement, he needed to model in a holistic way, and not just during campaigns, the kinds of behaviors and attitudes necessary for the success of a nonviolent movement for social change. Such leadership demanded a personal commitment to nonviolence, and so King made such a commitment.

It should be obvious how King's case challenges Narveson's conclusion that only universal pacifism can be principled. King did not believe that everyone was obligated to be a leader of a nonviolent movement for social change. He did, however, believe that it was a good thing that there *be* such leaders. He might also have reasonably believed that he had a duty to take a leadership role in the Montgomery Bus Boycott once it became clear how important it was for the campaign to move forward successfully and how uniquely situated he was to lead it, given the contingent facts of his personal history and the social forces in play in Montgomery at the time. Given the outcome of the boycott and his rise to social prominence as a civil rights leader, he clearly did conclude that he ought to continue in a leadership role in the burgeoning civil rights movement.

But even if King did not see himself as having a *duty* to become a leader in this nonviolent movement (given the threat such a role posed to his life, one might hesitate to attribute an obligation to adopt the role), one cannot doubt that he saw it as a morally good choice. Social circumstances and personal traits came together in such a way that King felt "called" to take on this role—in the sense of finding himself *distinctively* situated to do something that it would be good for *someone* to do. Even if one does not adopt a theistic notion of a "calling," the idea still has force in the sense that a social situation or historical moment may call for someone to take up an important role—and if you happen to be well situated to answer that call, perhaps better situated than most or even all others who might answer it, the "call" speaks to you in a distinctive way.

What I am sketching out here is a principled basis for vocational pacifism, which can be more formally laid out in terms of four conditions:

V1: Agent A is, for contingent reasons, well (or uniquely) situated to adopt role R.
V2: It would be morally good (if not obligatory) for someone well situated to adopt R to do so (even though it may not be morally good or obligatory for everyone to do so).
V3: The effective execution of R requires a commitment to abstain from violence, including defensive violence, even though such a commitment is not morally required of those who do not occupy R (or some other role with the same requirement).
V4: A has chosen to adopt R, in the sense of having voluntarily taken on R in response to the sense of "calling" generated by V1-V2.

When conditions V1-V4 obtain, A acquires an obligation to abstain from violence, an obligation distinctive to A but nevertheless principled. A distinctive set of contingent life circumstances combine with the life choice of an individual for whom these circumstances obtain to generate an obligation that does not obtain universally.

This is not a mere matter of personal taste or inclination, since the adoption of role *R* by *A* is taken to be morally good or praiseworthy if not obligatory (and hence is not merely a role that *A* happens to desire to occupy as a matter of personal taste), and abstaining from violence is a required dimension of faithfully executing *R*. Furthermore, *A*'s reasons for refraining from violence are ones that *A* would endorse for anyone who is similarly situated—even if few are similarly situated. But the selection of who the principle applies to is not based on membership in some arbitrarily chosen group. Instead, conditions V1-V4 provide a non-arbitrary basis for *A* possessing a duty to refrain from violence. Since these conditions will at least in theory apply to more than one individual, *A* can thus represent the group of individuals for whom V1-V4 obtain. Unlike the group of people over six feet high, there is a reason why members of *this* group are called to be nonviolent while others are not.

In short, Narveson's critique of what I am calling personal pacifism does not apply to its vocational form when V1-V4 obtain. When these conditions obtain, it would be appropriate for an individual to claim a duty to refrain from violence without asserting a general obligation for others to do likewise.

Such vocational pacifism, furthermore, appears to be as justified a basis for a claim to conscientious objector status as would be a belief in universal pacifism.[3] In any given case the claim that conditions V1-V4 actually obtain could be contested. That V4 obtains could be verified through investigating the agent's actual choices, but V1 is a matter of personal judgment while V2-V3 are matters of contestable moral principle. Perhaps the question of whether V1-V3 in fact obtain will always be controversial. But so is universal pacifism. At least in a politically liberal state where the state honors the right of individuals to live out reasonable comprehensive conceptions of the good life (to borrow John Rawls's language), establishing the truth of universal pacifism is not required for conferring conscientious objector status. It is sufficient that an individual sincerely ascribe to a reasonable comprehensive doctrine that implies universal pacifism. And if the state takes it that universal pacifism might be a sincerely held component of a reasonable comprehensive doctrine, there is little reason to think that one could not say the same of an individual who affirms conditions V1-V3 with respect to a role they have chosen to live out (thus meeting V4).

Hence, with respect to the vocational species of personal pacifism, it appears both that this form of pacifism is a moral position (not merely a matter of personal taste) and that it can serve as a basis for conscientious objection as well as universal forms can. But what about the more individual, non-vocational species of personal pacifism?

Individual Pacifism

King's decision to make a life commitment to nonviolence, based both on the role he occupied and on his judgment that the role demanded it, bears a clear resemblance to the vocational pacifism of the priesthood that Aquinas endorsed. But there are some important differences as well. For King, the disavowal of violence was not an entailment of formal vows made to a larger organization as part of adopting an established role within that organization. If King did indeed acquire a personal obligation to refrain from violence, it wasn't an obligation emerging out of explicit vows or promises. Nor was it tied to an already established office, created by an existing set of social institutions and carrying with it a set of clearly defined duties. Rather, King's vocational pacifism emerged out of his own evolving understanding of how best to live out his chosen path and mission with integrity.

In these respects, King's case offers a kind of *via media* between the more classic case of vocational pacifism and cases of what I am calling individual pacifism. In fact, King's case suggests that a clean line between the two species of personal pacifism cannot be drawn and that, therefore, recognizing the moral significance of vocational pacifism (and acknowledging its potential to warrant conscientious objector status) opens the door to recognizing the moral significance of more individual forms.

What King's case shows is that the vocational role that is taken to exclude violence can be one whose precise contours (its attendant responsibilities, characteristic activities, and prohibitions) needn't be established in advance by some existing institutional structures. A role can be created for a unique set of social circumstances, and its proper contours discovered by its occupant based on experience trying to live out that role with integrity. What is needed to justify vocational pacifism is not a prefabricated role that excludes violence. What is needed, rather, is for the individual called to vocational pacifism to discern (based on their sincerely held system of values) that (a) taking on the role would be morally good for them to do in part because of contingent personal and social realities (conditions V1-V2), and (b) faithfully executing that role would require refraining from violence in a systematic way (V3).

But if this is true for the adoption of a specified role, such as a leader in a nonviolent movement, couldn't it also be true of a *way of life*? It is pacifism understood as a personal "commitment or dedication" to a nonviolent "way of life"—one chosen because it is judged to be "morally more desirable" than other permissible ways of life—that Craig Ihara (1978: 370) has sought to defend against Narveson's arguments. For Ihara, the pacifist life choice is not a matter of whim or inclination but a judgment about what kind of life would be morally preferable (but not obligatory) for the agent to live. Ihara seems to posit the view that the nonviolent life is morally preferable for *everyone*, but one needn't adopt such a strong view. One could, in a manner analogous to what we found in the case of vocational pacifism, adopt the view that it would be morally good for some people to adopt this way of life, most notably those who are well positioned to do so because of contingent life circumstance (and so experience a "call"). Either way, Ihara suggests that once the pacifist has made the commitment to this way of life, the commitment may create, in the manner of a vow, an obligation that would not otherwise obtain (Ihara 1978: 371–372).

Ihara's thinking tracks well what we have said about vocational pacifism. To spell it out in parallel terms, imagine that an agent A discerns, based on sincerely held values, that the following conditions obtain:

I1: A is, for contingent reasons, well (or uniquely) situated to adopt way of life W.

I2: It would be morally good (if not obligatory) for someone well situated to adopt W to do so (even though it may not be morally good or obligatory for everyone to do so).

I3: Living out W with integrity requires a commitment to abstain from violence, including defensive violence, even though such a commitment is not morally required of those who do not adopt W (or some other way of life with the same requirement).

In short, A discerns that adopting W would be morally good for them (perhaps because of contingent life circumstances) and that living out this way of life with integrity would require refraining from violence in a systematic way. And then suppose that A makes the decision to adopt the way of life, such that the following condition obtains:

I4: A has chosen to adopt W, in the sense of having voluntarily taken on W in response to the sense of "calling" generated by I1-I2.

It appears that conditions I1-I4 could serve as a principled basis for individual pacifism just as V1-V4 serve as a principled basis for vocational pacifism. To recognize such a basis in the case of *vocational roles* but not *ways of life*, we would need to identify a morally relevant difference between roles and ways of life that could account for the distinction. One possibility is this: a role is, by its nature, bound up with a broader human enterprise, a collaborative project which that role helps to fulfill. A way of life, by contrast, needn't be integrally connected to such larger collaborative projects. Does this difference warrant treating vocational roles and ways of life differently when it comes to the issue at hand?

Consider an example. Someone might adopt an ascetic life characterized by extreme social isolation so as to focus on inner spiritual development. The ascetic might view this not as a general moral requirement, but as a way of life that it is good that some persons pursue because it brings into the world goods that would not otherwise be in the world. The ascetic may feel called to this life because of personal contingencies and may, furthermore, believe that violence displays a level of attachment to things of this world incompatible with spiritual asceticism. But even though this ascetic life is not part of a collaborative social project, and so is different from most vocational roles, it is far from obvious that this difference justifies denying conscientious objector status to the ascetic.

More importantly, however, not all ways of life are this cut off from collaborative social life and its collective aims. Sometimes, a way of life is chosen because it models some truth—some truth about the human condition, perhaps—that the one adopting it believes needs to be modeled for the sake of the social good. While not everyone needs to model this truth (perhaps it would be bad if everyone did), the ones adopting the way of life take themselves to be distinctively situated to "witness" to this truth. As a matter of personal witness, they adopt the way of life.

To add substance to this possibility, consider a case of individual pacifism that is something of an amalgam of individuals I have known (through my work with alternatives to violence training) who adopt a nonviolent life as a matter of personal witness. For the sake of simplicity, let us imagine a single individual: Mary.[4]

Although Mary affirms the right to use violence defensively, she distinguishes between the right to do so and the issue of whether doing it is wise or the best choice. She is convinced that on many of the occasions in which people exercise their right to defensive violence, their use of violence would not have been necessary had they cultivated certain skills—such as the ability to quickly assess the human dynamics of a situation and de-escalate conflict with appropriate humor, expressions of empathy, or assertions of dignity as the case demands. Mary believes these nonviolent skills make alternatives to violence available, alternatives that produce outcomes generally preferable to what violent defense generates. She is also convinced that the power and promise of these alternatives is underappreciated and underdeveloped. To change this reality, some individuals (who for reasons of personal history are well situated to do so) will need to model that power and promise by making a life commitment to nonviolence.

Mary is furthermore convinced that even though violence is sometimes justified, society exaggerates the extent to which this is so. The more routinely violence is used and treated as justified, the more this exaggeration is inflated. Even legitimate uses of violence pose the risk of contributing to this exaggeration. Furthermore, when the violence of unjust aggressors is met with violence, this often reinforces the aggressors' conviction that violence is the norm and is essential for getting on in life; whereas a nonviolent response may better highlight the unjustifiability of their aggression, awakening them to alternative ways of engaging with others in the world. While these possibilities do not make legitimate uses of violence illegitimate, they do imply that there is a cost to using violence—in terms of the risk of increasing the problem of violence in the world. This cost, Mary believes, is underappreciated just as the power and promise of nonviolence are underappreciated.

Mary believes that unless some people make a life commitment to cultivating nonviolence in all their interactions, the full potential of nonviolent alternatives will never be realized. Because facility with nonviolence in threatening situations is difficult to learn, and because resort to violence is a rather spontaneous human response to such situations, those who have not made a firm commitment to a nonviolent life are unlikely to strive for creative nonviolent solutions in these situations. Only when violence is off the table will the level of dedication and resourcefulness required to master nonviolence be fully brought to bear on the range of problems in which violence is commonly employed. And only once that level of dedication and resourcefulness is brought to bear will the full potential of nonviolent solutions be developed. And only when that potential becomes clear will humanity begin to be able to reduce the costs that all violence—even justified violence—can do.

Mary sees herself as well situated to make the relevant life commitment. She has witnessed the potential of nonviolence and the costs of violence. She has had teachers who have helped cultivate in her at least some of the skills that nonviolent engagement in threatening situations requires. Although she thinks parental duties to protect one's children would morally complicate a life choice to wholly eschew even defensive violence, she personally has no children. Hence, she feels "called" to become a witness to the power of nonviolence by making a commitment to a wholly nonviolent way of life. But making that commitment is incompatible with continuing to claim for herself the right to use violence, even defensively. And so she believes, once she has made this commitment, that it would be wrong for her to use violence. But she does not thereby think it would be similarly wrong for others who have not made the commitments she has made in response to the calling she has felt.

Mary's case is so closely analogous to vocational pacifism that it is hard to see how one could justify a stance that takes vocational pacifism seriously as a moral position (one that could warrant conscientious objector status), but does not similarly regard Mary's more individual commitment. Mary's commitment to nonviolence is principled, in the sense that she would endorse it for anyone similarly situated. And it springs from a comprehensive value and belief system that implies both the worth of making the commitment she has made and the incompatibility between doing violence and living out that commitment once she has made it. If we think that a similar vocational pacifist has, on these grounds, a claim on conscientious objector status, a similar conclusion seems warranted for Mary.

The Duty to Defend

One final issue with respect to personal pacifism lies with the common intuition that human beings have a duty to defend others, one which might be explicated as follows: (i) individuals have a moral duty to defend the vulnerable from unjust aggression, at least when they are uniquely positioned to do so (no one else is in a position to provide the needed defense) or called by a distinctive role to do so (such as being the parent of the victim or being a police officer whose occupational role calls for defending the victim), and (ii) the faithful fulfillment of this duty may on some occasions demand the use of violence—in cases, for example, when the defender, despite their best efforts to cultivate nonviolent skills, cannot in the moment when action is required discern an effective nonviolent means of satisfying the duty.

If this duty to defend obtains, one might argue that it rules out any commitment to a vocation or way of life incompatible with using violence, since one cannot know in advance of making such a commitment that one will never find oneself in circumstances wherein one has a duty to defend someone violently.

It needs to be noted that a duty of defense explicated in these terms is clearly at odds with *universal* pacifism. As such, were it true that personal pacifists have to deny that this duty obtains, to that extent they would be in *agreement* with universal pacifists on a matter of principle. In fact, we might assert that this matter of principle unites universal and personal pacifists while distinguishing both from non-pacifists—in which case Narveson would be mistaken when he says that non-pacifists can readily agree with the claim that "we may, if we wish, prefer not to resist violence with force." Non-pacifists might agree with this when it comes to *self*-defense (and perhaps select cases of the defense of others). But on this perspective it would be a distinguishing feature of *non*-pacifist ethics that it posits a duty to defend of the sort sketched out previously.[5]

But if we see personal pacifists as sharing with universal pacifists a rejection of the duty to defend, that rejection has no obvious bearing on the question of whether personal pacifists can legitimately claim conscientious objector status. If universal pacifists can claim such status, despite the controversial character of rejecting a duty of defense, then so can personal pacifists.

The more interesting and controversial case arises for personal pacifists who *accept* the view that some persons are obligated to use violence in defense of the vulnerable, but who exclude themselves from the scope of this obligation. Is such a position coherent? One possibility here is that personal pacifists construe the duty to defend others as a defeasible *prima facie* duty. They might argue that meeting conditions V1-V4 or I1-I4 provides the requisite defeater, such that they lack an all-things-considered duty to defend. This is the line that Ihara takes: any duty to defend is limited, and we don't generally have a duty to sacrifice life and limb in defense of others. But "requiring a pacifist to act violently is equivalent to forcing him to sacrifice that which is both most precious to him and that to which he has at least a prima facie right"(Ihara 1978: 373).

Rather than explore the complexities of this option, I would like to consider whether a personal pacifist could endorse a *collective* duty of defense—a duty borne by society as a whole that is discharged when some subset of the population takes on the burdens of military and police service. These personal pacifists would support a social obligation to wage wars in defense of victims of unjust military aggression and to provide law enforcement to defend victims of criminal violence. But since this collective obligation is satisfied when some subset of the population takes on the needed defensive roles (soldiers and police officers), personal pacifists might claim an exemption from being among those called to meet this obligation on the grounds that, based on their belief that V1-V4 or I1-I4 obtain in their own case, they have been called to a different, incompatible role.

As Kemp (1995: 31–38) has argued, at least *some* effort on the part of the state to accommodate the life choices of such individuals seems warranted. If the collective duty of waging a just war can be met without compromising these choices, respecting their choice would be fitting. However, accommodation of the nonviolent commitment need not preclude the state from requiring some alternative contribution to a war effort when broad societal contribution is needed and the pacifist believes the war is justified. In short, personal pacifists of this variety may object to adopting a *combatant* role, but not to serving the war effort in some non-combatant capacity. Thus, for example, Roman Catholic military chaplains might contribute to soldier morale, even instilling the courage to fight, while refusing to fight themselves.

Personal pacifists may also hold that some, by virtue of contingent life circumstances, acquire a personal duty of defense incompatible with vocational or individual pacifism. For example, they might think parents have a duty to defend their children. And while they might believe that such defense should be as nonviolent as they can possibly make it, they might also be convinced that sometimes, despite their best efforts to cultivate nonviolent skills, even the parents most committed to nonviolence will be unable to discern an effective nonviolent means to protect their children. In such cases, personal pacifists might believe that parents ought to resort to violence rather than fail to act in their children's defense. While they might be convinced that sufficient focus on developing nonviolent resources will reduce the frequency of cases like this, and that an ideal nonviolent agent would be so adept at nonviolent methods that no such cases arise, they may also believe that no actual person is such an ideal agent.

Personal pacifists who fit this description might think they are required to choose *between* personal pacifism and the role of parent. And should they become parents, they might perceive a moral requirement to modify their prior commitment to accommodate the parental obligation—with the result being a witness to nonviolence less potent than it might otherwise have been.

Clearly, personal pacifists who acknowledge such a parental duty but who are not themselves parents do not lose a claim to conscientious objector status in war based on the acknowledgement of this duty. They could readily hold that V1 or I1 would no longer apply to them *were* they parents—but, given that they are not, they remain well situated to adopt the nonviolent role or way of life that they are convinced it would be good for some to adopt.

The more interesting question is whether personal pacifists who acknowledge this parental duty and who then *become* parents lose their claim on conscientious objection. While this is a more complicated question, such parents may remain committed to being as *much* of a witness to nonviolence as is consistent with their perceived parental obligations. Since there is often only a remote likelihood of actually facing circumstances where parental obligations demand violence, such a witness could be quite powerful even given this singular (and possibly only hypothetical) exception—but would be fundamentally compromised by a requirement to serve in a combatant role. Hence, it is not obvious that such individuals have no claim on conscientious objector status.

Conclusion

It appears, then, that personal pacifism—both in its vocational and individual forms—can express a principled moral stance tied to a perceived "calling" to adopt a role or way of life incompatible with violence. Those who adopt such a role or way of life for the kinds of reasons addressed earlier are not merely expressing a disinclination to violence or a preference for this way of life. Rather, they believe, given their circumstances and life choices, that it would be wrong for them to use violence—even though they do not extend the same obligation to others. Furthermore, this belief is not incoherent. Any government prepared to extend conscientious objector status to universal pacifists based on their sincere beliefs would, it seems, be hard pressed to offer a compelling reason to withhold such status from personal pacifists who fit the profile described here. But depending on what the personal pacifists think about the justifiability of war, the state may be justified in requiring of these pacifists a non-combatant role within the war effort.

Notes

1 Of course, "whim" may not be the only basis for the emergence of such a personal obligation, a point I will take up in a later section.
2 For a detailed discussion of vocational pacifism for clergy, see Kemp 1995: 23–25.
3 This may explain the consistent policy, in the United States, to exempt clergy and seminarians from the draft—although this policy has faced some criticism (see Smith 1970).
4 I have previously sketched out both this and a second model of personal pacifism in somewhat different terms (Reitan 2000: 39–40).
5 Ihara (1978: 371) makes a similar point.

Works Cited

Aquinas, T. (1947). *Summa Theologica*, edited by Benziger Brothers, translated by Fathers of the English Dominican Province. Westminster, MD: Christian Classics. Available at: www.ccel.org/ccel/aquinas/summa.html

Atack, I. (2001). "From Pacifism to War Resistance." *Peace and Change* 26: 177–186.

Brock, P. (2001). "Personal Pacifism in Historical Perspective." *The Acorn: Journal of the Gandhi-King Society* 11: 53–59.

Ihara, C. (1978). "In Defense of a Version of Pacifism." *Ethics* 88: 369–374.

Kemp, K. (1995). "Personal Pacifism." *Theological Studies* 56: 21–38.

King, Jr., M. (1986a). "Nonviolence: The Only Road to Freedom," in J. Washington (ed.), *Testament of Hope: The Essential Writings and Speeches of Martin Luther King, Jr.* San Francisco: Harper Collins, 54–61.

King, Jr., M. (1986b). "The Social Organization of Nonviolence," in J. Washington (ed.), *Testament of Hope: The Essential Writings and Speeches of Martin Luther King, Jr.* San Francisco: Harper Collins, 31–34.

King, Jr., M. (1998). *Autobiography of Martin Luther King, Jr.*, edited by C. Carson. New York: Warner Books.

Lackey, D. (1989). *The Ethics of War and Peace*. Upper Saddle River, NJ: Prentice-Hall.

Narveson, J. (1965). "Pacifism: A Philosophical Analysis." *Ethics* 75: 259–271.

Reitan, E. (2000). "Personally Committed to Nonviolence: Towards a Vindication of Personal Pacifism." *The Acorn: Journal of the Gandhi-King Society* 10: 30–41.

Smith, J. (1970). "Ministerial Draft Exemption and the Establishment Clause." *Cornell Law Review* 55: 992–1003.

Further Reading

Kemp, K. (1993). "Conscientious Objection." *Public Affairs Quarterly* 7: 303–324. (Addresses conscientious objection from a just war perspective and defends selective conscientious objection.)

Kemp, K. (1995). "Personal Pacifism." *Theological Studies* 56: 21–38. (From a Roman Catholic perspective, considers and defends, with qualification, both vocational and individual pacifism.)

King, Jr., M. (1981). "Pilgrimage to Nonviolence," in *Strength to Love*. Philadelphia: Fortress Press, 146–153. (Reflection on King's journey towards a personal commitment to nonviolence.)

Reitan, E. (2000). "Personally Committed to Nonviolence: Towards a Vindication of Personal Pacifism." *The Acorn: Journal of the Gandhi-King Society* 10: 30–41. (Develops two philosophical foundations for personal pacifism.)

16

PACIFISM

Does It Make Moral Sense?

Jan Narveson

A huge amount has been written on this topic—a fact that should testify to its importance, since many of the writers are serious philosophers. In this essay, I will consider just what pacifism is, starting with ambiguities in the term. But there is a sort of "ur-thesis," what I call "General Pacifism": that we are not to use violence, no matter what, or at least with much heavier restrictions than most people think justified. I will then suggest that, for one thing, this ur-version doesn't really make sense, and second, narrower applications of it, especially to the context of international wars, really inherit the problems of the "ur-thesis." We are left with a kind of strong prima facie objection to using violence with which, surely, all reasonable people agree.

To begin with, then, there's the matter of definition. There is a great deal of unclarity about just exactly what the topic is. As an opening to this discussion, then, let's list some of the theses with which the term has been identified.

I'll use the term "Fundamentalist Pacifism" to refer to what we may call the Original Thesis of pacifism. (I called it "General Pacifism" in one of my papers on this subject.) On this view, no individual should ever use any kind of violence against anybody else for any reason whatever. It is the view apparently expressed in Christ's Sermon on the Mount, in which he says that we are to put up with not just one or seven blows but "seventy times seven" rather than fight back. It was approximately this sense of the term in which the popular movie *Friendly Persuasion* (1956, starring Gary Cooper and several other stars) was about pacifism. The movie depicts a Quaker family that really doesn't believe in violence—but it's set in the Civil War, and the family's cheerful life is interrupted by a Union officer who asks how the Quaker men can stand by when their houses will be looted and their families terrorized by approaching Confederate troops; to underline the point, explosions are heard in the distance, people's houses torched, and in general the horrors of war are made evident. The Original Thesis is severely tested by such things (and those Quakers don't pass); but we need to mention that while much has been said about it, most contemporary writers who support pacifism do not accept it. Very few of us, indeed, can "stand by" when our loved ones, not just ourselves, are threatened with violence by robbers, rapists, enemy soldiers, or terrorists.

"Fundamentalist" pacifism has been expressed as a strictly and narrowly ethical view about how individuals as such should behave. Are there any other views at this level that depart from the fundamentalist view and still deserve a special name, "pacifism," that distinguishes it from other views? One that won't qualify in that way is the view, simply, that violence is evil. Indeed it is, but to believe this is not special. Anyone who thinks that violence is not evil, or may even be good, is either talking paradoxically, or else has some sort of special thesis to push. For example, perhaps violence will be regarded as a challenge, or good for the soul, or some such.

As an example of the sort of thing that someone might have in mind along that line, consider violent sports such as boxing or, in its way, American football, or hockey. Those sports do involve a good deal of interpersonal banging around, and boxing indeed is increasingly recognized as damaging to the brain in the long run. Someone who liked boxing as a sport would be impressed by such findings, perhaps to the point of giving it up. But let's suppose that boxing did not have such negative after-effects. Its admirers, in that case, would not have to be worried in that way about it. But why do they enjoy it? Why, indeed, do the participants enjoy it? Most of us who write philosophical papers about such things are not like that. We are wimps! We don't like having our faces smashed, and we don't see how anyone else could either. But then, there are people who enjoy smashing other people's faces, and perhaps their view is a bit more understandable—though deplorable. Of course, if you engage in the sport, obey its rules, and encounter fairly equal opponents, you will soon enough find yourself being pummeled—it won't all be one way. And most likely, you will then have to decide whether the probability of being effectively and painfully pummeled is high enough to outweigh the pleasure, if that's what it is, of pummeling the other fellow.

What would really be strange, though, is taking the view that you had no right to (literally) hit back. In fact, your partner in the sport would wonder what on earth you were up to if you offered no similarly violent response. Pacifism in this context would strike most athletes, and their spectators, as unintelligible, odd, even slightly crazy. And that's something that the would-be pacifist needs to think about. Is there something wrong with the enthusiast for boxing? If so, just why? Here we would need to be especially careful to steer clear of any sort of assumption that people who enjoy boxing would be dangers to the public. They needn't be at all, and, I believe, usually aren't. They confine their violence to fellow voluntary participants.

Commonsense Opposition to Violence

So we need now to identify a view about morals that is, in fact, very familiar and widespread: that it is wrong to injure others, so long as they don't injure us. Where pacifism departs from common sense morality is precisely concerning that view. Most of us think that those who are ready to do violence to others are people whom we, the rest of us, have a perfect right to defend ourselves against, and also others who enlist our aid, and to do so by violence at least if it's "necessary."

Now, a pacifist might think that it never is necessary. That is an interesting idea, but on the face of it a dramatically implausible one, when we think of all sorts of familiar cases. The soldier on the front line, for example, facing an attack will be unlikely to attach much credence to it. And, to get down to earth in another way, consider the people in that movie whose houses are due for burning down by rampaging enemy soldiers; or think of a violent mob descending on your home with intent to do the same. Those on the scene are not likely to be impressed with a claim that violence is unnecessary at least in these actual cases. And it is about such cases that the ordinary moral belief that we are entitled to fight back is at its most compelling. I do not want my wife and children to be at the mercy of brigands, and if I can deal with them by shooting them, or superior swordsmanship or the like, then I will do so. In most communities we know of, people who might be able to use such means of defense and wouldn't would be thought very badly of by their fellows as well.

In summary so far, then: the view that violence is wrong is ambiguous. It might mean that it is wrong to use it no matter what—the fundamentalist view—or it might instead mean that aggressive violence, violence against the innocent, is what is wrong. And the very fact of aggression, with its intent to use violence to achieve other ends than defensive ones, is not only wrong, but wrong to the point that if no other means of dealing with it is readily possible on occasion, then the use of counterviolence on that occasion is permissible. Such is the thesis of the well-known position concerning war known as "just war" theory, to which we will turn our attention next.

Another type of pacifism is "War Pacifism." Ethical pacifism as applied to every particular individual at all times strikes most people as far-fetched, even crazy. But the war pacifist does not defend "fundamentalist" nonviolence. Instead, he is concerned with war in the standard sense of the term: namely, as large-scale, organized violence used by armies as means of political policy. His thesis then becomes that even defensive war is never justified. Question: why does the case of war seem to the war pacifist so different from the individual-versus-individual case?

When we speak of war in this usual sense, basic questions of political philosophy are raised. On the one hand, we have the question of why making war would ever be justified. In the millennium and a half since "just war" theory was first articulated (by St. Augustine, especially, in the fifth century C.E.), it has generally been agreed by thoughtful scholars that wars, if justified at all, are so because of expected benefit to the community on behalf of whom those wars are fought. But they have also tended to focus on just one general kind of benefit—namely, defense. Innumerable governments of many countries over the millennia have initiated wars of conquest, the point of which was, apparently, to seize the resources of their victims, and often to enslave the populace. They have been, in effect, national-level bandits. The philosophers I have in mind have reacted by insisting that that kind of war aim is not allowable, and wars fought for such purposes unjust. But they have also argued that war efforts to defend communities from such invasion are in principle just, or at least capable of being so. They might have agreed that if there was simply no hope in resistance—think Estonia versus modern Russia, for example—then for the leaders of the invaded country to insist on continued armed resistance would be not only futile but wrong, and wrong because futile. Now, why would that be? After all, for an individual to fight to the death in behalf of his own defense or that of his family would not as likely be so regarded. The difference, of course, is that a community is a whole lot of people, and those people are quite different from each other. Many of them would rather surrender than fight, at least if it looks as though the overwhelmingly likely outcome of fighting is their own death, along with that, or the enslavement, of their families. When that is their attitude, then the government, which after all is supposed to be doing its best for its people, cannot just barge ahead and try to make everyone into martyrs.

OK. But war pacifism, again, goes much farther. It doesn't just insist that we make a plausible estimate of the likelihood of success if we try to respond to invasion with military defense; it holds that even if the defense would probably be successful, then we still ought not to engage in it.

Or does it? Here things get rather thick. The temptation to assimilate the social case to the individual one is very strong, after all. If it is OK for an individual to try to defend himself with force, then why isn't it similarly OK for a community to do so? A "war pacifist" needs to answer that question.

A Matter of Degree

While it would be possible for a theorist to clench his fists and assert that no government is ever justified in making war against anybody for any reason, it is extremely unlikely, and to my knowledge, none actually does so. Nevertheless, some philosophers insist that they have a view that is properly called "pacifism" despite that. And if so, this suggests that pacifism is a matter of degree, even of nuance. Which kinds of war-aims, for example, will we allow and which not? The problem is that when we get into the real political world, it will not be so easy to say that X is definitely an "aggressor" while Y is definitely not. Consider the contemporary pressuring, as we see it, of the government of China in the South Chinese Sea area (at this writing in 2016). Here the Chinese have descended on tiny wisps of rock, scarcely even "islands," and built them up into islandlike places that support air landing strips, among other things. All the activity has been military: no civilian settlement, as such, is envisaged (or makes much sense, given the tininess of the places and their total lack of resources for civilian life). The islands in question are within the established 200-mile limit from other countries that has been internationally accepted as defining the legitimate areas of national jurisdiction over sea areas. So just about all of the nations bordering that sea are faced with military occupation by a foreign nation on what is internationally accepted as their waters. Still, those are bits of rock on which the presumed owners have done nothing in recent years, or ever. Does China have a claim, of a kind that makes sense and is accepted when made by individuals occupying hitherto unoccupied areas of land—first come, first served, it's yours? The international maritime court ruled otherwise. So, does pacifism say that the Chinese shouldn't do this? Perhaps. Does it say that either the small nations concerned—if they could—or the Americans—who clearly could if they wanted to—ought not to react in military ways? And if so, meaning what? For example, the American navy has made a point of routing ships within the much narrower, 12-mile limit of those islands, in order to make the point that these are international waters, waters in which all and sundry have a right to sail. (The Chinese have made considerable trouble for civilian fishermen trying to navigate in those very waters; but the American vessels are well armed and would make very big trouble for any ship, or for that matter land-based artillery, say, if the Chinese chose to try to chase them out by force.) How do we clearly identify what is "pacific" and what isn't in this kind of case?

Some politicians are labeled "doves" and some "hawks" because of their views about many specific international issues. But no one is hawkish enough to seriously advocate using nuclear weapons against any of the initiatives engaged in by any actors on the world stage today, major or minor. And on the other hand, no serious leader of a country that possesses nuclear weapons would propose unilaterally dispossessing their countries of those weapons. Would a war pacifist be committed to doing so? Does it not matter at all to such a theorist how many such weapons other nations had, or what their intentions seem to be about using them?

All those questions are designed to reinforce a general point: that it is very difficult to identify a serious position on international affairs that is clearly "pacifist" or "nonpacifist" in a flat-out way. Rather, it's a matter of how much of what kind of "pressure" a given country should be exerting on some or several other countries in regard to what kind of ventures those other countries initiate. Within fairly well-known limits, some will be more "hawkish" and others more "dovish" but neither of them is ready to make war about just anything—or indeed, about very much, nowadays—and neither of them is ready to back down all the possible way on much of anything.

Thus pacifism remains theoretical in the sense that we must not expect to be able to go straight from premises termed pacifist to conclusions about particular foreign-policy matters.

Relevant Variables

Some foreign policy initiatives are very likely to involve the country making them in shooting or bombing people, and some of those people will almost certainly be civilian. One possible pacifist might say: there must be no war that involves any avoidable civilian death.

But that idea, too, has a problem. What if it is argued that our not doing this now will result in many more civilians being killed, not by us but by, for instance, their own government (as in contemporary Syria), or by the government that is likely to replace the one "we" are currently supporting (as in Afghanistan, where the Taliban will be the next government if America allows it)? And too, it's not just a matter of killings. What if the alternative government will turn its people into virtual slaves, or will impose enormous limitations on allowable behavior in many respects, on pain of death? (For example, if women wear the "wrong" kind of attire in public.) Must a pacifist say that "we" have no business, on principle, in using military methods to prevent these horrific indignities (as we liberals regard them)?

A General Theoretical Argument

In my own earliest paper on these matters ("Pacifism—a Philosophical Analysis," 1965) I argue that pacifism was inconsistent. Here's how the argument went. The pacifist is against all violence. This is understood to mean that he himself will never use it. But suppose that if he doesn't, then someone else will use much more. (For example, if he doesn't shoot the terrorist now, then that terrorist will blow up 50 people, or 500, or whatever.) If opposition to violence is what motivates his nonviolence, then more violence will occur that he could have prevented. So his theoretical position is inconsistent with his prescriptions.

The pacifist could avoid this by insisting that his theory only applies to his own actions. Unfortunately, that doesn't help, since among those actions would be ones that would prevent certain other people from murdering many people. And why would he exempt those actions from among those his theory is about? In fact, almost everyone who considers situations such as this do "cave in" at some point: once the number who will be killed if he doesn't use violence against some specified persons rises above such-and-such, he will agree that he ought to use violence in that case.

And so it again becomes very much a matter of degree. If the pacifist is to specify that it's n people, then we should know why it is n rather than n/2, or n/50. And it seems very difficult to give a non-arbitrary answer to such questions.

Ordinary Morality

What is the alternative? Well, consider the view that seems to be implicit in ordinary morality, and made explicit by what are called "libertarian" theorists. Namely, that (a) there is no particular limit to the number of clearly evil persons, persons using violence for their own ordinary ends or any ends other than defensive ones, who may, if necessary, be killed in order to prevent any number of innocent people being killed by them; and (b) when we use violence for defense, then "collateral" damage, in the form of unintentional infliction of civilian death, should be zero, but if that is impossible, then it should be very small in comparison with the good, in the way of defense of innocent persons, being effected. Of course this latter is a problem of similar type to the one faced by the pacifist: just how many innocent persons may be unintentionally but foreseeably killed in order to prevent just how many innocent persons being intentionally as well as foreseeably killed by the "bad guys"?

The advantage of the ordinary view is that it's usually quite easy to live up to. For we are hardly ever performing any of the actions we are worrying about. It is very easy not to kill people; only on extremely special occasions are we faced with the options of either killing certain people, or else letting those people in turn kill still others. The libertarian view asks us to perform no actions that lead to the net harm of others. If we inflict any pain, it must be with the consent of those on whom it is inflicted, unless those persons are themselves in the process of inflicting horrible injuries, or deaths, on others. We are, in short, not to pursue our own good by inflicting evils on others. Beyond that, we have no actual, enforceable duty to do a lot of good, or save a lot of lives. We are permitted to save no lives, actually. But we want to save lives if we can, and we should and normally do regard as heroes people who do. The pacifist, however, seems to be saying that it is impermissible to take any lives even if doing so should be necessary in order to prevent greater evils, and even if those are the lives of the very people who will do the wrong things if we don't stop them.

Translating this back into the international sphere, then: one nation is not to make war against another for the purpose of adding to its own gross national product (say), let alone to conquer and enslave other people. More generally, no nation is to advance its own self-regarding interests at the expense of citizens in other nations. And it is to attempt to prevent other countries from doing likewise, and it is permitted to do so provided that it observes the familiar constraints, of not sacrificing innocent people if it is avoidable, and of sacrificing very few if it not. I take it that this principle is simply the application at the level of states of the general principle for individuals that they are not to interact with others in such a way as to impose uncompensated costs on those others, unless it is unavoidable. As with individuals also, this very principle entails a general right of self-defense against those who are attempting to impose those costs. The "costs" in question include, especially, the lives of the interactees in question, though they are by no means limited to their physical lives. We should take this to include damaging, stealing (including by defrauding their owners), or destroying their legitimately earned properties.

In earlier days, of course, what amounts to theft was a standard cause of war, as Country or Tribe A attempted to plunder Country or Tribe B by armed force. At present, no country would admit that that was its motive. It would invent some kind of pretext, such as that what it is taking belonged to it a thousand years ago. But we will ignore this diversion. The present point is simply that the libertarian view is not pacifist. It says we are not to make war against any innocent parties—where "innocence" is a matter of not making war on peaceable parties—but guilty ones are another matter, and that that goes for state actions as well as individual ones. So where does that leave us? It seems to leave pacifism in a bit of a jam. If it has a truly distinctive voice, as it is usually thought to have, then what that voice tells us is evidently incredible, since it tells us not to resist the one thing it's avowedly against—violence. And otherwise, its contribution is limited to taking the "dovish" side on issues that are distinguished by there being "hawks" and "doves" in disagreement about what to do. And there is such a distinction precisely because in so many cases it's really not obvious what to do—not obvious that the "doves" are necessarily in the right.

Up-to-Date Pacificness

Today's world is a lot more complicated than in any previous era. There is very rarely any question of out-and-out war-making of the traditional sort. The U.S. maintains an extremely powerful military establishment, and has every hope and intention of never seriously having to use it. The Americans have innumerable military bases all over the world and can get serious-sized armies to practically any place anywhere within a matter of a day or two. Their question would be—whenever, if ever, should they do it? Old-fashioned pacifism would presumably say that it must never use its military capabilities at all, at the level of shooting wars. But that view is surely not credible. What is far more credible is that America should be doing whatever it possibly can to see to it that things never get to that state. Its credibility, though, depends on just what the scope of the "whatever" is in that last sentence. In many cases, American power is intended to protect weaker allies, or, at least, states whose political record suggests that they are worthy of protection against states that we can reasonably describe as (more) seriously defective. Many of the states Americans protect or are allied with—such as Saudi Arabia—have plenty of serious faults from the liberal point of view: Saudi Arabia's treatment of women is notoriously awful, the degree of religious (especially), and other sorts of civil and political freedom it allows its citizens is far from beyond reproach—and it's just that its main regional antagonist, Iran, is arguably even worse and in any case, it is thought, far more dangerous. In such a confrontation, just what constitutes the "doing of whatever it possibly can" to maintain peace? Indeed, perhaps the main question is, just what constitutes "peace"? In particular, how are we at peace with a country that could be described as being continually at war with most of its own citizens? If America supplies armaments to Saudi Arabia, arguably assisting them in the oppression of their own people, is that justifiable if it helps to reduce the bellicosity of Iran?

The point here is not to get into actual political controversies and developments of the day. It is, instead, to press further the point about pacifism. If these actions are defended on the ground that they help to promote peace in the world, can a pacifist object, at any rate, to the principle behind the action? If, of course, it is argued that the policy initiative doesn't actually work, that is a legitimate complaint. But then the issue seems to be one of fact about whether the policy works, rather than a condemnation of its principle.

Some nations of the world do not profess similar principles. They insist that they have some kind of right to invade—as we see it—countries that they insist "belong" to them, even though people in those countries do not see it that way. And suppose we are right about this: suppose that their actions really are violations of the rights of those various people. Is it part of pacifism to insist that we should do nothing in the way of military action to try to prevent those invasions? But how can that be, if the prevention works and if otherwise many people would be in effect enslaved or perhaps killed by those expansionary nations? We might not be right, to be sure. But once again, it is unclear how there is a question of principle on which the pacifist stands on one side and "we" on the other.

Peace and the State

Pacifism is taken, nowadays, to be exclusively about state action, or at least the actions of groups aspiring to political power. While the state is taken for granted by nearly everyone, we should at least be aware of what we are taking for granted when we do so. Namely, states proceed by wielding political power, and that sort of power is inherently coercive. States make decisions on behalf of everyone, including many who do not agree with what they do. Those people don't have their choice. Government literally compels them to go along. One could almost say that the state is typically at some level of war with many or most or even all of its citizens. There is surely a general question whether and why this is all right. That general question, of course, is pretty much the basic reason for the existence of political philosophy, whose continuing question is whether and if so why the state is justified, either in general, or in regard to this or that particular program or policy. Always the question is whether coercive power may legitimately be wielded in that particular way, or ever.

There is one general answer—and it's a good one if it works. The state is claimed to be a protective agency: we are all supposed to be safer, more secure, because of its actions. It would be a good answer if it works because we all, surely, desire security. The state achieves this, insofar as it does, by hiring a lot of police, among other things, and going after those who murder, rape, assault, swindle, and more. And as we know, the state frequently gets the "wrong man"—punishing, or killing, the innocent and looking the other way, or worse, as the guilty ply their trade. Moreover, the modern state does a great deal more than that, much of which encounters the same problem: everyone is made to pay for its ventures, yet many don't approve of the programs for which they are paying. And yet, by and large, people view the state with approval, and even enthusiasm.

The would-be pacifist needs to clarify where he or she stands on these basic issues—not just war, but policing, criminal justice, prisons, and the like. If the pacifist thinks that general taxation for programs popular with few, or the state pursuing people not for harming others but for "harming" themselves, or doing simply what others don't like rather than what really violates their rights—as it certainly does, and frequently—are all acceptable, then it is hard to see how the blanket prohibition of war, as such, is to be sustained.

Conclusion

All of this is to say that a program recognizable as pacifism, as distinct from a general condemnation of violence when it is really wrong—done against innocent people—is extremely difficult even to define coherently, much less to sustain with plausible arguments. The world we live in does not come anywhere near to being the sort of place where thoroughgoing pacifism will not be counterproductive. And when that counterproductivity consists in people getting away with murder and the like, it has to count seriously by pacifist standards. No civilized person wants people to be able to murder, rob, maim, and otherwise damage their fellows, whether they do so as individuals or in large, highly organized—and extremely expensive—armies. But what are we to do to eliminate or at least minimize such behavior? No matter how we slice it, no program that is recognizably pacifistic seems to be the answer. We are left with a very general basic reluctance to use violence, which is surely something we should all share. Beyond that, some version of "just war theory" seems to be inescapable. So once again, the conclusion seems to be that either pacifism is a distinctive but unacceptable view, because it is downright incoherent, or else that it scarcely differs, apart from emphasis, from what we all—I hope—think: that military and other violence should be confined to defensive purposes, however that is construed.

Further Reading

Fiala, A. (2008). *The Just War Myth: The Moral Illusions of War*. Lanham, MD: Rowman and Littlefield. (A critical account of the just war theory.)
Holmes, R. (1989). *On War and Morality*. Princeton: Princeton University Press. (A sustained argument and critique of the morality of war when fought in modern conditions.)
Orend, B. (2001). "Evaluating Pacifism." *Dialogue* 40: 3–24. (An argument offering an evaluation of pacifism from the standpoint of just war theory.)
Ryan, C. (1983). "Self-Defense, Pacifism and Rights." *Ethics* 93: 508–524. (A skeptical account of the morality of killing in self-defense.)
Also see a number of articles/chapters by Narveson that offer the critique of pacifism, including:
Narveson, J. (1965). "Pacifism—a Philosophical Analysis." *Ethics* 75 (4), July: 259–271.
Narveson, J. (1968). "Is Pacifism Consistent?" *Ethics* 78 (2), January: 148–150.
Narveson, J. (1991–92). "A Comment on Filice's Defense of Pacifism." *Journal of Philosophical Research* XVII: 477–485.
Narveson, J. (2002). "Pacifism, Ideology, and the Human Right of Self-Defense." *Journal of Human Rights* 1 (1), March: 55–69.
Narveson, J. (2003). "Pacifism and Terrorism: Why We Should Condemn Both." *International Journal of Applied Philosophy* 17 (2): 157–173.
Narveson, J. (2006). "Is Pacifism Self-Refuting?" in B. Bleisch and J.-D. Strub (eds.), *Pazifismus: Ideengeschichte, Theorie und Praxis*. Bern, Stuttgart and Wien: Haupt, 127–144.
Narveson, J. (2012). "Is Pacifism Reasonable?" *Belgrade Philosophical Annual*, XXV: 143–154.

17
PACIFISM AS PATHOLOGY

José-Antonio Orosco

Opponents of pacifism usually employ two arguments against it. In terms of pacifism as an ethical position, critics typically attempt to reveal an inconsistency in taking a principled stance against the use of violence. For instance, they may try to demonstrate that some pacifists reject war, but would still revert to violence for personal self-defense, or to protect a loved one. Pacifists usually respond by pointing out that the inconsistency occurs when one assumes that there is only one form of pacifism, namely absolute pacifism. Yet there are a variety of pacifist views; some forms focus on the actions of institutions, some focus on the behavior of individuals, and within the latter there are some that allow for the use of violence for the protection of others or for self-defense by an individual (Ryan 2009). The second critique holds that pacifism, as a commitment to the use of nonviolent means for social conflict resolution, is ineffective in being able to deal with a particularly vicious, sadistic, or powerful foe. Here, pacifists respond by highlighting the growing body of empirical evidence that shows how nonviolent campaigns tend to be, on a whole, much more successful than armed struggle in achieving political transformation against dictatorial regimes in the twentieth century (Chenoweth and Stepan 2012).

However, a more recent line of argument presents a troublesome objection to pacifism that is not so easily dismissed. This objection claims that pacifism is a kind of pathological adherence to nonviolent strategies that are more, rather than less, likely to lead to the perpetuation of systematic forms of oppression. This essay will, first, reconstruct this argument as found in the work of George Orwell, Ward Churchill, and Peter Gelderloos. Each maintains that principled nonviolence, or what they call pacifism, is a morally irresponsible approach to a world structured by systematic forms of racial, gender, and colonial forms of domination. I then present two responses to the "pacifism is a pathology" perspective. The first holds that these critics fail to understand the ways in which pacifism deploys power, which may include the use of coercive force. The second holds that these critics fail to understand the full range of nonviolent tactics for social transformation, which may in fact include some destructive tactics such as property destruction. While I hold that the proponents of this idea have mischaracterized pacifism by failing to see it as a complex or "multipronged" theory about building and deploying nonviolent power, they nonetheless help to raise important issues about the appropriateness of nonviolent forms of social protest.

Pacifism as Pathology

The view that principled nonviolence is morally irresponsible begins with the assumption that in many contemporary societies oppression is a widespread condition in which victimized groups suffer violence, exploitation, marginalization, and so on, at the hands of dominant groups. This oppression is often institutionally inflicted and reinforced through the legal means of the state. Moreover, it is usually justified by appeal to ideological narratives or cultural traditions that demonize marginalized groups and make it seem as if the harm they receive is deserved.

In this line of thinking, pacifism is defined as the rigid insistence that the use of nonviolent methods is the only morally justifiable strategy for social justice struggles. Pacifism, the argument goes, typically operates by appealing to the moral conscience of the oppressor groups, or to the moral sympathies of bystanders in society. In general, pacifists try to avoid inflicting any kind of physical or psychological harm on the oppressor. But in a situation of systematic institutional and cultural oppression, this sort of appeal is often ignored by bystanders and by the dominant groups in control of the major institutions. Or worse, pacifism may trigger dominant groups to inflict more violence through state or paramilitary terrorism. If there is little or no evidence that principled nonviolence can offer relief from the threat of ongoing violence, or even from possible genocide, then, the argument goes, there is something morally wrong in insisting that oppressed groups are obliged to avoid armed resistance:

> Since improving the chances for social justice to flourish is usually a very high priority for pacifists, and is essentially linked with the activity of peacemaking itself for most of them, the possibility that a pacifist approach to oppression in a particular case could lead to worse consequences and more injustice for the oppressed would pose a serious dilemma for an advocate of this strategy.
>
> *Christensen 2010: 130*

George Orwell was perhaps the first to propose the idea that pacifism is a kind of pathology. In a letter from 1942 entitled "Pacifism and the War," Orwell called pacifism a "bourgeois illusion bred of money and security" (Orwell 1968: 101). He argued that British pacifists who took a public stand against the war in Europe were moral hypocrites. While they spoke out against the use of military force, they allowed themselves to take advantage of the food and security provided by the British naval personnel who were risking their own lives to violate the German blockades of the island.

Orwell believed that, in addition to this hypocrisy, pacifists simply did not understand the reality of politics, or how violent regimes like Nazi Germany work. Trying to resist an authoritarian government through nonviolent means did not elevate the moral standing of pacifists, it simply made them, and other marginalized groups, vulnerable to state violence: "Despotic governments can stand 'moral force' til the cows come home; what they fear is physical force" (Orwell 1968: 102). Orwell concluded that a commitment to nonviolent resistance when dealing with oppressive governments is almost a psychological disorder, a masochistic fascination with domination and submission:

> But though not much interested in the "theory" of pacifism, I *am* interested in the psychological processes by which pacifists who have started out with an alleged horror of violence end up with a marked tendency to be fascinated by the success and power of Nazism. Even pacifists who wouldn't own to any such fascination are beginning to claim that a Nazi victory is desirable in itself.
>
> *Orwell 1968: 102*

Native American rights activist and scholar Ward Churchill fills in more detail to this argument. He is the one who coined the phrase "pacifism as pathology" in 1986. Reflecting on developments in North American social movements, Churchill observes a widespread tendency among liberal activists to espouse principled nonviolence and to reject armed struggle as a tool for social transformation. By armed struggle, Churchill has in mind armed self-defense against state agents, as well as violence by organized groups against "offensive military operations," including the destruction of facilities and the targeted assassination of key figures in government or corporations (Churchill 2005: 38). The reason for this renunciation, according to Churchill, is the widespread faith among liberal activists that by rejecting armed struggle they can claim moral superiority against an oppressive state and thereby defeat it. Protest then becomes a morality play. If pacifists can, through nonviolent direct actions, prod the state to use violence to contain them, then they will have revealed the state's illegitimate and brute power and shown the just nature of their grievances against it. This willingness to endure these injuries inflicted by the state is a crucial part of this pacifist worldview. By accepting the suffering meted out by the unjust state, pacifists are somehow countering its force with an almost metaphysical understanding of power: "The teleological assumption here is that a sort of 'negation of the negation' is involved, that the 'power of nonviolence' can in itself be used to supplant the offending societal violence represented in the formation of state power" (Churchill 2005: 39).

The main issue for Churchill is that liberal activists believe these pacifist ideas without question, almost as articles of faith. If asked to produce evidence that pacifism works, liberal activists will point out "that it has been done, as the survival of at least some of the Jews, the decolonization of India, and the enfranchisement of Southern American blacks demonstrate" (Churchill 2005: 39). A closer look at these examples, Churchill claims, reveals exactly the opposite reality about pacifism's power. In the case of the Holocaust, Churchill believes that pacifism as pathology manifests itself in its most sinister form. Relying on the work of concentration camp survivor Bruno Bettelheim, Churchill argues that Jewish leaders counseled passive resistance in the face of the Nazi threat and, as a result, shepherded millions to genocide: "The mainly pacifist forms of resistance exhibited by the Jewish community played directly into the hands of their executioners" (Churchill 2005: 34).

In the other two cases of supposed pacifist victories, the success of nonviolent methods is simply exaggerated according to Churchill. For instance, in terms of Indian independence, it was not Gandhi's campaigns that forced the British to leave. Instead, Britain was an empire weakened by two world wars and an overextended military; it was simply too expensive and impractical to maintain control of India. Gandhi's feeble efforts were, in fact, "contingent upon others physically gutting their opponents for them" (Churchill 2005: 42). In the case of the U.S. civil rights movement, Churchill believes that the government conceded to demands from leaders, such as Martin Luther King, Jr., not because of pressure from nonviolent activism, but from the twin threats of a loss in Vietnam and the danger of black militant groups. Churchill holds that "without this spectre, real or perceived, of a violent black revolution at large in America during a time of war, King's nonviolent strategy was basically impotent in concrete terms" (Churchill 2005: 43). The correct conclusion to draw from these examples, according to Churchill, is not that pacifism works, but either that (1) pacifists are nonthreatening to oppressive state power or (2) that, if pacifists do somehow threaten oppressive state power using nonviolence, then they will quickly be defeated because of their refusal to use violence to defend themselves from the state, which has no moral qualms about using force against disobedient citizens.

The real danger is not simply that pacifism is ineffective. For Churchill, the issue is how readily pacifism has come to be accepted by liberal activists as a kind of dogmatic ideology about available strategies in the struggle for social justice. Pacifists, in their willful ignorance and adherence to nonviolence, fail to learn from the history of successes by armed guerrilla groups in the twentieth century. These examples teach that, in the face of industrialized military states, the best strategies are ones that refuse to obey standard military tactics and that keep the state confused and off balance. By remaining faithful to nonviolence, pacifists ensure defeat since their "actions become entirely predictable rather than offering the utility of surprise" (Churchill 2005: 89). For Churchill, principled pacifism is a naïve faith that ends up debilitating social justice movements by taking off the table the use of tactics that can effectively confront an oppressive state and protect the lives of the most vulnerable and marginalized members of society. Insofar as pacifists rule out armed struggle as an option, they stand in the way of achieving social justice. Moreover, pacifists are actually complicit in the atrocities perpetuated by oppressive groups by choosing a path that has no way of stopping state violence.

Radical community organizer Peter Gelderloos develops this last point further. He argues that principled nonviolence, in its ineffectiveness, reinforces systematic forms of oppression such as white supremacy, patriarchy, and homophobia. Pacifism is all the more dangerous, he believes, because its practitioners tend to prop up, rather than weaken, the authoritarian surveillance and control powers of the state.

Gelderloos thinks pacifism reinforces white supremacy, at least in the context of North America, in four ways. First, he maintains, like Orwell, that modern pacifism is paternalistic and hypocritical. Pacifism is mainly a commitment by white, privileged, middle-class activists who seek to impose on the social movements of non-white and working-class groups their understanding of social justice and transformation as the only moral or acceptable alternatives:

> Pacifism assumes that white people who grew up in the suburbs with all their basic needs met can counsel oppressed people, many of whom are people of color, to suffer patiently under an inconceivably greater violence, until such time as the Great White Father is swayed by the movement's demands or the pacifists achieve that legendary "critical mass."
>
> *Gelderloos 2007: 23*

Second, the effect of this epistemic privilege is the inability to understand violence in any form other than acts of direct harm to persons or property. This elitist understanding, according to Gelderloos, ignores structural violence, the kind of constant harm that is perpetuated disproportionately against communities of color by capitalist economic policy, and major institutions such as the police, military, and the prison system (Gelderloos 2016: 457). Next, liberal activists tend to whitewash history in order to find examples of social justice heroes, such as Gandhi, Martin Luther King, Jr., and Nelson Mandela, that support their pacifism while ignoring the examples of people of color that discount their theories (Gelderloos 2007: 24). In addition to this misunderstanding of these historical figures, white pacifists completely ignore, or are ignorant of, the role of other heroes in the social justice struggles of people of color. The white pacifist version of the Civil Rights movement, for instance, downplays the impact of militant leaders, such as Malcolm X, or Robert F. Williams, the author of *Negroes with Guns*. Both of these men advocated for the right of African Americans to engage in armed self-defense of themselves and their communities. Finally, pacifists discount the possible psychological benefits for people of color in resisting oppression more forcefully than through nonviolent demonstration. Here, Gelderloos relies on the work of Frantz Fanon and his studies on the effect of violence in anti-colonial struggles to ponder whether fighting back against state officials provides a psychological "uplift effect" for the oppressed (Gelderloos 2007: 37).

According to Gelderloos, pacifism also reinforces patriarchy rather than opposes it. For instance, Gelderloos finds absolute pacifism—a view that eschews all forms of violence, including that used in personal self-defense—to be unrealistic and immoral as a response to the kind of violence faced by individuals gendered as female:

> If we take this philosophy out of the impersonal political arena and put it in a more real context, nonviolence implies that it is immoral for a woman to fight off an attacker or to study self-defense. Nonviolence implies that it is better for an abused wife to move out than to mobilize a group of women to beat up and kick out her abusive husband. Nonviolence implies it is better for someone to be raped than to pull the mechanical pencil out of her pocket and plunge it into her assailant's jugular (because doing so would supposedly contribute to some cycle of violence and encourage future rapes). Pacifism simply does not resonate in people's everyday realities, unless those people live in some extravagant bubble of tranquility from which all forms of civilization's pandemic violence have been pushed out by the systemic and less visible violence of police and military forces.
>
> *Gelderloos 2007: 66*

Even less absolute forms of pacifism draw similar ire because they make, as a centerpiece of nonviolent direct action, the need for activists to be willing to accept the violence of the state without retaliation. For Gelderloos, the message that social justice activists must suffer for the cause coincides with the cultural narrative of the caretaker that patriarchy imposes on women. Patriarchal order depends on women internalizing a message that an authentic woman's role is to be submissive, passive, and willing to tolerate suffering for the good of men around her. What would overturn the patriarchal dynamic is not a theory that universalizes the pain of the subordinate gender, but one that upsets the system with an unexpected agency. Gelderloos thinks patriarchy must be confronted by those individuals gendered as women who reject suffering as a good or necessary part of their life and are willing to take on actions typically gendered as male, namely the use of violence for self-defense and retaliation against harm: "[W]omen reclaiming the ability and right to use force would not by itself end patriarchy, but it is a necessary condition for gender liberation, as well as a useful form of empowerment and protection in the short term" (Gelderloos 2007: 68).

Moreover, Gelderloos thinks that the pacifist emphasis on creating morality plays that pit a virtuous social justice movement against a brutal oppressor can foster an unhealthy environment that inhibits self-awareness of the ways in which sexism and gender violence operate within the social justice activist community:

> When your strategy's victory comes from "captur[ing] and maintain[ing] the moral high ground," it is necessary to portray yourself as moral and your enemy as immoral. Uncovering bigoted and oppressive dynamics among group leaders and members is simply counterproductive to your chosen strategy.
>
> *Gelderloos 2007: 70*

As an example of this harmful situation, Gelderloos refers to the manner in which Martin Luther King, Jr. exercised patriarchal power to silence women in the Southern Christian Leadership Conference, publically exhibited sexist stereotypes about women as mothers, and used his power to remove prominent gay leaders from roles in civil rights organizations. In a rush to construct a certain kind of moral narrative, pacifists downplayed or ignored these instances: "But then, why would these facts be widely available when making an icon of King entailed covering up any such faults and portraying him as a saint?" (Gelderloos 2007: 71).

Finally, Gelderloos thinks that pacifists are not just dangerous for promoting a largely ineffective understanding of the kinds of protest strategies needed to oppose systematic oppression, but they also have come to position themselves as "peace police" in a way that hampers powerful resistance to injustice. In his 2013 work *The Failure of Nonviolence*, Gelderloos provides a long list of prominent pacifist authors and activists, including Gene Sharp, Mark Kurlansky, Rebecca Solnit, Chris Hedges, and the Dalai Lama, as examples of people who have discouraged the use of any methods of social change other than principled nonviolence. Several of these pacifists adhere to the view that nonviolent methods are the only morally justified forms of protest. For instance, in analyzing the riots that occurred during the Occupy Oakland protests in 2011, journalist Chris Hedges referred to those who chose to engage in property destruction in pathological terms, calling them "sick," "beasts," or like "cancer" for a social movement (Hedges 2012). Many of these figures, according to Gelderloos, see their role in social protests as maintaining nonviolent discipline among participants during demonstrations and marches. They consider it their duty to police anyone who does not hold fast to nonviolence by isolating them or even physically apprehending them and turning them over to authorities for arrest and punishment (Gelderloos 2013: 126).

Rather than simply arguing in favor of armed struggle against oppressive governments as Churchill does, Gelderloos advocates for what he calls "the diversity of tactics." Social movement activists, in his view, should reject the pacifist moral constraint on the use of violence and instead think of direct action as a spectrum of tactics ranging from nonviolent protest to property damage and even to armed struggle against state authorities. In arguing for a diversity of tactics, Gelderloos is not trying to discount nonviolence as a method outright, but simply to make it one possible option among several. The choice of tactics should be based on pragmatic grounds about what will work best to protect marginalized communities from the state and systematic oppression (Gelderloos 2007: 3). Thus, a principled or absolute pacifism ought to be rejected since it cannot tolerate any form of protest that is not completely nonviolent and forces its practitioners to become accomplices of state violence against oppressed communities; but strategic nonviolence can be allowed as one choice among several:

> Nonviolence as an absolute philosophy has no place in a diverse struggle, because it is incapable of respecting the pluralistic nature of liberation. But people who personally favor peaceful tactics, and even those whose concept of revolution is to work for peace, who follow a philosophy of doing no harm, should be respected as part of the struggle.
> *Gelderloos 2013: 241*

Responses to Pacifism as Pathological

The positions of Orwell, Churchill, and Gelderloos seem to rest on two assumptions about what they are calling pacifism. The first assumption is that pacifism's only power for social transformation is through the moral persuasion of dominant elites or social bystanders. The second is that pacifism requires that protesters commit themselves to using only a narrow range of nonviolent tactics that avoid physically harming authorities, or vandalizing or damaging property. I will demonstrate how both of these assumptions about pacifism are mistaken. First, George Lakey's work demonstrates that nonviolence can deploy several forms of power, not just moral persuasion. Indeed, nonviolent tactics can deploy the kind of coercive force that critics believe only occurs though armed struggle, or movements that involve property destruction. Second,

Gene Sharp, Mark Engler, and Paul Engler reveal that even a principled pacifist, such as Gandhi, conceived of nonviolent struggle as involving a wide range of strategies, including nonviolent direct action protest, electoral politics, and alternative-community building to confront systematic oppression.

Orwell rejects pacifism because it relies on "moral force" and refuses to deploy "physical force" against even despotic and genocidal enemies. Churchill finds that pacifism's supposed historical victories were really the result of pressure put on unjust states by militant groups that were willing to employ armed resistance against them. Gelderloos agrees with Churchill's historical analysis, and while he does not outright dismiss nonviolent means as part of tactical diversity, he does think that pacifists underestimate "the role of confrontation and destruction in a revolution" (Gelderloos 2013: 241). Thus, the objection from the standpoint of pacifism as pathology is that pacifists have no other form of power available to them other than some kind of moral appeal to oppressing groups to stop their injustice. Indeed, Gandhi sometimes described nonviolence this way, fueling the impression that nonviolent direct action is either about morally shaming oppressors for their violence or inciting moral outrage at oppressors for the use of violence against oppressed groups:

> Since then the conviction to the people are not secured by reason alone but have to be purchased with their suffering. Suffering is the law of human beings; war is the law of the jungle. But suffering is infinitely more powerful than the law of the jungle for converting the opponent and opening his ears, which are otherwise shut, to the voice of reason. Suffering is the badge of the human race, not the sword.
>
> *Gandhi 1957: 185*

Yet, the worry is that oppressors are not likely to heed such calls to their conscience—after all, if they had a conscience they most likely would not be engaging to perpetuate systematic violence against the oppressed in the first place. In refusing to harm their opponents, even to the point that Gandhi recommended of refusing to think badly or speaking badly of them, pacifists simply fail to understand the reality of power in the world (Gandhi 1957: 189). It is only coercive force that will change the dynamic of oppression.

Lakey's analysis of nonviolent social movements demonstrates that this objection mischaracterizes the forms of power that exist and that are available to pacifists. Since 2011, Lakey and his students have compiled the Global Nonviolent Action Database, which contains over 800 nonviolent campaigns and studies the ways in which they implement strategies and tactics for social transformation. His research identifies at least three "mechanisms of change" that have been deployed successfully: *conversion, coercion, and accommodation* (Lakey 2013).

The first of these mechanisms, conversion, is the one that Orwell, Churchill, and Gelderloos seem to identify as pacifism itself—it is the attempt to convince an opponent that the pacifist position on an issue is correct, or to convert the opponent to adopt the demands and viewpoints of the pacifist campaign as their own. Interestingly enough, Lakey finds that this mechanism is, in fact, rare among nonviolent campaigns. It is one that Gandhi initially used against the British, but eventually abandoned in favor of other mechanisms. Lakey points out that Gandhi did realize that the British were not going to leave India merely because the Indians petitioned them or appealed to their sense of justice. Indeed, he came to the same conclusion as Churchill and Gelderloos—the British would only leave if coerced, and repeated attempts at conversion only perpetuated the oppression (Lakey 2013).

Coercion occurs when pacifists are able to force their opponents to change their position against their will. Orwell, Churchill, and Gelderloos argue that pacifists are unable to generate this kind of force. However, according to Lakey, Gandhi turned to this mechanism against the British. So did the revolutionaries that overthrew the shah of Iran in 1979. In both cases, grassroots social movements overwhelmed the oppressive state by not cooperating with orders and nonviolently resisting. In the end, both governments were forced to abandon their power in order to save face, to cut their economic and political losses, or simply to save their lives. Lakey finds nonviolent coercion in a variety of cases against dictators, but implies this mechanism is difficult to use since it requires massive mobilization on the part of pacifists in order to seize all the levers of power required to shut down a regime.

The mechanism that Lakey finds quite often in the database is accommodation. This occurs when pacifists are able to force their opponents to yield to their demands not because they have managed to convert, or convince, their opponents of the righteousness of their cause, but because the opponents realize that doing so would be in their own self-interest. One of the clearest examples, according to Lakey, is that of the suffragette campaign during World War I. Rather than back off on their efforts to pressure the government for the right to vote, many of the women, led by Alice Paul, continued their agitation during the war. Several of them were arrested and treated brutally in prison. When they were released, they continued their picketing of the White House, but they also went on national tours to speak about their suffering in prison. While many citizens and lawmakers did not approve of their activism during wartime, they were also appalled at the tales of harsh treatment endured by the suffragettes. Eventually, one representative stated: "While I have always been opposed to suffrage, I have been so aroused over the treatment of the women [in prison] that I have decided to vote for the federal amendment" (Lakey 2013). In this instance, it is not that the women were able to convert Congress to feminism, nor was it that the suffragettes were able to create a massive social movement that immobilized key sectors of the state and the economy. Instead, the campaign succeeded because it convinced federal lawmakers that to sustain the violence necessary to suppress the women was worse than to grant women the right to vote. The campaign did not require the men in Congress to have a moral conscience, it merely had to persuade them that suffrage, rather than continued persecution, was more likely to allow them to keep and enjoy their power in office.

Thus, Lakey's historical research reveals the power and flexibility of pacifism. Rather than being, as Orwell, Churchill, and Gelderloos repeatedly argue, a rigid worldview that can only respond to despotic power by engaging in passive and undignified supplication, pacifism turns out to be what I have called elsewhere "a multipronged theory about the means of building and deploying power" (Orosco 2008: 42). Pacifism is not a position trapped with having to appeal to the moral sentiments of political agents, but is itself a theory of how best to use nonviolent direct action to seize and pry open opportunities for change, depending on the social context and the organizing capacity of the pacifist movement. Sometimes that will mean using moral appeal, but it may also mean using coercive actions that force oppressive groups to give up their grip on power, or to realize that their continued standing depends on recognizing the demands from the grassroots.

Gelderloos advocates for a diversity of tactics in direct action because he feels that pacifists have imposed their normative understanding of violence and proper forms of protest on social justice activists today. Echoing Orwell, he thinks pacifism is a kind of "bourgeois morality" that actually seeks to quell radical dissent and to control the autonomy of activists during protests with invasive and unreasonable prohibitions on individual behavior. In particular, he has in mind popular demonstration guidelines distributed by the Veterans for Peace organization that forbid causing property damage, physically attacking persons, running, drinking, and insulting, as well as swearing at police (Gelderloos 2016: 453). By engaging in this kind of middle-class moralism, pacifists essentially render themselves ineffectual, and thereby offer no resistance to forms of systematic oppression such as sexism, homophobia, etc. Finally, Gelderloos thinks the only work pacifists do well is replicating the law enforcement work of an unjust regime:

> The order imposed by this framework privileges the normative and coercive functions of the state. The prohibition on running and "threatening motions" can reasonably be read as a law enforcement friendly measure.... In fact, in heterogenous crowds where not everyone has pledged to uphold the guidelines (or played any role in drafting them) "organizers" have occasionally turned dissidents over to the police.
> *Gelderloos 2016: 456*

The argument for diversity of tactics, then, is an attempt to break the pacifist stranglehold on the imagination of radical social activists that says there are only certain morally acceptable forms of confronting oppression.

Gelderloos not only misunderstands the varieties of pacifist power, but he also fails to realize that nonviolent direct action has many different strategies and tactics to express power; it is not limited simply to petitioning or marching in polite demonstration along officially approved routes. Gene Sharp, for instance, classifies nonviolent direct action into three categories: *protest and persuasion, noncooperation, and nonviolent intervention* (Sharp 2005: 49–63). Protest and persuasion—which seems to be the only form of direct action acknowledged by Orwell, Churchill, and Gelderloos—involves those actions that are meant to communicate a message about social injustice either to oppressing groups or social bystanders. This can take a variety of forms, including demonstrations, rallies, marches, and public speeches. Noncooperation involves the organized and deliberate withdrawal of cooperation or obedience in the social, economic, or political institutions of an unjust regime. This might include boycotts, labor strikes, or refusals to pay taxes. The aim of noncooperation is to disrupt the status quo by removing power or resources from the oppressive groups and institutions in society. Finally, nonviolent intervention involves those actions that are meant to deliberatively disrupt power relationships in society by targeting established traditions, ways of life, or legal policies. This may take the form of sit-ins, obstructions, nonviolent sabotage (which may include some forms of illegal and strategic property destruction), or paralyzing means of transportation. The goal of nonviolent intervention is to shock, destabilize, and make people uncomfortable with established social relationships so as to demonstrate how they maintain different forms of oppression.

Moreover, in order to describe the dynamics of successful nonviolent social movements in the twentieth century, Mark Engler and Paul Engler offer the concept of an "ecology of change" (Engler and Engler 2016: 251–279). Effective social movements, in their estimation, are able to find a balance between three different strategies: *protest and demonstration, institutionalization, and pre-figurative work*. The first of these involves activating people to show up in numbers to express dissatisfaction and call for social, political, or economic changes. A successful movement will be one that can harness that energy from mass mobilizations and then use it to build, or strengthen, lasting institutions that can affect long-term social gains.

An example of this shift of energy from protest to institutionalization comes from the famous sit-down strikes that began in automobile factories in Flint, Michigan, in 1936. Workers in General Motors plants were able to coordinate work stoppages in several plants that eventually spread nationwide to other auto factories, and even inspired workers in other industries to engage in sit-down strikes for their own grievances. As important as those strikes were for those particular autoworkers, perhaps more important was the fact that the national Committee for Industrial Organization, led by John L. Lewis, quickly moved to organize the workers, growing their union from thirty thousand members to a quarter million and becoming a bedrock of the U.S. labor movement for several more decades (Engler and Engler 2016: 269).

The final strategy in ecology of change involves what is called "prefigurative work." This involves the creation of countercultural groups and places such as communes, utopian communities, or "liberated public spaces, community centers, and alternative institutions" that actively embody the ideas and values of the activists and protestors (Engler and Engler 2016: 273). The main idea here is to create imaginative spaces that model the kind of ideal or future world in which activists would prefer to live. The benefit of prefigurative work is that it can help sustain social movements in the long haul by offering reminders of the values and relationships that activists hold dear, giving them a place to celebrate their ideals when a wider world might ignore or despise them, and serving as a community that can attract new members into the movement.

Gandhi was someone who was best able to nourish an ecology of change, according to the Englers. Rather than simply being locked into a mode of suppliant protest, he was able to engage in diverse actions that activated thousands, providing multiple ways for them to participate in the movement. He encouraged his followers to live with him in ashrams and other intentional communities in which they could learn a variety of forms of economic self-sufficiency and prefigure the mutual aid they would need to display for one another once independence was achieved. Gandhi's ashrams also became headquarters for planning his numerous bouts of civil disobedience and the ashram dwellers became reliable foot soldiers for protests. Furthermore, Gandhi played a leadership role in electoral politics by working to position the Indian National Congress as an organization that would institutionalize the gains achieved from demonstrations in a legal framework for an autonomous India. Clearly, Gandhi's movement was something that developed its own momentum and operated on many levels of power. It was far from a movement that relied entirely on gains made by more violent movements, or on a weakened British empire, in order to accomplish its gains, as argued by Churchill and Gelderloos.

Churchill and Gelderloos think that contemporary pacifists make unreasonable demands on the autonomy of activists and insist on such a restricted list of acceptable forms of direct action that they make themselves irrelevant to the deep kind of transformation needed to rectify social injustice today. They argue that in their ineffectiveness, pacifists allow systematic forms of injustice to fester in society. Thus, Churchill and Gelderloos recommend we ought to entertain a "diversity of tactics" as a guiding spirit for social justice movements today. We ought to make room for activists who may not be dedicated to principled nonviolence and not restrain those who choose to engage in property destruction or other forms of physical harm.

The historical analyses provided by Sharp and the Englers reveal that these critics offer a very narrow perspective about the options available to modern social activists in order to justify their own appeals to property destruction and armed struggle. Effective nonviolent social movements in the twentieth and twenty-first centuries utilize a wide range of strategies and tactics in order to make social change. Some of these tactics may involve the kind of nonviolent street protest and demonstration that Churchill and Gelderloos criticize as limited or useless. But it is clear that pacifists in modern social movements have not been restricted simply to participating in state-authorized marches and rallies or making public speeches. Indeed, successful nonviolent campaigns also involve some activists who have been able to directly defy state authorities and exercise coercive power through noncooperation, and even some forms of strategic property destruction and sabotage that Gelderloos claims are usually only part of so-called revolutionary movements (Case 2017).

Finally, rather than being mostly ineffectual, pacifist activists have been involved in electoral politics, building political organizations, and establishing alternative communities and civic spaces that prefigure new forms of social relationships. It is perhaps this last strategy that addresses the point that pacifism fails to resist systematic forms of oppression, such as racism, sexism, or homophobia. Through nonviolent alternative communities pacifists have tried to tackle these oppressions by maintaining organizations and activist spaces that model friendships and camaraderie built on non-hierarchal relationships that try not to replicate the white supremacist, bourgeois, patriarchal, and homophobic norms of mainstream society (Cornell 2011). The truth, however, is that these forms of oppression are endemic to most activist communities, including more revolutionary ones (Chen, Dulani, and Piepzna-Samarasinha 2016). Whether or not oppressive attitudes and behaviors fester in an activist setting is less a function of whether the group is pacifist or not, and more about whether the group has made an intentional and thorough commitment to interrogate its own power relations around class, race, gender, and sexual orientation (Crass 2013: 109–148).

Conclusion

Proponents of the "pacifism as pathology" critique argue that principled nonviolence is largely a useless way to bring out social transformation in a world pervaded by structural violence and inequality. Moreover, pacifism can actually be a dangerous perspective because it insists on misrepresenting historical social justice struggles to justify its reliance on (ineffective) methods of social change. Finally, pacifism is a regressive position because it is mostly a moralistic attitude that seeks to limit the freedom of activists to imagine and act on their own ideas of a better world. In this chapter, I have argued that these claims are mistaken and rely on flawed understandings of the history and dynamics of nonviolent social movements in the twentieth century. An examination of modern nonviolent social movements demonstrate that pacifist strategies and tactics have indeed been able to exercise coercive force against oppressive institutions and make social transformation happen even within extremely repressive regimes. It is indeed crucial to investigate whether or not nonviolence is an effective means for political transformation today, given changes in the global and national economy that intensify precarity and debt, the increase in the militarization of police forces worldwide, and the role of media in creating misinformation and public distrust (Meckfessel 2016; Schock 2015). Nevertheless, it is important to engage in such examination without relying on simplistic binaries such as violence/nonviolence or pacifist/revolutionary that abound in the work of both pacifists and their critics. The history of nonviolent movements is a rich and complicated one in which millions of people have participated in numerous acts of self-determination, autonomy, and imagination toward a better world.

Works Cited

Case, B. (2017)."Beyond Violence and Nonviolence." [online] Available at: https://roarmag.org/magazine/beyond-violence-nonviolence-antifascism/

Chen, C., J. Dulani, and L. Piepzna-Samarasinha. (2016). *The Revolution Starts at Home: Confronting Intimate Violence Within Activist Communities*. Chico, CA: AK Press.

Chenoweth, E., and M. Stepan. (2012). *Why Civil Resistance Works: The Strategic Logic of Nonviolent Conflict*. New York: Columbia University Press.

Christensen, K. (2010). *Nonviolence, Peace, and Justice: A Philosophical Introduction*. Ontario: Broadview.

Churchill, W. (2005). *Pacifism as Pathology: Reflections on the Role of Armed Struggle in North America*. Winnipeg: Arbeiter Ring Publishing.

Cornell, A. (2011). *Oppose and Propose! Lessons from Movement for a New Society*. Oakland, CA: AK Press.

Crass, C. (2013). *Towards Collective Liberation: Anti-racist Organizing, Feminist Praxis, and Movement Building Strategy*. Oakland, CA: PM Press.

Engler, M., and P. Engler (2016). *This Is an Uprising: How Nonviolent Revolt Is Shaping the Twenty-First Century*. New York: Nation Books.

Gandhi, M. (1957). *Selections from Gandhi*. Ahmendabad, India: Navajivan.
Gelderloos, P. (2007). *How Nonviolence Protects the State*. Boston: South End Press.
Gelderloos, P. (2013). *The Failure of Nonviolence: From the Arab Spring to Occupy*. Seattle: Left Bank Books.
Gelderloos, P. (2016). "Violence," in *Keywords for Radicals: The Contested Vocabulary of Late Capitalist Struggle*. Edited by Kelly Fritsch, Clare O'Connor, and A.K. Thompson. Chico, CA: AK Press, 455–462.
Hedges, C. (2012). "The Cancer in Occupy." [online] Available at: www.truthdig.com/report/item/the_cancer_of_occupy_20120206
Lakey, G. (2013). "Should We Bother to Change Our Opponents' Hearts?" [online] Available at: https://wagingnonviolence.org/feature/should-we-bother-trying-to-change-our-opponents-hearts/
Meckfessel, S. (2016). *Nonviolence Ain't What It Used to Be: Unarmed Insurrection and the Rhetoric of Nonviolence*. Chico, CA: AK Press.
Orosco, J. (2008). *Cesar Chavez and the Common Sense of Nonviolence*. Albuquerque: University of New Mexico Press.
Orwell, G. (1968). "Pacifism and the War," in *My Country Right or Left (1940–1943): The Collected Essays, Journalism and Letters of George Orwell*. Edited by Sonia Orwell and Ian Angus. London: Secker and Warburg, 220–229.
Ryan, C. (2009). *The Chickenhawk Syndrome*. Lanham, MD: Rowman and Littlefield.
Schock, K. (2015). *Civil Resistance Today*. Cambridge: Polity Press.
Sharp, G. (2005). *Waging Nonviolent Struggle: 20th Century Practice and 21st Century Potential*. Boston: Porter Sargent.

Further Reading

Churchill, W. (2005). *Pacifism as Pathology: Reflections on the Role of Armed Struggle in North America*. Winnipeg: Arbeiter Ring Publishing. (Important source for the claim that pacifism is a pathology of the privileged.)
Gelderloos, P. (2007). *How Nonviolence Protects the State*. Boston: South End Press. (Useful text for understanding the critique of nonviolence.)
Lakey, G. (2016). *Toward a Living Revolution: A Five Stage Framework for Creating Radical Social Change*. Eugene, OR: Wipf and Stock. (A book that examines nonviolent revolutionary theory and practice with a focus on contemporary examples.)
May, T. (2015). *Nonviolent Resistance: A Philosophical Introduction*. Malden, MA: Polity Press. (A philosophical text that examines the value of nonviolence such as respect for dignity and equality.)

PART III

Social and Political Considerations

18

THE TRIUMPH OF THE LIBERAL DEMOCRATIC PEACE AND THE DANGERS OF ITS SUCCESS

Fuat Gursozlu

Liberal democratic peace theory (henceforth LDPT) is based on two propositions:

1. Liberal democracies rarely fight each other.
2. Liberal democracies are as war prone as any other states in their relations with non-democratic states.

Immanuel Kant provided the first formulation of LDPT in his "Toward Perpetual Peace" (1795). LDPT has become immensely popular since the publication of Michael Doyle's two essays in 1983, which advanced the most sophisticated philosophical arguments in support of LDPT. Drawing on Kant's "Perpetual Peace," Doyle argues that the "dovishness" in relations between liberal democracies is the result of three pillars: liberal democratic norms dominant in these societies, liberal democratic institutions, and the shared commercial interests between liberal democracies. Together these three pillars establish grounds for peace among liberal states (Doyle 1986: 1162). There exists "a separate peace between liberal democratic states" (Doyle 1983a: 235).

There is now a consensus on LDPT. One commentator stated that "absence of war between democratic states comes as close as anything we have to an empirical law in international relations" (Levy 1988: 270). Another suggested that LDPT is "one of the strongest nontrivial or nontautological generalizations that can be made about international relations" (Russett 1993: 119–120). It is no surprise that such a successful theory has attracted the attention of policymakers. From Reagan to Obama, five different U.S. administrations have made statements including the core ideas of LDPT. Many commentators rightly pointed out that LDPT has made a significant impact on real-world politics. Reducing the complexity of LDPT to the single proposition that "democracies do not attack each other," policymakers argued that to achieve durable international peace it is imperative to spread liberal democracy (Owen 1994: 87). This popularized version of LDPT embraced by policymakers is based on the assumption that "the more democracies there are in the world, the wider the zone of peace" (Russett 1993: 4). This way of thinking, however, has "led to disastrous military interventions" (Layne 1994: 47) and "democratizing wars" with all the atrocities rationalized as means to build lasting peace (Fiala 2010: 66).

In this chapter, I examine the dangers of the triumph of LDPT. The problem with the success of LDPT is that it could lead to controversial wars and interventions against non-democratic

Doyle maintains that the three pillars of his LDPT provide the necessary and sufficient condition for democratic peace. Liberal peace rests on the combined effect of the three pillars and not on a single constitutional, international, or cosmopolitan element. When one of the pillars is absent, "pacific policy is underdetermined and undermined" (Doyle 2005b: 465). When all three pillars are present, "they plausibly connect the characteristics of liberal polities and economies with sustained liberal peace" (Doyle 1986: 1162). The "state of war" that defines international relations does not apply to the relationships between liberal democracies. Liberal states are fundamentally different and they exercise peaceful restraint in their relations with other liberals (Doyle 1983a: 235). As such, there is "a separate peace among liberal states" (Doyle 1986: 1156, and Doyle 1983a: 232). This separate peace has been maintained among liberal societies since the eighteenth century. Continuation of the separate peace together with the overall increase of the number of liberal states in the last 150 years gives the hope that by the gradual expansion of the liberal "zone of peace" an eventual world peace is a possibility (Doyle 1992).

The dyadic model advanced by Doyle—and also defended by the majority of proponents of democratic peace—is not the only strand of LDPT. The other major strand—the monadic model—affirms the dyadic proposition that liberal democratic states are peaceful in their relations with other liberal democracies, but it also defends a broader proposition that liberal democracies are generally more peaceful than undemocratic states (Doyle 1983b: 324; Russett 1993: 11). This is not to say that liberal democracies do not go to war; rather, the claim is that liberal democracies are "less prone to international violence and war" than undemocratic states (Rummel 1983). Although Rummel's (1983) monadic model is the most influential version, MacMillan has supported the monadic model of democratic peace theory and suggested that there is a recent monadic revival in LDPT (MacMillan 2003: 234–235). There is near consensus that the more plausible strand of democratic peace theory is the dyadic version, in part because it offers a well-developed theory supported by robust empirical evidence and in part because the proposition that liberal democracies are more peaceful than undemocratic states lacks a convincing theoretical foundation and the claim itself is not supported by "systematic evidence" (Doyle 1983b: 324, and Russett 1993: 11).

The dyadic model has been well supported by the empirical evidence that since the 1800s established liberal democracies have not fought with each other, but they have gone to war with nonliberal states. (See Doyle 1983a and 1983b. A survey of evidence is in Doyle 1983a.) However, the lawlike status of the dyadic model is not immune to challenges. Some researchers challenged the empirical basis of the dyadic model by arguing that attempts to explain the dyadic model are theoretically flawed (MacMillan 2003). Christopher Layne argues that democratic peace theory is a "myth" and the zone of peace defended by Doyle is a "peace of illusions" (Layne 1994). Layne's point is that there is no evidence supporting the proposition that liberal democratic peace is the result of some features of democracy. Neither the structural constraints nor the democratic norms explain democratic peace. Thus, Layne concludes, "democratic peace theory offers no convincing explanation of why democracies purportedly do not fight each other" (Layne 1995: 176). David Spiro questions the proposition that there is a separate peace among liberal democracies (Spiro 1994 and 1995). Spiro argues that given that both wars and democracies are rare, it is not surprising that there are not many wars between liberal democracies. Spiro contends that the proposition claim that democracies rarely fight with each other is supported by "tricky and highly contestable definitional issues" (Spiro 1995: 179–180). For Spiro, the argument for democratic peace depends on selective choice of definitions of key terms and data so that data analysis "always yields results favoring the Liberal Peace" (Spiro 1994: 55—for Doyle's and Russett's replies to Spiro and Layne, see Doyle 1995 and Russett 1995). It seems then that one's position on this debate depends on how one defines war and democracy. The important point for my purposes in this chapter is that despite the strong objections to LDPT, the hegemony of the dyadic model is intact and shapes the way we make sense of international relations. Liberal democratic peace is the new "conventional wisdom" (Russett 1995: 164).

Misuse of Democratic Peace

When writing on just war theory's contemporary triumph, Michael Walzer reminds us that just war theory, whose function is "to make war morally possible" by drawing a distinction between just and unjust wars, has historically been embraced by the rulers. The rulers of the world, Walzer writes, adopted the theory, "and did not fight a single war without describing it, or hiring intellectuals to describe it, as a war for peace and justice. Most often, of course, this description was hypocritical: the tribute that vice pays to virtue" (Walzer 2004: 4). In the post-Vietnam reinvention of just war theory, Walzer observes a similar tendency to misuse just war theory. Its categories have been used to justify contemporary wars from Kosovo to Afghanistan and the normative logic of the theory has gained a legitimate position in the political public culture. It is now taken over by politicians and generals to be used to explain and justify their actions.[2] Walzer's point is that when the generals sound like just war theorists, it is time for just war theorists to consider ways to reclaim the theory.

In many ways the fate of LDPT is similar to the fate of just war theory. One significant difference is that just war theory is normative theory whereas LDPT is supported by robust empirical evidence, which solidifies the hegemony of the theory and makes it more difficult to challenge. That's why LDPT has gained the status of law in international relations and its core ideas have deeply shaped the public political culture and influenced foreign policy. As Layne reminds us, democratic peace theory "has become a lodestar that guides America's post-Cold War foreign policy." Doyle's idea of a democratic "zone of peace" has often been used "in both official and unofficial U.S. foreign policy pronouncements" (Layne 1994: 45). Caranti notes that LDPT "today shapes the background knowledge, the conceptual apparatus, and the policy agenda" and the prospective view of major democratic powers (Caranti 2016: 447).

To be sure, there is a remarkable difference between defending peaceful promotion of democracy in the world in order to build a durable peace and calling for a crusade for democracy to expand the zone of peace. Some commentators find the idea of peacefully promoting democracy objectionable, but what really worries theorists is the aggressive interventionist approach encouraged by the latter position. LDPT could encourage or could be used to justify aggressive interventionist foreign policies. The aggressive foreign policy is the result of a belief in the idea that coerced democratization could bring about a peaceful world. As Andrew Fiala puts it, the hope for a peaceful world promised by LDPT "has a sort of mythic power that can seduce us toward" wars of forced democratization (Fiala 2010: 67).[3] LDPT could also be misused to legitimize war and mask the real motivation behind it. When political administrations talk the language of democratic peace, one cannot ignore this potential and the dangers it could bring about. The point is not that LDPT defends aggressive interventionism and forced democratization to achieve the dream of perpetual peace. Many defenders of LDPT argue against intervention as a way of promoting democracy and they emphasize that it is ineffective and morally wrong. However, some central ideas of LDPT "pander to impulses" that encourage aggressive interventionist policies (see Layne 1994; Doyle 1983b; Russett 1993). Thus, it is misleading to describe LDPT as a victim exploited by policymakers. LDPT may not be the author of these interventionist policies, but it is not as innocent as it has been suggested.[4] Theorists should recognize the destructive potential of LDPT and provide responses to reclaim the theory by offering ways to contain LDPT's destructive potential.

In fact, many scholars have pointed out the potential of LDPT to encourage aggressive policies toward non-democracies (Doyle 1983b; Russett 1993: 136). Recognizing that LDPT has great influence on policy, Russett emphasizes that a misunderstanding of LDPT "could encourage warmaking against authoritarian regimes, and efforts to overthrow them" (Russett 1993: 135). Doyle suggests that "the very constitutional restraint, international respect for individual rights, and shared commercial interests that establish grounds for peace among liberal states establish grounds for additional conflict in relations between liberal and nonliberal societies" (Doyle 1983b: 324). For Doyle, this is why liberal democracies are prone to war in their relations with nonliberal states. The norms of liberal peace do not apply outside the zone of peace since liberal democracies are caught in the anarchical nature of international relations.

According to liberal political philosophy, the legitimacy of a state depends on the consent of its citizens and whether it respects and effectively represents morally autonomous individuals. When states coerce their citizens and violate their basic rights, their right to be free from foreign intervention becomes questionable (Doyle 1983b: 325). Liberal democracies assume that because non-democracies do not rest on free consent, they are not just and because they are "perceived to be in a permanent state of aggression against their own people," they are necessarily aggressive (Doyle 1983b: 326). This deep lack of trust and disrespect pits societies against each other and determines the nature of the relations between liberal and nonliberal societies. As Doyle writes, "When the Soviets refuse to negotiate, they are plotting a world takeover. When they seek to negotiate they are plotting even more insidiously" (Doyle 1983b: 326). Doyle's example reveals the way the liberal discourse shapes the way the public perceive non-democracies. Doyle observes that "fellow liberals benefit from a presumption of amity; nonliberals suffer from a presumption of enmity" (Doyle 1983b: 337). This logic creates hostility against powerful nonliberal societies while exacerbating intervention against weak nonliberal societies.

By drawing a distinction between the "zone of peace" and the "zone of war" and proposing the existence of separate peace, LDPT inevitably creates a "mutual identity" among liberal democracies in a way that transforms its difference against which it defines itself to the "other." A constituent feature of this identity is a commitment to peaceful conflict resolution, which is a trait non-democracies lack. Liberal states should not just respect fellow liberal societies' security, but they also should enhance "each other's security by means of alliance" (Doyle 2005b: 465). Thus, "we"—liberal democracies—should protect each other from "them"—non-democracies. The main reason why the "zone of war" exists is because not all states are liberal democratic, and non-democratic states are by nature aggressive. "The end of history" represented by a liberal democratic and therefore a peaceful world is not beyond our reach. It is "them" who prevent the realization of the dream of perpetual peace. The final step of the argument is a normative position bound to be inferred from LDPT: if non-democracies are aggressive "troublemakers," and democracies are just, trustworthy, and peaceful states except when they have to deal with the potentially dangerous non-democracies, democracies will be truly secure and the world will be peaceful when every state becomes liberal democratic (Chan 1997; Xenias 2005). As such, LDPT's logic encourages an interventionist approach. This way of thinking suggests a simple solution to a complex problem: "fight them, beat them, and then make them democratic" for the noble goal of world peace (Russett 1993: 136). This logic is best expressed in a speech given by the thirty-eighth U.S. Secretary of State Elihu Root in 1917: "To be safe democracy must kill its enemy when it can and where it can. The world cannot be half democratic and half autocratic. It must be all democratic or all Prussian. There can be no compromise" (quoted in Russett 1993: 33). Many critics see this as a "recipe for 'perpetual war' rather than 'perpetual peace'" (Demenchenok 2007: 32). Proposed as a theory about democratic peace, LDPT has come to serve as a discourse used to justify aggressive foreign policies and military intervention.

Reclaiming Liberal Democratic Peace Theory

In 1990, Johan Galtung introduced the concept of "cultural violence" to explain direct and structural violence. Galtung defines cultural violence as "those aspects of culture, the symbolic sphere of our existence that can be used to justify or legitimize direct or structural violence" (Galtung 1990: 291). Cultural violence naturalizes and normalizes violence by presenting an account of reality that defines violence as reasonable, ordinary, and inevitable. Due to its core logic, main distinctions, and the account of reality it constructs, liberal democratic peace discourse has come to function as a discourse of cultural violence. To be sure, LDPT does not explicitly warrant aggressive interventionism and forcibly democratizing the world, but it encourages a way of thinking that leads to perverse inferences drawn from the theory. Because these illegitimate normative implications are encouraged by LDPT, and because as a hegemonic theory "DPT lends itself naturally to recommendations for the foreign policy of liberal states" (Caranti 2016: 467), there should be a stronger theoretical response to contain LDPT's potential to function as a discourse of cultural violence. Here I make four suggestions to respond to the misuse of LDPT.

1. Since Kant's "Perpetual Peace" is the founding document of LDPT, it would be useful to return to the origin and explore whether there are any ideas that may be used to prevent the misuse of LDPT. In the first part of the text Kant proposes six preliminary articles for perpetual peace among states. The fifth preliminary article explains Kant's position on intervention: "No state shall by force interfere with the constitution or government of another state" (Kant 1996: 319). The exception to the non-intervention rule is an internal rebellion, which divides a country into two camps, each claiming to represent the whole. In this case, Kant writes, "a foreign state could not be charged with interfering in the constitution of another state if it gave assistance to one of them (for this is anarchy)" (Kant 1996: 319). Kant qualifies this exception by noting that unless the internal dissension comes to this critical point an external interference would "infringe on the rights of an independent people struggling with its internal disease" (Kant 1996: 319–320). Having defined intervention as an offense that would render the autonomy of all states insecure, Kant emphasizes that preliminary article five is one of the three of the six preliminary articles that is of that strict kind "which hold regardless of circumstances (*leges strictae*)" and which demands prompt execution (Kant 1996: 319). This is not to say that moral condemnation of despotic states should be avoided (Caranti 2016: 463). But, moral condemnation and military intervention are radically different actions. Kant clearly rejects the latter. Kant's "Perpetual Peace" does not authorize military intervention or interfering in the internal states of authoritarian states. Moreover, it defends the non-interventionist position as a strict principle. Doyle notes that according to Kant conquest or imperial intervention is wrong. But, he adds, the practices of liberal states have not been so forbearing (Doyle 1983b: 324).
2. One reason why LDPT could function as a discourse of cultural violence is that it has been reduced to a simple formula. According to this formula the recipe for a peaceful and secure world is misleadingly simple: liberal democracies do not fight each other, therefore what needs to be done is to convert non-democracies to liberal democracies. Those who defend this formula fail to grasp the complexity of LDPT while assuming that democracy is simple and can easily be produced (Xenias 2005: 36). This approach assumes that once the proper institutions—such as free competitive elections and a liberal constitution—are in place, there is liberal democracy.

The problem with this approach is that it fails to recognize that democracy is more than a collection of institutions. Liberal democracy is a regime that includes a civic culture. Developing a civic culture and the political norms required to sustain democracy take a long time. Liberal democracy understood as a regime is already part of Doyle's and Russet's accounts of democratic peace. This is the main point of the normative model (Doyle's second pillar) that explains democratic peace. According to the normative explanation, it is the norms that constitute a liberal democratic culture, such as tolerance, autonomy, compromise, and commitment to peaceful resolution of conflict, that prevent the escalation of conflict into violence in liberal democracies. Liberal democracies follow these norms in their dealings with fellow liberal democracies because they believe that it is not right to fight one another and they should resolve conflicts by compromise and nonviolence (Russett 1993: 35). Russett notes that of the two main explanations of liberal democratic peace—structural model and normative model—there is greater empirical support for the normative model (Russett 1993). At this point, it is important to recall that according to Doyle's account, peace is the result of the working together of the three pillars. Having liberal democratic institutions would not be sufficient to bring about perpetual peace.

A democracy that lacks the culture of democracy would not necessarily be peaceful toward other societies. As Doyle recognizes, "a democracy of xenophobes or hyper-nationalists would externalize their preferences" (Doyle 2005b: 463). Liberal democracy as a regime develops spontaneously. The norms that constitute the regime slowly build up over time. Attempts to forcibly homogenize the world around liberal democracy are not only morally problematic, but also not prudent. As Russett rightly warns, "external military intervention, even against the most odious dictators, is a dangerous way to try to produce a 'democratic world order'" (Russett 1993: 136).

3. Many commentators indicate that the core logic of LDPT leads to a too-rigid distinction between liberal democracies and non-democracies. When the political realm is organized in accordance with the distinctions encouraged by LDPT—peaceful liberal democracies vs. aggressive non-democracies, the zone of peace vs. the zone of war—it creates "an absolutely insurmountable barrier" between liberal democracies and non-democracies (Demenchenok 2007: 30). It then appears reasonable to claim that non-democracies lack legitimacy and real sovereignty and have no right to be free from intervention. What follows is that liberal democracies have the right to feel threatened by non-democracies, they can be legitimately war-prone toward non-democracies, and the members of the pacific union should be prepared "to defend each other against this outside threat" (Doyle 1983b: 348). This is how liberal peace leads to perpetual war.

What needs to be done is to make the distinction between liberal democracies and non-democracies less rigid. Once more Kant's "Perpetual Peace" offers invaluable insights. Many commentators argue that the popularized version of LDPT that rests on an interpretation of Kant omits the crucial idea that Kant's pacific union is not an exclusively liberal club, but a federation of all states. When Kant says in the second definitive article, "The rights of nations shall be based on a federation of free states," he emphasizes the necessity of an international organization that would end the state of nature. Many liberal democratic peace theorists argue that only liberal democracies are allowed to enter the federation. However, nowhere in the text does Kant defend this view.

Commentators agree that Kant's hope for perpetual peace relies on nations gradually becoming liberal democracies as a result of the transformative force of international exchange. Those who criticize the exclusive view of the Kantian federation argue that excluding non-democracies from the federation would be against the spirit of Kant's project. For Kant, a mixed federation, and not a liberal democratic club, is "the most effective peace-promoting factor" (Caranti 2016: 453). Kant's idea of the pacific federation "does not exclude the other states seeking peaceful alliances" and should be "viewed as inclusive, not exclusive" (Demenchenok 2007: 11). The idea of federation we find in Kant's "Perpetual Peace" already denies the rigid separation between liberal democracies and non-democracies. However, in his 1983 articles, which have deeply shaped contemporary LDPT, Doyle takes for granted the exclusive view. Despite the "documented protests" by many Kant commentators, democratic peace theorists have followed Doyle's interpretation of Kant's position (Caranti 2016: 453).

Even when one opts for the "exclusive" interpretation, one need not encourage the rigid separation fueled by the popularized version of LDPT. The exclusive view of the federation of states, which suggests a division of the world into two zones, could be more inclusive. This is the model of Society of Peoples advanced by John Rawls in the Law of Peoples. Although the Society of Peoples is based on a rigid separation of the world in two main zones between those who follow the normative guidelines of the Law of Peoples in their mutual relations and those who do not, the Society of Peoples is more inclusive than LDPT since it is not limited to liberal democratic societies. "Decent hierarchical societies" who, by definition, are not liberal and may not be democratic are allowed to be members of the Society of Peoples. According to Rawls, a decent society does not "have aggressive aims" and honors the laws of peace while respecting the right to life, liberty, and property of their citizens.[5] Unlike liberal societies, a decent society does not affirm the idea that persons are citizens first and "have equal basic rights as citizens" (Rawls 2001: 66). Its political institutions do not recognize what Rawls calls reasonable pluralism—the existence of irreconcilable but reasonable comprehensive doctrines—and may be organized around one comprehensive doctrine such as a philosophical or a religious doctrine.

The reason why the Society of Peoples admits decent societies is similar to why Kant scholars insist on the inclusive account as the right interpretation. Rawls maintains that if the Society of Peoples only includes liberal societies and subject nonliberal societies to politically enforced sanctions, this would disrespect decent societies. Denying respect to decent peoples may wound their self-respect "and may lead to great bitterness and resentment" (Rawls 2001: 62). All societies undergo changes over time and by recognizing decent societies "as bona fide members of the Society of Peoples," liberal societies encourage decent peoples and "frustrate their vitality by coercively insisting that all societies be liberal" (Rawls 2001: 62). Rawls's point is that withdrawing respect may stifle such change while an inclusive approach may help a decent society "to recognize the advantages of liberal institutions and take steps toward becoming more liberal on its own" (Rawls 2001: 62). This is why decent peoples should be tolerated and included in the loose confederation of Society of Peoples.

An example of a decent people is the idealized Islamic people of the fictional "Kazanistan." In Kazanistan, Islam is the favored religion and there is no separation of religion and state. Other religions are tolerated and may be practiced freely, but "only Muslims can hold the upper positions of political authority and influence the government's main decisions and policies" (Rawls 2001: 75). It is important to notice that Kazanistan would be highly likely to be categorized as an aggressive state in the current political landscape shaped by the categories offered by the dominant version of LDPT. Approached from a Rawlsian perspective, however, Kazanistan deserves respect and equal treatment. Rawls recognizes that some may criticize him by arguing that his approach permits injustice without giving strong enough reasons. Rawls's response to his critics is telling: "I believe that there are such reasons. Most important is maintaining mutual respect among peoples. Lapsing into contempt on the one side, and bitterness and resentment on the other, can only cause damage" (Rawls 2001: 62).

4. To render the boundary between liberal democracies and non-democracies less rigid and to address the lack of trust and respect between the two camps it is important to recognize

that the ideological path followed by the West is not the only legitimate and possible one (Mouffe 2009: 558). Rather than trying to homogenize the world by imposing the Western model of liberal democracy worldwide as the only legitimate way of organizing human societies, which has already provoked "adverse reactions from those societies whose specific values and cultures are rendered illegitimate by the enforced universalisation of the Western mode," one should recognize that "the world is a pluriverse" (Mouffe 2009: 555). Non-Western societies have different historical experiences, cultural patterns, ideological underpinnings, and developmental goals (Pollis and Schwab 2006: 64). In many states in the world democracy in its liberal form and human rights as defined by the West "are rejected, or more accurately, are meaningless" (Pollis and Schwab 2006: 68). This does not mean that the ideas of democracy and human rights should be jettisoned. It means that democracy in its liberal form is not the only legitimate form of democracy. It also means that one should grasp the function human rights play in Western societies and see whether this function has been and could be fulfilled in different ways in other cultures. For instance, all societies, Pollis and Schwab point out, manifest conceptions of human dignity. Despite the divergences in the way different societies understand human dignity, there are shared commonalities. It is these commonalities such as "societal limits on the use of force or violence" and condoning "arbitrary and indiscriminate destruction of life or incarceration" that could lead to the formulation of a more universal notion of human rights (Pollis and Schwab 2006: 163).

Once liberal democratic societies take the idea of the world as a pluriverse seriously, acknowledge that human rights could be conceived in a variety of ways, and recognize that the West's interpretation of human rights and democracy are not the only legitimate ones, the separation between liberal democracies and other societies would become less rigid. This change of perspective may lead to a change of perception such that liberal democracies may recognize nonliberal or non-democratic regimes as legitimate and may not feel threatened by their existence. Liberal democracies may also recognize that many nonliberal or non-democratic societies are not inherently dangerous or aggressive. Recognizing the plurality of forms of democracy and understandings of human rights could create a more peaceful and stable world than enforcing liberal democracy as the only legitimate political organization that could bring about perpetual peace.

Conclusion

LDPT is not itself violent, but its main assumptions and distinctions construct an account of reality that represents non-democracies as potentially dangerous, aggressive states whose very existence threaten liberal democracies and prevent the realization of the dream of perpetual peace. For those who believe in the myth of democratic peace and those who feel threatened by non-democracies, supporting aggressive interventionism and democratizing wars can appear to be legitimate and reasonable. Moreover, LDPT could be exploited by those who need the support of the public in order to fight the morally problematic wars they aim to fight. As such, the success of LDPT contributes to the creation of a more violent world where violence against non-democracies is perceived to be acceptable.

It is important to recognize that for a more peaceful world it is imperative to offer ways to contain the destructive potential of LDPT. It is also important to recognize the seductive power of the myth of democratic peace and of the rhetoric of aggressive outsiders threatening our way of life. That's why in addition to formulating responses to the misuse of LDPT from within LDPT, such as bringing to the fore Kant's defense of the principle of non-intervention and the role of liberal democratic values and a civic democratic culture in explaining democratic peace, it is necessary to address the boundary between liberal democracies and non-democracies in order to render it less rigid. For Kant, liberal democracies and non-democracies should and could work together. The only way to achieve this peaceful coexistence is to build bridges between liberal democracies and non-democracies and address the sources of lack of trust and respect between them.

Notes

1 Kant's theory also contains both elements, but there are important differences between the two. I take up some of the differences between Kant's democratic peace theory and the contemporary version in the final section of this paper. For a detailed discussion of the differences between the two approaches see Caranti (2016).
2 Walzer's example is George Bush (the elder)'s use of just war theory to justify the Persian Gulf War—a war that failed to meet just war standards (Walzer 2004: 10).
3 Fiala's point is that to actualize the ideal of perpetual peace, "earnest ideals are willing to make moral compromises along the way" (Fiala 2010: 67). Fiala argues that the combination of LDPT and utilitarian thinking could lead to aggressive wars and atrocities.
4 Caranti states that "DPT is a victim, certainly not the author" (Caranti 2016: 459).
5 Rawls notes that a decent hierarchical society "secures for all members of the people what have come to be called human rights," including right to life, liberty, property, and "formal equality as expressed by the rules of natural justice" (Rawls 2001: 65).

Works Cited

Caranti, L. (2016). "Kantian Peace and Liberal Peace: Three Concerns." *Journal of Political Philosophy* 24 (4): 446–469.
Chan, S. (1997). "In Search of Democratic Peace: Problems and Promise." *Mershon International Studies Review* 41 (1): 59–91.
Demenchenok, E. (2007). "From a State of War to Perpetual Peace." *American Journal of Economics and Sociology* 66 (1): 25–48.
Doyle, M. W. (1983a). "Kant, Liberal Legacies, and Foreign Affairs: Part 1." *Philosophy and Public Affairs* 12: 205–235.
Doyle, M. W. (1983b). "Kant, Liberal Legacies, and Foreign Affairs: Part 2." *Philosophy and Public Affairs* 12: 323–353.
Doyle, M. W. (1986). "Liberalism and World Politics." *American Political Science Review* 80: 1151–1169.
Doyle, M.W. (1992). "Liberal Democracy and the Future of International Security." The Newsletter of PEGS 2(3): 12–13.
Doyle, M.W. (1995). "To the Editors (Michael Doyle on Democratic Peace)." *International Security* 19 (4): 180–184.
Doyle, M. W. (2005a). "Democratic Peace: To the Editors." *International Security* 19 (4): 180–184.
Doyle, M. W. (2005b). "Three Pillars of the Liberal Peace." *American Political Science Review* 99 (3): 463–466.
Fiala, A. (2010). *Public War, Private Conscience: The Ethics of Political Violence*. London: Continuum.
Galtung, J. (1990). "Cultural Violence." *Journal of Peace Research* 27 (3): 291–305.
Kant, I. (1996/1795). "Toward Perpetual Peace," in M.J. Gregor (ed.), *The Cambridge Edition of the Works of Immanuel Kant, Practical Philosophy*. New York: Cambridge University Press, 311–351.
Layne, C. (1994). "Kant or Cant: The Myth of Democratic Peace." *International Security* 19 (2): 5–49.
Layne, C. (1995). "Democratic Peace: On the Democratic Peace." *International Security* 19 (4): 175–177.
Levy, J. S. (1988). "Domestic Politics and War." *Journal of Interdisciplinary History* 18: 345–369.
MacMillan, J. (2003). "Beyond the Separate Democratic Peace." *Journal of Peace Research* 40(2): 233–243.
Maoz, Z., and B. Russett. (1993). "Normative and Structural Causes of Democratic Peace." *American Political Science Review* 87 (3): 624–638.
Mouffe, C. (2009). "Democracy in a Multipolar World." *Millennium—Journal of International Studies* 37 (3): 549–561.
Owen, J. M. (1994). "How Liberalism Produces Democratic Peace." *International Security* 19 (2): 87–125.

Pollis, A., and P. Schwab. (2006). "Human Rights: A Western Concept with Limited Applicability," in C. Koggel (ed.), *Moral Issues in Global Perspective*, vol. I. Peterborough, ON, Canada: Broadview Press, 60–71.
Rawls, J. (2001). *The Law of Peoples*. Cambridge, MA: Harvard University Press.
Rummel, R. (1983). "Libertarianism and International Violence." *Journal of Conflict Resolution* 27: 27–71.
Russett, B. M. (1993). *Grasping the Democratic Peace: Principles for a Post-Cold War World*. Princeton: Princeton University Press.
Russett, B. M. (1995). "The Democratic Peace: 'And Yet It Moves'." *International Security* 19 (4): 164–175.
Spiro, D. E. (1994). "The Insignificance of the Liberal Peace." *International Security* 19 (2): 50–86.
Spiro, D. E. (1995). "The Liberal Peace: 'And Yet It Squirms'." *International Security* 19 (4): 177–180.
Walzer, M. (2004). "The Triumph of Just War Theory (and the Dangers of Success)," in M. Walzer (ed.), *Arguing About War*. New Haven: Yale University Press, 3–22.
Xenias, A. (2005). "Can a Global Peace Last Even If Achieved? Huntington and the Democratic Peace." *International Studies Review* 7 (3): 357–386.

19
HUMAN RIGHTS AND INTERNATIONAL LAW

Robert Paul Churchill

Human rights and international law have been positive forces for global peace. Cosmopolitanism, the orientation taken in this essay, maintains that all human beings ought to receive equal respect and concern. Cosmopolitans hold that all agents are moral subjects. Heads of states, officials in multinational corporations, and international organizations such as the European Union are subject to the same moral demands and requirements that bind ordinary individuals. Cosmopolitans follow Kant (1724–1804), among the earliest advocates of an international federation in his *Perpetual Peace* (1795), in claiming that persons have *equal dignity*. Mere things have equivalents or substitutes, and thus have a price; by contrast, the dignity one has as a person is a value one has *in* oneself, not *for* others. Persons require respect; they must be treated as ends in themselves and never merely as means (Kant 2012).

Equal respect does not mean that every social group must accept the same values; quite the contrary, cultural diversity and moral pluralism are to be cherished. However, because persons are alike in possessing dignity, moral rules and laws are required to protect human beings everywhere from the violence of war and abuse, and to ensure, whenever possible, that human beings everywhere are provided with the necessities minimally required for a genuinely *human* life. To accomplish these ends, international affairs, along with intrastate affairs, must be subjected to the rule of law, to fundamental principles of justice, and to human rights norms. For these reasons, cosmopolitan objectives overlap extensively with those of pacifists and peace advocates. Indeed, the African Charter on Human and Peoples' Rights (1981) speaks explicitly about a "national and international human right to peace and security" (Article 23.1). In December 2016 the UN General Assembly affirmed a resolution proclaiming: "Everyone has the right to enjoy peace such that all human rights are promoted and protected and development is fully realized" (UN 2017: Article I).

This chapter provides an introduction to some important features of human rights and international law that might also be of interest for studies of pacifism, nonviolence, and peace activism. The essay has three general objectives. The first is to show that, despite appearances to the contrary, human rights and much of international law—international humanitarian law in particular—converge in support of cosmopolitanism and pacifism. It can be argued that there is a fundamental moral basis supporting both enterprises—human rights and international law. Second, I suggest that a proper understanding of the moral foundations for international law requires a version of pacifism known as *contingent pacifism*. Third, contrary to the common view that in international relations, as Thucydides (c. 460–c.400 BC) remarked, the powerful do what they want and the weak suffer what they must (Thucydides 1998), our world is one in which human rights are significant, and arguments for recognizing the human right to peace demonstrate the falsity of *realpolitik* and the erosion of the dominance of state powers. Human rights theories, appropriately understood, make it very difficult to justify war, allowing as exceptions only self-defense when under attack by aggressors, or humanitarian intervention to prevent genocide, ethnic cleansing, or other massive humanitarian crises. Moreover, even when justified as protecting human rights, because the violence of war necessarily violates human rights, a war may not rightly continue for political reasons, thus causing it to continue beyond what is minimally necessary to bring the rights violations of aggressors to an end.

Human rights and international law are mutually reinforcing. Why, then, do most specialists in international affairs, and especially self-styled "realists," regard international affairs, including international law, as an *amoral* arena in which states are free to pursue their own national interest unconstrained by concerns with human rights or other moral principles? There are two primary causes for the perception of international relations as an amoral arena and the supposed irrelevance in it of human rights. One cause has to do with a limited and one-sided view of the point, or purpose, of human rights. The other cause has to do with an equally limited and misguided view of the function of international law.

Historical Considerations

The flowering of human rights occurred during the Enlightenment and was spurred by the publication in 1689 of *Two Treatises of Government*, in which Locke (1632–1704) argued that far from pursuing the interest of a monarch or an elite, it was the responsibility of the government, based on a social contract, to protect and promote the natural rights of its citizens. The English Bill of Rights (1689), the US Declaration of Independence (1776), the French Declaration of the Rights of Man and of the Citizen (1789), and the US Bill of Rights (1791) are all fundamental human rights documents, and were all products of this new view of the relationship between government and its citizens. Indeed, the protection of individual dignity from arbitrary power has been a consistent theme in human rights discourse.

Despite the perennial concern that overweening state or private power (e.g. an undemocratic party) might violate human rights, human rights philosophy has had a major role in justifying governments. Jefferson (1743–1826) and the signatories of the Declaration of Independence and others, particularly Paine (1736–1809), held that natural rights justified the secession of a state from a tyrannical regime. At the same time, however, for Mason (1725–1790) and Madison (1751–1836), a justifiable government was one that was constitutional, or limited, and republican, that is, representative, or democratic, and "bills of rights" reserving certain rights to the people were to specify these limits. This line of political theory and philosophy can be traced back to Locke. Since Locke, an enormous body of work has been produced on this subject, including an ongoing and lively debate over whether or not human rights requires democracy (e.g. Christiano 2003; Gould 2004). There has also been considerable discussion of the "democratic peace thesis," namely, the thesis that democratic states do not make war on one another (Doyle 1997; Lipson 2003).

Despite the important role of human rights in checking government power, there is no necessary conflict between the two, and no reason, in theory, why the two need to be opposed. Human rights can justify and limit government power, and as far as government policy goes, legislators and executives can choose to respect human rights. In addition, governments can work together to vindicate human rights and bring pressure to bear on a state that is grossly violating its own people's human rights. One impressive example is the success of the total boycott of South Africa, including divestment of businesses, supported by a UN resolution in 1962, which led in 1991 to the abolition of apartheid in South Africa. This was an important example of how nonviolent tactics can be employed in the international arena.

Of course, a human right is a special kind of *moral* right, and thus, for the most part, specialists working in international relations did not see human rights as having a major role in the amoral international arena. Human rights were thought to apply to *intrastate* affairs, where constitutional clauses and legislative enactments could transform moral rights into legal rights. On the *interstate* scene, however, human rights could be effective only if state governments chose to emphasize them in foreign policy, but even so, national leaders who promoted human rights would find that there were no effective global mechanisms to enforce them. Thus, despite the eruption of philosophies of human rights during the Enlightenment, this dim view of the efficacy of human rights predominated before the founding of the United Nations. It still has its adherents today, especially among those whose thinking about interstate relations is dominated by a paradigm known as the Westphalian system.

Following the decline of the Catholic Church as the dominant transnational body in western Europe, and the collapse of most major multinational empires around the end of the Middle Ages and the early modern era, the entities remaining as dominant actors were warring monarchs and princes, each of which was sovereign over a territory roughly coinciding with a dominant nationality. This political arrangement was threatened by the savagery of the wars of religion, especially the Thirty Years' War, one of the bloodiest conflicts in European history. The exhaustion of the major contestants led to conclusion of the war with the Treaty of Westphalia in 1648, which imposed upon the population of a territory the religion of the *de facto* ruler of the state.

The Treaty of Westphalia was also known as the Peace of Westphalia, although "peace" was elusive: war continued between France and Spain until 1659 and the Dutch-Portuguese War continued until 1663. The real significance of "peace," in the context of the treaty, was that making war and concluding peace were now exclusively under the purview of heads of states. After Westphalia in 1648, any group able to exert *de facto* control over a defined geopolitical realm was recognized as a government and a *bona fide* member of the international order, whatever means had been used—fair or foul—to attain control. Only state actors possessed rights in the international arena, and states' rights were of great significance. Most important among these rights were the right of non-intervention, that is, the right to exercise exclusive control over the population under a recognized government's control, and the right of freedom in its internal affairs from the interference of other states. Hence, Westphalia marked the beginning of an international system in which realism, or *realpolitik*, came to dominate in terms of states each independently pursuing its own national self-interest, often in competition with other states.

The Westphalian, or state system, also critically endowed each state with the right of self-defense and self-help that enabled each state to be the sole arbitrator of when other states threatened its "vital" national interests, and whether or not it was militarily necessary to declare war in self-defense or in defense of national interests. Additional important states' rights included control of the natural resources within each state's own boundaries; control over membership, including closing the borders and determining who might enter; and the borrowing norm, which enabled a government to borrow from sources abroad, and thus to impose debts on its population, as well as, of course, to tax and to spend monies raised, including social welfare provisions or not, as government officials saw fit. The Westphalian system has continued to this day, despite considerable "erosion" and adaptation to the continuing influence of human rights, changes in international law, and cosmopolitanism (Shue 2014: 145–155).

The Westphalian system was not devoid of rights; however, all rights recognized within the system were states' rights, not the rights of individual persons. Insofar as there was a basis for peace, peace depended entirely on state governments' perceptions of mutual self-interest. This vision of "negative peace," namely, the absence of war as long as states are signatories to a treaty all agree to, is far different from the more robust vision of "positive peace," in which individual rights are respected. In the Westphalian system, individual persons were not recognized as having any standing whatsoever in international law. Thus, for the most part, whether or not individuals' human rights were protected and could be safely asserted and enjoyed depended entirely on one's membership in a state in which a bill of rights or a constitution was recognized as guaranteeing individual human rights. Of course, enjoying individual rights depended on whether those in power prosecuted violations of human rights and enacted legal measures, as needed, to enable the exercise of rights and to provide additional protection. For instance, despite its stature as a constitutional democracy with a bill of rights, the United States failed to respect many of the human rights of African Americans under the system widely known as Jim Crow. The Voting Rights Act of 1965 is one example of legislation intended to ensure that clauses of the Fourteenth and Fifteenth Amendments would provide equal access for all entitled to vote.

The second reason for the view that human rights did not belong in international affairs resulted from an overly narrow notion that much international law was created as a result of pacts between states, and thus has no explicit purpose beyond serving the interests of the state parties contracting. Before turning from the state system to treaties as expressions of national interests, it needs to be emphasized that major resistance to human rights has not been restricted to arbitrary power, or self-interest, whether of private entities or national groups. There are other forces that are, by their nature, opposed to the objectives of cosmopolitanism and human rights. For instance, patriotism, often regarded as virtuous, has the effect of giving one's loyalty to some particular subdivision of humanity above the common good. But the most virulent enemies of global human rights and peace are nationalism and the chauvinism that accompany ethnocentrism, racism, sexism, and intolerance. The movement known as Romanticism, and the Romantics' rejection of the Enlightenment emphasis on reason, arose while the Westphalian system was being consolidated. Because it valorized the supposed uniqueness of national groups, Romanticism reinforced the central tendencies of the new state system.

Romantics such as Johann Gottfried Herder (1744–1803) celebrated the German *Volk*, and argued that each "people" has its own distinct language, which shaped its thought and way of life and determined what a people could contribute to civilization (Herder 2007). Romantics such as Herder believed in national character and the perfection of individual character in the nation. Partly as a result of the French Revolution and the subsequent defeat of Napoléon's imperial ambitions, which required, for the first time, nationwide conscriptions into the armed services, the folk-philosophies of figures such as Herder turned into nationalism: the doctrine that the world is composed of discrete peoples who, in the form of nations, are entitled to rule themselves.

However, the right to self-determination, as it subsequently came to be called, was not a right to democratic government. Rather, it was a right to have a distinctive national collectivity not subjected to some other national or ethnic group. Moreover, nationalism appeared to justify the existence of *nation-states* without resorting to the reality of their *de facto* power. Georg W.F. Hegel (1770–1831) argued that the state, as defender of citizens' communal life, cannot surrender its sovereignty. For Hegel, the state, as the embodiment of freedom, or right, subsumes the family and civil society and fulfills them. Only through patriotism and membership in the state can the individual realize her true nature.

At its worst, Romantic and post-Hegelian ideologies propagated notions about the value of violence and war. Hegel's acquaintance Carl von Clausewitz (1780–1831), a Prussian general influenced by Romanticism, propounded in 1832 that war is the continuation of politics by other means (Clausewitz 1984/1832). Ideas about national character were combined with evolutionary theory to breed the false science of social Darwinism. According to the law of the "survival of the fittest," only those national groups and civilizations most "fit" would survive, according to adherents of this pseudoscience. Such thinking also gave rise to theories about eugenics, or the natural superiority of certain races—usually the "white man" or the "Aryan race"—and arguments were made about the way extreme trials among nations, such as those in warfare, could bring human character to its highest pitch. Yet, even in their less virulent form, Romanticism and nationalism were not sympathetic to the doctrine of human rights. Nationalists found human dignity residing not in the individual person, but rather in the person's contribution to the collective.

International Treaties and Agreements

The United Nations was brought into existence in 1945 "to save succeeding generations from the scourge of war" and to reaffirm "faith in fundamental human rights, in the dignity and worth of the human person and in the equal rights of men and women and . . . to promote social progress and better standards of life in larger freedom," as stated in the Preamble of the UN Charter. The United Nations was successor to the League of Nations, first imagined by Kant in *Perpetual Peace* and strongly advocated by American president Woodrow Wilson. However, the League had by 1935 no more than 58 members and lasted for only 26 years. Moreover, the League was destined to be ineffective because realist statesmen insisted that, notwithstanding the terrible carnage of World War I, serious international problems could best be solved by "power politics" as usual. The illusion that catastrophic war could be averted by politics as usual was exploded by World War II. When delegates to the United Nations met, there was no mistake that the militaristic regimes of Hitler, Mussolini, and Hirohito of imperial Japan had been most responsible for the gross human rights violations of World War II and the Holocaust. The UN set about to *make human rights a matter of international law* for the first time. Hence, the Universal Declaration of Human Rights became international law with adoption of the International Covenant on Civil and Political Rights (ICCPR) and the International Covenant on Social, Economic, and Cultural Rights (ICSECR). After being ratified by state members of the UN, these covenants, or treaties, entered into law in 1956, and the three documents have subsequently been known as the International Bill of Rights (IBR).

Some state members of the UN revised their own constitutions or legal codes to include provisions of the IBR. Since 1956, the admission of new states to the UN required that they include provisions of the IBR in their own constitutions. States meeting these conditions now comprise a majority of the General Assembly. It is nevertheless important to emphasize that while the UN has attempted to reach beyond the state system, it is also a creature of that system. In particular, the power to veto resolutions of the General Assembly is held by the permanent members of the UN Security Council—precisely the states most powerful in 1945 and, consequently, with the greatest vested interest in maintaining the state system. In addition, the UN was given little to no means of effective enforcement; instead, the UN has had to rely on the goodwill of members (often not forthcoming), as well as the willingness of members to finance and staff peacekeeping missions and to respect and implement human rights provisions within states' own borders. In particular, between 1956 and 1976 the UN Commission (now Committee) on Human Rights could receive only intrastate complaints about violations of human rights and not communications from individuals. This was surely a remnant of the worldview that individuals should not have standing in the international arena.

Among UN peacekeeping efforts, best known are peacekeeping missions intended to preserve truces negotiated between warring parties. By contrast, the UN has few options for *peacemaking*, and the absence of effective enforcement mechanisms for the IBR and other human rights covenants suggests to some realists that "international human rights law" is not really law. International law, they believe, concerns the ability of states to pursue their national interests. Examples include the North Atlantic Treaty Organization (NATO) that specifies the obligations of treaty members to promote mutual security, the North American Free Trade Agreement (NAFTA) to promote trade between Canada, Mexico, and the United States, and the UN Convention on the Law of the Sea Treaty (UNCLOs) to regulate navigation procedures, to set limits to territorial waters, and to stipulate agreed procedures for the mining of the deep seabed. These treaties can be said to confer rights, but on governments and not on individuals. For instance, the treaty setting up the World Trade Organization (WTO) specifies rights granted to states as trading partners as well as penalties to be paid by states that may violate WTO trading regulations. Complaints about violations of treaty obligations can be taken to the International Court of Justice that sits at The Hague. Again, however, difficulties arise due to remaining realities of the Westphalia system, particularly the absence—in a system in which every state is a sovereign of equal status—of some central law-enforcement body or instrument.

Some realist skeptics claim that international law is based on the rational self-interest of states. On this view, "international law can be binding and robust, but only when it is rational for states to comply with it" (Goldsmith and Posner 2005: 202). However, what must *rationality* mean if treaties are to have the binding and robust nature of law? "Rationality" cannot simply mean that following the law promotes a state's own self-interest, because this sense of rationality is completely consistent with a state's leaders deciding to violate the law if their national interests change. Hence, realists cannot make sense of why treaties come to be signed and followed at all; perhaps states might gain an advantage over others through deceit, but like lying promises, the net effect of this stratagem is to quickly destroy the value of relying on the word of others. Thus the realists' reductionist line of thought would, as Griffin says, "purge international law not only of ethics but also of explanatory capacity and action-guiding authority. It would gratuitously trivialize international law" (Griffin 2008: 206). Of course, these effects would also tend to undermine a stable and lasting peace.

Both the ICCPR and the ICSECR are now part of a large body of binding human rights treaties, or "instruments"—18 in all. They all have moral content and are in force because they require respect for human dignity whether or not they also advance signatories' interests, and because they make demands on states that can even be contrary to a state's interests. But the view that international law is divided into two parts is highly dubious. Even international laws designed to serve the parties' national interests, such as NAFTA or NATO, are based on a fundamental principle of reciprocity, and therefore have their foundations in moral concerns. Fuller (1902–1978) demonstrated that all coherent and logical legal systems must share an "internal morality" (Fuller 1969). This internal morality is required if law is to rationally guide behavior and it must have some minimal ethical content if law is to help humans achieve their objectives.

Even the Westphalian state system, which seems to be anarchical, respects principles of the internal morality of law. Among these principles are immunity from legal arrest and imprisonment for ambassadors and diplomats, a requirement necessary to enable heads of states to keep lines of communication open. Another principle requires that protocols for the making and amending of treaties be made and remain in effect. Others require that recognized states be treated, in formal relations, as equals; that the rights of neutral states be respected; and that belligerents not seek victories that will destroy the system itself.

Among the most basic elements of the internal morality of any system of rules is the rule of law. At a minimum, the rule of law requires that agents whose legitimacy depends on the rules of the system must also subject themselves to those rules. Thus the rule of law obligates rulers in the state system to explain how their behavior can be understood in terms of the rules of the system. Such explanations are made not as a matter of hypocrisy, but, as Brown notes:

> because failure to do so would, as it were, end the "game," and at the same time, end their capacity to claim the status of sovereignty since this status only exists by virtue of the existence of international society itself. Since most rulers do not wish to surrender their claim to sovereignty, they cannot simply declare that they could and would do anything they could get away with in order to further their own interest.
>
> Brown 2002: 36

In other words, rather than flatly saying that they disregard international law, heads of state will try to explain how their behavior is actually consistent with law, or will claim that their situations present a justifiable exception or excuse for violating the law. For instance, China is far more supportive of social and economic rights (protected in the ICSECR) than civil and political rights (protected in the ICCPR), but defends its position by arguing that civil and political rights can be implemented only after social and economic rights.

Further examples of internal morality pertain to the ways in which wars are to be conducted within the state system. In particular, "treacherous and perfidious" methods of waging war must be prohibited as thwarting the objectives of having "honest" tests of power. Perfidious methods to be avoided include using the flag of truce to feign defeat and having combatants wear the uniform of the enemy or use the badges of the Red Cross or Red Crescent. An additional principle prohibits methods of waging war that would undermine the possibility of concluding peace at the end of a war, and includes prohibitions on assassination attempts against heads of states, the poisoning of water supplies, the use of uncontrollable chemical or biological weaponry, or attacks on civilian populations that do not advance military objectives.

Many of the internal principles of the Westphalia system preceded the origins of the modern state and have histories reaching far back into the Middle Ages. Many of the moral requirements to be met before a state can go to war as well as limits on justifiable means of waging war make up the just war doctrine, while other principles have been codified as covenants in international humanitarian law, such as the 1925 Geneva Protocol prohibiting biological and chemical weapons, and reaffirmed by UN bans in 1976 and 1989 to include all "non-directed weapons" including napalm and nuclear weapons. Principles of the internal morality of law also restrict what can count as binding positive law, that is, law enacted by legislative bodies or decreed by a dictator. Hence, the Nuremberg Tribunal justifiably set aside defenses of Nazi war criminals that what they had done was legal in Nazi Germany, on the grounds that crimes of war, crimes against humanity, and crimes against peace were well established in customary law.

The Statute of the International Court of Justice announces (Article 38.1) that in settling disputes submitted to it, the Court shall apply (1) treaties, (2) customary law in the international sphere, (3) general principles of law recognized by civilized nations, (4) judicial decisions, and (5) the teachings of experts. The most basic of all customary law is *jus cogens* (Latin for "compelling law"), a body of peremptory norms that do not depend on consent for their force, and that cannot be violated by any state. In 1923 the Permanent Court of the International Court of Justice ruled that state sovereignty is not inalienable and the Vienna Convention of the Law of

Treaties (entering into force in 1980) claims under Article 53 that any treaty conflicting with *jus cogens* norms is void. Examples of these most preemptory norms include the prohibition on waging aggressive warfare, genocide, crimes against humanity, war crimes, apartheid, slavery, torture, maritime piracy, refoulment, and territorial aggrandizement.

The Nuremberg and Tokyo tribunals established precedents in holding high officials of government responsible for war crimes and crimes against humanity. The Treaty of Rome, which went into effect in 2002, established the International Criminal Court (ICC), at The Hague. The ICC, together with tribunals, has held heads of state responsible for crimes and also enhanced the ability of individuals to seek redress for human rights violations.[1] In this way, human rights concerns have influenced the international arena and contributed to international peace.

Among other critical developments, the doctrine of "conditional sovereignty" certainly should be cited. According to the doctrine, the sovereignty of a state depends on a satisfactory human rights record. This amendment of the most fundamental principle of the state system has been paired with an increased willingness to legitimate humanitarian intervention, as reflected in the General Assembly resolution of a Responsibility to Protect (R2P). When the internal morality of law, *jus cogens*, and international humanitarian law are taken together we must conclude that the present situation represents the *morality of states*—the expectation that states must relate to each other, to their own citizens, and to citizens abroad, in moral terms and not primarily as power-holders (Brown 2002: 33; Vincent 1986).

Natural Law Theory

This notion of a morality of states was first fully developed in natural law theorist Vattel's (1714–1767) *Law of Nations* (1758), in which he argued that there must be some reference point beyond which the laws and customs of states ought to be judged (Vattel 1915). Earlier natural law theorists Vitoria (1483–1546) and Suarez (1549–1617) defended the native peoples of the Americas and the Caribbean against the crimes of Spanish colonization by arguing that the natural law applies alike to all peoples and not just to Christians (Suarez 1944). Wolff (1679–1754) argued both that states comprise a society governed by natural law, and that there was a collective good—posited as a fictional collective sovereign, if necessary—that could declare and interpret the rules of the collectivity (Brown et al. 2002: 321).

Both the foundations of international law and those of human rights theory share a common origin in natural law theory going back to Augustine (354–430) before the collapse of the Roman Empire and to prominent figures such as Aquinas (1225–1274). Although Christian in origin, the natural law tradition was secular by the time Grotius (1583–1645), one of its major figures, published *On the Law of War and Peace* in 1625 (Grotius 1925). This shared ancestry is evident in Locke's and Jefferson's claims that human beings are "endowed by our Creator" with natural rights, a phrase that was changed to "human rights" in the UN Declaration of Human Rights to appeal to cultures outside the West. The notion that God has endowed humans with natural rights is a carryover of the idea that we were created in the image of God, as autonomous, moral agents, capable of self-creation. This view entered more secular Renaissance currents of thought by works such as Pico della Mirandola's *Oration on the Dignity of Man* (1486), in which Pico explains that, unlike the animals, God has given humans no fixed nature, enabling us to become whatever we will, including as like unto God as possible (Mirandola 2012).

To speak of human rights and natural law as "natural" meant, first, that human beings were equipped with the capacity to discover them and to achieve agreement on their content through rational discourse and logical argument. Thus, once appraised of the existence of human rights, men and women no longer required access to the will of God in determining what those rights were, and hence did not need religious scholars or other authorities. Second, because human rights were "natural" they were possessed by persons in virtue of their status as human beings and were not created or granted by governments or other human institutions. Third, understanding natural law opened up the possibilities for peaceful agreement. Hobbes argued in the *Leviathan* (1651) that a rational understanding of the laws of nature would lead individuals—otherwise liable to a continual state of war—to form a social contract, making peace possible. Locke went further, claiming in the *Second Treatise of Government* (1689) not only that individuals possess rights in the state of nature, but that governments exist to protect these natural rights.

It is hardly surprising that a similar emphasis on "the natural" lay behind international humanitarian law, which was conceived as prohibiting activity that was an outrage to the dignity of human beings, or shocking to conscience and decency. Finally, the emphasis on "natural" was understood to mean that, whatever their other differences, all human beings were morally equal. Equality in this sense meant both that all persons possessed the same human rights and that all persons possessed those rights equally, that is, to the same degree. Indeed, modern human rights theorists such as Griffin (2008: 9–28) insist on the historical and logical continuity of theories of natural law, natural rights, and human rights.

It can be said that the history of human rights and international law has not been linear but circular. It has already been observed that the major impetus for reaffirming the significance of human rights in the IBR came from the horrors of the Holocaust and the Second World War. The creation of new instruments was the beginning of an effort, continuing today, to provide for the *international* recognition of human rights. Recently some theorists have argued that human rights recognized by international treaties do not "mirror" human rights, but were created *sui generis* through the ratification of international covenants (Beitz 2009; Buchanan 2014). Such claims are not necessarily inconsistent with the naturalistic tradition (e.g. Griffin 2008) according to which these developments continue in the natural law tradition. Nevertheless, both sides hold that "internationalizing" human rights requires greater scrutiny of state behavior and justifies the work of new institutions, thus enhancing the practical effects of advocacy, legal promotion, and enforcement.

Natural law as the common source of both human rights and international law continues to exert considerable influence beyond the formation of international human rights. The natural law tradition maintains that standards for reason and ethics are naturalistic and global (Boylan 2014; Churchill 2006). This means that all political entities ought to pursue a common commitment to universal peace and to universal human rights. Although differences of interpretation or application might arise, these differences should be subject to agreed principles of debate and reasoning. There cannot be deep, incommensurable disagreements, because cultural or ethical relativism is unsupportable, and therefore, it is a mistake to believe that human rights norms apply differently in Iran or North Korea, say, than they do in Germany or the United States. It also follows from natural law that there cannot be different standards of morality depending on the type or arena of action. In particular, from the naturalistic orientation, it is false to assume, as some realists do (Morgenthau 1985; Niebuhr 2002), that there are different moral principles for statesmen or soldiers fighting in a war. Thus natural law principles limit what states can require of their citizens as well as permissible conduct in war.

Just War and Natural Law

Wars of aggression were outlawed in that part of natural law recognized as the just war doctrine.[2] The rules of *jus ad bellum* have been codified in international agreements. The idea of "just cause" is reaffirmed by the Kellogg-Briand Pact of 1928 that prohibits wars of aggression.

It has become a prominent feature of *jus cogens* and is inscribed in the UN Charter in Articles 1 (1) and 2 (4). Last resort is included in *jus cogens* as it calls for the "settlement of international disputes or situations that might lead to a breach of the peace" by "peaceful means." And, as May says, Article 51 "seems to call for a State to wait to see whether the United Nations will take action before the aggrieved State or its allies can use military force" (May 2008: 42): the UN's own peacekeeping missions and forces were among the alternative means to be used. Legitimate authority has increasingly been interpreted as requiring that citizens—those who must bear the actual sacrifices—agree that the war is just, a condition that entails some democratic process.

Even more important, as May notes, the rules of *jus in bello* (morality in waging war) fit within *jus cogens*.[3] The status of these rules in international law goes all the way back to Suarez's commandment in *On War* that "the method of its conduct must be proper" (quoted in May 2008: 35) and Grotius's dictum that just tactics must not violate the rights of the innocent (May 2008: 35). The principles of *jus in bello* entered modern international law through a series of Geneva Conventions and treaties at The Hague, and are now commonly referred to as "rules of war," as in the US Rules of Land Warfare.

The most significant feature of *jus in bello*, May claims, is the constraints it places on the application of *jus ad bellum* principles, "because it disrupts the separateness of these two branches of war" (2008: 35). Wars cannot be justifiably initiated and waged *unless* it is clearly foreseeable that justifiable tactics (those of *jus in bello*) can be employed. May correctly notes that the stringency of these requirements will result in a version of pacifism known as *contingent pacifism*.

May accepts the principle, quoting from Grotius, that "one cannot be rightly killed, in war or in capital punishment, for misfortune or for fault, but only for having done wrong" (in May 2008: 31). Soldiers conscripted against their will are certainly misfortunate, and at fault if forced to fight in an unjust war, but for those reasons alone, they do not commit wrongs. Wrongs are, as Grotius says, "things done purposely and with evil intent"; and thus, as Grotius adds, "it is necessary that he who is killed shall himself have done wrong" (May 2008: 32). Hence, as May says, "we must consider whether any given soldier has 'done wrong' as an individual before he may be justifiably killed" (May 2008: 32). A soldier who kills in self-defense while under enemy fire does so purposely, but not necessarily with evil intent.

Given the equal basic dignity and the universality of human rights, no one may legitimately violate the basic rights of others. Hence, only those who take the initiative as aggressors and violate the basic rights of others act with evil intent. However, because nearly all wars are impossible to wage without killing the innocent, states must accept contingent pacifism as a policy. For all practical purposes, contingent pacifism *ought to* require absolute anti-war pacifism, or a total ban on fighting war, at least until it is possible that weapons become so precise and intelligence so good that only those who have done wrong are singled out, and the use of violence against them is justified.

In general, we do not consider a violation of human rights morally justified *unless* the violation averts the violation of a more basic human right. For instance, if two parents can sustain the lives of their children in no other way than to appropriate sustenance from the excess supply owned by neighbors, then they may justifiably do so. Note that only the *necessity* of saving life justifies the violation of property rights. Self-defense may look to some very much like this paradigm case. What they want to believe is that our use of lethal violence is the lesser of two evils: deadly force is justifiably employed to prevent the violation of more basic rights. But most wars are not necessary in this sense; for example, consider that most wars in which the US engaged were not fought to prevent or avert imminent violations of citizens' basic human rights. Even when this is plausibly the case—e.g. the US's entry into World War II after the Japanese attack on Pearl Harbor—it almost never remains true throughout the course of a war. This is because, as noted previously, innocents are attacked and killed, but also because wars typically continue, as did World War II, long after adversaries are able to pose an imminent threat to human rights. We might also note that conscription poses a related threat to human rights.[4]

A Human Right to Peace?

The ongoing controversy over a human right to peace provides a fitting concluding topic here. In 1997 Federico Mayor, director-general of UNESCO, proclaimed that "lasting peace is a prerequisite for the exercise of all human rights and duties" (quoted in Said and Lerche 2006: 129). The African Charter on Human and Peoples' Rights asserts that all people have "the right to national and international peace and security" (Article 23.1). Griffin responds that this is a scarcely credible claim and it reflects the tendency of drafters to tack on to international rights what are only aspirations. Griffin asks further, "Would a country that decides to defend itself against invasion violate its citizens' rights?" (2008: 194). The presumption Griffin makes is that self-defense, if violent, is inconsistent with the human right to peace. Yet, the *point* of agreeing on human rights is, in large part, to set obligations on parties that otherwise would violate these rights. Thus the obvious point of a human right to peace is to reduce the likelihood of the scourge of war and the corresponding need for self-defense.

The human right to peace has been submitted for consideration of committees in the UN and debated for decades. When proposals do reach the General Assembly, as they did in 2016, a majority persists in declining to act. The simple fact is that implementing a human right to peace would require that states either dismantle or subject to international control weapons systems that, though proclaimed to be merely "defensive," necessarily have "offensive" war-fighting capabilities as well, such as Russia's intercontinental ballistic missiles, Pakistan's nuclear bombs, or the United States' armed but unmanned drones. But, of course, abandoning weapons systems would require that states surrender sovereignty, which they are unwilling to do.

The continuing aspirational status of the right to peace illustrates ongoing tensions in an international system in which state sovereignty continues to be eroded because of events beyond the ability of the strongest to shape (e.g. climate change) and because opportunities for the pursuit of parochial or one-sided national interests are increasingly constrained by international law and by a rich, increasingly complex and resilient human rights regime. We continue to be citizens of a world in which states violate law and human rights frequently, and sometimes with impunity. At the same time, we also inhabit a world in which a growing moral consensus indicates that, far from being required to accept Thucydides's dictum, acts of aggression are condemned and seen not as natural, but as unjust forms of cheating and advantage-taking. Occasional unchecked actions of immoral behavior should not lead us to believe that the moral force of human rights and international law is destined to fail any more than the occasional wrong decision by a court should lead us to be skeptical about the rule of law. Moreover, we should keep in mind that states are not agents possessing rights that entitle them to arbitrarily override human rights. The cosmopolitan view of international law as founded on ethics trumps the realist view of law as based upon power. We should continue to advance human rights discourse in international law, as a foundation for developing world peace.

Notes

1 Consider, for example, the arrest and indictment of Slobodan Milosevic for Serbian war crimes in Bosnia. The ability of individuals to seek redress for violations of human rights—and thereby create precedent—has been enhanced greatly by the work of the European Union of the Court of Human Rights (established in 1959 and made permanent in 1998), whose judgments are recognized as binding among EU members. A judgment of the Inter-American Commission on Human Rights (IACHR)

found that a US court violated the *jus cogens* prohibition against imposing capital punishment on a defendant who was a minor when the crimes for which he was convicted were committed. In 2005, a group of Inuit, who depend on seal hunting in the Arctic, petitioned the IACHR for a ruling that, as a major contributor to global warming, the US was threatening their existence. In 2007 the IACHR ruled that it did not have authority to compel the US to restrict its greenhouse gas emissions or compensate the Inuit. However, the IACHR also indicated that its parent body, the Organization of American States, should hold hearings including Inuit representatives of the Circumpolar Council to explore the legality of their complaints.

2 *Jus ad bellum* requires that six necessary conditions be fulfilled: just cause (the war must be for self-defense, defense of the innocent, or in aid of parties with whom a state has treaty obligations), legitimate authority (the war must be declared and conducted by legitimate authorities), right intention (the war must be waged to thwart aggression or vindicate human rights, and to restore peace), proportionality (waging war must not cause greater harm than would result if war were not waged), last resort (every less harmful means of attaining the just cause must have been exhausted), and reasonable chance of success (a state cannot use lethal violence if there is no reasonable chance of securing a just cause).

3 *Jus in bello* requires discrimination (or the immunity of noncombatants), humanity (the humane treatment of combatants who have surrendered, prisoners, and those detained), military necessity (use of least force to attain a legitimate military objective), and proportionality (with respect to specific strategies and tactics *within* war).

4 It might be said that if self-defense is necessary and justified, then a government has a moral obligation to make provision for the defense of its citizens. But can government officials require conscription of its citizens to bear arms? Perhaps most citizens will regard collective self-defense by the state and in which they participate as a special case of one's individual obligations to defend the innocent. If so, then perhaps they ought to volunteer their service rather than support a system of conscription that would require pacifists to fight as well. Many individuals would prefer to risk death rather than act in such a way as to knowingly cause the death of others. This claim has been corroborated by studies of men killed in combat (Grossman 1996; Marshall 2000), much to the alarm of militarists, as well as professed by absolute pacifists such as Leo Tolstoy (1828–1910). Other pacifists have claimed that even when self-defense is necessary, this does not give one a *right* to use *violent* self-defense. Civilian defense, or nonviolent national defense, is an option whose plausibility has been strengthened by empirical studies demonstrating the greater effectiveness of nonviolent struggle over violent methods (Chenoweth and Stephan 2011; Sharp 1990).

Works Cited

Beitz, C. (2009). *The Idea of Human Rights*. Oxford: Oxford University Press.
Boylan, M. (2014). *Natural Human Rights*. New York: Cambridge University Press.
Brown, C. (2002). *Sovereignty, Rights and Justice*. Cambridge: Polity Press.
Brown, C., Nardin, T., and Rengger, N. (eds.) (2002). *International Relations in Political Thought*. Cambridge: Cambridge University Press.
Buchanan, A. (2014). *The Heart of Human Rights*. Oxford and New York: Oxford University Press.
Chenoweth, M., and M. Stephan (2011). *Why Civil Resistance Works*. New York: Columbia University Press.
Christiano, T. (ed.) (2003). *Philosophy and Democracy*. Oxford and New York: Oxford University Press.
Churchill, R. (2006). *Human Rights and Global Diversity*. Routledge.
Clausewitz, C. (1832/1984). *On War*, translated and edited by M. Howard and P. Paret. Princeton: University of Princeton Press.
Doyle, M. (1997). *Ways of War and Peace*. New York: W.W. Norton.
Fuller, L. (1969). *The Morality of Law*. New Haven: Yale University Press.
Goldsmith, J., and E. Posner. (2005). *The Limits of International Law*. New York: Oxford University Press.
Gould, C. (2004). *Globalizing Democracy and Human Rights*. New York: Columbia University Press.
Griffin, J. (2008). *On Human Rights*. Oxford and New York: Oxford University Press.
Grossman, D. (1996). *On Killing*. Boston: Little, Brown.
Grotius, H. (1625/1925). *On the Law of War and Peace*, translated by F. Kelsey. Oxford: Clarendon.
Herder, J. (1784–91/2007). *Herder: Philosophical Writings*, edited by M. Clark and M. Forster. Cambridge: Cambridge University Press.
Hobbes, T. (1651/1994). *Leviathan*, edited by E.M. Curley. Indianapolis: Hackett Publishing.

Kant, I. (1792/2012). *Groundwork of the Metaphysics of Morals*, translated by M. Gregor and J. Timmerman. Cambridge: Cambridge University Press.
Kant, I. (1795/1991). "Perpetual Peace," in H. Reiss (ed.), and H. Nisbett (trans.), *Kant: Political Writings*. Cambridge: Cambridge University Press, 129–150.
Lipson, C. (2003). *Reliable Partners*. Princeton: Princeton University Press.
Locke, J. (1689/1988). *Two Treatises of Government*, edited by P. Laslett. Cambridge: Cambridge University Press.
Marshall, S. (2000). *Men Against Fire*. Norman: University of Oklahoma Press.
May, L. (2008). *Aggression and Crimes Against Peace*. Cambridge: Cambridge University Press.
Mirandola, P. (1486/2012). *Oration on the Dignity of Man*, edited and translated by F. Borghesi, M. Papio, and M. Riva. Cambridge: Cambridge University Press.
Morgenthau, H., and K. Thompson. (1985). *Politics Among Nations*. New York: McGraw-Hill.
Niebuhr, R. (2002). *Moral Man and Immoral Society*. Louisville: Westminster John Knox.
Said, A., and C. Lerche. (2006). "Peace as a Human Right," in J. Mertus and J. Helsing (eds.), *Human Rights and Conflict*. Washington: US Institute for Peace, 93–130.
Sharp, G. (1990). *Civilian-Based Defense*. Princeton: Princeton University Press.
Shue, H. (2014). *Climate Justice*. Oxford: Oxford University Press.
Suarez, F. (c.1610/1944). "On War," in G. Williams, A. Brown, and J. Waldron (trans.), *Selections from Three Works*. Oxford: Clarendon.
Thucydides. (c. 450/1998). *History of the Peloponnesian War*, translated by S. Lattimore. Indianapolis: Hackett.
United Nations. (2017). "Declaration of the Right to Peace Resolution Adopted by the General Assembly on 19 December 2016." Available at: www.un.org/en/ga/search/view_doc.asp?symbol=A/RES/71/189 (Accessed 14 July 2017).
Vattel, E. (1797/1915). *The Law of Nations*, edited by W. Fenwick. Washington: Carnegie Institute.
Vincent, R. (1986). *Human Rights and International Relations*. Cambridge: Cambridge University Press.

20
HOSPITALITY, IDENTITY, AND COSMOPOLITANISM
Antidotes to the Violence of Otherness

Eddy M. Souffrant

This chapter attempts to disentangle the violence that is embedded in nationalism. It proposes cosmopolitanism as a promoter of a global peace. The restrictive political philosophy of nationalism cannot take hold without the contribution of the foreigner. Nationalism is either internally inconsistent or willingly mistreats the foreigner as the emblematic other. Singular identity, the failure to recognize institutions as agents that significantly affect aspects of our lives, and the promotion of nationalism are some of the tools we use to establish otherness. These instruments tend to create 'othernesses' that found violence and are ultimately inconsistent with global peaceful coexistence. We would benefit from a revision of these exclusionary tendencies, and from adopting a robust cosmopolitanism. The theory and practice of nonviolence benefit from embracing hospitality and cosmopolitanism.

From Rwanda to Trump

The problem of violence, identity, and otherness can be seen in the work of the Rwandan performer Corneille. His 2007 song "I'll Never Call You Home Again" highlights the tensions that embody the forced cosmopolitanism of an artist who witnessed the assassination of his parents in Rwanda at the height of the genocidal agenda of that country's political leaders in the 1990s. Corneille was a victim of the genocidal nationalism that sliced through the vital members of the community. He had the political misfortune of being born of Hutu and Tutsi parents. He was thrust, after his family's massacre (and the luck of oversight, or the carelessness of an assassin) into the exodus that many Rwandans experienced out of Rwanda, and for some, into more hospitable environments. Corneille became a 17-year-old wanderer who had faith that his humanity would be recognized and accordingly properly gauged as dignified and worthy of succor. A few decades after the exodus, we find him wrestling in the previously mentioned song with the idea of home. Having experienced the violence of nationalism firsthand he hopes for a transformation, a nationalism purposed by care and duty to, at least, the nationals. These are no doubt laudable goals, but it remains that Cornelius Nyungura (Corneille) experienced a violence caused by the promulgation of false conceptions of identity (see Souffrant 2013: 245).

The conception of group identity that fueled the violence of the Rwandan nationalism of the 1990s understands identity formations to be ahistorical. It denied the truism that social groups and the identities they adopt are actually the results of historical mixtures. Communities and the identities they nurture "are constructed through emulation and exclusion, but present themselves as indigenous by ignorance or suppression of history" (Banerjee 2017). The tension that gave way to the Rwandan genocide took for granted that the hierarchies of group identities supported by Rwandan political structures were indigenous and homogenous. In reality, the violence in the Rwanda of 1994 embodied the worst emulations and exclusions. It mimicked that of a bygone period of colonization that nearly obliterated another historically native segment of the population.

Fortunately, Corneille was the beneficiary, despite his past trauma, of a form of hospitality that underscores his membership in a world human community. This indicates ambivalence regarding a) accepting the inhospitable national home and b) seeking the unmentioned hospitable "world house," to borrow a phrase from Martin Luther King, Jr. (King 1967). This ambivalence stems from the realization that, in our times, a fully cosmopolitan project cannot take hold without the recognition of national boundaries and without the infusion of cosmopolitan ideals within national boundaries and states. This practical hurdle does not contradict King's admonition in 1967 that our survival as a species depends on our ability to transform our living spaces on the globe from a sectarian ("neighborhood") world to a "world-wide brotherhood" (King 1967).

King believed, as I do, that hierarchical and political separations do violence and are, in the end, destructive. One need only to refer to his Nobel Lecture in 1964 to recall his broad argument that poverty of spirit, which includes racism, war, and socio-economic poverty, contrasted with humankind's wealth in matters of scientific and technological prowess. He sought to reveal and combat our persistent poverty of spirit with his two favored weapons of nonviolence and resistance/struggle. In the end, his project was fundamentally a moral one in which, as he saw it, the solution to the scourges of contemporary living would consist in counterbalancing our scientific progress with an equivalent and fitting moral progress. With the progress, we would furthermore learn and begin to practice living together and harmoniously (see King 1972).

For King then, harmonious and peaceful living involves the positive endeavor of transforming our global condition of war and spiritual and material penury into one of brotherhood and moral regards. It bears mentioning that brotherhood and family connections of themselves do not prevent violence. Some of our revered religious texts attest to this as they recount instances of patricide and fratricide, not to mention violence against women, whether sisters, wives, or perfect strangers. Thus, brotherhood or family relations are not sufficient for harmonious living. They both must be supplemented by will and moral guidance in order for us to live peacefully. The complement cannot be political for, perforce, this latter carves the public realm into those who belong to the political community and those severed from it.

But in itself, the exclusion from political membership constitutes violence that partitions the human community. Moreover, political exclusion risks perpetuating a replication of violence. It invites the excluded to seek political power of their own through political upheaval (revolution) or to practice, in turn, a similar type of exclusion through retribution, once they gain power. The need for a supplement is stark in the Rwandan case. The Rwandan community, on the verge of complete destruction, was already equipped with a moral supplement in the principle of "intore," even if it too was swept away, albeit momentarily, by the political violence. "Intore" (pronounced *EenOray* or *Eetoray*) translates loosely as "one of immense moral integrity, a lover of country." It is an attribution reserved for the ones of highest esteem. "Intore" is the highest compliment that one can receive as a Rwandan but it is also the "dance of heroes, traditionally performed by warriors coming home from battle" (Beharie 2017).

Intore is a perfectly suited concept for the challenge faced by the Rwandans (Hutu, Tutsi, Twa) of the latter part of the twentieth century who faced the battle of recovering from the genocide. The genocide undermined Rwandan unity to be sure, but the restoration of peaceful living in the community came to be established by a reactivation of the moral principle that encapsulated moral integrity. The moral ideal was suppressed by the political crisis, but in its aftermath, artists and performers reclaimed the spirit of "intore." Serving as a model for the entire community, these performers used the principle to heal themselves, and to restore the cohabitation and collaboration of the various members of their community in the wake of the atrocities. "Intore" as moral standard helped the community reject violence in order to restore itself. Its members channeled their pain into inspiration. They substituted violence with peaceful cohabitation.

The concept of "intore" can help the Rwandan people restore its place as an integral constituent of the global humanity. It does so not by political force or actions but by a reappropriation of its moral core, the rapprochement toward the other. Our interactions with others cannot simply be legislated. In the best of circumstances, it is morally motivated, duty bound. The duty however can be Kantian, rational or neo-liberal, i.e. individually (or atomistically) based, or organic, relying on a more discriminating sense of self. The Kantian sense of duty emanates from a specific interpretation of the Cartesian conception of identity that requires the self to be contained and complete and which makes interaction with others seem unnatural and artificial but necessarily duty bound because we do not live alone and we are prone to selfishness and violence. This Kantian or neo-liberal conception of duty contrasts with the sort of duty that draws from the recognition of our organic and metaphysical interconnection with others.

From the neo-liberal conception, violence and tension are natural. From a more communitarian perspective, violence is inconsistent with our organic and relational sense of self. In the former, the connection with others is artificial, if rational; with the latter, the link with others is organic. The antidote to violence, as King suggests, is a recognition that we are part of the same world community ("world house") rather than to presume an inherent disconnection with others, with whom we are expected to forge an alliance. The practitioners of "intore" have redefined, or perhaps better, recaptured the Rwandan conception of identity and have revealed a more relevant identity that is, on the whole, more fitting for the promotion of peace and conviviality not only in Rwanda, but prospectively the world over.

I consider Corneille as an example of a thought that haunts me. It is that the atrocities and the genocide seen in Rwanda can happen anywhere. We can think that it is endemic to the Rwandan people or to the Hutus to be exact. Rather, for me, such violence is always an option open to us humans. The rejection of that path is the challenge of humanity. To meet this challenge, we must revisit and be mindful of our oversights and silences. I find a potential source of violence to be the divorce that is encouraged between the governed and the governors. In a previously published work (Souffrant 2006), I warned of the potential alienation of the people from their governmental representatives and from governmental powers, arguing that the liberal tradition's silence on collective entities like corporations risks being filled by a capitalist and corporate model of political governance. In effect, the warning spoke of the pervasive tendency to grant corporations the right to control, or establish themselves for controlling, an entire nation or its affairs. That corporate understanding of political governance was at the time a purely speculative consideration on my part even if, in my view, that prediction was a logical extension of the transformation that I believe liberal institutions were undergoing. The governors in this scenario would be corporate authorities.

Some may even argue that we have reached this stage with recent political events in the US that have given way to the investiture of the current president, Donald J. Trump, but this suggests yet a different solution to the gap between governed and governors. In his inauguration speech, the president motioned in that direction. At first look, he would appear to solve the alienation problem of liberalism by favoring a more immediate and intimate conception of governance. Governmental powers in accordance to the liberal interpretation are distinct from the powers of the governed. Governmental powers in that tradition are justified, to the extent that they promote or sustain individual liberty (broadly speaking) and prevent harm to the individual or to society and any of its members. So, at one level, the president's proposal of a shift in governmental powers is an invitation to populism, and at another level, his proposal would also appear to buttress a nationalist, if an authoritarian, freehand, thereby risking some version of the Rwandan practice of otherness that gave way to the brutality we witnessed.

The Ethics of Hospitality and Nationalism

The ethical and political theory of hospitality provides an important resource for those who are interested in nonviolence and a more peaceful world. As an example, consider the work of Tracy McNulty, who explores the relationship between hospitality and enmity in human communal interaction (McNulty 2007). She reminds us that the Bible offers a precedent for clarifying the ambiguity around patriotism. She argues that the articulated tension between hospitality and enmity took shape for the first time through the acceptance of the Decalogue when this latter simultaneously assigned membership and exclusion. Those who subscribe to monotheism and the dictates of the Decalogue elicit a form of goodwill that is not open to the detractors of such dictates. But unlike the biblical theater, we live in a different world. In our contemporary world, it is no longer strictly the Decalogue but human decency to humanity, the interconnection with the rest of humanity, that motivates our acts of conviviality. So, an ethics of hospitality rather than one of enmity should motivate our interactions with the other.

The 'other' is by its very nature strange. To the extent that she is different and strange, we are justified in keeping her at bay. The wanderer, the different, the otherwise foreign to me, is potentially threatening if we adopt an infantile or primitive understanding of our identity and existence. In the primitive understanding of the self, the other undermines my integrity, my self-containment. Atomistic individualism, often associated with Descartes, is artificial. Alternatively, we have learned from Descartes onward that my identity depends on my presence with the other. Descartes himself argued that identity requires the postulate of God. Rather than think of identity as the integral self who is entirely self-constituted, we have with Descartes an alternative interpretation of identity. With Descartes to be sure, the self is self-contained and is uniquely integral, but for its integrity it relies on an intimate relation with the other.

McNulty believes that the other helps construct the self. Identity is not unitary but complex, or at least binary. McNulty argues even further that our identity harbors an element of unknowability that is akin to the opacity that the other could represent. If we think that the other is unknown or unknowable, our own constitution should encourage us to be as charitable to the other as we would be to ourselves. According to her, if the basis of our treatment of the other relies on our sense that he is unknown and thus a threat, we by our very constitution harbor an unknown too and as such harbor the same threat within us. Instead of threat or exclusion, the realization that we are also unknown to ourselves should encourage us to consider the unknowability of ourselves and of the other as familiar. Based on that familiarity, we are justified to treat the other more like a friend than a foe.

Recognizing that the other *is* like me does not preclude difference. The other is not me but she has qualities with which I am familiar. She is not me but that which would make her a threat, her unknowability, is familiar to me and as a result, she can be welcomed and not shunned. This intuition informs McNulty's argument for the ethics of hospitality. Her ethics of hospitality recommends that we welcome the stranger, and for her, the authentic act of hospitality requires celebrating the alterity of the stranger. She notices however that in the Hebrew Bible there is a shift from this notion of hospitality marked by the post-prophetic narrative.

From that point on, rather than openly welcoming the stranger, the ethics of hospitality requires that we know the stranger. Helped by the work of Gilles Deleuze and Felix Guattari, she understands that in the new version of hospitality the stranger, the de-territorialized other, the foreigner, comes to represent a threat to the state. The foreigner's movement defies the territorial logic of the state. The state as we know it circumscribes the subject's movement and maps "its identity within a closed system of signification" (McNulty 2007: 31). The foreigner thus destabilizes the hold of the state, questions the power of the state. It interrogates its ability to create and reward patriotic citizens.

The state, by contrast, aims to re-territorialize the individual through identity and the promise of protection. In the Abrahamic tradition, religion similarly re-territorializes the subject by excluding the nomad, and the stranger who is not a monotheist. Accordingly, for McNulty, hospitality precedes the law both historically and logically. Authentic hospitality practiced in monotheism puts the integrity of the self, the conception of identity, into question. It also challenges the notions of nationalism and patriotism especially as they put a price on state protection. The *quid pro quo* of nationalism is however compatible with yet another form of hospitality, the Kantian type of cosmopolitan hospitality.

Cosmopolitan hospitality constitutes a departure from the earlier conceptions of hospitality as an ethical act. I read Immanuel Kant here with Tracy McNulty, who maintains that in a world of nations, the ethics of hospitality presents a conflict for the host (Kant 1795). It is one in which he is to take in the other, the stranger, respect her foreignness, name her and acknowledge the stranger's illegibility, as outside the bounds of the home (however loosely or broadly construed). For Kant, the stranger has a right not to be treated with hostility. He holds that "[h]ospitality means the right of a stranger . . . [but] only a right of temporary sojourn, a right to associate, which all men have" (Kant 1795: Section II). The stranger is not identical to the host and it is outside of the bounds of amity secured through the state. The stranger does not belong to the nation-state. In the biblical interpretation, she is a non-believer. The ethics of hospitality, which directs laudable disposition toward the stranger despite his unknowability, is thus in conflict with the (national or religious) laws of hospitality. The latter presuppose a positive representation of identity. They expect the self and the other to be known quantities. In effect, they regulate from that platform, the interactions with others, and help as regulations, to order the polity.

Kant's search for a secular solution to the stranger subjects the hospitality relation to principles; i.e. he submits the foreigner, the stranger's "fundamental illegibility," to legislation in order to make him legitimate, thereby guaranteeing a universal and perpetual peace (McNulty 2007: 47). Kant's hospitality secures perpetual peace but his peace is not established by treaty (as merely political). Instead, it is grounded in universal moral maxims.

Kant recasts thus the problem of hospitality away from the problem of aggressive nationalism and its territorial gains and colonialism. Aggressive nationalism pursues interest beyond the borders of the nation. Agency for Kant has shifted from persons to nations and accordingly, he focuses less on the integrity of the host as person and instead emphasizes the host as nation. With that shift from individual to a collective or supra-individual body, he targets the increasing dispersion of people, the displacement of populations, and the need for some conceptions of a passive territorial and national sovereignty or integrity. The context he considers is partial or particular, but the conception of hospitality he develops rests on principles that apply to all peoples and individuals as subjects of national boundaries and laws.

Cosmopolitan Hospitality

The idea of cosmopolitan hospitality provides a resource for thinking about how we might promote peace and build a nonviolent future. From Kant's perspective, cosmopolitan hospitality responds to the conditions he has assessed prevalent in his time (displacement and dispersion). More specifically he replies to two threats to peace in a world of integral nations. The first threat is that the guest risks abusing or violating the integrity and sovereignty of the host nation. The second threat emanates from the host. Kant contends that the host must not impede the safe passage of the guest across its territory. The motivation for his contention is that national sovereignty must come to terms with the limitations of the finite space on earth. So, he feels a tension on the one hand, between what we hold in common and what is foreign, and on the other hand, between individuals and the nation-state. He believes that the integrity of the nation-state must be preserved and protected. This reaffirmation of borders runs counter to the practice of hospitality that, as McNulty understands it, usually implies a blurring of borders, exchange of property, and an invitation and welcoming of the guest.

For Kant, the nation is a moral person. It has integrity and cannot be bought or exchanged. It is possessed of a right to self-determination and cannot succumb to the whims of a host-patriarch (McNulty 2007: 50). The nation is not an appendage or property of the individual host and when it receives a guest, a visitor, it does so on its own terms. The nation is thus an emancipated moral person with its own rights. Nations, then, as distinct entities, cannot intermingle. Nations are self-contained and static. They have territorial integrity and given the rigidity of their borders, hostility, when it arises, results from the intermingling and transgression of the bounds of the nation. Conversely, when peace is reached, it is by means of mutual agreement or by means of a principle that binds the entities in question. The rational contract in which the nations engage is thus the best antidote to international hostility initiated by otherness.

The cosmopolitan life that Kant supports complicates the relation of host and stranger/foreigner because it acknowledges both the finitude of the globe and the necessity of trade. Commercialization between persons across the globe and the real threat that the strangers represent are for Kant impediments to the practice of hospitality. As a practical problem, hospitality is a secular challenge. The increasing cosmopolitan (global) nature of human relations requires a fitting conception of cosmopolitan hospitality that would protect guests and hosts at once. Kant's solution is thus twofold: first, he institutes a right of visit that does not involve a right of receiving or welcoming (initial constituents of an ethics of hospitality), and second, he placates notions of hospitality that would present risks and threats to the host. He thinks thereby to undermine the justifications to reject the foreigner.

In a realist world, nations are to look out for themselves. Their respective citizens must be patriotic and hold allegiance to the nation-state. In that atmosphere, every citizen is a threat to the nation other than its own, provided that he has one. To mitigate that threat, Kant suggests that we reach for universal values that can be formulated through universal principles. The principles ease commerce and limit nomadic travels because although the surface of the earth belongs to all, the territories are marked.

Kant's hospitality thus reduces the interaction between persons to a purely commercial interaction that would swallow human beings as well as goods. He eliminates the irreducible, unknowable, unforeseeable nature of the encounter with the other. He overlooks also the risk of personal loss and the generosity that interpersonal relations of nomadic hospitality necessitates. Kant's transactional and institutional hospitality replaces the pre- and post-Decalogue version. Hospitality is no longer mine to offer or not, but consists now of a right of the stranger.

Hospitality is a legal and principled contract rather than an encounter that transcends legislation or prediction. For him, the stranger is able to roam but the roaming cannot violate the integrity of national moral persons.

He thus transforms our understanding of the concept of hospitality. His analysis of hospitality leaves open the challenge that refugees, or individuals forced to flee persecution or natural disasters, pose to us in the contemporary period. All parties to the hospitality constitution that he advocates are autonomous but dependent on a commonly held, and presumably moral, law. The stranger has no right to asylum or permanent residence. In my understanding of Kant, the stranger is hostage to the nation-state as he is a fee-paying transient. Kant's formulation of hospitality simply undermines both cosmopolitanism and the hospitality that should sustain it. It practically and formally excludes the stranger and the foreigner. I do not know how Corneille would have survived his journey in a Kantian world.

The Foreigner

The determination of whether to be a welcoming or an excluding nation is an important component of contemporary political dialogue; it is also important for the thinking about the philosophy of peace and nonviolence. I follow Bonnie Honig's lead to discuss the role of the foreigner in contemporary and traditional democracy (Honig 2001). While McNulty informs our understanding of hospitality and confirms that Kant's commercial hospitality encourages a conditional cosmopolitanism, from my perspective, conditional cosmopolitanism is no cosmopolitanism at all. One is either at home or not. Commercial hospitality likewise is exclusionary and in fact, according to McNulty, it is no hospitality at all except if we think of it as conditional hospitality.

Commercial hospitality falls short of the hospitality that would motivate a cosmopolitan disposition or outlook. Cosmopolitan hospitality as commercial hospitality takes for granted that the nation is whole if it can determine its borders. It circles its members to exclude the foreigner in order to gain its own identity. Honig examines the philosophical ramifications of the role of the foreigner in the narrative of polity through the book of Ruth in the Hebrew Bible. To start, she argues that the foreigner who enters the polity is an outsider by definition and is also potentially a threat. To assuage the risk of threat, the foreigner proves herself a virtuous or worthy object of amity in various ways. Honig uses the figure of Ruth to show how the foreigner helps reinforce and found the nation.

So, the story goes:

> Elimelech and his wife Naomi leave Israel because of famine. They move to Moab, a flourishing nearby community. Soon after his arrival in Moab, Elimelech dies. His two sons Mahlon and Chilion marry two Moabites (Ruth and Orpah). All three violate the prohibition from Deuteronomy to marry Moabites. The sons too die (within ten years) leaving three childless widows.
>
> Naomi decides to return home having heard that the famine has ended in Israel. Her in-laws accompany her but she insists that they return home. Orpah reluctantly accepts her mother-in-law's command but Ruth persists. Arriving in Bethlehem, Naomi is welcomed by the women of the community. Naomi and Ruth live together. Ruth supports them by harvesting remnants from the field of Boaz, a relative of Naomi's. Ruth seduces Boaz and requests his protection in the form of marriage. Her alliance also helps recapture Naomi's inheritance from Elimelech. Boaz marries Ruth and they produce a son, Obed, who is given to Naomi to nurse. Obed, the progenitor of David and then eventually Jesus, initiates the kings of Israel.

> Elimelech's emigration and his marriage to the Moabite confirm that the Israelites have lost their social unity and cohesion. The move also reflects the porosity of proper boundaries/borders. Ruth redeems Israel, the ineffective nation, by adopting it. She restores its integrity by returning with Naomi and by founding a line of Kings in giving birth to Obed.
>
> *see Honig 2001*

The Book of Ruth considers the impact of the foreigner on a fully formed nation. Honig explains that the traditional readings of Ruth by Jewish readers are that she is the perfect example of virtuous devotion to either or both, God or her Israelite mother-in-law. By example, she turns the Israelites from corruption to their true spiritual path. Ruth is not a lawgiver per se, but the more distant and foreign she is, the clearer the objective positive value of (i.e. the more chosen) the people she joins.

Honig reads the Book of Ruth with the works of Ozick (Ozick 1996) and Kristeva (Kristeva 1991) to demonstrate that the story sheds light not only on the use of the foreigner as a significant constituent of the founding narrative of nations but also, in part, as a discourse on immigration and conversion. She holds that for Ozick, Ruth converts to Judaic monotheism and thus confirms the worthiness of the Jewish God. Ozick's Ruth exemplifies the appeal of monotheism by locating it in a state and establishing a royal lineage. Ruth's foreignness is absorbed through her conversion.

By contrast, Honig explains that for Kristeva, Ruth unsettles the order of things. She makes the Israelites more open to difference and to otherness. She prepares the way to a cosmopolitan identity. She is also a model for contemporary migrants (Muslim or otherwise) who are said to be resistant to the receiving regimes that purport to accommodate them. This reading foretells the ongoing attitude vis-à-vis the immigrant. The latter are valued but are such either for bringing us diversity or for giving us grounds to reappreciate our regime's virtues. They confirm that we are, as a nation, objects of desire.

For Honig however both Ozick's and Kristeva's interpretations are flawed because they understand Ruth on a single register. They see her as a friend that invigorates the collective or the nation. Her foreignness is domesticated. Therefore, against Ozick's and Kristeva's interpretations, Honig maintains that it is the foreignness that is to be valued, not the domestication, not 'the turning of the other into us.' With Honig, Ruth's foreignness engenders her influence as a founding agent to fuel a meaningful cosmopolitanism. She holds that Ruth's immigration and her status as a foreigner cannot be sublimated. Her 'Ruth' is at once friend and enemy. She thus invites a reconfiguration of the public space by triggering the question of how she might be accommodated in the public square.

Honig sees Ruth as an active agent who models a new kind of political agency. She represents those agents who make claims in advance of the categories that would legitimate such claims "in absence of proper legal standing" (Honig 2001: 61). Referring to Arendt's "right to have rights" attributed to those stateless persons who are always a step away from securing the rights granted by appurtenance in states or already protected by the apparatus of the state, Honig invites us to examine the status of the immigrant. We tend to parse the status of the immigrant as an object of charity or hospitality from its alternative status as "a full agent empowered to make claims on her own behalf" (Honig 2001: 62). Honig is clearly extrapolating from the book of Ruth, as she admits that Ruth never fully exhibits such agency and as such, Honig believes that her move away from Moab portends a normative and unconditional cosmopolitanism.

Honig does not deny that Kristeva favors a cosmopolitanism. In fact, Kristeva supports a cosmopolitanism that improves on Kant's initiative. Kristeva's cosmopolitanism situates the nation as a significant, but not exclusive, site of personal and political identity (Honig 2001: 63). Her cosmopolitanism is secured by a series of affective sets: self, family, community, homeland, continent, and humanity. At each level, these sets neatly inform and prepare the person for the next and more encompassing set. Identities, in Kristeva's view, cannot go beyond themselves unless they are asserted satisfactorily first, at an earlier level. This suggests a cumulative view of identity formation that would exempt refugees or wanderers like Corneille. One should also notice that this neat option of unfolding identities is not open to the very individuals that command immediately cosmopolitan values. Affirming identity before surpassing it is not an option accorded refugees or members of the immigrant communities, especially if these sets are contained within the nation-state.

We improve our national polity, and certainly our democracy, not by a conversion or a rejection of the foreigner, not by sending her back home where she came from, but rather, as Honig maintains, by facilitating various modes of collaboration, collective actions, and civic powers, and by remembering the past. In the example of Ruth proposed previously, Honig argues that such spaces for collaboration are open to Naomi because as she returns home, she is restored. She regains her full agency. Ruth, by contrast, has limited resources. She loses her transnational connections and is forbidden to mourn that loss for the sake of statal/communal stability. However, her loss permanently prevents the adopted community from becoming whole and integral. Ruth confirms the Israelites' identity as the chosen people as she also deeply threatens it. Ruth shores up enclosures and nationalism—but not democratic dialogue.

Conclusion: Cosmopolitanism and the State

Nationalism is practiced in the company of others. Identities are complex and multiple and one shapes one's identity with the help of at least one 'other.' As we have seen, nationalism thrives on identifying the foreigner to assert its boundaries. I have argued that nationalism mistreats the foreigner. Patriotism, as the adoption and support of national ideals, scapegoats the foreigner in various ways. The foreigner frightens and, as he is perceived as a risk, destabilizes the nation. To eliminate the threat, one expects him to shed his foreignness. The foreigner severs ties with his foreignness to rid himself of his difference or multiple identities. Thus, by its rejection of the foreigner, nationalism promotes a rejection of difference, of complexity, and of plurality. It creates and nurtures otherness, since it needs 'the other' against which it asserts national identity.

The ethics of hospitality familiarizes us with the opacity we find in ourselves and in 'the other.' It encourages amity in our interaction with the different. Versions of cosmopolitanism have attempted to articulate how to practice the ethics of hospitality. The recent planned and spontaneous demonstrations that publicly and globally resisted President Trump's early executive orders and his proposed policies regarding immigrants from certain nations help us identify a future for cosmopolitanism. These fraternal or sisterly coalitions displayed across the continent and the globe are the best antidote to a narrow, retrograde, and dangerous nationalism.

Honig would understand these marches as proofs or models of fraternal relations that bypass state structures and boundaries. The demonstrations do not carry out a single project. They enable people to cross over borders and national walls to empathize with the other. They show that people the world over develop a congruent sense of responsibility and 'at oneness' with the other (Honig 2001: 72). They help reassert values occluded by the statal machineries, especially authoritarian ones. In contrast with authoritarian and patriotic tendencies, such relations and demonstrations help reveal values common to our humanity.

I argue here for a cosmopolitanism that affirms an interconnected and interlaced world and which helps exemplify the concept of hospitality that keeps us from seeing the other as the enemy. Unification under a nationalist or patriotic vision is hostile to the contemporary environment in which we live. A world that advocates such a unification is antiquated regardless of whether it is practiced in the contemporary period. Furthermore, the observation that the practice is prevalent need not negate that it is in fact antiquated. Yes, folks are practicing it as they would practice many behaviors or modes of life that are no longer consistent or relevant for the world toward which we are progressing. The intransigence does not nullify the inevitable.

Honig helps me propose an alternative to the patriotic vision. She also reminds us that nationalism draws meaning against a background story and is developed for a particular purpose, i.e. the promotion of state institutions and the body politic. In view of this tendency, many of the liberal political thinkers who worked on the concept of government sought to justify the role of national government and the sustenance of the state apparatus.

The individual, the lynchpin of liberal political musings, needed convincing to accept state power. She needed to see that the state is an acceptable institution because after all, its purpose was to promote the individual's own viability and its own disposition. Patriotism aims to replace that focus on the protection of individual liberty. It rejects the liberal interpretation of the state apparatus as we reap the danger of the power ceded to the state out of fear. Reasonable though the fear of violence by foreigners may have been at the moment of the early implementations, it has given way to the uncritical acceptance of an authoritarian state. Anyone who purports to be constitutive of the state or receive its protection is expected to bend to it.

Rather than having the state justify itself for burdening the individual, it is now the individuals who are expected to justify themselves in order to be part of the state. The birth of the nation-state is consistent with the Westphalian moment, or with the rendition McNulty and Honig offer for the state of Israel. Both geneses set borders and exclude those who are unwilling to accept the unifying concept for these groups of individuals, whether it be God or the nation. Such agnostics or skeptics threaten the boundaries that determine the grounds from which we decide whom to accept or reject. The post-Decalogue and post-Westphalia worlds are, to be sure, worlds with borders but ones that exclude humanity. The world that the biblical environment spoke of is clearly not the world in which we live.

This truth we know: individuals are interconnected and interact with one another. Jettisoning the 'foreigner as threat,' I am inviting us to see patriotism as the threat that it truly is. We need a new way of interacting with one another and it cannot be through the prism of patriotism.

My proposal is that we shift the focus away from appropriated state and land, and focus instead on the need, the "right to have rights" of the traveling wanderer—of someone like Corneille who is displaced by violence from his home. Rather than erecting walls, doors instead ought to be opened. It is not for the individual to be *able to go* anywhere and feel at home. This disposition requires layers of familiarity. Indeed, it requires familiarity with travels, with different cultures, with different languages. It requires the comfort of being at home with difference in general. Yet that cultivated familiarity is not an option for those most in need of hospitality, those who are most in need of feeling at home.

Cosmopolitanism implies that we uphold the fundamental value of human viability everywhere. Pacifists and advocates of nonviolence ought to embrace a robust form of cosmopolitanism. The globe is indeed all of ours, so all of us have a responsibility to make it habitable and welcoming to every member of the globe, whether they are crossing borders—which are spurious concepts because they are consistent with nationalism, and especially in light of my preceding criticism of nationalism—or whether they are indeed staying put wherever they are. This is the burden of cosmopolitanism. It is a political as well as an ethical challenge. We must embrace or shoulder them both, regardless of whether we want to admit it or not. Our survival depends on our response.

Works Cited

Banerjee, C. (2017). "Identities, Diasporas, Cosmopolitanisms, and the Possibility of Global Humanities." *Institute for the Humanities- Simon Fraser University*. Available at: www.sfu.ca/humanities-Institute/contours/i4_p1.html (Accessed 20 October 2017).

Beharie, N. (host) (2017). *AfroPop: The Ultimate Cultural Exchange Program*: "Intore ('The Chosen')." PBS affiliate in Charlotte WNSC Channel 1030, originally aired 23 January 2017. Available at: www.pbs.org/video/2365934924/ (Accessed 30 March 2017).

Honig, B. (2001). *Democracy and the Foreigner*. Princeton: Princeton University Press.

Kant, I. (1795). "Third Definitive Article for a Perpetual Peace." *Perpetual Peace: A Philosophical Sketch* Section II. Available at: www.constitution.org/kant/perpeace.htm (Accessed 30 June 2017).

King, Jr., M. L. (1967). "The World House." Available at: http://pluralism.org/document/the-world-house-martin-luther-king-jr-1967 (Accessed 30 June 2017).

King, Jr., M. L. (1972). "The Quest for Peace and Justice," in F.W. Haberman (ed.), *Nobel Lectures, Peace 1951–1970*. Amsterdam: Elsevier Publishing Co. Available at: www.nobelprize.org/nobel_prizes/peace/laureates/1964/king-lecture.html (Accessed 30 June 2017).

Kristeva, J. (1991). *Strangers to Ourselves*, translated by L.S. Roudiez. New York: Columbia University Press.

McNulty, T. (2007). *The Hostess: Hospitality, Femininity, and the Expropriation of Identity*. Minneapolis, MN: University of Minnesota Press.

Ozick, C. (1996). "Ruth," in J. A. Kates and G. T. Reimer (eds.), *Reading Ruth: Contemporary Women Reclaim a Sacred Story*. New York: Ballantine, 211–232.

Souffrant, E. (2006). "Corporate Responsibility as Governance," in S. Servomaa (ed.), *Humanity at the Turning Point: Rethinking Nature, Culture and Freedom*. Helsinki, Finland: Renvall Institute Publications, 23 (2006), 433–440.

Souffrant, E. (2013). *Identity, Political Freedom and Collective Responsibility: Pillars and Foundations of a Global Ethics*. New York: Palgrave.

21

WARISM AND THE DOMINANT WORLDVIEW

Duane L. Cady

Warism is the position that war is morally justifiable both in principle and in fact. Some warists go so far as to say war is at times morally required, both for individuals and for their country. Warism can be expressed in a variety of ways. Always the basic notion is that war can be morally acceptable and thus that alternatives to war may be entertained only to the extent that they are likely to provide advantages over available war options. Pacifism, in contrast, is the view that war is morally wrong, by its very nature, and that we should be committed to peaceful resolution of conflict. Most pacifists oppose war itself, not merely this war or that; and pacifists work for positive peace, that is, social order that comes from agreement within and among groups, not negative peace, that is, order imposed by threat or force from the outside. There are many forms of pacifism—degrees of moral opposition to war and degrees of commitment to positive peace—but the general notion is the immorality of war and the goodness of peace.

Pacifists are a tiny minority. The overwhelmingly dominant attitude is simply taking war for granted as morally acceptable. War is what nations do, and pacifists are for the most part dismissed as well-meaning but misguided and hopelessly naïve. Warism is accepted almost universally and is the primary cultural obstacle to peace.

In every culture there are fundamental ideas, assumptions, concepts, and values that together form a frame of reference or cultural outlook through which members of the culture see the world. These fundamentals are so obvious from within that they are rarely recognized as having been taken for granted. Consider the Copernican Revolution as an example of a dominant cultural perspective that shapes how we experience the world. For more than a thousand years Europeans took for granted that the sun orbits the earth, but seventeenth-century science challenged the old earth-centered model of Ptolemy. Eventually the general perception of the mechanics of our solar system shifted to the now familiar sun-centered model of Copernicus, advocated by Galileo: we understand our weather patterns, seasons, and orientation to other planets and stars all to be consequences of how Earth orbits our sun. The way our solar system works did not change in the seventeenth century, but dominant perceptions did. And this change of basic outlook shook prevailing institutions to their foundations. Since we now take the sun-centered model for granted it is hard to imagine the fundamental conceptual shift involved.

Another example, but closer to our own experience, is our ongoing cultural adjustment over the theory of evolution. Cultures untouched by Western science find accepting modern scientific claims about human life emerging from less complex life forms to be impossible. Perceiving from within traditional understandings of divine creation makes an evolutionary development of human life beyond belief. Of course there are traditionalists within our culture as well as folks attached to traditional religious views but otherwise accepting of modernity. Both can get pretty defensive if their views are questioned. Some see the two models as compatible, thinking there's no reason for science and religion to be at odds. Others see evolutionism and creationism as diametrically opposed and accept one or the other. When the models are taken to exclude one another, fundamental differences in outlook are at stake. One's orientation to reality—even to the meaning of life—may depend on believing in a divine rather than a biological explanation of human origins, or vice versa. Challenging someone's view on this issue may be uncomfortable, even threatening, not only because they take their view seriously but because they take it as a "given."

Notions of race, gender, sexual orientation, class, and more can work in the same way. Without malicious intent—and without critical self-examination—people have taken for granted that black Americans were best suited for physical labor rather than the professions, that women interested in medicine were better suited to nursing than to becoming physicians, that men became corporate executives or heads of state while women were to remain secretaries or administrative assistants. Gay men, lesbians, and transgender folks were expected to keep their expressions of affection private despite the constant public display of heterosexuality. Poor people, expected to remain satisfied in "their place," were not supposed to aspire to positions of leadership as teachers, doctors, business leaders, or politicians. It should be obvious that unconscious assumptions about reality have significant implications for values as well as beliefs. Cultural "givens" are often like normative lenses; they shape and color much that we perceive and conceive. Resulting prejudices are exposed and addressed only after careful examination of presuppositions. Doing philosophy is, in part, making explicit the assumptions that stand behind our fundamental perspectives, values, and beliefs, as is questioning such assumptions and considering alternatives. The more basic the hidden presumptions, the more difficult their examination.

In our modern world, warism is a dominant outlook. Warists bear no special burden of justification for taking war for granted as morally justifiable; in fact, the greater burden of justification typically rests with those opposed to war. This fact alone qualifies warism as the sort of unconscious assumption we have been considering. It seems so obvious to most of us that we don't realize we're assuming it. As a result, pacifism rarely gets taken seriously; everybody "knows" it is naïve and unrealistic. Since we see war as normal and natural, all we can do is avoid it if possible and win if it can't be avoided. We even take for granted that it's morally right to threaten war in an effort to prevent it, and some accept "preemptive war."

Warism pervades not only politics but virtually all aspects of culture, including business, education, popular culture, and even religion. This is not a conspiracy; advertising, television programming, and school curricula all tend to reflect warism, from popular heroes like G.I. Joe, Rambo, and the galaxy of superheroes to a variety of role models like professional athletes and entertainers. Conflicts often become tests of superiority. Politicians express their seriousness on issues by declaring "war" on drugs, poverty, illiteracy, crime, and so on. Athletes are expected to go beyond winning; they must dominate, even humiliate their opponents with an "in your face" arrogance. Big games are battles, championships are wars. Even scholars try to be survivors of academic jousting, often embattled in verbal attack and rejoinder. The philosopher is a warrior fighting for truth, defending principle (and honor), exchanging linguistic blows in a struggle to defeat rivals and win arguments (see Burtt 1969). In all segments of society we see battles for superiority whenever conflict arises.

Individual autonomy, personal integrity, rights to privacy, property, and freedom from governmental interference, fighting for what we believe in against all odds, all are examples of fundamental values that are for the most part uncritically adopted. Warism is another, but less noticed and less often acknowledged. In political science and history classes in the US students learn, for example, about our nation: born in righteous violent revolution, expanded through wars with Native Americans, unified in civil war, a superpower preeminent after coming out on top in two world wars. School curricula routinely discuss battles, tactics, and military leadership, but pacifists, anti-war activists, and models of cooperation rather than military domination rarely arise in class lessons. This emphasis is no surprise given the warism taken for granted culturally.

Western culture traditionally attempts value-free public education and thus puts little emphasis on moral or political evaluation of current or past public policy. Public school teachers are supposed to teach facts or skills while values are left to parents, family, and religious institutions. Increasing realization that all teaching is laden with hidden values has made parents—and school boards—more likely to ban controversial topics in order to avoid introducing values incompatible with the mainstream, thereby reinforcing the status quo.

Warism is not only imbedded in popular culture; studies of academic philosophers' attitudes on war demonstrate that "the great bulk of philosophers who have spoken on the question of war have supported and defended it as an instrument of social change" (Steinkraus 1969: 3). Often academic philosophers justify war not in itself but as a means to some important end, like peace or self-defense. Warren Steinkraus describes philosophy professors' reactions to war, saying that "studied aloofness, which invariably means tacit acceptance" is the most common attitude, followed by "overt defense of a particular national policy." The next most common is "reluctant and even hesitant justification" with the least common being "direct criticism with or without consideration of alternatives" (Steinkrauss 1969: 6). This account could be extrapolated to describe academics generally.

Additional evidence that our common cultural disposition takes the moral justifiability of war for granted is the fact that pacifists are generally expected to defend their view whereas those accepting war as a normal and natural activity of nations rarely get asked to justify theirs. We, as a society, presume that the burden of proof rests on those morally opposed to war because warism is a cultural given, a general assumption in our contemporary world. This is not saying that all nations are belligerent; rather, it says that the war system, the standard practice of sovereign states constantly preparing for, threatening, and engaging in war, goes almost wholly unquestioned. People in and outside of government may disagree about whether and how to prosecute a particular war, but war itself is almost never challenged on moral grounds. The system is not in question. Given this context, it is understandable that those questioning the war system are met with hostility. Political candidates have no option but to present themselves as "tougher" than their opponents, and all candidates must be wary of being characterized as "soft on the enemy," "weak on defense," or hesitant to stand firm against adversaries. All of this reinforces the dominant warist attitude and belittles its critics. As a result, alternatives to the war system—pacifist views in particular—are not taken seriously because "everybody knows" how implausible pacifism is.

Warism may be held implicitly or explicitly. In its implicit form, warism takes war to be normal, natural, and morally justifiable. It never occurs to the holder that war in itself could be morally problematic. No other way of conceiving large-scale human conflict has ever come to mind. Like racism, sexism, and homophobia, warism is a prejudicial presumption that distorts judgments and beliefs with no awareness of bias by the holder. In its explicit form warism is deliberately chosen and openly articulated without apology. Explicit warists regard war as essential to secure justice and defend national security. In both forms warism misguides judgments and institutions by reinforcing the necessity and inevitability of war, thereby precluding alternatives and obstructing all challenges to the dominant conceptual framework of the culture, namely, taking the war system for granted. In this way warism is the single greatest obstacle to building a more peaceful world.

In *Just and Unjust Wars*, Michael Walzer explains that "war is always judged twice, first with reference to the reasons states have for fighting, secondly with reference to the means they adopt" (Walzer 1977: 21). But there is a third judgment of war that should be made prior to these two: might war in itself be morally wrong by its very nature? Walzer considers this question in an appendix, as an afterthought, and dismisses it as naïve. In a way we should not fault him for the dismissal; after all, his goal is to describe conventional morality and, as we have seen, it *does* take warism for granted. To this extent Walzer is right, and this is exactly the point: warist normative lenses blind us to the fundamental question, not whether this or that war is warranted or whether this or that behavior may be allowed in war, but whether war itself can be morally justified.

Our culture's slowly increasing awareness of racism, sexism, and homophobia, of ethnic, religious, class, and environmental oppression, and of group efforts at liberation offer hope that even the most deeply held and least explicit cultural predispositions may be recognized and examined. Perhaps those oppressed by warism may eventually begin to free us from accepting war as an inevitable condition of nature. After all, 200 years ago slavery was an accepted and established social institution taken for granted by most as a natural condition for beings considered inferior to the dominant group. Slavery was considered essential to the strength of the American economy. Yet within less than two centuries slavery is no longer tolerated. Although deep racial prejudices persist, slavery is universally condemned. This demonstrates that even the most deeply held values, allegedly essential to the survival of society and grounded in nature, *can* fundamentally change relatively quickly, with profound implications. John Dewey links this to warism: "War is as much a social pattern [for us] as was the domestic slavery which the ancients thought to be immutable fact" (Dewey 1946: 186). The civil rights era has helped us see that a racial hierarchy does not determine human worth. Feminism has taught us that dominant attitudes about people are more likely values we choose than innate features of human nature. Parallel to racial and gender liberation, pacifism questions taking war for granted, seeking to expose warism as racism and sexism have been exposed.

Warist bias routinely involves flip dismissal of pacifism, often confusing pacifism with passivism. "Pacifism," from the Latin *pax, pacis*, peace, originally a compact, plus *facere*, to make, means peacemaking or agreement making. "Passivism," from the Latin *passivus*, suffering, means being inert or inactive, suffering acceptance. Pacifists need not be passivists and vice versa. Often pacifists are activists committed to making peace, forging consensual agreement, contributing to harmonious social conduct cooperative from within rather than orderly by force from the outside. Pacifism is more than moral opposition to war; it includes active efforts to understand and make peace. As long as pacifism, working for cooperative societies through agreement without violence, is confused with passivism, appeasement and suffering acceptance, we will expect no alternative to forced and imposed social order. Warism reinforces the confusion between pacifism and passivism by blurring the distinction between them, something easy to do since the words sound alike. In fact pacifists typically reject passivism. Even Gandhi, the world's icon of pacifism since early in the twentieth century, says that when the only choice is between violence and giving in, he recommends violence, adding that the choice is rarely so clear and that nonviolent alternatives can be found if they are sought. Pacifism "does not mean meek submission to the will of evil-doer, but it means pitting one's whole soul against the will of the tyrant" (Gandhi 1951: 132).

Beyond the cultural predisposition to warism and the tendency to confuse pacifism for passivism is the warist's inclination to caricature anyone sympathetic to peaceful alternatives to war as a pacifist of the most extreme sort. Warism describes pacifism as monolithic and absolute when in fact there are many versions of pacifism along a moral restraint continuum between warism and the absolute prohibition of force always, everywhere, for everyone. Degrees of pacifism vary: pragmatically choosing nonviolence as a tactic (where violence is not likely to yield the desired result), rejecting mass violence while allowing even lethal personal self-defense, rejecting both mass and interpersonal violence while allowing capital punishment since it is adjudicated by law, rejecting all violence against human beings while allowing it against other forms of life, and so on. While a thorough discussion of the range of pacifist views cannot be undertaken here, it is important to note that not all pacifism is absolute even though warists often describe it as such (for more see Cady 1989/2010).

Warism results in a dominant attitude among many people that keeping the peace means preserving the status quo. Often those with this idea of peace are in privileged positions relative to those against whom they see violence as warranted.

Any threat to the status quo, the way things are, is seen to require "defense against aggression," usually without considering the possibility that their advantaged status may have oppressive implications for others. Whenever some humans enjoy disproportionate advantage, others are left at disproportionate disadvantage. If the population of the US is about 4 percent of the population of the world and if the US consumes about a third of what the world produces, then 96 percent of the people on earth are left with roughly two-thirds of global production. If North America and Europe together constitute 13 percent of the global population and together consume two-thirds of world production, then 87 percent of the world's population is left dividing roughly one-third of global production. The numbers here are not as important as the relative proportions of population and consumption. While there is a lot of talk about "undeveloped" nations, rarely do we hear talk of "overdeveloped" nations. Yet when population and distribution of goods and services are so imbalanced, tensions arise. The point here is that such tensions can result in conflict, and those in advantaged positions are inclined to "defend" their relative advantage against "aggression." The status quo, the way population and consumption are distributed globally in this example, may be accurate, yet the fact that things are as they are may not necessarily justify that things are as they should be. By encouraging an understanding of peace as the defense of the status quo, warism blinds us to possible injustice and obfuscates questions about the morality of war.

The pervasive view that keeping the peace means preserving the status quo leads to suspicion of those opposed to war. Emotional, intellectual, and moral strength are threatening to those used to dealing in physical, especially military, strength. So it's not surprising that those who see peace as preservation of the way things are tend to regard advocates of nonviolence as incompatible with "national security," insufficiently patriotic, or otherwise suspect. All of this grows out of warism. It is easy to forget that America's eighteenth-century freedom fighters were terrorists to King George III. Of course those in the relatively disadvantaged position may likewise consider peace as defense of the status quo and consequently reject peace since it locks in place their disadvantage. And those in the middle, between the relatively advantaged and disadvantaged, may see peace as defense of the status quo as well and side with the advantaged only to avoid ending up on the disadvantaged side. Change can be threatening because it promises the unfamiliar; at least the status quo offers relative stability. All of this is to say that social inertia favors conservatism unless conditions become extreme. Again, warism prevails.

We cannot set aside all of our preconceptions at will, but calling attention to the possibility that they may be prejudicial can open our minds and encourage us to begin examining warism.

Developing minds sufficiently courageous to question the most fundamental beliefs of our culture itself is difficult and dangerous. But such is necessary if we are to find our way to a more peaceful world, and warism may be our most formidable obstacle to that world.

Works Cited

Burtt, E. A. (1969). "Philosophers as Warriors," in R. Ginsberg (ed.), *The Critique of War*. Chicago: Henry Regnery, 30–42.

Cady, D. L. (1989/2010). *From Warism to Pacifism: A Moral Continuum*. Philadelphia: Temple University Press.

Dewey, J. (1946). *Problems of Man*. New York: Philosophical Library.

Gandhi, M. K. (1951). "The Doctrine of the Sword," in B. Kumarappa (ed.), *Nonviolent Resistance*. New York: Schocken, 132–143.

Steinkraus, W. E. (1969). "War and the Philosopher's Duty," in R. Ginsberg (ed.), *The Critique of War*. Chicago: Henry Regnery, 3–29.

Walzer, M. (1977). *Just and Unjust Wars*. New York: Basic Books.

22

THE MILITARY-INDUSTRIAL COMPLEX

William Gay

The military-industrial complex (MIC) is the informal, powerful, and entrenched network between the military establishment and the defense industry. This network, which has been explicitly identified since the 1960s, permeates the design, development, and procurement of weapons and military technologies, rallies public support for expansion of military budgets, and influences public policy on military need, spending, and operations. Military interests in continuous growth and corporate interests in increasing profits work together in the MIC in ways that are difficult to challenge, even though they can and often do run counter to national security and public interest.

Although the MIC and militarism are closely associated, they are not identical. Militarism can be defined as belief in and practice of constant preparation for war. Sometimes militarism is also associated with subordination of civilian control and interests to the military and its sympathizers. This latter feature can distinguish militarism from the MIC in which, by contrast, either coalescence occurs between civilian and military/governmental control or a decisive influence of industrial interests gains increasing dominance over military/governmental control. While militarism existed prior to and can exist apart from the MIC, in the MIC the influence of industrial interests and their motive for profit is distinctive. Early in the twentieth century Karl Liebknecht stressed the connections of capitalism and militarism to class society and class struggle (Liebknecht 2011). While these correlations are evident, most non-capitalist economies also display militarism and the influence of the MIC. As a consequence, the relevance of this perspective no longer captures the manner in which the MIC has transformed economic systems and militarism on a global scale.

Many groups are highly critical of the influence and dangers posed by the military-industrial complex. Because of their methods and goals, pacifists and advocates of nonviolence have taken especially strong stands against the MIC. Ethical and religious critics of the negative impact of the MIC stretch from the moral indictments of Martin Luther King, Jr. to the pleas of Pope Francis. King eventually broadened his social criticisms to include the violence and costs of war and preparation for war. In a similar vein, Pope Francis criticizes how the endless quest for profit sanctions war at the expense of peace and social justice. These and related criticisms of the MIC make clear that advancement of the work of pacifists and advocates of nonviolence requires a careful examination of and response to the MIC.

War and preparation for war have been around a lot longer than the military-industrial complex, but now efforts to end war or to reduce reliance on preparation for war cannot make much progress without confronting the military-industrial complex and its ties with capitalism. Advocates for a strong defense establishment, as well as advocates for largely unregulated capitalism, often at least accept or even support the alliance between the military and industry. Anti-militarists and peace activists typically want a critique of capitalism and the MIC and search for alternative approaches to security. While much critical and alternative literature is available theoretically, little progress has been made practically in relation to addressing the extensive influence of the military-industrial complex. Critical assessments of the role of capitalism often rely on parts of the analysis of capitalism developed initially by Karl Marx in the latter half of the nineteenth century and subsequently to efforts associated with C. Wright Mills, Seymour Melman, and others who have analyzed the military-industrial complex since the latter half of the twentieth century.

The free-market model of capitalism (laissez-faire economics) might seem to be less liable to entanglement in the MIC than either state-sponsored models of capitalism (Keynesian economics) or even explicitly non-capitalist (typically socialist) models. In practice, however, each of these economic models can be and has been co-opted by the MIC; so, this contrast is more theoretical than actual. Nevertheless, theoretically, the contrast is often made between unregulated free-market (laissez-faire) economies and planned (managerial) or command economies. For many decades, however, the global reality is more one of mixed economies that aim to preserve the benefits of free markets and at least some respect for the aims of human rights and social justice of planned economies. In the mixed economies that now operate globally, the MIC exercises a decisive influence on military spending and often on foreign policy (Gay and Alekseeva 1996).

President Dwight Eisenhower is generally credited with the introduction of the phrase "the military-industrial complex" (MIC) in his 1961 Farewell Address, in which he warned against its "unwarranted influence," but he had previously used this phrase and other uses of the term had occurred even earlier. Practices associated with what became known as the MIC date back at least to the efforts by Great Britain, France, and Germany starting in the 1880s that aimed to develop land and sea military supports for their respective empires, and such practices really have occurred throughout much of the history of the modern great powers, including in the United States (Koistinen 2003). In the nuclear age (to which Eisenhower, in part, was responding), the collusion between military and economic interests becomes quite visible, particularly in the enormously expensive military budgets during and subsequent to World War II. In brief, the MIC depends on war and promotes war—sometimes unintentionally, though too often intentionally. The impact of the MIC is felt throughout society. Beyond the obvious military and economic impacts, the MIC involves decreases in access to information by the public, in the amount of transparency by political and military leaders, and in the scope of democratic practices in a wide range of social institutions.

Estimates of MIC spending are difficult to determine and to assess. Some information is privileged. Reporting is not always candid. Dollars amounts listed are not always adjusted for inflation. Different sources cite different amounts, and the perspectives of many analysts affect their estimates and reports. Nevertheless, the economic scope of the MIC can be conveyed in general terms that are fairly reliable. In this regard, the example of the United States largely conveys the gargantuan economic scale of the MIC. The American Pentagon budget exceeds $700 billion a year and U.S. intelligence spending adds at least $80 billion more a year. Addition of the Department of State and the Department of Homeland Security brings the total closer to $1 trillion a year. Beyond these totals are the costs of the recent U.S. wars in Iraq and

Afghanistan. The total cost per U.S. soldier in wars like the ones in Iraq and Afghanistan is about $1 million a year. By comparison, at the same time, one in seven citizens in the United States lives below the poverty line, and spending on the U.S. infrastructure continues to decline. These and other similar correlations are not just coincidental. "Guns" and "butter" is much more myth than reality ("Military-Industrial Complex" 2003). In comparison to U.S. expenditures, the individual spending of any other nation or combination of nations has relatively little impact on the MIC and responses to it.

The MIC Formula and Its Scope

At the extremes are views that reject the MIC formula and views that expand it to include a very large portion of industrialized economic and cultural activity. To regard the term "the military-industrial complex" as a misnomer and characterize it as merely one aspect of the enormous industrial system that has emerged since World War II is myopic and misses the qualitative distinctiveness of this transformation within society. At the same time, the extension of the term should not be so great that it obscures the ability to focus on its most salient features. Still, some expansion on the term is appropriate, given the rapidly expanding influence of the military-industrial complex on so many facets of society. To the MIC formula some quite appropriately also add Congress to get the "military-industrial-congressional complex"—also known as the "iron triangle" ("Military-Industrial Complex" 2002). Eisenhower himself is reported to have had this phrase in an early draft of his Farewell Address but dropped it because of the political complications associated with explicitly linking Congress to this collusion. While the role of Congress or some other parliamentary body plays a role in democratic societies, the MIC pairs itself with whatever power brokers and influence peddlers help entrench and enrich it. Other terms are sometimes added as well, such as -educational (-scientific, -academic), -security, -internet, -media, -entertainment, and even -spiritual. As a consequence, the term can become so elastic as to obscure a connection with the military, such as "global industrial complex," which includes the criminal justice complex, prison complex, nonprofit complex, agricultural complex, medical complex, and even animal complex (Best et al. 2011). The use of "complex" with these terms at the least suggests the connection with big business and high profits, but this use of "complex" also entails forms of social and economic control that are often distinct from or only loosely associated with types of military operations. Such extension is also found in the term "disaster capitalism complex," which connects how private industries reap great profits from both war and natural disasters (Klein 2007). The shock of disasters, whether caused by war or by nature, allows for profits from "recovery" to go largely unchecked and also reduces the prospect of revolt by the masses of people who have lost their social safety nets. In addition and ostensibly as "safeguards," walls and concrete barriers of various sorts are erected and yield further profits for the industries involved in their construction and maintenance. Such military or military-like "fortifications" are now common around airports, embassies, and prisons and in fortified checkpoints and gated communities. (Such practices are sometimes termed "security apartheid," namely, the protection of the haves from the have-nots.) Nevertheless, even if these more far-reaching analyses conflate the MIC with other aspects of corporate greed, they point to problems with each and to the intertangling, if not the interdependence, of the two.

The phrase "military-industrial complex" is overall making a link between the military and the economy, especially capitalism. In this regard, two of the key historical theorists are C. Wright Mills and Seymour Melman. On the military side, in his 1956 *The Power Elite* Mills coined the term "military metaphysics" to express the thinking that perceives and treats international affairs from a military perspective (Mills 1956). He defines military metaphysics as "a military definition of reality" (198) and as "the cast of mind that defines international reality as basically military" (222). He also asserts, "During World War II, the merger of the corporate economy and the military bureaucracy came into its present-day significance" (212). Within philosophy, Duane Cady much later coined the similar term of "warism" to refer to the normative lens through which national security is viewed as requiring the capacity to wage war and hence the need to prepare for and to develop justifications of war (Cady 1989). On the economic side, Melman in the 1970s coined the terms "pentagon capitalism" and "permanent war economy" to express how war had become the dominating business nationally and internationally (Melman 1970, 1974). Of course, while capitalism has increasingly dominated globalization, other economic systems have had and continue to have similar complexes (materially and psychologically). The MIC or "iron triangle" has both national and international expressions (such as the ones in the United States and in the European Union), has little market competition, guarantees the profits for private firms, is inordinately expensive, and has questionable value in achieving national security. (The European Union relies heavily on NATO, which is itself influenced by the MIC; the same is true of other regional alliances around the world.) For the period between 1998 and 2003, the Center for Public Integrity analyzed over two million defense contracts totaling close to $1 trillion and summarized their findings. The top five recipients were Lockheed Martin ($94 billion), Boeing ($82 billion), Raytheon (close to $40 billion), Northrop and Grumman (close to $34 billion), and General Dynamic (also close to $34 billion) (Center for Public Integrity 2004). These contracts are not just for items such as weapons and delivery systems. They also include involvement from surveillance and interrogation to supplying toilet seats and other everyday supplies.

Perspectives on the fate of the MIC vary greatly—from it being at an end, to it being intractable, to it being amenable to policy changes. Theorists in the vein of Francis Fukuyama view capitalism as potentially eternal, while on some interpretations of Karl Marx other theorists view capitalism as eventually collapsing due to its own internal contradictions. Of course, from an empirical point of view, the fate of the MIC is an open question. The military-industrial complex is a social, political, and economic institution. Like all institutions, it is historical and is subject to change over time. Most theories of the MIC concede this point, even if they present mechanisms to delay or hasten its end.

In an influential 2014 article in *Foreign Affairs* William J. Lynn III (former U.S. deputy secretary of defense and former lobbyist for defense-contractor Raytheon) contends, from the perspective of a sympathetic insider, that the MIC may be coming to an end—at least in its classical expression (Lynn 2014). According to Lynn, the U.S. defense industry has gone through three phases and is now entering a fourth. During the first phase (1787–1941), government-owned arsenals and shipyards were predominant and commercial industry was utilized only during wars such as WWI. In the second phase (1942–1992), as a result of President Franklin Roosevelt's War Production Board, the largest industrial enterprises were conscripted to support the war effort but were not dismantled after World War II, and over time the defense industry became the nation's largest industry. During this period, leaders in the defense industry included Boeing and General Motors and later AT&T, General Motors, and IBM. This phase lasted until the end of the Cold War and is often the model associated with the MIC. The third phase (1993–2013) began when, because of shrinking budgets, Deputy Secretary of Defense William Perry called for consolidation within the defense industry, and this phase spans the post-Cold War period through the initial responses to the attacks of 9/11. The fourth phase, beginning in about 2014, is one in which commercial companies now are increasingly shifting their research and development (R&D) toward cutting-edge technologies that significantly exceed what is being provided to the Pentagon. For example, Microsoft and Toyota spend twice as much on R&D as the five largest U.S. defense contractors. So, in order to attract commercial companies, the Department of Defense might need to solicit and accommodate commercial industry through changes such as loosening intellectual property rules and streamlining auditing and accounting requirements (Strauss 2014). While such changes may further alarm critics of the MIC, advocates accept past and future accommodations between military and capitalist interests that maintain the dominance of the MIC—regardless of how it is named.

In contradistinction to positive establishment views on the MIC, economist Ismael Hossein-Zadeh, from the perspective of a critical outsider, refers to "parasitic capitalism," "parasitic imperialism," and even "parasitic military imperialism" in addressing the future of the MIC (Hossein-Zadeh 2006). This use of "parasitic" refers to the way in which the MIC "feeds" on the economic systems with which it is involved. Like a parasite, the MIC tends to appropriate more and more from its "host" at the expense to the host of its "vitality" or even "viability." In the case of the MIC, the tendency is to continue to draw to itself more and more of the wealth of the nation. This tendency tends to favor military contractors and weakens public capital and resources for maintaining social infrastructure and for responding to natural disasters and also weakens civil liberties and democratic values.

According to Hossein-Zadeh, two basic groups have competed in relation to those supporting the MIC. The first group is associated with historical expressions of imperial militarism that regard ongoing expansions in military spending and a permanent war economy as ultimately unsustainable. By contrast, the second group—sometimes referred to as permanent military Keynesianism—views military spending as stimulating the economy both on a short-term basis and on a long-term basis. Hossein-Zadeh contends the latter group has prevailed. As a result, in expanding its imperial influence the United States has entered into many international military alliances, including NATO and ten other joint military-commands of Unified Combatant Commands (UCC) in Africa, Europe, the Pacific, and elsewhere. At the same time that the MIC continues to be the largest item in the federal budget, national income and resources are redistributed in favor of the wealthy, with recent U.S. wars providing a boon to contractors. As a result the creation of public capital (both physical and human) has been undermined with major neglect to constructing and maintaining transportation infrastructures, facilitating disaster relief, promoting and advancing health and education, and protecting civil liberties and democratic values. Going beyond the usual contrasts, Hossein-Zadeh also stresses that the future of the current expansion of the MIC will be determined by the "politics of public finance"—unless an eventual internal revolt or international war settles the matter in a more violent manner. From this perspective, the future of capitalism and the MIC cannot be separated from how social forces are managed and how class struggle plays out (Hossein-Zadeh 2006: 255). Nevertheless, in the interim, these tensions allow for achieving some limits to the expansion of the MIC.

The MIC and the Nuclear Arms Race

Did the nuclear arms race cause the MIC? No. The influence of capitalism on the emergence of the MIC predates the development of nuclear weapons by many decades, and the profit motive of capitalism is one of the hallmarks of the MIC. Did the nuclear arms race entrench the MIC into the economies and policies of the nuclear powers? Yes. The nuclear arms race, which spans much of the history of the MIC, is closely associated with its rapid rise, expansion, and continuing global influence. While the history and aims of the MIC are broader in scope than the history and aims of the nuclear arms race, a detailed consideration of the nuclear arms race illustrates the challenges, milestones, and costs of the MIC and, by implication, can suggest how the impact of the MIC is repeated in other areas.

The history of the policies on and the production and deployment of nuclear weapons illustrates the vast expanse and enormous profits generated by the MIC (Gay and Pearson 1987). The various technological aspects are so exorbitantly expensive that few highly industrialized nations—let alone subnational groups—have adequate budgets and expertise. To obtain atomic or fission weapons, over a half dozen technological and industrial challenges must be met. These challenges include mining, milling, and enriching uranium (to a high percentage of fissionable U-235 or to the even more costly conversion of U-238 into plutonium—fissionable Pu239), fabricating the nuclear weapons, testing and deploying them, and managing (for hundreds, if not thousands, of years) the low- and high-level radioactive waste produced in these processes. Production of hydrogen or fusion weapons is even more difficult. (Hydrogen bombs require atomic detonators to yield sufficiently high temperature for fusion and involve even higher costs and technological and industrial sophistication.) Then, use of nuclear weapons presents even greater challenges for and drains on the environment and on societies and their economies. For each step in these processes very sophisticated and extensive industries are required. The MIC is inexorably linked to achieving and expanding these processes and the military strength and industrial profits that they generate. The expansion is not only quantitative but also qualitative. Nuclear powers not only produce more weapons but also continually search for innovations that generally are even more costly—and likewise profitable for private defense contractors. This drive is partly sustained by marketing to the public a fear of vulnerability—from Sputnik to bomber gaps, missile gaps, counterforce vulnerability, the Evil Empire, threats from space-based systems, rogue states, al-Qaeda, ISIS—and the list goes on, including various villains of the decade such as Stalin, Mao, Castro, Ho Chi Min, bin Laden, and Hussein. (Whether these fears are truly substantial is another matter.)

Some would go so far as to locate the catapulting of the MIC to the Manhattan Project by means of which the United States developed the first atomic weapons. This massive "project" employed over 130,000 people and cost about $26 billion (in 2016 dollars). From the time of the atomic bombings of Hiroshima and Nagasaki in 1945 until the first Soviet atomic test in 1949, the United States had a monopoly as the sole nation with nuclear weapons. The Soviet development of atomic weapons prompted President Harry S. Truman to expand U.S. nuclear weapons programs. The resulting weapons programs and strategies epitomized the shift toward the Cold War, in which the United States adopted military policies that aimed at containment of Soviet expansion into Eastern and Western Europe. Truman ordered production of the hydrogen bomb and other conventional and nuclear weapons. The United States tested its first hydrogen bomb in 1952, and the Soviet Union followed in 1953. While the United States maintained a nuclear monopoly in the 1940s and superiority throughout the 1950s, nuclear parity (or rough equality) of nuclear weapons and their means of delivery was reached in the 1960s. The already burgeoning connection of nuclear weapons with the MIC was largely complete as both nations developed their delivery systems for nuclear weapons. (The "Triad" of air, land, and sea means of getting nuclear weapons to their targets was based on the theory that at least one leg would survive a surprise attack and could launch a retaliation that would deliver a devastating second strike.) The Triad system relied on extensive and highly profitable defense contracts for large industrial corporations across the United States. During these years the MIC helped develop, produce, and deploy increasingly sophisticated types and numbers of aircraft, submarines, and missiles. Also, MIRVs (multiple independently targetable reentry vehicles) were added to ICBMs (intercontinental ballistic missiles) and SLBMs (submarine launched ballistic missiles), thereby enabling each missile to carry several warheads for delivery to separate targets. This entire system was matched by the Soviet Union, prompting Robert McNamara, secretary of defense in the administration of President John F. Kennedy, to characterize as MAD (Mutual Assured Destruction) the capability of the United States and the Soviet Union, even after a first strike by the nuclear weapons of the other, to deliver a similarly destructive second strike. Then, during the 1970s and 1980s, development of counterforce nuclear weapons (ones with accuracy that led some to believe they could be used in a successful first strike) and more sophisticated tactical nuclear weapons (ones with purported battlefield capability) led to the emergence of a policy sometimes termed NUTS (Nuclear Utilization Targeting Strategies). Whether or not the "Balance of Terror" maintained a precarious deterrence, it exacted an enormous economic toll that many analysts regard as a significant contributing factor to the disintegration of the Soviet Union in 1991. According to the Brookings Institution, since 1940, the United States alone has spent about $5.5 trillion on nuclear weapons (Wald 1998).

At the same time, nuclear proliferation expanded, despite the Non-Proliferation Treaty. Beyond the five major nuclear powers, at the least Israel, India, Pakistan, and North Korea have developed nuclear weapons and several other nations, particularly Iran, have tried or are trying to develop nuclear weapons. Also, some prospect exists that subnational groups could acquire the means for nuclear terrorism. Beyond these developments with nuclear weapons, other weapons of mass destruction (WMD), both chemical and biological, were (and often still are) produced and stockpiled (and occasionally used) by many nations around the world. Research on the production, testing, stockpiling, deployment, and hazardous waste management of most of these WMDs has involved the MIC. Beyond involvement with virtually all aspects of WMDs, the reach of MIC has extended since World War II into U.S. involvement in the Korean War, Vietnam War, the wars in Afghanistan and Iraq, and many other smaller military conflicts. Along the way, profits have flowed to major defense contractors such as Halliburton, Boeing, General Dynamics, and many others. (Over 80,000 private firms receive contracts.) Needless to say, the frequently redundant initiatives of the MIC consume a disproportionately large portion of global resources. Numerous books have been written on defense contractors—such as Lockheed Martin and Halliburton—detailing both their contributions to the military and their profits, waste, and scandals (Hartung 2011).

From 1950 (following the first Soviet nuclear test in 1949) until 1991 (with the dissolution of the Soviet Union), the Cold War had supplied a legitimating ideology for the MIC. Some analysts regard the more robust capitalism that supported the MIC in the United States as having enabled it to withstand these gargantuan drains on the economy. At any rate, during the 1990s (following the disintegration of the Soviet Union), some analysts suggested the United States would have a peace dividend, and some scholars even developed models for how to manage a decline of the MIC in a socially fair manner. However, throughout the closing decades of the twentieth century, no peace dividend was realized in large measure because of the MIC. Then, after only a ten-year gap that was too short to weaken the link, the events of September 11, 2001 (often referred to simply as "9/11") supplied a new legitimating ideology with the "war on terrorism" (which itself has spawned references to a military-industrial-security complex). Interestingly, Mills himself had suggested the complex could sustain itself over a decade when a clear threat was not present, but suggested a new one would by then need to be found. In this regard, a "terrorist threat" became a new flag raised to marshal the requisite fear needed to support another costly round of military spending—with a 50% increase in U.S. military spending over the first decade following 9/11.

Total global military spending underscores the central role of the nuclear arms race and the high cost that military strength has reached. These levels of spending also reflect the reach of the MIC and the profits it spawns. Globally, the top military spenders include the five major nuclear powers—the United States, Russia, the People's Republic of China, the United Kingdom, and France (and their status as the permanent members of the Security Council of the United Nations is no accident)—and among the top eight military spenders only Saudi Arabia and Japan are not nuclear powers. (India, Pakistan, Israel, and, marginally, North Korea are also nuclear powers.) According to the official Pentagon report, in 2015 the United States had 4,154 bases at home, 114 in U.S. territories, and 587 overseas—for a total of 4,855 (Department of Defense 2015). Outside sources generally put the total closer to 6,000. (Critics of the MIC who operate outside of government and its supporting organizations typically rely on formulas that take more factors into account and calculate totals that are considerably higher.) Constructing, equipping, and maintaining these bases and recruiting, training, and supplying these troops is very expensive. While world military spending totaled more than $1.6 trillion in 2015, the United States, the world's leading nuclear power, alone spent well beyond $600 billion and regularly accounts for about a third of the global total, with its military expenditures roughly equaling the size of the combined totals of the next seven largest military budgets around the world (National Priorities Project 2015). China, in second place, spent about $150 billion, while Saudi Arabia came in third at about $82 billion; the United Kingdom, Russia, and India each spent over $50 billion, and France and Japan spent over $40 billion (Perlo-Freeman et al. 2016).

After these leaders the rates of spending drop precipitously. While spending alone does not settle the issue, the high correlation between possession of extensive nuclear arsenals and high military spending is very telling. Also, with only a couple of exceptions, these levels of spending are closely associated with capitalism and its decisive role in the growth and influence of the MIC.

Beyond the MIC

Can anything be done to reduce the grip of the MIC? Yes. Advocates of pacifism and nonviolence can agree on the goal of ending war and militarism and, as an alternative, agree on the aim of employing nonviolent methods of response to conflict in the pursuit of positive peace. Finding effective means of advancing these goals is another matter, especially after the many decades of relentless expansion by the MIC. As far back as the 1960s, Herbert Marcuse highlighted how thought and behavior were becoming largely "one-dimensional" or uncritical under the political and economic systems of both the West and the East. Even earlier Max Weber had described the "iron cage" of bureaucratization and control in the modern world. However, despite the obstacles and challenges, neither of these theorists denied the possibility of any protest or change. The door to the "iron cage" of modern society has not been permanently locked shut, and some actions can slow and perhaps prevent it from closing. Nevertheless, in relation to the grip of the MIC under globalized capitalism, much of what can be done likely will be rather partial, unless somehow the making of profit can be excluded from the pursuit of military security.

A key issue concerns what can be done in relation to the "iron triangle" of military, economic, and political power and the "revolving door" that moves individuals from lucrative and influential positions in one of these spheres to positions of similar status in another of these spheres. Presently, military contracts are typically spread across as many congressional districts as possible in order to garner support from representatives in Congress who want to promote or protect MIC-related jobs in their districts. One concrete action would be to spread military contracts across as few congressional districts as possible so as to reduce the vested interest of congressional representatives in protecting jobs in their districts. Doing so could strengthen the prospects of legislative endeavors to defund many costly military programs. Nevertheless, at this stage in the MIC, defense contractors are so well integrated and are so highly influential that they no longer need to funnel much money directly to congressional representatives or lobbyists. In recent years, only Lockheed Martin and Boeing were among the major political contributors, and fewer than half of the other defense contractors expended funds on lobbyists (Center for Public Integrity 2004).

A more fundamental issue concerns how the MIC impacts federal budgets. In the post–Cold War period, federal budgets increasingly couple expansion of military expenditures with cuts in taxes on the wealthy. As a result, decreases in non-military public spending have accelerated. Critics, such as Hossein-Zadeh, argue that restricting military expansionism requires either an effort to force big businesses and wealthy individuals to pay their "fair" share in the escalating costs or an effort to pressure policy makers to curtail deficit financing of these costs (Hossein-Zadeh 2006: 256). Others support efforts at universal conscription (draft) as a means to share the loss of blood and life and thereby decrease the appeal of military expansion.

Of course, given the nature of capitalism, changing corporate behavior is very difficult. Under capitalism when profits fall in a particular industry, capital is moved to new areas where prospects for a larger market share and greater profits may be achieved. For example, in the related industrial complex of prisons the critique of the mass incarceration that was spawned by the privatization of prisons led to the shift of some of the same companies to the "treatment-industrial complex." Now, instead of seeking to expand prison populations in order to augment profit, some of these companies are seeking to privatize treatment and to profit from the transfer of many of the same former inmates and parolees (many of whom have serious mental health challenges) to "treatment centers" that may well do more to confine and retain their populations for extended periods than to treat and cure them (Issacs 2014). Would a similar pattern follow if nations shifted away from military defense and toward less provocative and less violent approaches to national security? (Civilian resistance is the most frequently cited non-military alternative.) Would private companies that currently manage military contracts try to shift to managing contracts for training, housing, and equipping civilians in a corps of nonviolent resisters? Such companies might pursue and secure government contracts that remain non-competitive and continue cost-plus practices. So, an aim to end the MIC could result in its replacement with a system that retains many of the same economic and political problems. Perhaps the analysis will come full circle with the realization that the solution requires a critique of the capitalist system that helps sustain the MIC and with the search for not only alternative security models but also alternative economic models that are more humane and less profit driven.

Throughout the nuclear arms race—in fact, throughout the history of warfare—philosophical and religious assessments of militarism and the MIC have been made. Not surprisingly, the persons who make these philosophical and religious assessments are almost never members of the strategic community or the political-military establishment. Nevertheless, philosophical and religious perspectives typically provide very relevant criticisms of the policies that govern military systems in relation to both the threat of use and the actual use of weapons.

In the religious responses, Martin Luther King, Jr. provided an exemplary view in his discussion of the "Giant Triplets" of racism, extreme materialism, and violence in the United States—and the rest of the world (King 1967). Reduction of the MIC obviously requires a critique of materialism (especially capitalism) and of violence (including militarism and warism). A critique of racism is also required—from the placing of toxic wastes of military projects in poor neighborhoods that are inhabited disproportionately by persons of color to the neo-colonialist and neo-imperialist practices of having persons of color as the victims of military actions. In relation to the iron triangle, since the military, economic, political, and racial dimensions are interconnected, a comprehensive response to the MIC involves all of these levels.

A wide range of religious leaders and theologians have made remarks similar to King's. Reinhold Niebuhr, a famous twentieth-century theologian, pointed out the mistake of equating the military-industrial complex and national interest. He favored arms control and arms reduction as ways to direct more scarce resources to the poor, sick, and downtrodden in society and to reduce the rising exploitation by the military-industrial complex. Contemporary theologian Ted Grimsrud, on the occasion of the fiftieth anniversary of the military-industrial complex, wrote on the moral legacy of WWII in relation to this growing influence of the MIC (Grimsrud 2011). More recently, Pope Francis stressed how capitalism sanctions war and violence because they make more money than peace and, like Niebuhr, called for stopping the arms trade that is closely associated with the MIC (Downie 2013).

Among philosophical treatments of issues of militarism, just war theory often receives the most attention. However, references to the MIC are generally absent in the analyses of just war theory. Critical attention to the MIC is more common during times of (relative) peace, since during war the additional fog of patriotism generally prevents consideration of effects of weapons use and profits from military spending. Even though between wars the MIC receives some consideration, just war theory is typically applied only just prior to or during war. Nevertheless, several aspects of the MIC could be addressed by this moral theory. For example, application of the criterion of "just cause" can be manipulated by economic interests of the private defense contractors, as can the principles of "right intent" (in relation to the real interests behind use of military force) and "proportionality" (in relation to likely "collateral damage" from use of many weapons). One exception in the literature from the just war perspective is the essay by Andrew Fiala on "Just War Ethics and the Slippery Slope of Militarism" in which he presents factors that make more likely our slipping into unjust wars. Arguing for giving more consideration to "the material conditions of war," he stresses the importance of examining "the influence of defense contractors, the pressure of pork-barrel polities, and the interests of lobbyists, military officers, and politicians who benefit from war" and concludes "the slope toward unjust war becomes slippery when it is lubricated by the interests of the military-industrial complex" (Fiala 2012). His call for examining the social and political preconditions of war brings into focus the role of the MIC in precipitating and justifying war. In brief, he exposes how economic concerns can displace moral intentions.

A large body of evidence suggests alternatives to military means are possible. Some of the political efforts include ones associated with nonviolent expressions of anti-globalism and its offshoot of "alterglobalism" that proposes a humanistic globalization strategy. Within peace studies stress is often placed on the successes of nonviolent methods, from those associated with Mahatma Gandhi to civilian resistance and similar strategies. These methods are not only possible but have been employed and have worked. In every decade of the twentieth century on all continents (except Antarctica) nonviolent social movements have succeeded (Ackerman and Duvall 2000). Not only does civilian resistance work, it also makes success of democracy more likely (Chenoweth and Stephan 2011). One advantage—beyond obvious moral ones—of nonviolent models of national security is that they are not capital intensive. Instead, they are labor intensive and rely on training large portions of the population in nonviolent resistance. Since capitalism relies on industry, which is capital intensive, nonviolent models of national security could undercut much of the cost of the MIC, though they also shift responsibility for defense from a relatively small professional army and its supports to a very large portion of the citizenry (Gay 1994). One step toward these goals can be found in efforts to reduce killing. The Global Center for Nonkilling notes few people ever kill another human being and proceed from this fact to develop strategies for seeking societies that no longer engage in war and other forms of killing human beings. Coupling their work with a shift from traditional approaches of conflict resolution and conflict management to cutting-edge efforts at conflict transformation offers additional hope. Within philosophy, further perspective and tactics can be drawn from William James's "The Moral Equivalent of War," John Dewey's involvement in the "Outlawry of War" movement, and, more recently, efforts by the professional association "Concerned Philosophers for Peace."

The future of the MIC revolves around two basic questions concerning whether it is necessary and whether it is unalterable. Is the MIC necessary? No. Is the MIC unalterable? No. In relation to the first question, the argument has been around for a long time that national security requires a strong military. Leaving aside the fact that nation-states are a product of modernity and are themselves historical, the argument for the need for a strong military has been challenged on its own terms. A strong military is not the only means (and perhaps neither the most effective nor most ethical means) for attaining national security. Moreover, even if a strong military is an effective means for attaining national security, it does not require militarism and the military-industrial complex. Less provocative and less costly military postures are feasible and could have comparable, if not greater, effectiveness. In relation to the second question, and perhaps most importantly for the next several decades, if the premise is accepted at least on pragmatic grounds that the pursuit of national security will continue to rely on the military-industrial complex, acceptance of the MIC need not allow—and advocates of pacifism and nonviolence would add "should not allow"—the interest in profit by the private sector to retain the current levels of influence over military policies and military operations. Even if a comprehensive critique of capitalism is not undertaken, at the least a critique is needed of the ways in which economic interests of private contractors have led to serious malpractice in the pursuit of security. The money spent, the profit gained, the resources consumed, the lives destroyed, and the environment degraded are each themselves threats to security that need to be exposed and criticized—and these threats can be reduced, if not eliminated, by changed policies and practices that break the grip of private, for-profit contractors.

Governmental desire to enhance the military led to reliance on industry and the rise of the MIC. Then, industry desire to increase profit led to reliance on government and the reversal of the relation between the military and industry in the MIC. The influence of industry on military policy led to the MIC being transformed from an arguably efficient means to a clearly self-perpetuating end. Would reversing this transformation in the MIC be enough to end its dangers? No. The fundamental dangers of the MIC of which Eisenhower initially warned would remain. The aim of technological enhancement of the capacity to wage war would remain, and private industry likely would continue to play a key role. The danger might shift from a profit imperative to a technological imperative. The toll on societies and the planet would continue, even if wars were to be increasingly avoided. Would ending governmental reliance on industry in the pursuit of national security eliminate the dangers? No. Direct (physical) violence would continue whenever war occurs and, regardless, direct violence (and other forms of violence) would continue elsewhere on an ongoing, pervasive, and massive scale. War and militarism, along with the many other purveyors of violence, are even more deeply entrenched in the contemporary world and in global history than the MIC. In the terminology of Johan Galtung, the structural violence of militarized and non-military institutions would continue, as would the cultural violence of warism and all the lesser -isms of cultural violence. Negative peace and social injustice would remain. The ultimate goals of pacifism and nonviolence are not only beyond the MIC and war; they are also beyond the structural and cultural violence that spawned the MIC and that sustain war.

Works Cited

Ackerman, P., and J. Duvall. (2000). *A Force More Powerful: A Century of Nonviolent Conflict*. New York: St. Martin's Press.

Best, S., R. Kahn, A. J. Nocella II, and P. McLaren. (eds.) (2011). *The Global Industrial Complex: Systems of Domination*. Lanham, MD: Lexington Book.

Cady, D. (1989/2010). *From Warism to Pacifism: A Moral Continuum*, 2nd ed. Philadelphia: Temple University Press.

Center for Public Integrity. (2004). "Outsourcing the Pentagon." Available at: www.publicintegrity.org/2004/09/29/6620/outsourcing-pentagon (Accessed 26 October 2016).

Chenoweth, E., and M. J. Stephan. (2011). *Why Civil Resistance Works: The Strategic Logic of Nonviolent Conflict*. New York: Columbia University Press.

Department of Defense. (2015). "Base Structure Report—Fiscal Year 2015 Baseline." Available at: www.acq.osd.mil/eie/Downloads/BSI/Base%20Structure%20Report%20FY15.pdf (Accessed 26 October 2016).

Downie, J. (2013). "Pope Francis's Stinging Critique of Capitalism." November 26. Available at: www.washingtonpost.com/blogs/post-partisan/wp/2013/11/26/pope-franciss-stinging-critique-of-capitalism/?utm_term=.8c403317dbae (Accessed 29 November 2016).

Fiala, A. (2012). "Just War Ethics and the Slippery Slope of Militarism." *Philosophy in the Contemporary World* 19 (2), Fall: 92–102.

Gay, W. (1994). "The Prospect for a Nonviolent Model of National Security," in W. Gay and T. Alekseeva (eds.), *On the Eve of the 21st Century: Perspectives of Russian and American Philosophers*. Lanham, MD: Rowman and Littlefield, 119–134.

Gay, W., and T. Alekseeva. (1996). *Capitalism with a Human Face: The Quest for Middle Road in Russian Politics*. Lanham, MD: Rowman and Littlefield.

Gay, W., and M. Pearson. (1987). *The Nuclear Arms Race*. Chicago: American Library Association.

Grimsrud, T. (2011). "The Military Industrial Complex and the Moral Legacy of WWII." *Peace Theology* January 16. Available at: https://peacetheology.net/2011/01/17/the-military-industrial-complex-and-the-moral-legacy-of-world-war-ii/ (Accessed 29 November 2016).

Hartung, W. D. (2011). *Prophets of War: Lockheed Martin and the Making of the Military-Industrial Complex*. New York: Nation Books.

Hossein-Zadeh, I. (2006). *The Political Economy of U.S. Militarism*. New York: Palgrave.

Issacs, C. (2014). "The Treatment Industrial Complex: How For-Profit Prison Corporations Are Undermining Efforts to Treat and Rehabilitate Prisoners for Corporate Gain." *American Friends Service Committee and Southern Center for Human Rights*. November. Available at: http://grassrootsleadership.org/reports/incorrect-care-prison-profiteer-turns-care-confinement (Accessed 24 October 2016).

King, Jr., M. L. (1967). "Beyond Vietnam." Speech of April 4 (NYC). Available at: http://kingencyclopedia.stanford.edu/encyclopedia/documentsentry/doc_beyond_vietnam/ (Accessed 3 March 2017).

Klein, N. (2007). *The Shock Doctrine: The Rise of Disaster Capitalism*. New York: Picador. (Contemporary geopolitical analysis of the MIC.)

Koistinen, P. A. C. (2003). "Military-Industrial Complex." *Directory of American History, the Gale Group Inc*. Available at: www.encyclopedia.com/topic/Military-Industrial_Complex.aspx (Accessed 24 October 2016).

Liebknecht, K. (2011). *Militarism and Anti-Militarism*. Montreal: Black Rose Books.

Lynn, W. J., III. (2014). "The End of the Military-Industrial Complex: How the Pentagon Is Adapting to Globalization." *Foreign Affairs* November-December. Available at: www.foreignaffairs.com/articles/united-states/end-military-industrial-complex (Accessed 26 October 2016).

Melman, S. (1970). *Pentagon Capitalism: The Political Economy of War*. New York: McGraw-Hill.

Melman, S. (1974). *The Permanent War Economy: American Capitalism in Decline*. New York: Simon and Schuster.

"Military-Industrial Complex." (2002). *Britannica Online Encyclopedia*. Available at: www.britannica.com/topic/military-industrial-complex (Accessed 24 October 2015).

"Military-Industrial Complex." (2003). *Dictionary of American History*. The Gale Group. Available at: www.encyclopedia.com/social-sciences-and-law/political-science-and-government/military-affairs-non naval/military-1 (Accessed 24 October 2016).

Mills, C. W. (1956). *The Power Elite*. New York: Oxford University Press.

National Priorities Project. (2015). "U.S. Military Spending vs. the World." Available at: www.nationalpriorities.org/campaigns/us-military-spending-vs-world/ (Accessed 26 October 2015).

Perlo-Freeman, S., A. Fleurant, P. Wezeman, and S. Wezeman. (2016). "Trends in World Military Expenditures, 2015." *Stockholm International Peace Research Institute (SIPRI)* April. Available at: http://books.sipri.org/files/FS/SIPRIFS1604.pdf (Accessed 10 March 2017).

Straus, M. (2014). "The Innovation Economy Is Killing the Military Industrial Complex." Available at: http://io9.gizmodo.com/the-innovation-economy-is-killing-the-military-industri-1649364098 (Accessed 26 October 2016).

Wald, M. L. (1998). "U.S. Nuclear Arms' Cost Put at $5.48 Trillion." *New York Times* July 1. Available at: www.nytimes.com/1998/07/01/us/us-nuclear-arms-cost-put-at-5.48-trillion.html (Accessed 4 November 2016).

Further Reading

Hartung, W. D. (2011). *Prophets of War: Lockheed Martin and the Making of the Military-Industrial Complex.* New York: Nation Books. (Illustrates the influence of one of the key private defense contractors.)

Hossein-Zadeh, I. (2006). *The Political Economy of U.S. Militarism.* New York: Palgrave. (A contemporary analysis of the MIC by an economist.)

Melman, S. (1974). *The Permanent War Economy: American Capitalism in Decline.* New York: Simon and Schuster. (A classic text on the MIC.)

23
FEMINISM AND NONVIOLENT ACTIVISM

Danielle Poe

This chapter will focus on the overlap between two political stances: feminism and nonviolence. While feminism has evolved over the years (an evolution that I will explain in the following paragraph), those who are part of this political position turn their attention to the ways in which women's actions, thoughts, and contributions have been subordinated to those from men. Feminism brings to light the ways in which women's perspectives are different than men's and provides new ways of thinking and new forms of justice that are covered over when men's actions and ideas are held up as the universal standard by which everything else is judged. While not all feminists are committed to nonviolent action, feminism as a movement has example after example of women who responded to violence with nonviolence: Sojourner Truth, Harriet Tubman, Dorothy Day, Jane Addams and the Women's International League for Peace and Freedom, Audre Lorde, Wangari Maathi, Shirin Ebadi, Jody Williams, Aung San Suu Kyi, Leymeh Gbowee, and Malala Yousafzai. While this list is long, it is not exhaustive and will hopefully inspire readers to learn about the many different ways that women live out feminist, nonviolent practice.

In order to understand why feminism includes such a variety of women, it is helpful to understand its history. Feminism as a political movement can be understood in terms of "waves"; the first two waves focused on goals that feminists had in common. First wave feminism (mid-1800s and early 1900s) focused on the fight for women's right to vote, which entailed a number of recognizable forms of nonviolent action: marches, petitions, rallies, speeches, hunger strikes, disruptive political action. Second wave feminism (1960s through the early 1990s) focused on equal rights for women and again used nonviolent action to promote its cause. These early forms of feminism focused on common issues, but since the 1990s feminism has expanded to include many issues and has led to disagreement about what is rightly called "feminist" or "feminism."

Unlike the first two waves, third wave feminism (1990s through today) addresses a wide range of injustices that impact all people. This third wave arose as a critique and expansion of second wave feminism. The critique is that feminism was promoting a single image of women; namely, feminism was focusing on the experience of white, middle-class, U.S. women. The critique of feminism's narrowness led to an expansion of feminism, as it embraced women from across the globe, as well as across lines of race, religion, ethnicity, and class. What makes all of the third wave movements feminist is that they are organized, led, and developed by women who are using their experiences as women to craft their critiques, responses, and vision (Coleman 2009; Orr 1997; Bailey 1997; Kinser 2004; Snyder 2008).

This chapter will focus on third wave feminism by drawing on the work of feminist groups and individual women to illustrate the wide variety of influence that feminists and feminism have had on nonviolent activism and also the ways in which they have created more justice in the world. Feminist nonviolent activists—like all other feminists—include a wide variety of philosophical commitments and political affiliations. But what they all share in common is that their identity as women is central to their leadership as they address social and political injustices, especially those injustices that disproportionately impact women.

To begin this chapter, I will focus on two individual women, Leymah Gbowee and Arundhati Roy. Gbowee won the Nobel Peace Prize in 2011 for her role in ending the civil war in Liberia and bringing democracy to the country. She continues her activism as part of the Nobel Women's Initiative, which brings together the women who have won the Nobel Peace Prize in order to work collaboratively on projects that improve the lives of women and children around the world. My focus in this article will be on Gbowee's activism that brought down Charles Taylor, a violent dictator responsible for widespread violence and suffering in Africa.[1]

Next, I will analyze the work of Arundhati Roy, who rose to prominence when her book *The God of Small Things* was published in 1997. In this work, Roy brings to light the many forms of social injustice that the people of India suffer as a direct result of their colonized history. The success of her book elevated her to international, near-celebrity status. Roy felt compelled to use her prominence to speak out against injustice on behalf of those whose voices otherwise would not be heard. She has since addressed the corruption of governments, big business, and individuals.

I will also examine the activism of two organizations, Code Pink and Madres de Plaza de Mayo. Code Pink formed in the U.S. in 2002 in order to bring women together to publically demonstrate against a U.S. invasion of Iraq. Since that time, the group organizes public protests against war, occupation, and unjust business practices. They are particularly adept at showing the relationship between U.S. business interests and global social injustice. Code Pink uses a combination of social critique, public demonstrations, and satire to draw attention to their causes. Their ability to ground their work in gender and national identity in relationship to global issues illustrates a powerful performance strategy that other feminist groups and individuals use as well.

Finally, I will discuss Madres de Plaza de Mayo. From 1977 through today, this organization has brought Argentinian women together to fight for transparency and human rights. The Madres began informally in 1977, when mothers would walk daily around a public square in order to share information about their children who had been disappeared by the military dictatorship. Over time, they became a formal organization that worked together to challenge the oppression, torture, and injustice of the military regime. Even after the government became democratic in 1983, the women continued their activism (although the original group splintered into two groups) in order to facilitate a peace process and to advocate for other social justice issues.

The four case studies in this chapter will introduce the reader to the range of nonviolent activism initiated and sustained by women around the world. I characterize all of these movements as feminist, even when their activism is on behalf of all people, because the women understand their activism as explicitly connected to their identity as women. This is not to say that there is something about being a woman that makes women nonviolent. Rather, my argument is that women who are committed to feminism and nonviolence use their experiences to inform their political beliefs and actions. Their experiences include an intersection of differences: religious, class, ethnic, national, racial, and sexual to name a few. For each group and each woman, the access to power and experience of vulnerability comes out of the intersection of differences. The emphasis on difference comes out of feminist philosophy and the emphasis on addressing injustice through nonviolence is a political commitment, and it is this overlap that will be examined. The feminists covered in this chapter are not an exhaustive accounting of feminist nonviolent activism; rather, they are illustrative of the many ways in which feminism is informing nonviolence and bringing about peace and justice. Readers are invited to take this chapter as inspiration to do further research on contemporary feminist nonviolent activists and groups.

Leymah Gbowee

Nobel Laureate Leymah Gbowee provides an important example of how someone who faced extensive violence joined with other Liberian women to confront that violence with nonviolence. Her story is important because it illustrates the effectiveness of nonviolence against violence, and the power that women have to create the conditions for peace when they explicitly use their identity as women in their activism. Not only does she use her experience as a woman and as mother to inform her activism, but she also uses her education, her political commitment to interreligious dialogue, and her work with humanitarian groups to promote nonviolent change.

In her book *Mighty Be Our Powers* and in the film *Pray the Devil Back to Hell*, Gbowee describes the bloody war in Liberia that began on Christmas Eve 1989 when Charles Taylor began an attack on the Liberian government (Gbowee and Mithers 2011; Reticker 2008). From the moment that Taylor began his campaign to take over Liberia, his leadership was marked by terror and cruelty. For example, Gbowee describes hearing about the death of a friend in the early days of the war:

> And I heard about Koffa, my high school friend, the joker with the perfect handkerchief, who dreamed of becoming a US Marine. His father had enemies who were also in the military, and under the guise of war they came for him one day. He hid, so they killed the rest of the family and laid their bodies in the street. Koffa's body …
>
> Gbowee and Mithers 2011: 24

Gbowee ends this passage with "Koffa's body …", an incomplete thought that emphasizes just how traumatic the violence in Liberia is and that no one is safe during this war. Although the soldiers came looking for Koffa's father, they killed the family when they couldn't find their target. Not only were Taylor and his forces responsible for indiscriminate killing, rape, and looting, but the Liberian government, led by President Samuel Doe, was also responsible for killing civilians and refugees who were thought to be sympathetic to the rebels (Beck and Hendon 1990; Boateng and Hilton 2011; Graham and Khor 1995; Huband 1990; Huband 1991). While all accounts of war are filled with suffering and violence, the war in Liberia was particularly disturbing in its use of children:

> It was "Papay" Taylor who first brought children into the Liberian war with his Small Boy Units, although eventually all the rebels used them. Tens of thousands fought, some of them as young as eight, carrying AK-47s they were barely strong enough to lift. They were a nightmare vision of childhood, these soldiers, desperate to please and too young to understand what they were doing, taken away from their families and kept high on alcohol and drugs until they became the most merciless killers of all.
>
> Gbowee and Mithers 2011: 90

Gbowee was trying to raise her four small children who were between the ages of 6 years and 7 months old during the time period in which she recalls her first work with Taylor's boys.

Within Gbowee's narrative of the war in Liberia, the immediate suffering from the war takes place between 1989 and 2003. However, it should be clear from the previous descriptions that the impact of this violence continues long after the war stops, long after the arrest of Charles Taylor on March 29, 2006, and long after his conviction for war crimes on May 30, 2012.

One basic idea of nonviolence is that means and ends should be linked; the reason for this belief is that nonviolence is both practically and morally superior when confronting violence and pursuing peace. Practically, Gbowee is the mother of small children, which immediately limits the kinds of actions that will make sense for her. In order to continue to care for her children, she does not have the option of taking up arms and fighting violence with violence, since that is far more likely to result in her death than it is to result in ending the violence. Further, all sides in the conflict are inflicting harm on women, children, and civilians, so adding more violence continues to escalate violence instead of creating the conditions for peace. Morally, as a mother, Gbowee wants her children to grow into adults who value peace and justice. For that to happen, they need to develop those habits and capacities as youth. Because they are surrounded by violence in their society, Gbowee will have to provide another example, an example of acting for peace and justice.

Next, one can consider the objection that nonviolent direct action is too risky and so as a mother Gbowee should not confront the violence surrounding her. But Gbowee is surrounded by risk whether she does something or nothing. Throughout her memoir, Gbowee describes her work with women in internally displaced persons camps where she helps them to tell their stories of suffering during the war. Just one of these stories reveals the horror of the war:

> The soldiers came into the displaced persons camp they said, "Give us all the money you have!" I did. I gave them everything. Then they said, "Take off your clothes!" I did what they told me. They all had sex with me. All but one. He was the last one and he said, his penis was too good for me. And so instead, he used his knife.
>
> *Gbowee and Mithers 2011: 106*

The experience of this woman is representative of the experience of thousands of women during the war; the soldiers systematically stripped women of their possessions, their well-being, and their dignity at every opportunity. The violence, shame, and grief that Gbowee helped women to address in her work with women in displaced person camps stretches across the whole of Liberia. Roughly 200,000 people were killed and another 600,000 people were displaced during the Liberian civil war. The extent of violence at the time meant that standing by and doing nothing was also a threat to Gbowee and her children's safety.

In the 2000s Gbowee would help to inspire other mothers to confront the violence in their country. Gbowee describes the inspiration for her action as coming from a dream that she had after the day that I described in the previous section, when she thought that neither she nor the fifty women gathered together could take any more pain: "*I didn't know where I was. Everything was dark. I couldn't see a face, but I heard a voice, and it was talking to me—commanding me: 'Gather the women to pray for peace!'*" (Gbowee and Mithers 2011: 122; italics in original). In order to act on her vision, Gbowee began to network with other women's networks, trying to cast as wide a net as possible in order to gather women from across all walks of life and across the wide religious divide between Christian and Muslim women. Gbowee describes the women sitting, all in white T-shirts "to signify peace," day after day from "dawn to dusk" under the burning sun where they chanted, prayed, and held signs demanding an end to violence and for peace. Women were there by the hundreds to be visible to the warlords as they supposedly engaged in peace talks. While Charles Taylor and the other rebel leaders paid lip service to the women's demand for peace, the war raged on, heaping more suffering on the people of Liberia.

This impasse and her willingness to risk everything for peace led Gbowee to lead the women to a dramatic protest that changed the course of negotiations. Just in time for the lunch break of those who were supposed to be negotiating for peace, Gbowee led 200 women, wearing their white T-shirts, into the building, and they all sat in front of the door to the hall, effectively blocking the participants from leaving the hall for lunch. To explain their purpose, she gave the men inside a note that read, "*We are holding these delegates, especially the Liberians, hostage. They will feel the pain of what our people are feeling at home*" (Gbowee and Mithers 2011: 161; italics in original). This, of course, outraged the men inside, and they threatened to have Gbowee arrested:

> I was so angry, I was out of my mind. "I will make it very easy for you to arrest me. I'm going to strip naked." I took off my hair tie. Beside me, Sugars rose to her feet and began to do the same. I pulled off my *lappa*, exposing the tights I wore underneath.... I was beside myself desperate. Every institution that I'd been taught was there to protect the people had proved evil and corrupt; everything I valued had collapsed. These negotiations had been my last hope, but they were crashing, too. But in threatening to strip, I had summoned up a traditional power. In Africa, it's a terrible curse to see a married or elderly woman deliberately bare herself.... For this group of men to see a woman naked would be almost like a death sentence. Men are born through women's vaginas, and it's as if by exposing ourselves, we say, "We now take back the life we gave you."
>
> *Gbowee and Mithers 2011: 161–162*

The result of her actions was that negotiations became serious and the war began to end and processes for peace began. Gbowee describes her action as a spontaneous response to her outrage at the luxury accommodations provided for the representatives of the political factions responsible for inflicting terrible suffering on the people of Liberia, her disgust at being threatened with arrest for interfering with people who had proved evil and corrupt, and her determination to speak out against these injustices. Although her act was spontaneous, she remained true to nonviolent direct action; her actions over many years had created a mindset of nonviolence such that she was able to take advantage of an opportunity using local knowledge and tradition.

Ultimately, Gbowee's act and the protests by other women successfully brought democracy to Liberia in 2003. Taylor was indicted for war crimes and was eventually convicted in 2012 by special international court in The Hague. Gbowee was awarded the Nobel Peace Prize in 2011 and now uses her influence to advocate for girls' education around the world.

Arundhati Roy

As a feminist peace activist, Arundhati Roy confronts the inequity in the world that we all live in today. Roy's feminism is part of her work in two important ways: a legacy that has paved the way for her activism and a political movement entwined with other movements against injustice, particularly the injustice perpetrated by capitalism. With respect to the legacy of feminism, Roy's interview with Aishwarya Subramanyam is instructive because Roy states:

> Every freedom we have today, we have because of feminists. Many women have fought and paid a huge price for where we are today. It didn't all come to us only because of our own inherent talent or brilliance. Even the simple fact that women have the vote, who fought for that? The suffragettes. No freedom has come without a huge battle.
>
> *Subramanyam 2016*

Roy's point is important for understanding contemporary feminism: women's voices and experiences are part of the conversation because other women have paved the way for contemporary women to express themselves, to vote, to access the media, and to access education. Roy, then, is a feminist because her perspective is formed by the convergence of being a woman, being Indian, being a writer, experiencing poverty, and experiencing affluence.

One place in which Roy's critique of capitalism and her perspective as a feminist is explicit is when she warns against the co-opting of feminism so that it focuses on women's bodies rather than on coercion:

> When, as happened recently in France, an attempt is made to coerce women out of the burka rather than creating a situation in which a woman can choose what she wishes to do, it's not about liberating her but about unclothing her. It becomes an act of humiliation and cultural imperialism. Coercing a woman out of her burka is as bad as coercing her into one. It's not about the burka. It's about the coercion. Viewing gender in this way, shorn of social, political, and economic context, makes it an issue of identity, a battle of props and costumes.
>
> *Roy 2014: 36*

Roy is keenly aware in her work that the harmful effects of capitalism and neoliberalism disproportionately impact women, but an explicit focus on feminism as the primary lens for analysis carries the risk that her audience will get pulled into debates about women's bodies rather than focusing on the source of harm for women. Roy's primary concern is to draw attention to capitalism and coercion and its effects on people. Feminism, then, is the historical legacy by which Roy has a voice and platform to raise her concerns and it permeates her critique of capitalism.

Her activism is both focused on local struggles of the poorest people in India and focused on a global critique of capitalism because "of *course* India is a microcosm of the world. Of *course* versions of what happens there happen everywhere" (Roy 2001: 3). Whereas other activists in this chapter use nonviolent direct action, Roy's activism is primarily academic and intellectual. She has brought her message to India and to the world through fiction, journalism, academic articles, and university speeches, and in radio and television interviews. As she explains in *Power Politics*, "It is the writers, the poets, the artists, the singers, the filmmakers who can make the connections, who can find ways of bringing it into the realm of common understanding" (Arundhati 2014: 32). It is also important to remember that when Roy writes about or talks about the poorest people in India and elsewhere, women are disproportionately part of this group (Arundhati 2014: 34).

Roy's career as an activist started unexpectedly when her book *The God of Small Things* came out in 1996. The book was a work of fiction, but it powerfully captures the struggles of Indian people who were being forgotten in the push for development in India. Through that work, Roy became a well-known global author. And, through the combination of her celebrity and her face-to-face contact with suffering people in India, Roy describes herself as compelled to act:

> Sometimes you can't control what you have to do. As in, I can't live with myself every day knowing that I have earned myself space in public. I can make a difference. I can say what I'm thinking. And, when you know that space is there it's very hard to walk past it. I long to walk past it, to tell you the truth. I long to walk past these things. I'm not someone who enjoys controversy.
>
> *BBC Interview 2016: 17:30*

When Roy refers to "these things," she is referring to the injustice that she witnesses globally, and especially the injustice in India. In this particular interview, she is referring to the Indian government's dam projects, which according to her calculations have displaced 33 million people (BBC Interview 2016: 5:55). She had to use her own calculations because the number of people displaced by these projects is not tracked by the government. Roy's research has also uncovered that these projects are primarily (if not exclusively) benefitting the interests of the sugar industry (BBC Interview 2016: 8:12), while the people who are being displaced are reaping none of the benefits. Because Roy asked questions about the dam projects, discovered real harms to the most vulnerable people in India, and knows that false information is being disseminated by the Indian government, Roy feels an obligation to speak out because she has a public voice and recognition that allows her to be heard in a way that those who are directly harmed are not heard. Even though speaking out causes controversy, name-calling and threats against her, Roy speaks out because she feels she must.

One of Roy's most powerful books is her analysis of capitalism, *Capitalism: A Ghost Story*, in which she critiques the irrationality of an economic system that measures the wealth of a nation but fails to measure the cost of that wealth for the poor, and the systematic violence used to protect those who have the wealth. Roy sites the 2010 statistic from *Forbes Asia* which documents the fact that "in a nation of 1.2 billion, India's one hundred richest people own assets equivalent to one-fourth of the GDP" (Roy 2014: 7). And, in the United States of America, 400 people own half of the wealth (Roy 2014: 94). The point of these statistics is to show that while a country may have a continually growing GDP and may look healthy from the perspective of GDP, the growth may actually be harming more people than it's benefitting. If most of that wealth is owned by very few people, then we should look more closely in order to determine how the rest of the people are doing and the violence used to consolidate that wealth.

Roy does the work of finding out what is happening to the rest of the population. She traces the ways in which the production of wealth for some is at the expense of others and is deliberately hidden both by businesses and the media. The wealthy are able to protect their interests through favorable media coverage and media that simply does not report on potential scandals and irregularities because the media outlets are owned by big business and also because the media outlets have shares in business (Roy 2014: 14–20). Further, businesses are able to build their public reputation by sponsoring education, the arts, and festivals (Roy 2014: 65–66). While sponsoring things that serve the public interest would seem to indicate that big businesses and the wealthy care about the common good, these investments are actually minimally beneficial and are mostly effective as a smokescreen to hide the environmental and financial harms being committed.

Roy's critique of the ways in which big business has infiltrated the media, education, and the arts also applies to non-governmental organizations (NGOs). NGOs are most widely known for their role in the world community as non-state responders to humanitarian crisis. Roy's analysis, though, reveals that the funding for NGOs tends to come from major capitalist foundations that give money to NGOs who will perpetuate capitalist values (Roy 2014: 34–36, 42, 54). Instead of funding NGOs to respond to humanitarian crises in ways that are compatible with what people on the ground are requesting, the NGOs are coming into countries with preformed ideas about what sorts of economic and political ideals should be instilled in the people. For Roy, this is the newest form of colonialism.

While it may seem that these critiques of capitalism and NGOs fall outside of the concerns of feminism, Roy's work documents the violence perpetrated against women especially. The most common form that this violence takes is sexual violence and rape (Roy 2014: 12, 64, 73,

90). The documentation of rape is critical to Roy's other critiques because women are not protected from sexual violence, are blamed when they are victims of it, and are victims of this violence because of the institutions that should protect them. Because police and the soldiers are not investigating or punishing rape (and worse, are themselves raping), women are subject to an institutional silencing of their voices and their perspectives. Roy, though, has a voice and international platform to expose this violence and to critique the institutions and structures that create the violence.

Roy's critiques of capitalism clear a space for "demands" that will make way for a more just future:

> One: An end to cross-ownership in businesses. For example: weapons manufacturers cannot own TV stations, mining corporations cannot run newspapers, business houses cannot fund universities, drug companies cannot control public health funds./ Two: Natural resources and essential infrastructure—water supply, electricity, health, and education—cannot be privatized./Three: Everybody must have the right to shelter, education, and health care./Four: The children of the rich cannot inherit their parents' wealth.
> *Roy 2014: 93*

Roy's demands are an important mixture of limits and support. She limits the ways in which corporations and the wealthy can accumulate power and wealth by calling for an end to cross-ownership and an end to inheritance of wealth. Her second demand is both a limit and a support. By stating that natural resources and infrastructure cannot be privatized, corporations' right to own these is limited, but the access to both are extended to everyone, which in turn lays the groundwork for people to realize their rights.

Roy's championing of rights for all people, particularly the poor, means that she not only critiques the consolidation of power by the rich and by big businesses, but she is also a fierce critic of governments and those who claim to promote peace but fail to address structural inequality. Her critiques that may be most surprising to her readers are those that target Nobel Peace Prize recipients. She critiques Nobel recipients Barack Obama and Mohammed Yunus because they ultimately fail to bring about peace because they are only using the structures that are currently available, and in both cases that reinforces injustice rather than moving closer to peace. While Obama received the Nobel Peace Prize in recognition of his potential to bring about peace, Roy uses Kashmir as an example of Obama's failure. Before he became president, Obama pledged to support Kashmir's fight for independence, but as president he privileged his Afghanistan war efforts and the U.S.'s relationship with Pakistan and turned his back on Kashmir (Roy 2014: 69–75). Obama's failure to support Kashmir's independence paved the way for greater violence there.

In the case of Yunus, many peace activists know the story of the Grameen Bank, which created micro-lending opportunities for the poorest of the poor in India. But Roy traces the full impact of people's participation in capitalism: "Microfinance companies in India are responsible for hundreds of suicides—two hundred people in Andhra Pradesh in 2010 alone" (Roy 2014: 27). While the micro-loans allowed some people to escape poverty, those who struggled to make payments were subject to pressure and ostracism within their communities. For many, the social isolation and inability to make payments is so inescapable that people commit suicide.

Roy uses her status, her research, and her writing to tell the complete stories instead of focusing on the façade that is presented. Roy's work to expose injustice and to tell the complete story is work that carries a great deal of risk since many of the journalists who have critiqued the

Indian government have been subject to harassment, imprisonment, and even mysterious deaths (Roy 2014: 57–66). She is aware of these risks, but continues to speak out on behalf of the dead:

> One day in Dantewanda [an Indian district which has been subject to much violence between local people who are opposed to the destruction of their land and the government] too the dead will begin to speak. And it will not just be dead humans, it will be dead land, dead rivers, dead mountains, and dead creatures in dead forests that will insist on a hearing.
>
> *Roy 2014: 65*

Because of Roy's activism, the dead are already speaking of the injustice that has destroyed them, and the living can begin to create a more just future.

Madres de Plaza de Mayo

Just like the other narratives of feminist nonviolent activism, the story of the Madres de Plaza de Mayo begins with a story of violence and oppression against which the mothers organized and responded. From the 1970s through 1983, Argentina's military engaged in systematic kidnapping, torture, and murder of people who disagreed with the military dictatorship or who in some way were viewed as a threat to the dictatorship. While the military officially came to power on March 24, 1976, they had begun their campaign of terror in 1974. Once they had officially gained control of the government, the level of repression and violence in the country escalated dramatically (Benedetti 2013; Bustos et al. 2009; Carlson 2000; Schmidli 2012).

At this time it was not only dangerous to question the government, it was also dangerous to meet in groups and give the appearance of organizing against the government. Thus, the strategy of the Madres de Plaza de Mayo to meet in a public square and to walk together each day was effective for building solidarity, for raising public awareness about their plight, and for helping to bring an end to the military dictatorship.

For some writers, the activism of the Madres de Plaza de Mayo is impressive human rights work, but not accurately characterized as feminism. For example, in her entry "Feminist Activism in Latin America," Julie Shayne states:

> The women who organized their committees did so as mothers, wives, grandmothers, sisters, daughters, etc. of the "disappeared" men in their lives; they were in no way making a feminist statement. Rather, their efforts lay firmly in a human rights agenda which called for the end of dictatorships and their tactics of summary torture, kidnapping, and incarceration.
>
> *Shayne 2007: 1687*

For Shayne, groups such as the Madres de Plaza de Mayo are not feminist organizations because their goals are not targeted toward equal rights or some other social good for women. A wider understanding of feminism would include those groups who work to challenge injustice and to establish peace through their identity as women, which is precisely how these women effectively agitated for political change that was ultimately successful. This section will analyze the ways in which the Madres' identity as women influences their nonviolent activism.

In the article "The Madres de Plaza de Mayo and Three Decades of Human Rights' Activism: Embeddedness, Emotions, and Social Movements," Fernando J. Bosco examines how this group has been able to maintain their group identity and activism since 1977. For Bosco, the

Madres have continued to have a strong political presence and identity in spite of internal conflict because of a shared "embeddedness," which he defines "as a process that develops and intensifies over time, and its assessment should give attention to the shared emotional attachments that bind people together in social networks, rather than simply to the frequency of interactions" (Bosco 2006: 347). Bosco's analysis of embeddedness and effectiveness emphasizes the kinds of interactions that the women have had, and the ways in which their emotional investment in their cause, in their shared past, and in their commitment to each other all create a network of activism that continues today.

Bosco's analysis of the emotional ties between the women as a source of cohesion is important when we consider their origins. These are mothers whose sons and daughters have disappeared; they felt isolated and scared. By coming together weekly to exchange information and to offer support, these women—most of whom had never met before becoming Madres de Plaza de Mayo—found women who understood their suffering and became sources of care for each other. Bosco writes:

> For the Madres, the emotional is not and was never just a strategic façade (though the Madres do recognize that they took advantage of this in the past) but rather it runs deep into the core of the interpersonal relations among the Madres themselves and defines the nature of their activism.
>
> Bosco 2006: 354

Bosco is describing the way in which the Madres' emotions have always characterized their interactions with each other as well as their activism. Their early activism was characterized by a very public show of their tears and their grief, a way to draw international attention to the repression and violence of a state that kidnaps and disappears citizens who oppose them. But this passage also expresses the way in which the Madres actively cultivate their relationships to each other through their hugs, laughter, and support.

Another perspective on the Madres de Plaza de Mayo's activism is detailed by Julio Etchart in "'Not One Step Backwards!'" She chronicles the continued work of the Madres in the thirty years since they began their protests. The first victory came in 1983 when democracy was restored in Argentina. Unfortunately, Presidents Raúl Alfonsin and Carlos Menem granted amnesty to the police, dictators, clergy, and civilians who had disappeared, tortured, and murdered Argentinians. It was not until 2003 that President Néstor Kircher began the process of overturning amnesty. Now:

> as of March of this year [2013], a total of 250 people have been found guilty; 22 have been absolved, 790 cases are proceeding and 35 suspects have gone into hiding. So far, many of those tried have been armed forces and police personnel. But the net has been cast wider and civilians too are being investigated and brought to justice.
>
> Etchart 2013: 24

Because the reach of oppression ran so deeply through Argentina, the Madres continue to protest and agitate for justice and accountability. They are seeking to bring charges and convictions against the companies and clergy who provided spiritual and financial support to the government. They are seeking a change in the actions of the police and unions because they continue to be populated by those who were formed during the dictatorships and those who were formed in this way continue to respond violently and oppressively. And they are seeking new laws and protections for women, children, and other vulnerable Argentinian people.

For the Madres de Plaza de Mayo, solidarity comes from their shared experience as women who have devoted time, energy, and love to the care and well-being of their children, and through that experience they have a respect for the dignity of all human life. Their respect for all human life leads them to continue to advocate for extensions of justice to all people who are oppressed. In "The Mothers of La Plaza de Mayo: A Peace Movement," Viviana M. Aberu Hernandez quotes Hebe de Bonafini, one of the mothers who continues to be involved in the protests today:

> The child of one of us is the child of all of us, not only those who are missing, but the ones who are fighting for their rights today. We learned this from our guts, not from philosophic concepts. We are aware that before everything comes the defense of life.
>
> *Abreu Hernandez 2002: 401*

For these mothers, the Roman Catholic imperative to defend life was much more than a political directive against abortion; rather, it was a call to speak out for those who had been disappeared and to demand an accounting for all of their lives. And, even when Argentina's government became a democracy and stopped the systematic disappearances, kidnapping, torture, and murder, the mothers continued to defend life by agitating for human rights.

Code Pink

The final group that illustrates the variety of feminist activists and feminist organizations who are active in nonviolent activism is a U.S. group, Code Pink. This group walks many different activist lines; they walk between the reactive and creative, the humorous and serious, and national and international concerns. Code Pink's origin comes from the line between being reactive and creative. The three founders of the organization—Medea Benjamin, Jodie Evans, and Gael Murphy—were all involved in peace and justice work that promoted environmental, social, and political rights. In 2002 they joined together to protest against the possibility of a second Iraq War, which in fact began on March 19, 2003.

Code Pink's linking of the humorous and the serious directly relates to their origins as both proactive and reactive. Code Pink may be best known for their humorous public protests, which have included the use of lingerie (a giant "pink slip" for George W. Bush to protest the Iraq War), pig snouts (an elegant party to raise awareness and critique Haliburton's contracts in Iraq: "Halibacon" profiting off the war and suffering in Iraq), sparkly vagina costumes (a protest in front of a Republican National Convention to emphasize the number of platform policies that undermined U.S. women's rights), and pussyhats (endorsed by Code Pink as part of the 2017 women's march to protest Donald Trump's inauguration and a reminder of his statements encouraging violence and subordination of women). These protests have gained national and international attention and raised awareness about violations of human rights, militarism, and environmental destruction. Alongside of these highly visible protests are the proactive acts of Code Pink that allow viewers to imagine what a just and peaceful world would entail. One example of this work is detailed by Linda Milazzo in her article "Code Pink: The 21st Century Mothers of Invention":

> Code Pink coordinated the historic "Families for Peace Delegation." On this trip the three Code Pink founders, and a member of UPJ [United for Peace and Justice], accompanied Fernando [a father whose son, an American soldier, was killed in Iraq by an American cluster bomb], his wife Rosa, several relatives of fallen American soldiers, and families of "9/11" victims to Amman, Jordan. In an inspiring act of humanity and

generosity, they brought with them $650,000 in medical supplies and other aid for the Fallujah refugees who were forced from their homes when the Americans destroyed their city.

Milazzo 2005: 103

The blend of critique with peace-building is part of the success of Code Pink. When something is identified as unjust, such as the destruction of a city by American forces, Code Pink acts to support those who are harmed and to provide survivors the support that they have available. This act recognizes a certain unavoidable complicity that U.S. citizens have in the acts carried out by our military and our government. But their act also points to a deeper relationship that is possible between U.S. citizens and people around the world: a relationship of compassion and mutual support.

Many of the commenters on Code Pink's work note the line that this organization walks between embracing femininity and challenging the norms of femininity. For instance, Rachel V. Kutz-Flamenbaum, in her article "Code Pink, Raging Grannies, and the Missile Dick Chicks: Feminist Performance Activism in the Contemporary Anti-War Movement," quotes the Code Pink founding document: "Women have been the guardians of life—not because we are better or purer or more innately nurturing than men, but because the men have busied themselves making war" (Kutz-Flamenbaum 2007: 93). In their mission statement, the founders draw on a common social experience rather than making a claim that it is an essential feature of all women to be nurturers and guardians of life. In "Pink Thongs and Patriarchy," Liza Featherstone makes a similar distinction when she writes, "Code Pink and projects like it resist essentialism by making a joke of femininity, even while honoring it. It is a delicate balance, which somehow mostly works" (Featherstone 2009: 12). For the women of Code Pink, that which binds them together is a belief that war and militarism are harmful, and their socialization as women provides powerful means to speak out against militarism's destruction. Ultimately, their blend of humor and serious critique, which characterizes both their protests and constructive action, work to create a space that draws people into comforting norms that they recognize (such as women as "guardians of life") even while challenging other social norms (such as the conflation of security and militarism).

Code Pink, the Madres de Plaza de Mayo, Arundhati Roy, and Leymah Gbowee come from different experiences and backgrounds, but they all are attentive to the needs of their social context and address those needs out of an awareness of their own social formation as women. In the twenty-first century, feminism embraces its global context and makes connections between women's experiences and social injustice that harms others. Feminism no longer focuses only on issues that harm women since it is by forming alliances between people and recognizing patterns of oppression that structural violence can be addressed and undone. This chapter has introduced just four examples of nonviolent feminism and hopefully has inspired the reader to continue to look for more examples in their local contexts and around the world.

Note

1 This section is adapted from my article "Responding to Violence and Injustice Using Nonviolence: Martin Luther King, Jr., Leymah Gbowee, and Dorothy Stang." *Global Change, Peace and Security*, 26 (2), 177–193, 2014.

Works Cited

Abreu Hernandez, V. M. (2002). "The Mothers of La Plaza de Mayo: A Peace Movement." *Peace and Change* 27 (3): 385.

Bailey, C. (1997). "Making Waves and Drawing Lines: The Politics of Defining the Vicissitudes of Feminism." *Hypatia* 12 (3): 17.
Beck, R. and Hendon, D. (1990). "Notes on Church-State Affairs: Liberia." *Journal of Church and State* 31 (3): 581–623.
Benedetti, M. (2013). "The Disappeared: The Triumph of Memory." *NACLA Report on the Americas* 46 (4): 78–80.
Boateng, A. and Hilton, J. (2011). "The First Home Visit: The 'Return' Experiences of Liberian Refugee Women in Ghana." *Association of Third World Studies* 28 (1): 115–138.
Bosco, F. J. (2006). "The Madres de Plaza de Mayo and Three Decades of Human Rights' Activism: Embeddedness, Emotions, and Social Movements." *Annals of the Association of American Geographers* 96 (2): 342–365. doi: 10.1111/j.1467-8306.2006.00481.x
British Broadcasting Corporation (BBC). (2016). "Arundhati Roy Interview-Agenda BBC World Service." Available at: www.youtube.com/watch?v=dhMWHTMeZW8 (Accessed 21 July 2016).
Bustos, A. M., D. Webb, and G. J. Fairbairn. (2009). "(Un)Covering the Silence During the Argentinean Coup d'Etat." *Peace Review* 21 (2): 155–159. doi: 10.1080/10402650902877377
Carlson, E. S. (2000). "The Influence of French 'Revolutionary War' Ideology on the Use of Torture in Argentina's 'Dirty War'." *Human Rights Review* 1 (4): 71.
Coleman, J. (2009). "An Introduction to Feminisms in a Postfeminist Age." *Women's Studies Journal* 23 (2): 3–13.
Etchart, J. (2013). "'Not One Step Backwards!'" *New Internationalist* 463: 23–24.
Featherstone, L. (2004). "Pink Thongs and Patriarchy." *The Women's Review of Books* 12: 11–12.
Gbowee, L., with C. Mithers. (2011). *Mighty Be Our Powers: How Sisterhood, Prayer, and Sex Changed a Nation at War*. New York: Beast Books (Perseus).
Graham, C. and Khor, J. (1995). "National Notations: Liberia." *Peacekeeping and International Relations* 24 (5): 18.
Huband, M. (1990). "The Scars of War." *Africa Report* 36 (2): 47–50.
Huband, M. (1991). "Doe's Last Stand." Africa Report 35 (3): 47.
Kinser, A. E. (2004). "Negotiating Spaces For/Through Third-Wave Feminism." *NWSA Journal* 16 (3): 124–153.
Kutz-Flamenbaum, R. V. (2007). "Code Pink, Raging Grannies, and the Missile Dick Chicks: Feminist Performance Activism in the Contemporary Anti-War Movement." *NWSA Journal* 19 (1): 89–105.
Milazzo, L. (2005). "Code Pink: The 21st Century Mothers of Invention." *Development* 48 (2): 100–104. doi: www.palgrave-journals.com/development/archive/index.html
Orr, C. M. (1997). "Charting the Currents of the Third Wave." *Hypatia* 12 (3): 29.
Reticker, G. (2008). *Pray the Devil Back to Hell*. Warren, NJ. Passion River Films.
Roy, A. (2001). *Power Politics*. Cambridge, MA: South End Press.
Roy, A. (2014). *Capitalism: A Ghost Story*. Chicago, IL: Haymarket Books.
Schmidli, W. M. (2012). "Human Rights and the Cold War: The Campaign to Halt the Argentine Dirty War." *Cold War History* 12 (2): 345–365. New York: Routledge
Shayne, J. (2007). "Feminist Activism in Latin America," in G. Ritzer (ed.), *The Wiley Blackwell Encyclopedia of Sociology*. Hoboken, NJ: Blackwell Publishing, 4: 1685–1689.
Snyder, R. C. (2008). "What Is Third-Wave Feminism? A New Directions Essay." *Signs: Journal of Women in Culture and Society* 34 (1): 175–196.
Subramanyam, A. (2016). "I Get So Annoyed When 'Cool' Young Women Say They Are Not Feminists: Arundhati Roy." *Elle India*. Available at: www.huffingtonpost.in/aishwarya-subramanyam/arundhati-roy_b_10770790.html (Accessed 14 February 2017).

Further Reading

Bosco, F. J. (2004). "Human Rights Politics and Scaled Performances of Memory: Conflicts Among the Madres de Plaza de Mayo in Argentina." *Social and Cultural Geography* 5 (3): 381–402. doi: 10.1080/1464936042000252787
Poe, D. (2015). *Maternal Activism: Mothers Confronting Injustice*. Albany: SUNY Press.
Roy, A. (2003). *War Talk*. Cambridge, MA: South End Press. (Arundhati Roy's reflection on war and politics, after September 11.)
Yousafzai, M., and P. McCormick. (2013). *I Am Malala: How One Girl Stood Up for Education and Changed the World*. New York: Little Brown. (This is a book about the struggle of the youngest recipient of the Noble Peace Prize.)

24
QUEER OPPRESSION AND PACIFISM

Blake Hereth

This chapter argues that considerations arising from queer oppression can furnish support for pacifist positions. The first consideration concerns the nature and strength of the moral presumption against violence. Violence undermines a victim's agency, coercing them to betray their identities, not unlike "reparative therapy." The second consideration concerns the moral presumption against conscription. Current conscription policies are cisgender-normative, threaten to coerce queer citizens to fight for unjust states that oppose their basic rights, and coerce queer citizens to risk their lives and welfare on behalf of queerphobic citizens. These considerations serve to deepen criticisms of violence.

The Pink Pistols, Equal Defensive Rights, and Pacifism

We teach queers to shoot. Then we teach others that we have done so. Armed queers don't get bashed.... The Pink Pistols are the ones who have decided to no longer be safe targets. They have teeth. They will use them.[1]

This blurb from the website of the Pink Pistols provides a direct and fascinating introduction to the topic of queer oppression and pacifism. According to the website:

We are dedicated to the legal, safe, and responsible use of firearms for self-defense of the sexual-minority community. We no longer believe it is the right of those who hate and fear gay, lesbian, bi, trans, or polyamorous persons to use us as targets for their rage. Self-defense is our *right*.[2]

As the quote indicates, members of the LGBTQ—or, in brief, *queer*—community are frequently oppressed by violent means. The Federal Bureau of Investigation in the United States estimates, in their 2015 Hate Crime Statistics findings, that 1,263 individuals were targeted because of their sexual orientation and 122 individuals were targeted because of their non-cisgender gender identity.[3] Brandon Teena was murdered with a gun in Nebraska in 1993, and Matthew Shepard suffered torture and was beaten to death with a gun in Wyoming in 1998. In a more recent case from California in 2013, Sasha Fleischman was set aflame on a school bus as a demonstration of opposition to Sasha's gender identity.[4]

The Pink Pistols link the right to own and use firearms to the pervasive violence against queer persons. In a word, they maintain that this right is grounded in the right to *self-defense*. In a recent paper, C'Zar Bernstein, Timothy Hsiao, and Matt Palumbo use this strategy. Their argument, in brief, is that because "firearms are a reasonable means to self-defense" and because "people have a *prima facie* right to be allowed to own" things that provide them such a reasonable means, persons have a right to own firearms.[5] Concerns such as these motivate not only the view that queer persons should have reasonable access to firearms and firearm training, but that the exercise of that training against unjust aggressors is morally permissible in an array of cases.

Indeed, given the pervasiveness of violence against queer persons, it might be that queer persons have an even *stronger* moral right to own and use firearms in self-defense.[6] For example, suppose Ariam will be attacked by an unjust aggressor with a loaded firearm and Bill will be attacked with a fist and that you can provide a loaded firearm to exactly one of these individuals. It seems obvious that Ariam has the stronger claim to use of the firearm, since without it her odds of successfully self-defending are compromised. Said another way, persons have a right to reasonable means of self-defense, and part of what determines whether a means is reasonable is the degree or frequency of risk faced by the person acting in (legitimate) self-defense.

The point can be pressed more strongly from the angle of other-defense. Whereas the right to self-defense is generally characterized in terms of a Hohfeldian *liberty* (that is, persons with a right to self-defense are permitted but not obligated to self-defend), the defense of others, or *other-defense*, is often characterized as a *duty* (see Rodin 2010: 17–34 or Frowe 2016: 26).

Firearms and other weapons can be used not only in defense of oneself but also in defense of others, and it's the latter sort of cases that arguably provide the strongest case for the conclusion that groups like the Pink Pistols are right to encourage firearm ownership and defensive training. In a paper defending the moral permissibility of drone usage, Bradley Strawser argues that such usage is a duty, other things being equal. The reason, in short, is that:

> it is wrong to command someone to take on *unnecessary* potentially lethal risks in an effort to carry out a just action for some good; any potentially lethal risk must be justified by some strong countervailing reason.
>
> *Strawser 2010: 344*

Strawser calls this the Principle of Unnecessary Risk. He utilizes the principle to show that since drones reduce the risk that just combatants would otherwise face in modern warfare, their use is obligatory, other things being equal. Fundamentally, the Principle of Unnecessary Risk aims to protect the rights of just combatants. Although Strawser is concerned with minimizing the risk to just combatants in warfare by restricting the commands military leaders are permitted to give, it is not difficult to see how similar considerations apply to more domestic cases of other-defense. Consider, for example, the following case:

> Josh and Corbin are two gay neighbors living in a suburb of Atlanta. The area is known to be highly unsafe for gay men. One day while jogging, Josh sees two men assault Corbin. Josh knows that he can intervene at very little risk to himself, and he sees a gun nearby that he might use, but he refuses to use it to help Corbin.

Did Josh act wrongly in failing to assist Corbin? It might seem so, at least if we accept the view that other-defense is morally required. To do otherwise is to expose them to unnecessary risk, or at least to fail to take seriously their right to defensive assistance. What the case of Josh and

Corbin shows is that queer persons have reason to arm themselves in order to protect each other, as the Pink Pistols claim.

What goes for self-defense and other-defense in domestic cases goes similarly for *national defense*.[7] Until 1994, when "Don't Ask, Don't Tell" was instituted by the Clinton administration, queer persons were forbidden from serving in the United States military. Afterwards, queer persons were permitted to serve, but not openly. Finally, in 2011, "Don't Ask, Don't Tell" was repealed by the Obama administration and replaced with a policy that permitted queer persons to serve openly in the armed forces. What is intriguing about the former two policies—the outright ban of queer persons and the mitigated, closeted ban—is that they forbade queer persons from engaging in national defense. The more contemporary consensus, of course, is that such bans were reflective of a broadly queerphobic culture unwilling to accept the full inclusion of queer persons in modern society. What's somewhat surprising is that such policies ever managed to get off the ground given their counterintuitive implications. Consider, for example, the following scenario:

> Genevieve and Hamdi are lesbian partners living in a rural neighborhood during the Third World War. The Russians have invaded the United States and President Putin commands the Russian military. Without him, the Russians would be forced to retreat. It just so happens that Putin is near the home of Genevieve and Hamdi, and they are given an opportunity to kill him during a battle.

In such a scenario, few Americans would object to Genevieve and Hamdi killing Putin. But if Genevieve and Hamdi did so, they would be acting as *de facto* combatants on the side of the United States.[8]

Or consider a variation on this example in which Genevieve and Hamdi are *already* members of the United States military fighting against the Russians, and are attacked in their home by Russian operatives and threatened with rape—a war crime. Plausibly, no one would object to Genevieve and Hamdi defending themselves against rape, but then why object to them serving more generally as members of the military? Perhaps the objection is that when Genevieve and Hamdi defend themselves against rape, they are not defending themselves *qua combatants*. But that implies that if their intentions were not simply to defend *themselves* against rape, but also to do so *as a means of achieving military victory over the Russians*, then they would be acting qua combatants and thus acting impermissibly. Such a conclusion can hardly be believed.

What, then, was the central objection to persons like Genevieve and Hamdi serving more generally as members of the military? The worry at the time was that partial or full inclusion of queer persons in the military would be disruptive to military cohesion and would threaten national defense. Thus, it was thought that the rights of American citizens (including queer American citizens) would be *undermined* by permitting queer persons to fight for them. The argument for bans, then, went something like this:

(1) American citizens have a right to defense against their enemies.
(2) If American citizens have a right to defense against their enemies, then they have a claim against those who would undermine American chances of success in defending against their enemies.
(3) The partial or full inclusion of queer persons in the American military would undermine American chances of success in defending against their enemies.
(4) Therefore, American citizens have a claim against the partial or full inclusion of queer persons in the American military.

The centrally controversial premise is (3). The initial, speculative psychological basis for belief in the premise has long been discredited (see MacCoun 1996; Moradi and Miller 2010). The motivating moral premises, however, again appeal to rights to reasonable means to successful defense: in the same way that it's impermissible to take away someone's gun when they are being lethally attacked, so also it's impermissible to permit people to join the military if they will do little more than undermine the defensive capacities of that military (the gun example comes from Huemer 2003: 307).

Suppose, however, that we *accept* (3). That is, suppose we accepted the (false) view that the partial or full inclusion of queer persons in the American military would result in others failing to defend themselves successfully. Does it follow from this that such inclusion is impermissible? Not obviously. Consider the following example:

> Adolf, who has an axe, is lethally and unjustly threatening Mikhail, Vlad, and Joseph. Mikhail is Adolf's first and current target, after which he will move on to Vlad and Joseph. As the axe swings towards his head, Mikhail evaluates his defensive options: He could duck, but then the axe would strike (and kill) Vlad. He could punch Adolf, but that would only further anger Adolf, resulting in the deaths of Mikhail, Vlad, and Joseph. Or, lastly, he could permit the axe to strike his head, killing him.

In such a case, it is not obvious that Mikhail is *obligated* to choose the third option. That is, it is not obvious that he is obligated to permit himself to be killed.[9] After all, Adolf's attacks against him are just as unjust as they are against the others, and thus he has an equal right to defend himself against unjust aggression. It is difficult to see how Mikhail has an *equal* right to self-defense if, in choosing between his life and others' lives, he is obliged to prioritize *their* lives over his own life.[10] But then perhaps the claim American citizens have against others described in (2) is not always overriding: there *can* be cases in which persons are permitted to defend themselves even if doing so undermines the self-defending efforts of others. Or, alternatively, perhaps (2) is false. Either way, it seems that (3), even if it were true, is not obviously sufficient to render impermissible the partial or full inclusion of queer persons in the military.[11]

Against the Pink Pistols and defenders of the moral permissibility of violence in defense of individuals, principles, or property, *pacifists* of virtually all varieties maintain the violence is less often permissible than is typically believed. For example, the species of contingent pacifism defended by Robert Holmes maintains that a modern war is permissible only if the number of non-combatants killed in that war is zero (See Holmes 1989: 181; see also Bazargan 2014). This is a high bar that virtually no modern war will meet, and thus virtually no modern war is permissible—a conclusion at odds with the widespread view that *some* modern wars, such as the one waged defensively by the Allied powers against the Axis powers in the Second World War, were permissible. Other pacifists, such as absolute pacifists, hold that the wrongness of violence is *necessarily* wrong (see Ryan 1983; Reader 2000; Hereth 2017). But in all its forms, pacifism maintains that violence is less often permissible than is typically believed.

We have seen that there are reasons to believe that the use of violence is permissible, and perhaps sometimes even obligatory, for queer persons. What I shall explore in the remainder of this paper is whether there are considerations arising from queer oppression that lend credence to some version of pacifism. I defend the view that there *are* such considerations. First, I shall explore the moral presumption against violence, arguing that the wrong-making properties of violence are shared by other coercive activities, such as "reparative therapy." This illustrates that what makes violence wrong is also what makes "reparative therapy" wrong, and vice versa.

Second, I address military conscription and the ways in which it wrongs queer persons *qua* queer persons. In particular, I argue that the highly cisgender-normative procedures for selecting persons for the draft contribute to the oppression of queer persons, and that there are strong moral concerns with coercing queer persons to fight either for nations or citizens who don't defend (or, worse, *oppose*) their interests. What this shows is that military conscription can be morally objectionable for reasons beyond those traditionally given—reasons that, while perhaps not unique to queer oppression, are nonetheless grounded in the realities of that oppression.

The Presumption against Violence

There is a moral presumption against violence, at least when it is directed at individuals with a particular kind of moral status. One sort of moral status that guarantees such presumptive protection against violence is being a *rights-bearer*, and a commonplace right is the right not to be subjected to unjust violence.

Of course, that construal might make it seem as if there is no moral presumption against violence, but only a presumption against *unjust* violence. But there is a sense in which violence itself is presumptively unjust: namely, it is a pro tanto welfare diminishment and thus requires sufficiently good reason to inflict. In cases where causing such welfare diminishment is done for sufficiently good reason, violence is permissible, but otherwise not. Thus, there is a presumptive *badness* to violence, one that must be overcome by the right sort of moral considerations.

There are a number of accounts as to what makes violence presumptively wrong, and I shall not here attempt to summarize them. Instead, I shall examine accounts of the wrongness of violence that are morally intertwined with particular wrongs committed against queer persons. To see this, consider first Sissela Bok's comparison of violence with deceit:

> Deceit and violence—these are the two forms of deliberate assault on human beings. Both can coerce people into acting against their will. Most harm that can befall victims through violence can come to them also through deceit. But deceit controls more subtly, for it works on belief as well as action.
>
> *Bok 1999: 18*

Here, Bok maintains that deceit and violence share a common wrong-making feature: coercion. She rightly notes that deceit controls more subtly than violence, since it is easier to see how violence is coercive. One transparently coercive kind of violence is torture. Arguing against the moral permissibility of torture, Bob Brecher makes the following remarks:

> This is exactly what torturers aim for: to break a person, to make them into only a body. It is worth pausing here to emphasize that this is why interrogational torture—as contrasted with torture used to intimidate, terrorize, punish or dehumanize—has to require extraordinary skill. The torturer has to get the person they are torturing to "pour out their guts," but to do so in that precise moment just before the response to "any request the torturer might make" becomes just that, an unthought response, rather than an action. Otherwise they are no longer *able* to give the torturer what they want, namely a truthful answer to the question, "Where's the bomb?" What could be a more complete negation of a person than to break them, to make simply an object of them?
>
> *Brecher 2014: 268–269*

The central wrong-making feature of torture, according to Brecher, is that it reduces persons to mere objects (see Kellenberger 1987: 135–140).

In this respect, it's coercive since it opposes the autonomy of the tortured individual—usually by means of capture, restraint, and the infliction of profound pain—to the extent that it has an eliminative effect on their autonomy. The concerns about autonomy, moreover, do not end here, as David Sussman observes:

> Torture does not merely insult or damage its victim's agency, but rather turns such agency against itself, forcing the victim to experience herself as helpless yet complicit in her own violation. That is not just an assault on or violation of the victim's autonomy but also a perversion of it, a kind of systematic mockery of the basic relations that an individual bears both to others and to herself.
>
> *Sussman 2005: 30*

Sussman's characterization of the tortured individual's agency (or autonomy) as turning against itself is distinct from Brecher, who characterizes the agency as disappeared. Nevertheless it is clear that, for Sussman, these persons are coerced and that violence is the coercive tool. (For a critique of Sussman's views on the distinctive wrongness of torture, see Kamm 2013: 9–12.)

Of particular interest with Sussman's account is the notion of agents being coerced to turn against themselves in some fundamental sense. Frances Kamm considers a case in which torturing an agent will violate that agent's values:

> But what if A would prefer to be killed rather than (predictably) act to betray his important mission of killing B just to stop the torture, when it does not directly incapacitate him? Betraying his cause to stop the torture may be a fate that, given his values, he would regard as worse than death. Given his values and assuming he will give in, it does not seem that he could reasonably share the purpose of torturing rather than killing him.
>
> *Kamm 2013: 20*

Kamm raises this case in order to deepen the apparent impermissibility of torture. However, she ultimately concludes:

> The interest of his that he has a claim on us to consider is his survival, whose value does not depend on his personal conception of it, rather than the protection of his honor whose value, like the value of a monument to one's god, depends on his conception of it.
>
> *Kamm 2013: 21*

Thus, since A's cause has value that depends on A's conception of it, it lacks the kind of value that would confer a claim on us to act differently so as to respect its value. Kamm therefore maintains, as many do, that because certain individuals are morally liable to be harmed (including tortured) and lack special claims on us that we not harm them in particular ways (such as torture), it's permissible to torture them.

But what of individuals who are *not* morally liable to be harmed but are nonetheless harmed in part because of valuable facts about them—facts whose values *don't* depend on their personal conception of them? Consider one such example:

> David is a teenager whose parents learn that he's gay. They disapprove and want him to change, so they send him to "reparative therapy," where specialists work day after day to

get David to deny his sexual orientation and to adopt another one. David is devastated by this, as he loves being gay and values his relationship with John, his partner.

David is coerced into betraying himself and what he values. Unlike the tortured individuals described by Brecher, Sussman, and Kamm, David is not morally liable to such harm and there is no justification for it. He is therefore wronged by everyone whose aim it is to change his orientation coercively. The same is true of Alan Turing, who was subjected to chemical castration in order to "cure" his sexual orientation.

What these cases suggest is that what's wrong with violence is also what's wrong with rejecting queer identities by means of "reparative therapy" and other coercive measures aimed either at *changing* those identities or *repressing* them. Thus, Judith Butler appears to be right in her concern that cisgender-heteronormativity shares in the wrongness of violence by sharing (some of) the same wrong-making features of violence:

> [Violence against queer persons] emerges from a profound desire to keep the order of binary gender natural or necessary, to make of it a structure, either natural or cultural, or both, that no human can oppose, and still remain human. . . . The violent response is the one that does not ask, and does not seek to know. It wants to shore up what it knows, to expunge what threatens it with not-knowing, what forces it to reconsider the presuppositions of its world, their contingency, their malleability.
>
> *Butler 2004: 35*

Butler maintains that coercing persons to change or repress their identities is itself an instance of violence, but it's not necessary to share that view in order to see that one of the central wrong-making features of violence is coercion. There are therefore at least two possible views here. The first view is that cisgender-heteronormativity, when acted out (e.g., in David's case), is *necessarily* another instance of violence. The second view is more modest and maintains only that cisgender-heteronormativity, when acted out, shares a common property with violence that contributes to the wrongness of both.

The Draft and Protected Identities

In the United States and many other countries, military service can be conscripted. Persons, often men, are forced to leave their homes or families, don a uniform (effectively painting themselves as targets), travel to another country, and fight for causes with which they may not agree. The methods of identifying men/males are not only profoundly cisgender-normative,[12] but also profoundly *essentialist*. Men/males are drafted and women/females are not because it is believed that, on some deep level, violence is an appropriate activity for men/males in a way that it isn't appropriate for women/females.[13] Thus, the selective nature of the draft furthers essentialist attitudes and, with it, features of the gender binary that, as discussed in the last section, share some of the same wrong-making properties that make violence wrong.

That drafts tend to select only males for service ("Selective Service") makes them something of an easy moral target. Were the draft to select only persons of color for service, it would provoke rightful outrage on the grounds that it arbitrarily exposes persons of color to greater risks than white persons—that is, it is racist. Since the draft chooses only males for service, it is sexist.

However, the draft might be executed differently than it is in many contemporary states. A draft might, for example, choose persons irrespective of their sex or gender, thereby avoiding singling only males for military service. In doing so, it might evade the charge of sexism.

Such a move might open the draft to other charges, however, such as coercing certain groups of persons to fight (or fill positions that, in principle, could require them to fight if certain conditions are met) who are oppressed by the state. Queer persons are one such group, at least relative to the United States, where state and federal protections for sexual orientation and gender identity are few and far between. As of 2016, most states in the United States do not include non-discrimination protections for gender identity. Because these non-discrimination protections safeguard fundamental interests such as equal opportunity in employment and housing, queer individuals forced to fight for their nation or home state would often be (and in the past, were *always*) forced to fight for a nation or state in which they are not equals. This is one of many reasons why, during the American Civil War, it was impermissible for Confederate states to coerce slaves into fighting for the Confederacy: because the Confederacy failed to represent the fundamental moral interests of the slaves.[14]

As with the charge of sexism, however, it might be thought that this objection to the draft is an objection to how it is *contingently* designed. We might either design a draft that does not select members of state-oppressed or state-unprotected groups, or design a draft that does draft its citizens equally but only when the citizens enjoy full political and social equality.

But these suggestions are problematic. The former option has the moral upshot of avoiding further burdening members of oppressed or unprotected groups, but the burdens associated with warfare are steep—arguably far steeper than the burdens unfairly placed on queer persons in contemporary society. Lacking equal opportunities to legally adopt children, for instance, is an unjust burden that many queer persons are forced to face, but that burden seems considerably far less severe than the burden faced by combatants in contemporary warfare. Thus, requiring only members of unoppressed or protected groups to serve as combatants during wartime seems to shift the burden to an unjust extent. However, it might be argued that some of the burdens placed on queer persons—for example, lacking equal opportunity to housing—can (and sometimes does) surely place queer persons, and particularly minors, in dire straits, as is the case with the risks of homelessness, which include serious health risks and death.

Moreover, it's not obvious that every member of an unoppressed or protected group is morally liable to shoulder the burdens associated with being a combatant in contemporary warfare. Consider reliable allies: persons who are cisgender and straight who advocate daily for the full political and social equality of queer persons, sometimes sacrificing their own interests for equality. It appears implausible to suppose that persons such as these would be drafted as a morally preferable alternative to drafting queer persons.[15] And it's not clear how the state would go about reliably distinguishing these persons from persons who are not reliable allies.

The alternative—designing a draft that drafts its citizens equally but only when they enjoy full political and social equality—has problems of its own. A seemingly basic requirement of full political and social equality is that the state provides protections and opportunities in ways that aren't merely formal. For example, in San Francisco during the 1960s and 1970s, queer persons were afforded a number of basic legal protections in the formal sense, like the right not to be subjected to extrajudicial killing. But these rights often went unenforced by the city's law enforcement. In cases like these, queer persons are *de facto* unequals even if they are *de jure* equals. Thus, for a draft to be permissibly instituted on this view, queer persons must be the *de facto* equals of non-queer persons. Again, as a contingent matter, this standard seems very difficult to achieve, and it's not obvious that any contemporary state meets it.

Furthermore, the draft requires a person to fight not only for the state but also for all the *members* of the state. Presumably, while it's contingently true that some citizens of the state generally fail to respect the rights and dignity of queer persons, it is highly likely that any state will always have at least *some* such citizens. We might inquire, then, whether it's permissible to coerce any queer person to fight for citizens who fail (whether personally or in principle) to respect their rights and dignity.

One might think that the answer is no, but that this is not due to the discriminatory nature of the queerphobic citizen. Rather, it's due to the fact that it's impermissible to coerce anyone to fight for someone else when doing so would put the coerced person at serious risk of harm.[16]

What this position entails, however, is that the queerphobic citizen's claim on the queer citizen to defensively assist them is *not substantially weakened by* their queerphobia. Consider the following case:

> Nolan is a neo-Nazi who would kill Michael, a Jew, if he had an opportunity to do so, and Michael knows this. Fortunately, Nolan is unlikely ever to meet Michael. One day, Nolan runs into trouble: he slips by the side of a pool, hitting his head and knocking him unconscious, and falls into the pool. From a great distance, Michael can save Nolan by hitting a button that drains the pool. But hitting the button is very dangerous, since it often electrocutes people who touch it.

In this scenario, is Michael obligated to push the button in Nolan's defense? It seems not, and for two related reasons. The first is that Michael isn't obligated to risk his own life.[17] The second reason is related to the first: by saving Nolan, Michael would be putting himself at *greater* risk of unjust harm than if he failed to save Nolan. This is because although Nolan does not represent a *likely* threat to Michael, he does represent a *non-zero* threat to him. Thus, if Michael is not obligated to risk his own life at the level of pushing the button, he is even less obligated to risk his own life at the level of pushing the button *for Nolan*.[18] Said another way, it would be morally *worse* to coerce Michael to do the latter than the former. By implication, it's on balance worse to coerce queer persons to expose themselves to great risk on behalf of queerphobic citizens than it is to coerce persons to expose themselves to great risk.

There are two further reasons not directly related to the first two. The first concerns the likely event of coercing queer persons to fight for causes in which they do not believe or, worse, causes that oppose their fundamental interests as queer persons. We are already familiar with conscientious objectors who for religious or philosophical reasons object to participating in warfare either full stop or as combatants. In the United States, these individuals are sometimes allowed to avoid military service altogether or at least avoid particular kinds of military service (e.g., as a combatant). However, "a man's reasons for not wanting to participate in a war must not be based on politics, expediency, or self-interest."[19] Suppose now that a gay man were drafted into the United States military prior to the federal legalization of same-sex marriage and other federal protections for gay individuals, and that he applied for conscientious objector status on the grounds that he objected to risking his life for a state in which he was a second-class citizen in important respects. This man's objection is plausibly a *political* one, and thus its invocation disqualifies him for status as a conscientious objector. Or suppose that the same gay man, after 40 years of waiting for the federal legalization of same-sex marriage, was finally able to marry his lifetime partner, but was then conscripted and objected on grounds of *self-interest*, citing his long-term desire to marry his partner and not die tragically in warfare. In both of these cases, the interests at stake are fundamental to these men in ways central to their identities as gay men. Indeed, in some ways, they are fundamentally *bound up in* their identities as gay men. Thus, to require them to fight for a homophobic state or to risk losing their spouses is to force them to act in ways that violate their identities. In this way, the draft seems in some morally serious respects comparable to "reparative therapy," forcing queer persons to risk serious harm to themselves and turn against interests central to their identities.

A second worry concerns hate crimes. What is a hate crime? Claudia Card's account is helpful here. She characterizes criminal offenders who commit hate crimes as individuals "who intentionally select as their victims members of certain groups who are especially vulnerable to oppression on the basis of their race, color, sexual orientation, disability, or other deviance, or perceived deviance, from social norms" (Card 2001: 196).

Thus, as Marcia Baron comments, on this account "*X* counts as a hate crime only if the victim is a member of a group that is especially vulnerable to oppression," and "*X* does not count as a hate crime if the offender selects as a victim a member of such a group . . . *without regard to* the fact that the victim is a member of that group" (Baron 2016: 505). Leaving aside questions about whether hate crimes are worse than, or ought to be punished more than, non-hate-crimes of a similar nature, it's generally agreed that hate crimes are very serious wrongs.[20]

Imagine that a queerphobic citizen desires the eradication of queer persons in their country and sees a dangerous war as an opportunity to achieve this. This citizen knows that not all queer persons will voluntarily sign up to serve as combatants in the war, and that some further measure will therefore be required. To accomplish their evil intentions, this citizen goes about drumming up popular support for a draft—but leaves their own reasons a secret. The draft is instituted and would have been instituted even *without* this particular citizen's efforts. Many queer (and many non-queer) citizens are then drafted as combatants and subsequently die in warfare.

Are these queer persons victims of a hate crime? Perhaps the answer is yes since they are selected and victimized by the queerphobic citizen on the basis of their queer identities. But there are two potential problems with this view. The first is that since hate crimes require certain *intentions* and it's *not* the queerphobic person who drafts queer citizens, it remains possible that the state drafts queer persons for reasons that are not queerphobic. The second is related. The state might draft queer persons for morally good reasons: for example, because the state and its citizens have been subjected to unjust aggression from another state and a larger military force is needed to defend the state and its citizens. These reasons suggest, at the very least, that if these queer persons are victims of a hate crime, they are not victims of a *paradigmatic* hate crime.

Might they nonetheless be victims of a hate crime in some non-paradigmatic way? Certainly it seems true that the queerphobic citizen *intends* something that is very much like a hate crime. If the queer citizen is permissibly drafted and forced to risk their life on behalf of the queerphobic citizen, they will be morally *forbidden* to act in opposition to the intention of the queerphobic citizen. Said another way: they will be effectively *obligated* to fight for the queerphobic citizen even if doing so will result in giving the queerphobic citizen exactly what they want, namely, the death of the queer citizen.

Notes

1 From "About the Pink Pistols," emphasis mine. Link: www.pinkpistols.org/about-the-pink-pistols/.
2 From "About the Pink Pistols," emphasis mine. Link: www.pinkpistols.org/about-the-pink-pistols/.
3 See U.S. Department of Justice, Federal Bureau of Investigation, 2015 Hate Crime Statistics at the following link: https://ucr.fbi.gov/hate-crime/2015/topic-pages/victims_final.
4 As the *New York Times* reports, Fleischman's case was, like Teena's and Shepard's, tried as a hate crime. Link: www.nytimes.com/2015/02/01/magazine/the-fire-on-the-57-bus-in-oakland.html.
5 Bernstein, Hsiao, and Palumbo (2015: 345). Cf. David Rodin's account of permissible self-defense in Rodin (2010: 37). Rodin does not explicitly appeal to a right to own firearms, but it isn't difficult to see how his more basic, correlative account of rights is similar to the one utilized by Bernstein, Hsiao, and Palumbo.
6 This is not to say that the queer community *uniquely* possesses this stronger right. Other communities, such as communities of color, are also at greater risk of unjust violence. There is evidence that the

intersectional nature of hate crimes is sometimes overlooked by the queer community at large. See, for example, Meyer (2012).
7 Here, I pass over the controversy between reductive individualists (who maintain that the moral rules governing domestic self-defense and international warfare are fundamentally the same) and collectivists (who maintain that the moral rules are fundamentally different) about war. For an overview of the debate, see Frowe (2016: 31–41).
8 This assumption is controversial. However, the example can be tailored to fit different conceptions of what constitutes a "combatant." For example, perhaps the United States armed forces maintain a policy during the Third World War that anyone willing to fight against the Russians is automatically deemed a combatant, or perhaps Genevieve and Hamdi are already combatants serving in the armed forces.
9 Cf. Whitley Kaufman's (2010) similar argument that because a duty of martyrdom is implausible, so too is the position that it's impermissible to kill innocent aggressors.
10 Indeed, the logical coherence of such a suggestion is dubious. If Mikhail has such an obligation, then so do Vlad and Joseph. But then they are obligated to prioritize Mikhail's life over theirs, and thus lack a claim on Mikhail that Mikhail prioritize their lives over his own.
11 It might be objected that the case of Mikhail is not really a counterexample to (2), since (2) is concerned with cases in which the defensive actions of someone like Mikhail undermine *everyone's* defensive rights. For example, suppose that Adolf will kill Mikhail no matter what Mikhail does, but that either Vlad or Joseph will be spared if Mikhail intentionally sacrifices himself. Here again, however, it is not obvious that Mikhail is obligated to do so.
12 The methods are cisgender-normative insofar as they promote or rely upon cisgender-normative assumptions about whether someone is male or female. For example, persons are drafted if their official state documents identify them as male, and it tends strongly to be the case that those documents identify someone as male only if medical professionals determined around the time of birth that someone was male on the basis that the individual had a penis, testes, and the like.
13 Cf. Sjoberg's (2006: 10–11) claim that the identification of women with pacifism "denies women's agency in choosing political alternatives," since it relies on misogynistic conceptions about what is appropriate for women to do during warfare.
14 None of this is meant to suggest that the condition of slaves in the nineteenth-century United States is on a moral par with queer persons in the twenty-first-century United States, only that they share one significant wrong-making property.
15 Alternatively: it is morally preferable since they are less oppressed and more protected, but not *sufficiently* morally preferable to justify exposing them to the horrors of war.
16 This might not be true in cases where the person coerced to put herself at risk of harm is morally responsible for the fact that someone else stands in need of assistance.
17 This is why non-queerphobic citizens lack a general right to coerce queer persons to defensively assist them in warfare. Moreover, even if non-queerphobic citizens had a claim on queer persons to fight on their behalf (thus making it permissible to draft them), queer persons would have *the same claim* on non-queerphobic citizens.
18 This is true even if we assume that the risk Nolan *alone* poses to Michael would be insufficiently strong to permit Michael not to save Nolan. Recall that the issue here is whether it's permissible to require queer persons to wage war on behalf of queerphobic citizens *on top of* the risks already imposed by fighting in warfare.
19 U.S. Selective Service System. Link: www.sss.gov/consobj.
20 For worries about hate crime legislation, see Hurd (2001). For a positive view, see Wellman (2006).

Works Cited

Baron, M. (2016). "Hate Crime Legislation Reconsidered." *Metaphilosophy* 47 (4–5): 504–523.
Bazargan, S. (2014). "Varieties of Contingent Pacifism in War," in H. Frowe and G. Lang (eds.), *How We Fight*. New York: Oxford University Press, 1–17.
Bernstein, C., T. Hsiao, and M. Palumbo. (2015). "The Moral Right to Keep and Bear Firearms." *Public Affairs Quarterly* 29 (4): 345–363.
Bok, S. (1999). *Lying: Moral Choice in Public and Private Life*. New York: Vintage Books.
Brecher, B. (2014). "Torture and Its Apologists," in A.I. Cohen and C.H. Wellman (eds.), *Contemporary Debates in Applied Ethics*, 2nd ed. Malden, MA: Blackwell, 260–271.
Butler, J. (2004). *Undoing Gender*. New York: Routledge.

Card, C. (2001). "Is Penalty Enhancement a Sound Idea?" *Law and Philosophy* 20: 195–214.
Frowe, H. (2016). *The Ethics of War and Peace: An Introduction*, 2nd ed. New York: Routledge.
Hereth, B. (2017). "Against Self-Defense." *Social Theory and Practice* 43 (3): 313–635.
Holmes, R. (1989). *On War and Morality*. Princeton, NJ: Princeton University Press.
Huemer, M. (2003). "Is There a Right to Own a Gun?" *Social Theory and Practice* 29 (2): 297–324.
Hurd, H. (2001). "Why Liberals Should Hate 'Hate Crime Legislation'." *Law and Philosophy* 20: 215–232.
Kamm, F. M. (2013). *Ethics for Enemies: Terror, Torture, and War*. New York: Oxford University Press.
Kaufman, W. (2010). "Self-Defense, Innocent Aggressors, and the Duty of Martyrdom." *Pacific Philosophical Quarterly* 91: 78–96.
Kellenberger, J. (1987). "A Defense of Pacifism." *Faith and Philosophy* 4 (2): 129–148.
MacCoun, R. (1996). "Sexual Orientation and Military Cohesion: A Critical Review of the Evidence," in G.M. Herek and J.B. Jobe (eds.), *Out in Force: Sexual Orientation and the Military*. Chicago: University of Chicago Press, 157–176.
Meyer, D. (2012). "An Intersectional Analysis of LGBT People's Evaluations of Anti-Queer Violence." *Gender and Society* 26 (6): 849–873.
Moradi, B., and L. Miller. (2010). "Attitudes of Iraq and Afghanistan War Veterans Toward Gay and Lesbian Service Members." *Armed Forces and Society* 36 (3): 397–419.
Reader, S. (2000). "Making Pacifism Plausible." *Journal of Applied Philosophy* 17 (2): 169–180.
Rodin, D. (2010). *War and Self-Defense*. New York: Oxford University Press.
Ryan, C. (1983). "Self-Defense, Pacifism, and the Possibility of Killing." *Ethics* 93 (3): 508–524.
Sjoberg, L. (2006). *Gender, Justice, and the Wars in Iraq: A Feminist Reformulation of Just War Theory*. Lanham, MD: Lexington Books.
Strawser, B.J. (2010) "Moral Predators: The Duty to Employ Uninhabited Aerial Vehicles." *Journal of Military Ethics* 9 (4): 342–368.
Sussman, D. (2005). "What's Wrong with Torture?" *Philosophy and Public Affairs* 33 (1): 1–33.
Wellman, C. H. (2006). "A Defense of Stiffer Penalties for Hate Crimes." *Hypatia* 21 (2): 62–80.

Further Reading

Conrad, R. (ed.) (2014). *Against Equality: Queer Revolution, Not Mere Inclusion*. Oakland, CA: AK Press, Part 2. (An anthology of work focused on gay and lesbian concerns.)

PART IV

Applications

25
CARE THEORY, PEACEMAKING, AND EDUCATION

Nel Noddings

"Peace" is best described as a desirable state of human relations—not merely as the cessation of hostilities. Peacemaking, as we will see, is the process of describing, building, and maintaining that desirable state. Care theory, as a relational approach to ethics and moral education, provides advice on this process, especially on the forms of communication involved in caring relations. This chapter starts with a brief overview of care theory, moves on to a discussion of the centrality of communication in establishing and maintaining peace, and concludes with some recommendations on what we might do in schools to foster peacemaking.

Care Theory

Care ethics (Noddings 2013a) is a relation-based moral theory. It is meant to guide us toward the establishment, preservation, and deepening of cooperative human relations. It is concerned, too, with the quality of relations between humans and all other living things, but its roots are firmly grounded in the human-to-human relation. Care ethics is a needs-based theory. It is concerned primarily with needs, not rights. At its simplest, the caring relation is described as the interaction or series of interactions between two parties, carer and cared-for, in which the carer attends to, listens closely to, the expressed needs of the cared-for. The carer tries to understand those needs, reflects on them, and feels something—is moved by the expressed needs. He or she then either acts to meet the need or to somehow transpose it; in the latter case, the carer, while rejecting the need as presented, responds in a way meant to preserve the caring relation. The cared-for plays an essential role by responding, by recognizing the efforts of the carer as caring. Without this response, there is no caring relation despite the efforts of the carer.

Notice that both parties contribute to the relation. The relation cannot be described as caring unless the response of the cared-for indicates that caring has been received. Unlike virtue ethics, care ethics does not look only at the acts and motives of the carer. Notice, too, that the carer listens for *expressed* needs. We often engage with others on the basis of *assumed* or *inferred* needs. Indeed, teachers today are hard pressed—even ordered—to address needs assumed in the stated curriculum, and they are often discouraged from listening to the needs that might be expressed by their students. We will return to this topic in the last section of the chapter.

In equal-to-equal relations, carer and cared-for regularly exchange positions. In adult relations, we expect to see such exchanges quite often, and their absence may lead us to assess the overall relation as in some danger of failing. In adult to infant (or young child) relations, there can be no such exchange; the adult is always in the position of carer. But even here, the infant contributes substantially as cared-for to the relation—coos, smiles, extends arms, sighs in contentment, wriggles with delight. When an infant is severely handicapped and unable to respond expressively to a parent's loving efforts to care, the relation is sadly diminished, and the parents may suffer greatly. Parents in such situations need the care of other adults to support them.

Some relations are formally defined: doctor, patient; lawyer, client; teacher, student. By definition, exchanges of position in these caring relations are rare. When such exchanges are frequent, the relation moves from one formally defined to one better described as friendship.

Now and then, when we look at a relation that is usually characterized by mutual caring, we see that it has gone quiet; that is, there is a substantial decrease in interactions of any sort. This sometimes happens in marriages, friendships, and even parent-child relations. It is often a sign that participants are afraid that interactions might turn unpleasant, even conflictual, and—if the silence or emptiness is brief—it may be a very good strategy. When interactions resume, when things "blow over," the hope is that there will be a renewed commitment to caring. If the silence is mutually embraced as a cessation of hostilities, it may be regarded as a prelude to genuine peace, a condition marked by mutual caring, one that must be continually renewed.

Many of our day-to-day interactions are guided by cultural expectations of civility and politeness; there is no moral demand for the specific acts of caring described in care ethics, and care ethics recognizes this. Moral educators working from the care perspective envision a society in which citizens are *prepared* to care when a need arises. Normally, for example, we expect to exchange friendly greetings with our neighbors, but if we detect unusual sadness, fear, or worry, the interaction becomes one of caring. The empathetic attention required of carers must be cultivated in those who would be carers. Such empathetic attention and communication should also be activated in interactions within and across groups, communities, and nations.

In his discussion of the search for the "great community," John Dewey argued that not only must individuals within groups communicate effectively but groups, too, must do so, and "different groups [must] interact flexibly and fully in connection with other groups" (Dewey 1927: 147). We do not communicate with others only to attain our own objectives but to understand and help others to attain theirs.

So far we have been talking about what might be called "natural caring." In such cases, we respond as carers because we are naturally moved by the expressed need of the cared-for. This sensitivity is sharpened by the close physical contact we have with relatives and friends. Because the response characteristic of natural caring is central to our lives, we are led to ask whether we are obligated to respond with care to strangers and others who are not closely connected to us. Can we—should we—embrace an ethic of care? Should we move beyond natural caring to ethical caring? And what does this mean?

Natural caring endows us with a spontaneous feeling of "I must." I must relieve my child's hunger, my friend's depression, the accident victim's pain. The spirit of ethical caring develops in response to a remembrance of natural caring:

> The memory of our own best moments of caring and being cared for sweeps over us as a feeling—as an "I must"—in response to the plight of the other and our conflicting desire to serve our own interests.
>
> *Noddings 2013a: 80*

We may or may not act on this initial feeling. We may start with the feeling, "I must do something," and then switch to "something must be done." In that case, we have given up the

"I must." Openness to this ethical "I must" is cultivated by the intense experience of natural caring and encouragement to seek within ourselves for memories of caring and being cared for. As we reflect on this experience, we develop an ideal of caring and are better prepared to care for those who address us.

Care ethics makes an important distinction between caring-for and caring-about. When we move from "I must do something" to "something must be done," we have moved from the possibility of caring-for to merely caring-about. Caring-about is synonymous with concern. We care-about many people unconnected with us and situations in which we are not directly involved. For example, most of us care-about people in Syria and other parts of the Middle East who endure bombing, homelessness, and hunger. But unless we have some form of direct contact, we cannot *care-for* them. That does not mean that we should do nothing, but, without some direct response from those we try to help, a caring relation cannot be established; we cannot be sure that our attempts to care have been received. Caring-about is important and should be encouraged, but it has another limiting feature. We must often be directed by assumed needs; without direct contact, we do not receive the expressed needs of those we would help. We are thus doubly constrained in our efforts to care; we are not sure what the needs are, and we are often unsure whether they have been met. The distinction between caring-for and caring-about will be very important in our discussion of communication in attempts at peacemaking.

Communication and Peacemaking

In her discussion of maternal peacemaking, Sara Ruddick contrasts the mere cessation of hostilities with the genuine task of peacemaking, noting that it requires staying-with, giving, receiving, and renewing communication: "The peacemaker asks herself and those she cares for not what they can afford to give up, but what they can give, not how they can be left alone, but what they can do together" (Ruddick 1989: 181). In what follows, we will explore the need for staying-with and renewing communication.

The silence that often accompanies a cessation of hostilities can be both hopeful and worrisome. To generate *peace* those involved in a disagreement or lack of trust must work to build or restore caring relations, a condition in which they can work together, and such relations require effective communication. This is true not only of formerly warring nations but also of individuals and competing groups within nations that have fallen into contention. Historically, classes within a society have often experienced difficulty in communicating with each other, and a long cold silence may actually increase both misunderstanding and smoldering animosity. Then, too often, the solution is sometimes achieved by finding a common enemy. The current revival of nationalism in the U.S. may be a product of this sort of misunderstanding across classes, and it should worry us. In what follows, I will use "class" as it is usually defined in economic or educational terms, but most of what is said may well apply to religious and racial classes as well.

George Orwell spoke openly and usefully in the mid-1930s about the problems of communicating and understanding across classes: "To get rid of class-distinctions you have got to start by understanding how one class appears when seen through the eyes of another" (Orwell 1958: 131). Both must see themselves clearly as the others see them. Orwell criticizes the well-meaning "do-gooders" who would assist the poor through a process of "leveling up"—that is, of making the poor more like their betters. It is not enough for the better-off class to work at "improving" the other according to its own standards—in Orwell's words, "by means of hygiene, fruit-juice, birth-control, poetry, etc." (Orwell 1958: 162). This does not mean that we should forsake all thoughts of improving the condition of those less fortunate. It means, rather, that we should communicate respectfully with them, listen to their expressed needs, and work cooperatively with them. We may give to them, they may give to us, and together we may achieve deeper understanding.

This advice is echoed by Michael Walzer in his discussion of the relationship between liberators and those they want to liberate. He, too, notes dramatic class differences:

> The relationship simultaneously encompasses deep sympathy and deep hostility. Sympathy, because the liberators don't just resent the foreign rulers and hope to replace them; they really want to improve the everyday lives of the men and women with whom they identify: *their* people (the possessive pronoun is important). Hostility, because at the same time the liberators hate what they take to be the backwardness, ignorance, passivity, and submissiveness of those same people.
>
> *Walzer 2015: 68*

Walzer describes the disappointment of liberators when the formerly oppressed turn away from their partially realized freedom and return to forms of autocratic governance from which they had been freed. But, again, it may be that the liberators operated on assumed needs—surely these people want to live freely just as we do—and failed to communicate with them on a level that would allow them to express the full range of their felt needs. In the cases discussed by Walzer, the liberators failed to hear and understand that the oppressed rejected the secularization that accompanied the program to liberate them. It is not easy to understand that people are sometimes attached—even devoted—to some feature of their oppression or to some prior commitment, such as religion, that has survived and sustained them throughout their oppression. Again, open-hearted communication is required if the liberators and oppressed are to work together. We cannot allow caring-for to degenerate into caring-about.

Today in the U.S., class differences are growing, and this presents another problem in communication. Thomas Frank tells us:

> Today, the American class divide is starker than at any time in my memory, and yet Congress doesn't seem to know it. Today, the House of Representatives is dedicated obsessively to the concerns of the rich—to cutting their taxes, to chastising their foes, to holding the tissue box as they cry about the mean names people call them.
>
> *Frank 2016: 19*

He goes on to advocate more careful evaluation of the economic advice offered by financial experts and bank lobbyists who "bamboozle members of Congress" (Frank 2016: 166) with the claim that *they* should be trusted because *they* understand the system whereas both the Congress and the people do not. Even the "caring-about" seems insincere.

This troubling class divide has alienated both the "new poor" and the traditionally poor, and it has angered a class of people who are not seeking to acquire a status they have never had but, rather, to regain the status and respect they have long held but see slipping away from them. Arlie Hochschild writes that an empathy wall has been erected between the flourishing middle class and those recently pushed out of it, and she notes that "an empathy wall is an obstacle to deep understanding of another person, one that can make us feel indifferent or even hostile to those who hold different beliefs" (Hochschild 2016: 5). Her remarks underscore the emphasis that care ethics places on listening to expressed needs and feelings in order to understand.

In all three of the examples just cited, we see a troubling failure of communication and resulting lack of understanding. Orwell's suggested solution—one by which he lived—is for people from different classes to live and work together on at least a few common projects. In doing so, both sides gain a better understanding of the other and of themselves. Orwell learned to poke fun at the snobbishness of his own class, but he also acknowledged a certain idealism in the tenacity with which it held onto its language and manners.

We see a similar form of holding on to customs and traditions in the situations described by Walzer. It is often interpreted by "helpers" or "liberators" to be a stubborn, even stupid, resistance to self-improvement. Again, this paradox of assumed need and resistance is at least partly rooted in lack of understanding. Perhaps this explains the somewhat greater effectiveness of NGOs over government agencies in improving the lives of those in need. Representatives employed by the NGOs live and work with those assumed to be in need, and they listen and respond to *expressed* needs.

Hochschild spent several years studying the people of Louisiana oil country, trying to get some understanding of the logical paradoxes that characterize the thinking of so many hardworking people living in worsening economic conditions. Baffled by the frequent emergence of contradictory beliefs and actions, she finally put aside logical arguments and probed for what she calls the deep story. "A deep story," she writes, "is a *feels-as-if* story—it's the story feelings tell, in the language of symbols" (Hochschild 2016: 135). Pursuing this deep story, she learned that many hardworking, friendly, religious people despise the federal government they believe is supporting lazy, incompetent people—some "blacks, women, immigrants, refugees"—and these less deserving people are coming closer to the American Dream than they are despite their hard work and devotion to tradition. They feel betrayed.

All of these accounts affirm the central tenets of care theory. When we are prepared to care, we listen to what the other thinks and feels, we allow ourselves to feel in response, and we resolve to work together either to meet the expressed needs or to find some mutually satisfactory alternatives. Listening and working together on some community projects will not remove class differences, but such an approach may well reduce violence and foster respect for the deepest beliefs and legitimate complaints of each class. This is peacemaking at work.

To Teach Peacemaking

Most of what we teach today about peace in our high school courses is connected to war. In the two high school social studies textbooks on my shelf, "peace" appears in the index of one as "Peace Corps" and not at all in the other. Both list the equivalent of several index pages to war. "Peace" in most school texts is simply the end of war. But we are interested here in peacemaking, in building a caring environment in which conflict can be reduced or used in a nonviolent way to produce cooperation and the betterment of all involved. It might be useful, then, to start our discussion of peacemaking in the curriculum by asking how we handle conflict.

Conflict occurs in every social setting of human life—in families, among friends, in communities, in schools, and among nations. How have philosophers and other social theorists thought about conflict and its resolution? I will suggest three general approaches that might profitably be discussed with high school students.

The first, with which we are all familiar, is to focus our discussion on the end of hostilities, to making peace at the end of conflict. It usually means success for one party in the conflict and defeat for another. Indeed, history itself has often been described as the record of war and military competition. War has been glorified; it has been described as the workplace of heroes:

> War is evaluated in an oddly ambivalent way. On the one hand, we say that we dread it, and our leaders claim that no one wants war. On the other hand, we invoke the word *war* to emphasize seriousness of purpose. We have launched wars on drugs, on poverty,

and on terrorism. War, for all its horrors, takes on a positive connotation when it is conducted against some perceived evil.

Noddings 2012: 13

The glorification of conflict in the name of good, right, and justice extends to civil and even personal conflict. We admire those who fight for what they (and we) believe is right. Timothy Garton Ash describes Christopher Hitchens as a possible example of such a hero, a defender of free speech:

> Hitchens exemplified courage. . . . [He] was outspoken, outrageous, never afraid to offend, impressively undeterred by Islamist death threats. He was also almost never prepared to admit that he had been wrong, nimbly shifting his ground to defend, with equal vehemence, whatever contrarian position he chose to adopt at a particular moment. But he was brave, and utterly consistent in his defense of free speech.
>
> Garton Ash 2016: 375

This willingness to fight selflessly and heroically has motivated war stories and poetry even when the writing has condemned war: "Whatever may have been the actual desire to end war of the various soldier-poets of the Great War, one of their paradoxical effects was to render their war experience as something fatally attractive to younger men" (Goldensohn 2003: 31). The reading of war poetry, then, should be followed by critical discussions of contradictory reactions. Why has this work inspired both love and hate for war? Goldensohn remarks, "War's worst murder is the destruction—dulling, blunting—of our capacity to care" (Goldensohn 2003: 81). And, of course, it is just this capacity to care that we are trying to develop in our students.

We can expect that paradoxical reactions will result from our reading and teaching of war novels and poetry, and we should conscientiously add to the paradox by including biographical accounts to our readings. It is not enough to read Wilfred Owen's *Dulce et Decorum Est*; students should also learn that Owen died in that war and that angry criticism was directed at him by another poet, the Nobel Prize winner W.B. Yeats. The glorification of war should be a major topic in our discussion of war and peace, but I will not pursue it further here because the main topic in this chapter is peacemaking. War is a way of approaching conflict, but it is not a form of peacemaking.

Principled objection to war—even after it is underway—is another approach to conflict and it is one that should be discussed in some depth. *Pacifism* as a word describing the rejection of war and commitment to the preservation of peace is just a little over a hundred years old (Cortright 2008). It was not construed as the mere rejection of war but, rather, as an active commitment to peacemaking, but even today there is substantial disagreement over exactly what the term should mean. For present purposes, we might prefer an emphasis on active peacemaking, not merely the rejection of violence in the resolution of conflicts. The history of pacifism should certainly be studied. It should be recognized, however, that it is not feasible to take a position of absolute pacifism; most of us acknowledge that we would fight—resist physically—if we or our children were under actual attack (Fiala 2008).

Another way of rejecting conflict is to withdraw from it. The withdrawal can take several forms. As already mentioned, people may adopt pacifism as their own individual approach to violence. In another way, people give up individual personal control over their lives by pledging themselves to a religious order. Notice that this is an autonomous decision to give up a host of other autonomous decisions. Isaiah Berlin writes:

> This is the traditional self-emancipation of ascetics and quietists, of stoics or Buddhist sages, men of various religions or of none, who have fled the world—I retreat into my

own sect, my own planned economy, my own deliberately inculcated territory, where no voice from outside need be listened to, and no external forces can have effect.

Berlin 1969: 135–136

But, of course, this "retreat to the inner citadel" is made after much deep thinking and a carefully considered commitment.

A far shabbier form of this escape—of opting out—is made by people who just give up and refuse to be involved in the many social/political conflicts that surround us. As educators, we cannot endorse this option, but we must try to understand it, and this prompts a return to our earlier discussion about the communication gap between the educated and uneducated classes. Walzer mentioned the sad assessment of "backwardness, ignorance, passivity, and submissiveness" among the oppressed; Orwell derided attempts to make the poor "more like us"; and Hochschild struggled to solve the "great paradox" that pushes people to work against their own interests. People sometimes give up because they feel helpless. Paulo Freire described a fear of freedom that often afflicts the oppressed:

One of the basic elements of the relationship between oppressor and oppressed is *prescription*. Every prescription represents the imposition of one man's choice upon another, transforming the consciousness of the man prescribed to into one that conforms with the prescriber's consciousness.

Freire 1970: 31

We are reminded here of the crucial difference between "caring-for" and "caring-about." As a result of the "uplifting" practices described by Orwell, Walzer, and Hochschild, the oppressed sometimes become oppressors themselves. Often, however, they simply retreat from the struggle and take refuge in some element of their oppressed lives—religion, the companionship of their fellows in misery, their shared contempt for the oppressors. They understand neither the ways of the oppressors nor the ways of the liberators, and the would-be liberators do not understand them. The methods described by Hochschild in her search for the deep story offer some hope of coming to understand one another. Understanding how others *feel* is a central requirement of caring and peacemaking, and promoting that understanding is an essential function of education.

Now the question arises where this material might be taught. Certainly, our history/social studies texts are loaded with content on war, and our literature classes add to the accounts and praise of heroism in war and other conflicts. But to get at the problems of communication being addressed here, we will have to provide student discussion groups and/or seminars. Readers should keep this in mind, and we will return to the "how to" topic after addressing a third way to approach conflict.

The third way to approach conflict is central to academic life—to keep the lines of communication open, to talk to and listen to others when a conflict arises or threatens to arise. At the conclusion of his analysis of free speech, Timothy Garton Ash reminds us that it would be naïve to attempt to eliminate conflict:

That will never happen and if it ever did, the result would be a sterile, faded world. But our inevitable, indispensable, creative human conflicts can be conducted peacefully, by making jaw-jaw rather than war-war.

Garton Ash 2016: 381

This is the very heart of real peacemaking in families, communities, and the world. Students should hear John Stuart Mill on the power and necessity of approaching conflicts in this way:

> He who knows only his own side of the case, knows little of that. His reasons may be good, and no one may have been able to refute them. But if he is equally unable to refute the reasons on the opposite side; if he does not so much as know what they are, he has no ground for preferring either opinion.
>
> *Mill 1993: 43*

His chapter "Of the Liberty of Thought and Discussion" should rank high on the list for teachers' reading.

Isaiah Berlin, an admirer of Mill's work, also wrote powerfully about the need for tolerant discussion, free speech, and the value of well-informed individual choice:

> Pluralism, with the measure of "negative" liberty that it entails, seems to me a truer and more humane ideal than the goals of those who seek in the great, disciplined, authoritative structures the ideal of "positive" self-mastery by classes, or peoples, or the whole of mankind. It is truer, because it does, at least, recognize the fact that human goals are many, not all of them commensurable, and in perpetual rivalry with one another.
>
> *Berlin 1969: 171*

"Negative" liberty, on Berlin's definition, is the freedom for each adult individual to decide for him or herself what constitutes the good life and how to live it. "Positive" liberty is defined as the freedom to live as the most rational, authoritative thinkers have determined. In the latter case, it is claimed that all fully rational people will embrace a universal view of what they should believe and how they should live. Berlin spoke eloquently for negative liberty. Negative liberty is consonant with caring-for; positive liberty is more closely aligned with caring-about.

Advocates of both positive and negative liberty recognize that elements of the positive view must be used in raising and teaching children; clearly, they must be guided toward socially acceptable behavior by kindly, intelligent adults. But even children must be encouraged to make choices, and those of us who agree with Berlin's negative liberty are keenly aware that our guidance must increase the capacity of young people to decide on their own ideals and goals for life and to respect those of others.

It is this spirit we should encourage in those we teach and in those we want to help. Garton Ash says of Berlin:

> [He] was one of the most eloquent, consistent defenders of a liberalism which creates and defends the spaces in which people subscribing to different values, holding incompatible views, pursuing irreconcilable political projects . . . can battle it out in freedom, without violence.
>
> *Garton Ash 2016: 375*

This illustrates the basic lesson in peacemaking that should guide what we do in schools.

Teaching Peacemaking

We should not forsake discussion of war and peace; indeed, we should extend that discussion to include much more about the critical history and literature of war and its horrors, minimizing heroism and excitement (Noddings 2012). We should also be alert to the need to keep civic interest alive in students who might easily fall into the "opt-out" group. Here, however, I want to emphasize the third approach to handling conflict because of its potential power to encourage peace in every facet of our lives. This is the approach advocated by Mill and Berlin and also by care theory. The idea is to maintain tolerant, open conversation aimed at understanding ourselves and others, to maintain caring relations. It is especially important today when we are increasingly afflicted by group polarization (Putnam 2015; Sunstein 2009).

There is much work for educators in combatting this polarization. We need not agree with James Campbell, who has remarked:

> To put it bluntly, the pathologies often ascribed to polarization are not so much the result of too many people being liberals and conservatives, but of too many of these polarized people being a bit too pig-headed, narrow-minded, unrealistic, disrespectful, and ill-informed.
>
> *Campbell 2016: 241*

Rather, we—with Orwell, Walzer, and Hochschild—would like to hear the deep story of all groups, including the pig-headed and ill-informed, reduce the number of such citizens who graduate from our schools, and teach our kids to persevere in discussion with one another.

The question that arises immediately is *where* in the curriculum we would place such a topic. Standard procedure in American high schools is to assign every concept or topic to one of the already established subjects. This is a mistake we should rectify. If our study of conflict is assigned to English/language arts, it may well deteriorate into debate preparation; if it is assigned to social studies, it may be challenged by those critics constantly on the lookout for questionable political topics. Students of education know that "progressive" or "problem-oriented" texts and curriculum additions have been attacked repeatedly by critics who often brand critical studies as anti-American or anti-intellectual (Evans 2006; Thornton 2005).

The best answer is to teach it everywhere—in all of our main disciplines—as a logical companion to critical thinking (Noddings 2013b, 2015; Noddings and Brooks 2017). Even soundly embedded in the whole curriculum, it will come under attack. There are many who accept—and will try to enforce—Berlin's description of "positive" liberty. Remember the Professor in *Erewhon* who advised:

> It is not our business to help students to think for themselves. Surely this is the very last thing which one who wishes them well should encourage them to do. Our duty is to ensure that they shall think as we do, or at any rate, as we hold it expedient to say we do.
>
> *Noddings 2015: 107*

To promote the third approach advocated by Mill, Berlin, and care theory, we need to increase interdisciplinary studies. The disciplines, highly specialized and sharply separated from one another, give us little help with social problems and everyday concerns. Almost 100 years ago, John Dewey spoke convincingly about the shortcomings of disciplinary knowledge:

> The astronomer, biologist, chemist, may attain systematic wholes, at least for a time, within his own field. But when we come to the bearing of special conclusions upon the conduct of social life, we are, outside of technical fields, at a loss.
>
> *Dewey 1960, 1929: 312*

Today, E. O. Wilson presses the case for interdisciplinary studies:

> What was once perceived as an epistemological divide between the great branches of learning is now emerging from the academic fog as something far different and much more interesting: a wide middle domain of mostly unexplored phenomena open to a cooperative approach from both sides of the former divide.
>
> *Wilson 2006: 136*

Continuing on the middle domain, Wilson adds:

> It, moreover, addresses issues in which students (and the rest of us) are most interested: the nature and origin of life, the meaning of sex, the basis of human nature, the origin and evolution of life, why we must die, the origins of religion and ethics, the causes of aesthetic response, the role of environment in human genetic and cultural evolution, and more.
>
> *Wilson 2006: 136*

One easily accessible and powerful way to join the disciplines in matters of broadly human interest is through the use of biographies. It is dismaying to talk with high school math students who have never heard the name of a mathematician other than Euclid. If some attention were given to Bertrand Russell (perhaps during lessons on sets), opportunities would arise to talk about pacifism, atheism, nuclear disarmament, socialism, John Stuart Mill (Russell's godfather), women's rights, and world government. Mention of G.H. Hardy could lead to a discussion of friendship and collaboration across international lines and, again, of pacifism and hatred of war. Discussion of Isaac Newton could lead beyond his scientific genius to his attempt to establish an accurate chronological account of the Bible stories. Many more examples could be introduced to enliven lessons and make the connections sought in interdisciplinary studies.

If we want adult citizens to communicate openly and effectively with one another, we should provide many more opportunities in our high schools for them to learn how to do this. Faculties, working with students, must find a way to bring students together in discussion. As it is, we seem to produce too many of the unrealistic and ill-informed citizens criticized by Campbell. I have suggested creating seminars or discussion groups composed of students from all programs—honors, arts, standard college-prep, remedial, vocational—that should meet regularly to discuss social/political questions (Noddings 2013b, 2015; Noddings and Brooks 2017). Notice that this recommendation does not specify details on how often the seminars should meet, how many participants there should be in each group, how teachers will be selected, or what topics should be addressed. These should be local decisions. I do recommend that the seminars continue with the same participants throughout the high school years and that there should be no tests, no grades. The object is for the students to learn and to practice the open, intelligent, tolerant conversation that we hope they will exercise as adult citizens. The crucial factor is the composition of the participants. If we want to produce adult citizens who will communicate across class differences, we should give them adequate experience doing so while they are in high school. We want them to leave school prepared to care.

Under current practices, we may actually be contributing to class differences. We seem to think that those differences are reduced by putting many more students in college-prep programs. This practice may, however, actually aggravate class differences. By failing to provide excellent vocational courses from which students can proudly make choices, we deny the respect that true equality demands. To make matters worse, those enrolled in academic work are usually separated into honors, advanced, standard, and remedial classes, and this practice sets up its own standard of class differences. We should find a way to recognize differences in academic talents and interests (and there clearly are such differences) without stigmatizing the recipients of our attempts at equality (Noddings 2015).

Peace education should be a central topic in secondary education. In this troubling time of increasing polarization in America, the emphasis should be on peacemaking. Drawing on care theory and supported by the advice of John Stuart Mill and Isaiah Berlin, this chapter urges an approach to peacemaking that emphasizes open, tolerant, critical communication across social classes. This approach is designed to produce citizens who are prepared to care and to work collaboratively in a participatory democracy.

Works Cited

Berlin, I. (1969). "Two Concepts of Liberty," in I. Berlin (ed.), *Four Essays on Liberty*. Oxford: Oxford University Press, 118–172.
Campbell, J. E. (2016). *Making Sense of a Divided America*. Princeton: Princeton University Press.
Cortright, D. (2008). *A History of Movements and Ideas*. Cambridge: Cambridge University Press.
Dewey, J. (1927). *The Public and Its Problems*. New York: Henry Holt.
Dewey, J. (1960). *The Quest for Certainty*. New York: G.P. Putnam's Sons. Original work published 1929.
Evans, R. W. (2006). *This Happened in America*. Charlotte, NC: Information Age Publishing.
Fiala, A. (2008). *The Just War Myth*. Lanham, MD: Rowman and Littlefield.
Frank, T. (2016). *Listen, Liberal*. New York: Metropolitan Books.
Freire, P. (1970). *Pedagogy of the Oppressed*, translated by M.B. Ramos. New York: Herder and Herder.
Garton Ash, T. (2016). *Free Speech: Ten Principles for a Connected World*. New Haven and London: Yale University Press.
Goldensohn, L. (2003). *Dismantling Glory*. New York: Columbia University Press.
Hochschild, A. R. (2016). *Strangers in Their Own Land*. New York: New Press.
Mill, J. S. (1993). *On Liberty and Utilitarianism*. New York: Bantam Books. Original work published 1859.
Noddings, N. (2012). *Peace Education: How We Come to Love and Hate War*. Cambridge: Cambridge University Press.
Noddings, N. (2013a). *Caring: A Relational Approach to Ethics and Moral Education*. Berkeley: University of California Press.
Noddings, N. (2013b). *Education and Democracy in the 21st Century*. New York: Teachers College Press.
Noddings, N. (2015). *A Richer, Brighter Vision for American High Schools*. Cambridge: Cambridge University Press.
Noddings, N., and L. Brooks. (2017). *Teaching Controversial Issues: The Case for Critical Thinking and Moral Commitment*. New York: Teachers College Press.
Orwell, G. (1958). *The Road to Wigan Pier*. San Diego: Harcourt. Original work published 1937.
Putnam, R. D. (2015). *Our Kids: The American Dream in Crisis*. New York: Simon and Schuster.
Ruddick, S. (1989). *Maternal Thinking: Toward a Politics of Peace*. Boston: Beacon Press.
Sunstein, C. R. (2009). *Going to Extremes: How Like Minds Unite and Divide*. New York: Oxford University Press.
Thornton, S. (2005). *Teaching Social Studies that Matters: Curriculum for Active Learning*. New York: Teachers College Press.
Walzer, M. (2015). *The Paradox of Liberation: Secular Revolutions and Religious Counterrevolutions*. New Haven: Yale University Press.
Wilson, E. O. (2006). *The Creation: An Appeal to Save Life on Earth*. New York: W.W. Norton.

Further Reading

Cortright, D. (2008). *Peace: A History of Movements and Ideas*. Cambridge: Cambridge University Press. (A definitive overview of the history of peace activism and nonviolence.)

Noddings, N. (2012). *Peace Education: How We Come to Love and Hate War.* Cambridge: Cambridge University Press. (A critical examination of contemporary education systems that calls for more and better education for peace, including critiques of nationalism, hatred, certain forms of masculinity, religious extremism, and so on.)

Thornton, S. (2005). *Teaching Social Studies That Matters.* New York: Teachers College Press. (A book that contributes a Deweyan perspective on teaching and curriculum in social studies.)

26
BECOMING NONVIOLENT
Sociobiological, Neurophysiological, and Spiritual Perspectives

Andrew Fitz-Gibbon

Writers on pacifism and nonviolence share an implicit assumption that to become nonviolent, as societies, groups, or individuals, is actually possible. However, the dominant narrative of human history has focused on violent actions—what historian Francisco A. Muñoz termed "violentology" (Gay 2016). This dominant historical narrative is unremittingly deterministic. In other words, that humanity might choose a pacifistic or nonviolent future is unlikely based on human history. As with all deterministic ideologies—whether religious, biological, sociological, or historical—free will, the ability to make choices that might result in differing future outcomes that are not predetermined, is a chimera. If the narrative is true, and if it can be demonstrated that the human animal is, in fact, determined for violence rather than nonviolence or pacifism, then the work of nonviolent philosophy and activism is futile.

Historical determinism has been buttressed by biological positivistic frameworks that have suggested that the human animal is, in fact, hardwired for aggression and violence and no amount of wishful thinking will change that fact of nature (Wilson 1975, 2015; Dawkins 1989). I will offer, later, a more hopeful prognosis. I suggest that the possibility of becoming nonviolent is a warranted assumption based on recent studies in the psychology of peace (Christie, Wagner, and Winter 2001; MacNair 2003) that humanity has the potentiality and resourcefulness for empathy and nonviolence (Midgley 1995; Rifkin 2009; Pinker 2011; Krznaric 2014), and that a spiritual practice of the habituation of nonviolence suggests a realistic hope for a nonviolent future (Simpkins and Simpkins 2011, 2012). This is, however, not a deterministic viewpoint and the future remains open. I will not suggest that a nonviolent future is inevitable—humanity may yet destroy itself, and much of the planet with it—but rather, and more modestly, that humanity has the potentiality for nonviolence that is often obscured by the dominant violentological narratives.

However, before that I look briefly at the sometimes conflicted findings of sociobiology, and the more recent field of neurophilosophy, that have presented the most serious challenge to the assumption that humanity might choose nonviolence over violence.

Sociobiological and Neurophilosophical Perspectives

In common with the dominant historical narrative, sociobiology has suggested that humanity is biologically determined to be violent. In 1975, Harvard biologist E.O. Wilson presented a shift in the field of biology with the publication of his now classic *Sociobiology*. In it he argued that all human behavior can be traced to the evolutionary process of natural selection, and that scholars in disciplines such as moral philosophy ought to focus their ethical quest not on the traditional philosophical understanding of motivations and values, but more directly on the emotional control centers of the hypothalamus and limbic system of the brain. In Wilson's words, "Sociobiology is defined as the systematic study of the biological basis for all human behavior" (Wilson 1975: 4). Thus, morality—the choice of nonviolence over violence as a moral decision—has an evolutionary explanation. Wilson presents evolutionary biology as deterministic of human moral behavior. In other words, genes determine ethical decisions. So, for Wilson, suggestions, such as philosopher Immanuel Kant's that the moral life consists of following one's duty, on the basis of a "good will" (an autonomous will that determines itself in accordance with the moral law), are profoundly erroneous, as are any ethical schemes that assume the human will is, in some sense, free. Toward the end of *Sociobiology*, Wilson suggests, "Scientists and humanists should consider together the possibility that the time has come for ethics to be removed temporarily from the hands of philosophers and biologicized" (Wilson 1975: 562).

In his explanation of his proposed biologicization of ethics, Wilson demonstrates that though he is a fine biologist, he is a poor philosopher, suggesting, for example, that modern moral philosophy from Locke, Rousseau, and Kant to John Rawls (and presumably all philosophy before that) is all alike "intuitionist." For instance, Rawls's conception of "justice as fairness" is, Wilson says, an "ideal state for disembodied spirits," but is unsuited for human beings because it is neither explanatory nor predictive of human behavior. For Wilson, the evolutionary trajectory has been one of "extreme unfairness." He seems to suggest that, if natural selection has been a process of unfairness, any human attempt to introduce the notion of fairness flies in the face of evolutionary biology and is thus doomed to fail. Human beings are ruthlessly competitive, destined to be so because the gene is ruthlessly competitive. Given his assertions about competition in human behavior, it is little wonder that the politically and economically right wing has often applauded Wilson's notions while those on the left radically disagree with him. If the ruthlessly competitive gene is predictive of human behavior, then the ruthlessness of free-market capitalism better fits the human condition than welfare socialism.

In his latest book, Wilson summarizes his life's work and clarifies his understanding of the human propensity toward violence. He says:

> Almost all groups compete with those of similar kind in some manner or other. However gently expressed and generous in the tone of our discourse, we tend to think of our own group as superior, and we define our personal identities as members within them. The existence of competition, including military conflict, has been a hallmark of societies as far back in prehistory as archeological evidence can be brought to bear.
> *Wilson 2015: 25*

To search for nonviolent or pacifistic solutions to human problems would, thus, run counter to sociobiology. Wilson does, however, allow for some altruism in natural selection. He summarizes his research: "Within groups selfish individuals beat altruistic individuals, but groups of altruists beat groups of selfish individuals" (Wilson 2015: 33). If we translate his ideas from the world of ants—Wilson's primary field of research—to that of humanity, the implications seem to be that, say, within the United States the best policy (one that agrees with sociobiology) is to encourage selfish individualism as the way to "win." However, should the United States be at war, it is more likely to "win" if citizens demonstrate altruism and self-sacrifice. If the enemy has greater stores of these, then the likelihood is that the United Sates will "lose." Wilson does not attempt a reconciliation of the psychological difficulties of having citizens whose primary motivation is selfish individualism, yet who must also be altruistic self-sacrificers against external enemies in order to survive. Therein lies his problem: humans are not ants. The ant as machine—so far as we know—programmed through genes, and the self-conscious person, conflicted by myriad motivations and needs, are too dissimilar for meaningful comparison.

Nonetheless, in terms of human violence and nonviolence, the implications of a deterministic sociobiology seem clear. If, from the biological evidence, we can determine that human beings are biologically programmed for violence, then attempts to move individuals, groups, or society toward nonviolence or pacifism fall at the first hurdle.

A year after Wilson published *Sociobiology*, working on similar issues, Oxford biologist Richard Dawkins published *The Selfish Gene* (Dawkins 1989). Dawkins's project was to present a social theory based on natural selection, and to "examine the biology of selfishness and altruism" (Dawkins 1989: 2), based on the notion that human beings are "machines created by our genes" (Dawkins 1989: 3). Successful genes are of necessity selfish genes, for only selfish genes survive in the competitive world of natural selection:

> This gene selfishness will usually give rise to selfishness in individual behavior. . . . Much as we might wish to believe otherwise, universal love and the welfare of the species as a whole are concepts that simply do not make evolutionary sense.
> *Dawkins 1989: 3*

However, Dawkins expresses a greater appreciation of moral philosophy than does Wilson. He says, "I am not advocating a morality based on evolution" (Dawkins 1989: 3). He says further:

> Be warned that if you wish as I do, to build a society in which individuals cooperate generously and unselfishly towards a common good, you can expect little help from biological nature. Let us try to *teach* generosity and altruism, because we are born selfish. Let us understand what our selfish genes are up to, because we may at least have the chance to upset their designs, something that no other species has ever aspired to.
> *Dawkins 1989: 3–4, italics original*

Eighteenth-century Scottish philosopher David Hume had long since warned of the difficulties (some would say the impossibility) of deriving moral ideas from nature—the naturalistic fallacy. What is the case, in human behavior, does not tell us anything about what ought to be the case. If nature determined morality, then the human tendency toward racism and xenophobia would be morally acceptable, as would the human male tendency toward misogyny. What ought to be the case (that is, the moral quest if it is to make sense at all) derives from the complex interaction of the innate motivations and desires of human nature, tradition and culture, together with values and reasoning. Dawkins seems to appreciate this, though many who read his work reach different conclusions, seeing the moral quest as impossible given the deterministically selfish nature of the human genome.

A more helpful way to appreciate the work of sociobiology is to realize that the moral dimension of humanity is a result of the process of evolution; that the human ability to think and act ethically, to make choices, to consider consequences of actions, and to possess virtues is developed to a greater degree in the human animal than other species precisely because of natural selection. Problems arise when that evolutionary perspective becomes deterministic of human behavior in a reductive and mechanistic sense. It is "I," as a rational, emotive, moral agent, who decides not to return vengeance for harm caused, not my genes, selfish or otherwise.

For much of their career Wilson and Dawkins shared a similar approach. However, in 2014, growing differences came to a head, with Dawkins dismissing Wilson's later work, and Wilson calling Dawkins a mere "journalist" (Johnson 2014). Wilson had changed his mind on some of his earlier conclusions, notably that the selfish gene theory is too simplistic, and that a multi-level selection theory better fits the facts. Dawkins remains with the selfish gene theory. The jury is still out as to which biological theory will win the day.

However, despite the popularity of sociobiology, it is far from certain that its central story is a good one. Biologist Frans de Waal, in a critique of Wilson and Dawkins, states, "Genes can't be any more 'selfish' than a river can be 'angry,' or sun rays 'loving.' Genes are little chunks of DNA" (de Waal 2009: 39). British philosopher Mary Midgely, in *Beast and Man*, has a sustained critique of the findings of sociobiology. While Wilson and Dawkins admit that their language referring to genes as "selfish," "spiteful," and "manipulative" is metaphor, in usage, and most certainly in the popular understanding of sociobiology, the language takes on a literal meaning. She comments, "The words *God* or *Providence* can be substituted for *natural selection* in these Just So stories without changing the sense at all" (Midgely 1995: XXI, italics original). In other words, though Wilson and Dawkins are militantly atheistic, decrying any sense of a god or gods determining the world, they substitute the immortal gene, and give to that gene the kind of agency traditionally ascribed to the gods, or god, and that we find in the human person as a thinking, feeling, choosing individual. Midgely states:

> Scientific reductionism is thus still a powerful and irrational force hindering our thought about freedom and responsibility, making it hard for us to accept our situation as active citizens of the physical universe.
>
> *Midgely 1995: XXIX*

Midgely does not, however, continue the age-old error that humanity is, in some sense, other than animal—more god-like than animal-like. Her argument is that the human animal is truly animal, but rational, sentient, and moral in ways differing in degrees from other animals, and that difference, itself, is a product of the process of evolution.

In the twenty-first century neurophilosophy, or neuroethics, has added complexity to the issue. In brief, neuroethics suggests that it may be possible to discover the neural basis of ethical reasoning; meaning, effectively, that consciousness, free will, and ethical choices can be analyzed, and perhaps predicted, by a more complete understanding of brain functions. In other words, the traditional critical disciplines of philosophy and ethics can be reduced to biological functions. Doubtlessly, neuroscience will greatly enhance our understanding of the functioning of the brain in the ethical process. However, the danger, much like the danger of sociobiology, is a positivistic reductionism that sees brain-mind function as fixed and unalterable. Spanish philosophers Sonia París Albert and Irene Comins Mingol comment:

> [T]he use of an essentially reductionist method, the Galilean tradition, for the analysis of an essentially complex reality such as the human being, will lead to understandings of the human being, and of the world and life of the human species, which will not be holistic, but unavoidably partial.
>
> *Albert and Mingol 2013: 67*

For example, much of the experimental work of neuroethics relates to the functioning of the brain when faced with dilemmas, as if the whole of ethics relates to solving such hypothetical problems. Aristotle, among many of the ancients, helped us realize the moral life is inextricably complex, as the human-social animal makes sense of the Good, and at least since David Hume philosophers have understood that the passions, or emotions, are a deep and intricate aspect of morality. The moral life is always more than a detached mathematical or experimental process and involves the whole human person—thinking, feeling, choosing—and is shaped by nature and nurture, genes, brain functions, society, education, and culture. Nonetheless, and quite helpfully, neuroscience is beginning to demonstrate that, contra to either historical or biological determinism, the human animal is not destined or merely programmed toward violence. Violence and nonviolence remain ever-present possibilities, despite a dominant violentology perspective. Albert and Mingol again:

> The new neurological perspectives place neurological transmission and learning in the framework of theories which are more favorable to sociability (mirror neurons), [which see below] positive emotions, or moral commitments, among them the commitment to make peace.
>
> *Albert and Mingol 2013: 73*

Psychological Perspectives

In the twenty-first century, in psychology—most especially social psychology and positive psychology—the human potential for empathy has been given greater emphasis. Whilst barely a hundred years old, psychology has mostly focused negatively on human neuroses, aggression, and disease. Perhaps as a sign of coming of age, the discipline has broadened to include the whole of human behavior and potentialities—hence positive psychology (though psychologist Abraham Maslow was the pioneer of the field in the mid-twentieth century). Positive psychology deals with the classical philosophical category of human happiness—*eudaimonia*—and how human persons can achieve well-being. Though not directly relevant to nonviolence, redeeming the human species from unremitting neuroses and violence is surely helpful in considering the possibility of a nonviolent future. Social psychology, too, has helped us understand human motivations, and in the context of the present discussion, motivations for violence and toward peace.

Psychologists have been aided in the task of positive psychology by the work of primatologists, and other ethologists, Frans de Waal among the foremost (de Waal 2009, 2016). In keeping with the historical violentology perspective, we have generally assumed that animals are primarily aggressive. The human tendency toward violence has been perceived as the "animal nature" within the human person. A violent person is compared to a "savage beast," or "mad dog." In response to a tale of human violence the hearer says, "He's such an animal!" De Waal and others have begun to demonstrate, on the contrary, that animals are not merely aggressive, but have extraordinary potential for empathy. Empathy is necessary for the human animal's moral commitment to the principle that is nonviolence. Both aggression and empathy are shared in different degrees by many animals, including the human animal. De Waal presents much evidence that the human empathic response is as "preprogrammed" as the much-vaunted aggressive response. He wonders:

> Why did natural selection design our brains so that we're in tune with our fellow human beings, feeling distress at their distress and pleasure at their pleasure? If exploitation of others were all that mattered, evolution should never have gotten into the empathy business.
>
> *de Waal 2009: 43*

De Waal's conclusion is reached through a thorough investigation of primate and other animal behavior and its corresponding human behavior. His conclusion is inescapable that the "animals are merely aggressive to selfish ends" narrative is as false for humans as it is for other animals.

Much of the development in the change of thinking among natural and social scientists with regard to the nature of human nature was gathered magpie-like, and popularized, by economist and social theorist Jeremy Rifkin in his widely read, yet controversial, *The Empathic Civilization*. He comments:

> Recent discoveries in brain science and child development are forcing us to rethink the long-held belief that human beings are, by nature, aggressive, materialistic, utilitarian, and self-interested. The dawning realization that we are a fundamentally empathic species has profound and far-reaching consequences for society.
>
> *Rifkin 2009: 1*

Contrary to the violentological perspective, Rifkin states, "Although life as it's lived on the ground, close to home, is peppered with suffering, stresses, injustices, and foul play, it is, for the most part, lived out in hundreds of small acts of kindness and generosity" (Rifkin 2009: 10). He argues that this is so because the core of human nature is empathic, and that this empathic side to humanity is the result of evolution. To demonstrate his argument, Rifkin uses the change in psychology post-Freud from an understanding of human nature as aggressive—driven by libidinal and thanotic needs—to one in which the need for relationality is paramount (Rifkin 2009: 66–81).

In making his argument that humanity is *homo empathicus*, Rifkin makes much of the fairly recently discovered phenomenon of "mirror neurons." In brief, "mirror neurons allow humans—and other animals—to grasp the minds of others 'as if' their thoughts and behavior were their own" (Rifkin 2009: 83), and that grasping occurs through feeling rather than thinking. It is this biological mechanism that makes relationality possible. For example, when a friend tears up because of some distress, our own response is to feel that distress (caused by mirror neurons) and we feel empathically for our friend. Quite literally, in this instance, "I feel your pain." In other words, Rifkin argues that the human animal is hardwired for empathy, or perhaps more accurately, becomes hardwired for empathy through socialization. Rifkin comments:

> What [researchers] are finding is that the biological circuitry becomes activated by social exercise. In other words, parental and community nurture of infants is essential to trigger mirror neurons' circuitry and establish empathic pathways in the brain.
>
> *Rifkin 2009: 86*

However, in arguing positively that mirror neurons offer a biological explanation for the development of empathy, Rifkin skates over the corollary that the plasticity of the brain in early childhood means that with inadequate and even violent care, the mimetic nature of mirror neurons suggests that the brain can be hardwired for aggression. Much, then, depends on the quality of nurturance and care that the child receives as to the development of mirror neurons (Krznaric 2014: 14–16).

Harvard psychologist Steven Pinker has urged caution at overinflating the role of mirror neurons, as if the discovery of mimetic behavior given a biological cause is a panacea for all the ills of the world. He states:

> Empathy, in the morally relevant sense of sympathetic concern, is not an automatic reflex of mirror neurons. I can be turned on and off and even inverted into counter-empathy, namely feeling good when someone else feels bad and vice versa.
>
> Pinker 2011: 577

And further:

> The problem with building a better world through empathy, in the sense of . . . mirror neurons, is that it cannot be counted on to trigger the kind of empathy we want, namely sympathetic concern for others' well-being. Sympathy is endogenous, an effect rather than a cause of how people relate to one another. Depending on how beholders conceive of a relationship, their response to another person's pain may be empathic, neutral, or even counterempathic.
>
> Pinker 2011: 378

However, despite the disputes that this new science has engendered, of interest for the possibility of nonviolence is that this latest research suggests that the human brain is not necessarily hardwired for aggression, as previously thought.

Steven Pinker, who cautions against an overemphasis on mirror neurons as the be-all and end-all of an empathic response, is nonetheless optimistic about the present and future reduction of violence in the world. In his *The Better Angels of Our Nature* Pinker argues that, over the last 500 years, violence has been in decline. This counterintuitive assertion is demonstrated by an impressive dataset in which Pinker looks at a large number of variables, measuring differing types of violence per 100,000 of the population. For example, with regard to European homicide decline, in the thirteenth century homicides were between 50 and 90 per 100,000 of the population, for differing countries. Today, in all European countries homicides are less than one per 100,000 (Pinker 2011: 63). In the United States the decline has also been great, though not quite as impressively as in Europe. From the 1830s, when the rate was around 100 per 100,000, the homicide rate is down to below ten. The data is equally impressive with regard to the decline of deaths in warfare, which again seems counterintuitive given the bloodbath which was the first half of the twentieth century. Pinker considers the major wars in human history, and adjusts the death toll based on population equivalency to the mid-twentieth century. Though in actual deaths, the Second World War ranks highest, its adjusted rank, based on deaths per numbers in the population, is nine in the history of warfare. The largest percentage death toll was the An Lushan Revolt of eighth-century China (Pinker 2011: 195). While not dismissing the massive death tolls of recent wars, the data demonstrate that humanity has not been getting worse in its waging of warfare. Killing in war has been a constant. Even so, since the end of the Second World War—what Pinker calls the "Long Peace"—the world's superpowers have not engaged in war, there have been no more nuclear attacks, and none of the world's traditional great powers have waged war with each other, nor have the countries of Europe. No major developed countries have waged war, no major countries have expanded territories through conquest, and no major state has gone out of existence because of war or conquest (Pinker 2011: 249–251). A long peace is not a perpetual peace, and the nations of the world may yet wage war again.

Pinker suggests that the reason for the decline in violence has been the civilizing process begun in the humanitarian revolution of the modern period; that is, the decline in violence coincides with the Enlightenment of modernity. Pinker's critics point out that he ignores and minimizes too much of the violence of the last 500 years. They point out, too, that the imperialism and colonialism of Western Europe—born at the time of Europe's turn to humanism—resulted in devastation for the world's indigenous populations who were exterminated and enslaved by the Europeans. Even so, the humanitarian revolution has resulted in a very different view of violence, evidenced in the United Nations Universal Declaration of Human Rights, the International Criminal Court, the Geneva Conventions, and the unacceptability of violence in everyday life. Doubtless, the debate about Pinker's findings will continue. However, at the very least, Pinker's thorough analysis of the data on violence suggests that the future is more open than determined on prospects for a less violent world.

Spiritual Perspectives

Spirituality might be considered part of psychology, perhaps that area of psychology that deals with the natural impulse toward the transcendent, what Sigmund Freud—borrowing from a correspondent—called the "oceanic feeling." Freud states:

> This feeling was a purely subjective fact, not an article of faith; no assurance of personal immortality attached to it, but it was the source of religious energy that was seized upon by the various churches and religious systems, directed into particular channels and certainly consumed by them. On the basis of this oceanic feeling alone was one entitled to call oneself religious, even if one rejected every belief and illusion.
>
> *Freud 1961: 11*

Popularly, something like Freud's oceanic feeling is likely meant when people speak of being "spiritual, but not religious." In this way, being "spiritual" distances oneself from being "religious," with its negative connotations, while accepting that to be human is, in some sense, to be positively spiritual.

However, though it might be contained within psychology, spirituality, with its millennia of traditions, practices, and complex understandings, is sufficiently distinct to be an area of inquiry on its own. So far as we know, the human animal has always exhibited a natural impulse toward the experience of transcendence. Religions, with their worldviews, dogmas, traditions, and rituals, seem to be humanity's imperfect attempt to come to terms with, and make sense of, that experience. The spiritual, then, has often been sustained by religion, yet religion without spirituality can also become merely one more expression of culture.

Though religions have often been directly involved in and legitimated human violence, historically most pacifists and nonviolentists have been so for religious reasons. This presents a quandary in analyzing spirituality and nonviolence. Historian of religion Karen Armstrong suggests that the difficulty can be understood, to some degree, by the development of the human brain (Armstrong 2014: 7). From the old reptilian brain—the fight, flight, feed, and reproduce function—some 120 million years ago, the mammalian limbic system of the brain developed. This new system produced the empathic emotions that facilitated protection and nurture of the young and the forming of alliances. A mere 20,000 years ago, the "new brain," the neocortex, developed with new powers of reasoning and self-awareness, allowing the human animal to stand back from its primitive impulses. The complexity of human life, an admixture of selfishness, fellow feeling, and rationality, was the fertile soil in which religion and spirituality grew.

However, religion has never been far removed from violence, at time providing legitimation for wars—holy and otherwise—crusades, pogroms, jihads, and genocide. Early religions assumed that the transcendent required sacrifices to placate it. In time, human sacrifice was replaced by the sacrifice of animals, redirecting violence to other species, echoing the reality of life in hunter-gatherer societies. Armstrong comments:

> Much of what we now call "religion" was originally rooted in an acknowledgment of the tragic fact that life depended on the destruction of other creatures; rituals were addressed to help human beings face up to this indissoluble dilemma.
>
> *Armstrong 2014: 9*

Christianity, for example, exemplifies and continues this proximity to violence. Its central narrative has Jesus as nonviolent mystic and visionary, as well as the Christ who is at once the "lamb of God who takes away the sin of the world" and the judge who will condemn the ungodly to unending torture in hell. Christianity's central act of Eucharist, or Holy Communion, is a repeated remembrance and reenactment of the suffering and execution of Jesus. The admixture of violence and nonviolence is dizzying, and Christians have found solace in the nonviolent Jesus as well as the executor of judgment.

There is, then, a paradox at the heart of religion—and all religions share it to some degree—that the human animal, *homo religiosus*, is both violent and empathic, and that religious dogma and ritual provides a legitimization of both violence and nonviolence. Religion, then, merely reflects the central dilemma that is the human condition.

Nonetheless, pacifists and nonviolentists have found their pacifistic rationale in the teachings of religion, and their moral strength through the spiritual practices of religion. Despite sacred texts containing the most egregious examples of wanton violence, there is within all sacred traditions a core of compassion. Karen Armstrong, having written extensively on sacred violence in all religions, still reminds us:

> All faiths insist that compassion is the test of true spirituality and that it brings us into relation with the transcendence we call God, Brahman, Nirvana, or Dao. Each has formulated its own version of what we sometimes call the Golden Rule, "Do not treat others as you would not like them to treat you," or its positive form, "Always treat others as you would wish to be treated yourself." Further, they all insist that you cannot confine your benevolence to your own group; you must have concern for everybody—even your enemies.
>
> *Armstrong 2010: 4*

It is to that compassionate core that religious pacifists and nonviolentists have appealed, often distancing themselves from the violent aspects of their own religious traditions (in much the same way that nonreligious humanists appeal to the humanitarian impulses of modernity, while distancing themselves from its darker and troubling violent practices).

However, it is not merely the teachings of a tradition to which religious nonviolentists resort, but to the spiritual practices that sustain a pacifistic approach to life. Spiritual practices—meditative, yogic, contemplative—are often at the heart of religious pacifism. Though there is much in common with all spiritual practices, in the East spiritual practices were often somatic, that is, they were not merely mental exercises but bodily practices too. The paramount spiritual exercise of meditative breathing focuses on the physicality of breath, and the body's natural rhythm. These somatic practices were, perhaps paradoxically, often entwined with the martial arts—swords, spears, staffs, and unarmed martial arts like *taijiquan*, *baguazhang*, and *xingjiquan*—as well as other somatic practices such as tea ceremonies and painting. All alike helped the practitioner become a different, kinder, less violent person.

While practitioners have advocated the benefits of spiritual practice for millennia, recent research has added scientific veracity to their claims. Psychotherapists C. Alexander Simpkins and Anellen M. Simpkins offer evidence that spiritual practices affect brain states. They state:

> Neuroscience has provided evidence for some of the ancient claims about meditation. Clearly, meditation does bring about measurable changes in the brain and nervous system.
>
> *Simpkins and Simpkins 2012: 31–32*

In simple terms, the habituated somatic practice of breath meditation, the slow physical movements of *taijiquan*, or various yogic postures affect emotional and mental states for the better. In their research, Simpkins and Simpkins found that Zen breath meditation and yoga positively affected issues such as anger, anxiety and depression, as well as helped the practitioner form healthy, loving relationships (Simpkins and Simpkins 2011, 2012). In short, spiritual practices derived from various religious traditions do help change the human person.

If spirituality is the human response to the experience of transcendence, the Freudian insight is that spirituality is not, then, conditional on any dogma, or religious perspective. In other words, spirituality is part of the human condition, shared by all, and need not be linked to any worldview or religious dogma. Spiritual practices, too, then need not be linked to a "belief in" god or the following of a particular faith. This notion is confirmed by the ready acceptance, for example, of breath meditation practices, yoga, and such by people of all faiths and none. One does not need to be a Buddhist to practice *zazen*. This amounts to a secularization of spiritual practice. If the insight is true, that such spiritual practices bring change to the practitioner—in reducing anger and in becoming less violent, for example—then hope of a nonviolent future is a possibility, at least on an individual level.

In moral philosophy, since Alasdair MacIntyre's *After Virtue* (1985) neo-Aristotelian perspectives have gained currency. Aristotle's notion was that the good of human life was *eudaimonia*—well-being—and that the eudemonic life was a life of virtue. Virtue, in its turn, was produced through habituation of practice. For example, for Aristotle, a virtuous, hence eudemonic, life would be a life of courage. The virtue of courage was fostered by many courageous actions over time; that is, the daily practice of courage produced a courageous person. Simply put, you become what you most often do. Of significance for the possibilities of a nonviolent future is that the neo-Aristotelian perspective suggests that the repeated practice of nonviolence might produce nonviolent people. This hopeful understanding is very similar to the understanding of practices in the spiritual traditions, as well as positive psychology, in cultivating habits of happiness and probably peace (Cohrs et al. 2013).

Summary

I began by noting that for the task of nonviolent, or pacifistic, philosophy and practice to be meaningful, it must be possible for individual people, groups, and society actually to choose nonviolence. The historical violentological perspective, with its unrelenting focus on human aggression and violence, suggests, rather, that humanity is destined to continue in its unremittingly violent course. This deterministic narrative has been buttressed by the sociobiological narrative of the selfishness of the human gene, and, hence, the violence of the human animal.

However, I have suggested that these deterministic narratives have been challenged in philosophy, psychology, and from within the biological sciences. It turns out that the human animal is not merely hardwired for aggression as previously thought. The new science suggests rather that the human brain is more plastic, that possibilities for both aggression and empathy are contained within, and that the future, in terms of freedom and choices, is more open than fixed. This does not guarantee a nonviolent or pacifistic future, but leaves the question open. In other words, humanity is not bound by a programmed biological nature, nor by a cultural determinism.

This conclusion is in line with the wisdom of the ancients, of both East and West, who suggested that much depends on the virtues or vices that each person develops through virtuous or vicious habits. This account suggests that nonviolentism, or pacifism, is most helpfully sustained by practice, in the neo-Aristotelian sense. Habits of nonviolence build the virtues of nonviolence, which produce nonviolent people who help shape culture in nonviolent ways. Nonviolent culture in its turn, through education and socialization, reinforces the hope of a more nonviolent, and less violent, future. In other words, people change and cultures change. Steven Pinker's hopeful analysis of violence over the past 500 years supports this conclusion.

Works Cited

Albert, S. P., and I. C. Mingol. (2013). "Epistemological and Anthropological Thoughts on Neurophilosophy: An Initial Framework." *Recerca* 13: 63–83.
Armstrong, K. (2010). *Twelve Steps to a Compassionate Life*. New York: Alfred A. Knopf.
Armstrong, K. (2014). *Fields of Blood: Religion and the History of Violence*. New York: Anchor.
Christie, D. J., R. W. Wagner, and D. D. Winter. (2001). *Peace, Conflict, and Violence: Peace Psychology for the 21st Century*. Upper Saddle River, NJ: Prentice Hall.
Cohrs, J. C., D. J. Christie, M. P. White, and C. Das. (2013). "Contributions of Positive Psychology to Peace: Toward Global Well-Being and Resilience." *American Psychologist* 68 (7): 590–600.
Dawkins, R. (1989). *The Selfish Gene*. Oxford: Oxford University Press.
de Waal, F. (2009). *The Age of Empathy: Nature's Lessons for a Kinder Society*. New York: Three Rivers Press.
de Waal, F. (2016). *Are We Smart Enough to Know How Smart Animals Are?* New York: W.W. Norton.
Freud, S. (1961). *Civilization and Its Discontent*. New York: W.W. Norton.
Gay, W. C. (2016). "Pacifism, Feminism, and Nonkilling Philosophy: A New Approach to Connecting Peace Studies and Gender Studies." A talk presented at Concerned Philosophers for Peace at St. Bonaventure University.
Johnson, C. (2014). "Biological Warfare Flares up Again Between EO Wilson and Richard Dawkins." *The Guardian* November 6.
Krznaric, R. (2014). *Empathy: Why It Matters, and How to Get It*. New York: Random House.
MacIntyre, A. (1985). *After Virtue*. London: Gerald Duckworth.
MacNair, R. (2003). *The Psychology of Peace: An Introduction*. Westport, CT: Praeger.
Midgley, M. (1995). *Beast and Man*. New York: Routledge.
Pinker, S. (2011). *The Better Angels of Our Nature: Why Violence Has Declined*. New York: Viking.
Rifkin, J. (2009). *The Empathic Civilization: The Race to Global Consciousness in a World of Crisis*. New York: Jeremy P. Tarcher.
Simpkins, A. M., and C. A. Simpkins. (2011). *Meditation and Yoga in Psychotherapy: Techniques for Clinical Practice*. Hoboken: Wiley.
Simpkins, C. A., and A. M. Simpkins. (2012). *Zen Meditation in Psychotherapy: Techniques for Clinical Practice*. Hoboken: Wiley.
Wilson, E. O. (1975). *Sociobiology*. Cambridge, MA: Belknap Press.
Wilson, E. O. (2015). *The Meaning of Human Existence*. New York: W.W. Norton.

Further Reading

Fitz-Gibbon, A. (2012). *Love as a Guide to Morals*. Amsterdam: Rodopi. (A theory of ethics based in love and described through philosophical dialogue.)
Gan, B. L. (2014). *Violence and Nonviolence: An Introduction*. Lanham, MD: Lexington. (An overview of philosophical and ethical issues related to nonviolence and the philosophy of peace.)

27
THE DEATH PENALTY AND NONVIOLENCE

Justice Beyond Empathy

Lloyd Steffen

The death penalty is a lethal instrument of social control that political entities use to assert power over the lives of those deemed undesirable and disposable for some reason. Those on whom the death penalty is visited could be criminal law breakers, political adversaries or simply members of a dispossessed group in a particular society. Death by execution is a direct and intentional killing and as such raises serious moral questions. The death penalty ought to be an important topic for consideration for those who are interested in pacifism and nonviolence.

Given that imposing the death penalty permanently and irretrievably places any chance to redress an error or injustice beyond moral reach, both supporters and opponents of the death penalty hold very strong opinions on the subject. This is to be expected given that reasonable people of goodwill do not want to entertain doubts and experience uncertainty as to the justice of directly and intentionally killing a fellow member of the moral community. No global consensus of opinion has developed concerning the fundamental rightness or wrongness of the death penalty, although voices of opposition from across the globe have included advocates of nonviolence and pacifists, as well as numerous legal authorities, writers, artists, social justice activists, religious organizations and prominent religious leaders like the Dalai Lama and Pope Francis. The death penalty is legal in fifty-eight countries, led by China, Iran, Pakistan, Saudi Arabia and the United States in that order, and 141 nations, a majority, have abolished the death penalty in law or practice (Smith 2016; Amnesty 2016).

The death penalty derives from a political community of some sort claiming authority and asserting the power to render a human life "disposable" to some end. Sovereign states can sanction a death penalty process through law and statute, but also through dictatorial decree if that is how the power flows in a particular political community. An extralegal community that gathers to eliminate outsiders deemed threatening to the social order and undeserving of legal protections can also claim the execution power, as occurred with lynchings in the American South. The power of a political collective to deprive a human being of life by a direct act of killing is perhaps the most awesome and frightening power human beings can exercise. Whether human beings have the right to claim such a power is a troubling moral question at the heart of the death penalty, and it informs the political debate over the death penalty as social policy.

Disposable Persons and Power

The discussion that follows will focus on the death penalty as a moral issue as well as a political and social policy question. Bibliographic resources that address these aspects of the death penalty are legion, so this discussion will attempt to limit the range of issues by focusing on the views of those who oppose the execution practice on principle, especially pacifists and advocates of nonviolence.

For the purpose of context and terminological understanding, I shall refer to pacifists as individuals who are committed to nonviolence and who oppose warfare on principle. Not all pacifists are the same, however, and the variations can be striking. For instance, pacifists can commit to nonviolence either absolutely or conditionally. An absolute pacifist would staunchly oppose any use of violence and could interpret any form of governmental action as coercive violence not to be condoned. Leo Tolstoy, perhaps the most famous pacifist absolutist, did just that. Interpreting any action of government as necessarily coercive, he objected to police protection, property and taxes, aid to the poor, and anything governmental tax money supported, which could include everything from the military to road repairs and the postal service (Steffen 2007: 155). Absolute pacifism is rare. Those who advance such a perspective are usually deeply committed to uncompromising and unqualified religious principles.

Conditional pacifism can take different forms. For instance, some pacifists will assert their opposition to killing but not necessarily to all uses of coercive force. Yet another type of pacifist will adopt a personal stance against violence but then refuse to insist that others do likewise: adopting an anti-war, anti-violence stance is not framed as a universal ethical call but as an act of personal conscience. And yet a third form of pacifism has grown up around opposition to "just war" thinking and the political and ethical realism that supports it. No war yields positive benefits and no war ever satisfies the demands of being just, these pacifists hold, and they will argue that the just war criterion of "last resort" is always short-circuited and never pushed so far as to open up realistic alternatives to war and violence. Those who argue that no wars—or other state-sponsored acts of violence like the death penalty—are or can be just could be included as conditional pacifists. Also to be included as pacifists are those who understand nonviolence to be a particular kind of force, "love force," that can be used to oppose injustice and advance peace. Nonviolent resisters like Mohandas Gandhi and Martin Luther King, Jr. are thus appropriately included in the category of pacifist. Including nonviolent resistance under the umbrella of pacifism demonstrates that the term "pacifism" is not univocal or without nuance or breadth of meaning. What can be said with some reliability is that "pacifists" have in common an opposition to uses of lethal force even when such force is proposed as a means to some positive political or social end. We usually identify pacifism with anti-war stances, but pacifists also object strenuously to the use of lethal force at the heart of the death penalty.

Pacifists and nonviolence advocates share a principled opposition to the central act involved in the death penalty—a killing. They object to the destructive violence the death penalty levels at human life; they affirm that all human lives are valuable, even those that political authority or popular opinion in a particular community might deem "undesirable." They would also deny that a political entity could claim the power to subvert human dignity by rendering human life disposable as a means to some end. Pacifists and advocates of nonviolence cannot grant the death penalty moral justification.

This assessment of the moral meaning of the death penalty will command the assent of death penalty opponents who identify as either secular or religious pacifists. John Howard Yoder identified twenty-nine different forms of religious pacifism (Yoder 1992); and religious pacifists who are theists, such as one finds in Mennonite, Amish and other Anabaptist Christian traditions, would oppose the death penalty on the grounds that such power over human life as is exercised in an execution rightly belongs only to God. Martin Luther King, Jr. expressed his religiously grounded opposition to the death penalty this way: "I do not think God approves the death penalty for any crime—rape and murder included.... Capital punishment is ... above all else, against the highest expression of love in the nature of God" (King 1957: 305). Secular-minded or humanistic pacifists, on the other hand, would assert respect for the good of life, holding that life is a preeminent good in that all other goods depend upon it for the possibility of their enjoyment. They will hold that the good of life must be preserved and protected, thus disallowing any claim that a human life is or can be viewed as "disposable" to some end, even if the end sought appears to be a good end. Along with pacifists and advocates of nonviolence, opponents also include those who support certain limited uses of force in certain circumstances yet who object to the death penalty on principle for reasons related to justice. This latter view will be discussed in more detail later.

Justice and Empathy

A 2016 Pew Research poll showed that Americans are divided in their attitudes toward the death penalty, with 49 percent supporting it and 42 percent opposing it, the highest opposition numbers since the early 1970s (Oliphant 2016). A long-term trend toward broader acceptance of abolition is discernible in the United States since "only" twenty executions were carried out nationwide in 2016, a year in which federal crime statistics reported 15,696 murders (FBI News n.d.). The death penalty thus appears to be an unusual punishment even for heinous crimes, which begs the question about how the death penalty is meted out and to whom. Both sides of the death penalty debate share a common concern for relevant moral questions such as the limits and extent of retributive justice, fair sentencing, discrimination in imposition, methods of execution, wrongful capital convictions, and even cost concerns. Yet supporters and opponents interpret questions about the moral meaning of the death penalty in quite different ways, and it is appropriate to ask why that is the case.

Two critical issues affect how people arrive at a position on the fundamental rightness or wrongness of capital punishment. The first issue is a debate over the meaning of justice in the wake of an aggravated murder, the crime for which a death sentence is usually sought. Death penalty supporters argue that society demonstrates how deeply it cherishes life by requiring a comparable loss from the one who unjustly takes a life, so that to commit an act of murder is to render one's own life forfeit. This position, often expressed as "an eye for an eye," which is as old as the Hammurabi Code and the Hebrew Bible, seeks justification in various ethical theories, including deontological perspectives on just retribution as well as in utilitarian defenses that appeal to preservation of the social order. The utilitarian argument usually invokes deterrence, namely, the idea that the good of society as a whole is advanced when the fear of losing one's own life prevents an individual from wrongfully taking the life of another. Harsh and unpleasant as the death penalty is, this argument sometimes goes, it functions to yield positive consequences for the greater good by preventing deadly crimes.

Opponents of the death penalty, on the other hand, will point out that executing an individual offender involves the legal system and, by inclusion, a whole society in an act of violent killing that mistakenly perpetuates the idea that violence can solve societal problems. They will argue that killing a killer lowers society to the level of the killer, thus disrespecting life, and that the death penalty erodes social respect for the value of life while subjecting those who are selected for execution to various forms of discrimination and cruelty.

Opponents and supporters of the death penalty may fail to acknowledge each other's particular understanding of which justice concern should have decisive weight in debate—a possible reason for that is my next point in this discussion—but there is no doubt that justice concerns are central to both sides. Each side is convinced of the rightness of its position even if the reasons supporting that position emphasize different factors, all of which may have truth to them, but neither side seems able to make an argument so compelling that it persuades the other side to change its position on the rightness or wrongness of the death penalty.

The reason that opponents and supporters of the death penalty fail to convince one another of the strength of their respective arguments about justice issues rests elsewhere than in rational argument. This leads me to the second issue of importance when considering the death penalty. Supporters of the death penalty as well as opponents are persuaded by appeals to emotion, particularly to empathy.

Yale psychologist Paul Bloom has argued in his book *Against Empathy: The Case for Rational Compassion* (Bloom 2016) that empathy is a serious problem for devising fair social justice systems. This is due to the way empathy spotlights individual incidents and tempts people to lose sight of larger ethical issues that affect the well-being of communities and societies. Empathy, Bloom argues, affects individual ethical responses and works against forming ethical views based on reason. The emotion-related issues revolving around empathy heighten the possibilities for harsher retribution and even increase the likelihood of expanding injustice, for, as Bloom notes, it seems a now indisputable psychological datum that "the more empathetic people are, the more they want a harsher punishment" (Bloom 2016: 195).

Empathy creates the conditions for reconstructing the emotional meaning of a crime and its aftermath. Empathy can cause people to react to the details of crimes eligible for the death penalty by imagining such a loss themselves and thus feeling what a real victim's family member experiences in the face of a tragic, devastating and often cruel loss. Most morally attuned human beings can imagine how such a loss would affect them. In the wake of confronting through empathy the emotional meaning of terror and loss, people can find themselves supporting the death penalty while resisting rational arguments about systemic injustices in the criminal justice and death penalty administration systems. To step back and offer a rational policy objection to the death penalty amid such empathic emotional arousal can easily misfire, as happened in an American presidential campaign. In 1988, presidential nominee Michael Dukakis arguably lost his bid for the nation's highest office when in debate he responded to a question asking him how he would react if his wife, Kitty, were a victim of rape and murder. He sidestepped the emotional point of the question, failed to show any empathic outrage, and proceeded to respond by restating his long-standing rational opposition to the death penalty. His failure to address the emotional question reinforced the perception that he was too rationalistic, too unfeeling and too much the policy wonk to actually take on the demands of leading and inspiring a nation.

Alongside the primary concern for justice, then, attention must be given to the role played by emotions, especially empathy, in thinking about the fundamental rightness or wrongness of the death penalty. These emotion-related issues are especially important for prosecutors now that the capital trial system allows victim impact statements to be made at sentencing hearings with the purpose of informing a jury that a particular offender should receive the death penalty because of the specific pain caused by the specific crime committed by a specific person. Allowing such statements at sentencing is evidence that the law has evolved to allow the pull of emotion to play an essential role in gaining a capital conviction. A sentencing system based on reason would disallow such statements because they unfairly enflame hostility toward the offender while arousing empathy for the crime victim who has lost a loved one. I say "unfairly" because in a rational ethical system, the fact that a human life has been taken wrongfully and with malice should suffice to convey all the foundation needed for assessing the moral horror of a crime and determining a fair sentence. Disparities in sentencing due to race may go to the point that white juries are much quicker to empathize with white victims and their families if the accused perpetrator is black, and race of victim has long been a core death penalty statistic: blacks accused of killing whites are disproportionately likely to receive the death penalty.

By raising the empathy issue, I do not mean to suggest that it is relevant only to those who wind up empathic toward crime victims and their loved ones. Empathy affects opponents of the death penalty as well. Opponents of the death penalty can experience the appeal to empathy when they focus attention on those death row prisoners who have reformed, or those who are suspected or proven innocent of the crime that got them to death row. Sometimes the simple fact of a condemned person's hopelessly helpless situation arouses empathy. In his famous "Reflection on a Guillotine" essay, Albert Camus focused on the change that overcame his father after he had witnessed the beheading of a man who killed a farmer and his family, including several children. Camus noted that his father, after witnessing the execution, which he wanted to see because the crime had so outraged him, returned home terribly affected by the condemned man's fate: "Instead of thinking about the slaughtered children, he could think of nothing but that quivering body that had just been dropped onto a board to have its head cut off" (Camus 1960, 1963: 132). And George Orwell, who, incidentally, was no friend of pacifism, perhaps reflects how much more difficult it is to support executions when they are carried out right before one's eyes. At a hanging he witnessed, Orwell was moved to comment on a condemned man who stepped aside to avoid a mud puddle while on the way to the gallows. Orwell's epiphany was that a man about to be hanged was indeed a fellow human being like himself:

> It is curious, but till that moment I had never realized what it means to destroy a healthy, conscious man. When I saw the prisoner step aside to avoid the puddle, I saw the mystery, the unspeakable wrongness, of cutting a life short when it is in full tide. This man was not dying; he was alive just as we were alive. All the organs of his body were working—bowels digesting food, skin renewing itself, nails growing, tissues forming—all toiling away in solemn foolery. His nails would still be growing when he stood on the drop, when he was falling through the air with a tenth of a second to live. His eyes saw the yellow gravel and the grey walls, and his brain still remembered, foresaw, reasoned—reasoned even about puddles. He and we were a party of men walking together, seeing, hearing, feeling, understanding the same world; and in two minutes, with a sudden snap, one of us would be gone—one mind less, one world less.
>
> *Orwell 2016: n.p.*

Condemned persons, then, can also arouse empathy and affect the decisions even non-pacifists like Orwell make about the justice and moral meaning of the death penalty.

The prospect of executing an innocent person also makes an emotional appeal. The moral horror of such a prospect is made real by the fact that since the United States Supreme Court lifted the moratorium on executions in 1976, close to 160 persons have been released from death row due to wrongful conviction and in some cases actual exoneration. Average citizens whom we must include in a large class of "innocent" people, meaning by that a class of persons who have not committed a capital crime, can without too much strain imagine persons like themselves—innocent persons—being wrongly convicted of a capital crime and condemned to death. The release of wrongfully convicted persons from death row is still a newsworthy event, and release from death row because of a mistake and a wrongful conviction can arouse an empathic reaction. Evidently, the thought of such powerlessness as a condemned person would experience along with the rational concern about the impossibility of correcting an injustice if one's life were irretrievably lost can likewise make an emotional appeal. Empathy works this side of the aisle also.

Although many opponents and supporters of the death penalty can appeal to rational arguments and statistics in support of their positions, a cluster of emotional influences, especially those related to empathy, can affect how people settle the moral issue of rightness or wrongness. Advocates of principled nonviolence typically avow that violence does not solve problems but inevitably adds to them—where once there was one grieving family there are now two; and they may of course feel empathy for victims and offenders, even for one over the other. Their stance on executions, however, is not determined by those feelings but is grounded in a rational perspective committed to the ethical view that human beings must be treated with dignity and respect. The act of execution violates this ethical view, for intentionally killing a person, for whatever claimed good reason, is not an obvious way to show that person respect and avow that person's dignity.

Advocates of nonviolence and pacifists find nothing in the death penalty to support. Commitment to nonviolence is itself a principled and rationally defensible stance that attends to issues larger than those that focus attention on a particular crime or a particular offender's situation. Commitment to nonviolence transcends empathy, surmounting it with a concern for justice both in terms of broader issues affecting the welfare of communities and in terms of peaceable outcomes. Reasonable people will always prefer the nonviolent outcome. They will support the nonviolent process of engagement that affirms the message that violence is not an appropriate way to resolve conflicts or societal problems.

So two clusters of issues guide the decision people make to determine a moral interpretation of the death penalty, namely, those related to justice and those arousing deep emotional connections to the persons directly involved in actual death penalty dynamics. The justice issues are moral as well as social and political. The emotionally charged issues involve incompatible targets of empathy. Disagreements about justice questions and the emotional issues at play with respect to empathy affect how people wind up on one side or the other of the question about the moral meaning of the death penalty. Advocates of nonviolence and pacifism will take a principled stand opposing the killing and violence involved in the death penalty, which they believe violates essential respect for the value of human life. It may therefore be inferred that for advocates of nonviolence, empathy plays less of a role—and concern for justice principles more of a role—in establishing grounds for a rational moral opposition to the death penalty.

Principled Opposition to the Death Penalty: The Natural Law Approach

The death penalty is a killing, and the violence involved in such a killing cannot be hidden no matter how sanitized or, as in lethal injection, "medicalized" the method of dispatch. Pacifists and advocates of nonviolence will inevitably oppose the execution power, and they will ground their opposition in life-affirming principles. Pope Francis appealed to religious scruples upholding the sanctity of life when he remarked, "[The death penalty] is an offence to the inviolability of life and to the dignity of the human person; it likewise contradicts God's plan for individuals and society, and his merciful justice" (San Martin 2016: n.p.). Recognizing human persons as inviolable centers of meaning and value through a humanitarian commitment to peace and nonviolence may also serve as the basis for opposition to the death penalty. In either case, opposition to the death penalty will be *principled*, which means that opposition is not a matter of objecting to this or that use of the death penalty in an individual case due to some problem in, say, legal procedure. Principled opponents deny moral sanction to any use of the death penalty on the view that it violates cherished values, especially the value of life, and that it affronts the core moral affirmation that no human life is disposable. The pacifist would hold that it is a grievous moral wrong to think that it is ever useful to kill a person, no matter what the offense.

Pacifists and advocates of nonviolence will clearly oppose the death penalty as inconsistent with their core beliefs regarding nonviolence, but that opposition is a consequence of the core commitment to nonviolence rather than the result of a reasoned moral analysis of the execution practice itself. The question yet to consider is whether another route to principled opposition to the death penalty is available. Is there a foundation for opposing the death penalty on principle for reasons other than pacifism or a holistic philosophical or religious commitment to nonviolence? Such a foundation can be found in an unexpected and ancient philosophical resource—natural law ethics.

Natural law ethics has a long history. It is a philosophical perspective that was common to the ancient Greeks, the Stoics and even Christian philosophers. The Roman Catholic Church to this day employs natural law as a philosophical framework for moral theology. Natural law thinking, despite this tradition, is not about religion, and religion enters in for some natural law theorists mainly because of questions about human nature. Some natural law theorists turn to religion to avow that human beings are the way they are because God made them so. Natural law, however, does not insist on a religious affirmation of divine revelation, only on the idea that human beings share a common and universal nature. It is the fact that human beings are by nature what they are rather than why or how this nature came to be that is critically important.

Given this qualification, the central affirmation of natural law ethics is that human beings share a natural endowment common to all human persons—reason. Because reason enables human beings to discern moral meaning and determine right and wrong, a route to principled opposition to the death penalty opens due to moral affirmations held in common by all reasonable persons of goodwill. Natural law ethics recognizes that reason must articulate and adjudicate moral issues as human beings engage with one another and sort out questions about moral meaning. That disagreement in moral matters is a hallmark of any approach to ethics, so too is it in natural law ethics, and this is the case despite the natural law affirmation that human beings share a common nature in the universal human capacity for moral discernment grounded in reason. Reasonable people of goodwill can take up different perspectives on a whole variety of moral issues, the death penalty included. As noted earlier, differing views about justice and even different ways of applying empathy and emotion to death penalty issues can affect how moral disagreements come about.

Given the controversy surrounding the moral meaning of the death penalty, a natural law theorist would recognize the divisive nature of this issue yet still ask if there is a reasonable moral agreement to which both supporters and opponents could assent. There is. It is both a simple and obvious moral statement but one vital to affirm, which is this: *Both sides of the death penalty debate can affirm that a state or political authority ought not ordinarily be about the business of killing its citizens.* That this "common agreement" is empirically observable can be affirmed by noting that there is a serious reluctance to execute citizens in a death penalty country like the United States. Recall that of the over 15,000 homicides committed in the United States in 2015, "only" twenty persons were executed. Obviously, the general principle of moral retribution housed in the idea of "a life for a life" is not observed in light of these numbers. In addition, even death penalty supporters are not demanding the execution of every person responsible for committing a homicide.

The natural law theorist, however, does not stop with the common agreement that states ought ordinarily not kill citizens. If that is so, and disagreements exist between death penalty supporters and opponents, the next question to ask is whether it is *ever* justifiable for the state to authorize the killing of a citizen. To this question many reasonable people would answer that exceptions can be made. An example might be the police officer who uses lethal force to save innocent lives at risk of being unjustly killed in, say, a robbery-hostage situation. Using lethal force to save innocent lives would seem to many people a just cause for using such force if every effort had been made to avoid doing so and it was done only as a last resort. If such an exception can be granted, the claim that the state ought ordinarily not kill its citizens is not on this natural law view the absolute prohibition we can associate with a particular pacifist stance. Natural law allows us to envision reasonable exceptions. Natural law ethics accepts that reason can affirm common moral agreements but also consider possible exceptions due to the press of circumstance.

Reasonable people would grant that some uses of force could be morally justified in certain situations. Gandhi held that *satyagraha* or "love force" was always superior to armed force, but even he allowed that:

> when a woman is assaulted, she may not stop to think of himsa or ahimsa. Her primary duty is self-protection. She is at liberty to employ every method or means that come to her mind in order to defend her honour. God has given her nails and teeth. She must use them with all her strength and if need be die in the effort.
>
> *Gandhi 2009: 215*

If situations involving saving innocent lives, or self-defense, or humanitarian intervention in the face of genocide allow reasonable people to grant an exception to the use of lethal force, the question arises whether the death penalty is also a possible exception to the common moral agreement involved with the death penalty, namely, that the state ought not ordinarily kill its citizens. Can the killings that take place by means of the death penalty be morally justified?

Natural law ethics addresses such a question through a particular mode of analysis important for thinking about difficult ethical issues, the paradigm model for it being the idea of just war. "Just war" thinking affirms that ordinarily force should not be used to settle conflicts—this is the common moral agreement reasonable people of goodwill can affirm without controversy. The ethic then goes on to establish on the basis of reason several criteria related to justice concerns, each of which would have to be satisfied if the moral presumption against war were to be lifted and a use of force proceed. Just war is a model of natural law thinking—it avoids absolutism, makes room for possible exceptions to common moral agreements and allows human beings to apply reason to situations and contend with one another over what should be done given reason's demand for constraint on the use of force. Those constraints are articulated in various justice concerns, also known as the criteria of just war, which include such matters as right authority, just cause, right intention, last resort, proportionality and others. All of the criteria must be satisfied, not just some, and it is difficult to satisfy them, so difficult that the argument has been made that just war is actually a means to achieve practical pacifism without being committed to the inflexibility of theoretical pacifism (Steffen 2012).

Natural law ethics can approach the death penalty on this model of analysis. Since the appeal is to reason and not to religion or to ideology or to an identity-encompassing commitment to a core value like nonviolence, the ethics issue is whether there could be "just execution." The claim that executions can be morally justified would have to satisfy several justice-related criteria:

- Just authority.
- Just cause.
- Motivation must be justice and not vengeance.

- Fair imposition.
- The method of execution must not be cruel or torturous.
- Execution must be a last resort.
- Executions must preserve respect for the value of life.
- The end of execution must be to restore an equilibrium upset by an offender's crime.
- Proportionality must be observed so the punishment fits the crime.

Detailed discussions of these criteria are available elsewhere (Steffen 1998, 2006, 2012), but a brief mention of the kinds of issues that attend two of these criteria will at least show how the natural law mode of analysis functions. Consider first "just authority."

Although Americans think of the death penalty as the result of a legal process, many uses of the execution power throughout human history have been conducted by political authorities acting extralegally. Executions have been conducted by all kinds of political partisans and governments to eliminate political enemies through assassinations, death squads and government-sponsored murder (Amnesty International 1983). Thinking through legitimate authority requires consideration of the broader execution power claimed by political entities and the moral appropriateness of such claims. This criterion also requires consideration of flawed justice-dispensing systems, one of the most notorious being vigilantism. Vigilantes have in different places and times dispensed death sentences with no regard for legal protections, and the case could be made that the death penalty exists today as the result of a sublimated and legalized form of vigilantism in some communities.

Franklin Zimring has investigated the lynching culture of the American South and concluded that it reflects an essential vigilantism that has been historically directed against community outsiders, usually black males (Zimring 2003). Communities under the sway of white supremacist cultural values claimed the right to eliminate blacks suspected of transgressing social barriers or committing crimes whether or not evidence of the accused's guilt was established. The lynching culture, born of the vigilante tradition, has not disappeared, Zimrung argues, but it has changed form and is present today in the legalized procedures that comprise the death penalty system. The law now sanctions executions in those states—and often in the specific counties—that have a strong vigilante history, and high-execution-rate states and counties today correspond to jurisdictions with a historically strong vigilantism tradition. In these areas, executions continue to fall disproportionately on minorities and persons deemed "outsiders" to the community majority. In support of Zimring's research connecting yesterday's vigilante justice traditions with today's high-execution-rate states, the Death Penalty Information Center has provided an analysis of execution by county that further demonstrates that execution-friendly counties have a history of vigilante-lynching justice (DPIC, "Top 15 Counties" n.d.).

An execution that takes place outside of law fails to satisfy the criterion of just authority, and although lynchings and vigilante justice fail to satisfy the just authority criterion, so do some systems of legal justice. Thus did Martin Luther King, Jr. comment in his "Letter from a Birmingham Jail" that "we should never forget that everything Adolf Hitler did in Germany was 'legal' and . . . [it] was 'illegal' to aid and comfort a Jew in Hitler's Germany" (King 1963: n.p.). Legal though they might have been, the wrongful deaths compiled under Hitler's reign of terror point out that where an execution power is in place and operational, just authority requires that the law satisfy moral requirements, not the other way around.

Just authority raises issues about the moral foundation for the power to execute citizens. The death penalty system as a legalized means of killing is error-prone, even broken by some legal critics' viewpoints (Gelman et al. 2004), yet it is also beyond the pale of reasonableness to ask that such a system achieve perfection and never make mistakes. The moral problem, however, is that system perfection is required in order to avoid the horror of executing an innocent person. System perfection would require no errors in the investigation of a crime, no errors in charging an individual with a capital crime and no mistakes in prosecuting a crime. To deny the need for this standard of perfection would lead to the conclusion that the death penalty is so important to have that it is morally acceptable to tolerate a few unfortunate mistakes that cost innocent persons their lives. If an "acceptable losses" perspective is, in fact, unacceptable, it is because any innocent person could become subject to it; if that is the case then it ought to be unacceptable for the innocent person wrongly subjected to a state-sponsored sentence of death.

These are concerns that attend reflection on the criterion of just authority. The criterion of "fair imposition" is another criterion that raises serious issues, for various analyses of the death penalty system demonstrate that racial, class and gender discrimination seem to infect that system. Race of victim, for instance, is often an indicator of unequal application of the death penalty. Statistical evidence shows that 50 percent of murder victims are white, but more than 75 percent of executions involve a white victim (DPIC "Fact Sheet"). Race appears to be a factor in who is charged with a capital crime and who is finally put to death. One study in Louisiana showed that the chance of receiving a death sentence was 97 percent higher if the victim was white than if the victim was black, and in the state of Washington jurors were three times more likely to impose a death sentence on a black defendant than on a white defendant in a similar kind of case (DPIC "Fact Sheet"). If race affects decisions about who gets executed, and if racial biases emerge from community values in a particular area of the country, and if financial resources secure good lawyering to avoid a death sentence when such resources are not available to the poor—then such factors point to discrimination and unfairness in the administration of the death penalty system.

A cursory examination of just two of those criteria has raised serious issues that should give pause to one trying to decide whether the death penalty is an exception to the common agreement that states ought not ordinarily kill their citizens. The problems raised under "fair imposition" alone would be sufficient to halt executions and dismantle the system, and as has been shown elsewhere, serious problems can be shown with all nine of the criteria (Steffen 2006).

Based on this kind of examination, a person committed to a natural law ethic could oppose the death penalty *on principle* since it is so flawed a practice that it cannot reasonably meet the standards of justice. Because a natural law ethics cannot justify the killing that occurs in a state-sponsored execution, we can include persons who adopt such an ethical stance—along with pacifists and other persons committed to nonviolence—among those able to adopt a *principled* stance against the death penalty.

Conclusion

The execution power is dangerous. Executions have spilled innocent blood across the spans of human history and culture as political and even religious institutions have eliminated enemies and used executions to shore up power. Pacifists and advocates of nonviolence have historically resisted this power, and they have themselves become the object of execution—conscientious objectors in wartime have not only faced prison but death sentences and actual execution. In 2007, Pope Benedict XVI declared blessed Franz Jägerstätter, an Austrian conscientious objector who was executed for refusing to support or fight for the Nazi regime (Mathis 2007). The Nazi political regime inflicted the execution power on individual resisters like Jägerstätter as well as on millions of persons, including all those exterminated in the "final solution" program of the Holocaust.

The death penalty has long been defended as a just and equitable response to the worst thing a human being can do, which is to take another person's life unjustly. But capital punishment is no longer defended solely as a retributive punishment. Today, the defense of capital punishment focuses on the claim that only an execution can bring closure to the surviving victims of a terrible crime, especially the family of a murdered loved one. The defense of the death penalty in such a situation rests on a strong appeal to empathy—because people can imagine what such an experience of loss would be for them. The appeal to empathy is powerful and persuasive, and victim impact statements, as already noted, have reinforced how important the appeal to emotion is in capital cases and how the law acts to bias juries toward a death sentence through emotional appeals.

Such an appeal to empathy turns attention away from rational consideration of the death penalty's many shortcomings, obscuring the fact that the death penalty, while it fails to protect society or meet reasonable standards of justice and fairness, also perpetuates the very act of lethal violence—the intentional and direct killing—it condemns. Aside from these considerations, there is every good reason to be suspicious of claims that a victim's loved ones receive emotional closure through execution. Families of victims are often so caught up in the legal process leading up to the execution of the person who has killed their loved one—the trial and years-long appeals—that they evade a full confrontation with their loss. Once the prosecutor contacts and public interest go away after an execution finally takes place, family members find themselves left alone with a long-postponed grief. Closure in the face of such heartache and anguish becomes a vain and idle fancy.

Executing a murderer does not bring a wrongfully killed loved one back to life—the balance of justice in such a situation cannot be restored. In the face of that imbalance, pacifists and advocates of nonviolence support restorative justice alternatives to incarceration and retributive punishment. "The Journey of Hope" moves this approach into the arena of murder and justice for victim families as it brings the families of loved ones lost to murder together with their loved one's killer. This program has brought about change and built relationships between perpetrators and victims' family members; and hard as that process may be, the effort to effect healing for family members proceeds by the explicit repudiation of violence and hatred (Journey of Hope 2017). Pacifists and nonviolence advocates cannot demand that those who have lost loved ones to murder forgive those whose crimes have caused tragic loss, but they can hope for a killer's transformation and redemption, and that is a process that requires life, not death, even for the hope of such change to come about.

Sentencing a murderer to life without chance of parole satisfies the call for a harsh retributive punishment for a terrible crime like aggravated murder, but this "death by incarceration" option also requires a moral analysis. To open up the issue of alternatives to the death penalty and life sentences calls for an examination of decarceration and restorative justice practices, both of which advocates of nonviolence and pacifists would heartily endorse. Opting for imprisonment over the death penalty recognizes the value of life by preserving life and holding open the opportunity for transformation and personal redemption. It also sends the message that the problem of criminal killing in a society is not solved by more killing. That society cannot solve its problems through violence—killing the killer—is a legacy of pacifism. That legacy exerts a powerful influence on reflection about the moral meaning of the death penalty; and that pacifist viewpoint has the potential to change societal attitudes toward the death penalty and eventually bring about its abolition.

Works Cited

Amnesty International. (1983). *Political Killings by Governments 1983*, London: Amnesty International Publications.

Amnesty International. (2016). *The Death Penalty 2015: Facts and Figures* April 6. Available at: www.amnesty.org/en/latest/news/2016/04/death-penalty-2015-facts-and-figures/ (Accessed 18 January 2017).

Bloom, P. (2016). *Against Empathy: The Case for Rational Compassion*. New York: HarperCollins.
Camus, A. (1960/1963). "Reflections on the Guillotine," in J. O'Brien (trans. and intro.), *Resistance, Rebellion and Death*. New York: Modern Library, 131–179.
Death Penalty Information Center (DPIC). "Fact Sheet." Available at: www.deathpenaltyinfo.org/documents/FactSheet.pdf (Accessed 22 April 2017).
Death Penalty Information Center (DPIC). "Top 15 Counties by Execution Since 1976." Available at: www.deathpenaltyinfo.org/executions-county (Accessed 15 January 2017).
FBI News (n.d.). "Latest Crime Statistics Released." September 26, 2016. Available at: www.fbi.gov/news/stories/latest-crime-statistics-released (Accessed 12 December 2016).
Gandhi, M. K. (1951). *Non-Violent Resistance*. New York: Shocken Books.
Gandhi, M. K. (2009). *India of My Dreams*. Delhi, India: Rajpal and Sons.
Gelman, A., J. Liebman, A. West, and A. Kiss (2004). "A Broken System: The Persistent Patterns of Reversals of Death Sentences in the United States." *Journal of Empirical Legal Studies* 1 (2): 209–261. Available at: www.stat.columbia.edu/~gelman/research/published/jels.pdf (Accessed 23 January 2017).
"Journey of Hope . . . From Violence to Healing." (2017). *Journey of Hope*. Available at: www.journeyofhope.org/who-we-are/murder-victim-family/bill-pelke/ (Accessed 17 January 2017).
King, M. L., Jr. (1957, 2000). "'Advice for Living' Ebony: 106," in C. Carson, S. Carson, S. Englander, T. Jackson, G.L. Smith, (eds.), *The Papers of Martin Luther King, Jr.*, vol. 4. Berkeley: University of California Press.
King, M. L., Jr. (1963). "Letter from a Birmingham Jail [King, Jr.]." African Studies Center, University of Pennsylvania. Available at: www.africa.upenn.edu/Articles_Gen/Letter_Birmingham.html (Accessed 23 January 2017).
Mathis, C. (2007). "Vatican to Beatify Austrian Conscientious Objector." *Catholic News Agency* October 18. Available at: www.catholicnewsagency.com/news/vatican_to_beatify_austrian_conscientious_objector/ (Accessed 22 April 2017).
Mazhar, K. (1999). *Gandhi and the Indian Freedom Struggle*. New Delhi: APH Publishing Corporation.
Oliphant, B. (2016). "Support for Death Penalty Lowest in More than Four Decades." *Pew Research Center* September 29. Available at: www.pewresearch.org/fact-tank/2016/09/29/support-for-death-penalty-lowest-in-more-than-four-decades/ (Accessed 3 December 2016).
Orwell, G. (2016). "A Hanging." Available at: www.online-literature.com/orwell/888/ (Accessed 28 January 2016).
San Martin, I. (2016). "Pope Francis Calls for World 'Free of the Death Penalty'." *CRUX: Taking the Catholic Pulse* June 21. Available at: https://cruxnow.com/vatican/2016/06/21/pope-francis-calls-world-free-death-penalty/ (Accessed 25 April 2017).
Smith, O. (2016). "Mapped: The 58 Countries That Still Have the Death Penalty." *The Telegraph* September 1. Available at: www.telegraph.co.uk/travel/maps-and-graphics/countries-that-still-have-the-death-penalty/ (Accessed 3 December 2016).
Steffen, L. (2006). *Executing Justice: The Moral Meaning of the Death Penalty*. Eugene, OR: Wipf and Stock Publishers.
Steffen, L. (2007). *Holy War, Just War: Exploring the Religious Meaning of Religious Violence*. Lanham, MD: Rowman and Littlefield.
Steffen, L. (2012). *Ethics and Experience: Moral Theory from Just War to Abortion*. Lanham, MD: Rowan and Littlefield.
Yoder, J. H. (1992). *Nevertheless: Varieties of Religious Pacifism*, 2nd ed. Scottsdale, PA: Herald Press.
Zimring, F. (2003). *The Contradictions of American Capital Punishment*. Oxford: Oxford University Press.

Further Reading

Beck, E., S. Britto, and A. Andrews. (2007). *In the Shadow of Death: Restorative Justice and Death Row Families*. New York: Oxford University Press. (First-person accounts of capital offenders' family members and application of restorative justice principles to capital crimes.)
Ingle, J. B. (1990). *Last Rights: 13 Fatal Encounters with the State's Justice*. Nashville: Abington Press. (A Christian minister who worked on death row presents up-close stories about thirteen known death row inmates who were executed.)
Johnson, D. T., and F. E. Zimring. (2009). *The Next Frontier: National Development, Political Change and the Death Penalty in Asia*. New York: Oxford University Press. (Death penalty issues in a global political context.)

Radelet, M. L. (ed.) (1989). *Facing the Death Penalty: Essays on Cruel and Unusual Punishment*. Philadelphia: Temple University Press. (Important collection of essays from experts who reveal what it is like to live under sentence of death.)

Steffen, L., and D. Cooley. (2014). *The Ethics of Death: Religious and Philosophical Perspectives in Dialogue*. Minneapolis: Fortress Press. (A philosopher and a religion scholar engage a dialogue about the death penalty, including discussion of the natural law perspective.)

Zimring, F. (2003). *The Contradictions of American Capital Punishment*. New York: Oxford University Press. (Insightful analysis of American belief in violent social justice and vigilantism as a means of local control against outsiders and execution, legal and non-legal, as safeguard of community values.)

28
ECOLOGY AND PACIFISM

Mark Woods

What ecological insights can we bring to bear on pacifism and nonviolence? In what follows, I explore different ways of looking at wars, military activities, and nonviolence through a lens of ecology and what we might call an environmental ethic of war and peace.

Perhaps the clearest link between ecology and nonviolence is what Randall Amster (2015) has called *peace ecology* or what Martin Ceadel (1987) identifies as *ecological pacifism*. Ecological pacifism is a moral opposition to wars and armed conflicts grounded in ecological considerations. Michael Fox (2014: 122–125) develops an anti-war argument along these lines. He argues that because the fates of *Homo sapiens* and other species are interrelated, we have moral obligations to nonhumans. War makes it difficult to fulfill these obligations, and we thus have a moral obligation to oppose war. This should make us ecological pacifists.

It is not difficult to see why one might be an ecological pacifist. There are many negative environmental impacts of conventional military forces at war and at peace (Cahill 1995; Biswas 2000; Fidler 2000; Leaning 2000; McNeely 2000; Woods 2007a; Machlis and Hanson 2008). Consider the following: (1) defoliation, deforestation, degradation, and destruction of natural areas, (2) killing (direct and collateral) of animals and plants and habitat loss, (3) surface water and groundwater contamination, (4) crater formation and the compaction, contamination, and erosion of soils by bombs, missiles, and military vehicles and their hazardous and toxic residues, (5) various forms of land pollution such as garbage dumps, latrines, land mines, and unexploded ordnance, (6) air pollution and atmospheric emissions of CO_2 and NO_x, (7) use of high-intensity sonar that can lead to erratic behavior, internal tissue damage, and death of cetaceans, and (8) noise of 140 decibels or more from low-flying aircraft and weapons that can lead to long-term hearing impairment in people and animals. Following armed conflicts, there can be further environmental harms for people, such as (1) damage and destruction of croplands, marine fisheries, and pasturage and the resulting loss of agricultural products and other foodstuffs, (2) damage and destruction of water storage and distribution systems, waste and wastewater treatment facilities, and sewer systems, and (3) damage and destruction of human structures such as buildings and power grid systems. These kinds of environmental harms in turn can lead to wider impacts such as the following: (1) disruption or destruction of economic and social infrastructures, (2) dislocation of human populations, and (3) creation of new opportunities for the spread of infectious diseases. Following the end of armed conflicts, there can be further negative impacts as people expand from damaged and destroyed areas into undamaged natural areas and waterscapes (Hart and Hart 2003).

As pacifists such as Duane Cady and Robert Holmes point out, wars do not operate in isolation: wars necessitate and are preceded by extensive war systems that have numerous impacts (Cady 1989; Holmes 1989). Asit Biswas estimates that worldwide military use accounts for about 6% of global petroleum consumption, 8% of global lead use, 9% of global iron consumption, and 11% of global copper consumption. He notes that the total energy use by militaries in wartime can increase by factors of five to twenty times over peacetime levels of use (Biswas 2000). Gary Machlis and Thor Hanson estimate that war preparations during peacetime utilize up to fifteen million square kilometers and that militaries at peace produce as much as 10 percent of all global CO_2 emissions (Machlis and Hanson 2008). It is estimated that US military consumption of oil for combat operations in Iraq in 2008 alone was the equivalent of approximately 1,210,000 cars on the road in the US of that year (Watson Institute 2015). As Joni Seager provocatively claims, military forces are "privileged vandals" (Seager 1999: 163).

Examples of the environmental impacts of non-conventional military weapons include the nuclear winter effects of a thermonuclear war during the Cold War between the US and the Soviet Union (Harwell 1984; Dotto 1986), defoliant use of Agent Orange by the US in the Second Indochina War (Westing 1984; Hay 2000), oil fires and oil pollution of the 1991 Persian Gulf War (El-Baz and Makharita 1994; Omar et al. 2000), and use of depleted uranium during the 1991 Persian Gulf War (Rostker 2002; Giannardi and Dominici 2003) and in subsequent conflicts in Iraq and Afghanistan. Unfortunately, this list will probably grow.

How might an ecological pacifist champion protecting the environment from the ravages of military activities and armed conflicts? One possible way might be to build environmental constraints into military thinking itself via the just war tradition. While ecological pacifism certainly stands in contrast to just war thinking, an ecological pacifist might consider turning just war thinking against itself in order to protect the environment. How might this be done?

A number of just war philosophers have attempted to build environmental considerations directly into just war thinking. Merrit Drucker uses the *jus in bello* (justice in war) principle of distinction—noncombatant immunity—to protect the environment. The environment is a noncombatant because, like other noncombatants, it poses no direct threat to combatants, and, unlike combatants, it has no choice to be involved with fighting. Drucker also claims that the environment is similar to noncombatants such as chaplains and medical personnel who do not fight and instead nurture and heal people. He argues that the environment has inherent worth because species have inherent worth (Drucker 1989).

Gregory Reichberg and Henrik Syse combine the *jus in bello* principles of proportionality and discrimination to champion protection of the environment. In relation to projected military gains, environmental destruction can destabilize ecosystems and have severe, negative, and long-term environmental consequences and thus violate proportionality—especially given that many environmental impacts will likely outlast military campaigns—and be indiscriminate because environmental destruction often destroys natural resources upon which civilians depend. As the environment for Reichberg and Syse consists of natural resources for human use, ecosystems, and natural objects, their environmental ethic is neither exclusively anthropocentric (human-centered) nor nonanthropocentric (non-human-centered); they argue that the ethic stems from the claim that people have duties toward nature as per the stewardship tradition of St. Thomas Aquinas (Reichberg and Syse 2000).

Following Drucker, and Reichberg and Syse, I have argued for regarding the environment—especially populations of nonhuman organisms and ecosystems—as a noncombatant and attacks that damage or destroy the environment as violations of the principle of discrimination or noncombatant immunity (Woods 2007a). When such attacks are not proportionate to military gains, the attacks also can violate *jus in bello* proportionality. To add more bite, I have argued that if it can be foreseen that a war is likely to cause environmental harm and thus violate noncombatant immunity and/or proportionality, this should count as a reason not to go to war when deliberating about whether or not a war will satisfy *jus ad bellum* (justice of going to war) principles. Foreseen environmental harm might violate the likelihood of success principle if destruction of the homeland counts against winning and the proportionality principle if overall the war is not likely to result in environmental benefits over harms. If the just cause principle is construed in terms of self-defense of a homeland, foreseen environmental harm also might violate this principle if the home*land* is harmed by self-defense military activities. Robin Eckersley argues for a new kind of just cause principle that would justify armed humanitarian interventions in order to prevent environmental degradation and harm (Eckersley 2007). In response, I have questioned armed ecological interventions because the negative environmental impacts of military activities will probably outweigh the good consequences of supposedly protecting the environment (Woods 2007b). I have also argued that environmental harm can count against just settlements in ending a war and thus violate one or more *jus post bellum* (justice after war) principles (Woods 2007a). Finally, environmental harm can count against a just war subdivision Harry van der Linden has called just military preparedness (van der Linden 2010) that I have called *jus potentia ad bellum*—justice of the potential of going to war (Woods 2007a)—when peacetime training and preparations for war cause environmental harm.

Military necessity presents the greatest challenge to using just war thinking to develop some kind of an environmental ethic of war and peace. No matter how well aimed and informed environmental protection is, military necessity probably will override environmental protection. From a military commander's point of view, fighting is first and foremost about following orders, winning battles, and keeping one's troops alive. If an action will significantly contribute to the success of a mission, then such an action is militarily necessary, as long the action is not a violation of the legal rules of war. In the eyes of the military, environmental damage and destruction become justifiable collateral damage. To move beyond regarding the environment as such justifiable damage, the ecological pacifist more than likely will need to move beyond the just war tradition. One possible remedy might be to regard environmental destruction as a type of action that is *mala in se*—evil in itself—and thus violates the just war tradition. An example of a *mala in se* action is genocide in that genocidal actions are never justifiable. No one has attempted to classify environmental destruction as *mala in se*, but perhaps this is a route to get around military necessity within the just war tradition.

Beyond the just war tradition, what other possible directions might an ecological pacifist take to protect the environment? One way might be an appeal to international humanitarian law (Diederich 1992; Grunawalt, King, and McClain 1996; Richards and Schmitt 1999; Falk 2000; Schmitt 2000).

There are three international treaties that contain environment-specific language about the conduct of war: (1) the ENMOD Convention (United Nations Convention on the Prohibition of Military or Any Other Hostile Use of Environmental Modification Techniques of 1976), (2) Protocol I (Protocol Additional to the Geneva Conventions of 12 August 1949 and relating to the Protection of Victims of International Armed Conflict 1977), and (3) the Rome Statute of the International Criminal Court (1998). Article I of the ENMOD Convention prohibits "military or any other hostile use of environmental modification techniques having widespread, long-lasting or severe effects as the means of destruction, damage or injury to any other State Party" (UN 1976, n.p.). Environmental modification is defined in Article II of ENMOD as manipulating natural processes of the biota, atmosphere, hydrosphere, or lithosphere into weapons of war. ENMOD was originally drafted in response to the widespread use of herbicides, including Agent Orange, by the US in the Second Indochina War. For the second environment-specific convention, Article 35(3) of Protocol I prohibits warfare that can "cause widespread, long-term and severe damage to the natural environment." Article 55(1) prohibits damage to the natural environment that "prejudice[s] the health or survival of the [human] population," and Article 55(2) prohibits using attacks against the natural environment as reprisals (ICRC 1977). For the third environment-specific convention, Article 8.2(b)(iv) of the Rome Statute defines causing "widespread, long-term and severe damage to the natural environment" as a war crime (ICC 1998).

While the world community of nation-states has made noble attempts to regulate the conduct of war, the track record of regulation so far has been less than impressive. There are at least three practical problems with attempts to use environment-specific international laws to regulate the conduct of war. First, the environment-specific laws seem to have little real bite. The ENMOD Convention is designed to prevent modifications of the environment for military purposes and not to protect the environment *per se*. Protocol I, in contrast, is directed toward protection of the environment. In the 1991 Persian Gulf War, Iraqi forces released approximately eleven million barrels of oil into the northern Arabian Gulf, and the fires caused from the sabotage of more than 800 oil wells spewed approximately six million gallons of crude oil into the atmosphere. The US claimed these actions violated neither the ENMOD Convention nor Protocol I in spite of the fact that these activities seemed to clearly be environmentally destructive. Second, there is considerable scientific and economic uncertainty in regard to measuring military damages to the environment and legal uncertainty about enforcement and punishment of offenders. Third, international conventions only govern the actions of signatory parties. It's difficult to see how the environment is protected during wartime when the world's largest military power—the US—has not ratified Protocol I and when a number of countries—again including the US—have not ratified the Rome Statute.

There are at least two conceptual problems with attempts to use environment-specific international laws to regulate the conduct of war. Consider first the threshold for environmental damage: widespread, long-lasting, and severe. In an "Understandings Regarding the Convention" text meant to accompany the ENMOD Convention, widespread is defined as "encompassing an area on the scale of several hundred square kilometers," long-lasting is defined as "lasting for a period of months, or approximately a season," and severe is defined as "involving serious or significant disruption or harm to human life, natural or economic resources or other assets." This means that environmental disruption or damage must cover an area almost half the total size of the US state of Rhode Island, last for a minimum time period of at least three months, and/or be severe, simply redefined as serious or significant. The definition of severe is ambiguous, and many environmental impacts that fail to meet the spatial and temporal criteria might not count as environmental damage. The second conceptual problem is the most worrisome. Damage to and destruction of the environment, whether it is civilian property or the nonhuman natural world, is permissible when it is done in the name of military necessity and offers a military advantage. As long as military commanders believe that they are doing what they must do to win a battle and are not intentionally trying to damage or destroy the environment for the sake of damaging or destroying it, almost any form of environmental collateral damage seems to be permissible. Much like when attempts are made to build environmental constraints into just war thinking, international humanitarian law runs up against a wall of military necessity.

The ecological pacifist needs to think beyond this wall. What is needed is something Randall Amster has called "peace ecology." Peace ecology focuses on how to move beyond wars and war ecologies in positive ways. It asks the question: how can environmental issues become catalysts for peace instead of for war? (Amster 2015).

One way to answer this question is to examine *environmental security*. Because environmental change might contribute to (or possibly cause) violent conflicts and wars, resource conservation and environmental protection can become important or necessary steps for environmental security. Environmental security discourse became prominent in the early 1990s after the end of the Cold War, but what became known as the environmental conflict thesis can be found in the World Commission on Environment and Development's 1987 report *Our Common Future*: "Environmental stress is both a cause and an effect of political tension and military conflict" (WCED 1987: 290). In 1994, Robert Kaplan's influential article "The Coming Anarchy" predicted that population growth, resource scarcity, and environmental degradation were leading us into a bifurcated world in which the global North would have to wall itself off from fascist-tending mini-states, totalitarian regimes, and road-warrior cultures in the global South (Kaplan 1994). For Kaplan, the environment itself was a hostile power and would become *the* national security issue of the twenty-first century. In *Environment, Scarcity, and Violence*, Thomas Homer-Dixon uses empirical research to support his thesis that "scarcity of renewable resources . . . can contribute to civil violence, including insurgencies and ethnic clashes" (Homer-Dixon 1999: 177). Environmental scarcity occurs when powerful groups within societies shift the distribution of resources in their favor—resource capture—and prevent less powerful groups from accessing and/or using the resources—ecological marginalization. Such scarcity can then interact with what Homer-Dixon calls contextual factors—physical characteristics of a given environment and localized human social relations and institutions—to increase the probability of violence, particularly within developing countries (Homer-Dixon 1999: 80). In addition to the resource scarcity thesis, there is a contrary resource curse thesis: wars are fought over resources like rare minerals in countries such as Angola and the Democratic Republic of Congo, oil in countries such as Nigeria, and timber in places such as the island of Borneo (Renner 2002; Le Billon 2005). The global distribution of resources such as oil and freshwater supposedly will be important in the military policies of nation-states and other political actors (Klare 2002). There are a variety of theoretical frameworks that have been developed by social scientists to explain the relationships between violent conflicts and environmental conditions (Renner 1989; Baechler 1999).

There are several problems with the resource scarcity, resource curse, and general environmental conflict theses. First, there is considerable diversity in the empirical research upon which these theses ride. Here is a sampling: armed conflict cannot be reduced to greed-driven resource wars, but the control of local resources does influence the agendas and strategies of warring parties, and the political economy and specific geography of resources can exacerbate conflicts (Le Billon 2001). Lootable resources like gemstones do not make conflict more likely, but they do tend to lengthen existing conflicts (Ross 2004). There is little empirical support for the claim that population pressures themselves on resources make civil wars more common (Urdal 2005). There is little explanatory power for the resource scarcity thesis, but high levels of land degradation can increase the risk of civil conflicts (Theisen 2008). Natural resources do play important roles in armed conflicts because of the opportunities and incentives they present to belligerents, and the duration of conflict is doubled if there are extractable, natural resources in the zone of conflict (Lujala 2010). There is little empirical support for the resource scarcity thesis, but there is some evidence for the resource curse thesis (Koubi et al. 2014). It would appear that verdicts have yet to be rendered on the resource scarcity, resource curse, and general environmental conflict theses. It is a similar story with respect to the "climate change will increase the risk of violent conflicts" thesis. For example, the following theses have been defended: climate-related natural disasters lead to a lower risk of civil wars (Slettebak 2012), there is no consensus on whether or not climate change will lead to armed conflicts (Salehyan 2008), there is only very limited support for the climate change and violent conflicts thesis (Gleditsch 2012), and climate change will lead to a new era of violent conflicts (Dyer 2010; Parenti 2011).

A second type of problem with the resource scarcity and resource curse theses is how solutions to these theses have been articulated. Early discourse in environmental security was understood in terms of a military model in which threats to national security and political governance were synonymous with environmental insecurity (Finger 1991). This military model focused on the general environmental conflict thesis and largely ignored the environmental impacts of militaries and armed conflicts. This led to new reasons why militaries are needed to prevent and wage war. In terms of national security, the environment needs military protection rather than the environment needing protection from military activities. A good example of this type of environmental security thinking is the US report *National Security and the Threat of Climate Change*. The main argument of this report—written by a blue-ribbon panel of eleven retired US admirals and generals—is that climate change presents a serious threat to the national security of the US because over the next thirty to forty years it would have "the potential to disrupt our [American] way of life and force changes in the way we [Americans] keep ourselves safe and secure" (Military Advisory Board 2007: 6). While the panel does recommend that the US military use more energy-efficient technologies and fewer nonrenewable sources of energy, recommendations are directed toward mitigating the consequences climate change will have on US national security and military capability. As per the report, climate change is likely to exacerbate already marginal living standards for people in Africa and Asia, leading to weak and failed governments, authoritarian and radical movements, more intrastate conflicts, and a greater likelihood of terrorist threats. The US will have to react militarily to assist people overseas and to protect the home front. The irony is that climate change is caused in part by the greenhouse gas emissions of the American lifestyle, and the authors of the report call for more military impacts—including more greenhouse gas emissions—to protect that lifestyle.

The military model of national security might be giving way to a new model of human security (Peou 2014). Under this new model, military force is more specifically directed toward protecting human individuals—or identifiable groups of individuals—as opposed to protecting the supposed interests of nation-states. The guiding ideal is to protect human rights, especially freedom from fear and freedom from want. The degree of collateral damage tolerated under the old national security model is no longer acceptable, including environmental impacts that affect people. This new model of human security, however, still seems to rely upon military intervention in many cases as a solution to environmental security problems. How can environmental or human security move beyond such military intervention?

The ecological pacifist reexamines resource conflicts to see how solutions to the conflicts can be catalysts for peace. Not all resource conflicts lead to violence, and conflicts can be solved through cooperative and collaborative resource-sharing. An example of this is the relationship between India and Pakistan concerning sharing the Indus River basin (Swain 2002: 61–62). Water wars are relatively rare, as the majority of the world's 263 international, shared river basins are governed by agreements, treaties, and other mechanisms (Amster 2015: 154). Shared water resources can provide a catalyst for peaceful and cooperative management schemes (Dinar, Dinara, and Kurukulasuriya 2011), yielding "the most likely candidate for successful environmental peacemaking programs" (Parker, Feil, and Kramer 2004: 10).

Beyond water resources, a number of people have proposed what might be called "peace parks" (Ali 2007) as a way to solve conflicts. The central idea is that shared concerns over the conservation or preservation of a natural area becomes a way for conflicted parties to focus on something beyond their conflict. Borderlands are strong candidates for peace parks. One example is the biodiversity hotspot of the demilitarized zone on the Korean Peninsula and the adjacent Civilian Control Zones in North and South Korea, now inhabited by rare and endangered species of Asiatic black bears, leopards, lynx, and red-crowned cranes (Machlis and Hanson 2008: 732). Another example of a peace park is linking together three adjacent parks into a transfrontier park: Kruger National Park in South Africa, Limpopo National Park in Mozambique, and Gonarezhou National Park in Zimbabwe (Spenceley and Schoon 2007). While South Africa, Mozambique, and Zimbabwe have not been at war with each other, the central goal is to strengthen nature-based tourism in the region as a way to alleviate poverty. Peace parks need not always be borderlands. There could be a cluster of protected areas with or without intervening land or a protected area on one side of a border with sympathetic land use on the other side of the border. The embodiment of a continental-scale peace park is, of course, Antarctica, where environmental protection and conflict avoidance go hand in hand, beginning with the 1963 Antarctic Treaty (Zebich-Knos 2007); subsequent treaties have transformed Antarctica as a common heritage into the world's largest protected wilderness area (Rolston 2002). There is much to admire here for the ecological pacifist.

Amster notes that an operative principle is transforming environmental conflicts into opportunities for peace when it can be shown that there is more to be gained by cooperating rather than competing and when "peaceful cooperation transcends the interests and aims of nation-states that are generally focused on security as a function of resource control" (Amster 2015: 144). Resource control is a dominant operative principle today because it is races for what is left of untapped oil, mineral reserves, and other natural resources that can lead to armed conflict in the first place (Klare 2012). While some people champion top-down solutions to resource conflicts such as corporate social responsibility, it is often top-down control that is the very problem. Resource conflicts are partially driven by the roles that corporations and economic systems play in shaping desires for and acquiring resources. Solving resource conflicts will thus require, in part, reshaping how global economies function. This parallels the general pacifist need to reshape how global economics function in creating and maintaining military economies.

The ecological pacifist champions environmental dispute resolution, environmental peacemaking, environmental peacekeeping, and environmental peacebuilding. Environmental conflict resolution consists of facilitation, mediation, and conflict resolution drawn from indigenous systems and various models of justice that can deal with disputants in a holistic manner that engages them within the context of their communities and cultures (Caplan 2010: 94). Similar to this, environmental peacemaking consists of practices and processes, set within an environmental context, that help remediate or resolve specific disputes. Environmental peacekeeping consists of environmental initiatives offered after a conflict that helps keep the peace. Environmental peacebuilding focuses upon environmental and structural conditions that are necessary to create a peaceful society before, during, or after a conflict.

These structural conditions will most likely include environmental protection, environmental justice for people, and environmental sustainability. Environmental sustainability in turn is linked to other forms of sustainability, namely economic and social sustainability. Current levels of resource consumption of much of the global North and the elites of the global South are not sustainable, and this is exacerbated by the disproportionate use of resources utilized by military economies, as outlined earlier in this chapter. The ecological pacifist points out that environmentalists who call for sustainability thus must address military consumption and pollution. Environmental philosophers who articulate the values of nature have been largely remiss in addressing the environmental impacts of armed conflicts, military activities, and military economies, and they need to develop something that I have called the environmental ethics of war and peace (Woods 2007a). In addition to the protection of nonhuman nature, such an ethic must address concerns of environmental justice for people. Such justice will often be linked to military activities. There is, for example, the case of the island of Vieques in Puerto Rico, where residents were forced to relinquish their lands to the United States Navy during World War II and then had to live with parts of their island serving as an artillery range for decades (Yelin and Miller 2009). Gregory Hooks and Chad Smith develop the idea of a treadmill of destruction by showing how Native Americans living on reservations disproportionately reside near military facilities, many of which are dangerously polluted from decades of military use (Hooks and Smith 2004). David Bronkema et al. argue that peacemaking will require just and sustainable economic development that focuses on helping the poor as one way to remove inequalities that can lead to conflicts (Bronkema, Lumsdaine, and Payne 2004). Those who champion the Environmental Justice Movement should see themselves as allies of the ecological pacifist. The non-governmental organization (NGO) Greenpeace is a good example of this. Greenpeace came into existence in the early 1970s originally as a protest against nuclear weapons testing on Amchitka Island in Alaska and is now a premier global environmental justice NGO.

While there are exceptions, such as the Unabomber (Ted Kaczynski), most environmental activists are committed to nonviolence against people. This is something they share in common with peace activists. This can be seen in acts of civil disobedience when activists attempt to educate the public, persuade it that their cause is just, and work toward changing the law so that it aligns with justice. On September 9, 1980, eight people from the Ploughshares Movement trespassed onto a nuclear missile facility in Pennsylvania, damaged nuclear warhead nose cones, poured blood onto files and documents, and were openly arrested. Numerous environmental and animal activist groups such as Earth First! and the Animal Liberation Front have engaged in violent activities against inanimate property since the early 1980s. Such activities have included spiking trees, destroying equipment, and, for animal activists, "liberating" test animals. More radical actions include the Earth Liberation Front's burning down of ski resorts and condominiums. One major difference between peace activists and environmental/animal activists who engage in militant, violent actions against inanimate property is that the former usually openly take responsibility for their actions, while the latter usually do not.

What lessons can the ecological pacifist draw here? First, there is the question of whether violence against inanimate property should be justifiable. The peace activists are committed to nonviolence against people, while the environmental and animal activists are committed to nonviolence against living beings. Does the target of violent actions morally matter? Christopher Manes argues that because living beings have more value than inanimate objects, damage and destruction of the latter is justifiable if it is done in the interests of protecting the former (Manes 1990). Would the ecological pacifist agree? Would this justify damage and destruction of military objects to protect living beings from military damage and destruction? Second, there is the issue of whether or not activists should take open responsibility for their actions. The main argument from environmental and animal activists might be that their actions can be more effective if they are done in the dark of night. That is, more meaningful damage and destruction of inanimate objects can be accomplished that in turn will more effectively protect living beings from damage and destruction. Would the ecological pacifist agree?

What the ecological pacifist seems to have in common with radical, militant environmental and animal activists is a basic commitment to rethinking human relationships to nature. Nature is typically conceptualized as a thing that needs to be protected, or, more commonly, as a commodity to be used. The dominant capitalist or consumerist mindset toward nature is what we might call *economism*. This is an ideology that reduces the world to people and commodities, uses economics as the framework to make many or most public policy and political decisions, elevates economic or monetary values above other values, and changes us from *Homo sapiens* into something we might call *Homo economicus*. The central problem with economism is that it sanctions a domination of nature. Nature is a passive object that awaits human use and has no value beyond its instrumental use value for people. There are two related ways to rethink this human-nature relationship. First, entities in nature can be reconceptualized as active subjects with their own ways of being, independent from humans (Woods 2017). Second, the value of entities in nature can be reappraised as some form of non-instrumental value; nature thus has its own intrinsic value, or people can intrinsically value nature. Rethinking the human-nature relationship in terms of nature's non-instrumental value or active presence stands as a counter to the domination of nature. There are numerous ways to do this rethinking in terms of zoocentrism (Jamieson 1998)—animal-centered ethics, biocentrism (Taylor 1986)—ethics centered on living organisms, and ecocentrism (Rolston 1988)—ethics centered on holistic environmental entities such as species and ecosystems. The ecological pacifist has many resources to draw upon from environmental ethics in order to articulate the non-instrumental values of nature.

Bringing together ecology and pacifism offers much promise. For the ecological pacifist, a critique of war and military activities by itself is as incomplete as a critique of the human relationship with nature without a critique of war and military activities. Whatever else, a green world will require peace and justice.

Works Cited

Ali, S. H. (ed.) (2007). *Peace Parks: Conservation and Conflict Resolution*. Cambridge, MA: MIT Press.
Amster, R. (2015). *Peace Ecology*. Boulder: Paradigm Publishers.
Baechler, G. (1999). "Environmental Degradation and Violent Conflict: Hypotheses, Research Agendas and Theory-building," in M. Suliman (ed.), *Ecology, Politics and Violent Conflict*. London: Zed Books, 76–112.
Biswas, A. K. (2000). "Scientific Assessment of the Long-Term Consequences of War," in J.E. Austin and C.E. Bruch (eds.), *The Environmental Consequences of War: Legal, Economic, and Scientific Perspectives*. New York: Cambridge University Press, 303–315.
Bronkema, D., D. Lumsdaine, and R. A. Payne. (2004). "Foster Just and Sustainable Economic Development," in G. Stassen (ed.), *Just Peacemaking: Ten Practices for Abolishing War*. Cleveland: Pilgrim Press, 109–130.
Cady, D. L. (1989). *From Warism to Pacifism: A Moral Continuum*. Philadelphia: Temple University Press.
Cahill, K. M. (ed.) (1995). *Clearing the Fields: Solutions to the Global Land Mines Crisis*. New York: Basic Books.
Caplan, J. A. (2010). *The Theory and Principles of Environmental Dispute Resolution*. Environmental Dispute Resolution USA.
Ceadel, M. (1987). *Thinking About War and Peace*. New York: Oxford University Press.
Diederich, M. D., Jr. (1992). "'Law of War' and Ecology—A Proposal for a Workable Approach to Protecting the Environment Through the Law of War." *Military Law Review* 136: 137–160.
Dinar, S., A. Dinara, and P. Kurukulasuriya. (2011). "Scarcity and Cooperation Along International Rivers: An Empirical Assessment of Bilateral Treaties." *International Studies Quarterly* 55: 809–833.
Dotto, L. (1986). *Planet Earth in Jeopardy: Environmental Consequences of Nuclear War*. Chichester: John Wiley and Sons.
Drucker, M. P. (1989). "The Military Commander's Responsibility for the Environment." *Environmental Ethics* 11: 135–152.
Dyer, G. (2010). *Climate Wars: The Fight for Survival as the World Overheats*. New York: Oneworld.
Eckersley, R. (2007). "Ecological Intervention: Prospects and Limits." *Ethics and International Affairs* 21: 293–316.
El-Baz, F., and R. M. Makharita. (eds.) (1994). *The Gulf War and the Environment*. New York: Gordon and Breach Science Publishers.
Falk, R. (2000). "The Inadequacy of the Existing Legal Approach to Environmental Protection in Wartime," in J.E. Austin and C.E. Bruch (eds.), *The Environmental Consequences of War: Legal, Economic, and Scientific Perspectives*. New York: Cambridge University Press, 137–155.

Fidler, D. (2000). "War and Infectious Diseases: International Law and the Public Health Consequences of Armed Conflict," in J.E. Austin and C.E. Bruch (eds.), *The Environmental Consequences of War: Legal, Economic, and Scientific Perspectives*. New York: Cambridge University Press, 444–466.
Finger, M. (1991). "The Military, the Nation-State and the Environment." *The Ecologist* 21: 220–225.
Fox, M.A. (2014). *Understanding Peace: A Comprehensive Introduction*. New York: Routledge.
Giannardi, C., and D. Dominici. (2003). "Military Use of Depleted Uranium: Assessment of Prolonged Exposure." *Journal of Environmental Radioactivity* 64: 227–236.
Gleditsch, N. P. (2012). "Whither the Weather? Climate Change and Conflict." *Journal of Peace Research* 49: 3–9.
Grunawalt, R. J., J. E. King, and R. S. McClain (eds.) (1996). *International Law Studies, Volume 69: Protection of the Environment During Armed Conflict*. Newport, RI: Naval War College.
Hart, J., and T. Hart (2003). "Rules of Engagement for Conservation." *Conservation in Practice* 4: 14–22.
Harwell, M. A. (1984). *Nuclear Winter: The Human and Environmental Consequences of Nuclear War*. New York: Springer-Verlag.
Hay, A. W. M. (2000). "Defoliants: the Long-Term Health Implications," in J.E. Austin and C. E. Bruch (eds.), *The Environmental Consequences of War: Legal, Economic, and Scientific Perspectives*. New York: Cambridge University Press, 402–425.
Holmes, R. L. (1989). *On War and Morality*. Princeton: Princeton University Press.
Homer-Dixon, T. F. (1999). *Environment, Scarcity, and Violence*. Princeton: Princeton University Press.
Hooks, G., and C. L. Smith. (2004). "The Treadmill of Destruction: National Sacrifice Areas and Native Americans." *American Sociological Review* 69: 558–575.
International Committee of Red Cross (ICRC). (1977). "Protocol Additional to the Geneva Conventions of 12 August 1949, and Relating to the Protection of Victims of International Armed Conflicts (Protocol I), 8 June 1977." Available at: https://ihl-databases.icrc.org/applic/ihl/ihl.nsf/INTRO/470 (Accessed 10 July 2017).
International Criminal Court (ICC). (1998). "Rome Statute." Available at: www.icc-cpi.int/nr/rdonlyres/ea9aeff7-5752-4f84-be94-0a655eb30e16/0/rome_statute_english.pdf (Accessed 10 July 2017).
Jamieson, D. (1998). "Animal Liberation is an Environmental Ethic." *Environmental Values* 7: 41–57.
Kaplan, R. D. (1994). "The Coming Anarchy." *Atlantic Monthly* 273: 44–76.
Klare, M. T. (2002). *Resource Wars: The New Landscape of Global Conflict*, 2nd ed. New York: Henry Holt and Company.
Klare, M. T. (2012). *The Race for What's Left: The Global Scramble for the World's Last Resources*. New York: Metropolitan Books.
Koubi, V., G. Spilker, T. Böhmelt, and T. Bernauer. (2014). "Do Natural Resources Matter for Interstate and Intrastate Conflict?" *Journal of Peace Research* 51: 227–243.
Le Billon, P. (2001). "The Political Ecology of War: Natural Resources and Armed Conflicts." *Political Geography* 20: 561–584.
Le Billon, P. (2005). *Fuelling War: Natural Resources and Armed Conflict*. New York: Routledge.
Leaning, J. (2000). "Tracking the Four Horsemen: The Public Health Approach to the Impact of War and War-Related Environmental Destruction in the Twentieth Century," in J.E. Austin and C.E. Bruch (eds.), *The Environmental Consequences of War: Legal, Economic, and Scientific Perspectives*. New York: Cambridge University Press, 384–401.
Lujala, P. (2010). "The Spoils of Nature: Armed Civil Conflict and Rebel Access to Natural Resources." *Journal of Peace Research* 47: 15–28.
Machlis, G. E., and T. Hanson (2008). "Warfare Ecology." *BioScience* 58: 729–736.
McNeely, J. A. (2000). "War and Biodiversity: An Assessment of Impacts," in J.E. Austin and C.E. Bruch (eds.), *The Environmental Consequences of War: Legal, Economic, and Scientific Perspectives*. New York: Cambridge University Press, 353–378.
Manes, C. (1990). *Green Rage: Radical Environmentalism and the Unmaking of Civilization*. Boston: Little, Brown and Company.
Military Advisory Board. (2007). *National Security and the Threat of Climate Change*. The CNA Corporation. Available at: www.cna.org/cna_files/pdf/national%20security%20and%20the%20threat%20of%20climate%20change.pdf (Accessed 2 July 2016).
Omar, S. A. S., E. Briskey, R. Misak, and A.A.S.O. Asem. (2000). "The Gulf War Impact on the Terrestrial Environment of Kuwait: An Overview," in J.E. Austin and C.E. Bruch (eds.), *The Environmental Consequences of War: Legal, Economic, and Scientific Perspectives*. New York: Cambridge University Press, 316–337.

Parenti, C. (2011). *Tropic of Chaos: Climate Change and the New Geography of Violence*. New York: Nation Books.

Parker, M., M. Feil, and A. Kramer. (2004). "Environment, Development, and Sustainable Peace: Finding Paths to Environmental Peacekeeping." Report based on Wilton Park Conference 758, in cooperation with Adelphi Research (Berlin) and the Woodrow Wilson International Center for Scholars (Washington, DC).

Peou, S. (2014). *Human Security Studies: Theories, Methods and Themes*. Singapore: World Scientific Publishing Company.

Reichberg, G., and H. Syse. (2000). "Protecting the Natural Environment in Wartime: Ethical Considerations from the Just War Tradition." *Journal of Peace Research* 37: 449–468.

Renner, M. (1989). *National Security: The Economic and Environmental Dimensions*. Washington, DC: Worldwatch Institute.

Renner, M. (2002). *The Anatomy of Resource Wars*. Washington, DC: Worldwatch Paper 162.

Reuveny, R., A. S. Mihalache-O'Keef, and Q. Li (2010). "The Effect of Warfare on the Environment." *Journal of Peace Research* 47: 749–761.

Richards, P. J., and M. N. Schmitt. (1999). "Mars Meets Mother Nature: Protecting the Environment During Armed Conflict." *Stetson Law Review* 28: 1047–1090.

Rolston, H., III. (1988). *Environmental Ethics: Duties to and Values in the Natural World*. Philadelphia: Templeton University Press.

Rolston, H., III. (2002). "Environmental Ethics in Antarctica." *Environmental Ethics* 24: 115–134.

Ross, M. L. (2004). "What Do We Know About Natural Resources and Civil War?" *Journal of Peace Research* 41: 337–356.

Rostker, B. (2002). *Depleted Uranium: A Case Study of Good and Evil*. Santa Monica: RAND.

Salehyan, I. (2008). "From Climate Change to Conflict? No Consensus Yet." *Journal of Peace Research* 45: 315–326.

Schmitt, M. N. (2000). "Humanitarian Law and the Environment." *Denver Journal of International Law and Policy* 28: 265–324.

Seager, J. (1999). "Patriarchal Vandalism: Militaries and the Environment," in J. Silliman and Y. King (eds.), *Dangerous Intersections: Feminist Perspectives on Population, Environment, and Development*. Cambridge, MA: South End Press, 163–188.

Slettebak, R. T. (2012). "Don't Blame the Weather! Climate-Related Natural Disasters and Civil Conflict." *Journal of Peace Research* 49: 163–176.

Spenceley, A., and M. Schoon. (2007). "Peace Parks as Social Ecological Systems: Testing Environmental Resilience in Southern Africa," in S.H. Ali (ed.), *Peace Parks: Conservation and Conflict Resolution*. Cambridge, MA: MIT Press, 84–105.

Swain, A. (2002). "Environmental Cooperation in South Asia," in K. Conca and G.D. Dabelko (eds.), *Environmental Peacemaking*. Washington, DC: Woodrow Wilson Center Press, 61–85.

Taylor, P. W. (1986). *Respect for Nature: A Theory of Environmental Ethics*. Princeton: Princeton University Press.

Theisen, O. (2008). "Blood and Soil? Resource Scarcity and Internal Armed Conflicts Revisited." *Journal of Peace Research* 45: 801–818.

United Nations (UN). (1976). "Convention on the Prohibition of Military or Any Other Hostile Use of Environmental Modification Techniques (ENMOD)." Available at: www.un-documents.net/enmod.htm (Accessed 10 July 2017).

Urdal, H. (2005). "People vs. Malthus: Population Pressure, Environmental Degradation, and Armed Conflict Revisited." *Journal of Peace Research* 42: 417–434.

van der Linden, H. (2010). "From Hiroshima to Baghdad: Military Hegemony versus Just Military Preparedness," in E. Demenchonok (ed.), *Philosophy After Hiroshima*. Newcastle upon Tyne: Cambridge Scholars Publishing, 220–231.

Watson Institute for International and Public Affairs. (2015). "Environmental Costs of War." Available at: http://watson.brown.edu/costsofwar/costs/social/environment (Accessed 22 June 2016).

Westing, A. H. (ed.) (1984). *Herbicides in War: The Long-Term Ecological and Human Consequences*. London: Taylor and Francis.

Woods, M. (2007a). "The Nature of War and Peace: Just War Thinking, Environmental Ethics, and Environmental Justice," in M.W. Brough, J.W. Lango, and H.V.D. Linden (eds.), *Rethinking the Just War Tradition*. Albany: State University of New York Press, 17–34.

Woods, M. (2007b). "Some Worries About Ecological-Humanitarian Intervention and Ecological Defense." *Ethics and International Affairs* 21: Online Symposium on Ecological Intervention. Available at: www.cceia.org/resources/journal/index.html (Accessed 30 June 2016).

Woods, M. (2017). *Rethinking Wilderness*. Peterborough: Broadview Press.

World Commission on Environment and Development (WCED). (1987). *Our Common Future*. New York: Oxford University Press.

Yelin, J. C., and D. S. Miller. (2009). "A Brief History of Environmental Inequity and Military Colonialism on the Isle of Vieques, Puerto Rico." *Environmental Justice* 2: 153–159.

Zebich-Knos, M. (2007). "Conflict Avoidance and Environmental Protection: The Antarctic Paradigm," in S.H. Ali (ed.), *Peace Parks: Conservation and Conflict Resolution*. Cambridge, MA: MIT Press, 164–183.

Further Reading

Ali, S. H. (ed.) (2007). *Peace Parks: Conservation and Conflict Resolution*. Cambridge, MA: MIT Press. (Discussion of how to solve conflicts and achieve peace through nature protection.)

Amster, R. (2015). *Peace Ecology*. Boulder: Paradigm Publishers. (Thoroughgoing treatment of how ecological issues map into peace movement issues.)

Austin, J. E., and C. E. Bruch (eds.) (2000). *The Environmental Consequences of War: Legal, Economic, and Scientific Perspectives*. New York: Cambridge University Press. (Discussion of the environmental consequences of war.)

Conca, K., and D. Dabelko (eds.) (2002). *Environmental Peacemaking*. Baltimore: John Hopkins University Press. (Discussion of how environmental cooperation can lead to conflict resolution.)

29
ANIMALS, VEGETARIANISM, AND NONVIOLENCE

Christopher Key Chapple

This chapter examines nonviolence in regard to human-animal relations through the prisms of worldview, normative ethics, and personal choices. Three competing worldviews will be considered. The first regards animals as important for their use to human beings, deeming animals to be instruments to be used for human nutrition, entertainment, and comfort. This worldview deems it acceptable to kill and consume animals. The second, appealing to what might be characterized as the "logic of the humane," suggests that animals have a rich interior life, that animals suffer, and that it does not make sense to harm animals for selfish human benefit. Both of these views consider the human and animal realms to be distinct from one another. The third worldview, found within traditions that arise in India, holds that animals and humans are part of the same continuum. Animals must be protected not only for their own sake but out of self-interest and empathy. Each animal has the potential for human birth and each human, according to the doctrine of rebirth, has lived a prior life as an animal. Whereas biblical narratives clearly proclaim human dominion over creatures, lore and archaeological remains from India that predate biblical times indicate a relationship of deep affection with animals.

This chapter will present a few select examples of human-animal relations in Hinduism, Buddhism, and Jainism. It considers Gandhi's sources and influences. And it points toward sources in Western religion, including Adventists and other nonviolent Christianities. The chapter concludes by reflecting on the convergence of worldviews that is helping a new global ethic of nonviolence to emerge in regard to animals and their relationship with the human order.

Animals

Animals have no voice. Animals have been subjected to human exploitation since the beginning. For the first few hundred thousand years of human-animal relations, humans were as much prey as predator; even today in places like India, hundreds of humans lose their lives each year to marauding elephants and hungry tigers. For the most part, however, few people face the risk of being killed by an animal. In contrast, billions of animals each year succumb to satisfy human desires.

Human desires take many forms. As outlined in the gripping 2005 online documentary *Earthlings*, animals die to provide food, clothing, entertainment, pets, and scientific research for human sustenance and comfort.[1] On the one hand, this usage can be seen as natural and even beautiful. All life forms rely upon other life forms for food; many humans have survived frigid weather with the warmth provided by animal pelts; leather shoes keep feet warm and protected from injury; animals provide delight through their companionship and antics; many life-saving procedures have been perfected through laboratory testing. On the other hand, the proportionality of benefit often exceeds reasonability and scale.

In 1975, Australian ethicist Peter Singer published *Animal Liberation: A New Ethics for Our Treatment of Animals*. This book, which has sold millions of copies, brought awareness to the systematic abuse to which animals have been subjected. Coming as it did upon the heels of the movements for Women's Liberation and Black Liberation, he opens the book with an eloquent appeal to the arguments made by Mary Wollstonecraft in her *Vindication of the Rights of Women* (1792) and Sojourner Truth in the 1850s on behalf of their respective advocacy that dignity be accorded to women and black slaves. Singer's book called into question the use of animals in scientific experimentation and the maltreatment of animals in "factory" farming. He urges vegetarianism as the most ethical personal way to address human domination over animals. Singer coined the term "speciesism" as he pleaded for the end of our "indefensible" and "ruthless" exploitation of animals (Singer 1975: 258). Nonviolence toward animals is inspired by Singer's call that we must recognize this unwarranted tyranny. In the spirit of Gandhi we must find the wherewithal to make changes, even and especially small changes that can effect lasting change. We begin with an examination of Gandhi's commitment to vegetarianism.

Gandhi and His Influences

Gandhi was born into a family that practiced vegetarianism, as remains common among Vaishnavite Hindus and Jainas throughout the subcontinent. During his study of law in England from 1888 to 1891, Gandhi came to understand his vegetarianism and commitment to nonviolence in a modern context. He was a mere 19 years old when he embarked on this journey. It was a time of remarkable self-discovery which undoubtedly shaped ideas and attitudes that took form over the course over several years, culminating in the publication of his core work, *Hind Swaraj*, in 1909.

Three primary written sources were influential on Gandhi during his years in London that helped shape his views toward the role of vegetarianism in the development of personal ethics: Henry Salt's *A Plea for Vegetarianism*, *The Ethics of Diet* by Howard Williams, and *The Perfect Way of Diet* by Anna Kingsford. Gandhi became deeply involved with the Vegetarian Society while in England and contributed nine articles to a periodical titled *Vegetarian* (Sethia 2012: 17).

When Gandhi landed in England, he endured hunger, not knowing where to find food that would sufficiently provide complementary nutrition. Finally, he learned of a vegetarian restaurant on Farringdon Street. It was here that he discovered the works of Henry Salt. More than fifty years later (on November 20, 1931), Gandhi delivered a speech to the London Vegetarian Society. Salt himself, an octogenarian, was present. Indicating Salt, Gandhi said, "He showed me why it was a moral duty incumbent on vegetarians not to live upon fellow-animals."[2] The tract that so inspired Gandhi with its elegant, elevated, engaging, and entertaining prose sets forth an argument for vegetarianism that Gandhi found quite bracing. Salt wrote, "Future and wiser generations will look back with amazement on the habit of flesh-eating as a strange relic of ignorance and barbarism" (Salt 1886: 20). Gandhi, in his early twenties, no doubt took solace in this affirmation of the lifestyle in which he was raised. At the same time, Salt acknowledged that vegetarianism, though the norm in many Indian households, ran counter to mainstream British sensibilities at the time, noting that many regarded it to be an "impious absurdity and dangerous hallucination of modern times, to be classed with Mormonism, Spiritualism, Anglo-Israelism,

Socialism, and possibly Atheism itself" (Salt 1886: 10). The rhetoric employed by Salt was simultaneously humorous and insightful, demonstrating the truly countercultural aspects of the vegetarian lifestyle.

Gandhi visited Howard Williams on the Isle of Wight in 1891. He wrote of being moved by Williams' research into the historical aspects of vegetarianism. Williams published *The Ethics of Diet* first as a series of articles in a journal titled *The Dietetic Reformer and Vegetarian Messenger* (1878ff), and it was later published as a book in 1883 and issued in several subsequent editions. Tolstoy wrote the preface to the Russian edition of 1892.[3] The book provided details regarding eighty-four men (and one woman) throughout history who have written positively about the practice of vegetarianism. These include Hesiod, Buddha, Pythagoras, Empedokles, Plato, Asoka, Ovid, Seneca, Apollonius of Tyanna, Plutarch, Tertullian, Clement of Alexandria, Porphyry, Rousseau, Adam Smith, Jeremy Bentham, Schopenhauer, Shelly, Byron, Lamartine, Wagner, and Thoreau. In 1896 he added a detailed profile of the next major influence on Gandhi's view on vegetarianism and vivesectionism, Anna Kingsford.

Kingsford was born into a wealthy merchant family, was highly educated from childhood, and married an Anglican priest at the age of twenty-one. She converted to Catholicism with his blessings at the age of twenty-six. At the age of twenty-eight, Kingsford traveled to Paris in order to receive medical training. She took a strong stand against vivisection. She was only the medical student at that time to earn her degree without performing animal dissection.

Her dissertation, "De l'Alimentation Vegetal che l'Homme," was translated into English and published as the book *The Perfect Way in Diet: A Treatise Advocating a Return to the Natural and Ancient Food of Our Race*. Its fifth edition was published in 1892. It opens with a "Proem," a lengthy verse quote from Edwin Arnold's *Light of Asia* recounting the episode in which the Buddha forbids animal sacrifice: "Henceforth none shall spill the blood of life nor taste of flesh, seeing that knowledge grows, and life is one, and mercy comes to the merciful" (Kingsford 1892: XII). Her argument for vegetarianism begins with an anatomical analysis of the human mouth, noting its similarities to "orangs, chimpanzees, and the gorilla" whose teeth stomach, and saliva are adapted for a herbivorous, frugivorous diet (Kingsford 1892: 5–16). She devotes several pages to the dietary habits of various peoples, including Romans, Hindus, Buddhists, Egyptians, Chinese, "Indians of the New Spain," the Turks, the Chinese, and the Algerians, extolling the vegetarian diet in each instance. She writes that in regard to Palestine, "the diet of both Christian and Muslim is strictly vegetarian" (31). She describes in great detail suffering inflicted on cattle and warns of the dangers of parasites in meat. She gives several case examples of cures brought about by changing to a vegetarian diet. She also writes about the superior farming efficiency gained by the cultivation of vegetables rather than the grazing and feeding of animals (100–104). In short, she advances various scientific and social reasons for adopting a vegetarian diet, all in colorful, elegant rhetoric. She closes the book as it begins, with a poem that concludes: "Let your mouths be empty of blood, and satisfied with pure and natural repasts" (121).

These three thinkers affirmed for Gandhi the principles and premises of India's long-standing commitment to nonviolence and vegetarianism. Although Gandhi's family had followed Hindu and Jaina customs in their eschewal of meat, these authors gave Gandhi a sense of being part of a larger global history of vegetarianism. In a sense, Salt, Williams, and Kingsford legitimated his lifestyle through the modern categories of history and science.

Some aspects of Indian thought that informed Gandhi's natal worldview can be summarized as follows. The Vedas, the Sanskrit literature that arose from 1500 B.C.E., articulate an unformed foundation, a realm of nonexistence (*asat*), a mist from which arise distinct worlds, depending upon human desire. Through desire, humans craft their world, creating boundaries and distinctions, separating heaven from earth, light from darkness. In this constructed world, sustained by sacrifice, meditation, and prayer, individuals gather into community, moving from the unformed to the formed. Intention and desire direct communities and individuals to select various options, symbolized by various deities, all seen as provisional tools for attaining a goal, whether worldly or sublime. This process connects the individual with the cosmic flow of life (*rta*). Practitioners of Yoga in its various forms strive for an elevated sense of connection, known as *samadhi*. For both the worldly and the spiritually inclined, five precepts must be followed: nonviolence, truthfulness, not stealing, sexual propriety, and non-possession. These guarantee harmony between the ongoing flux or flow between the unspeakable realm of origin, the *asat*, and the realm of manifest activity. These precepts, observed by Vaisnavas, Saivas, Jainas, Buddhists, and Sikhs in India, include respect for all forms of life, a mandate to be truthful and honest, and caution against the dangers of greed and lust. These precepts shaped both Gandhi's personal and social ethics.

Drawing from this worldview, Gandhi championed nonviolence and a commitment to truth, as well as non-possession. In his life work, he constantly reminded his followers of the importance of *satyagraha* (holding to truth), *ahiṃsā* (nonviolence), and *aparigraha* (non-possession). For Gandhi, appropriate action can only take place from a place of direct encounter with a transcendent reality, of the sort described in the Vedic term *rta* and the Yoga meditation term *samadhi*. By seeing our unity with the adversary, we can hope to understand, empathize with, and convert that enemy. For Gandhi, the adversary was not only the British but also any form of injustice toward the downtrodden, whether impoverished low-caste Hindus, women of all faiths, or disadvantaged Muslims.

For Gandhi, nonviolence entailed kindness to animals, both human and nonhuman. Gandhi's nonviolence required vegetarianism as well as a willingness to engage and converse with and ultimately have compassion and even love for one's antagonists. Gandhi advocated a village economy. This involves the consumption of local foods and the wearing of clothes spun and woven by each individual. He also encouraged small-scale technologies, which, for instance, involve solar cookstoves, locally generated electricity, and self-transport using bicycles.

Gandhi, as a vegetarian, considered the life of animals to be sacred and advocated for the protection of animals. He was a vocal anti-vivisectionist. He wrote of vivisection: "No religion sanctifies this. All say that it is not necessary to take so many lives for the sake of our bodies. These doctors violate our religious instinct" (Gandhi 1997: 64). He called all physicians to abjure vivisection: "It is better that bodies remain diseased rather than that they are cured through the instrumentality of the diabolical vivisection that is practised in European schools of medicine" (Gandhi 1997: 65). For Gandhi, protection of animals underscored his commitment to nonviolence, the key precept that he observed and taught throughout his lifetime.

Animal Stories in Hindu Tradition

India has nurtured numerous religious traditions, including forms of Hinduism that include Vaishnavism, Shaivism, and Advaita Vedānta. Early images from the Indus Valley cities of Mohenjadaro and Harappa (ca. 3000 B.C.E.) depict humans surrounded with animals, fierce and domestic. Terra-cotta sculptures show humans imitating the countenance of animals, most notably the tiger. The earliest image of what might be deemed a proto-Yogi shows a cross-legged figure sitting upon an animal skin, adorned with a headdress that includes horns from a buffalo or antelope. Yoga postures, often in imitation of animals, emerged as a distinct expression of religious devotional practice in several of these traditions over the course of many hundreds of years in India.

Starting around 1500 B.C.E., a body of literature in Sanskrit known as the Vedas was composed and transmitted orally, establishing the ritual and philosophical traditions of Hinduism.

The oldest of these texts, the Rig Veda, extols the cow in dozens of hymns, likening the beneficence of the cow to the dawn, to speech, to the rain clouds, and creation itself. Eventually the cow was granted sacred status and it remains taboo for a Hindu to eat beef.

In the Upaniṣads (ca. 800 B.C.E.) animals find frequent mention. In the story of Satyakāma found within the *Chāndogya Upaniṣad*, a young seeker called Satyakāma obtains knowledge and wisdom from his encounters with animals.[4] A bull gives Satyakāma the first of four teachings about the nature of Brahman. He alerted Satyakāma to the four directions: east, west, south, and north, resulting in an experience of all the areas and spaces in which light shines (*prakāśa*). The bull indicated that his next teaching would come from the fire. That night, the fire instructed Satyakāma about the worlds to be found in the earth, the atmosphere, the sky, and the ocean. A swan came in the evening and told him of the fourfold nature of the luminous: fire itself, the sun, the moon, and lightning. A diving bird gave Satyakāma the final teaching, a fourfold analysis of that which supports experience: the breath, the eye, the ear, and the mind.

Through these four remarkable encounters, Satyakāma learned the importance of locating oneself within the four directions. He also grasped the vast expanse of the earth below, the surrounding air, the largeness of space, and the unfathomable ocean. He moved on to understand the many manifestations of fire and light and then discovered the inner working of the human being, living in a body through the senses and the mind. His forest teachers were not human. He received instruction from a bull, a fire, a swan, and a diving bird, creatures of the earth, fire, water, and the air.

This story highlights the special nature of particular animals. The bull, the swan, and the diving bird of the story of Satyakāma, though sparingly described, each convey a sense of their species' special gifts. The bull would know the range and spread of the directions as delineating space. The swan, with its white radiance, would know the nature of light in its various forms. The diving bird, with its penetrative skills and knowledge of what lies beneath the surfaces of the waters it pierces, would understand the origins of things in their relationship with the body and the senses and the mind. This sense of intimate knowledge conveyed by animals underscores the sense of kinship at the heart of India's core sensibility, a key aspect of the teachings on nonviolence. Animals are seen as kin, as teachers, and hence merit respect and protection.

The Upaniṣads also introduce the idea of reincarnation into Hinduism, with the *Kaushitaki Upaniṣads* stating that "[one] is born again here according to [one's] deeds (*karma*) as a worm, or as a moth, or as a fish, or as a bird, or as a lion, or as a wild boar, or as a snake, or as a tiger, or as a person" (Hume 1921: 303). Several hundred years later, the *Yogavāsiṣṭha*, a Sanskrit text of more than 29,000 verses, uses tales of reincarnation to bring solace to a grieving son and brother. In the story of Punya and Pavana, two brothers grapple with the death of their parents. This narrative suggests that because all humans have once been animals, insects, and even trees, we can feel empathy for each of these life forms. Through reflecting on these other existences, we can lessen our attachment to this particular precious human birth. By feeling this sense of kinship, one gains a rapport with the natural world that also brings solace to interpersonal relationships.

Punya, the older brother, has attained the state of spiritual liberation (*jīvanmukti*) and accepts the death of his parents with equanimity. Pavana, the younger brother, is inconsolable in his grief. Punya instructs him regarding the fleeting nature of the body and eventually frees his brother from his affliction, bringing him to liberation through tales of birth and rebirth. His teachings urge Pavana to remember his past births as a myriad of beings. By reflecting on the joys and pains of various past births, Punya prompts his brother to gain a new perspective on his current circumstance. Ultimately, this insight liberates Pavana. Specifically, Punya reminds Pavana that he has been a deer, a swan, a gander, a tree, a fish, a monkey, a raven, a donkey, a dog, a partridge, and various insects (see Mitra 1998: 254–260). By seeing his connections with past animal embodiments, Pavana gains the dispassion needed to heal his grief and engage the world through a state of equanimity. Through moving himself away from self-concern by reflecting on animals, Pavana becomes free to act again within the world without depression or fear, important lessons for the young Rama.

Puṇya's friendly advice to his grieving brother outlines a way of understanding human emplacement within the round of birth, death, and rebirth. Kinship defines this story in a radical way: brothers deal with the passing of their parents each in his unique way, with Puṇya expanding the definition of kinship to include all manner of beings: trees, ants, beetles, bees, mosquitoes, scorpions, frogs, crocodiles, cranes, parrots, hawks, swans, eagles, donkeys, deer, camels, elephants, tigers, and lions. By connecting with the broader web of life, Pāvana moves from despair to calm, a starting point for living in a spirit of nonviolence.

Animals were not only past incarnations and beloved companions, but they themselves became elevated to deity status in Hinduism, such as the eagle Garuda, the monkey Hanuman, and the elephant-headed Ganesh. Each anthropomorphic deity has a well-known companion animal, including Ganesh's rat, Durga's lion, Saraswati's peacock, Lakshmi's elephant, and Siva's bull.

In the medieval period, detailed Yoga manuals were composed that provide instruction on how to mimic the stance and mood of specific animals. Many postures (*āsana*) carry the names of animals. The *Haṭha Yoga Pradīpikā*, written by Svātmarāma in the fifteenth century, lists several poses named for animals, including the Crow, the Cow's Head, the Tortoise, the Rooster, the Peacock, and the Lion. Later Yoga manuals such as the *Gheraṇḍa Saṃāita* include several additional poses named for animals, including the Serpent, the Rabbit, the Cobra, the Locust, the Eagle, the Frog, and the Scorpion.

Hinduism developed and maintained an attitude toward and relationship with animals in stark contrast with the mechanistic view of animals asserted by Aristotle and reinforced by Bacon and Descartes. An animal holds great mystery, a mystery unlocked by sustained reflection upon their powers and a willingness to acknowledge their presence and agency. Through imitation of animals in Yoga postures and through the telling and imagining of one's own past lives of animals, Hinduism cultivates a sense of intimacy with the other-than-human realm, as well as a sense of playful awe. At its core, Indian nonviolence or *ahiṃsā* arises from an emotion grounded in shared kinship, a reluctance to do harm to those beings whose place within the universe can be seen as interchangeable with one's own.

Animal Stories in Buddhism and Jainism

Like Hinduism, Buddhism and Jainism both teach the doctrine of rebirth or reincarnation. Many of the teachings of the Buddha were couched in allegories drawn from his past lives, often embodied as an animal. He told his followers about the goodness of the tigress who sacrificed her own flesh for the sake of her young, about an elephant who threw himself off a cliff to save starving travelers, and a rabbit who jumped into a fire to provide food for a Brahmin. In each instance, animals manifest compassion for others. The great Buddhist emperor Aśoka (ca. 274–232 B.C.E.) erected pillars throughout the subcontinent mandating protection of animals (see Chapple 1986). The Dalai Lama restates this Buddhist commitment of nonviolence to animals as follows:

> Life is as dear to a mute creature as it is to a man. Even the lowliest insect strives for protection against dangers that threaten its life. Just as each one of us wants happiness and fears pain, just as each one of us wants to live and not to die, so do all other creatures.
>
> *Gyatso 1980: 78*

The Jaina tradition, older than Buddhism, also uses animal allegory as a prime teaching device. Jainism provides the earliest and most plaintive call for nonviolence as the basis for its religious teachings in the *Ācārāṅga Sūtra*, ca. 350 B.C.E.:

> Injurious activities inspired by self-interest lead to evil and darkness. This is what is called bondage, delusion, death, and hell. To do harm to others is to do harm to oneself. "Thou art he whom thou intend to kill! Thou art he whom thou intend to tyrannize!" We corrupt ourselves as soon as we intend to corrupt others. We kill ourselves as soon as we intend to kill others.
>
> *Jacobi 1887: I.1.2*

Because of their adherence to nonviolence, all Jainas are strict vegetarians and avoid all professions that cause harm to animal life in any way. They see all life forms as not different in essence from their own. The *Ācārāṅga Sūtra* proclaims: "All beings are fond of life; they like pleasure and hate pain, shun destruction and like to live, they long to live. To all, life is dear" (Jacobi 1887: I.2.3).

Jaina animal stories emphasize the continuity of life from incarnation to incarnation. Elephants become reincarnated again as elephants, and elephants become humans, and humans become monks, and monks become angels. Along the way, many other animals cross paths: antelope, deer, lions, jackals, cattle, and rabbits. One's actions toward other life forms determine one's status in the lives to come. If, even in the midst of a natural calamity such as a forest fire, one can seek to spare the lives of others, a reward will be gained.

The story of the prince who, having remembered his past lives as different elephants and having then become a monk, demonstrates the layered complexity of ethical decision-making in Jaina tradition.[5] Human beings sometimes innately know the correct path to follow. This story suggests that from the classical Indian perspective this knowledge arises from lessons learned both in this life and in prior lives. Because he had fallen victim to a ferocious fire in a prior birth, the elephant who became a prince created a meadow of protection through which he saved many beings, even at his own peril. Because he had become aware of the sufferings endured by all beings, the prince renounced his worldly life, symbolized by the forest fire, in order to gain a heavenly reward after practicing years of asceticism. Ingenuity and kindness arose from horrific experiences. This created a sensitivity within the prince. This tenderness paved the way for a life dedicated to nonviolence and the protection of life in all forms.

In the Indian system of reincarnation, all beings are said to be equal. As famously stated in the *Bhagavad Gītā*, "People of learning view with equal eye a Bramhin of knowledge and good learning, a cow, an elephant, and even a dog and an outcaste" (*BGV*:18). Just as it would unthinkable to condone cannibalism, so also from the logic of Indian nonviolence, it would be unthinkable to for a Jaina to eat a fellow animal.

Building on a legacy of kindness toward and respect for animals, India maintains an extensive network of religious organizations that advocate animal welfare, including shelters for unwell and elderly cattle. Thousands of Jaina Pinjrapoles give shelter, food, and medical care to countless birds and animals each year. The most famous animal activism movement in India, the Bishnoi, was founded by Jambheśvara in Rajasthan in 1485 for the protection of human well-being, animals, and plants. In modern times, Bishnoi have established the All India Jeev Raksha Bishnoi Sabha, a wildlife protection organization, and the Community for Wildlife and Rural Development Society (see Jain 2011).

Humans maintain a remarkable intimacy with animals on the Indian subcontinent. Cows, water buffalo, goats, camels, and elephants ply the same roadways with humans. They continue to provide labor that in the developed world has been replaced with machinery. In their honor, animal celebrations are held each year, such as Pongal, when animals are given a special day of rest and decorated with brightly colored dots and patterns. No place in the world can claim a more pervasive and diverse vegetarian cuisine, a practice that has been inspired by the commitment of *ahiṃsā*, to do no harm.

Vegetarianism for All?

The poet, philosopher, and Zen Buddhist icon Gary Snyder, in his provocative book *The Practice of the Wild*, suggests that eating animals is fine as long as we, as humans, encounter those animals directly, thank them for their sacrifice, and kill them, skin them, disembowel them, carve them, and cook them directly (Snyder 1990). Snyder, in a certain sense, invites humans to return to the hunter-gatherer days, a time when the playing field was more level, and humans were as likely to be preyed upon as to prey upon others. For Jainas and Buddhists and Hindus, this logic would be unimaginable. Hunting and the eating of meat would be a sign of utter barbarism, certain to lead to a future life of misery.

How much difference can an individual animal make? Those who have been in a relationship with a cat or dog often comment that their pet knows them better than anyone else, even, sometimes, better than themselves. Companion animals console, cajole, and prod humans to be better, to be more caring, to be more responsible. To harm a pet would be unthinkable. Pets deepen and enrich humanity. Berry commented that as species go extinct, human consciousness itself becomes diminished. He urged that we heed his call to understand that we live in a communion of subjects, not a collection of objects (Berry 2006: 5–10). It is important to note, however, that Berry, born and raised in the American South, never became a vegetarian. In the Western tradition, affection for animals does not necessarily mandate adoption of vegetarianism.

Animals, Intimacy, and an Ethic of Nonviolence

This chapter began with a reflection on the status of animals as objects of utilitarian use in the mainstream of Western civilization. By way of contrast, we examined the reasons given by Gandhi for his own vegetarianism, which sees a link between the treatment of animals and the treatment of one's own body. We also explored how the view toward animals in Hinduism, Buddhism, and Jainism has been shaped by a worldview, a metaphysics that sees continuity between human experience and the experience of nonhuman animals. This worldview generates a narrative of empathy toward animals, and, by extension, to fellow human beings. By seeing oneself as not different from other beings, feelings of care and concern arise spontaneously. This feeling of fellowship lies at the heart of the practice of nonviolence and, in the case of Hinduism and Jainism, generally also entails vegetarianism.

Studies of school shootings have revealed that the perpetrators of this senseless violence began their path of violence by torturing and killing animals. Callous disregard for animals can lead to disregard for humans as well. In order to cultivate a healthy, loving sense of self, one place to begin is to develop relationships with animals. Animal therapy has been demonstrated as an effective means to reconnect with one's sense of well-being, whether through dogs who are trained to visit the sick and elderly in hospitals, or horses through which autistic individuals learn skills of nonverbal communication. By connecting with the life force of another species, one learns to reconnect with one's own vitality.

The religious traditions of India have developed tools to cultivate nonviolence that begin with a foundational regard for animals, nurtured through instructional narratives of past lives, development of a vegetarian diet, and the performance of movement and meditative practices that literally position one to view the world through the body and senses of an animal. This empathetic approach broadens and deepens a gentle, friendly way of manifesting nonviolence in daily life.

The question may be raised, what is the relationship between nonviolence, animal protection, and pacifism? Does someone who advocates for the protection of animals by definition oppose all forms of violence? From Gandhi's perspective, we know this not to be the case. Although Gandhi staged a massive and successful nonviolent campaign that resulted in the overthrow of British colonial rule after decades of persistent action, Gandhi refused to reject the nobility of fighting for a noble cause, and often put his own well-being at risk. Similarly, even members of the Jaina community will participate in military service if required. The Jaina tradition states that violence in defense of self or family or society might be unavoidable, but only as a last resort. However, even the most fervent Jaina would not assent to disruptive or violent behavior to protest maltreatment of animals. The usual Jaina strategy would be to periodically buy animals headed for slaughter and arrange their public release, in an attempt to gain sympathy for the cause of nonviolence.

In Western history, some of the most famous groups of pacifists, deeply committed to nonviolence, include the Quakers and the Mennonites. However, neither group categorically advocates vegetarianism. Furthermore, American Quakers were very successful and prosperous whalers in the eighteenth and early nineteenth centuries. Other American religious movements did advocate vegetarianism, though they did not necessarily align themselves with nonviolence or pacifism, including the early members of the Church of the Latter-day Saints (meat was only to be eaten in winter). The Seventh Day Adventists, however, were both vegetarian and pacifists, opting to pay the commutation fee to avoid military service during the Civil War, though some in recent years have entered military service (see Morgan 2003).

The question may be posed: must all pacifists be vegetarian? It is important to distinguish between vegetarianism, pacifism, and nonviolence, which often entail distinct individual and societal narratives. First, not all vegetarians are nonviolent toward other human beings. One of the most notorious vegetarians was Adolf Hitler, who was directly responsible for millions of deaths. Nor are all pacifists vegetarian, as seen in the example of the Quakers. For some adherents to a vegetarian diet, a consistency might be detected that would extend compassion toward animals to human animals as well. However, not all vegetarians are committed to nonviolence, and some may adopt vegetarianism exclusively for health reasons.

It is well documented that vegetarians have a longer life span than meat eaters. The city of Loma Linda, California, home to many Seventh Day Adventists, has been designated as a "Blue Zone," meaning that the average resident of Loma Linda will live seven years longer than the "ordinary" meat-eater. Based on extensive scientific studies, Dr. Dean Ornish and others promote vegetarianism as a key to human health, not necessarily as a moral response to the maltreatment of animals.

Animal rights organizations such as People for the Ethical Treatment of Animals have taken up animal advocacy and advocacy of vegetarianism. More anarchic movements take direct action to bring attention to the plight of animals, and have released minks, made threats against animal researchers, and caused extensive property damage to research laboratories. This form of criminal behavior has resulted in the condemnation of such movements as terrorist and some individuals have received harsh sentencing as a result. Nonetheless, the moral commitment on the part of many animal advocates has been particularly effective in creating a public awareness and conscience in regard to animal abuse. White's book *In Defense of Dolphins* contributed significantly to the decision by Sea World to phase out entertainment programs that feature captive dolphins performing tricks in their amusement parks (White 2007).

This chapter began with reference to a widely disseminated documentary, *Earthlings*, that focuses on the exploitation of animals for the sake of food, clothing, entertainment, pets, and other forms of non-essential human benefit. Though more comprehensive than most, this film is part of a fully developed genre of films that problematize human dominance over animals. Other films include *Knives Over Forks*[6] and *Cowspiracy*,[7] which focus more directly on the eating of animal flesh, asserting that a carnivorous diet shortens the human life span. Not only does the eating of animals do harm to animals, it also causes direct harm to the human body, resulting in increased rates of heart disease and various forms of cancer, particularly colon cancer. The Humane Society of the United States has widely distributed a light educational video advocating vegetarianism titled *Eating Mercifully* that reaches across all economic and social strata.[8] Many evangelical Christians have taken up this cause, as well as related environmental issues.[9]

The Jaina community has also expanded its internal conversation regarding food acceptability. The traditional Jaina diet relies upon a complement of dairy (milk, soft cheeses, and yogurt) and legumes combined with rice to provide sufficient protein. Appalled by the brutality of commercial dairy farming worldwide, including in India, many Jainas have now switched to a vegan diet, eschewing the inclusion of milk-based foods. Veganism has become widespread, creating some rifts within the broader community of vegetarians.

This brings us to the larger issues of worldview, normative ethics, personal choices, and the greater good. We have outlined three competing worldviews in regard to animals. The first regards animals as important for their use, deeming animals to be instruments to be used for human nutrition, entertainment, and comfort. This worldview deems it acceptable to kill and consume animals. The second, appealing to what might be characterized as the "logic of the humane," suggests that animals have a rich interior life, that animals suffer, and that it does not make sense to harm animals solely for human benefit. Both of these views share the premise that the human and animal realms are distinct; the reason to cultivate kindness toward animals arises to human beneficence, not necessarily from a view of innate animal goodness. The third worldview, found within traditions that arise in India, holds that animals and humans are part of the same continuum. Animals must be protected not only for their own sake but out of self-interest and empathy. According to Jainism, if one harms an animal, a mass of karmic material will cloak one's life energy, predisposing one to commit future acts of violence, and inviting future retribution. By avoiding harm toward animals, one purifies this karmic impulse, setting the stage for continued acts of benevolence and kindness. Jainas not only avoid flesh foods, they will periodically fast to avoid harm to grains and vegetables, and have for centuries encouraged monastic and laypersons toward the end of life to consciously enter death through a process of ritualized fasting and dehydration (see Chapple 2010).

Even the Jainas, who have for millennia held the edge when it comes to making radical lifestyle choices, are now being asked to reconsider their time-honored observances. New forms of social analysis have revealed the difficulties inherent in large-scale agricultural practices. No longer do cows roam freely to graze, but even in India they are confined to feedlots and connected to machines at milking time. Additionally, India has now become the leading exporter of cattle for slaughter, including the many "excess" young bulls who will never produce milk.

In some ways, globalization has blurred the borders between worldviews. Animal ethology has revealed the presence of a rich emotional life within nonhuman animals, reversing previously held European and American assumptions. Nutritional research has allowed for the emergence of veganism as a viable dietary choice. In the former instance, Westerners are being challenged to acknowledge and appreciate the feelings of animals. In the latter instance, vegetarians worldwide are being challenged to consider the vegan option. Nonviolence in regard to other-than-human animals requires a willingness to take a longer look at human-animal narratives and at consumer choices at multiple levels, including food, clothing, and entertainment.

Notes

1 *Earthlings*. Narrated by Joaquin Phoenix. Link: Nationearth.com. 2005.
2 Gandhi, "The Moral Basis of Vegetarianism" at International Vegetarian Union. Link: https://ivu.org/news/evu/other/gandhi2.html (Accessed 17 July 2017).
3 At International Vegetarian Union. Link: https://ivu.org/history/williams/ (Accessed 17 July 2017).
4 During the early period when India was lightly settled, cow herders were sent out into the forests and meadows to tend to flocks in distant quarters. One such young drover, Satyakāma Jābāla, achieved great spiritual insight while in the wild, learning profound truths from the elements of nature and from animals. The young Satyakāma asked his mother about his father, seeking indirectly to learn of his caste or varṇa. She responded that she does not know which man caused her pregnancy, and hence he is known as Satyakāma (desirous of truth), son of Jābāla, his mother's name. He sought out the renowned teacher Haridrumata Gautama and, when asked about his family origins, shared guilelessly the story told by his mother. Satyakāma's honesty earned him accolades from Haridrumata Gautama, who proclaimed him to be a Brahmin and agreed to teach him. First, however, work needed to be rendered. The teacher charged the young man with tending a herd of 400 cattle. Rising to the task, Satyakāma vowed not to return until the herd grew to a thousand head. He retreated into a landscape of forests and meadows for a period of years and then encountered four experiences that transformed him into a sage, a man of wisdom.
5 Here is the story of Meghkumar, the Cloud Prince, as found in the Gyātasūtra of the Jaina canon. This story weaves past-life memories in such a way that not only does a prince gain insight into his current state of affairs, but also in his immediate prior incarnation he recalls a lesson from an incarnation prior to that. Prince Meghkumar was born after his mother Dharinī recalled two dreams: one of a white elephant who came down from the sky and entered her womb through her mouth, and the second of an insatiable desire to ride through the city on a white elephant on a cloudy day. The king Shrenik and his queen consequently named their beloved son Cloud Prince and provided the happiest life possible for him, including his marriage to eight princesses.

Some years passed. The Tīrthaṅkāra Bhagavan Mahavir, the twenty-third great teacher of Jainism (ca. 800 B.C.E.), came to the capital of Shrenik's kingdom of Magadha, the city known today as Rajagriha. After hearing the Bhagavan speak, Prince Meghkumar decided to leave behind his wives and princely comforts to take up the life of a Jaina monk. The day before his initiation his father arranged for him to be king for a day, lending even greater weight to the significance of Meghkumar's renunciation. After the ceremony initiating Meghkumar into monkhood was completed, the former prince settled on the floor to sleep. As the most junior monk, he was required to sleep near the door. All night long, the monks came and went in order to relieve themselves in the field, disturbing his sleep. He tossed and turned, receiving no rest. He fell into a deep sadness and yearning for his prior life.

In the morning he approached Bhagavan Mahavir and asked to be released from his vows. Using his powers of omniscience, the Bhagavan told two stories of Meghkumar's prior lives when he lived as an elephant. In one story he was an elderly pure white elephant named King Sumeruprabh. A forest fire swept through his domain, forcing all the animals to flee. Because of his advanced age, Sumeruprabh stumbled and fell into a muddy lake bed. A younger elephant took advantage of his plight and gored him to death. The elephant was reborn again, this time as a bright red elephant named Meruprabh, with four tusks, also king of his clan. While witnessing a fire from afar, he recalled the plight of his prior birth and urged his fellow elephants to clear an eight-mile meadow that would be safe in case of fire. Eventually, the summer fires came to the forest and all the animals, including antelope, deer, lions, jackals, cattle, and rabbits, crowded into the meadow. Meruprabh lifted his foot to scratch his itchy stomach. A rabbit scampered into the space underneath his leg. For fear of killing the rabbit, Meruprabh stood on three legs for two and a half days. By this time, the fire had died down, but Meruprabh's leg had stiffened and he tumbled to the ground. He lay prone for three days, unable to move, suffering from pain, hunger, and thirst. However, because of the compassion he had manifested in order to save the rabbit, he felt peace even amidst the pain and took rebirth in the womb of Dharinī and was born as Prince Meghkumar. Having been reminded of this act of compassion, Meghkumar renewed his religious zeal and after twelve years of monastic life ascended to Mount Vipulchal, where he engaged in a final fast, attaining a heavenly state as an angel in his next life (see Vijayi 1952 or Jaini 2000).

6 Link: www.forksoverknives.com/
7 Link: www.cowspiracy.com/
8 Link: www.youtube.com/watch?v=L-Va6F3iQFc
9 Link: www.evangelicalsforsocialaction.org/creation-care/animals/video-eating-mercifully/

Works Cited

Berry, T. (2006). "Loneliness and Presence," in P. Waldau and K. Patton (eds.), *A Communion of Subjects: Animals in Religion, Science, and Ethics*. New York: Columbia University Press, 5–26.

Chapple, C. K. (1986). "Noninjury to Animals: Jaina and Buddhists Perspectives," in T. Regan (ed.), *Animal Sacrifices: Religious Perspectives on the Use of Animals in Science*. Philadelphia: Temple University Press, 213–236.

Chapple, C. K. (2010). "Eternal Life, Death, and Dying in Jainism," in L. Bregman (ed.), *Religion, Death, and Dying*. Santa Barbara: Praeger Perspectives, 115–134.

Gandhi, M. K. (1997). *Hind Swaraj and Other Writings by M.K. Gandhi*, edited by A.J. Parel. New York: Cambridge University Press.

Gyatso, T. (the 14th Dalai Lama). (1980). *Universal Responsibility and the Good Heart*. Dharamsala, India: Library of Tibetan Words and Archives.

Hume, R. E. (1921). *The Thirteen Principal Upanishads*. Oxford: Oxford University Press.

Jacobi, H. (1887). "Ācārāṅga Sūtra I.1.2," in H. Jacobi (ed.), *Jaina Sūtras*. Oxford: Oxford University Press, 18.

Jain, P. (2011). *Dharma and Ecology of Hindu Communities: Sustenance and Sustainability*. Farnham, UK: Ashgate.

Jaini, P. S. (2000). *Collected Papers on Jaina Studies*. Delhi, India: Motilal Banarsidass.

Kingsford, A. (1892). *The Perfect Way in Diet: A Treatise Advocating a Return to the Natural and Ancient Food of Our Race*. London: Kegan Paul, Trench, Trubner, and Co.

Mitra, V. H. (1998). *The Yoga-Vāsiṣṭha of Valmiki, Sanskrit Text and English Translation*, Vol. II., *Sthiti Prakaraṇa, Upaśama Prakaraṇa*, edited by R.P. Arya. Delhi, India: Parimal Publications.

Morgan, D. (2003). "Between Pacifism and Patriotism." *Adventist Review*. Available at: http://archives.adventistreview.org/2003-1535/story5.html (Accessed 17 July 2017).

Salt, H. S. (1886). *A Plea for Vegetarianism and Other Essays*. Manchester: Vegetarian Society.

Sethia, T. (2012). *Gandhi: Pioneer of Nonviolent Social Change*. Boston: Pearson.

Singer, P. (1975). *Animal Liberation: A New Ethics for Our Treatment of Animals*. New York: Avon Books.

Snyder, G. (1990). *The Practice of the Wild*. New York: North Point Press.

Vijayi, M. S. P. (1952). *Inspiring Story of Meghkumar* in *Jnatadharmakathanga (Nyayadhammakaao)*. Mumbai: Mahavir Seval Trust.

White, T. I. (2007). *In Defense of Dolphins: The New Moral Frontier*. Malden, MA: Blackwell.

Williams, H. (1883). *The Ethics of Diet*. London: F. Pitman.

30
CHILDREN, VIOLENCE, AND NONVIOLENCE

Jane Hall Fitz-Gibbon

Children suffer violence at rates far higher than any other definable social group. The literature on child abuse—physical, sexual, and emotional—is extensive (for examples, see Finkelhor 1979, 1983, 1986; Gerbner, Ross, and Zigler 1980; Briere 1992; Straus 2001; Straus, Gelles, and Steinmetz 2006, 2014). Stories of egregious child abuse often make headlines, yet these stories are only the tip of a very large iceberg. In contemporary society children are hurt through abuse and neglect at an alarming rate. In 2014 (the last statistical year at the time of writing), the United Nations Children's Fund (UNICEF) stated that 70 million young girls between the ages of 15 and 19 reported being victims of physical violence—a quarter of all girls in that age group. One hundred and twenty million females under the age of 20 are subject to rape or other forced sexual acts, while 95,000 children and young people under the age of 20 were the victims of homicide (UNICEF 2014, 1–6). In the same year, in the United States, 702,000 children were proven victims of abuse and neglect, out of over three million Child Protective Services (CPS) investigations, while 1,580 children died at the hands of their caregivers—nearly half of these less than a year old (U.S. Department of Health and Human Services 2014).

Why violence against children is a moral issue is perhaps too obvious to state. Like all violence, violence against children causes harm and produces no good results in the long term (Fitz-Gibbon 2017: 103–117). Yet, in an anomaly in the literature on pacifism and nonviolence, there is no in-depth treatment of the possible nonviolent responses of society, parents, caregivers, and schools concerning children as the victims of violence. The cycle of violence often begins in the home, and for a comprehensive response to violence in society, theories of nonviolence must take the phenomenon of violence in the home seriously. If nonviolence can be taught and modeled by parents and caregivers, then perhaps children will become adults who have internalized nonviolent principles. An important solution, therefore, is to develop a theory and practice of nonviolent parenting. Globally there is a movement away from corporal punishment for children, arising in Sweden and elsewhere. This development is an important part of the project of building a culture of peace.

The violence against children that takes place in the home and in school is often hidden under the guise of discipline. In this chapter, therefore, I consider the effect and harm done to children through socially accepted corporal punishment, together with a possible nonviolent response. (For a more detailed treatment of corporal punishment in schools see Fitz-Gibbon

2017; for an analysis of violence that necessitated CPS intervention and nonviolent responses, see Fitz-Gibbon and Fitz-Gibbon 2016).

Children are generally considered to be the most vulnerable members of society, yet they remain some of the least safeguarded citizens. Spanking children in their own homes—the place where they should be most protected—is not banned anywhere in the United States, and only 31 states have a restriction on physical punishment in schools. The latest UNICEF report on the violence against children comments, "Most violence against children occurs at the hands of the people charged with their care or with whom they interact daily—caregivers, peers and intimate partners" (UNICEF 2014: 169).

Society has not usually considered the corporal punishment of children as a violent action, but rather a parent's, or school's, right to discipline wayward children in ways deemed appropriate. Violence is an ambiguous word. Sociologist Murray A. Straus defines violence as "an act carried out with the intention, or perceived intention, of causing physical pain or injury to another person" (Straus 2001: 7). In these terms, the physical punishment of children is unequivocally violent. However, such violence against children is often hidden in euphemisms and socially accepted ways of hiding actual violence. Children's rights advocate Peter Newell notes that contemporary society lends "its support to a whole vocabulary of violence against children." He elaborates:

> Whether couched in comfortable words like "smacking", "spanking", "cuffing", or stronger terms like "beating", "belting", "thrashing", and "caning", all forms of physical punishment of children entail the deliberate infliction of physical pain by one—large—person on another generally smaller, sometimes very much smaller, person.
> *Newell 1989: IX*

Furthermore, many of the major scholars and activists associated with nonviolence have, to date, not offered much consideration to violence against children. For example, there is little in the writings of Martin Luther King, Jr. about children. It seems to have been something of a blind spot in his philosophy. Although King did not personally spank his own children, the home was not nonviolent, with his four children receiving corporal punishment from their mother and grandparents (Fitz-Gibbon 2017: 104).

Data on Spanking

Data drawn from 190 countries show that worldwide almost a billion children between the ages of 2 and 14 are subject to physical punishment on a regular basis by their caregivers (UNICEF 2014). The report comments, "Violence remains an all-too-real part of life for children around the globe—regardless of their economic and social circumstances, culture, religion or ethnicity—with both immediate and long-term consequences" (UNICEF 2014: 6).

Globally the movement to prevent corporal punishment is gaining momentum, with 52 nation-states now having a complete ban on physical punishment in all settings. Furthermore, 129 states fully prohibit the use of it in school. Although the new awareness of the harm caused by corporal punishment is to be applauded, still only 10 percent of the children in the world are fully protected from this form of violence (Global Initiative to End All Corporal Punishment 2017a).

The Harris Poll conducted two surveys in the United States on approval and usage of corporal punishment. These show that although corporal punishment has declined, still more than half the population remain in favor of it. The two polls were conducted in 1995 and in 2013 respectively (Harris Poll 2013). In 1995, 87 percent of those polled agreed that spanking is sometimes appropriate; in 2013 this declined slightly to 81 percent. The figures do show a more significant decline with the question, "Have you ever spanked your children?" regardless of whether the child was currently living in the home or not. In 1995, 80 percent had spanked their children, with a drop to 67 percent by 2013. This reduction in corporal punishment was mainly reflected in respondents 18 to 36 years old. This shows that younger parents discipline their children by methods other than spanking. It is likely that this trend will continue, bringing about a further decline in the practice.

The most prevalent form of corporal punishment is spanking. The Harris Poll included a question about whether participants had been punished physically in ways other than spanking. Only 23 percent said they had experienced other means of corporal punishment. This data masks, however, what "spanking" means in different contexts. For example, in the United States, spanking most often means hitting a child with an implement, a paddle or a switch. In Europe, spanking usually refers to the open hand. Clearly, other things being equal, the potential harm caused by a wooden implement is greater than an open hand. Much depends on the person carrying out the corporal punishment. Presumably, a large physically strong male could cause more harm with his hand than a smaller female with a switch. Yet even to argue the case is to miss the point. All violence against children is morally wrong.

Practitioners of physical punishment have varying opinions about whether it is preferable to use a hand or an implement to administer the punishment. The conservative Christian group *Focus on the Family* advocated always using an implement. Their reasoning was that hands were for loving caresses and therefore an inanimate object should always be used for punishing a child (Ingram n.d.). The buttocks have long been preferred as the area where spankings are administered, the pretext being that they are soft and fleshy and contain no major organs; however, medical doctor Lesli Taylor refuted this. Recent research has shown that the buttocks are a sensitive area with a profusion of nerves. Spinal damage to the coccyx is also a possibility (Taylor and Maurer n.d.).

The Harris Poll asked also, "Were you spanked by your own parents?" The results were the same for respondents in both 1995 and 2013, with 86 percent admitting that they had been spanked as children. Furthermore, of those who had experienced physical punishment as a child, 95 percent had in turn spanked their own children.

Psychologist Steven Pinker notes a possible inaccuracy in the polls on corporal punishment, as polls for violence against children largely consist of self-reports by perpetrators rather than from victims. Although in the past it may have been acceptable for a parent to leave a bruise or mark when physically punishing a child, in contemporary times this is less acceptable. A positive response by a perpetrator could be seen as an admission of wrongdoing. Therefore, the reported decline of corporal punishment could be a result of fewer parents owning up to corporal punishment (Pinker 2011: 439). UNICEF also noted that the polls may not reflect the severity of the situation:

> Over the past decade, recognition of the pervasive nature and impact of violence against children has grown. Still the phenomenon remains largely undocumented and underreported. This can be attributed to a variety of reasons, including the fact that some forms of violence against children are socially accepted, tacitly condoned, or not perceived as being abusive. Many victims are too young or too vulnerable to disclose their experience or protect themselves.
>
> *UNICEF 2014: 1*

Professor and historian of family Philip Greven is in agreement that much physical punishment of children goes unnoticed:

> Most children suffer the pain of punishment inflicted by adults within their own families and households, without public knowledge, concern, or protection. Occasionally, however, the assaults and violence against children done in the name of discipline become public knowledge, and the courts, or other public officials intervene to protect the interests of the child or children being assaulted and abused in the guise of discipline.
>
> *Greven 1992: 32*

Despite the concern about underreporting, Pinker cites various studies that show a steady decline in child abuse. A new awareness of children and the harm done to them, plus legal ramifications for perpetrators, may well have been significant factors in this decline.

While the reduction shown in the data can be applauded, there is still a significant form of violence done to children under the guise of corporal punishment. In her book *Breaking Down the Walls of Silence*, psychologist Alice Miller quotes from a letter she sent to an editor in 1986. She wrote:

> You are living in a country in which two-thirds of the parents interviewed by the magazine *Eltern* (Parents) regard the physical punishment of children as necessary and correct. What this means is that millions of children are endangered, because they have not been taught to regard such behavior as dangerous.
>
> *Miller 1997: 56*

It is salutary that 30 years later Miller's statement still reflects the situation regarding physical punishment.

Spanking in the Home

A 2015 Florida case, reported in the media, highlighted the use of spanking in the home. A parent wanted to spank his 12-year-old daughter using a paddle. He was concerned that he would spank his daughter to the point where he would get into legal trouble for abuse. Therefore, he called the local sheriff's office and requested that an officer come to witness him administering corporal punishment. A sheriff's deputy duly witnessed the punishment and concluded it was not abusive. The deputy wrote:

> (He) wanted me to stand by while he spanked her with the paddle. . . . I stood by as (he) spanked (her) four times on the buttocks. Since no crime had been committed this case is closed.
>
> *Grisham 2015*

In a later interview the sheriff's department said that although they did not advertise this service they had provided it on request to about a dozen families. Many of the comments in various media forums supported the father's action. One comment in an ensuing news article from a neighbor who wished to remain anonymous said that "people don't hit their kids because of consequences from the authorities" (Robinson 2015).

The girl's offense was that she had fought with her sister. Apparently, the fight had been particularly vicious, and clearly there was a need for parental intervention to show the child that her actions were wrong. However, evidence is mounting to suggest that such corporal punishment is the cause of physical and psychological trauma to its victims (as discussed later in this chapter).

On occasions when parents who have spanked their children face charges, in many cases the charges are not upheld. Such was the case of a 13-year-old in Newark, Ohio. The teenager was caught stealing—again something that any responsible parent might want to address. His parents made the decision to use corporal punishment. The father used part of a cutting board as a paddle and hit his son four or five times. The next day the boy's wrestling coach saw the ensuing bruises and called the authorities. Ultimately, the father was charged with domestic violence. He was acquitted by Licking County Municipal Court. The father stated that he was angry about being charged for something that he believed was his right to do, punish his son with a spanking (Lecker n.d.). In the United States, reasonable corporal punishment by parents is allowed. However, what amounts to being reasonable is open to question; "reasonable" changes as cultural mores change.

Clearly, the parents of these children believed they were acting in the child's best interest. They used spanking to try to correct their children's behavior, presumably for the child's own good. Straus comments there is "the widespread belief in the United States that spanking reduces delinquency" (Straus et al. 2014: 110). In addition, parents face social pressure to use corporal punishment to be considered good parents. Straus notes:

> Friends and relatives expect parents to use corporal punishment if a child persistently misbehaves. . . . The non-spanking parents frequently had to defend their child-rearing methods to skeptical neighbors and relatives, often with great difficulty.
>
> *Straus 2001: 7*

However, the evidence is increasingly showing that although spanking may have an immediate effect, there are no long-term benefits. To the contrary, the harm caused by spanking can cause problems later in life (as discussed later in this chapter).

Spanking at School

In the United States, corporal punishment at school is legal in 19 states. This usually takes the form of a spanking on the buttocks using a wooden paddle that is about four inches wide. Paddling is not just reserved for teenagers, and children as young as five have been paddled. In 2016, a video, which was repeatedly shown in the media, pictured a small boy who was about to be paddled by two school administrators. His mother had secretly filmed the event on her phone. It was a complex situation, as the mother had believed if she did not consent to corporal punishment she could be jailed. Although the actual paddling was not shown, the fear and confusion of the child in the minutes leading up to the physical punishment were evident (Hezakya News 2016).

In some cases, injuries have occurred that required medical attention. Human Rights Watch notes, "The Society for Adolescent Medicine has documented serious medical consequences resulting from corporal punishment, including severe muscle injury, extensive blood clotting (hematomas), whiplash damage, and hemorrhaging" (Human Rights Watch 2009).

I consider European issues later in this chapter. In the United States, when parents have objected to the severity of the beating there is little legal recourse. After the landmark case of

Ingraham v. Wright (U.S. Supreme Court 1977), where it was upheld that paddling did not violate either the Eighth or the Fourteenth Amendment, the courts have been unwilling to adjudicate in school cases. In this case, in 1970, 14-year-old James Ingraham (a student at Charles R. Drew Junior High School, Dade County, Florida) received 20 strokes of a paddle by the principal, Willie J. Wright. Ingraham had been slow to leave the auditorium. He was held in place by two assistant principals while he was paddled. The ensuing injury necessitated medical attention and 11 days' leave from school. Another student, Roosevelt Andrews, who had been paddled for not being quick enough walking to class, joined the case against Wright, the two assistant principals, Lemmie Deliford and Solomon Barnes, and Edward L. Whigham, the district superintendent. The families of the boys contended that the severity of the corporal punishment violated the Eighth Amendment, "cruel and unusual punishment," as the paddling was excessive. The punishment also violated the Fourteenth Amendment, "due process," because they weren't given the opportunity to be heard before the paddling was administered. In a 5–4 vote the United States Supreme Court ruled that public schools can administer corporal punishment to students without a hearing, and that the cruel and unusual punishment clause was not applied to schools, only to those convicted of a crime (Lee 1979; Fitz-Gibbon 2017: 30–33). This law still stands.

Though schools are *in loco parentis*—in place of a parent—in several cases the injuries caused by paddling would have resulted in a call to Child Protective Services, had they happened in a home setting. Therefore, a teacher or administrator can cause harm to children that is beyond that which would be legally acceptable in the home. School psychologist Irwin A. Hyman notes, "The incidences of educator-induced violence far exceeds that of offenses committed by students" (Hyman and Snook 1999).

Race, Disabilities, and Patriarchy

Corporal punishment in schools is administered at a higher rate to students who are Black, male, or covered by the Individuals with Disabilities Education Act. The Hechinger Report (April 14, 2014) looked at the disparities in corporal punishment for Black students. It assessed the situation in Mississippi, the state that has the largest percentage of students paddled. In Mississippi, half the students are Black, yet, in 2012, 64 percent of those paddled were Black (Carr 2014). This bias toward using corporal punishment more often for Black students is also reflected in the national figures (Fitz-Gibbon 2017: 33, 39, 49, 123). Developmental psychologist Elizabeth Gershoff comments:

> It is clear that racial disparities are present in all forms of school discipline, and the fact that they have persisted for decades points to a need for a major change in the school discipline system.
>
> *Gershoff and Grogan-Kaylor 2016: 31*

The American Civil Liberties Union and Human Rights Watch produced a paper in 2009 that looked at physical punishment and students with disabilities. The document begins with the stories of two boys who received paddling, and the deleterious effect it had on their well-being and education. Other stories cited show the severity of the physical punishment, and that corporal punishment is administered at a higher rate for children who have disabilities than for the general student body. The conclusion was:

> Corporal punishment, which is never appropriate for any child, is particularly abusive for students with disabilities whose medical conditions may be worsened as a consequence of the punishment itself.

> These discriminatory, abusive, and ineffective practices should be abolished in US schools. There are better methods of providing effective school discipline, including positive behavioral support systems that enable educators to respond to children's individual needs. It is past time for US states to ban paddling and all other forms of physical punishment, and provide adequate protection and a decent education for students with disabilities.
>
> ACLU 2009: n.p.

In addition, there is a gender disparity. Boys receive corporal punishment at a higher rate than girls, both in the home and at school. Straus offers several reasons why this may be so. Boys, who are often more active, may be perceived to misbehave more. Culturally it is encouraged for boys to be daredevils, even becoming a matter of pride for parents. In contemporary society we hold an underlying assumption that boys should be tougher than girls. Using corporal punishment helps reinforce this process. In addition, girls are perceived to be more easily injured. Society tends to assume that girls do not need to grow up to be as physically aggressive as boys. Although gender stereotypes are decreasing, Straus' research shows that stereotypes remain among the reasons why boys are paddled at a higher rate than girls (Straus 2001: 31).

The Religious/Political Argument

Kyoto, Japan, saw more than 800 religious leaders convene for the eighth world assembly of Religions for Peace (Religions for Peace 2006). Leaders were drawn from every region of the world and all major religious traditions. Incorporated into the declaration issued from the assembly was an acknowledgement that religious communities had failed to protect children from violence: "Through omission, denial and silence we have at times tolerated, perpetuated and ignored the reality of violence against children in homes, families, institutions and communities, and not actively confronted the suffering that this violence causes" (Dodd 2011: 4). The attendees further stated their intention to be part of the solution of violence against children in their religious communities.

As European countries have largely secularized over the last century, little data on religion, children, and violence is available. One small survey done in England and Wales showed that while 59 percent of parents agreed that the law should allow corporal punishment only 5 percent of respondents cited religious practice as a reason to use it (Ipsos 2007).

In the United States, the Harris Poll (mentioned earlier) also delineated its results by political party and philosophy. Of those who self-identified as Republicans and conservative, 87 percent believed it was appropriate to use corporal punishment. A lower 78 percent of those who self-identified as Democrat, and 71 percent of those who considered themselves liberal, also approved of physical punishment. The more religious South and the Midwest—an area colloquially known as the Bible Belt—polled a higher approval rate for corporal punishment than the West or East (Fitz-Gibbon 2017: 49). The place of religion in the support of corporal punishment is significant. For those who have strong religious convictions, it is necessary to find ways of interpreting sacred texts that do not conflict with their deeply held views yet allow them to support alternatives to corporal punishment.

There are only a few biblical texts that talk about training and punishment for children, mainly in the book of Proverbs. These short passages have been used to justify harm done to children. Greven comments:

> For centuries, Protestant Christians have been amongst the most ardent advocates of corporal punishment. The Bible has provided fundamental texts that have served

successive generations as primary guides to child-rearing and discipline. These ancient writings, in both the Old and New Testaments, have justified and shaped the practices of corporal punishment in the discipline and rearing of children.

Greven 1992: 46

Over the last two decades, scholars have begun to look at the issue of corporal punishment and those religious texts that have been used to support it (Greven 1992; Webb 2011; Fitz-Gibbon 2017). These have included the new ways of interpreting texts, such as the usage of the word translated "rod," as in the popularized phrase "spare the rod and spoil the child." For example, the word translated "rod" is used in various biblical texts to denote care and guidance, rather than as a rod to punish.

Essentially the religious discussion around the need for the corporal punishment of children reflects an understanding of the nature of humanity. The argument is that either people are born inherently sinful, with the concomitant need to beat the child to break her will, or that children are born *tabula rasa* at birth and need care to be molded into responsible adults. John Locke (1632–1734) and Jean-Jacques Rousseau (1712–1778) posited the latter understanding, although its roots can be traced to Aristotle. Locke expounded his theories in *An Essay on Human Understanding* (1689) and Rousseau in *Emile* (2009). This different understanding of human nature suggested a different approach to children. Though in most respects men of their time, Locke and Rousseau came into direct conflict with the Puritan understanding that suggested "physical punishment, discipline, strict routines and Christian training to rid children of evil habits were some of the characteristics associated with Puritan approaches" (Grieshaber 2004: 3). For example, Rousseau stated, "Children should never receive punishment as such; it should always come as a natural consequence of their fault" (Rousseau 2009: 83).

Religious advocates of corporal punishment tend to use the Christian Old Testament. However, the Gospels, the primary Christian texts, do not refer to spanking or to the punishment of children. Greven again:

> Jesus never advocated any such punishment. Nowhere in the New Testament does Jesus approve of the infliction of pain upon children by the rod or any other such implement, nor is he ever reported to have recommended any kind of physical discipline of children to any parent.
>
> *Greven 1992: 51*

On the contrary, the teaching of Jesus recorded in the Gospels is more likely about the kind of love and compassion that necessitates the acceptance of children, in ways unusual for the then contemporary society.

Similar debates are happening in other religions. Islamic religious leaders are contending that the Qur'an does not support striking a child, but emphasizes nonviolence. Chris Dodd, author of *Ending Corporal Punishment of Children: A Handbook for Working with and Within Religious Communities*, which was produced in conjunction with Save the Children, Churches Network for Nonviolence, and End All Corporal Punishment, quoted from a publication that provided guidance on the care and upbringing of children:

> Given that it is not permissible to incur harm, no parent (or teacher, or employer) has the right to smack a child; this would inevitably inflict psychological as well as physical damage. Both psychological and physical damages have been banned by the Islamic

Sharia. In handling children the Sharia urges us to embrace them, and show them love and compassion.

Dodd 2011: 39

Dr. Jayaraman, head of the Bharatiya Vidya Bhavran, reasoned that corporal punishment could not be justified in the Hindu scriptures. In 1998 in *Hinduism Today* he wrote, "My personal view, and that of the Bhavran, is completely against corporal punishment" (Dodd 2011: 40).

The Sikh Awareness Society developed a resource for parents. It contains the words:

Avoid harsh discipline. Of all the forms of punishment a parent uses, the one with the worst side effects is physical punishment. Children who are spanked, hit or slapped are more prone to fighting with other children.

Dodd 2011: 46

These are just a few examples of faith-based support for eliminating corporal punishment. The desire for children to be treated with compassion, living lives free from violence, can be found in most other world religions (Dodd 2011: 27–47).

Spanking and Harm

According to the Global Initiative to End All Corporal Punishment of Children (GIEACPC):

There is no need to look for evidence of the negative effects of corporal punishment in order to know that it must be prohibited in law and eliminated in practice—just as there is no need for research to show that violence against women is harmful before efforts are made to end it.

GIEACPC 2013: 1

Nonetheless, many studies suggest that corporal punishment causes actual harm to children. In a review of 150 studies, the GIEACPC found "associations between corporal punishment and a wide range of negative outcomes" (GIEACPC 2013: 2). The report contends that "most child abuse is corporal punishment—adults using violence to control and punish children" (GIEACPC 2013: 1), and further, that "the purported distinction between 'ordinary' physical punishment and 'abuse' is meaningless: no line can or should be drawn between 'acceptable' and 'unacceptable' violence against children" (GIEACPC 2013: 2).

In 2016, Elizabeth T. Gershoff and Andrew Grogan-Kaylor offered a meta-analysis of corporal punishment based on the work of four previous meta-analyses from 2002, 2004, 2005, and 2013. Collectively these meta-analyses contained several hundred studies. In the 2016 study physical punishment is defined as "noninjurious, open-handed hitting with the intention of modifying child behavior." Of significance is that the study does not include incidences of corporal punishment that had potential to cause injury—that is, punishment using implements such as the paddle or a switch. Although the several meta-analyses had different outcomes depending on their focus, all determined a correlation between corporal punishment and harm, including mental health issues, failure to graduate from high school, marital violence, and an increase in aggression and socially unacceptable behaviors. Research from other sources reached the same conclusion:

A major study by the University of Texas and the University of Michigan last year on physically punishing children concluded that smacking could lead to mental health problems, lower cognitive ability and a risk of accepting physical abuse as a norm later in life.

Samuel 2017

In *Beating the Devil Out of Them*, Straus gives in-depth results of a number of studies. The evidence is stark. For example, there is a correlation between the percentage of people who had suicidal thoughts and the number of times they were spanked as teens. For those who had never experienced corporal punishment, about 2.5 percent of males and 4 percent of females had considered killing themselves. This rose to about 24 percent of women and 17 percent of men for those who had experienced physical punishment over 20 times. Other markers such as depression, spousal abuse, abusing a child, striking a sibling, delinquency, assault, student violence, masochistic sex, and failure to achieve academically all showed similar percentage increases for those who had experienced corporal punishment.

The European Direction

In 1979, after a lengthy process and much debate, Sweden banned the use of corporal punishment, the first country to do so. The Swedish Parenthood and Guardianship Code was amended to contain the words:

> Children are entitled to care, security, and a good upbringing. Children are to be treated with respect for their person and individuality and may not be subjected to physical punishment or other injurious or humiliating treatment.
>
> *Durrant 1996*

Sweden had abolished corporal punishment in schools more than 20 years previously. The new law required a widespread public relations exercise and was widely publicized in the media. A 16-page pamphlet, *Can You Bring Up Children Successfully Without Smacking and Spanking*, was delivered to all households with children. It was published in several languages to ensure all areas of the population were reached. In addition, the information was printed on milk cartons for the ensuing few months.

The effectiveness of the campaign was assessed by Professor Adrienne Haeuser in 1981 and 1988. She noted:

> The law continues to be discussed in parent education classes which are available to all expectant parents, in child health clinics used by "99.99 percent" of all parents and as appropriate in the public health nurse's mandatory home visit during a baby's first month. It may also be discussed in the mandatory health screening of all four year olds.
>
> *quoted in Newell 1989: 76*

In addition, Haeuser found that the law, and its origin, was taught as part of the ninth-grade curriculum. She also noted changing attitudes, even between 1981 and 1988. She commented, "Whereas in 1981 parents reported 'thinking twice' before using any physical punishment, in 1988 parents simply said they do not use it" (Newell 1989: 85).

The law was intended to educate rather than to criminalize parents. Therefore, no punitive action was taken for violations, unless abuse was proved. However, it was clear that hitting children was no longer socially acceptable.

In 2011, CNN covered a story about a generation who had never experienced corporal punishment. Part of the story featured a young boy, Ian Swanson, who at the age of 5 had moved to

Sweden with his parents. He remembered getting the occasional spanking from his parents and the resultant visit from his kindergarten teachers to talk about, what they termed, "the abuse." It was explained to them about the differences in child discipline in Sweden and the policy of not using corporal punishment. A return to the United States some years later also came as something of a culture shock to Swanson. He says:

> Kids would say things like "My dad's going to whup my ass when he gets home" and I sort of didn't really believe that was a possibility. The first time I actually saw one of my American peers being spanked my jaw hit the floor.
>
> *Gumbrecht 2011*

The experience of the Swedish nonviolent approach changed him. When asked whether he would spank his own children Swanson was quite clear that he would never use corporal punishment.

Sweden was followed by Finland in 1983, after which many more countries followed the Swedish example. Mongolia, Paraguay, and Slovenia all banned corporal punishment in all settings in 2016. On December 22, 2016, France legislated a ban on corporal punishment, becoming the fifty-second country to do so. France had an already existing ban on corporal punishment in schools, but not in the home.

The campaign for the physical punishment ban was initiated by Dr. Gilles Lazimi, who leads the Ordinary Educational Violence Observatory (OEVO), a French watchdog for violence against children. Lazimi explained about the new law:

> This law is a very strong symbolic act to make parents understand just how all violence can be harmful for the child. Above all, it removes the notion of a threshold: there is no small or big violence. There is violence, full stop.
>
> *Samuel 2017*

The French amendment, Egalité et Citoyenneté (Equality and Citizenship), not only seeks to prevent physical violence, but orders parents and caregivers to "abstain from all forms of violence: physical, verbal and psychological" (Samuel 2017).

The United Nations Special Representative on Violence against Children, Marta Santos Pais, welcomed the bill. In a statement, she said:

> The adoption of this new legislation marks a very important commitment towards the protection from violence of more than 14 million children living in France. Ending cruel, degrading or humiliating treatment is an indispensable component of a comprehensive national strategy for the prevention and elimination of violence against children. It lays the foundation for a culture of respect for children's rights; safeguards children's dignity and physical integrity; and encourages positive discipline and education of children through non-violent means.
>
> *Pais 2016*

The Lithuanian parliament voted unanimously on February 14, 2017, to prohibit corporal punishment. Article One of the bill gives a definition of corporal punishment as "any punishment in which physical force is used to cause physical pain, even on a small scale, or otherwise to physically torture a child" (GIEACPC 2017b). Article Four states, "Children have the right to be protected from all forms of violence, including corporal punishment, by their parents, other legal representatives, persons living with them or other persons" (GIEACPC 2017b).

An earlier law that recognized the parental right to discipline their children is amended in Article Five, making it clear that corporal punishment is no longer acceptable as a means of discipline. It states:

> Parents and other legal representatives of the child may appropriately, according to their judgment, discipline the child, for avoiding to carry out his duties and for disciplinary infractions, with the exception of corporal punishment and any other form of violence.
> *GIEACPC 2017b*

Opposition to legislation by the state with regard to corporal punishment usually takes the form that parents should not be told how to handle their own children. This was expressed in the case of Klein (mentioned previously); after he was acquitted he commented, "We should be running our own children and our own families." Rudy Cannon, one of the jurors on the case, agreed, "The government needs to keep its nose out of this" (Lecker n.d.). Steven Pinker summarizes this common argument:

> In one frame of mind, this meddling is a totalitarian imposition of state power into the intimate sphere of the family. But, in another, it is part of the historical current trend toward a recognition of the autonomy of individuals. Children are people, and like adults they have a right to life and limb (and genitalia) that is secured by the social contract that empowers the state. The fact that other individuals—their parents—stake a claim of ownership over them cannot negate that right.
> *Pinker 2011: 437*

Pinker cites other areas where the state exercises authority in areas of family life where there is less debate, such as "compulsory schooling, mandatory vaccination, the removal of children from abusive homes, the imposition of lifesaving medical care over the objections of religious parents, and the prohibition of female genital cutting by communities of Muslim immigrants in European countries" (Pinker 2011: 437).

The United States, with no ban on corporal punishment in the home, no ban on corporal punishment in private schools, and 19 states still allowing corporal punishment in public schools, lags behind Europe, and now other parts of the world, in legislation to prohibit the use of corporal punishment.

Where Now?

> International human rights law is clear that children have a right to legal protection from all corporal punishment in all settings of their lives.
> —*GIEACPC 2013*

The United Nations Convention on the Rights of the Child was adopted on November 20, 1989. At the time of writing the United States is the only United Nations state not to have ratified it (UNTC 2017). On the twenty-fifth anniversary of the passing of the convention the *Washington Post* reported:

> Twenty-five years ago this week, 190 member countries of the United Nations passed the Convention on the Rights of the Child, a landmark agreement that stands as one of the most ratified human treaties in history. . . . It includes the right to protection

from discrimination based on their parent's or legal guardian's sex, race, religion and a host of other identifiers.

Attiah 2014

President Bill Clinton signed the UN Treaty in 1995, but it has never attained the two-thirds majority in a Senate vote to enable it to be ratified. In Articles 19, 28, and 37 the treaty can be interpreted as prohibiting corporal punishment (GIEACPC 2017c). Ratifying the Convention on the Rights of the Child would be a positive step forward in prohibiting violence against children.

It is likely, as happened in Sweden, that should a law be passed to abolish the use of corporal punishment in schools and homes, the practice would diminish over time. As children mature and eventually have their own families, corporal punishment would cease to be their first thought as a form of discipline. Child clinical psychologist Jean Durrant noted this change of opinion: "Over the course of three decades, public attitudes have undergone a major shift; whereas a majority of Swedes believed in the necessity of corporal punishment in 1965, only a small minority support its use today" (Durrant 1996).

One common response to the abolition of corporal punishment in both schools and homes is that it remains a necessary last resort in the disciplining of children. Straus debunks this, and many of the common myths surrounding the use of corporal punishment, in his chapter "Ten Myths That Perpetuate Corporal Punishment" (Straus 2001: 149–162). He claims that these myths are "grounded in society's beliefs that spanking is effective and relatively harmless" (Straus 2001: 162).

Psychologists and educators have written increasingly on ways of child discipline that are nonviolent. Collectively these scholars make suggestions of methods and philosophies that, in their experience, have proved effective (see Aldridge and Aldridge 1987; Arnall 2007; Brendtro, Brokenleg, and Bockern 2002; Curwin and Mendler 1997; Mackenzie 2001; Noddings 2002, 2005, 2007; and Rosenberg 2003, 2005a, 2005b). These methods are helpful to any caregiver or educator wishing to embrace nonviolence. Yet, as helpful as methods are, a social, personal, intentional, and determined commitment to be nonviolent toward children is paramount. In this regard, a neo-Aristotelian understanding of the habituation of nonviolent actions, together with the development of nonviolent character traits for parents and caregivers, is essential (Fitz-Gibbon and Fitz-Gibbon 2016: 121–132).

Conclusion

Violence toward children is always an emotive subject. Pictures and stories of children who have suffered abuse always evoke strong feelings. In this chapter I have exposed a more insipid type of violence, the hidden legalized violence of corporal punishment, including spanking, hitting, and paddling—all actions used with the intent to cause pain.

The UNICEF report reminds us that it is the task of everyone to try to reduce violence against children: "Violence against children is widespread but not inevitable. Bringing it to an end is a shared responsibility" (UNICEF 2014). In 2001, Straus was hopeful that one day there would be an end to the practice:

> We can look forward to the day when children in almost all countries have the benefit of being brought up without being hit by their parents; and just as important, to the day when many nations have the benefit of the healthier, wealthier, and wiser citizens who were brought up free from the violence that is now a part of their earliest and most influential life experiences.

Straus 2001: 215

At the time of writing, 16 years later, many nations around the world have moved to a more humane treatment of children. Steven Pinker in his *The Better Angels of Our Nature* argues that as general violence is slowly and steadily on the decline in society, our better angels suggest that violence against children, too, ought to have our attention (Pinker 2011: 415ff). However, in the United States, much remains the same, and children remain the single most violated group in society. It is time for philosophers of nonviolence and activists alike to turn their attention to this neglected facet of nonviolence.

Works Cited

ACLU. (2009). "Impairing Education: Corporal Punishment of Students with Disabilities in Public Schools." Available at: www.aclu.org/impairing-education-corporal-punishment-students-disabilities-us-public-schools-html (Accessed 19 March 2017).
Aldridge, B., and J. Aldridge. (1987). *Children and Nonviolence*. Pasadena, CA: Hope Publishing House.
Arnall, J. (2007). *Discipline Without Distress*. Calgary: Professional Parenting Canada.
Attiah, K. (2014). "Why Won't the U.S. Ratify the U.N.'s Child Rights Treaty?" *Washington Post* November 21. Available at: www.washingtonpost.com/blogs/post-partisan/wp/2014/11/21/why-wont-the-u-s-ratify-the-u-n-s-child-rights-treaty/?utm_term=.be670ca267d6 (Accessed 2 April 2017).
Brendtro, L. K., M. Brokenleg, and S. V. Bockern. (2002). *Reclaiming Youth at Risk: Our Hope for the Future*. Bloomingdale, FL: National Education Service.
Briere, J. N. (1992). *Child Abuse Trauma: Theory and Treatment of the Lasting Effects*. Newbury Park: Sage.
Carr, S. (2014). "Why Are Black Students Being Paddled More in the Public Schools?" *The Hechinger Report*. Available at: http://hechingerreport.org/controversy-corporal-punishment-public-schools-painful-racial-subtext/ (Accessed 26 March 2017).
Curwin, R. L., and A. N. Mendler. (1997). *As Tough as Necessary: Countering Violence, Aggression and Hostility in Our Schools*. Alexandria, VA: Association for Supervision and Curriculum Development.
Dodd, C. (2011). *Ending Corporal Punishment of Children: A Handbook for Working with and Within Religious Communities*. Nottingham: Russell Press.
Durrant, J. E. (1996). "The Swedish Ban on Corporal Punishment: Its History and Effects." Available at: www.nospank.net/durrant.htm (Accessed 14 March 2017).
Finkelhor, D. (1979). *Sexually Victimized Children*. New York: Free Press.
Finkelhor, D. (1986). *A Sourcebook on Child Sexual Abuse*. Newbury Park: Sage.
Finkelhor, D., and L. Jones. (2006). "Why Have Child Maltreatment and Child Victimization Declined?" *Journal of Social Issues* 62 (4): 685–716.
Finkelhor, D., R. J. Geles, G. T. Hotaling, and M.A. Straus. (1983). *The Dark Side of Families: Current Family Violence Research*. Thousand Oaks: Sage.
Fitz-Gibbon, J. H. (2017). *Corporal Punishment, Religion and United States Public Schools*. New York: Palgrave Macmillan.
Fitz-Gibbon, J. H., and A. Fitz-Gibbon. (2016). *Welcoming Strangers: Nonviolent Re-Parenting of Children in Foster Care*. New Brunswick: Transaction.
Gerbner, G., C. J. Ross, and E. Zigler. (1980). *Child Abuse: An Agenda for Action*. Oxford: Oxford University Press.
Gershoff, E. T., and A. Grogan-Kaylor. (2016). "Spanking and Child Outcomes: Old Controversies and New Meta-Analyses." *Journal of Family Psychology* 30, June: 453–469. Available at: www.ncbi.nlm.nih.gov/pubmed/27055181 (Accessed 14 March 2017).
Global Initiative to End All Corporal Punishment of Children. (2013). "Review of Research on the Effects of Corporal Punishment: Working Paper." Available at: www.endcorporalpunishment.org/assets/pdfs/research-summaries/Review-research-effects-corporal-punishment-June-2016.pdf (Accessed 7 March 2017).
Global Initiative to End All Corporal Punishment of Children. (2017a). "Countdown to Universal Prohibition." Available at: www.endcorporalpunishment.org/progress/countdown.html (Accessed 14 March 2017).
Global Initiative to End All Corporal Punishment of Children. (2017b). "Prohibition of All Corporal Punishment in Lithuania." Available at: www.endcorporalpunishment.org/progress/prohibiting-states/lithuania.html (Accessed 14 March 2017).

Global Initiative to End All Corporal Punishment of Children. (2017c). "Convention on the Rights of the Child." Available at: www.endcorporalpunishment.org/prohibiting-corporal-punishment/hrlaw/crc/ (Accessed 14 March 2017).

Greven, P. (1992). *Spare the Child: The Religious Roots of Punishment and the Psychological Impact of Physical Abuse*. New York: Vintage Books.

Grieshaber, S. (2004). *Rethinking Parent and Child Conflict*. New York: Routledge Farmer.

Grisham, L. (2015). "Father Requests Police Presence When Spanking Child." Available at: www.abc10.com/news/father-requests-police-presence-when-spanking-child/183539459 (Accessed 24 January 2017).

Gumbrecht, J. (2011). "In Sweden, a Generation of Kids Who Have Never Been Spanked." *CNN*. Available at: www.cnn.com/2011/11/09/world/sweden-punishment-ban/ (Accessed 14 March 2017).

Harris, P. (2013). "Four in Five Americans Believe Parents Spanking Their Children Is Sometimes Appropriate." Available at: www.theharrispoll.com/health-and-life/Four_in_Five_Americans_Believe_Parents_Spanking_Their_Children_is_Sometimes_Appropriate.html (Accessed 16 January 2017).

Hezakya News. (2016). "Georgia Principle Paddles 5-Year-Old, Threatens Boy's Mom with Jail if She Interferes." Available at: www.youtube.com/watch?v=752gpRNPSRw (Accessed 14 March 2017).

Human Rights Watch. "Impairing Education: Corporal Punishment of Students with Disabilities in US Public Schools." August 10, 2009. https://www.hrw.org/report/2009/08/10/impairing-education/corporal-punishment-students-disabilities-us-public-schools

Hyman, I. A., and P. A. Snook. (1999). *Dangerous Schools: What We Can Do About the Physical and Emotional Abuse of Our Children*. San Francisco: Jossey-Bass.

Ingraham v. Wright. (1977). "U.S. Supreme Court." Available at: https://supreme.justia.com/cases/federal/us/430/651/case.html (Accessed 7 March 2017).

Ingram, C. (n.d.). "Discipline with Action and Words." Available at: www.focusonthefamily.com/parenting/effective-biblical-discipline/effective-child-discipline/discipline-with-action-and-words (Accessed 22 May 2017).

Ipsos, M. (2007). "A Study into the Views of Parents on the Physical Punishment of Children for the Department for Children, Schools and Families (DCSF)." Available at: http://dera.ioe.ac.uk/6886/8/Section%2058%20Parental%20Survey.pdf (Accessed 29 May 2017).

Lecker, K. (n.d.). "Court Case Over Son's Spanking Still Stings Dad." Available at: www.calesariclaw.com/Articles-Table-of-Contents/Court-Case-Over-Son-s-Spanking-Still-Stings-Dad.shtml (Accessed 14 March 2017).

Lee, V. (1979). "A Legal Analysis of Ingraham v. Wright." Available at: www.corpun.com/usscr5.htm (Accessed 12 March 2017).

Locke, J. (1689). *The Works of John Locke*, vol. 1: *An Essay Concerning Human Understanding*. Available at: http://oll.libertyfund.org/titles/locke-the-works-vol-1-an-essay-concerning-human-understanding-part-1 (Accessed 24 March 2017).

Mackenzie, R. J. (2001). *Setting Limits with Your Strong-Willed Child*. New York: Three Rivers.

Miller, A. (1997). *Breaking Down the Walls of Silence: The Liberating Experience of Facing Painful Truth*, translated by S. Worrall. New York: Meridian.

Newell, P. (1989). *Children Are People Too: The Case Against Physical Punishment*. London: Bedford Square Press.

Noddings, N. (2002). *Educating Moral People: A Caring Alternative to Character Education*. New York: Teachers College Press.

Noddings, N. (2005). *The Challenge to Care in Schools: An Alternate Approach to Education*. New York: Teachers College Press.

Noddings, N. (2007). *Philosophy of Education*. Boulder, CO: Westview Press.

Pais, M. S. (2016). "Violence Against Children." Available at: http://srsg.violenceagainstchildren.org/story/2016-12-28_1522 (Accessed 14 March 2017).

Pinker, S. (2011). *The Better Angels of Our Nature: Why Violence Has Declined*. New York: Viking.

Religions for Peace. (2006). "The Kyoto Declaration on Confronting Violence and Advancing Shared Security." Available at: http://rfp.org/sites/default/files/pubications/Kyoto%20Declaration%20-%20Final%20Draft.pdf (Accessed 29 May 2017).

Robinson, B. (2015). "Sheriff's Deputy Called to Home to Witness Father Spanking His Daughter with a Paddle to Make Sure He Wasn't Committing a Crime." Available at: www.corpun.com/15archive/usd01501.htm#25837 (Accessed 24 January 2017).

Rosenberg, M. B. (2003). *Nonviolent Communication: A Language of Life*. Encinitas, CA: PuddleDancer Press.

Rosenberg, M. B. (2005a). *We Can Work it Out: Resolving Conflicts Peacefully and Powerfully*. Encinitas, CA: PuddleDancer Press.

Rosenberg, M. B. (2005b). *Raising Children Compassionately: Parenting the Nonviolent Communication Way*. Encinitas, CA: PuddleDancer Press.

Rousseau, J.-J. (2009). *Emile*, translated by B. Foxley. LaVergne, TN: BookJungle.

Samuel, H. (2017). "France Bans Smacking, Raising Pressure on UK to Follow Suit." Available at: www.telegraph.co.uk/news/2017/01/03/france-bans-smacking-raising-pressure-uk-follow-suit/ (Accessed 14 March 2017).

Straus, M. A. (2001). *Beating the Devil Out of Them: Corporal Punishment in American Families and Its Effects on Children*. New Brunswick: Transaction.

Straus, M. A., E. M. Douglas, and R. A. Medeiros. (2014). *The Primordial Violence: Spanking Children, Psychological Development, Violence and Crime*. New York: Routledge.

Straus, M. A., R. Gelles, and S. K. Steinmetz. (2006). *Behind Closed Doors: Violence in the American Family*. New York: Routledge.

Taylor, L., and A. Maurer. (n.d.). "No Vital Organs There, So They Say." Available at: http://nospank.net/taylor.htm (Accessed 22 May 2017).

UNICEF. (2014). "Hidden in Plain Sight: A Statistical Analysis of Violence Against Children." Available at: www.unicef.org/publications/index_74865.html (Accessed 22 March 2017).

United Nations Treaty Collection. (2017). "Human Rights: Convention on the Rights of the Child." Available at: https://treaties.un.org/Pages/ViewDetails.aspx?src=IND&mtdsg_no=IV-11&chapter=4&clang=_en (Accessed 2 April 2017).

U.S. Department of Health and Human Services. (2014). "Child Maltreatment 2014." Available at: www.acf.hhs.gov/sites/default/files/cb/cm2014.pdf (Accessed 17 March 2017).

Webb, W. J. (2011). *Corporal Punishment in the Bible: A Redemptive-Movement Hermeneutic for Troubling Texts*. Downers Grove: IVP Academics.

31
PEACE PEDAGOGY FROM THE BORDERLINES

Renee Bricker, Yi Deng, Donna A. Gessell, and Michael Proulx

This chapter is about our combined experience teaching about peace in a course that was funded by a grant from the National Endowment for the Humanities focused on "Enduring Questions." One enduring question is "What *is* peace?" It may seem that the answer is self-evident, only its path to realization tangled, obscure, and impossible to sustain. That is certainly the assumption of our students. Yet the question "what is peace" is an enduring one, without a single answer. Therefore, the underlying assumption of the course we have developed is that concepts of peace are mutable: they change with time, as well as with cultural, religious, and geopolitical perspectives. Our challenge is to resist the urge to arrive at a final definition, or even to develop a map for constructing peace in a modern conflict. Rather, we and our students repeatedly ask ourselves what peace is as we try to unpack its variegated meanings. Our task together is critical, made acute because this will be the only course about peace our students will ever encounter during their tenure at our university. Our goal, at once modest and ambitious, is to instigate thought about peace; to provoke discussion, and exploration; to render peace worthy of seriousness, challenging the old-fashioned stereotypes many of our students may share that peace is a mere relic of a bygone Vietnam "hippie" era or an unobtainable fantasy.

Instead, and together with them, we scrutinize many of the linguistic and historical conditions of peace amid the lacunae of the broader strokes rendered by wars that comprise so much of recorded history (Boulding 2000: 16). Like war, peace happened, too. This startles many students. Often history or political science courses ignore, or fail to make explicit, the reality that many accomplishments in history require freedom from direct violence. Because peace, unlike war, lacks a narrative arc, it often *seems* more difficult to grasp. Peace can seem ambiguous or even irrelevant, for example, often muted in survey history courses.

Further complicating our questioning of peace, our students are a homogeneous group young enough to have grown up in an America always at war with an elusive enemy characterized popularly by its religious and ethnic identity as Muslim-Arab. So, we begin our guided intellectual journey with surprise as they discover that peace, as a concept, might be defined differently across chronology and cultures. For example in the Western world, countries are assumed to be at peace unless they declare war; in Islamic history, countries are assumed to be at war unless peace is made through respectful recognition. At first, students are bewildered to learn that there is more than one kind of peace. Even more so, that there is more than one kind of violence seems revelatory at the course's beginning. By uncovering the multivalence of violence, we and our students can begin to identify and grapple with the potential fault lines of sustaining peace.

Our experience provides a microcosm of some challenges in peace education. This course was offered in a university environment without a formal peace studies program, on a campus that is also oriented toward military culture. "Visions of Peace in the East and West," as we call our course, and the Enduring Questions proposal to the National Endowment for the Humanities that funded its creation in 2014, is rooted in controversial observations by peace theorist Johan Galtung. For instance, among what he defines as structural and cultural violence, he identifies high school JROTC and ROTC programs, while noting that the integration of the military into American education is particularly egregious (Galtung 1969). This clashes with our institutional climate, for our university—the University of North Georgia—is one of the six senior military colleges in the United States. Our students certainly do not share Galtung's equation of campus military with structural and cultural violence; therefore, this provides a departure point for asking our students whether, and how, their experiences comport with Galtung's assumptions.

Likewise, in the same essay, Galtung suggests that disciplinary "borderlines" ought not demarcate the field of peace research. Peace, he argues, is too crucial to global fate and "attractive to the inquisitive mind" (Galtung 1990). We interpret this as a challenge that is also an invitation, "to new disciplines to join the quest for peace" (Galtung 1990). In this Galtungian spirit of curious minds along the borderlines, we seize his invitation to cross disciplinary boundaries into the field of peace studies inspired, in equal parts, by his observations about a militarized campus culture, and the urgent attraction of peace.

We offer lessons learned as non-specialists engaging in questions about peace with skeptical students. These include experiences of course structure and its content comprised of documentary encounters with peace, as well as our own development as faculty and scholars. Moreover, we contribute to a current conversation in peace education scholarship that seeks to de-center Western peace paradigms and insist on "critical education," defined as interrogating assumptions, including our own, and contexts (Spencer and Shogimen 2014; Borg and Grech 2017). As teachers concerned with global encounters within our respective disciplines, we affirm the conviction that a peace course must include non-Western sources. Therefore, what follows is a discussion of course contexts and its description, including activities, student engagement with peace, and finally our reflections.

Course Context: Our Teaching and Learning Environment

Our learning environment is central to understanding what the course does as well as its limitations. The utility of our example is in what it may suggest about structure and content for peace courses absent institutional programs of peace education, and for students who do not view peace as either complex or a realistic goal. Neither do many of our students see themselves as political or historical actors; many of them are at university with modest dreams to make a better life for themselves.

The exposition developed in this chapter proceeds from Galtung's remarks and is twofold, each with its own set of challenges. First, our geographic setting is that of a public, southern United States, primarily traditional undergraduate university that draws from mostly middle-class exurban students. Like many U.S. communities in our post-9/11 culture, ours does not usually question the infrastructure of violence. Military and police are heroized. The U.S. Constitution's Second Amendment is venerated.[1] This matters because affection for the right to bear arms is one that is commonly accepted, both in daily life with concealed carry as customary and pastimes such as hunting and shooting normalized, and in popular cultural representations of brutal savagery such as in films and video games, with settings both domestic and international (Darder 2017: 98–99). In these aspects, our institutional experience is much like others in that our students do not question violence.

However, secondly, an even larger influence on all that we do is our designation as a senior military college. Though cadets comprise fewer than 10 percent of one of our five campuses, military culture shapes and defines the institution. The military drill field is at the center of the campus with classroom, administrative, dining, and dormitory buildings encircling. Cadet events bookend the academic year, with FROG (Freshman Recruit Orientation Group) week at each semester's beginning and the ceremony to commission new officers during commencement at each semester's end. Daily reveille and taps, flag raising and lowering, and the discharge of the howitzer that begins and ends the workday are rituals for us all, as we stand motionless and in silence when outdoors during these ceremonies. As rituals these create and affirm, in this instance, the military culture of our state-designated leadership institute. The effect may be amplified in the small environment of this campus surrounded by the foothills of the Appalachian Mountains, creating a kind of intimacy reinforced by the Army values of loyalty, duty, respect, selfless service, honor, integrity, and personal courage. These values are practiced in competitive leadership experiences combining formal classroom instruction and tactical simulations, within a 24-7 living and learning community setting. With this perspective, even while practicing violence, cadets are taught its role—its time and place—and are often introduced to ways of questioning more sophisticated than those of their civilian peers. We groom military officers, women and men who, even if they do not commission, nevertheless bring this background into their lives and careers. Civilian students share in this military culture too, many choosing to attend the institution because the cultural values permeate both the co-curricular and the academic.

In this environment, it would not be an exaggeration to state that the students who enroll in our seminar do so either because they know and appreciate the faculty members involved, or because of expediency in that it meets scheduling and curriculum requirements. They are also curious: Why would a whole course be devoted to the examination of peace? What could it possibly be about? Doubtless this would not be an uncommon reaction of students elsewhere. It is in this intellectual context that we ask our students, repeatedly, the seemingly "outlandish question," as one cadet originally put it: "What is peace?" And, more ridiculously, "How might peace be obtained, then sustained?" In short, most of these students, perhaps like many others, are not harboring a driving passion to understand and wage peace. These are all reasons why we thought we *needed* to engage in a conversation about it with our students, who, though in possession of the inquisitive minds Galtung anticipated, do not begin their quest imagining that peace or violence are more complicated than "whether or not bullets are flying."

Because none of us has an academic background in peace education, or studies, we perhaps approach our driving question, "What is peace?," with a certain disciplinary naïveté. We each come to this subject from the vantage of our respective humanities fields: English, history, and philosophy. Grounded in their correspondent disciplinary tools of close reading, textual analysis, contexts of production and reception of texts, and iconography, our students, mostly juniors and seniors, join us on an intellectual quest to interrogate peace first conceptually, and then in practice. Our approach responds to current calls for critical education and interdisciplinary approaches to peace studies, for example in recent work by Carmel Borg and Michael Grech, and elsewhere in this volume by Nel Noddings (Borg and Grech 2017). Therefore, ours is an inquiry from across the academic borderlines, as well as from the perspectives of future military officers and uncertain civilian undergraduates.

Course Description: Structure

Despite being a course that purports to be about peace, the syllabus is nevertheless organized according to categories of violence and war. Thus, its structure betrays our assumption that peace and violence are dependent upon each other for definition and distinction. We are aware, therefore, that we have at its outset built in an implicit dichotomy. Arranged according to four topics representative of the kinds of violence we identify as important to us, the course starts with approaches to war that address the psychological, biological, philosophical, and intercultural. The second topics, religion and violence, and third topics, politics, culture, and violence, culminate with the fourth, non-violent resistance. Each of these is further subdivided into global geographical and chronological areas that begin with the ancient classical worlds of China, India, Greece, and Rome through medieval Europe, the early modern era, and European Enlightenment, culminating in contemporary non-violent resistance. We point out that the periodization we use makes little sense outside of the West; for example, Chinese history is demarcated according to dynasty, thus it makes no sense to speak of its medieval period. Current debates about peace and violence bookend the course because we find it useful to start with the familiar, to begin with where students are themselves in time and place. Our weekly discussions also consider relevant current events in light of course materials.

We assume students need a base from which to begin their course inquiry. Primary sources such as philosophical treatises, declarations, letters, images, literary texts, and early books are the main grist for reflection and discussion. Yet engagement with these is enhanced with some preparation. To build an introduction to the landscape of peace and aggression, students begin with selections from David Barash's reader to provide a contemporary general overview of peace studies and exploration of human behavior (Barash 2013). These are complemented by excerpts from Douglas P. Fry's provocative collection of essays, which at once lay out and destabilize evolutionary assumptions of human aggression (Fry 2015). While these are not fixed choices in every iteration, the objective to prepare students to undertake the demands of the course remains constant.

It may seem obvious to include, but initially we overlooked violence as a category of preparation to study peace. This oversight stemmed from our assumptions that students would be alert to violences in society besides war. We assumed, that is, that they see the violence we see in the world that surrounds us. In response, we asked ourselves, what do our students need to know about violence to study peace?

Course Description: From Violence to Peace

In an early course offering, one student complained that "for a course on peace, we really spend a lot of time examining and talking about violence." This is true and, as we were startled to learn, necessary. Notably, violence seems more familiar, perhaps because of a combination of popular culture and histories of war that dominate the study students experience in history, political science, and international relations courses. This presumption of acquaintance with violence occurs even though students overwhelmingly describe their individual lives as peaceful. War is often a default response to foreign enemy action because "tough action" can seem to be a matter of national honor, masculine identity, and paternalism.[2] A reflex to war rests comfortably with the cultural violence Galtung identifies as reinforced by popular articulations that glorify war and violence in movies, cartoons, music, and other types of popular media. But direct violence is only its most patent expression, not an explanatory device. *Why* can violence seem irresistible, inevitable, or necessary, while peace can seem irrelevant, impossible, or dull? We have embarrassed discussions about this. Some of the faculty and students alike guiltily confess liking an action adventure film where people perhaps get killed and things explode. Uncovering this attraction, related to what Julia Kristeva calls the "power of horror," is the provenance of another field of study (Kristeva 1982: 3–5). Yet violence *must* mean something more than its blatant expressions.

But this gets ahead of things. Our first challenge is to dislodge students' confidence about meanings of "peace" and "violence." We realize a need to replicate with our students some of what we experienced ourselves in our preparation and development of this course. An example of how we meet this challenge is our use of Galtung and Arendt, and, perhaps less predictably, in offering Hobbes as a departure point.

As with the apparent acquaintance with violence, Hobbes is familiar enough to students that they recognize his words because of their prior experiences with Western Enlightenment sources. For students, Hobbes provides safe ground in an otherwise unfamiliar world of non-Western source material. In different iterations of this course, some students take refuge in his pronouncement of the natural state of human nature as basically corrupt. Questions of why peace was not sustainable in a particular historical context, such as why the ancient Greeks understood war as a "zero-sum" endeavor, are dismissively answered with recourse to Hobbes' explanations of human nature and the lack of peace in the world: human beings are just plain bad, and Hobbes proves it. Many easily express this confidence that the old man hit the nail on the head, so to speak. Moreover, Hobbes' conclusion corresponds with many of their religious views of a fallen and sinful humanity, so his verdict seems an obvious truth. Yet, is it so obvious, or true?

Ironically, Hobbes provides a constructive inauguration to modern thinking about violence and peace. While it is true that Hobbes did not think highly of human nature, students' recollections invariably strip the context from his most famous quotations from *Leviathan*. Helpfully recalling his historical context—that he had in mind his own experiences of the seventeenth-century English Civil War—we return Hobbes' insights and concerns to their context. This shifts how students view his pronouncements on human nature: he was witness to life in a state of war and violence. Hobbes, it turns out, was not quite the man many of them thought they knew.

For instance, of fighting he said that were three main reasons: competition, lack of self-confidence (diffidence), and glory (see Hobbes 1651: 95). When they read Hannah Arendt's declaration that "power and violence are opposites . . . violence appears where power is in jeopardy," she seems to echo his observation that diffidence is a reason people fight (Arendt 1969: 21). What restrains these impulses are a common power, for "without a common Power to keep them all in awe, they are in that condition which is called Warre" (Hobbes 1651: 96). Students' discussions and papers show that many agree with enthusiasm that global peace is only possible with one strong world government, although a global government is certainly not what Hobbes had in mind. Curiously, none of them wants to live under a single global authority. How do they deal with this contradiction? What students believe about human nature—leaving aside debates about its validity as a category—is central to how they react to peace as ideal and as experience. Hobbes reassures some of them because he seems to validate many of their conclusions about human behavior and remedies.

In the same section where he enumerates reasons for fighting, he raises peace: "The Passions that encline men to Peace, are Feare of Death; Desire of such things as are necessary to commodious living; and a Hope by their Industry to obtain them" (Hobbes 1651: 96). Here the door opens to discussion of negative and positive peace (Galtung 1969). Does Hobbes seem to suggest that to maintain peace, people need assurances of what modern audiences might identify as issues of social justice and political stability? In this same section, he seems to say that there can be no such thing as a just war. To join these two words together—just war—presents both an illogical language construction and a manifestly impossible reality. Why? Because a state of war itself is lawless: without a common (to the combatants) power there can be no law; without law there can be no right, or wrong; and without this measurement, there cannot be justice, or injustice. Therefore, it makes no sense to speak of war as "just." He then makes perhaps his best-known—and most misunderstood—pronouncement: in a state of war there can be no industry, art, innovation, farming, learning: "[W]orst of all [is] continual fear and danger of violent death; *And the life of man solitary, poor, nasty, brutish, and short*" (Hobbes 1651: 96, italics added). This final pronouncement is not Hobbes' assessment of human life generally, but—and this is crucial—*life in a state of war*. Many students are astonished because the quotation is often taken to represent Hobbes' stark assessment of humanity and human nature. However, its context alters that association. They learn that, for Hobbes, peace is such an urgent goal that he advocates some surrender of personal liberties to obtain it. Thus Hobbes proves to be a springboard for discussion of kinds of peace.

To complicate matters we pivot next to Arendt and Galtung on violence and power. In contrast, Arendt seems to define violence narrowly in terms of what Galtung calls direct violence. Once again this equation is familiar to students. Yet, her distinction between power and violence, the latter a means to the former, or reaction by the former to a perceived diminishment, presents an intellectual challenge because many students want to argue instead that violence *is* a sign of power (Arendt 1969: 1, 15). Galtung and Arendt agree, for different reasons, that violence is not the opposite of peace. For Arendt, violence is a means that uses implements, or tools: think weapons. For Galtung, violence is triangular. It includes killing and maiming, the direct violence that Arendt considers and that students largely see as its only definition; but, it is also the repression inherent in structural violence, and the facets of cultural context that make violence "seem, if not right, at least not wrong" (Galtung 1990: 291).

Related to parsing violence is comprehending toleration. After all, is not toleration a path to peace? Here George Carey's definition, echoed by Susan Mendus, undermines that conclusion (Mendus 2000: 3). First, there are conditions that no society ought to tolerate; but second, and just as important, toleration requires discomfort or disapproval (MacIntyre 2000: 136, 151; Mendus 2000: 3). Here, we tread close to the boundary of conflict resolution; but wrestling with what defines peace, violence, and tolerance shows that none of these fit into neat interpretive compartments. Now students are confronted with definitions of violence that make questions of peace vexing to answer. With some grounding in discourses of violence, students are ready to think about it as polymorphous; thus, they are better prepared to think that peace could, did, and does mean many things. Also, they are ready to consider that every peace may not be a peace worth maintaining.

Course Description: What *Is* Peace?

Students read Eastern and Western sources of peace that mostly follow a chronological pattern; however, a thematic approach is at work as well. As professors in humanities fields, we approach each source with our students asking the usual questions about author, audience, context, reception. Put another way, we ask the old-fashioned "Five Ws" to examine texts: who, what, when, where, and why (and how). Then, we ask students to think about how the ideas in the texts interact with one another. In other words, we ask that they imagine conversations between the texts, the authors, the ideas. As the semester progresses, students come to do this on their own.

In addition to discussion, students write a research paper, and they work on a reading project, choosing to do so either collaboratively or individually, on their choice of books from a provided list including novels, with the task of answering what its message of peace is. Most students have questioned the attainability of peace in reality, especially when they consider the nature of peace and its relation to conflict. From the preparation they receive on violence, our students learn that "conflict" does not merely refer to war or physical violence, but also includes value disagreement and direct confrontation. Thus, they use concepts developed by Galtung and Arendt as heuristic frameworks for parsing sources they encounter. Debates on human nature and aggression are lively, and the problem of "in-group amity, out-group enmity" adds to their wrestling with constructions of peace. In their reading projects, they connect, for example, issues of our inner states of peace and conflict with a book project chosen from among *Slaughterhouse Five*, *Fiasco: The American Military Adventure in Iraq*, *Jarhead*, *Beasts of No Nation*, and *Generation Kill*. They can also focus on psychological experiments, such as the Stanford prison and Milgram experiments.

Even without thematic orchestration, on their own in research projects, students often juxtapose thinkers from different times and places with one another. For example, we encourage students to consider how the contextual conditions for peace can unsettle political and social relationships. This is a particular challenge because our student population is not especially diverse. Thus, we depend on a wide variety of sources to inspire them to consider other ways of seeing and thinking. This approach is also valid for more diverse learning environments that nonetheless often privilege Western paradigms of war and peace. At course's end, students have some tools to describe, in personal terms, individual, social, and cultural values that have influenced aspects of violence and peace.

Some general themes emerge from students' reflections on the definition of peace: the multiplicity of perspectives, the need to respect those differences, and the challenge to do so as well as to ascertain whether any of them is more attainable and sustainable than the others. As the course begins, the many perspectives of peace seem strange. However, students appreciate a variety of viewpoints on the concept of peace in differing historical and cultural contexts. Especially intriguing to them are those far from their original backgrounds: for example, Greek *eirene*, Confucian harmony, Daoist spontaneity, *pax Romana*, Christian pacifism, Hindu *dharma*, Islamic *jihad*, Gandhi's *ahimsa*. Some of these, *pax Romana*, Christian pacifism, or Islam's *jihad*, for instance, students believe they already know. Yet confrontation with the primary sources, whether the patristic authors of Christianity, who debated Jesus' meaning of "turn the other cheek," or excerpts from the Qu'ran that explicitly restrain violence in war, disturb what they feel sure about.

Adopting comparative methods encourages students to use journals as a platform to seek their own definitions of peace through responses to the readings. They constantly compare and contrast different cultures, societies, and historical periods organically as they wrestle with what peace means at different times to different people. Taken a step further, questions arise about the validity of, or applicability of, those sometimes contending ideas in other contexts. For example, what does peace mean in Athens and Sparta, or Christianity and the Roman Empire? Students assume Christianity is more peaceful than Islam until confronted with scriptural texts from each.

Does Confucianism or legalism, Hinduism or Buddhism offer better notions of, and paths to, peace than Western ideas? Would those ideas work in the West, and why? Where are they similar? What happens when Machiavelli is arranged next to Dr. Martin Luther King, Jr. and Malcolm X, as one student did in a research project? This is a particularly nettlesome juxtaposition because students believe, as with Hobbes, that they know Machiavelli, or Dr. King. Machiavelli opens a door to rhetoric that points to a way to attend to how concepts are framed and the importance of words. Reading Dr. King's "Letter from a Birmingham Jail," for example, or Malcolm X's "Confronting White Oppression," through the eyes of Machiavelli's use of language, one student observed that it was not simply the words the two men used, but how they framed their thoughts and movements (King 1963). Although this would be obvious to academics, perhaps, this student changed from thinking peace impossible to realizing that rhetoric has both the power to provoke and legitimate war, and the power to inspire people to non-violent reform, and peace. Again, this may seem obvious, but our student came to this independent of instructor persuasion.

Many students are also certain that peace is only possible with a strong leader, a single global government. However, the matter of peace is further complicated with Bentham and Kant, Gandhi and the *Laws of Manu*, Athenian democracy and Enlightenment democracy, Roman glory and Hindu *dharma*. In this course we displace Western texts to compel engagement with the non-Western. Students respond well to this because they like encountering what is less familiar.

Significant Learning Experiences: An Example

Mining Eastern and Western, as well as ancient and contemporary, sources, our students make new connections among elements of peace to discover universal concepts of peace that could unite the global experience, always negotiating assumptions and expectations. Perhaps the most significant learning experiences are the comparative opportunities between notions of governance, its ideals, and its purposes.

An extended example illustrates how we negotiate with our students three areas of interest in ancient differences: (1) Mediterranean civilizations and China, (2) how these geographically separate regions formulated an understanding of peace in terms of communal identity, and (3) how they perceive others beyond as members of their communities. Early modern comparative works between Machiavelli and Huang Zongxi that deal with the establishment of the ideal ruler and, therefore, a peaceful state reveal curious similarities, challenging us to discuss the limits of establishing a peaceful world.

In our discussions, our desire to see ourselves in ancient Greek and Roman civilizations is largely brought to sobering correction: many of us are willing to acknowledge that we have embraced their cultural worldviews. Contrary to preconceived expectations, these Mediterranean societies reflect a narrower view of community, absent of concepts of modern peace promoting cultural egalitarianism. Our search for any such modern ideals of a universal peace finds no such perspective among Greeks and Romans. Insentient competition and internal discord (*agon*) and strife (*eris*) between states hamstrung ancient Greek society to the point that victory was driven by a view of "zero-sum" by most. A popular story of a Greek farmer in competition with his neighbor illustrates the point: when the farmer finds out that his neighbor produces twice as much as whatever he does, he prays to a god to pluck out one of his own eyes in the hope that his neighbor will experience his fortune double-fold. Likewise, Homer's epics are filled with the tragic moral lessons that this behavior produces, and the deep sense of undercutting one another remains a constant theme in Greek history. In fact, Greek states fought more of their wars against each other than against the Persians. Thus, we discover that this culture of internal antagonism plaguing the Greek world came to an end only from external intervention in the late fourth century BCE by Philip of Macedon; his conquest of Greece produced the closest concept of a universal peace among the city-states. His unification platform was achieved, in part, by promoting himself as a unifier with plans to invade Persia. The solitary concept of universal peace among Greek cities was conceived through both egotism and the prism of war against another culture.

Romans differed little from the Greek experience in their insular view of peace. Although our students recognize the concept of individual self-sacrifice for the purpose of communal cohesion in Roman concepts of duty to the family and state (*pietas*), they have to acknowledge that the purpose of Roman duty was to galvanize the community against its enemies. In the earliest foundation period, these were against Rome's immediate Latin-speaking neighbors, a practice eventually extended to all groups. Although our students see that the eventual Roman practice of naturalized citizenship, a unique concept in world history, breaks down some ancient barriers of communal identity, they realize that naturalized citizenship was usually gained only after serving nearly three decades in the military. Therefore, even this seemingly egalitarian model of citizenship was driven by violence. For the Romans, war against a perceived threat was a core element that bound a unified community.

Students' takeaway from understanding the intercommunal Greek *agon* and Roman *pietas* finds resonance in similar ideas of self-sacrifice for the communal good. Requiring, and even demanding, that individuals submit themselves to a greater ideal of war to defend the community becomes our enduring connection to the ancient Mediterranean world. We discuss how governmental systems seem different in name only, as they function today according to our own social values. Students realize that sacrifice for the purpose of defense against an external threat is a shared value with an ancient past rather than a differentiation. As a historical continuity, it remains a great challenge to break from this ancient past principle as we confront contemporary human relationships with war and peace.

We change up the discussion by introducing a possible way to consider a solution to these ancient challenges: to consider some advice from some ancient and early modern scholars. In the first millennium BCE, Eastern values promoted a divine mapping of the terrestrial world that linked a sense of universal humanity. *T'ian Ming* principles emphasize no singular claim of a chosen people by any government; rather, it broadcasts the unifying concept of "what Heaven ordains" (deBary 1999: 43). Confucian principles embodied in the model leader (*Junzi*) urge those in power to view themselves as fathers, responsible for all subject peoples under their rule as a father is responsible for his family. Similarly, members of society must recognize their place in the social order and responsibility to it (deBary 1999: 44–61). This model, constructed around the central principles of relationships between human groupings, provides the earliest representation of a peace with which we might most identify. For Confucius and many of his contemporaries, social harmony and peace are possible only through the recognition and willful submission to one's place in society. Although this seems to counter our American tradition of individualism, it invites discussion about the limits of our rhetoric of freedom, especially given the current climate of political and social upheaval. Moreover, some students who self-identify as Christian find resonance in Confucian ideas of filial piety and virtue, ignoring or perhaps blind to the inherent renunciation of self in his thought. Peace, they argue, is possible on a small level beginning with the individuals who cultivate inner virtue and devotion to family, friends, and humanity. Otherwise, a few of these same students maintain that global peace would only occur with the Second Coming of Christ.

In our discussions, we acknowledge this perspective of a foundation from which one can identify with an ancient continuum of peace, set apart from its contemporary civilizations when the organizing principles in Mediterranean societies are questioned. We help students make a general set of distinctions between a more rigid Mediterranean concept of zero-sum victory and an Eastern ideal of harmony among peoples. In our pedagogical framework, these dichotomies provide some insight for exploring modern political studies of liberalism and realism.

Achieving Peace in a Postmodern World

What can we learn from this? One of the most enlightening observations we gain from our course readings is an understanding of the paradigms of leadership between Western and

Eastern ideals. The role of government and model rule comes into high relief when considering the early modern mindset of Machiavelli's *The Prince* and the principles of ethical leadership of the neo-Confucian scholars in the Ming dynasty. We are cautious to remind ourselves of the baggage that Machiavelli brings to the establishment of the realpolitik of sixteenth-century Florence and Italian affairs; his work must be understood within the context of the fall of the republic and the establishment of Medici authority. Notwithstanding, Machiavelli's chilling perspectives about power and governance permeating *The Prince* must always be balanced with his earlier humanist writings on the positivist nature of humankind and the promise of a republican form of government. We remind students that these humanist tendencies appear in the work when he advises princes on how to maintain peace with those he has conquered: never change their traditions and customs, never seize their property, never take their women. Students come to appreciate that, given the Medici style of rule, Machiavelli's advice reflects a new realism of European thought: princes have the supreme authority over their populations, and thus impose a kind of violent peace from above. They can, and should, manipulate religious traditions to their benefit, and they must punish with extreme prejudice those who oppose them. However, if the prince wishes to maintain his position of authority, he must respect the traditions of society and his subjects. Peace can be more easily gained by respecting those under one's rule.

Through comparison, students learn that this element of Machiavelli's reaction to the new order in Florence stands on familiar ground with the ethical considerations of leadership of his near contemporary, Huang Zongxi, who lived in a time of great change. In his seminal work, *Waiting for the Dawn*, Huang criticizes the dynastic imperial system of the late Ming dynasty and, like Machiavelli, he fought against the establishment of a new order of power: the Manchu conquest of China (de Bary 2000: 6–17). Corruption, government strife, and war plagued Huang's view of a peaceful state, and he identifies the prince as the source of that instability. For Huang, gone are the halcyon days of Han rule when Confucian values balanced the state. By this time in the course, students are wise enough to question any golden age in Chinese history, but the ideals that permeate the discussions over the proper way to rule are never in doubt. Huang calls upon his contemporary scholar statesmen to advise the prince with truth. In order to end the cycle of self-aggrandizement, one must resist becoming an imperial yes-man who seeks only to better his own position with the emperor for the sake of securing his own family fortune. In an early modern sense, Huang calls upon his fellow statesmen to put their nation above their own selfish motives. We discuss how this call rings true for many today, when one considers the extent of what those in power have done for themselves as opposed to what they have done for the country as a whole. Students find that these two perspectives on improving chances for peace from the perspective of advice are relevant to our larger discussion.

However, we find that the most challenging observation students raise deals with the modern era of identity politics. The writings of the United Nations Declaration of Human Rights (UNDHR), Gandhi, Martin Luther King, and Malcolm X enshrine model ideals for sustainable peace, while exposing what is perhaps the single most influential factor that prevents any concept of peace between peoples: racism. The open sore of racism forces all of us to question our own definitions of peace and any possibility of achieving it at even the most basic levels of activity and organization. The UNDHR seeks to codify our responsibility to one another as global citizens, but global history since its inception has shown that its implementation may be impossible. Nevertheless, students learn that a hard fight through non-violent protest may provide some possibilities.

Gandhi's *satyagraha* elicits spirited debate about the willful use of non-violent confrontation as a means to achieve peace through passive resistance by challenging the British Crown with its own value of liberal human rights. And Martin Luther King's blend of sacred eloquence to touch the human spirit and non-violent action to expose the brutality against the body stands as a testament of humanity finding its moral center in America. However, Malcolm X's surgical speeches remove the veil that may be called racial harmony in America. Most students—but not all—believe that the current state of politics in America reflects this perspective that race, as we define it, is the greatest impediment to achieving a concept of enduring peace as defined in the UNDHR.

The emergence of the Black Lives Matter movement, protesting tragic and shocking police and civilian shootings of unarmed black men in the last decade, betrays any claim of social harmony. Consequently, racism has been stoked by fear of terrorism and the disappearance of manufacturing jobs to automation and cheap overseas labor. With no change in rhetoric or action, we can attest that few things in American discourse are post-racial. After we remind students that it was once heralded in 2008 that this nation had achieved a "post-racial America" given the praise for electing President Barack Obama, we discuss how these tensions had some real effect in the political revolution of 2016, with its scapegoating of immigrants and the demonization of Muslims.

Lessons Learned and Shared

Pursuing the question "What is peace?" critically shapes how we individually and collectively approach other urgent issues, especially those with values conflicts, within our scholarship and teaching. These involve collaboration and the transfer of pedagogies across disciplinary lines. Although we teach this course individually, our work as an interdisciplinary team to prepare the course helped us to understand how powerful the approach is. We are reminded of the need and the value of bringing Chinese philosophy to current discourse, developing dialogues with other peace theories, and collectively seeking solutions to contemporary problems, especially in the global domain. Thematic comparisons across disciplines improve how teachers and students seek solutions to problems and recognize our own prejudices, through developing dialogues with different cultures, societies, powers, and disciplines.

Reflection on our collaborative experiences shapes how we teach other classes, making us alert to opportunities for integrating peace issues there. With an insertion of a selection of documents, a film, or a novel, students can be asked to identify its message of peace. For example, Albert Camus' *The Plague* offers an opportunity to use a bifocal approach that discerns how a town fights bubonic plague, while metaphorically examining how a group of engaged citizens can fight fascism and its attendant structural violence. Another short exercise uses the Edict of Nantes in 1598, which orders forgetfulness as a path to peace while acceding judicial and property rights and freedom of worship to French Protestants and Catholics. Juxtaposed against the call to never forget, as in the case of 9/11, this offers a spirited exercise in debating paths to peace that begin with asking how we can achieve a cease-fire. For another course requirement, students present a poster encapsulating their open research papers and craft a final reflection requiring them to come to terms with the central question of the course. Using pedagogy with similar outcomes from those envisioned for our course, students are forced to reflect on what has become, through their research and learning, singularly most important.

To return with our students to our framing question, "What is Peace?," we recognize that there is no static response. But we also realize with them that that is not the point. The response to defining peace, our cross-cultural, cross-chronological inquiry leads us to conclude, is that the answer requires fluidity, flexibility, and persistence: an inquisitive mind. Our students generally concur that world peace is not possible or sustainable. That too is beside the point. Instead, this significant discursion leads us all to ask further and different questions about violence and peace. For both, what we achieve is the disturbed equilibrium of comfortable assumptions.

Notes

1 As of this writing, we now join the list of American states that allow guns on college campuses and in classrooms.
2 For example, these interpretations can be found in recent scholarship about the Napoleonic Wars and women by John Tone and Charles Esdaile, and in the military history of the French Revolution, and more controversially on Haiti, by Jeremy Popkin.

Works Cited

Arendt, H. (1969). "Reflections on Violence." *Journal of International Affairs* 23 (1): 1–35.
Barash, D. (2013). *Approaches to Peace: A Reader in Peace Studies*, 3rd ed. Oxford University Press.
Borg, C. and M. Grech (eds.) (2017). *Pedagogy, Politics and Philosophy of Peace*. Bloomsbury Critical Edition Series. London: Bloomsbury Press.
Boulding, E. (2000). *Cultures of Peace: The Hidden Side of History*. Syracuse, NY: Syracuse University Press.
Carey, G. (2000). "Tolerating Religion," in S. Mendus (ed.), *The Politics of Toleration in Modern Life*. Durham: Duke University Press, Chapter 4.
Cortright, D. (2008). *Peace: A History of Movements and Ideas*. Cambridge: Cambridge University Press.
Darder, A. (2017). "Dreaming of Peace in Culture of War," chapter six in Borg, C. and M. Grech (eds.), *Pedagogy, Politics and Philosophy of Peace: Interrogating Peace and Peacemaking*. Bloomsbury Critical Edition Series. London: Bloomsbury Press.
de Bary, W. T., and I. Bloom (eds.) (1999). "Confucius and the Analects," in *Sources of Chinese Tradition*, vol. 1, 2nd ed., *Introduction to Asian Civilizations*. New York: Columbia University Press, 41–61.
Fry, D. P. (2015). War, Peace, and Human Nature: The Convergence of Evolutionary and Cultural Views. Oxford: Oxford University Press; Reprint Edition.
Galtung, J. (1969). "Violence, Peace, and Peace Research." *Journal of Peace Research* 6: 167–191.
Galtung, J. (1990). "Cultural Violence." *Journal of Peace Research* 27 (3): 291–305.
Hobbes, T. (1651/1909). *The Leviathan*. Oxford: Clarendon. Available at: https://archive.org/details/hobbessleviathan00hobbuoft
Huang Zongxi. (2000). "Waiting for the Dawn," in William Theodore de Bary and Richard Lufrano (eds.), *Sources of Chinese Tradition*, vol. 2, 2nd ed. New York: Columbia University Press, 6–17.
King, Martin Luther. (1963). "Letter from a Birmingham Jail." Available at: https://web.cn.edu/kwheeler/documents/Letter_Birmingham_Jail.pdf
Kristeva, J. (1982). *Powers of Horror: An Essay on Abjection*. New York: Columbia University Press, 3–5.
MacIntyre, A. (2000). "Toleration and the Goods of Conflict," chapter nine in S. Mendus (ed.), *The Politics of Toleration in Modern Life*. Durham: Duke University Press.
Mendus, S. (2000). "My Brother's Keeper: The Politics of Intolerance," chapter one in S. Mendus (ed.), *The Politics of Toleration in Modern Life*. Durham: Duke University Press.
Spencer, V., and T. Shogimen. (eds.) (2014). *Visions of Peace: Asia and the West*. New York: Routledge.
X, Malcolm (1965). "Confronting White Oppression." Available at: http://thespeechsite.com/en/famous/MalcolmX-3.pdf

Further Reading

Borg, C., and M. Grech. (eds.) (2017). *Pedagogy, Politics and Philosophy of Peace*. London: Bloomsbury Press. (A useful volume of essays that summarize current debates in peace pedagogy and advocate for critical education that resists privileging Western concepts.)
Govier, T. (2006). *Taking Wrongs Seriously: Acknowledgment, Reconciliation, and the Politics of Sustainable Peace*. New York: Humanity Books (imprint of Prometheus Books). (An examination of work to create peace and reconciliation based in global examples from Rwanda and elsewhere.)

Nepstad, S. E. (2011). *Nonviolent Revolutions: Civil Resistance in the Late 20th Century*. Oxford: Oxford University Press. (Neptad pairs three sets of twentieth-century successful non-violent revolutions with three unsuccessful non-violent revolutions against repressive governments and analyzes the reasons for each.)

Spencer, V., and T. Shogimen. (eds.) (2014). *Visions of Peace: Asia and the West*. New York: Routledge. (This collection of essays explores global traditions of peace from the ancient world to the nineteenth century, making it useful for preparation for teaching and providing contextual background for primary sources in the classroom.)

AFTERWORD

Nonviolence and the Non-Existent Country

James M. Lawson, Jr.

Introduction (by Veena R. Howard)

Reverend James M. Lawson, Jr. (1928–) is widely recognized as a pioneer of nonviolence in the American Civil Rights Movement. Lawson is a living icon embodying the power of nonviolence in securing justice and peace. His work has been highlighted in the book and documentary *A Force More Powerful* (Ackerman and Duvall 2000), which shows Lawson's strategic workshops to train students to confront segregation in lunch counter sit-ins in Nashville, Tennessee, in the 1960s.[1] This successful movement became a paradigm for nonviolent activism.

In his life and work, Lawson has been deeply influenced by Mohandas Gandhi's method of nonviolence and truth-force. Lawson draws connections between Gandhi's ideas and Jesus' doctrine of unconditional love. But Lawson also credits the early inspiration of his mother. When he responded with his fists to violence and racial slurs in his childhood his mother told him, "There must be a better way." Calling this episode a "numinous experience," Lawson recalls, "I said to myself, 'Never again will I use my fists on the playground when I get angry or when someone else gets angry with me.' And I heard myself saying, 'I do not know what the better way is, but I will find out'" (Wong et al. 2016: 6). Lawson's search for a better method led him to study Gandhian nonviolence, including passive resistance and civil disobedience. As a college student Lawson met civil rights activists A.G. Muste and Bayard Rustin, who introduced Lawson to Gandhi's ideas. Muste, the head of the pacifist Fellowship of Reconciliation, discussed Gandhi with Lawson. During the Korean War, Lawson became a draft resister. He believed that "the draft was antithetical to his faith and his sense of justice" (Wong et al. 2016: 8). For this he was tried and sentenced to prison for three years. After his release from prison, he went to India in 1953, where he had firsthand experience with leaders of India's independence movement. He visited Gandhi's ashrams and read books on the method of nonviolence. This became foundational for his work in the American Civil Rights Movement.

Even though Lawson was influenced by Gandhian methods of resistance and civil disobedience, he developed his own unique tactics, including lunch counter sit-ins. Gandhi emphasized that nonviolent struggle requires training and preparation. Lawson also understood the importance of strategic training in self-sacrifice for the cause. He held workshops to train student activists, teaching them how to remain nonviolent when faced with the abuses and acts of violence, through role-playing sessions.

Martin Luther King, Jr. called Lawson a great tactician of nonviolence. In his last speech, "I Have Been to the Mountaintop" (April 3, 1968), King commended Lawson for his work in the struggle. King was gunned down the next day. But the struggle continued. Lawson developed a four-step program of nonviolent action based on Gandhian principles: (1) focus, (2) negotiation, (3) direct action, and (4) follow-up.

In workshops, which he continues to offer every month in Los Angeles, Lawson identifies ten steps of Gandhi's teachings: (1) investigation, (2) negotiation and arbitration, (3) preparation of the group for direct action, (4) agitation, (5) issuing an ultimatum, (6) economic boycott and forms of strike, (7) non-cooperation, (8) civil disobedience, (9) usurping functions of the government, and (10) parallel government (Sharma in Wong et al. 2016: 20). This categorization provides activists with concrete strategies to be utilized in various situations.

Lawson did not confine his work to African American civil rights. He has dedicated himself to securing peace and justice for workers in fields and hotels, including working alongside Cesar Chavez and Elena Durazo. In the 1990s, he trained the organizers of the hotel workers' movement under Durazo's leadership. Durazo recalls the value of Lawson's training workshops: "Reverend Lawson put it all in context. . . . What it was to get arrested, what it was like to get kicked, to get spit on, to get beat up" (in Wong et al. 2016: 92). Lawson's unique strategy of role-playing exercises prepared activists for nonviolent resistance in the face of physical and verbal abuses. Such training and broad community alliances resulted in the Los Angeles living wage ordinance. Lawson continues to be active in offering workshops and fighting against various forms of exploitation and injustices in the US. He still teaches at California State University, Northridge and at UCLA's center for labor, research and education.

Lawson's essay provides an overview of the philosophy of nonviolence in the American Civil Rights movement, demonstrating a debt to Gandhi as "the father of nonviolence." Lawson resists using the term "pacifism." Rather, he emphasizes the method of nonviolent resistance along with what he calls here soul force, the force of truth, the force of love, and the power of the spirit. He highlights the Gandhian axiom that "means and ends must be consonant," finding its resonance in Christian ideas. He celebrates nonviolence as the greatest discovery of the twentieth century—an idea that has given people an extraordinary tool for securing justice, dignity, and equality. In his remarks, Lawson repeats the phrase "I am a citizen of a country that does not yet exist," to emphasize that nonviolence points us toward an ideal world that is beyond negative forces such as racism, sexism, violence, and plantation capitalism. He commemorates Rosa Parks and Martin King—founding figures of what he calls "the second American Revolution"—whose work and lives demonstrate the power of nonviolence and the gift and energy of life.

James Lawson's Speech, February 23, 2017

One of the lessons that I have learned across the years is that human beings are human beings wherever they are. After college I decided I wanted to live outside the country in order to shed some of the stuff of USA culture and in order to learn about and come to recognize another set of people. I was in prison for 13 months for conscientiously refusing to serve in the Korean War, in 1951 and '52, where I discovered that all kinds of men were incarcerated for many reasons. There were people who were considered dangerous in the cellblock where I was confined for five months because I was a troublemaker. But even those human beings are fundamentally the same. Our similarity is in our DNA. But we have allowed, for too long, certain kinds of mythologies to keep us from acknowledging our basic humanity and from pushing to make our true humanity the common birthright of us all.

There was once a revolutionary member of a self-determination party, I do not know where, but he was a poet in Africa—and a part of that group of people in the late '50s, early '60s, beginning to try to see how they can move toward self-determination—it's a magnificent story that has not yet really been told for the world to know. At any rate this poet, a man of inspiration, said something like this at a gathering:

I am a citizen of a country that does not yet exist.[2]

And all who want the different sort of nation, a different sort of Fresno, or California, or a different sort of Delta of Mississippi—all who aspire must have that sensibility, if they are going to struggle. The sense that "I am a citizen of a country that does not yet exist." I see it, in some of your faces. I see it in people across the earth. I see it in struggles that are at the local level in many ways. I hear it. I sense it in some political aspect in Europe and elsewhere. I see it in the United States, trying to appear.

But there are forces in our nation that I call the forces of spiritual wickedness. They are determined that the nation rooted in equality and liberty and justice and the beloved community for every boy and every girl everywhere, those forces of spiritual wickedness are determined that it will not happen in the United States of America. That it will be pushed back. That's the meaning of the motto "making America great again."

Making America great again. Do they hold that slavery was a great period of life? That the hanging of women in 1637 as witches in Salem, Massachusetts, and elsewhere, was greatness? That the decimating of 11 million indigenous populations—until in less than 200 years they were all in open-air concentration camps . . . that's greatness? The Civil War represents greatness? Not at all.

Rosa Parks' Struggle: Martin King and the Second American Revolution

Let's begin with Rosa Parks' struggle and our changing society. I want to add a sub-note to it, "Opposing Trumpism"—which is about getting back on the track of creating a society of equality and justice for all. We should not allow "Trumpism" and the divisiveness in our country to stop ordinary people like ourselves from dreaming large dreams and engaging in the twenty-first century in the experiment of being a people who are self-governing. We must recognize that the forces of history that we have come through are forces that continue to want to prevent us from making that experiment work. We know the extent to which the USA experiment since 1776 is the most important event of history. It began to challenge the idea that we human beings must be governed from the top down by patriarchy, monarchy, and tyranny. It began to challenge the idea that we human beings cannot be trusted to know who we are, to discover who we are, and to use that knowledge for the pursuit of a society—of small societies, large societies, and families—that can reflect the magnificence of the gift of life. And so that's my topic, Rosa Parks' struggle, and I could say then, in shorthand, *our* struggle.

I use this term, "Rosa Parks' Struggle," because I want you to separate what I say from the way in which the nation and many academics have considered what's called "the Civil Rights Movement." I maintain—as one who was in the middle of it for nearly 70 years—that using the term "Civil Rights Movement" is a way of trying to preserve a kind of racism, because it allows too many American people, too many people in this land, to see what happened between 1953 and into the '70s, '80s, and '90s—to see that as pertaining only to people of color, only for black

Americans ... and not to the whole nation. I use the term "Rosa Parks' Struggle" to indicate the extent to which that movement was a massive umbrella movement under which there were many facets and many dimensions. I have in my own study, reading, and reflection isolated at least 20 different dimensions of that struggle, of which the one that I represent—Martin King represents, Rosa Parks represents—was but one dimension. And ours was perhaps by far the most essential dimension because it involves moving out of the way of thinking primarily in terms of legal desegregation, legal ways of delegitimizing segregation under the Constitution, which was an important strategy.

There were of course, before '53, cases of school desegregation where black parents insisted, in various parts of the country, that public education needed to do some basic reform concerning the way they approach black youngsters (and other youngsters as well). But the "Rosa Parks' Struggle" offered a variation of enormous importance. It was this: women in Montgomery, Alabama, insisted that bus segregation needed to be changed. They reported on the indignity of that system of segregated busing. They reported on the way in which, because of the segregation laws and customs and spirituality, they were treated with such hostility: in riding the bus to shop, riding the bus to go to work, riding the bus to go to the schools and whatnot. They insisted before 1955. But this indignity was the heart of the problem of the racism of the United States. That was a different kind of an agenda from the constitutional challenges to legal segregation.

Rosa Parks was a key to it. She was, before 1955, an organizer, a devoted member of the AME (African Methodist Episcopal), from St. Paul AME Church in Montgomery. She was an organizer for the NAACP. She was a consulate to the youth branch of the NAACP. She organized one of the task forces that protested in the Montgomery area against the rape of black women (especially the rape of a young housewife and mother just a few miles outside of Montgomery). She was bold enough, with a gentle spirit that I witnessed many, many times across those years and up through her death. She was a gentle spirit, but it was a gentle spirit with a stubborn will—that declared that it was not right to subjugate some people to all sorts of indignities and fears and animosities and prohibitions on what they can do, what they can be, where they can live, and the rest of it.

She never compromised with the notion that the United States of America was on the wrong track with Jim Crow Law, which began at the end of the nineteenth century and into the twentieth century.

You need to understand that the United States basically deserted the creed of the Declaration of Independence: We hold these truths to be self-evident, that all are created equal, that all are endowed with certain inalienable rights, that among these are life, liberty and the pursuit of happiness. That was literally deserted at the end of the nineteenth century and into the twentieth century because segregation and dark codes and discrimination became a part of a major social thrust of the people of our land who felt that they were superior to women, that they were superior to people of color, that they were superior to the poor, that they were superior to the people who did not share their Christian religion. That [white supremacy] was a movement that pushed hard—harder than what the nation would like to acknowledge. Six thousand black men were tortured and lynched in the United States publicly across the land, especially in the Southeast and also in the part of the world where I grew up, in the Midwest. Six thousand! That excludes those who were incarcerated and killed by the police in the '30s and the '40s and the '50s. Black people were knocked off-balance after Reconstruction by that.

Rosa Parks' Struggle represents, then, the explosive spark that became the first organizing and emerging campaign to push back against segregation and hopelessness for millions of people. It was the first organized campaign. And you need to understand it. That is why I call it "the

Second American Revolutionary movement," why some historians (black historians) call it "the Black Freedom Movement," why I insist that that movement began because of the aspirations and the visions and the hearts and minds and spirits of many people like myself who knew that segregation was in contradiction to the path of history, that it was in contradiction to the way of God, and that it was in contradiction to the deepest philosophies of life, both here and around the world, both modern and ancient.

So the Rosa Parks' ignition was to develop under the emergence of what I now call "the Nonviolent Movement of America"—or "the Soul Force Movement of the United States." Her strength of character became the key that pulled the feelings of many people together. Rosa Parks' colleague and friend Mary Joe Robinson, at the first notice of Rosa Parks' arrest, on December the first of 1955, spent the night mimeographing 8 × 11 sheets that she cut in two. She and a number of her friends did this all night long so that on Saturday morning they were starting to pass out these leaflets around the Montgomery area saying let's boycott on Monday the fifth of December. They thought it would only be a one-day boycott. They met Monday afternoon and there they decided to form structures to run the boycott, to make it happen. That movement and that dimension of the movement, I maintain, was a beginning place.

So they nominated Reverend Martin Luther King, Jr. to become the advocate of the effort. And there emerged this phenomenal person, Martin King, who became the advocate. And Rosa Parks, as she went home December the fifth of that year, after the massive meeting around the Hope St. Baptist Church, where King spoke for the first time to 5,000 people around the church—Rosa said, it looks like we've selected the right man, the right person to do this task with us.

So that was the first plunge. I like this month, February 2017, because it represents the sixtieth year since Dr. King and I shook hands, February the sixth, 1957, at Oberlin College in Oberlin, Ohio. That was when we had a chance to have our first face-to-face. I was in graduate school, having just returned from my work in India of three years. He was brought to the campus to speak to the campus and community. I was a part of a small group that was to meet him for lunch at noontime. It was a small dining room on campus. I walked in the door. Martin King walked in shortly after me. And I turned to him and we stopped and talked and had our first face-to-face.

It was a momentous moment for me because I had been studying nonviolent struggle out of Gandhi's *Autobiography* in '47, which confirmed what I had been trying to do as a person, a high school person, a college person. As we talked and visited together, I expressed the fact that someday—when I finished one or two graduate degrees in theology—I would probably move south to work. And Martin said something like this: "Don't wait, come now—we need you now."

It was one of those luminous moments in my life. I didn't know how that decision was going to be confirmed. But I heard myself say, "I will come as soon as I can."

And so I dropped out of graduate school and moved in January of 1958. So I was in on the organization of the Southern Christian Leadership Conference and its development—and all of the first structures that grew out of that wing of what you call the Civil Rights Movement.

In 2013, on the fiftieth anniversary of the march of 1963, *Time* magazine called Martin Luther King, Jr. a founding father of the nation. *Time* had a beautiful essay on why he should be called a founding father: as the first advocate of social change in the United States, who tried to make his understanding, his biblical Christian understanding, of Jesus relevant to the social political scene. He was the first advocate in Western civilization of nonviolence as an effective force—as a way that this can be done, as the only way this can be done. He spent the remainder of his 13 years in campaign after campaign in and across the southern part of the country, helping folks to understand that we have power in our hands. If we understand that power and use that power, we will be astonished at what can be accomplished.

I stand here now in 2017 at age 88—and I am astounded. I am astounded by what we were able to accomplish—and how, in fact, we did begin to move this country away from becoming a citadel of injustice towards letting government become for the people, of the people, and by the people. We're a long ways from that. But that movement and that dimension of the movement, I maintain, was a beginning place.

Nonviolence, Love, and the Four Sources of Evil

You know nonviolence is a great way to talk about love. That is the love of God, the love of life, the love of one another. The love that many of us have met in our families from the very beginning. That's my case indeed. Gandhi meant this, in fact, when he coined the term *nonviolence*—so Gandhi can be called the father of nonviolence but not the inventor. He can be called the father of the science of nonviolence. And most people don't recognize that we have today sufficient evidence, sufficient theses, axioms that can be documented. We have a sufficient history of the twentieth century alone. Yes, that ought to verify the reality that when we are in trouble with a social scene—or an emotional scene in a family or a congregation or a union or a city or a campus—you do not have to imitate that social scene in its wrongness. That in fact to do that is to escalate the wrong, and to give the wrong a victory over yourself and over others. This is a cardinal principle that Gandhi and others raised. It is a science of how you resist and fight back.

Take for example the present state of great activism in the United States.[3] But let me suggest to you that too much activism for the sake of activism and not for the sake of changing ourselves and changing our land—too much of it—so that in these marches, that have been going on where people are wearing "the pussy hat" or wearing some signs—"He is not my president." That only reflects opposition. It does not reflect a struggle that is going to offer new glimpses of the country that does not yet exist.

"End and the means," Gandhi said, "must be consonant." But a more ancient figure, Jesus, said, "You can't get grapes from a thistle bush nor figs from the thorn bush." Gandhi suggested that this is a law of social history and personal history. The consonance of ends and means is a law, like the law of gravitation. You break the law, you sow the consequences, you gain the consequences.

In the twentieth century we understand the power of law. We fly today not because of breaking the laws of force, power, wind, or gravitation, but because we obey them. The same is true in the matter of social and political events. There is no way our nation, with 800 military bases in more than 100 countries in the world, can create progress toward a peaceful world. Can any of those military bases create a better world, a safer world, or a world that includes every boy and girl anywhere in the world? There is no way that that can happen. For the method itself has within it the seeds of destruction. And surely it's time for us and our land to be rid of the enemy that is called violence and that is called war.

One of the ways in which I broke with some of the peace movement efforts in the '60s and '70s is this: I did not see war as the major tragedy for this country and its wars and rumors of wars. I saw domestic violence, racist violence, the violence of structures of injustice as the larger problem. Consider the violence of saying to ordinary people, "You work, but you do not deserve adequate pay for your work. Little pay is enough, you don't need more than that."

So I come then to the forces of spiritual wickedness that want our society to go towards tyranny. And I do not say fascism, deliberately, because it's our homegrown tyranny, our homegrown oppression, our homegrown injustice [that is the problem].

Here are four forces that influence American policy and practice more than we know, causing confusion and turmoil: racism, sexism, violence, and plantation capitalism. These are the four. Each of them can be talked about for quite a bit of time, but all of them share two major elements.

First of all, they share the element which insists that some people are not human and should not be treated as human. That some people are not equal; therefore they should be subjugated to the rest of us. Each has a mythology: a mythology that is very ancient in our own country, the mythology, "The only good Indian is a dead Indian."

Violence shares the mythology that certain people cannot understand ordinary human discourse. The only way they can be managed or controlled is through violence. Sexism shares the ideology that more than half of the *Homo sapiens* species is inferior to the other portion. Plantation capitalism takes the point of view that a slave is not a human being. A slave needs no attention in humane and loving forms. A slave is property. A slave is a piece of wealth. All across our land under the power of plantation capitalism we have extreme disparities of economic injustice.

In California, a year or so ago, lawyers won cases in the courts that called for employers to pay ordinary working people $26 million of back wages that they were not paid. This is not just true for California, it's epidemic. Our present economic scene insists that some people should only earn a pittance: not a living wage, not benefits, and not sufficient economic well-being from their work that they can care for themselves and for their families—and that they can care for the environment in which they live—that they can work as full human beings to create a sustaining world, a sustaining nation. That's plantation capitalism.

One year ago, unions of California got a $15 minimum wage in various places. The opponents were almost entirely the chamber of commerce, business, big business, who could not see and did not sense that to be a democratic society there must be economic justice, economic opportunity, economic access. Poverty as a structure of oppression must be dealt with and wiped out. Homelessness and shelterlessness, living in the streets, is a product of modern society which we do not need and which we are smart enough and wealthy enough and ingenious enough to abolish and delete. But instead we tolerate it because we are still too much in the mythology of plantation capitalism.

These four forces, the bitter enemies, these four forces are what produced Donald J. Trump as president of the United States. He is the embodiment of the worst of the American experience, not the best. He is the personification of what tyranny is about. And you cannot fight tyranny with more tyranny—you have to learn a new language. And the language we need to learn is that the community of people who want change must somehow learn the language of compassion and community and understanding—one with another. What is the value of protesters who say Donald Trump is not our president? Trump is not our president only if we, therefore, refuse to accept our democratic process, spirit, and experiment.

Whether we like it or not racism, sexism, violence, plantation capitalism all represent our inheritance as USA people. No, we did not make those decisions 10 years ago, or 50 years ago, or 100 years ago, or 300 years ago, or 400 years ago. But we live now with the consequences of our past. We don't need to feel guilty about it, we just need to try to understand in the most profound way that we've inherited, and we need to change it in our own lifetime for the distance that we can go.

The King movement, the Rosa Parks movement, the Fannie Lou Hamer campaign represent the hope of our country. Soul force, the force of truth, the force of love. The power of the spirit.

It is these elements that represent the untapped power of the human family to discover itself and to discover the countries that we need, that do not yet exist.

Martin Luther King, Jr.'s final book was called *Where Do We Go from Here: Chaos or Community?* This funny little question—a question of the struggle that he represented and led so very, very well, and strategized for 13 years: *Where Do We Go from Here: Chaos or Community?* What King was saying in that book was something like this: that society will become more chaotic, unless we see the truth of the nonviolent movement of America. Using Congressman John Lewis' words, unless America sees—unless the USA sees—the vision, the power, the energy, and the truth, and the justice of the nonviolent struggle in the United States, the country will simply increase its own turmoil and chaos.

And so, the challenge for each one of us is: on which side are we willing to be? Struggle may be chaotic. I recognize that, through 17 or 18 or 20 various campaigns. But in the midst of the chaos there is an energy and a purpose and a vision that again and again can help us see and feel and know that we are on the right trail for ourselves and for others.

Chaos or community? If it's community, friends, then there is only one way. We have to find the language and the tools and the means to construct and build—block by block—community: persons, family, immediate, or extended family, congregation, union, camps. Then we need campaigns that can embrace all of Fresno and the world. Campaigns that can help lead the way for the movements that we need in the twenty-first century, that we must have if our nation is to exist. But not just for the nation to exist, but to find itself at its best in the experiment, that we hold these truths that all are created equal.

Each one of us has the gift of life. Biologists from the twentieth century have written that each of us has in us the debris of the Big Bang, the debris of the very beginning of our galaxy, our universe. A well-known biologist by the name of Ernst Mayr has said that in the 4 to 5 billion years in the existence of the Earth, some 50 billion living species have existed. We are destroying them incidentally at a rate of about 100,000 every year or every 50 years—or so I'm told. But Mayr said that of these 50 billion living species, the human species is the only one that has learned to sing and dance and use language and create intimate families, raise children—to be fully human—the only species that has learned to fly, to build skyscrapers, to build houses, and the rest of it. That speaks to me of the power of the gift of life that each one of us represents.

And at the heart of nonviolent power is the power in your own soul and life—what Gandhi called the will, the capacity to determine that in the midst of evil I will walk humbly with compassion and care. In the midst of chaos, I will know who I am, and I will make who I am significant for my own life and the life of my family and others. In the midst of racism, I will be a non-racist, I will be a sister or a brother of everyone around me and of all humankind. In the midst of sexism, I will tear off the chauvinism that is hurting the debate in public life in our land so very, very much. And I will see and can be a person who knows full well the equality and the necessity of all human life both genders, all genders. In the midst of injustice, I will work for justice. When I see the hungry I will want to see politics and policies that feed the hungry, not feed the bomb. When I hear hate slurs I will try to respond with care and humanity. That means I will live, each of us will live, as a citizen of a country that does not yet exist. I will live with other human options than the one of the status quo—not because I expect to be effective or successful, but because I want to be alive and human and full of the energy of living.

Acknowledgments

This essay is based on a speech delivered by Reverend Lawson entitled "Nonviolence: Then and Now," at Fresno State University on February 23, 2017. The audio was recorded by Fresno

State media communication and journalism student Corey Rudolf and initially transcribed by Jarrett M. Ramones. Further edited by Veena R. Howard and Andrew Fiala. Introduction by Veena R. Howard.

Notes

1 "A Force More Powerful" is a two-volume documentary directed by Steven York (1999/2000).
2 One likely source for this quotation is from some remarks of Dr. Vincent Harding. Link: www.huffingtonpost.com/marian-wright-edelman/dr-vincent-hardings-call_b_5420254.html
3 Lawson is referring here to massive nonviolent protests that occurred as Donald Trump was inaugurated president in January 2017.

Works Cited

Ackerman, P., and J. Duvall. (2000). *A Force More Powerful*. New York: Palgrave.
Sharma, P. (2016). "The Philosophy of Nonviolence," in Wong, J.K., A.L. Gonzales, and James M. Lawson, Jr. (2016). *Nonviolence and Social Movements: The Teachings of Rev. James M. Lawson, Jr.* Los Angeles, CA: UCLA Center for Labor Research and Education.
Wong, J.K., A. L. Gonzales, and James M. Lawson, Jr. (2016). *Nonviolence and Social Movements: The Teachings of Rev. James M. Lawson, Jr.* Los Angeles, CA: UCLA Center for Labor Research and Education.

INDEX

Abernathy, Ralph 70
Adams, John 17
Addams, Jane 15, 23–24, 30, 31, 125, 268
Adolf, Antony 15–16
Africa: ancient, medieval and early modern North Africa 66–68; ancient Egypt 65–66; concept of nonviolence 65; twentieth-century South 72–74; twentieth-century West 68–72
African Charter on Human and People's Rights 225, 235
African Life and Customs (Blyden) 64
Against Empathy: The Case for Rational Compassion (Bloom) 321
Agent Orange 332, 334
Age of Enlightenment 12
ahimsa 90–91; Buddhism 83–85; Hinduism 85–86; Jain concept of 83
al-Baghdadi, Abu Bakr 60
Albert, Sonia París 310–311
Alcott, Bronson 31
Alexander I (Czar) 109
Alfonsin, Raúl 277
American Civil Liberties Union 360
American Civil Rights Movement 4, 384–385
American Civil War 132, 288
American Revolution 17, 107; Parks, King and second 386–389
Amish 20, 320
Amnesty International 51
Amster, Randall 331, 334–335, 337
Anabaptists 11, 20, 128, 320
Angell, Norman 25
Animal Liberation (Singer) 344
Animal Liberation Front 338
animals 343–344; ethic of nonviolence 350–353; Gandhi and vegetarianism 344–346; stories in Buddhism and Jainism 348–350; stories in Hindu tradition 346–348; vegetarianism and 350
Annan, Kofi 158
Anscombe, Elizabeth 38, 39, 45
Aquinas, Thomas 38, 44, 47, 48, 49, 182, 232, 332
Arendt, Hannah 245, 375–377
Aristophanes 8–9
Aristotle 10, 168–172, 176n1–2, 177n16, 177n4, 316, 348
Armstrong, Karen 314–315
Arnaud, Émile 32
Arnold, Edwin 345
Assmann, Jan 65
Augsburger, Myron 37
Augustine 10, 38, 66–67, 76n4, 125, 127, 130, 133, 232
Aung San Suu Kyi 84, 268
Azad, Maulana 60–61, 62

Baba, Ahmad 75n1
Bahá'í 20
Bakunin, Mikhail 22
Balou, Adin 31
Banna, Hassan-al 60
Baptists 20
Barash, David 374
Baron, Marcia 290
Bazargan, Saba 142, 151
Benedict XV (Pope) 20
Benedict XVI (Pope) 327
Benjamin, Medea 278
Bentham, Jeremy 31, 345
Berlin, Isaiah 300–301, 302, 305
Bernstein, C'Zar 282
Berrigan, Daniel 37, 51

Index

Berrigan, Philip 37, 51
Bettelheim, Bruno 201
Better Angels of Our Nature, The (Pinker) 313, 368
Bhagavad-Gita, The (Hindu synthesis) 8, 86–90
Bible 2, 44–46, 361–362
Bin Laden, Usama 60
Biswas, Asit 332
Black Consciousness Movement in South Africa 74
Black Lives Matter 381
Bloom, Paul 321
Blyden, Edward Wilmot 64, 75n2
Boaz, Frantz 110–111
Boersema, David 116–124
Boer War 24
Bok, Sissela 285
Bonhoeffer, Dietrich 36–37
Borg, Carmel 373
Bourne, Randolph 32, 125, 135
Breaking Down the Walls of Silence (Miller) 358
Brecher, Bob 285
Bricker, Renee 371–383
Brock, Peter 43
Bronkema, David 338
Buber, Martin 36
Buddhism 20, 43, 80, 91, 377; *ahimsa* as ethical precept 83–85; animal stories in 348–350
Burritt, Elihu 18
Bush, George W. 278
Butler, Judith 287

Cady, Duane L. 7–14, 106, 124, 249–254, 258, 332
Campbell, James 303
Camus, Albert 322, 381
Capitalism: A Ghost Study (Roy) 274
Card, Claudia 290
care theory, ethics 295–297
Carey, George 376
Carnegie, Andrew 26, 31
Cassin, René 131
Catholicism 20, 43
Ceadel, Martin 331
Chan, David K. 168–178
Chapple, Christopher Key 343–354
Chavez, Cesar 3, 37, 385
Child Protective Services (CPS) 355–356
children: European direction for raising 364–366; race, disabilities and patriarchy 360–361; religious/political argument for training 361–363; spanking and harm 363–364; spanking at home 358–359; spanking at school 359–360; spanking data 356–358; treaty of United Nations for 366–367; violence against 355–356, 367–368
Chinese Revolution 133
Christadelphians 20

Christianity 10, 11, 20, 25, 38, 43, 377; advent of social 20; Biblical background of pacifism 44–47; just war theory 46, 47; negative formulation of rational defense 47–48; positive formulation of rational defense 48–52
Churchill, Robert Paul 225–237
Churchill, Ward 199, 201–202, 204–208
Churchill, Winston 175
Church of the Brethren 20
Church of the Latter-Day Saints 351
Cicero 9, 10
Civil Disobedience Movement in India (Rao) 70
Clausewitz, Carl von 106, 126, 132, 229
Clinton, Bill 158, 283, 367
Code Pink 269, 278–279
coercive power 53
Cold War 30, 38, 123, 125, 133, 258, 332, 335
collective morality 108–110
collectivities: value of 107–108; war as undertaking 106–107
communication, peacemaking and 297–299
Complaint of Peace (Erasmus) 11, 12
Concerned Philosophers for Peace 4
Concert of Europe 17–18, 136
Condorcet, Nicolas de 17
Confucianism 377
Confucius 379
Congregationalists 20
Consciencism (Nkrumah) 69
Considine, Craig 59
Constantine (Emperor) 10
contingent pacifism 225, 234, 284; defending 144–146; defining 142–144; extending 149–151; military service as transformative experience 146–149; objections to 151–153
Contingent Pacifism (May) 146
Cooper, Gary 191
Cooper, Sandi 16, 27
Copernican Revolution 249
Corneille, Rwandan performer 238–240, 244, 246, 247
corporal punishment: European direction for 364–366; Harris Poll 356–357, 361; race, disabilities and patriarchy, 360–361; *see also* children
Cortright, David 16, 26–27
cosmopolitan hospitality 243–244
cosmopolitanism, state and 246–247
Crimean War 125, 132
Crito (Plato) 9–10
Crusades 11, 127–128
Cryptonomicon (Stephenson) 163

Dalai Lama 3, 39, 204, 318, 348
Danish resistance, response to intervention 161
Dawkins, Richard 309, 310
Day, Dorothy 37, 51, 268

death penalty and nonviolence 318, 327–328; disposable persons and power 319–320; justice and empathy 320–323; principled opposition to death penalty 323–327
de Bloch, Jan 25
Deegalle, Mahinda 84
De Indis (Grotius) 125, 128
democratic peace *see* liberal democratic peace
Democritus 114
Deng, Yi 371–383
Descartes, René 75n1, 241, 348
de Vattel, Emer 131, 232
de Waal, Frans 310, 311–312
Dewey, John 30, 31, 32, 265, 296, 303
dharma, notion of 80–81
Dialogue of a Man and his Soul (anonymous) 65
Diderot, Denis 17
Dodd, Chris 362–363
Doe, Samuel 270
Dombrowski, Daniel A. 43–53
"Don't Ask, Don't Tell" policy 283
Doukhobors 20
Doyle, Michael 213, 215–216, 218
draft, protected identities in 287–290
Drucker, Merrit 332
Duc de Sully (Maximilien de Bethume) 12
Dukakis, Michael 321
Durazo, Elena 385

Earthlings (documentary) 343
Ebadi, Shirin 268
Eckersley, Robin 333
ecology and pacifism 331–339; environmental impact of war and peace 331–332; environmental security 335; environmental sustainability 337–339; impacts on populations 332–333; international treaties 333–334; peace ecology 334–335; resource management 335–337
Edeh, Emmanuel 72
education, teaching peacemaking 302–305
Egypt, ancient 65–66
Einstein, Albert 1, 30, 33, 35, 36
Eisenhower, Dwight 135, 256, 257
Elshtain, Jean Bethke 38
empathy, justice and for death penalty 320–323
Engels, Friedrich 22
Engler, Mark 205, 207
Engler, Paul 205, 207
Enlightenment 12, 126, 132, 143, 226–228, 313, 374–375, 378
ENMOD Convention 333–334
Environmental Justice Movement 338
equality and justice, peace 121–123
Erasmus, Desiderius 11–12, 31, 125, 126
Etchart, Julio 277
ethics: care theory 295–297; *see also* virtue ethics
Ethics of War and Peace, The (Lackey) 181

European direction, corporal punishment 364–366
Evans, Jodie 278

Failure of Nonviolence, The (Gelderloos) 204
Fanon, Frantz 70–71, 76n10
Female Auxiliary Peace Societies 18
feminism and nonviolent activism 268–270; Arundhati Roy 272–276; Code Pink 278–279; Leymah Gbowee 71, 270–272, 279; Madres de Plaza de Mayo 276–278, 279
Fiala, Andrew 1–4, 30–42, 142, 143, 217, 223n3, 264
Finland 365
First Hague Peace Conference of 1899 23
First World War *see* World War I
Fitz-Gibbon, Andrew 307–317
Fitz-Gibbon, Jane Hall 355–370
Fleischman, Sasha 281
foreigner, hospitality and 244–246
Fourier, Charles 22
Fox, George 44
Fox, Michael 3, 15–28, 331
France 365
Francis (Pope) 39, 255, 264, 318
Francis, Michael Kpakala 71
Franco-Prussian War 19, 125
Frank, Thomas 298
Frankena, W. K. 111
Franklin, Benjamin 17
Freire, Paulo 301
French Declaration of the Rights of Man and the Citizen 226
French League of Public Good 21
French Revolution 17, 20, 107, 382n2
Freud, Sigmund 314
Friendly Persuasion (movie) 191
Fry, Douglas P. 374
Fukuyama, Francis 39, 258
Future of War in Its Technical, Economic and Political Relations, The (de Bloch) 25

Galtung, Johan 30, 40, 117–118, 123, 219, 265, 372–377
Gan, Barry L. 3, 93–101
Gandhi (film) 94
Gandhi, Mohandas K. 1, 2, 3, 15, 18, 24, 31, 36–37, 39, 51, 60, 61, 72, 73, 93, 319; King and *Satyagraha* 99–100; on Lawson 384–385; notion of *dharma* 80–81; peace 116; politics and Indian National Congress 208; reading of the *Bhagavad-Gita* 86–90; *satyagraha* as way of life 94–95, 325; *satyagraha* as weapon 95–97; social justice heroes 202; term nonviolence 389; vegetarianism influence 344–346
Garibaldi, Giuseppe 19
Garton Ash, Timothy 300, 301, 302

Gay, William 255–267
Gbowee, Leymah 71, 268, 269, 270–272, 279
Gelderloos, Peter 199, 202–208
Geneva Conventions 132, 139, 234, 314, 333
genocide 167n1, 167n5; Rwandan 157–158, 159
George III (King) 253
Gershoff, Elizabeth 360, 363
Gessell, Donna 371–383
Ghaffar Khan, Khan Abdul 61–62
Gier, Nicholas F. 81, 84
Global Initiative to End All Corporal Punishment of Children (GIEACPC) 363, 365–367
God Has a Dream (Tutu) 74
Goldmann, Emma 33
Govier, Trudy 76n11
Great War 25, 32, 300
Grech, Michael 373
Greven, Philip 358, 361–362
Grimsrud, Ted 264
Grogan-Kaylor, Andrew 363
Grotius, Hugo 125, 128, 130, 139, 232, 234
group identity, conception of 238–239
Gulf War 135, 137, 223n2, 332, 334
Gursozlu, Fuat 213–224
Gyekye, Kwame 69

Haeuser, Adrienne 364
The Hague 23, 26, 230, 232, 234, 272
Hague Conventions 132
Hamer, Fannie Lou 390
Harari, Yuval Noah 148
Hardy, G. H. 304
Hartshorne, Charles 52
Hauerwas, Stanley 37
Hedges, Chris 204
Hegel, G.W.F. 27, 34, 64, 75n1, 228–229
Heraclitus 8, 114
Herder, Johann Gottfried 228
Hereth, Blake 281–292
Heston, Charlton 44
Hinduism 20, 43, 80, 91, 377; *ahimsa* as yogic discipline 85–86; animal stories in tradition 346–348
Hitchens, Christopher 300
Hitler, Adolf 36, 37, 133, 154, 175–176, 229, 326, 351
Hobbes, Thomas 12, 34, 130, 214, 233, 375–377
Hochschild, Arlie 298–299, 301, 303
Holmes, Robert L. 1, 36, 105–115, 332
Holocaust 162, 201, 229, 233, 327
Holy Alliance 107, 109
holy war, ideal of 127–128
Homer-Dixon, Thomas 335
Honig, Bonnie 244–247
Hooks, Gregory 338
hospitality: cosmopolitan 243–244; ethics of 241–242; foreigner and 244–246

Hossein-Zadeh, Ismael 259, 263
Howard, Veena R. 80–92, 384–385
Hsiao, Timothy 282
Huang Zongxi 378, 380
Hugo, Victor 18
Hull House 23
Humane Society 352
humanitarian intervention: against 154–156; Danish resistance 161; enabling escape 163–164; in favor of 156–157; pacifist intervention 162–163; pacifist response 160–161; Responsibility to Protect (R2P) 158–160; Rwandan genocide 157–158
human rights: historical considerations 226–229; international law and 225–226; just war and natural law 233–235; natural law theory 232–233; peace 235
Human Rights Watch 359, 360
Hume, David 309, 311
Hutterites 20

ibn Abi Talib, Ali 57
ibn Ali, Husayn 57
Ihara, Craig 179, 185, 188
imperialism 129–131, 133, 136, 155, 259, 273; American 31; anti- 133; British 87; European 314; free-trade 128; Western 138
individual morality 108–110
individual pacifism 184–187
Individuals with Disabilities Education Act 360
Ingraham v Wright (1977) 360
Institute of International Law 19
Inter-American Commission on Human Rights (IACHR) 235–236n1
International and Permanent League of Peace 19
International Bill of Rights (IBR) 229
International Court of Justice 230
International Covenant on Civil and Political Rights (ICCPR) 229, 230, 231
International Covenant on Social, Economic, and Cultural Rights (ICSECR) 229
International Criminal Court 158, 232, 314, 333
international law: human rights and 225–226; just war and natural law 233–235; natural law theory 232–233; treaties and agreements 229–232
International League of Peace and Liberty 19
International Olympic Committee 19
International Peace Bureau 20
intervention *see* humanitarian intervention
intore, concept of 239–240
Iraq wars 112, 278
Islam 11, 20, 54–55, 62–63; modern figures of nonviolence in 59–62; roots of peace and nonviolence in 55–57; term 54; violence and nonviolence in history 57–59

Isoo, Abe 25
Izutsu, Toshihiko 55

Jägerstätter, Franz 327
Jahanbegloo, Ramin 54–63
Jainism 7, 20, 80, 91; animal stories in 348–350; nonviolence as highest vow 81–82
James, William 1, 26, 30, 32, 265
Japanese Society of International Law 25
Jaurès, Jean 131
Jeffers, Chike 66
Jefferson, Thomas 17, 226, 232
Jesus of Nazareth 10, 44–47; cleansing of temple 46–47
Jim Crow Law 228, 387
John Paul II (Pope) 38, 39, 67
Johnson, James Turner 38, 135
Johnson, Mordecai 93
Judaism 20, 56
jus ad bellum (justice of going to war) 47–48, 134, 139, 175, 233–234, 236n2, 333
jus in bello (justice of war) 38, 47–48, 134, 139, 175, 234, 236n3, 332–333
Just and Unjust Wars (Walzer) 125, 126, 135, 136, 145, 156, 252
justice: corrective 123; distributive 122; empathy and for death penalty 320–323; peace 121–123; procedural 122; retributive 123; substantive 122
just war theory 109, 113, 114; Christianity 46, 47; natural law and 233–235, 325; virtue ethics pacifism and 174–176
just war tradition 125–127; contemporary thinking 134–135; future questions 139–140; genealogy of thinking 127–128; of nineteenth century 131–132; revisionist critiques of 138–139; of twentieth century 132–134; Walzer's revival 135–138; war, states and state system 128–131

Kaczynski, Ted (Unabomber) 338
Kamm, Frances 286
Kant, Immanuel 12–13, 15, 20–21, 31, 64, 131, 155, 308; hospitality 242, 243–244; liberal democratic peace theory (LDPT) 213; "Perpetual Peace" 213–215, 219–221, 225, 229
Kantianism 114
Kanzō, Uchimura 25
Kaplan, Robert 335
karma, concept of 85
Kennedy, John F. 261
Khan, Abdul Ghaffar 39
Khartoum (movie) 44
Khidmatgar, Khudai 62
Khomeini, Ruhollah 60
killing: in self-defense 173–174; virtue and 170–171
Killing in War (McMahan) 148

King Martin Luther, Jr. 1, 2, 3, 4, 31, 37, 39, 51, 93, 125, 134, 155, 255, 319; civil rights activism 97–99; corporal punishment 356; death penalty 319–320, 326; individual pacifism 184–185; on Lawson 385; peace 377–378; racism, extreme materialism and violence 263; Rosa Parks and second American Revolution 386–389; social justice heroes 201–203; vocational pacifism 182–183; "world house" 239
Kingsford, Anna 344
Kling, Jennifer 154–167
Koka, Ntate 74
Kosovo 159, 167n2, 217
Krishna 86–89
Kristeva, Julia 245–246, 375
Kurlansky, Mark 17, 204
Kutz-Flamenbaum, Rachel V. 279

Lakey, George 204–206
Lao Tzu 7
Law of Karma 85
Law of Nations, The (Vattel) 232
Lawson, James M. Jr. 2, 4, 31, 37, 97, 384–392; speech (February 23, 2017) 385–386
Layne, Christopher 216
Lazimi, Gilles 365
League of Nations 36, 133, 136, 229
League of Universal Brotherhood 18
learning *see* peace pedagogy
legalism 377
Lemonnier, Charles 19
Lenin, V. I. 22
Leo XIII (Pope) 20
Let My People Go (Luthuli) 73
Leviathan (Hobbes) 12, 233, 375
Lewis, C.S. 38
Lewis, John L. 207
liberal democratic peace: foundations of 214–215; Kant's "Perpetual Peace" 213–215, 219–221, 225, 229; misuse of 217–218; rise of 215–217; zone of peace 213, 216–218, 220; zone of war 218, 220
liberal democratic peace theory (LDPT) 213–214, 222–223; reclaiming 219–222
Liebknecht, Karl 32, 255
Locke, John 17, 226, 308, 362
Long, Edward 75n1
Lorde, Audre 268
Luban, David 150
Luther, Martin 12
Luthuli, Albert 72–73
Luxemburg, Rosa 22, 32
Lynn, William J. III 258
Lysistrata (Aristophanes) 9

Maathi, Wangari 268
Machiavelli, Niccolò 130, 377–378, 380

Index

Machlis, Gary 332
McMahan, Jeff 146, 148, 150
McNamara, Robert 260
McNulty, Tracy 241–244, 247
Madison, James 226
Madres de Plaza de Mayo 269, 277–278, 279
Mahabharata (trans. by Dutt) 80, 85–91
Mahavira, Vardhmana 7
Maimonides, Moses 58
Malcolm X 202, 377, 380–381
Mandela, Nelson 3, 72–73, 117, 172, 202
Manhattan Project 36, 260
Marcuse, Herbert 262
Marx, Karl 22, 256, 258
Maslow, Abraham 311
Mason, George 226
Masque of Anarchy, The (Shelley) 18
Mawdudi, Maulana 60
May, Larry 142, 143, 145, 160
Mayor, Federico 235
Mayr, Ernst 391
Mays, Benjamin 93
Melman, Seymour 256, 257, 258
Mendus, Susan 376
Menem, Carlos 277
Mennonites 11, 20, 31, 125, 320, 351
Merton, Thomas 37, 51
Methodists 20
Mexican-American War 18
Midgely, Mary 310
Milazzo, Linda 278–279
militarism 143, 255
military-industrial complex (MIC) 255–257; beyond the 262–265; formula and its scope 257–259; nuclear arms race and 259–262
military service: draft and protected identities 287–290; as transformative experience 146–149
Mill, John Stuart 21–22, 154–155, 156, 302, 304, 305
Miller, Alice 358
Mills, C. Wright 256–257, 261
Milosevic, Slobodan 235n1
Mingol, Irene Comins 310–311
Mohammad (Prophet) 57
Montesquieu, Baron de 17
Montgomery Bus Boycott 97–99, 183
moral dilemmas, virtue ethics 171–173
morality: concept of 105, 110–113; individual and collective 108–110; individual perspective 113–115; pacifism and 105–106; pacifism and ordinary 195–196
Moravians 20
Morrow, Paul 142–153
Mother Teresa 39
Mumford, Lewis 135
Muñoz, Francisco A. 307
murder, virtue and killing 170–171

Murdoch, Iris 49
Murphy, Gael 278
Muste, A. J. 37, 70, 134, 384
Mutual Assured Destruction (MAD) 123

Napoléon Bonaparte 17, 24
Napoleonic Wars 109, 128–129, 131–132, 134, 148, 382n2
Narveson, Jan 1, 181–185, 188, 191–198
National Council of Churches 20
National Endowment for the Humanities 371, 372
nationalism 238; cosmopolitanism and the state 246–247; ethics of hospitality and 241–242
natural law theory 232–233; principled opposition to death penalty 323–327
Nazi Germany 161, 175, 200, 231
Nazism 34, 35, 36, 161, 175–176, 200
negative peace, term 117
Negroes with Guns (Williams) 202
Newell, Peter 356
Newer Ideals of Peace (Addams) 23
Newton, Isaac 304
Nicomachean Ethics (Aristotle) 10
Niebuhr, Reinhold 38, 264
Nietzsche, Friedrich 34
Nihon Heiwa-Kai 19
nineteenth century: contributions to world peace 25–27; evolving peace movement 18–20; global view of nonviolence and pacifist activity 24–25; just war tradition 131–132; overview of period 15–18; peace pioneers of 20–24
Nkrumah, Kwame 69–70, 76n9
Nobel Peace Prize 19, 20, 23, 26, 27, 71, 72, 100, 269, 275
Noddings, Nel 295–306, 373
nonviolence 1–4, 20; ancient, medieval and early modern North Africa 66–68; ancient Egypt 65–66; animals, intimacy and ethic of 350–353; on becoming 307, 316–317; definition of 16; Lawson's speech 385–386; love and sources of evil 389–391; nineteenth-century global view 24–25; psychological perspectives 311–314; sociobiological and neurophilosophical perspectives 307–311; spiritual perspectives 314–316; twentieth-century South Africa 72–74; twentieth-century West Africa 68–72; vow in Jainism 81–82; *see also* death penalty and nonviolence; feminism and nonviolent activism
nonviolentism 3, 39, 317
North Africa, ancient, medieval and early modern 66–68
North American Free Trade Agreement (NAFTA) 230
North Atlantic Treaty Organization (NATO) 108, 159, 167n2, 230, 258–259
North Korea 233, 261–262

nuclear arms race, military-industrial complex and 259–262
Nuremberg Tribunal 231, 232
Nyungura, Cornelius 238; *see also* Corneille
Nzegwu, Nkiru 72

Obama, Barack 275, 283, 381
Obenga, Theophile 75n3
Ordinary Education Violence Observatory (OEVO) 365
Origen 67, 76n5
Orosco, José-Antonio 199–210
Orwell, George 38, 199–200, 202, 204–207, 297–299, 301, 303, 322
Osman, Mohamad Fathi 58
Osterhammel, Jürgen 27
Ottoman Empire 18, 132
Owens, Richard 22
Owens, Wilfred 300

pacificism 31, 32, 106
pacifism 1–4, 20; beyond twentieth century 39–40; Biblical background of 44–47; definition of 16; degree of 193–194; duty to defend and 187–189; early twentieth century 31–35; ecology and 331–339; fundamentalist 191–192; general argument 195; as global perspective 106; individual 184–187; modes of approach to 50; nineteenth-century global view 24–25; ordinary morality and 195–196; as pathology 200–204; peace and the state 197–198; personal 126, 179, 180, 181; political 126; relevant variables 194–195; responses to, as pathological 204–209; response to intervention 160–161; Second World War and beyond 35–39; term 142; universal 179, 180, 181, 183–184, 188; up-to-date 196–197; virtue ethics, just war and 174–176; vocational 181–184; war 193; warism *vs* 249, 252–254; *see also* contingent pacifism; queer oppression and pacifism
Paine, Thomas 17, 226
Pais, Marta Santos 365
Pal, Amitabh 59
Palumbo, Matt 282
Papal Postulatum (1870) 125
Parks, Rosa 385, 386–389, 390
Passy, Frédéric 19
pathology, pacifism as 200–204
Paul, Alice 206
Paul, L. A. 142, 147–149, 150, 151
peace: achieving in postmodern world 379–381; action and agents 118–119; basic conceptions of 116–118; care theory 295–297; equality and justice 121–123; human rights and 235; negative 117; peacemaking 299–302; positive actions 119; promoting 123–124; rights 119–121; secondary concept 117; state and 197–198; teaching "What Is Peace?" 376–378; *see also* liberal democratic peace
Peace: A World History (Adolf) 15–16
peacemaking 299–302; communication and 297–299; education teaching 302–305
Peace of Westphalia (1648) 159, 227
peace pedagogy: achieving peace in postmodern world 379–381; answering What Is Peace? 376–378; combined experiences in teaching peace 371–372; course structure 374; learning experiences 378–379; lessons learned and shared 381–382; teaching and learning environment 372–373; from violence to peace 374–376
Peckover, Priscilla 19
Peloponnesian War 8, 9
Penn, William 12
People for the Ethical Treatment of Animals 351
"Perpetual Peace" (Kant) 13, 213–215, 219–221, 225, 229
Perry, William 258
personal pacifism 179, 180; case against 181; duty to defend 187–189
persuasive power 53
Peterloo Massacre 18
Phenomenology of Mind, The (Hegel) 75n1
Pinker, Steven 40, 312–314, 357–358, 366
Pink Pistols 281–285
Plato 9, 89
Poe, Danielle 268–280
Politics (Aristotle) 10
Politics of Nonviolent Action, The (Sharp) 124
Poor People's Campaign 99–100
Potonié-Pierre, Edmond 19
Practice of the Wild, The (Snyder) 350
Praeg, Leonard 74
Praise of Folly (Erasmus) 12
Presbey, Gail M. 64–79
Presbyterians 20
Prince, The (Machiavelli) 380
Protestantism 20, 31
Proulx, Michael 371–383
Puritan Revolution 131
Pythagoras 114

Quakers (Society of Friends) 20, 31, 44, 351
queer oppression and pacifism: draft and protected identities 287–290; Pink Pistols 281–285; presumption against violence 285–287
Qur'an 55–58, 60–62, 362
Qutb, Seyyed 60

Radhakrishnan, S. 85
Ramose, Mogobe 74
Ram-Prasad, Chakravarthi 76n8
Ramsey, Paul 38, 45, 134

Index

Rawls, John 51, 142, 152, 221, 308
realism 8, 9, 37, 109, 136, 227, 319, 379, 380
Red Cross 19, 231
Reformation, the 11, 128
Reichberg, Gregory 332
Reitan, Eric 179–190
Republic (Plato) 9, 89
Responsibility to Protect (R2P) 158–160, 232
Rifkin, Jeremy 312
rights, peace and 119–121
Robillard, Michael 149
Robinson, Mary Joe 388
Rodin, David 139, 144–146, 151–152, 290n5
Roosevelt, Theodore 27
Root, Elihu 26, 218
Rousseau, Jean-Jacques 12, 13, 17, 130, 131, 308, 362
Roy, Arundhati 269, 272–276, 279
Ruddick, Sara 297
Russell, Bertrand 1, 30, 32–34, 35–36, 304
Russell-Einstein Manifesto 36
Russian Revolution 133
Russo-Japanese War 25
Rustin, Bayard 76n9, 384
Rwanda: Corneille 238–240, 244, 246, 247; genocide of 157–159, 238–240
Ryan, Cheyney 1, 125–141, 142, 143

Sacred and Profane Love Machine, The (Murdoch) 49
Salt, Henry 344
Salt March 95–97
Sartre, Jean-Paul 76n10
satyagraha: Gandhi's 94–95; philosophy of nonviolent resistance 94; as way of life 94–95; as weapon 94–97
Scheler, Max 34–35
Schweitzer, Albert 39, 51, 87
Second Indochina War *see* Vietnam War
Second Treatise of Government (Locke) 233
Second World War *see* World War II
securing survival 127
self-defense 236n4; just war thinking 127–128; killing in 173–174
Selfish Gene, The (Dawkins) 309
September 11, 2001 tragedy 54
Seventh Day Adventists 343, 351
Shakers (United Society for Believers in Christ's Second Appearing) 20
Sharp, Gene 22, 40, 124, 162, 204, 205, 207
Shayne, Julie 276
Shelley, Percy Bysshe 18
Shepard, Matthew 281
Shifferd, Kent 26
Shue, Henry 120–121
Siddhartha Gautama 83
Sikh Awareness Society 363
Sikhism 20

Simpkins, Anellen M. 316
Singer, Peter 344
Smith, Adam 345
Smith, Chad 338
Snyder, Gary 350
social Darwinism 132
social ontology 107–108
Society of Friends (Quakers) 20, 31, 44
Society of Peoples 221
Sociobiology (Wilson) 308
Socrates 2, 9, 10
Sojourner Truth 268, 344
Solnit, Rebecca 204
Souffrant, Eddy M. 238–248
South Africa, twentieth-century 72–74
spanking: data 356–358; harm and 363–364; Harris Poll 356–357, 361; at home 358–359; at school 359–360; *see also* children
Spengler, Oswald 34
Sri Aurobindo 87, 89
Starr, Ellen Gates 23
Steffen, Lloyd 318–330
Steinkraus, Warren 251
Story of My Experiments with Truth, The (Gandhi) 24
Straus, Murray A. 356, 359, 361, 364, 367
Strawser, Bradley 149, 282
Stride Toward Freedom (King) 93
Subramanyam, Aishwaraya 272
Sufism 54
Sussman, David 286
Sutherland, Bill 76n9
Sweden 364–365
Swedish Parenthood and Guardianship Code 364
Syse, Henrik 332

Taipang Rebellion 131
Taoism 7
Tao Te Ching (Lao Tzu) 7
Tarpeh, Etmuniah 71
Taylor, Charles 71, 270, 271
teaching *see* peace pedagogy
Teena, Brandon 281
Tenzin Gyatso *see* Dalai Lama
terrorism 40, 74, 164, 195, 200; America's war on terror 30, 123, 127, 261; terrorist groups 115n2; *see also* war on terrorism
Thich Nhat Hahn 39
Thirty Years' War 128–129, 227
Thoreau, Henry David 18, 31, 87
Thucydides 8
Thurman, Howard 93
Tilak, B.G. 87
Tocqueville, Alexis de 18
Tolstoy, Leo 1, 22, 30, 31, 131, 132, 236n4, 319, 345
Treaty of Westphalia 129, 227
Treitschke, Heinrich 109

Trojan Women, The (Euripides) 8
Truman, Harry S. 260
Trump, Donald J. 240, 246, 278, 390, 392n3
Trumpism 386
Tubman, Harriet 268
Tutu, Desmond 73–74
twentieth century: beyond 39–40; early, from Tolstoy to Second World War 31–35; just war tradition 132–134; pacifism 30–31; Second World War and 35–39; South Africa 72–74; West Africa 68–72
Two Treatises of Government (Locke) 226

Unabomber (Ted Kaczynski) 338
UN Convention on the Law of the Sea Treaty (UNCLOs) 230
Unitarians 20
United Nations 16, 21, 26, 36, 51, 133–134, 136, 157, 227, 229, 234, 366
United Nations Charter 133, 136
United Nations Children's Fund (UNICEF) 355–357, 367
United Nations Convention on the Rights of the Child 366–367
Universal Declaration of Human Rights 131, 158, 229, 232, 314, 380
universal morality 111
universal pacifism 179, 180, 181, 183–184, 188
US Bill of Rights 226
US Civil War 20
US Declaration of Independence 226

van der Linden, Harry 333
vegetarianism, Gandhi and his influences 344–346
Vietnam War (Second Indochina War) 84, 100, 125–126, 134–135, 137–138, 261, 332
Vindication of the Rights of Woman (Wollstonecraft) 107
violence: commonsense opposition to 192–193; presumption against 285–287
virtue ethics: just war and pacifism 174–176; killing 170–171; killing in self-defense 173–174; moral dilemmas 171–173; neo-Aristotelian 168–169
Virtue of Nonviolence, The (Gier) 81
Vlastos, Gregory 10
vocational pacifism 179, 180, 181–184
Voerword, Wilhelm 76n11

von Suttner, Bertha 22–23
Voting Rights Act (1965) 228

Waghid, Yusef 74
Walesa, Lech 3
Walzer, Michael 125–126, 135–139, 145–146, 150, 155–157, 162, 175, 217, 252, 298–299, 301, 303
war *see* just war theory; just war tradition; warism; war pacifism
warism 106, 249–254
War of Indian Independence 131
War on Terror, America's 30, 123, 127, 261
war pacifism 8, 9, 193
Washington, George 17
weapons of mass destruction (WMD) 40, 50, 108, 115n2, 261
Weigel, George 38
Weiss, Paul 35
West Africa, twentieth century 68–72
Where Do We Go From Here: Chaos or Community? (King) 391
Why Men Fight (Russell) 34
Williams, Howard 345
Williams, Jody 268
Williams, Robert F. 202
Wilson, E. O. 304, 307–310
Wilson, Woodrow 32, 109, 229
Wiranthu 84
Wollstonecraft, Mary 107, 344
Women's International League for Peace and Freedom 23
Women's Peace Party 23, 32
Woods, Mark 331–342
World Trade Organization (WTO) 230
World War I 17, 19, 20, 23, 25, 30, 33–34, 48, 125, 128, 132–133, 135, 148, 229
World War II 30, 33–34, 35, 47–48, 128, 132–133, 136, 148, 161, 164, 229; military-industrial complex 256–258

Yeats, W.B. 300
Yoder, John Howard 37, 125, 319
Yousafzai, Malala 268
Yunus, Mohammed 275

Zahn, Gordon 135
Zimring Franklin 326
Zionism 107

Taylor & Francis eBooks

Helping you to choose the right eBooks for your Library

Add Routledge titles to your library's digital collection today. Taylor and Francis ebooks contains over 50,000 titles in the Humanities, Social Sciences, Behavioural Sciences, Built Environment and Law.

Choose from a range of subject packages or create your own!

Benefits for you
- Free MARC records
- COUNTER-compliant usage statistics
- Flexible purchase and pricing options
- All titles DRM-free.

Benefits for your user
- Off-site, anytime access via Athens or referring URL
- Print or copy pages or chapters
- Full content search
- Bookmark, highlight and annotate text
- Access to thousands of pages of quality research at the click of a button.

Free Trials Available
We offer free trials to qualifying academic, corporate and government customers.

eCollections – Choose from over 30 subject eCollections, including:

Archaeology	Language Learning
Architecture	Law
Asian Studies	Literature
Business & Management	Media & Communication
Classical Studies	Middle East Studies
Construction	Music
Creative & Media Arts	Philosophy
Criminology & Criminal Justice	Planning
Economics	Politics
Education	Psychology & Mental Health
Energy	Religion
Engineering	Security
English Language & Linguistics	Social Work
Environment & Sustainability	Sociology
Geography	Sport
Health Studies	Theatre & Performance
History	Tourism, Hospitality & Events

For more information, pricing enquiries or to order a free trial, please contact your local sales team:
www.tandfebooks.com/page/sales

Routledge — Taylor & Francis Group | The home of Routledge books

www.tandfebooks.com